Public Money

Kaoru Yamaguchi · Yokei Yamaguchi

Public Money

The Systems Solution to End National Debt, Banking Crisis, Built-In Inequality, Inflation and Control by CBDC

Springer

Kaoru Yamaguchi
Japan Futures Research Center
Sumoto, Hyogo, Japan

Yokei Yamaguchi
Japan Futures Research Center
Sumoto, Hyogo, Japan

ISBN 978-981-97-6563-8 ISBN 978-981-97-6564-5 (eBook)
https://doi.org/10.1007/978-981-97-6564-5

This Springer imprint is published by the registered company Springer Nature Singapore Pte Ltd.
The registered company address is: 152 Beach Road, #21-01/04 Gateway East, Singapore 189721, Singapore

As a result of trying to pose as a science, the field of economics has become substantially detached from real-world behavior, and has tended toward a closed theoretical discipline disconnected from the world it tries to explain.

Instead of being a science, I suggest that economics should become a systems profession. As a systems profession, economics would be parallel to management, engineering, and medicine, each of which is based on underlying sciences.

An economics systems profession would be based on underlying sciences such as psychology, decision-making, and nonlinear feedback dynamics. As a systems profession, economics would then reach beyond its basic sciences to understand and redesign economic systems.

—Jay W. Forrester (2003)[1]

---

[1] This book is dedicated firstly to Jay W. Forrester [1918–2016], who has inspired us to learn system dynamics on which the paradigm shift in economics presented in this book is based. The quotation is from his plenary address delivered at the 2003 International System Dynamics Conference held in New York City entitled "*Economic theory for the new millennium*" (Forrester, 2013, p. 27). A systems solution proposed in this book would not have been attainable without the scientific discipline of system dynamics pioneered by Dr. Jay Forrester.

A major problem to understanding money is that, because so much power is exercised through monetary systems, those who control the systems and receive special benefits have protected those privileges by shrouding the monetary concepts in secrecy and confusion.

These smoke screens, applied for centuries, have actually caused many of the principles of the science of money to be lost, as various arts and sciences disappeared during the dark ages. These principles are lost to the general public, and to many in the economics profession, some of whom have further confused the monetary picture [p. 3].

When society loses control over the money system, it loses whatever control it might have had over its destiny. It can no longer set priorities and the policies for achieving them. It can't solve problems, which then develop into crisis and continually mount up [p. 656].

Over time, whoever controls the money system, controls the nation.

—Stephen A. Zarlenga (2002)[2]

---

[2] Secondly this book is dedicated to Stephen A. Zarlenga [1941–2017], the founding director of the American Monetary Institute (AMI), who has carried the torch of *Monetary Reform* on the American soil. The first two quotations are from his magnum opus entitled "*The Lost Science of Money*" (Zarlenga, 2002) and the last sentence is adapted from the AMI's website. Without his unswerving vision on monetary reform and intellectual guidance on the history of money, our present book might not have seen the light of day this early.

Preface

What is economics? When Kaoru–the first author–was a freshman in college (1965), he learned in one of the lectures on economic history that the word "economics" in Japanese comes from an abbreviation of a passage from the Chinese classic, which literally means "Govern the World and Save Our People." While a doctor's mission is to save the patient, an economist must have a mission to cure the society's diseases. As an 18-year-old who knew nothing about the world, Kaoru remembers himself ruminating about the purpose of economics, saying, "To study economics is to become a social doctor as opposed to a medical doctor." And the lesson learned from that lecture has never left his mind.

More than half a century have passed since. Technologies improved our modes of production and increased productivity. And the world has become much more connected over the Internet. Yet poverty and hunger still persist globally. And many of the economic problems carried over from the twentieth century have yet to find a solution. The purpose of writing this book is to restore the original purpose of economics and help people realize that there is a prescription to fix our economy and address the major problems indicated in the subtitle of this book.

What is the prescription, then? In short it is the *monetary reform*. When the blood in our body becomes dirty and the blood flow remains stagnant, various complications and illnesses occur in our body. If pure and healthy blood (public money) are injected into the system, the blood begins to flow smoothly, cells become active and the circulatory functions will be restored. Consequently, our immune system and innate self-healing power begin to be enhanced and the symptoms will be alleviated (our economy and the society will be revitalized).

For the past 250 years, however, economics has effectively served to camouflage the legal nature of money and diminished the fourth function of money as a *means of control*. Readers may be surprised to learn that since Adam Smith, the father of economics, money has not been incorporated properly into the economic theory and analysis. When the Great Depression in the 1930s hit the world, the two leading economists at the time each proposed a remedy to rescue the economy and prevent it from happening again. They were Irving Fisher's *100% Money* (Fisher, 1935) and John M. Keynes's *General Theory* (Keynes, 1936).

Keynes's theory has become what we today call "macroeconomics" and served as the rationale of fiscal and monetary policies implemented by governments and central banks around the world. However, Fisher's theory and prescription, which called for the revival of the 100% reserve requirement on demand deposits, was deemed politically unacceptable to the Wall Street international bankers, as it would have ended their financial alchemy through their practice of fractional reserve banking. As this book will highlight, the role of commercial banks as creators of 99% of money was diminished in economics textbooks and teachings after the WWII and eventually made a *taboo* subject by the economics establishment. Consequently, the proposals of 100% reserve banking in the 1930s were largely ignored by most textbooks on the history of economic thoughts.

In fact, Kaoru has heard directly from a well-known economist in the UK that a Nobel Prize winner in economics who is still active today once advised his students to "NEVER TOUCH THE MONEY ISSUE" if they wanted to get a job at a university. And that issue is the current debt-based money system where private banks are legally allowed to make loans by creating new *fictitious* deposits out of thin air and charge interests on them. Until the Lehman shock in 2008, Kaoru had never heard of the *Chicago Plan for Banking Reform* proposed by the founders of the Chicago School of Economics in 1933, or Fisher's *100% Money*. In this sense, he was completely ignorant of the issue until he met with Stephen A. Zarlenga in 2010, who was leading monetary reform movement in the United States as the founding director of the American Monetary Institute (AMI) with his colleagues and the Congressman Dennis J. Kucinich.

Whether they are aware of this issue or not, academic economists employed by universities still do not challenge this fundamental issue. As a result, not only is mainstream economics incapable of providing a proper diagnosis of the major economic problems but its intellectual edifice has completely collapsed with the onset of the Global Financial Crisis since 2008, which was caused by the same debt-based money system again after the Great Depression of the 1930s.

Touching on this issue, Kaoru was suddenly removed from teaching economics, saying, "Your economics is biased," and unilaterally forced to leave his post as a full professor at the Business School of Doshisha University in Kyoto in the spring of 2013. This unprecedented ouster took place despite the presence of his graduate students and international government-sponsored students who were in the midst of their doctoral dissertations under his supervision.

Despite these circumstances, the results of his decades of research have continued to inspire him for scientific truth in the name of academic freedom, to brake the fear of touching the taboo of economics and eventually led him to succeed in integrating the theories of Fisher and Keynes in his new textbook titled: *Money and Macroeconomic Dynamics—Accounting System Dynamics Approach* (Yamaguchi, 2013). As a general introduction to this integrated economic theory, he then published a Japanese book titled: *Public Money: Modern Version of the Chicago Plan that Liquidates Government Debts* (Yamaguchi, 2015).

The purpose of the present book, however, is not to explain the Accounting System Dynamics (ASD) modeling method itself, but to introduce to students and general readers the findings of the new economic prescription obtained from such scientific method in as simple a manner as possible. This book therefore brings money back to the forefront of the economic science, revives the Fisher's *100% Money* based on the ASD method and proposes *Public Money System.*

After Kaoru published his books on public money, Yokei–the second author–joined the research with his background in system dynamics and fintech. And our joint research on *Electronic Public Money* (EPM) has evolved since. During these times we were particularly inspired by the vision of *Peer-to-Peer Electronic Cash System* proposed by Nakamoto (2008). Subsequent developments in blockchain and decentralization technologies allow new ways of organizing our institutions and economy on top of the EPM as a new national payment infrastructure designed to protect our privacy and freedoms at the system level.

With today's information technology and communication infrastructure, our governments can and must issue EPM as the true form of *electronic cash* against Central Bank Digital Currency (CBDC) that will lead to a total surveillance and dystopian futures. Core nodes of the new EPM payment network should be maintained and operated jointly by the government and the private sector. This will prevent an excessive concentration of power in either the government or the private sector participants, while ensuring availability and scalability of EPM as a critical national economic infrastructure. Such decentralized system architecture will also prevent EPM system from becoming another instrument of statecraft as the existing payment systems are used to impose sanctions against foreign nations and even target their own citizens to silence political dissidents.

EPM system would then enable us to introduce a new *Uniform Tax* (UT) proposed concurrently in this book, which would greatly simplify the present highly complex and inefficient tax system that suffers from various loopholes into a single, direct and fully-flat uniform tax rate that is automatically collected on every payment transactions as public service fees. This way, the privacy of individuals and businesses will be fully preserved, the inequitable system of wealth deprivation through the present porous tax system would be ended, while the role of government will radically shift from that of a powerful arbitrator in the game of market-based economic exchange to that of disinterested ticket taker, performing minimum functions such as diplomacy, defense, groundwork research in science, and maintenance of social security and public infrastructure.

This uniform tax will also free our society from the enormous costs and labor expended on administering the current national tax system. Thus, it is not only the fairest, simplest, most neutral and transparent form of taxation but also the most ideal form of tax that can fully adapt to the digital economy, while solving the problems of double taxation and tax evasion by multinational enterprises.

Therefore, both EPM and UT systems, which can be implemented in parallel with minimum cost, must be the basis of our collective effort in rebuilding an ideal system of government for the twenty-first century, where everyone can enjoy the true fruits of our freedom and prosperity in proportion to individual contributions to our collective societies.

Taking into account of our joint research in the subsequent years, we have completed the system design of EPM with the publication of our joint book titled: *Introduction to Public Money* (Yamaguchi and Yamaguchi, 2021b). However, our previous books on public money were written in Japanese and there has been no English book that explains what is public money, why we need it and how to transition from the present debt money system. This book is the first English translation that explains them with updated data and analyses.

This book turns out to be a outcome of the unexpected invitation of Kaoru to the Social Sciences University of Ankara in Turkey (2018–2022) where he taught two courses: Special Topics in Economic Dynamics (doctoral course) and Monetary Theory (masters course). We are very thankful to the faculty members of Economics Department for this opportunity. Graduate students who participated in Kaoru's lectures were from the government offices, Turkish Central Bank, public and private organizations and international graduate students from Middle Eastern countries.

During this period, Kaoru also participated in the TUBITAK Project for constructing a Turkish ASD macroeconomic model directed by Dr. Syed F. Mahmud (Economics Department), together with Yokei as an external research collaborator. Earnest weekly discussions with the project members as well as graduate students have been reflected into the contents of this book, for which we are very thankful. We are now convinced that the public money system is also fully compatible with the principle of Islamic banking and Sharia-compliant finance, which forbids usury, and that it would rather start being practiced from these Islamic nations.

Your feedbacks are most welcome. If you are in a position to teach, we would be happy to jointly explore how to incorporate the "paradigm shift" discussed in this book into your curriculum. It is by unchaining ourselves from the wheel of endless debt that our world can aspire to higher levels of social evolution. Thus, educating the next generation is the key and the most effective leverage point to break the cycle of debt bondage, to redirect economics for the better, and to unleash our full potential as one human race.

Finally, it is our great pleasure if this book serves as an introduction to public money and as a catalyst for the paradigm shift in *economics as systems science*, because both of them would be necessary to build mutual understanding, move beyond the current divisiveness, and bring peace and unity in our life on earth.

Awaji Island, Japan
June 2024

Kaoru Yamaguchi, Ph.D.
Yokei Yamaguchi, M.Phil., M.Sci.

Contents

About the Authors

Kaoru Yamaguchi Ph.D. in Economics, University of California, Berkeley, 1985. Director at the Japan Futures Research Center. Former Professor at the Graduate School of Social Sciences University of Ankara, Turkey (2018–2022). He held academic posts at California State University, Hayward, University of San Francisco, University of Hawaii, Manoa, then in Japan at Osaka Sangyo University, and Doshisha University (Business School) in Kyoto. He was a visiting scholar at Sloan School of Management, MIT (1998, 1999), Hawaii Futures Research Center, University of Hawaii (2001), Haas School of Business, University of California, Berkeley (2003), and Victoria Management School, Victoria University of Wellington, New Zealand (2009). He was invited to present MuRatopia economy in China (1988), Russia (1998), etc., and to the System Dynamics Macroeconomic Workshop in Ankara (2015), then to the Turkish TUBITAK project of developing Turkish macroeconomic model (2017–2019). He has served as the president of Economics Chapter of the System Dynamics Society (2008), and received Advancement of Monetary Science and Reform Award from the American Monetary Institute (2010).

Yokei Yamaguchi M.Phil., M.Sci., Erasmus Mundus Joint Masters in System Dynamics, 2017 (University of Bergen, Norway, University of Palermo, Italy, and Radboud University, the Netherlands). He has previously worked as a director of the Institute of Money and Economic Systems at Soramitsu–a Japanese fintech company specialized in blockchain-based solutions and decentralized applications. He has publications in peer-reviewed academic journals and books. As a researcher at Japan Futures Research Center, he is currently leading the development of Accounting System Dynamics (ASD) macroeconomic models and Electronic Public Money (EPM) system proposed in this book.

List of Figures

List of Tables

Chapter 1
Introduction

> The "100% Money" proposal–to raise reserve requirements against checking deposits from 10%, or thereabouts, to 100%–may at first seem startling. But it is an historical fact that, in the earliest days of deposit banking, a 100% reserve was required.
>
> The revival now of this ancient 100% system, with the readjustments demanded by modern conditions, would effectually restrain the monetary inflation and deflation incident to our present system; that is, would actually stop the irresponsible creation and destruction of circulating medium by our thousands of commercial banks, which now act like so many private mints. For these and other reasons, the 100% system would be a great boon, even to bankers.
>
> — Irving Fisher, *100% Money* (1935), Preface to First edition.

Hello Mr. Lincoln

In proposing the Public Money, we may begin by sharing the Kaoru's personal anecdote related to Abraham Lincoln, the 16th President of the United States of America. It was around 1979 when he was a PhD student at the University of California, Berkeley. One day on the campus, a stranger suddenly said to him, "You look a lot like President Lincoln." Several years later, after a concert at the San Francisco Civic Center, a stranger suddenly approached him near the exit and said, "You look just like President Lincoln," again from a stranger. Kaoru knew that President Lincoln was assassinated at Ford's Theatre in Washington D.C. So he just thought that the stranger, knowing it or not, was simply joking to him as if to say "You are lucky to be alive." Since it was the second time, as soon as he returned to the International House in Berkeley, he took out a five-dollar note and compared it with himself in front of a mirror. Figure 1.1 is a portrait of President Lincoln engraved on the five-dollar bill.

Kaoru did grow a beard at that time. But other than that, there was any resemblance between the two. His knowledge of Lincoln at that time was also limited to what he was taught in high school, that he was a great leader who led the Union Army to victory in the Civil War and freed the slaves in the South.

K. Yamaguchi and Y. Yamaguchi, *Public Money*,
https://doi.org/10.1007/978-981-97-6564-5_1

Fig. 1.1 President lincoln on $5 bill–federal reserve note

In 1985, Kaoru was finishing his doctoral dissertation in economics and was staying at a hotel in New York City for a college job interview that was being held simultaneously at the site of American Economic Association (AEA) conference. One afternoon, just as he jumped on the hotel elevator, a stranger suddenly called out to him, "Hello Mr. Lincoln." The third time happened. Of course Kaoru still remembers joking back, "I don't want to be assassinated yet."

Because of these experiences, Kaoru gradually developed a personal affinity for President Lincoln and began researching his life. He eventually come to learn that Lincoln did not fight to free the slaves in the South, as he had been taught in high school; that Lincoln fought for the unification of the United States to keep the constitutional republic against those who sought to divide it and weaken its economic power; and that in order to finance the war effort, Lincoln rejected the loan sharking by bankers and financiers, and instead issued the interest-free government money in the form of Greenbacks.

The victory achieved by the issuance of legal tender notes (greenbacks) is said to have triggered Lincoln's assassination on April 14, 1865. Many Americans still call dollars as "bucks." We do not know why people started calling them that way. However, we cannot help but to think that they started calling them "bucks" out of nostalgia for the national currency that saved the USA, and in memory of the President who had successfully led the war, by superimposing "bucks" on the "back" of the greenbacks, which were printed in green.

About a decade ago, at a high school reunion that Kaoru had not attended in many years, a charming woman (classmate) with a good aesthetic sense suddenly approached him with a glass of wine in her hand and whispered something completely unexpected into his ear. "I have an artistic sense," she said, "and good at getting people's impressions. Your impression is just like that of President Lincoln." Kaoru was so surprised that he almost dropped his beer glass. This time she was a Japanese. Kaoru wondered why, since he was already thinning and his beard was turning white. Since then, he began to joke in conferences that "If President Lincoln were alive today, he would probably look like me."

Fig. 1.2 President lincoln on $5 bill–United States note

Following the Lincoln's lead, the 35th President John F. Kennedy issued the Executive Order 11110 on June 4, 1963 to issue a similar government-issued money, almost 100 years later. Figure 1.2 shows the five-dollar note issued in 1963. At first glance, this five-dollar note appears almost identical to the five-dollar note in Fig. 1.1 with President Lincoln on the front and the Lincoln Memorial on the back. However, there is one difference: FEDERAL RESERVE NOTE at the top has been replaced by UNITED STATES NOTE.[1] About six months later, President Kennedy was shot to death in Dallas, Texas, on November 22.

Kaoru was a high school student when JFK was assassinated. And he still remembers the shock of the event. It was the day when Japan and the US conducted the world's first experiment in satellite broadcasting. Sadly, the very first news that arrived from the US was the news about President Kennedy. Since then rumors persist that one of the reasons for the assassination was the issuance of these interest-free legal tender notes. After the death of President Kennedy, these United States Notes were largely taken out of circulation, while Federal Reserve Notes continued to serve as legal tender of the United States.

Is there a direct causality between the issuance of interest-free government currency and assassinations of the US presidents? After being called "Hello Mr. Lincoln"

---

[1] The overall design of five-dollar US Note shown in Fig. 1.2 followed a similar design from the earlier US Notes series 1928 and 1953. Although the 1928 series originally had a red seal of the Treasury, the US Notes series 1953A (Silver certificates, public money) had a Treasury seal in blue and 1953B (legal tender, public money) had a red Treasury seal, while $5 Federal Reserve Notes (legal tender, debt money) that were circulating at the time had Treasury seals and serial numbers all in green. Similarly, the only noticeable difference between the US and Fed Notes issued in 1963 was the color of the seals. The Federal Reserve Notes issued in 1963 (Fig. 1.1) after President Johnson succeeded JFK had a Treasury seal and serial numbers both in green, a signature of the Secretary of the Treasury (Henry H. Fowler) as well as a district seal of respective Federal Reserve Banks on the left, while the United States Note issued in 1963 (Fig. 1.2) had a seal of the Treasury and serial numbers both in red, a signature of the Secretary of the Treasury (Clarence Douglas Dillon) on the right, and a signature of the Treasurer (Kathryn O'Hay Granahan) on the left. By the way, Federal Reserve Note in Fig. 1.1 is a "star note." The star suffix attached after the serial number is used to identify notes that serve as replacements during the production process. Image source: Author's possession.

three times by strangers in the US and once by his Japanese high school classmate, Kaoru felt strange and became curious at the connection between the two. Why should a president elected by the people be assassinated simply by replacing "FEDERAL RESERVE" with "UNITED STATES"? Is not the Federal Reserve a government institution? Why doesn't the US government let its own Bureau of Printing and Engraving create its currency as UNITED STATES NOTES, but instead borrows from the Federal Reserve and commercial banks in the form of treasury securities at interests? What would happen if the lettering "NIPPON GINKO" (Bank of Japan) on the 1000-yen banknote were replaced with "NIPPON" (Japan) without changing the overall design at all? Would Japanese Prime Ministers suffer the same fate as Lincoln and Kennedy?

These simple questions about money kept coming up one after another. However, none of the economics textbooks that he has looked at clarified these questions. When Kaoru was forced to leave from teaching, one of his graduate students told him, "Mr. Lincoln of Japan was *academically* assassinated!"

Fisher's 100% Money (1935) and Tabooed Economics

16 years after the 28th President Woodrow Wilson signed the Federal Reserve Act in 1913, the New York stock market crashed in October 1929. This led to a financial panic and plunged the US economy from the Roaring Twenties to a depression. The stock market continued to fall through 1932, when the Dow fell approximately 90% from its peak and reached below 42 dollars. The market crash caused fear and uncertainty among investors and transmitted to the real economy as consumers lost their life savings. Businesses slowed production and furloughed workers. National income, tax revenues and prices all fell.

The Great Depression of the 1930s also plunged the world into an unprecedented downturn, and is said to have reduced international trade by more than 50%. Unemployment rate in the US peaked at over 20% around 1933. The Depression also affected Japan, plunging the country's economy into a state of crisis and caused the most severe depression in the prewar Japan.

The Great Depression occurred when neoclassical economics and Marxian economics, which had given birth to the Soviet Union in 1917, were in conflict. However, the economic reality brought about by the Great Depression radically undermined the teachings of (neo)classical economics up to that point. Specifically, it was proven that the economy was not equipped with any self-regulating ability of the market by the God's invisible hand and exposed it to be a complete fiction.

Ironically, this incident left the world with only one option: socialism and communism based on Marxian theories (Marxism). Fearing the possibility of the communization of America, and in an attempt to prevent the Depression from happening again, the two leading economists at the time each proposed a remedy in the same year of 1935: the Irving Fisher's *100% Money* (Fisher, 1935) and John M. Keynes's *General Theory* (Keynes, 1936).[2]

Fisher's *100% Money* proposal was not radical and designed to achieve the maximum effect with minimal change in the banking system through seamless transition. Yet it was deemed *politically* unacceptable to the Wall Street international bankers and was successfully replaced by the more lax Banking Act of 1933, commonly referred to as the Glass-Steagall Act. The details of monetary reform programs proposed in the 1930s will be explained in the succeeding chapters (Chap. 9 in particular). In essence what they all shared in common was to (1) raise the legally required reserve ratio on checking deposits to 100%, and (2) authorize and direct "Currency Commission" *á la* Fisher (1935) to provide interest-free government currency, and to use those money to redeem treasury securities held by the Federal Reserve Banks and replace their Federal Reserve Notes, which had only been in circulation for about 20 years at the time.

Requiring a 100% reserve ratio on demand deposits would have ended the fractional reserve banking, under which commercial banks finance new loans by creating new "deposits" out of nothing. Accordingly, banks will become genuine intermediaries of existing funds between savers and borrowers in the economy, thus greatly increasing resiliency, safety and stability of the financial system. In Chap. 3 we will explain how banks lend money they do not possess and the legal mechanism behind such *sleight of hand* perpetrated against the public.

The second arrangement would have replaced all *debt money* (such as Federal Reserve Notes) with interest-free *public money* (such as United States Notes) and made all bank deposits backed by the legal tender. Much of our national debts would have been liquidated as a byproduct during the system transition, freeing nations from financial servitudes imposed by compounding interests on public debts, which are collected through income and other federal taxes.[3]

The Glass-Steagall Act instead established the Federal Deposit Insurance Corporation (FDIC) and separated the banking business from the securities business. This Banking Act, to all intents and purposes, kept the American economy from experiencing a major financial panic, and the economy progressed steadily thereafter until the Clinton administration repealed the act in 1999.

And the History Repeated Itself

Keynes's *General Theory*, on the other hand, analyzed that the lack of demand caused the Depression based on disequilibrium analysis, which was a completely new approach compared to the dominant (neo)classical thinking. In essence, Keynes

---

[2] The General Theory was published in 1936. Its preface, however, was drafted on December 13, 1935, while Fisher's 100% Money (first edition) was published in 1935. Therefore the two leading economic thinkers at the time wrote their books in the same year coincidentally.

[3] Let it be reminded that US federal income tax was introduced in 1913, the same year as the Federal Reserve Act was passed. Whether this was a coincidence is an open question.

proposed the importance of government's fiscal stimulus as a countercyclical policy in times of recession. Keynes's theory soon replaced (neo)classical economics and served as the rationale of fiscal and monetary policies.

In the 1970s, however, a phenomenon called stagflation emerged, in which inflation and recession progressed simultaneously. As a result, Keynesian theory was also considered to have reached its limits and anti-Keynesian revolutions (such as monetarism led by Milton Friedman) began to take hold. And the Glass-Steagall Act was repealed in the midst of these battles in economics.

On the political front, the globalization was on the rise. Kaoru studied mathematical economics at Berkeley in the early 1980s, just as Keynesian theory was declining and neoclassical theory was making a comeback. In other words, the world entered an era of *market fundamentalism*, accompanied by deregulation of the financial sector also known as the financial Big Bang. Thus, by the 2000s, neoclassical economics regained its dominance over the Keynesian economics.

In terms of economics, at this point, the same situation that existed prior to the Great Depression had re-emerged. As a result, the history repeated itself on September 15, 2008 when the Lehman Brothers bankruptcy triggered a global financial crisis. The 2008 crisis should be referred to as the Second Great Depression because it was repeated with the same underlying cause as the Depression of the 1930s. If we call it a "financial crisis" this time and use a different name from the Great Depression, it will create the impression that the two events occurred through different mechanisms.

In this way, the Second Great Depression once again knocked out neoclassical economics, or so it seemed. Economists have begun to return to the old neoclassical economics, as if the proverb says, "Danger past, God forgotten." This phenomenon was ironically expressed in a book published by Quiggin (2012) titled "*Zombie Economics*". When the world was hit by the First Great Depression in the 1930s, there was an alternative theory of Marxian economics. Since then, however, socialist countries and the Soviet Union disappeared one after another in the 1990s and Keynesian economics were losing its influence.

Thus, after the Lehman Shock, a complete academic vacuum emerged in economics with no alternative theory. After the First Great Depression, two economic reform policies were proposed as mentioned earlier. This time, however, since no such reform proposals have been put forward by economists, *i.e.*, no alternative economics has been proposed, economists have begun to fill this vacuum by resurrecting the once-dead zombie of neoclassical economics. Therefore, to stop this resurgence and to prevent the next Third Great Depression, "it is necessary to provide an alternative to zombie economics of market liberalism" (Quiggin 2012, p.240). Will economics succeed in doing so this time?

The Birth and Proposal of Public Money System

Figure 1.3 illustrates these history of battles in economic thoughts. In 2003 Kaoru came up with an integrated analytical method that combines the theoretical and methodological foundations of social and natural sciences and systematized it as a new modeling framework under the concept of "Accounting System Dynamics

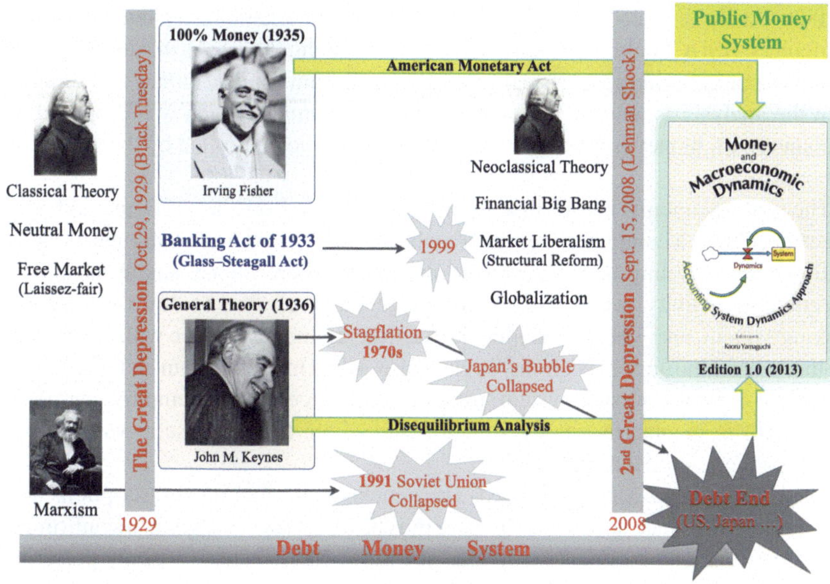

Fig. 1.3 Debt money system and the birth of public money system

(ASD)" (Yamaguchi, 2003). Although it was originally conceived as an integrated modeling method for corporate business strategy and financial analysis, Kaoru soon realized that if the method is effective for corporate financial modeling, it should also be effective for macroeconomic modeling of a country as an aggregate of micro-level economic agents.[4]

At that time, he was deeply disappointed with economics, especially the methodology of mathematical economics that had wandered into the world of abstraction, and had determined never to return to the field after finishing his graduate studies at Berkeley (see Chap. 9). However, the fact that he established the ASD method somehow became an self-encouragement to him and breathed life back into his economics research. From there, Kaoru began a series of macroeconomic modeling step-by-step (Yamaguchi, 2004b, 2005, 2006, 2007) and completed it in the summer

[4] Using the Accounting System Dynamics modeling framework, students above K-12 can easily visualize and understand the accounting system in a unified manner by using the stock-flow concept of system dynamics. Needless to say, an accounting system is a recording technique based on the principles of double-entry bookkeeping to calculate profit and loss accruing as a result of various transactions. It is a basic yet most systematically completed theory in the *social sciences*, which has stood the test of time since the merchants of Venice in medieval Italy. System dynamics, on the other hand, is a methodology for numerically solving differential equations by computer, which began in the 17th century with Newtonian mechanics as a fundamental theory of dynamics in the *natural sciences*. All economic transactions are analyzed based on double-entry bookkeeping principle, and macroeconomic activity as a totality of these transactions cannot be captured without regard to it. Thus, the ASD framework provides the most robust and reliable analytical foundation for economic simulation analysis.

of 2008 with the open economy model reported at the International System Dynamics Conference (ISDC) held in Athens, Greece (Yamaguchi, 2008). As discussed in Part II of this book, in the neoclassical general equilibrium model, money is excluded from the analysis as neutral, and in Keynesian economics, which was proposed as its counterpart, money is given as an exogenous variable controlled by the monetary authority.

The open economy model that he developed based on the ASD method was constructed from a completely new approach that differed from conventional models; it allows for modeling that is grounded in reality, where money sits at the center of economic activity, where money is endogenously created or destroyed by the banking system, and where economic transactions cannot take place without money. In other words, the current economy is viewed as a debt money system and it becomes possible to analyze how such system structure causes recessions, unemployment, debt crises, built-in income inequality, inflation and so on. In this sense it was the first macroeconomic model of its kind.

Then, the Lehman Shock occurred. The neoclassical economic prescriptions that came back to life since around 1980s were thus beaten back once again, reconfirming that the current debt money system does not work. Nevertheless, the only prescription that was left with to escape from the shipwreck was to rely on the traditional fiscal and monetary policies based on Keynesian theory. In other words, the western governments mobilized fiscal stimulus. Yet the effects on the real economy were disappointing and the government debt surged.

Conversely, if the government cut spending to avoid the debt ceiling or raised taxes in an effort to keep the public debt in check, the economy would fall off a cliff. Ben Bernake, chairman of the Federal Reserve at the time, used the term "fiscal cliff" to warn of its potentially serious negative impact not only on the US but also on the global economy. Therefore, following Japan's experiment after the burst of the bubble in the 1990s (detailed in Chap. 4), quantitative easing (QE) policies were adopted by the Federal Reserve and European Central Banks as the last resort to absorb the ballooning debts. Under the present system the only way to keep the business going is to continue to increase someone's debts.

Faced with the situation, Kaoru started simulation analysis of the government debt crisis and presented his results at the ISDC in Seoul in 2010 (Yamaguchi, 2010) and then in Washington DC in 2011 (Yamaguchi, 2011). During these periods, Kaoru has struggled in the search for a cure to avoid the next crisis and succeeded in integrating the Fisher's *100% Money* and Keynes's *General Theory* based on the ASD modeling method. In particular, his research findings presented in Washington DC showed that transition to public money system would allow governments to pay down their debt without causing a fiscal cliff recession, unemployment, wage reduction, inflation or contagious recessions.

The series of ASD macroeconomic modeling was later published as a new textbook titled: *Money and Macroeconomic Dynamics–Accounting System Dynamics*

Approach (Yamaguchi, 2013).[5] Based on these results, Kaoru proposed an alternative system of public money designed to overcome the inherent problems of the debt money system, which have caused the First and Second Great Depressions. In essence, public money solution was proposed as the alternative to the flawed mainstream economic policies applied under the present debt money system.

Neoclassical Economics As the Ideology of Globalism

Let's take a closer look at the situation from the 1980s onward, when neoclassical economics came back to life. Under the slogan of deregulation and privatization, the wave of globalization gained its momentum and has fundamentally transformed the structure of our economy, not only in the financial sector, but also in water, food, agriculture, education, medicine, health care, postal services, local governments, military, and the list goes on. Industries and markets have since become increasingly concentrated into the hands of multinational enterprises.

According to one study on the global network of corporate shareholders (Vitali et al., 2011) , which will be discussed in Chap. 10, 146 firms (0.02%) among 43,060 transnational corporations (TNC) controlled 40% of total TNC operating revenues and 737 firms (0.123%) controlled a whopping 80%. Yet not one of these well-known TNCs were among the list of top 50 control holders.

Who controls the global economy, then? Surprisingly or unsurprisingly, all of the top 25 control holders were the international big banks and financial institutions, who have caused the Second Great Depression themselves after the repeal of the Glass-Steagall Act allowed them to structure and speculate on mortgage-backed securities. Yet the Federal Reserve Banks, whose shares were held by none other than these *too-big-to-fail* banks, stepped in and provided trillions of dollars with a flick of a keyboard, while letting some institutions go bankrupt like controlled demolition of buildings.

These group of international banking syndicate nestled in the core of the "network of global corporate control" in turn hold the shares of the rest of non-financial TNCs. And collectively, they are in a position to exert great decision-making power over the global economy through their fraudulent scheme that allow these private banks to create fictitious "deposit" out of thin air with a flick of a keyboard. Imagine a Monopoly game where one player (bankers) can print money, dictating the rules while others play by their standards. This reflects our real-world financial system where a few hold immense power over the economy, and the rest of society simply play along. This is the nature of financial oligopoly facing the world today.

[5] In response to the limitations identified in Dynamic Stochastic General Equilibrium (DSGE) models grounded on the general equilibrium theory (discussed in Sect. 9.2 in Chap. 9), alternative modeling approaches have gained renewed attention such as Agent-based (AB), Stock-Flow Consistent (SFC) and System Dynamics (SD) modelings. From the ASD modeling perspective, the term "stock-flow consistent" is redundant as accounting is a system of bookkeeping that captures both stock and flow variables by construction. See Yamaguchi and Yamaguchi (2021a) for a brief discussion of the similarities and differences between AB, SFC, and ASD modeling approaches.

The outcome is ever increasing inequality between the rich and poor, and extreme concentration of wealth and power into the hands of private shareholders who ultimately control these international banks. This is what the neoclassical ideology of market fundamentalism has brought on us. When we analyze the current situation in this way, it also becomes clear that the economic problems facing our world today are no longer problems that can be alleviated at the classical microeconomic level such as price mechanism, free competition, etc.

How can we end this cycle of trillion-dollar bailouts and make money and finance work for the rest of the society? Since these problems are the symptoms of a deeper systemic failure, they can be solved only by eliminating the root cause of the problems; the debt money system.

Total Failures of Keynesian and Neoclassical Economics

Japan was no exception to this wave of Globalism promoted by international bankers and financiers. Japanese companies achieved remarkable growths during the postwar period and led the world in many fields by 1980s, especially in manufacturing industries such as machineries, automobiles and semiconductors. However, after the burst of the bubble in the early 1990s, the economy has not recovered as expected for the next 30 years despite the bold implementation of all economic policies suggested by the mainstream economics.

Structural reform based on neoclassical economics has encouraged cheap labor policies and increased the number of low-wage, non-regular workers, while fiscal and monetary policies based on Keynesian economics gave rise to the national debt hell of over 1,000 trillion yen. In other words, theoretical flaws of the mainstream economics were brought to light again. This time in Japan.

The collapse of the bubble caused bankruptcies of local credit unions and banks serving small and medium-sized enterprises. A series of mergers among major city banks have greatly changed the structure of financial system that was decentralized and the backbone of Japan's industrial complexity and the source of international competitiveness. In the meantime, concentration of industries and markets have progressed. Through various deregulations, shares of Japanese blue-chip companies, which had been held by domestic sectors, were acquired by foreign financial institutions after the burst of the bubble.[6]

As a result, many of Japan's leading companies and banks are now incorporated into the network of global corporate control. Thus, Japan's highly successful economic model, which had taken the world by surprise, was also successfully broken down by the structural reform of neoclassical ideology. And Japanese people are now suffering from the fallout of decades-long stagnation.

In our previous book (Yamaguchi and Yamaguchi, 2021b), we estimated that the Japanese government debt will reach 1,674 trillion yen in 2036 and its debt-to-GDP ratio, currently the world's worst at 234% as of 2019, will reach a level exceeding 300% or, to be exact, three years' worth of its nominal GDP. In 2050 the government

[6] See Fig. 11.5 for changes in foreign sector's ownership of Japanese equities.

debts will be at 2,193 trillion yen and its debt-to-GDP ratio will reach 400% as detailed in Chap. 6 of this book. If this situation continues, Japan will face one of three catastrophic scenarios: (1) systemic banking crisis (financial meltdown), (2) monetary crisis (hyperinflation), or (3) government default (sovereign debt crisis). Any of the above scenario will have serious consequences on the domestic economy and the global supply chain.

Pandemic, Wars ... Is the World Prepared for the Next Crisis?

Looking at other OECD countries, although their national debts are not as severe as in Japan yet, their economic growths have slowed down, the aging society are accelerating and income disparities are widening. In the mean time, the coronavirus (SARS-CoV-2) reported in 2019 in Wuhan, China, quickly spread the world. And the WHO declared the public health emergency of international concern (PHEIC) on January 2020 and global "pandemic" on March following the explosion of positive PCR-test cases. Governments around the world took drastic measures in response, causing demand and supply economic shocks.

Supply chain disruption and surge in energy prices caused rampant inflation while the global economy has not fully recovered from the fallout of the Second Great Depression (global financial crisis) since 2008. Even before the pandemic, there was a growing concern that other nations would get trapped into a similar situation as in Japan–a phenomenon called "Japanification" or "Japanization."

With the collapse of Chinese real estate bubble, the socialist market economy, which is said to be the only example of Marxism that has successfully cohabited with capitalism, is now experiencing the same symptoms as post-bubble Japan with low growth, deflation, population decline and public debt crisis. Chinese bubble was also the result of the debt money system. That is why the disease and its symptoms are similar. Together with on-going trade conflict with the US, uncertainty in global supply chain is increasing, and the ballooning debts, both in private and public sectors, are reaching levels unprecedented in history.

These economic factors, entangled with international conflicts that have deepened due to the genocides in Ukraine and Palestine, are inducing structural reconfiguration in the geopolitical system of the postwar era. Since the abolishment of unilateral convertibility of the Dollar with gold in 1971, the US government has been similarly increasing its debt and now facing debt crisis. As our systems analysis in Chap. 6 indicates, the US is likely to be in an even more serious *debt hell* than Japan. While the US dollar still maintains its dominance in international trades and financial transactions, if the debt problem is not addressed now, sooner or later, the loss of confidence in the currency will accelerate the on-going shift away from the US dollar as the international reserve currency, giving rise to a whole range of issues that undermines the economy and American way of life.

National Debt Clocks are Ticking

When we analyze the current situation more closely, the Japanese government is also the world's largest holder of the US Treasuries. In other words, the US and Japan, which are the first and third largest economies that have maintained close trade relationship and military alliance, are carrying the world's biggest *time bombs* in the form of national debts. To make the situation worse and unsettling, our analysis also indicates that it is impossible, by design, to stop the hands of the debt clocks, let alone reversing the situation by turning them back. Indeed the world economy as of 2024 is gradually heading towards *debt end* and beginning to look like an eve of another *Third Great Depression*.

An inevitable collapse of the dollar, which would likely induce a simultaneous collapse of the Yen, will have devastating impacts on the global economy, financial system and international order. The endless wars since WWII instigated by the military-industrial-congressional complex have taken countless innocent lives and now become a quagmire. The Washington Consensus has lost its credibility and the global hegemony with the US as a main vehicle of neoimperialism is now reaching its capacity. With the exchange of violence, social destruction and the resulting cycle of hatred, the world is still in the midst of deep unrest.

The fiscal and monetary policies proposed by mainstream economics have all failed and economists are now feeling as helpless as a doctor who cannot come up with any prescription for a terminally ill patient. However, just as it is a doctor's mission to save the patient, economists have a mission to identify the root cause of the society's diseases in order to cure them properly.

What is the prescription, then? In short, it is the *monetary reform*. The only solution that will end national debts, banking crises and built-in inequality and inflation is to (1) transition from the debt money system, which is at the base of current global power that is depriving people of their freedom and destroying national sovereignties, into the public money system, and (2) establish the MuRatopia economy out of the present Globalism, immediately. The purpose of this book is to unravel the root cause of these economic problems and to present the solution with a focus on the Japanese and US economies. Hence, the keywords of this book are: Public Money *vis-à-vis* Debt Money, and MuRatopia *vis-à-vis* Globalism.

Public money restores the power of issuing currency under legislative control, reestablishing a system of government of the people, by the people, and for the people. MuRatopia economy liberates workers from the control of Globalism, restores freedom and democracy at their workplaces and brings back prosperity for all nations. However, our previous books on public money was available only in Japanese and there has been no English book that explains what is public money, why we need it and how to make the system transition. This book explains them all. If these messages resonate with you, then this book is for you. Please start reading and begin your own journey towards *MuRatopia*.

Structure of the Book

Part I Evidence

Chapter 2. In the Beginning was Definition of Money

This book starts with the precise definition and classification of money. Obverse definition is discussed in terms of who issues money, according to which different types of money is classified as *public money* issued without interest and *debt money* issued at interest. Next, reverse definition is introduced in terms of legal status, according to which money is classified as *legal tender* (currency) enacted by law and as *functional money* that can function as currency only during normal times. Then, examples of public money in the Eastern and Western history are briefly explained. In this way our journey begins with an overview of how public money was taken over by debt money along the course of the long history of money.

Chapter 3. 99% of Your Money is Someone's Debt

The world economy is currently operating under the debt money system. This chapter first focuses on the composition of money in the present day. Specifically, monetary data from Japan and the US are examined according to our definition of money. Then, it is shown that total money stock in Japan and the US are approximately equal to total debts of non-banking sectors such as households, firms and the government. That is, 99% of your money is someone's debt. To understand the structure of the debt money system, the legal mechanism of fractional reserve banking is analyzed. Finally, surprising findings from our monetary decomposition analyses in Japan and the US are presented. Specifically, private debts end up with time deposits (savings) while government debts supply M_1.

Chapter 4. Debt Money System is Design Failure–Lessons of Japan's Lost 30 Years

Since the burst of the bubble in the early 1990s, Japan has been suffering from stagnation with almost zero economic growth–a phenomenon called the *Lost 30 years*. By briefly reviewing its postwar economic history, this chapter analyzes the root cause of Japan's decade-long stagnation based on the findings obtained in Chap. 3. While the Japanese case tends to be viewed as a special case with the world's fastest aging society and a declining birthrate, it was the result of honest implementation of prescriptions suggested by the mainstream economics. Taking Japan as a case study, this chapter provides analyses of what we think is the reason behind its economic struggle and draws a lesson that the debt money system is a design failure. Ironically the lesson from Japan turned out to be the same lesson that was once learned by the American economists during the Great Depression but later made a taboo subject and gradually forgotten.

Part II Analysis

Chapter 5. Collapse of the Mainstream Economics

To bring the economy back from the post-bubble recession the Japanese Government and policy makers at the Bank of Japan have implemented structural reforms of neoclassical economics, and monetary and fiscal policies suggested by Keynesian economics. However, all of them failed to revitalize the economy. In this chapter we will examine what went wrong with them one by one. Our analysis reveals that these policy failures are deeply related with the flawed view of mainstream economics that money is exogenously supplied by the monetary authority. For countries whose economies are currently on a growth path or in the midst of post-bubble recession, the Japanese case provides a crucial lesson about what would happen if the policies of mainstream economics are blindly applied.

Chapter 6. Debt Money System is Debt End

Under the debt money system our government is destined to accumulate debts to maintain the nation's money supply. This chapter analyzes how serious government debts are in Japan and the US, then poses a question: What would happen if our government continues to accumulate more debts? By applying systems thinking, we will discuss three devastating scenarios that Japan may face, that is, financial meltdown, hyperinflation and government default. These scenarios may also apply to other OECD countries with heavy debt burdens; It is concluded that current debt money system is indeed "debt-end" due to its system design failure.

Chapter 7. Paradigm Shift in Macroeconomics

Concerning the causes of the Great Depression, the two opposing hypotheses have been presented and discussed by mainstream economists; deficiency of effective demand by John M. Keynes and monetary contraction by Milton Friedman. Using the standard IS-LM model, Professor Mankiw accepts the Keynes's view called *spending hypothesis* in one of his popular textbooks, while rejecting the Friedman's proposition called *money hypothesis*. In this chapter we will first examine both hypotheses based on the endogenous money IS-LM model and discuss that Mankiw (2016) drew a wrong conclusion as a result of his own misinterpretation of Fisher's debt-deflation theory. We then analyze that the failures of Keynesian economics are due to the flawed assumption of the IS-LM model itself that money is exogenously supplied by the monetary authority. Furthermore, the endogenous money IS-LM model can explain the cases of the Great Depression and Japan's Lost 30 Years under the *endogenous money spending hypothesis*, which turns our to be consistent with Fisher's original analysis (Fisher, 1933, 1935). Our model suggests that Japan can recover from the stagnation by transitioning to the public money system and implementing policies that stimulate private investment instead of blindingly increasing fiscal expenditures through national debts. These new insights obtained in this chapter serve as a paradigm shift in macroeconomics, and become the rationale of our policy recommendations presented in Part III.

Chapter 8. Mathematical Analysis of the Paradigm Shift

The purpose of this chapter is to present the paradigm shift model discussed diagrammatically in Chap. 7 with mathematical equations and develop the corresponding System Dynamics (SD) and Accounting System Dynamics (ASD) models. First, our simulations show that both spending and money hypotheses fail to explain the Great Depression under the exogenous money IS-LM model.

This has led us to revisit the Fisher's debt-deflation and 100% Money theories and build the endogenous money IS-LM model by introducing the *endogenous money spending hypothesis*. The endogenous money IS-LM model thus developed can explain the Great Depression as well as Japan's Lost 30 Years in a manner consistent with data. The revised model is robust enough to capture the above two historical cases, making it suitable for the paradigm shift model.

Chapter 9. There Exist Only Four Monetary Theories

Monetary theory seems to be complicated and diverse at first glance. According to our classification, it turned out that there are only four monetary theories: (1) public money theory, (2) mainstream neoclassical theory, (3) mainstream Keynesian theory and (4) endogenous debt money theory. Mainstream neoclassical theory has served to support the market fundamentalist policies of deregulation and privatization in practice. Mainstream Keynesian theory, which is embraced by standard economics textbooks, assumes that the supply of money is exogenously controlled by the central bank and banks are merely financial intermediaries between savers and borrowers. Yet Keynesian models based on this theory failed to explain the cases of the Great Depression and Japan's Lost 30 Years, demonstrating that this theory is fundamentally flawed. On the other hand, the endogenous debt money theory reflects the role of banks as creators of money and conforms with the economic reality. The Chicago Plan, Fisher's 100% Money and other monetary reform proposals are based on this theory, which brings us to the public money theory. Out of four monetary theories thus examined, only two theories have survived; public money theory and debt money theory. Which one would readers support?

Chapter 10. Debt Money As a Means of Control

Accordingly we are left with two choices: public money vs. debt money. Before discussing the solution in Part III, identifying the stakeholders and mechanism of Globalism is crucial. Hence, this chapter focuses on the fourth function of money as a *means of control*, which is overlooked by the standard economics textbooks. The driving force of control is the power of exponential growth applied to the collection of compound interest on loans. Specifically, the law of doubling time is explained with numerical examples. Then, by applying systems thinking, two feedback loops of control are identified: (1) outer loop of control exercised through compound interest under the debt money system, and (2) inner loop of control through equity ownership of the capitalist system. Based on this institutional framework, the inner loop of control is further analyzed based on the study on the "Network of Global Corporate Control." The reality emerges where a handful of international banks exert a disproportionate control over the global economy through equity ownerships and interlocking directorates. Power structure analysis developed in this chapter highlights the root cause of the merger of corporate and state power (Globalism) and forms the basis of our solution presented in Part III.

Chapter 11. MMT Hides System Design Failures of Debt Money

The global financial crisis has discredited the mainstream monetary theories and left a gaping hole in the field of economics. The fiscal expansion to counteract the post-bubble recession increased debts further and forced governments to turn to fiscal austerity. The root cause of growing inequality and social distress may be that the austerity policy promoted by mainstream economics has been fundamentally wrong. Driven by such doubts and dissatisfaction with existing monetary theories, Modern Money Theory (MMT) has recently attracted attention as if it is the alternative theory that can break through and overcome the failures of monetary and fiscal policies by mainstream theories. In this chapter we will point out the falsity of MMT by grouping its falsehoods into seven themes. Our analysis reveals the deceptive nature of MMT as if it were a propaganda devised to conceal the system design failures of debt money.

Part III Solution

Chapter 12. Transition to Public Money System

Debt money system has design failures. Therefore, unless the system structure is fixed, we will continue to suffer from national debt, banking crisis, built-in unfair income distribution and inflation. Transition to the public money system will eliminate these problems from the ground up. Moreover, the transition is easy once the political will is firmly established. This chapter describes the process of transition from the current debt money system. First, we explain three goals of transition and then outline the seven-step transition process based on macroeconomic balance sheet of the Japanese economy as an example. We then describe new economic landscapes that will emerge after the transition. If this roadmap is followed, national debts can be reduced to zero immediately. All nations with technical capacity to issue their own currencies can apply the same transition steps described in this chapter.

Chapter 13. Electronic Public Money and Uniform Tax System

Money is information of value carried by its media, whose technology has developed over the course of history. Today money has developed into digital form stored on electromagnetic memory, through which EPM (Public Money) or CBDC (Debt Money) can be issued. In this chapter we compare the two different types of digital currencies and claim that EPM is the money of the future that protects our privacy and freedom while achieving financial inclusion. EPM thus envisioned must meet seven system design requirements listed in this chapter. Among these, uniform tax rate is further analyzed as a new tax system that radically simplifies taxation, save administrative costs and renders tax evasion impractical.

Chapter 14. Public Money Initiative

What can we do with public money, then? Following the publication of *Public Money* (Yamaguchi, 2015), a group of readers gathered and proposed the Public Money Initiative as a comprehensive economic policy to save Japan from the lost 30 years. By applying systems thinking, this chapter explains five major programs proposed by the initiative and analyzes how each program will work in synergy to transform the economy. Specifically, we have identified four positive feedback loops that can drive Japan's economic growth; regular employment loop, living environment loop, growth engine loop and participatory workplace loop. We have then analyzed that Japan's lost 30 years were caused by the balancing feedback loop of "non-regular employment" introduced in the 1980s and 90s. By using causal loop diagrams, it becomes clear that Japan's bright future can only be attained by regaining the four loops that enabled its postwar economic success. The spinning of these loops will stop the declining birthrate and labor force. Consequently, it will reduce the need for immigrants to fill in domestic labor shortages, thus eliminating cultural frictions in the workplace and preventing social fragmentation and polarization. Lubricated by subsidies and allowances with public money, these five positive feedback loops reinforce each other to make the nation prosperous again. These problems are not unique to Japan and there are common issues that other countries are beginning to experience such as lack of investments in infrastructure and education due to austerity. Therefore, we believe the discussion here will be of great interest to readers outside Japan.

Chapter 15. MuRatopia Economy

This final chapter presents MuRatopia economy as a new socioeconomic system design beyond the failures of capitalism, socialism, communism and the present globalism. MuRatopia economy consists of four pillars: (1) public money system, (2) self-managed businesses, (3) free & laborless market and (4) sustainability. In this book much of our energy is spent on how to end the outer loop of control identified in Chap. 10 by transitioning to the public money system. In this chapter we will focus on why the inner control loop of equity ownership must also be eliminated to end inequality and regain democracy at workplaces. Its elimination inevitably leads to the pillars (2) and (3). Finally, our concept of MuRatopia is presented as a vision towards a holistic society that unifies the Eastern and Western civilizations. MuRatopia thus envisioned as a network of self-sufficient green villages will achieve the pillar (4) of long-term sustainability.

This is the overview of this book. Without further ado, let's begin our journey!

Part I
Evidence

Chapter 2
In the Beginning was Definition of Money

It is therefore necessary that all commodities shall be measured by some one standard, as was said before. And this standard is in reality demand, which is what holds everything together, ... But demand has come to be conventionally represented by money; this is why money is called nomisma *(customary currency), because* ***it does not exist by nature but by custom*** *(nomos), and can be altered and rendered useless at will.*

– Aristotle, *Nicomachean Ethics*, ca. 350 BCE.

Everyone knows money. It is one of the most familiar things we all use everyday. We therefore tend to think that everyone shares the same concepts. However, once we start talking about money, we do so with our own images and preconceptions. Even if the same terminology is used, its definition may be completely different in the other person's mind, and our discussions often become out of control. This confusion also arises among economists and practitioners who study money as their profession. If we get the definition of money wrong, we'll get the entire science built upon it wrong. Thus it is extremely important to set the foundation rock-solid. Therefore, we will begin this book by properly defining the confusing terms and nomenclature related to money.

2.1 Definition of Money

Money in this book is generally defined as unit information of value and their media as a whole that can be exchanged for goods and services. Of course, it is assumed that its unit and type of media are legally established beforehand as Aristotle observed above. Figures 2.1 and 2.2 are *mandala* of money that we have arrived at after many years of research. The figures show classifications of money in Japan and the US, respectively. Historically, monetary systems took various forms in different regions in different times. However, all nations today have come to adopt similar

K. Yamaguchi and Y. Yamaguchi, *Public Money*,
https://doi.org/10.1007/978-981-97-6564-5_2

monetary standards based on decimal system with Hindu-Arabic numerals (0, 1, 2, ...). Accordingly, readers can apply this classification table to your own countries. Here, all Japanese Yen (JPY) and United States Dollar (USD) that were circulating as of the end of 2018 and 2022 are organized, respectively. Whenever readers get confused on their way, they can come back to this table and sort out the concepts of money, then continue their journey in this book. Unless otherwise mentioned, this book will proceed with discussions based on this definition of money. It is our hope that the classifications presented here will serve as a basis for discussion about money.

2.2 Public Money Versus Debt Money

Let's take a closer look at Figures 2.1 and 2.2. Here, money is defined from two sides, *obverse* and *reverse*, just like the US dimes and quarters are made like metal sandwiches made up of the outside layers (nickel-copper mix) and the filling (copper) in between, known as "clad" coins. Instead of two metal layers, however, our classification table has two definitions; *obverse* and *reverse* definitions, according to which various types of money struck in the middle are classified. In Fig. 2.1 all JPY circulating as of 2018 are depicted in the middle, with obverse side pushed (classified) downward from the top and reverse side pushed upward from the bottom. Figure 2.2 classifies USD in the same manner.

Unit: Trillion JPY (¥)

Issuance (Obverse Def.)	Public Money 4.8	Debt Money (99.7%) 1420.9 (≈ Total Debts of Producers, Households and Government)			
Types of Money in Japan (As of 2018)	Government Coins 4.8	Bank of Japan Notes 107.6	Reserves 393.9	Functional Money (Mf) 324.9	
Base Money (M_0)	506.3				
Money Stocks (As of 2018)	Cash 112.4		Demand Deposits 718.8		Time Deposits 594.5
M_1	831.2				
M_3	1,425.7				
Fiat Status (Reverse Def.)	Legal Tender (35.5%) 506.3			Expanded Functional Money (M_F) (64.5%) 919.4	

Data Source: Bank of Japan (2019). Monetary Statistics & FFA data.
Image Source: Lydian electrum (Wikipedia); WadoKaiho-gin (Wikipedia).

Fig. 2.1 Classification table of money in Japan—Debt money system

Unit: Billion USD ($)

Issuance (Obverse Def.)	**Public Money** 51.4	**Debt Money** (99.8%) 20,648.6 (≈ Total Debts of Producers, Households and Government)			
Types of Money in the U.S. (As of 2022)	**Government Coins**	**Federal Reserve Notes**	**Reserves**	**Functional Money (Mf)**	
	51.4	2,257.6	3,359.1	1,211.6	
Base Money (M_0)	5,668.1				
Money Stocks (As of 2022)	**Cash**		**Demand Deposits**		**Time Deposits**
	2,309.0		4,570.7		13,820.3
M_1	6,879.7				
M_2	20,700.0				
Fiat Status (Reverse Def.)	**Legal Tender** (27.4%) 5,668.1			**Expanded Functional Money (M_F)** (72.6%) 15,031.9	

Source: Federal Reserve (2023) Financial Account of the United States.

Fig. 2.2 Classification table of money in the US—Debt money system

Public Money Versus Debt Money (Obverse Definition)

The obverse definition is a classification according to the nature of money, which is closely related to its issuer. Hence, money consists of *public money* and *debt money*. As this book emphasizes, both definitions are equally important when we analyze the socioeconomic and political functions of (the system of) money.

Public Money are interest-free money issued by the governments or public authorities of the time, such as the reigning monarchs in the Europe, the emperor or the shogunate in Japan. Historically, public money took various forms both in the East and West–from commodities such as shells, stones, precious metals, to papers. In the beginning we defined that money is a unit of value information and its media as a whole. When we classify different kinds of money that existed in the past, however, it becomes useful to distinguish the information component of money (Yen, Dollar, etc.) and its media that carries the value information. Today, about 90% of money stock (M_3 in Japan and M_2 in the US) consists of bank deposits, which are issued and exists as digital (electronic) information. We will discuss the classification of money according to the types of media in Table 13.1. First, let's focus on the differences between public money and debt money.

Although 99% of the money we use today is debt money, this is only a recent development. There are many examples of public money in the long history of human civilizations. The Lydian *electrum*, for example, which was made of a natural alloy of gold and silver, is the oldest coin in the world from *Lydia*, the powerful kingdom existed in the western Asia Minor (Anatolia) in the 7th century BC. As shown in Fig. 2.1, electrum is the world's oldest known example of public money. Lydia was known for its commercial prosperity, but was later destroyed by Cyrus II of Persia. The Greek city states issued their own coins and the practice of metal coinage was carried over to the Roman Empire, whose currencies consisted of gold, silver, bronze and copper.

The world's oldest paper money was introduced during the *Song* Dynasty (960–1270) in today's China. The paper currency later issued by the Yuan Dynasty around 12th century is one of the oldest form of fiat paper currency that circulated as public money. Historical examples of public money circulated in North America include the Spanish silver dollars, the early American coins, paper currencies circulated in the British colonies called the continental currency, and more recently, the United States Notes (Greenbacks) issued during the Civil War. The United States Notes, which were issued in denominations ranging from $1 to $1,000, were authorized under the Legal Tender Act of 1862 (12 Stat. 345)[1] signed by the 16th President Abraham Lincoln.

Greenback Dollars (Public Money) saved the USA

At the time of Civil war, the US did not have a central bank. In fact the country had opposed to the idea of central banking for a century (Zarlenga, 2002). To finance the war effort, Lincoln rejected loan sharking and approved the issuance of legal tender backed by the credit of the government. It was Elbridge G. Spaulding [1809–1897], a lawyer and the former Treasure to the State of New York and the Republican member of the House of Representatives at the time, who figured out, out of necessity as the chair of the House Ways and Means subcommittee, that the government needed to introduce national paper currencies to succeed and drafted the Legal Tender Act. After the war, Spaulding (1869) recounted the time of national peril and stressed as follows:

> The United States, at the breaking out of the rebellion, had no national bank currency, and no gold or available means in the Treasury, or Sub-Treasury, to carry on the war for the Union, and consequently the means to prosecute the war had to be obtained upon the credit of the government, and by taxation. The fundable legal tender currency was the most available form of credit which the government could use in crushing the rebellion. It was at once a *loan* to the government without interest, and a *national currency*, which was so much needed for disbursement in small sums during the pressing exigencies of the war. It was indispensably necessary, and a most powerful instrumentality in saving the government and maintaining the national unity (p.5; Emphasis original).

Thus, there were two types of US notes authorized by the Legal Tender Acts passed during the civil war: (1) interest-bearing notes, as in the early colonial paper currencies, in order to make them readily acceptable, and (2) non-interest-bearing notes. Strictly speaking, the latter falls under the genuine type of public money in the sense that no interest is involved in the issuance.

Gold and silver certificates were also issued by the US government sporadically during the late 19th and early 20th centuries. They were convertible notes issued against deposits of monetary gold and silver held physically in the Treasury. Since

---

[1] The original title is: *An Act authorizing the Issue of United States Notes, and for the Redemption or Funding thereof, and for Funding the Floating Debt of the United States.*

these legal tender notes did not bear interest, they were also public money. Accordingly they are classified as "Public Money Notes" in Table 13.1. Gold and silver redemptions were finally suspended in 1968, during a time in which all US currencies (coins and paper currencies such as the US and Federal Reserve Notes) were turned into fiat money. Today, most US treasury currencies still circulating are in the process of retirement, except government coins. Therefore, these US treasury currencies are collectively classified as "Government Coins" in Fig. 2.2.

Treasury Currencies (Public Money) saved the UK

In the United Kingdom, one of the recent examples of public money issued in paper form was the *Currency Notes* issued by the Treasury during the Financial Crisis of 1914. These currency notes were issued as one of the emergency measures taken by the Government to ease the run on the sovereign gold coins (a British pound) and contain the unprecedented crisis. These public money notes were made convertible to gold sovereigns, issued in the denominations of one pound and 10 schillings, given full legal tender status for any amounts, and remained so until 1928 as authorized by the Currency and Bank Notes Act (4 & 5 Geo 5, c.14, 6th August).

The UK's Treasury Currency Notes were declared to be legal tender for any amount, whereas the Bank of England Notes authorized under the Act of 1833 were legal tender in England and Wales only for amounts over £5. Issued to supplement £5 banknote, which was the smallest denomination among circulating banknotes at the time, the treasury note was suitable for daily transactions, and its circulation increased about seven times compared to that of the banknotes in the first few years. These treasury notes came to be called 'Bradburys' after Sir John Bradbury, the Permanent Secretary to the Treasury, whose signature appeared on them. Upon their retirement in 1928, treasury notes were made convertible to banknotes and transferred to the Bank of England. Gold coins were also withdrawn from circulation in the UK from 1915, and the first gold fixing took place at New Court offices of the N M Rothschild & Sons. The country left the gold standard in 1931 and the Bank of England's note issue became entirely fiduciary backed by the government debt securities (treasury bonds).

Japan's Oldest Coin were Public Money

Historical examples of public money in Japan include the oldest *Wadō-kaichin* coin made of copper (and later silver) issued in the first year of Wadōera (708) as shown in Fig. 2.1. From 17th century onward, the oval-shaped gold coins were introduced including the first *Keichō* gold coins minted by the *Ieyasu Tokugawa*, who made a victory in the Battle of Sekigahara in 1600 and became the first *Shogunate* of Edo period, uniting the country under its rulership.

Ieyasu ordered the excavations of silver mines all over the country, including Sado Island located in the eastern part of the Sea of Japan. And by around 1620 Japan was the world's top silver-producing region, second only to South American colonies of Spain at the time. With ample productions of gold within the territory, and together with silver and other metal coins, all these coins minted under the Tokugawa coinage circulated as public money of the early modern period of Japan. The gold coins in particular were called *koban*, which literally means a small oval-shaped coin in Japanese. Though the exact size, weight, and purity of the gold kobans differed depending on the time of issue, each coin was accepted as a single *ryo* throughout the Edo period, and they had a fixed denomination under the quaternary system.[2]

In addition to these metal coins, paper notes called *hansatsu* were issued by feudal clans throughout the country to compensate the lack of small denomination. And some of them circulated locally and outside the clan as public money. It is estimated that the population of Edo, today's Tokyo Metropolitan area, exceeded 1 million, surpassing that of Paris and London during the Kyohō period (1716–1736). Later the new Meiji government began issuance of *Dajōkan-Kinsatsu* since 1868, which was the first nation-wide fiat paper currency circulated as public money. Therefore, almost all Japanese money until the Bank of Japan was established in 1882 were public money.

Today, only six types of coins–1, 5, 10, 50, 100 and 500 yen–are issued by the Japanese government as public money, together with other commemorative coins since 1964 (they are also legal tender of Japan). As Fig. 2.1 shows, Japanese coins as of 2018 account for only 0.3% or 4.8 trillion yen of total money stock (M_3) of 1,425.7 trillion yen. The difference that accrues when the face value of public money exceeds its production cost is called *seigniorage* and recorded as net asset (profits) of the issuer. Today coins in other nations are also issued by the government at interest-free. Thus, they are modern examples of public money.

Debt Money Issued by Private Banks

Debt Money, on the other hand, are the other type of money issued as interest-bearing debts by private institutions other than the issuer of public money, such as central banks and commercial banks. Thus, debt money are essentially borrowing certificates or IOU of the borrowers to these banks. Borrowers of these debt money include (non-banking) businesses such as producers, households, and the government.

Historical examples of debt money include the oldest banknote in Europe issued by the Stockholms Bank in 1661. After having issued notes more than the amount the bank had received from its customer as their deposits, the Stockholms bank ran out

[2] *Ryo* was a counting unit of currency (not for weight or purity) used exclusively for gold coins. One *ryo*, *i.e.*, one piece, of gold koban was defined as four times that of one *Bu* (a unit for silver coins) and sixteen times that of one *Shu* (or one sixteenth of one ryo). However, the actual exchange rate fluctuated constantly in the market.

of cash and collateral, became insolvent, and soon went bankrupt in 1667. Sveriges Riksbank, the central bank of Sweden, is known as the oldest central bank that is still in existence, and perhaps best recognized today as the awarder of the *Nobel Memorial Prize in Economics*.[3] It is, however, not widely known that its lineage goes back to the infamous Stockholms bank that failed from lending money that they did not possess–a fictitious scheme that still continues to this day as the *fractional reserve banking*.

Under the fractional reserve banking system, deposits are, both legally and practically, IOUs representing indebtedness of banks to their depositors, and simultaneously, the indebtedness of borrowers to the banks. We will discuss the underlying mechanism and legal construct allowing such counterfeiting of a grand scale in Chap. 3. There is a false argument that banknotes issued by central banks will also generate *seigniorage* as in the issuance of public money. However, it is clear that there will be no such gains on issuance of debt money, because, by definition, the central bank notes are not public money. The term seigniorage originates from the Old French *seigneuriage*, meaning the right of the lord (*seigneur*) to mint public money as interest-free currencies. Only interests and dividends are generated through the issuance (lending) of debt money.

Our latest empirical studies (presented in the next Chap. 3) demonstrate that these debt money are almost equal to the total debts owed by non-banking private sectors (mainly producers and households) and the government. In Fig. 2.1 the total amount of debt money in Japan is 1,420.9 trillion yen. In other words, based on the obverse definition, we have obtained indisputable facts that virtually all types of money (99.7%) are issued as someone's *debts* from banks at interest.

It should be noted here that the distinction between public and debt money is not drawn by the ownership status of the issuers. This is particularly relevant today since not all of the central banks are privately-owned. The Governor and Company of the Bank of England, for instance, was incorporated as a joint stock company in 1694 by the Royal Charter. However, the whole of the the bank's capital stock was acquired by HM treasury under the Bank of England Act 1946, and is now held by the Treasury Solicitor on behalf of the Treasury. Accordingly, the bank is considered to be a "public sector" body. Nevertheless the Bank of England continues to issue debt money against, among other things, the treasury securities (UK gilts), which are nothing more than debts of the public.

[3] Officially named "Sveriges Riksbank Prize in Economics Sciences in Memory of Alfred Nobel" since 2006. The original "Nobel Prizes" established by Alfred B. Nobel's will and legacy have been awarded annually since 1901 in five categories: physics, chemistry, physiology or medicine, literature, and the promotion of peace. While some Nobel's descendants are known to be critical of the economics award, the memorial prize has been awarded since 1969 with a donation from the Swedish central bank to commemorate the 300th anniversary of the bank. Consequently, very few of the Riksbank prize winner have openly criticized the fractional reserve banking. In Chap. 9 we will discuss why the Chicago Plan or any similar version of monetary reform has been made a politically taboo subject and how some of these Nobel Memorial Prize laureates have played a central part in the systematic obfuscation of the role of commercial banks as creators of money through their popular economics textbooks.

Another example is the Bank of Japan. The central bank, which was modeled after the National Bank of Belgium, was established initially as a joint stock company, whose shares were held by the Japanese Imperial household, private individuals as well as banks. Today 55% of its shares, or "prioritized investment securities" as the bank wished to be referred to, are held by the Government of Japan. The rest is held by private persons (40.4%), financial institutions (2.0%) and others (2.6%) as of March 2020.[4] The shareholders receive annual dividends but not entitled to exercise voting rights. Accordingly the bank is often seen and explained as a government agency. However, the Bank of Japan issues notes and reserves against interest-bearing government bonds on its balance sheet, just like the Bank of England. Therefore, the Bank of Japan are issuing debt money.

The Federal Reserve System–the central bank of the US created in 1913 by the Federal Reserve Act– consists of the Board of seven governors, Federal Open Market Committee (FOMC), and the 12 regional federal reserve banks, which are chartered as private corporations. Shares of the regional banks are owned by its member banks, *i.e.*, private commercial banks. The Fed increases reserves when purchasing treasury securities, on which it earns interests in its portfolio just like the Bank of England, Bank of Japan and other central banks. Thus, the Federal Reserve System also issues debt money. As many central banks around the world are now preparing to issue Central Bank Digital Currency (CBDC), our classification of money by the obverse definition becomes useful to understand the CBDC's nature as debt money. We will discuss the classification of CBDC in Table 13.1.

2.3 Legal Tender Versus Functional Money

From the reverse definition of money, that is, whether it is legally enforceable as a means of settlement or not, money can be broadly divided into *legal tender* and *functional money*. Legal tender is money authorized by law as the means of settlements, and no one can refuse it in payment of debts both private and public, unless otherwise specified in contracts. For example, the issuance of government coins in Japan is stipulated by the Act on Currency Units and Issuance of Coins 44(Act No. 42 of 1987), and the issuance of the Bank of Japan (BoJ) notes is authorized under the Bank of Japan Act (Act No. 89 of 1997). Therefore, the currency of Japan is: Currency = Government Coins + BoJ Notes. Currency thus defined becomes legal tender.

[4] Similar to the National Bank of Belgium, whose shares are listed on the stock exchange (previously the Brussels Stock exchange, now Euronext since 2002), the Bank of Japan's investment securities are listed on the Tokyo Stock Exchange (8301:TYO) since November 1983.

Legal Tender Versus Functional Money (Reverse Definition)

The term *currency* is used strictly in Japanese law to specify money in a narrower sense. Currency is called *cash* in our daily language. Furthermore, reserve deposits are deposits of banknotes that the Bank of Japan accepts mainly from commercial banks. Reserves are used among financial institutions for their transaction settlements. In this sense reserve deposits are considered equivalent to BoJ notes, and have payment finality as currency. Therefore, reserves that will be withdrawn by commercial banks as the BoJ notes in the future must also be regarded as legal tender in a broader sense of the term.

When banknotes are returned to the central bank as reserves of commercial banks, the banknotes outstanding will be reduced on the liability of the BoJ's balance sheet and reserves will increase by the same amount. Therefore, the reserves literally become the BoJ notes that have already been issued (or subject to future withdrawals). In summary, the legal tender of Japan consists of Currency and BoJ reserves, which amounts to 506.3 trillion yen as of the end of 2018. This amounts to 35.5% of total money stock M_3 as shown in Fig. 2.1.

Functional Money (M_f), on the other hand, is a new type of classification that we utilize in this book. As Fig. 2.1 shows, it is defined as the part of demand deposits that is not secured (backed) by reserves. The broader definition of functional money is further defined as the sum of Functional Money and Time Deposits. This *Expanded Functional Money* (M_F) was 919.4 trillion yen as of 2018. That is, 64.5% of total money stock (M_3) has been created by private banks out of thin air in Japan. In the US, M_F accounts for 72.6% of total money stock (M_2). These are the types of money that are not backed by legal tender. In this sense functional money could also be interpreted as *fake money* or *counterfeit money*.

Until around 1930s when the *Chicago Plan* and Fisher's *100% Money* were proposed, economists made a strict distinction between currency and functional money (bank deposits). As we will see in Chap. 3, history teaches us that functional money is a part of money stock that will disappear when banks fail. We should all be aware that our economy is currently operating under these unstable, fake, and interest-bearing debt money.

Public Money Taken Over by Debt Money

Figure 2.1 is a cross-sectional snapshot of the Japanese money as of 2018 in its long monetary history. Next let's take a brief look at how such Japanese money has changed over a longer time span.

The first public money in Japan was the *Wadō-kaichin*, which was issued in 708 by the order of the Empress *Genmei* (the 43rd). To put this in a global context, the Monnaie de Paris (Paris Mint), the oldest continuously operating mint in France, was founded in AD 864, roughly 160 years after the *Wadō-Kaichin* was minted. This oldest public money in Japan was deeply involved in the national redevelopment project of *Heijo-kyō*, which was a new square-shaped Imperial capital measuring 4.3 km east to west and 4.8 km north to south, built on the northern edge of the present-day Nara Basin in central Japan.[5] After that, public money with 12 kinds of copper coins starting with the *Wadō-kaichin* had been minted and distributed one after another until 958.

In the Edo period, gold coins such as *Keichō* (1601) and *Bunsei Koban* (1819) were casted, and the Japanese version of the gold standard system was established. During the Edo period the Tokugawa government minted number of gold coins, with each series having a certain purity and fixed face value. They were exchanged with silver coins under the quaternary system. In 1868, the first year of the Meiji Restoration, a new public money called *Dajōkan-satsu* were issued as non-convertible fiat paper money, and valid for the next 13 years. In 1871 the new Meiji government finally adopted decimal system with the New Currency Act to reform the monetary system from the Edo period, and introduced the new currency units *yen*, *sen* (tenth of a *yen*) and *rin* (the hundredth of a *yen*) by issuing new gold, silver and copper coins based on minting technology adopted from the Europe. As shown in the classification table of Fig. 2.1, Japan has maintained its economy and society under the public money system for 1,160 years since the issuance of *Wado-kaichin* in 708.

However, since the establishment of the Bank of Japan in 1882, the nation's economy has been taken over by the debt money system devised by the bankers in Europe. As a result, public money in Japan has now shrunk to just 0.3%, and interest-bearing debt money is occupying 99.7% of the total money in circulation.[6]

---

[5] This national project can be briefly summarized as follows. First, the Prince *Nakano-Ohe* defeated *Soga-no-Iruka*, the head of Soga clan, and became the 38th Emperor *Tenji* (reign: 668–672), unifying the nation. Then the emperor carried out the *Reforms of Taika* with his younger brother, Prince *Oamano*, later the 40th Emperor *Tenmu* (673–686). Specifically, the emperor issued an imperial edict of reformation centering on public land reform aimed at curbing private ownership of land by aristocrats and local powerful families and securing tax revenue for the state, establishment of local administrative organizations, and creation of family registers. Next, the *Taihō Code*, the first law governing the new nation, was enacted in 701 by Empress *Jito* (the 41st and wife of Emperor *Tenmu*), including criminal, administrative and procedural laws. Then, the Empress *Genmei* (the younger sister of Empress *Jito*) succeeded to the 43rd throne. The *Wado-kaichin* was issued during her reign (707–715) in 708 to pay wages to the construction workers for the national development project. In 710, the 3rd year of *Wado* period, the empress moved the capital from *Fujiwara-kyō* (located in today's central *Nara*) to *Heijo-kyō* (in northern *Nara*) and completed this national reconstitution. In this way, public money was used constructively to establish a new nation in ancient Japan.

[6] The conversion of government-issued notes (public money) into Bank of Japan notes (debt money) began from 1885 at the initiative and direction of Masayoshi Matsukata [1835–1924], then Minister of Finance, who was behind at the creation of the Bank of Japan (BoJ). In 1859, there was a significant outflow of gold from Japan due to arbitrage by foreign traders, who exploited the different conversion rate between gold and silver in the Japanese and overseas market. Therefore, the BoJ notes were first made convertible to silver specie. They were later made convertible to gold specie from 1897 with the increased reserves from the reparation of the Sino-Japanese War. By 1899 the conversion was completed, and all public money were suspended thereafter, except government-issued coins. The gold standard in Japan was suspended and resumed several times until 1941 when the specie reserve system was eventually abolished just before the Second World War. The BoJ's largest shareholders at the time of its establishment included the heads and founders

There is nothing wrong with this debt money system if it is functioning well and serving the public interests. However, there are fundamental design failures in the present system. As a result, we have faced numerous economic crises; inflation and deflation, depression, unemployment, war, income inequality, and so on. The Japanese government has now fallen into debt hell, and the global economy is now on the verge of another systemic crisis.

Transitioning to the Public Money System

This book propose a transition from the current debt money system to the public money system. Why is this transition necessary? We hope the readers will use this book as a guide and think deeply about the reasons. If we compare this journey to a mountain climbing, we are aiming at the summit of a new economic futures under the public money system. In order not to get lost on the way, we would like readers to first imagine a beautiful view of the sunrise that can be seen from the summit at the beginning of this journey.

First, according to the obverse definition of money, 99% of money is issued as interest-bearing debts owed by producers, households and governments both in Japan and the US. And they are destined to disappear when those debts get repaid or default in recessions. Under the public money system, on the other hand, all money is put into circulation as interest-free stable currencies issued by the Public Money Administration (PMA). Accordingly, the instability such as booms and depressions or bank runs, will be prevented and eliminated. As Chap. 12 will explain in detail, the PMA is an independent monetary authority that will be established under the legislative branch of the government, such as the Congress in the US, National Diet in Japan, or the Parliament in the UK. Thus, the PMA will become the sole issuer of national currency in place of the central bank and private banks as currently structured.

Next, according to the reverse definition of money by fiat status, 64.5% of total money in Japan (72.6% for the US dollar) are currently created out of nothing by private banks. These functional money under the debt money system are destined to disappear when banks go bankrupt. In contrast, every money in circulation under the public money system becomes legal tender, *i.e.*, currency. Therefore, they are always legally secured and the supply of money becomes stable since the governments (PMA) will be fully in charge of monetary policy through control over its total quantity. As a result of this system transition, the classification table of Fig. 2.1 will now look like Fig. 2.3 in the Japanese case.

In other words, all money will be public money (highlighted in green) issued by the government, and all money becomes legal tender (highlighted in purple). This

---

of Japan's major zaibatsu families such as Mitsui, Kawasaki, Yasuda, Mitsubishi, and Sumitomo, as well as the head of the former major samurai clans (such as Tokugawa and Shimazu) who were given titles after the Meiji restoration.

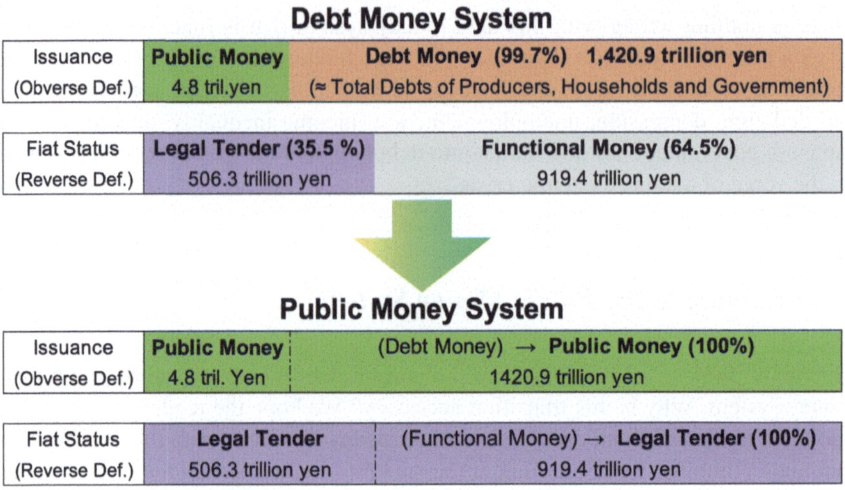

Fig. 2.3 Transition from debt money system to public money system

is what Fisher meant when he said "100%" in his *100% Money*; that is, all (100%) of money becomes legal tender in terms of the reverse definition. Consequently, all debt money (red) and functional money (gray) under the present system will be eliminated. This transition will enable us to enjoy immeasurable benefits and open up unprecedented opportunities as detailed in Part III. Using this book as a guide, we hope readers will embark on their own journeys toward bright futures while thinking deeply about the merits of public money system.

Chapter 3
99% of Your Money is Someone's Debt

Money classification tables presented in Chap. 2 are snapshots of total money stock M_3 in Japan and M_2 in the US. Where did those 1,420.9 trillion yen of debt money, which accounts for 99.7% of M_3 in Japan, come from? What about M_1, consisting of cash and demand deposits? M_1 is the most basic type of money we all need for daily payments. Mainstream monetary theories explain that banks are *financial intermediaries* who collect deposits from savers and lend them out to borrowers in cash. However, Figs. 2.1 and 2.2 show that cash is just a fraction of M_2 or M_3. If banks are only intermediaries who circulate cash or base money (M_0) around, where did the other 919 trillion yen (M_F in Fig. 2.1) come from, which is the difference between M_3 and M_0? In this chapter let's solve these mysteries and uncover the true nature of debt money system.

3.1 Money Stock Data by the Bank of Japan

In order to answer these questions about money, our research began with a quest for reliable data. Specifically, we first obtained M_1 and M_3 data from 1980 to 2019 published by the Bank of Japan (BoJ). As Fig. 3.1 shows, however, they were subdivided into three discontinued periods: (1) 1980–1988, (2) 1988–2008, and (3) 2003–2019. There were significant discrepancies between 1980–1988–2008 and 2003–2019. For example, M_1 surged 111 trillion yen in 2008, while M_3 fell 186 trillion yen. In fact, a huge amount of money, equivalent to one or two times the national budget of Japan, have increased and decreased suddenly at these disconnections. Business managers and investors who have made their strategies based on the BoJ's monetary statistics might have been confused by these discrepancies. Which data should be used in our analysis?

Since reliable research cannot be performed with such inconsistent time series, we sought an alternative data source and arrived at the Flow of Funds Accounts

K. Yamaguchi and Y. Yamaguchi, *Public Money*,
https://doi.org/10.1007/978-981-97-6564-5_3

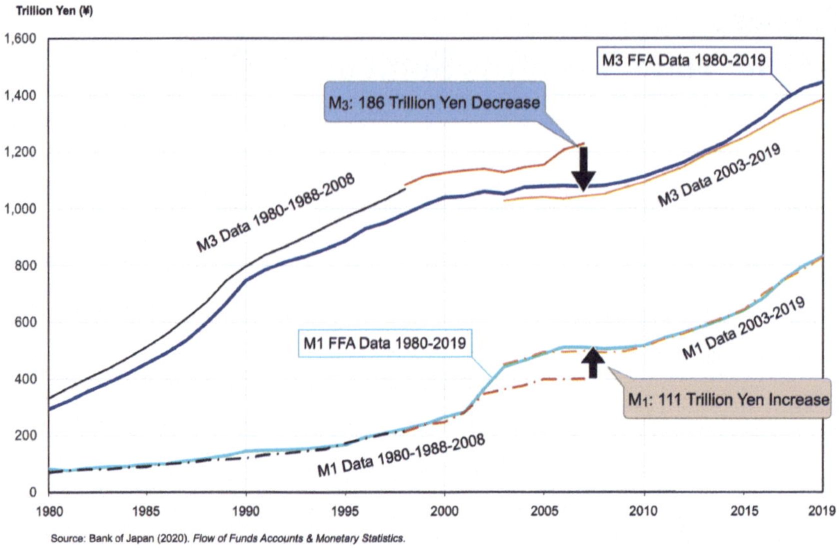

Fig. 3.1 Comparison of M_1 & M_3 data published by bank of Japan

(FFA) published also by the BoJ. The latest data available for our research was time series starting from 1980 until the end of 2022 (or the beginning of 2023). However, the BoJ's FFA data are enormous, consisting of 45 macroeconomic sectors and 51 transaction items. The data for one year alone consist of 2,295 matrix cells. Since each sector has assets and liabilities, the total number of data points for 40 years period from 1980 to 2019 becomes 183,600 (= 45 × 51 × 2 × 40) data. The quarterly data becomes 734,400 data points. Therefore, we have developed a dedicated "FFA Data Analysis Model" using system dynamics (SD) software and imported all these FFA data.

Based on these FFA data, we have recalculated M_1 and M_3 according to the definition by the BoJ. Unfortunately, money stock obtained from FFA data did not match the money stock data. We therefore shifted the obtained FFA data by one year over the entire period. The reason for this adjustment is because we judged that the discrepancies between the two time series originated from time lag that occurs when calculating stock values.[1]

As Fig. 3.1 shows, for M_1 data, the disconnections in time series seem to be explained after the adjustments. Hence, we have determined that M_1 obtained from FFA data ("M_1 FFA Data 1980–2019") are tentatively reliable.

Next, we have similarly compared the two time series for M_3. Yet they just did not fit as they did in M_1. M_3 obtained from the FFA data ("M_3 FFA Data 1980–2019" in Fig. 3.1) are already shifted by one year. As we can see, M_3 FFA data goes between

[1] Stock values are calculated at the beginning of the period in the SD software used in our research, while the original BoJ's FFA data are published as the end of each period.

the three disconnected "M_3 Data." Thus, for M_3, we have also decided to use the time series obtained from FFA data.

3.2 Money Stock Data by the Federal Reserve

How about money stock data in the US? The appropriate indicator for total money stock in United States Dollar (USD) is M_2. Similarly, there are two approaches to obtain data. One way is to directly use the money stock data published by the Fed. Another way is to calculate M_2 based on the FFA data, which are also available from the Federal Reserve Economic Data (FRED) website.

The FFA data published by the Fed is called Financial Accounts of the United States (FAUS). We have similarly obtained M_2 based on the FAUS data (M_2-*FAUS*) and compared it against M_2 time series available from the FRED (M_2-*FRED*).[2] To examine their reliability as money stock data, Fig. 3.2 compares these two time series. Note that M_2-*FRED* starts from Q1 1959.

Both lines are plotted on quarterly basis. As we can see, M_2-*FAUS* is generally higher than M_2-*FRED*, except for the period between 1998–2003 and 2020 when M_2-*FRED* is higher. The discrepancy between the two time series becomes the widest at 1,068 billion dollars in 2007. Although there may be several factors causing these discrepancies, there are no significant gap between the two, making M_2-*FAUS* thus

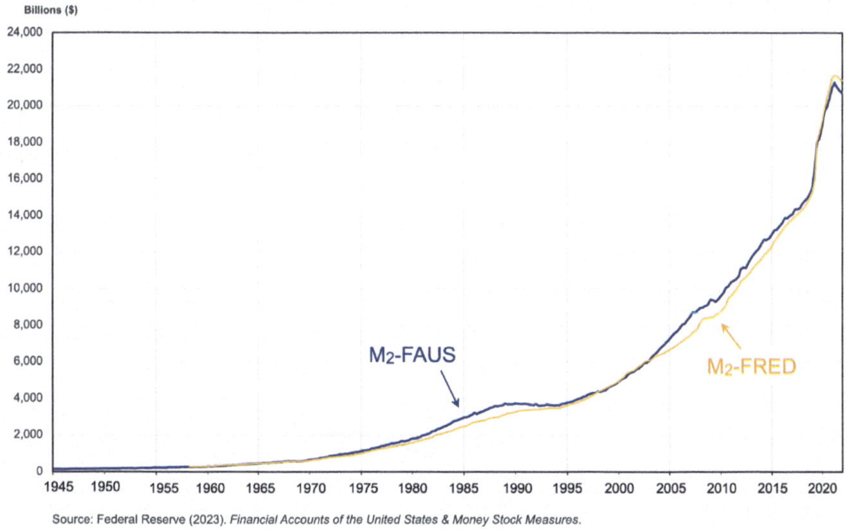

Fig. 3.2 Comparison of M_2 data by the federal reserve: 1945–2022

[2] Board of Governors of the Federal Reserve System (US), M2 [M2SL], retrieved from FRED; https://fred.stlouisfed.org/series/M2SL, September 26, 2023.

defined reliable for our analysis. Accordingly, we will proceed with our discussion based on this M_2-*FAUS* elsewhere in this book unless specified otherwise.

3.3 Money Stock ≃ Total Debts

The essence of the debt money system is that virtually all money are supplied into the economy as interest-bearing debts. Where do those money come from? Howe are they issued? Now that we have obtained money stock data from Japan and the US, let's take a closer look at them to answer these questions.

$M_2 \simeq$ Total Debts (Case of US Dollar)

Figure 3.3 compares M_2 and Total Debts. Just by visual inspection, we can observe that total debts have historically approximated total money stock in the USD case. Here the debt money analysis was performed since 1945 when FAUS data becomes available. Indeed, *99% of our money is someone's debt*. The widest gap between M_2 and total debts was at 1,132 billion dollars observed in Q1 2021, where M_2 exceeded total debts. The classification table of money in the US (Fig. 2.2) indicates that 99.8% of M_2 or 20,648 billion dollars were circulating as debt money as of 2022.

There are different types of "debt" held by various economics entities. What we are focusing here are specific type of debts that create new money. These *money-creating debts* (liabilities) owed by non-banking private sectors are in turn recorded

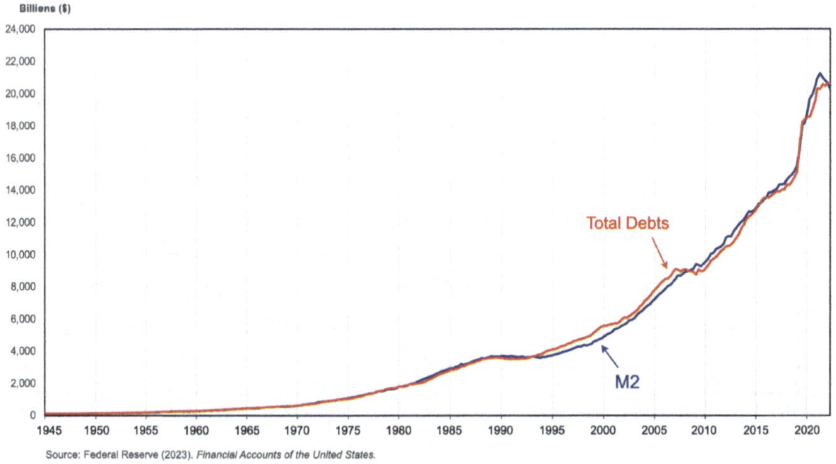

Fig. 3.3 Money stock $M_2 \simeq$ total debts–case of USD (1945–2022)

as loans (assets) of banks in the FFA statistics. Similarly, money-creating debts owed by the US government are largely held by banks and the Fed as their treasury security holdings (assets). Accordingly, total debts are estimated as the sum of transaction items recorded on the asset side of the banking sector and the central bank in the FFA datasets. Therefore, total debts in Fig. 3.3 is depicting the historical growth of these dollar-denominated money-creating debts over the last 75 years.

Most strikingly, the postwar trend in total debt and money stock is exponentially increasing in the United States. Especially, we can see that the rate of growth in total debts have accelerated from 2000 onward, which was a period leading up to the 2008 financial crisis. Furthermore, there is a sudden and significant increase in both Total Debts and M_2 in 2020. This recent deviation from the long-term trend of debt money relationship in the US coincided with the period when COVID-19 pandemic struck the economy, and the US government mobilized fiscal expenditures, followed by the Fed's asset purchase operations. As we will discuss in more detail in Fig. 3.9, this precipitous increase in M_2 was largely caused by the increase in federal government debts.

$M_3 \simeq$ Total Debts (Case of Japanese Yen)

Similarly we have performed the debt money analysis on the case of Japanese Yen (JPY). Line 1 in Fig. 3.4 shows Japan's M_3 data. Line 2 (red) shows the historical changes in the total debts obtained from the FFA data published by the Bank of Japan. In the JPY case, debt money analysis was performed since 1980 when FFA data becomes available. We can similarly notice that growth in M_3 in Japan has been approximated by total debts for at least over the last 40 years.[3]

Possible Explanations for the Divergence in JPY Case

Theoretically, M_3 and Total Debts should also match precisely (excluding 0.3% of public money). However, an intermediate divergence is observed during 1994–2015. Specifically, total debts underestimate M_3, or *vice versa*. This period corresponds to the time when a huge amount of non-performing loans became problematic due to the burst of the Japanese bubble in the 1990s, and as a result, many financial institutions went bankrupt. On the intermediate discrepancies observed in the JPY case, Yamaguchi and Yamaguchi (2021a) have submitted three hypotheses as follows:

[3] Debt money analysis on the JPY case presented in this section is a follow up of our previous research (Yamaguchi and Yamaguchi 2021a, Chap. 4). See the original chapter for further details on the methodology, data source, and definitions of money stocks and total debts. Debt money analysis on the USD case was first reported by Yamaguchi (2021). See the original paper for details on the methodology, data source, and definitions in the USD case.

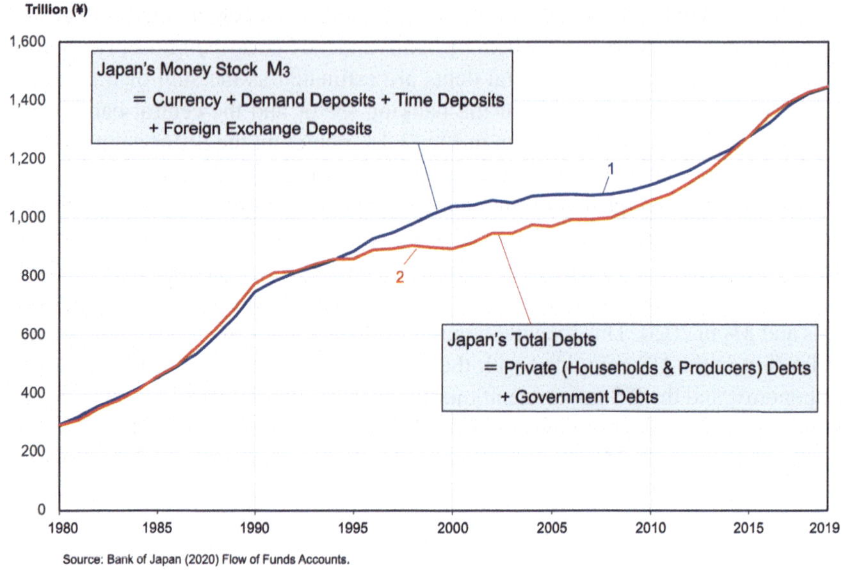

Fig. 3.4 Money stock $M_3 \simeq$ total debts–case of JPY (1980–2019)

Hypothesis 1 Total Debts are underestimated due to missing items that should have been included in the definition (estimation error).

Hypothesis 2 M_3 is overestimated because some of transaction items that make up M_3 in the FFA statistics are duplicated (estimation error).

Hypothesis 3 FFA statistics published by Bank of Japan itself contains inaccurate data, thus either one of the two time series overestimates or underestimates the other (error in BoJ's FFA statistics).

Hypotheses 1 and 2 both assume that the divergence is due to our own fault in obtaining correct values for M_3 and Total Debts. Hypothesis 3, on the other hand, points to the possibility that inaccurate values are contained in the original FFA statistics. Given the accuracy and precision of our debt money analysis demonstrated in the USD case, Hypothesis 3 deserves a priority in future investigations.

Linear Regression on M_3 (Japanese Yen)

Next, we performed a simple linear regression analysis to obtain a statistical result on the JPY case. The correlation coefficient between M_3 and Total Debts was determined as follows:

$$M_3 \simeq \text{Total Debts} \quad \text{(Correlation Coefficient = 0.9881)} \tag{3.1}$$

The correlation coefficient (R) between the two variables turned out to be high. Furthermore, our simple linear regression analysis yielded the following result (in billions of yen) where coefficient of determination (R^2) is close to one:

$$M_3 = 5,201 + 1.032 * \text{Total Debts} \quad (R^2 = 0.976) \tag{3.2}$$

The regression coefficient became almost close to one, indicating a strong positive correlation where an increase or decrease in total debts coincided with an alsmost equal amount of increase or decrease in M_3. The macroeconomic relationship such that Money Stock $\simeq$ Total Debts is now verified in the JPY case.

Linear Regression on M_2 (US Dollar)

We have similarly performed a simple linear regression analysis on the USD case. As expected, correlation coefficient between M_2 and Total Debts turned out to be significantly high for the period between 1945–2022:

$$M_2 \simeq \text{Total Debts} \quad (\text{Correlation Coefficient} = 0.9985) \tag{3.3}$$

Furthermore, the above linear regression analysis yielded the following result (in millions of dollars):

$$M_2 = -82,671 + 1.0152 * \text{Total Debts} \quad (R^2 = 0.997) \tag{3.4}$$

The coefficient of determination (R^2) is almost one and the coefficient of above regression function (3.4) is 1.0152, indicating that an increase in debt increases almost the same amount of M_2.

These results indeed demonstrate that *99% of Our Money is Someone's Debt* in the US and Japan. All money are supplied as interest-bearing debts of producers, households and the government, except 0.3% of public money circulating as coins. The reality of debt money system has now emerged where people and their companies must pay a huge amount of interests each year to sustain the level of money supply they need. If the overall net interest rate was at 1%, the annual interest payments to the banking sector would be roughly 207 billion dollars (= 20,700 billion × 0.01 per year) for the US economy, and 14 trillion yen (= 1,400 trillion × 0.01 per year) in Japan. This is how the present system is designed.

So long as someone keeps borrowing from banks, there is money to be earned. If these debts are paid off, 99% of our money will disappear and the economy will come to a complete halt. According to the regression analysis above, Japan's M_3 would be reduced to just 17 trillion from 1,400 trillion yen. Given the volumes of USD and JPY used in international trades and financial transactions, these results have fundamental implications to both economic theory and policy.

These empirical results also provide important implications on the issue of income distribution and economic inequality. Through this debt-based system, a huge amount of interest is transferred from debtors to creditors. And they are ultimately siphoned off by the shareholders (owners) of international banks through dividends, rents and so on. Through this financial mechanism, together with corporate control under the equity ownership system discussed in Chap. 10, creditors have largely controlled the major Western media and news outlets, food, energy supplies, medical and pharmaceutical industries. This is the driving force of globalism the world is currently facing, and the root cause of the merger of corporate and state power, which will be analyzed in detail in Chap. 10.

Availability and Reliability of FFA Statistics

We have searched for FFA data in other cases including Canada (CAD), Mexico (MXN), China (CNY), Taiwan (TWD), United Kingdom (GBP) and the Euro area (EUR). In terms of data availability, however, we have faced with difficulties in obtaining appropriate time series that are comprehensive and accurate enough to examine the debt money relationship in these economies.

For instance, the European Central Bank publishes monetary data and sectoral balance sheets. Yet they are somewhat aggregated and available periods are relatively short due to its time of existence. In any case, the more detail and accurate data becomes available, the more precise relationships should be observed in other economies. In this respect, the FAUS provides a benchmark for data reliability required for FFA statistics. Economists should first examine the debt money relationship as a separate reliability test in addition to the balance sheet and flow-of-funds consistency followed by the publishers of FFA statistics before conducting any type of research involving these time series data.

3.4 Alchemy of Fractional Reserve Banking

How and from whom do banks raise such huge amounts of money and lend them to debtors? Whenever we borrow money from banks, we know that amount of "deposits" are added to our bank accounts. So we tend to think that banks are providing us with real money. If banks were acting as financial intermediaries between savers and borrowers in the economy, *i.e.*, if they were conforming to a 100% reserve requirement on customer's deposits, banks can only lend from excess funds (savings) they had collected prior to making additional loans.

If we look at Fig. 2.1, however, there exists no cash or base money (M_0) in Japan worth about 1,400 trillion yen that should cover the total amount of bank loans (total debts) outstanding in the economy. The same applies to the US as shown in Fig. 2.2. Indeed, when banks grant loans, they do not provide us with cash over the counter, especially when loans involve a large sum of money. Then, the question becomes, what are banks really lending to their customers?

Banks are Lending Money They Do Not Even Possess

The answer is that banks are not lending money or anything. They are simply making promises, or entering into loan contracts, that they will prepare the *currency* (cash) upon requests. Legally, what banks are doing is they are instituting creditor-debtor relationships with their customers by creating new "deposits" and credit (add) them into their customer's deposit accounts.

Realizing this fradulent nature of fractional reserve banking, Fisher (1935) tried to explain to the American public how banks began to practice this "*sleight-of-hand*" using a simplified illustration as follows:

> On, say, June 1 a bank is started—the only one, let us suppose, in the community—with one million dollars of capital consisting of actual money in vault. This bank then proceeds to lend this money. The first customer borrows, say, $10,000, giving his promissory note. The $10,000 of actual money is, let us suppose, actually pushed through the teller's window to the customer; but the customer immediately pushes it back again, that is, "*deposits*" it. The same is done by other customers, so that, by the end of the day, the whole million has been lent out and redeposited.
>
> Thus far the bank has lent only its own capital to its customers; and its customers, after receiving it (the million dollars), have redeposited it.
>
> These customers now think of it as *their* money. And, at this stage, it practically, though not legally, is there money rather than the bank's; for they are secured by a 100% reserve against the million dollars of deposits recorded on the stubs of their check books.
>
> Our imaginary bank, then, has one million of deposits (which are its *liabilities* due to the depositors) and it has assets of two millions—one million consisting of deposited cash, the other consisting of promissory notes.
>
> If the cash can be called the property of the depositors, the promissory notes must be considered as the property of the bank. It is true that *legally* both millions belong to the bank, but *practically*, as just indicated, the former—the million of cash in vault—belongs to the depositors. It may be thought of as, in effect, held in trust for them, by the bank.
>
> The depositors can, by check, shuffle about, from person to person, their respective shares in this million dollars, in payment for groceries and everything else for which checks customarily circulate. So far, the situation is almost exactly like that of the old Bank of Amsterdam before the period of its secret manipulation [that is, when the bank was still operating on the 100% reserve principle].
>
> On June 2, the same thing happens as on June 1. That is, the bank proceeds to loan out actual money from its vaults to the second day's borrowers—*the very same million dollars*, the million which practically belonged to yesterday's depositors, though legally to the bank; and then these borrowers of today, like those of yesterday, as fast as they get it, redeposit that money—*the same million dollars*. At the end of the day there are bank liabilities of two millions (recorded as cash on the stubs of check books) and assets of three millions—namely, one million of cash and two millions of promissory notes representing the two days' loans (pp. 36–38; emphasis original).

Figure 3.5 illustrates the community bank's balance sheet at the end of June 2. Because the bank has relent the same one million cash to other borrowers, the bank's current reserve ratio became 50% as of the end of its second business day. That is, one million of *vault cash* held against two million of deposits.

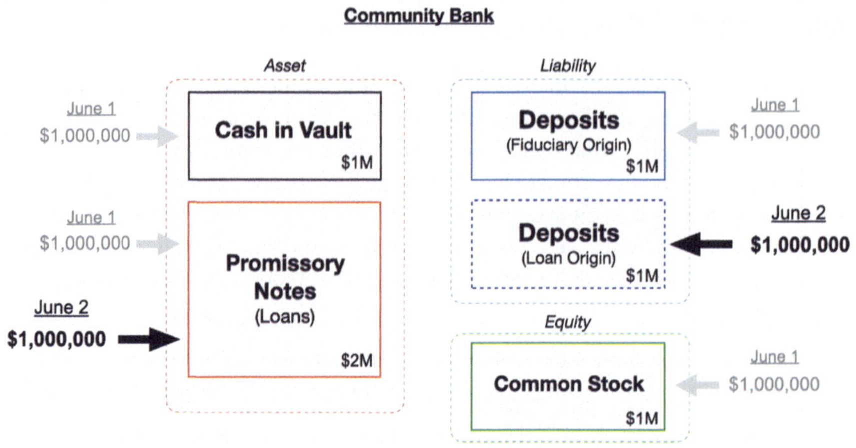

Fig. 3.5 Balance sheet of the community bank as of June 2

Fisher (1935) continues:

> Here the danger has begun. The deposits are now two millions but the assets, though they are three millions, include only one million of *cash*. The bank has done what the Bank of Amsterdam did surreptitiously, replaced cash with promissory notes. Half of the deposits are now backed by these promissory notes. Yet the two millions of deposits count for cash so far as the depositors are concerned. They have on the stubs of their check books a total of two million dollars, and call all of it their "cash in bank"; they circulate this entire two millions by check, just as if it were real pocket-book money, turning it over, according to estimates, at about the rate of once a fortnight.
>
> The bank is no longer in the position of a mere custodian. It has assumed a more serious responsibility—that of furnishing cash which it does not possess. It is in the position of a person who has sold a commodity short. It trusts to good management (and to good luck) to get that commodity, cash, when needed. As already noted, legally the million of cash, as well as all the other assets, belongs to the bank. The depositors' ownership of two millions of "cash in bank" has become a fiction. It is not even there in trust. It is not there at all. The depositors do not own two millions of cash, although ordinarily they think they do and their books say so. All they really own is the right to demand cash—two millions of it.
>
> By allowing the second set of depositors to circulate by check what is not real money, the bank has, in effect, manufactured (by mere promises to furnish cash on demand) a million dollars of new circulating medium. Each dollar of the deposits is a mere promise to furnish a dollar on the demand of the depositor. These promises to pay its depositors *instantly* are made partly on the strength of the counter-promises of the borrowers to pay the bank *sometime*. These latter, the promissory notes of the depositors, are the basis for half their deposit, the other half being backed by the solitary million of cash (pp. 38–39; emphasis in original).

Thus, from the customer's point of view, bank deposits are monetary claims that also function as cash, and simultaneously their debts (liability) owed to banks. From the bank's point of view, customer deposits are debts (liability), which banks incurred as a result of extending loans (acquiring promissory notes).

> On June 3 the bank lends out that solitary one million of cash for the third time and again receives it back as the borrowers redeposit it.

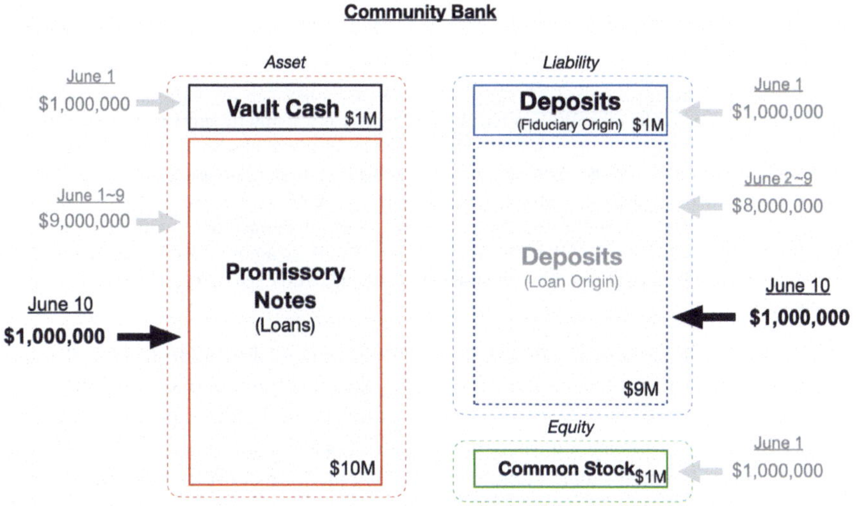

Fig. 3.6 Balance sheet of the community bank as of June 10

> In practice, of course, the cash seldom really passes through the teller's window and back again, but simply stays undisturbed in the vaults. All that usually happens is that the depositors are told to record the successive "deposit"—the proceeds of loans—on the stubs of the check books, and each is assured that he may feel safe in drawing checks against it up to the full amount of *his* particular deposit.
>
> On June 4, the million is lent and deposited a fourth time; on June 5, a fifth time; and so on, until June 10, inclusive, when the deposits became $10,000,000 while the cash is still $1,000,000 (and the promissory notes are $10,000,000). Then (if the bank hasn't stopped earlier) the law steps in—the legal limit of 10 per cent reserve has been reached[4] (pp. 39–40; emphasis in original).

As a result of additional loan and deposit transactions the community bank has made "surreptitiously," the bank's balance sheet now looks as Fig. 3.6. Would a bank approve a loan to a company doing such a shady business on a shoestring? Yet

[4] "Strictly speaking, the example given does not fully apply to an individual new bank in a community in which there are other deposit banks. The million, when lent and then transferred by check to others, would not all be redeposited in the same bank; and the other banks, as they receive their part, would draw out some of the million from the vaults of the new bank into their own vaults. This spilling over of the reserve from one bank's vault to another's hides the fact above stressed of relending the same money many times over—usually hides it even from the banker.

The multiple lending is more evident when there is only one bank to consider. But, even when there are many banks, the same fact holds true for them all *as a group*. The spilling over from one bank to others merely shift to these others parts of the additional lending.

This banking paradox by which what is true for banks as a whole is not true for the individual bank was first clearly pointed out by Chester Phillips, now Dean at the University of Iowa" (Fisher 1935, p. 40, n. 6; emphasis in original).

this is exactly how banks are legally allowed to operate under the fractional reserve principle. Fisher (1935) summarizes the story:

> With a 10% reserve, only 10% of the check-book money can properly be called real deposits of money. The other 90% of check-book money is a synthetic substitute for pocket-book money, created by a sort of slight-of-hand. The customer thinks he has obtained a loan of pre-existing money of the bank and then deposited that money. He does not see that the "money" he deposited was, in effect, created by the bank out of his loan itself—his own debt. He has helped the bank manufacture money and this manufacture of money concerns not only himself and the bank but the whole nation exactly as a gold miner's manufacture of money when he takes his gold to the mint concerns the whole nation (p. 43; emphasis in original).

As Fisher indicated, in the practice of banking, the cash seldom passes through the teller's window and back again. As is now clear from the above illustration, for banks operating under the fractional reserve requirement, lending means to simultaneously increase monetary claims called "loans" (asset) and debts called "deposits" (liability) on its balance sheet. Then, from the day the loan contract takes into effect, banks start collecting interests from the debtors. As a result, 99% of our money stock exists as interest-bearing debts. This is the reason why total debts approximates M_2 in the United States (Fig. 3.3) and M_3 in Japan (Fig. 3.4). Total debts corresponds to promissory notes of ten million dollars in Fig. 3.6, and money stock is ten million dollars of deposits.

Legal Mechanism of Bank Deposit Creation

It is understandable from the Fisher's illustration how banks began to create "deposits" on their books instead of lending with real cash. However, if they do so, are they not in turn committing a fraud on their customers? Banks are charging interests on loans they made with the money they did not possess, while calling them "deposits" even though not all of them were collected as deposits of real cash. How can banks create deposits out of thin air and still *legally* call them "deposits" on their financial statements? Readers may wonder.

Indeed, it is *physically* impossible for anyone to lend something he or she does not possess. It is also extremely unethical to pretend as if there were actually something to lend. In fact, nations have prohibited such fraudulent acts under their criminal laws. Back in the days, forgery and counterfeiting of currency were crimes worthy of capital punishment.[5] However, what has been strictly prohibited is exactly what banks are still allowed to engage. While people make fortunes by producing goods and services with real economic value, banks have been engaging in such *alchemy* all the time. How? It is almost like a wordplay.

---

[5] For instance, the Sveriges Riksbank, the central bank of Sweden, the world's oldest of its kind and the awarder of the "Nobel Prize in Economics", writes a short article on the criminal case from 18th century where two female banknote counterfeiters (Susanna Ekström and Ingeborg Jönsdotter) were sentenced to death according to the transcriptions of judgements from the Svea Court of Appeal preserved in the Riksbank's archives. Source: www.riksbank.se/en-gb/about-the-riksbank/history/historical-timeline/1700-1799/counterfeiters-sentenced-to-death/ [accessed: April 15th, 2024].

Let's take the Japanese Law as an example, The secret is in the application of what is known as *deposit of fungibles* contract (Article 666 in the Japanese Civil Code) under the fractional reserve requirement on bank deposits. To understand this, we need to first distinguish the two distinct concepts that describe the act of depositing: (1) *bailment* and (2) *deposit of fungibles*.

If deposit is done as a bailment, for example, when Alice deposits her cash with Bob, then the bailment agreement between the two parties is established when Bob received the contractual object from Alice. That is, Bob, as the *bailee*, is obliged to keep that very object *as it is* for Alice as the *bailor* of that thing. Therefore, Alice is the rightful owner of her own money—the very same cash that Alice entrusted to Bob on, say, June 1 in the Fisher's illustration above.

If Alice and Bob had agreed to do this as deposit of fungibles, then Bob can take the contractual object (cash) that Alice had entrusted to him and use it at his will. It is sufficient for Bob to return a thing of the same kind, quality, and of the same amount at a later date. That is, Bob can now *consume* it instead of safekeeping it. As long as he can meet the obligation to Alice for the return of the thing, he is not violating any deposit contract with her. Under this deposit contract, therefore, the ownership of the contractual object is considered to be transferred from the original depositor (Alice) to the depositary (Bob).

Who really owns your money in the bank, then? As Fisher said, legally they are no longer yours. You, as the depositor, is no longer the legal owner of the money, but merely a creditor. As stated above, bank deposits are a typical example where the deposit of fungibles contract are applied under the Japanese civil codes, which were influenced by German and French Laws (which were in turn intellectualized within the framework of Roman Law).

One can imagine that a similar logic is also applied under the common law such as in the UK and US jurisdictions. Therefore, a correct description of bank deposit is that depositors are not depositing money for safekeeping (as in bailments), but are actually *lending* money to banks. In fact, since deposit of fungibles are similar to a *loan for consumption*, the provisions of Loan for Consumption (Article 587 of Japanese Civil Code) apply *mutatis mutandis*.[6]

Therefore, when banks accept deposits in cash, they are not obliged to simply store them in their vaults and return them as they were originally brought in to the bank. All they have agreed with their depositors is to return them with the same kind, quality, and of the same amount, with the presumption that they can be used for whatever purposes banks wish to do, such as lending money (that originally belonged to you but no longer yours) to someone else at interest.

---

[6] Two types of loan contracts need to be distinguished here; (1) loan for *use*, and (2) loan for *consumption*. Loan for Consumption, as the name suggests, is a type of loan contract where one party would lend on the premise that the object in question will be consumed by the other party. In Roman law, for example, the loan for use is called *commodatum*, whereas loan for consumption is called *mutuum*. Under commodatum, a person entrusts (gratuitously) the contractual object, which is to be used but must be returned in the very thing loaned. Mutuum is the one in which a person lends a thing to the other party who is obliged to return (or restore) a thing of the same kind, quantity, and quality.

This is why banks pay interest to depositors as borrowing fees rather than charging them for safekeeping. If depositors kept their money with their banks as bailments, it would be strange for them to receive interests from banks on those deposits. It would be the depositors who should pay 'service fees' to banks.

The application of *Loan for Consumption* also eliminates the inherent nature of deposits that would otherwise arise from different origins. Thus, deposits accrued from the acceptance of cash ("fiduciary origin") and deposits generated through lending ("loan origin") need not be legally identified nor distinguished operationally. For this reason, banks can now regard deposits of fiduciary and loan origins as the same indistinguishable "deposits" altogether.[7] And finally, together with the fractional reserve requirement, banks can readily increase customer's deposit account balance without having to actually collect or possess cash prior to making loans (and without violating any contracts or laws).

Once we understand the legal and operational mechanism behind bank's deposit creation, the question naturally arises: Does the Generally Accepted Accounting Principles (GAAP) and International Financial Reporting Standards (IFRS) permit these deceptions? Indeed, accountants criticize such bank accounting is in violation of IFRS (see Schewmmann 2015 for instance).[8] Under the 100% reserve requirement, bank's loan transaction must be a *switch* between assets, instead of creation of assets and liabilities as presently done. Thus, its balance sheet must show a reduction in "vault cash" (held as excess reserves by banks beyond 100% reserve ratio) and a corresponding increase in "loans". This is the proper double-entry bookkeeping for loan transactions under the public money system.

In any case, what we call "deposits" under the present system are nothing more than monetary claims and debts that exist between (1) depositors (as creditors) and

---

[7] Notice the distinction we made in the stylized bank's balance sheet in Figs. 3.5 and 3.6. Economists also call these newly created deposits of loan origin as *credits* as in the "credit creation." In the double-entry bookkeeping terminology, the left hand side of account items are called *debits* and the right hand side as *credits*. In fact the journal entry for loans in bank bookkeeping is nothing more than increasing the balance of credit of deposit account, which is a liability on bank's balance sheet. However, using the term "credit creation" to students who have not taken accounting course only confuses them. Even if students take accounting courses, most of them study commercial and industrial bookkeepings, and it is rare for them to learn bank bookkeeping and accounting. In either case, banks generate *deposits* on their balance sheets against loans granted or other assets purchased. Hence, the term *deposit creation* is not only intuitive than *credit creation*, but also conforming with bank accounting terminology. Recently, the expression such as "money creation" is getting popular (see Mcleay et al. 2014 for example). However, by money creation, it lacks specificity as to which money is referred to in our classification tables (Figs. 2.1 and 2.2). Therefore, we will prioritize the term "deposit creation" in this book unless we need to quote others.

[8] Schewmmann (2015) argues that receivables (loans) acquired by the bank do not meet the requirements of an asset as defined in the IFRS; that is, a resource controlled by the entity, as a result of a past event, from which future economic benefits are expected to flow to the entity. Specifically, Schewmmann (2015) argues that "[A] mere promise to pay obtained by the bank without a cost basis, is not an economic resource, is not the result of a past event, but the event itself through bookkeeping, the interest being an economic benefit, provided that the first two criteria can stand, which they cannot" (p. 26). Therefore, the corresponding deposits recorded on the liability also "falls to the ground" (*ibid.*) and fail to meet the accounting standard.

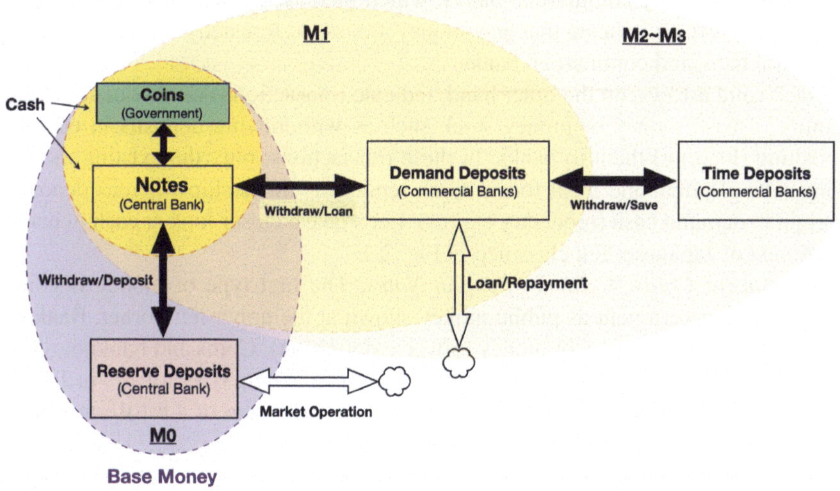

Fig. 3.7 Monetary aggregates (M_0-M_3) under the debt money system

banks (as debtors) and (2) banks (as creditors) and borrowers (as debtors). This is why those fictitious "deposits" created by the banking system beyond what can be covered by base money (cash and reserves) are called *functional money* in our classification tables. If depositors rush to withdraw their money all at once, banks cannot fulfill their promises (debt obligations). This is why banks keep failing because the fractional reserve requirement allows them to lend money they do not even possess nor exist anywhere in the economy.

3.5 Types of Public Money and Debt Money

Figure 3.7 illustrates the definition of monetary aggregates (M_0-M_3) discussed so far and financial transactions that increase or decrease them.[9] Different types of money classified in Figs. 2.1 and 2.2 are rearranged here from the perspective of how they are issued and circulating in the economy.

White blank arrows indicate transactions that directly increase or decrease base money (M_0) or money stock ($M_1 \sim M_3$). Examples of such transaction include open market purchase operations conducted by central banks, which increase reserves, or

[9] Adapted from Fig. 1.3 of Yamaguchi and Yamaguchi (2021b). Note that foreign currency-denominated deposits are excluded from the illustration.

new loans granted by commercial banks, which increase demand deposits. Clouds connected to arrows indicate that new money are issued (created) out of nothing by the central bank and commercial banks.

Black solid arrows, on the other hand, indicate transactions that do not affect the quantity of base money or money stock such as withdrawing deposits in cash or depositing (loaning) them to banks. In these transactions, only the existing money changes its physical and legal forms. Cash represents ownership whereas deposits are right to demand cash (monetary claims). Let's take a closer look at each items in the context of Japanese Yen classified in Fig. 2.1.

Government Coins ⇆ Bank of Japan Notes. The first type of money is coins issued by the government as public money shown at the upper left corner. Bank of Japan notes are issued as debt money (obverse definition). Coins and banknotes are all legal tender (reverse definition). Although coins make up 0.3% of M_3 in Japan, cash are still widely used in retail payments. Cash is the sum of 4.8 trillion yen of government coins and 107.6 trillion yen of BoJ notes.

Bank of Japan Notes ⇆ Reserves. Whenever we withdraw deposits at ATM, or transfer them to another banks, our banks need to make sure they have enough cash in order to meet their obligations. Accordingly banks must keep a certain amount of cash in vaults or at the central bank as deposits. These deposits in turn become central bank reserves shown at the bottom left corner. These reserves are also used as a means of settlement among commercial banks and to meet their reserve requirement. When banks withdraw their reserves from the central bank, banknotes are considered to be "issued" at this point.

In addition to banknotes, central banks issue reserves through purchases of treasury securities and other financial assets in the conduct of monetary policy. Thus, the origin of all central bank money (BoJ notes and reserves in Japan) can be traced back to the fact that most of them were issued against national debts. Although not explicitly shown in Fig. 3.7, the government's deficit expenditure financed by banks through treasury securities also increase money stock as examined in the debt money analyses above. Thus, any repayment of private and public debts owed to banks decrease money stock conversely.[10]

In other words, our government is forced to use "deposits" issued by the central bank under the present debt money system instead of issuing their own interest-free

---

[10] Fiscal laws generally prohibit central banks from underwriting treasury securities and providing loans directly. Therefore, central banks purchase (marketable) securities from banks through their open market purchase operation. Some countries exceptionally allow central banks to directly underwrite treasury bills (maturity of one year or less), which are issued to cover short-term fiscal needs. Treasury bond purchases by central banks, whether they are bought directly or indirectly, are in effect fiscal finance. Reserves will increase whenever a central bank purchases securities and other assets from depository institutions. However, money stock will increase *only* when the government spends those newly borrowed funds back into the economy. Money stock decreases when the government redeems its bonds accordingly. We will explain why this is the case using double-entry bookkeeping exercises in Chap. 11.

currency as public money. Today, central bank reserves are issued digitally with no convertibility with commodities such as gold and silver.[11]

Base Money. Cash (coins and notes) and reserves are collectively called base money (M_0) in the sense that these cash and reserves serve as the base for deposit creation by commercial banks. Reserves in Japan have increased significantly when the BoJ purchased a large amount of treasury bonds under the quantitative easing (QE) policy since 2013 (see Fig. 4.5 in Chap. 4). According to Fig. 2.1, base money was 506.3 trillion in 2018. At the end of 2022, the BoJ reserves became 480 trillion yen and base money has grown to 600 trillion yen, exceeding the Japan's nominal GDP. However, prior to the zero interest rate policy implemented in the late 1990s, M_0 used to be only about 50 trillion yen, of which reserves were about 3∼5 trillion yen.

Money Stocks ($M_1 \sim M_3$). Based on M_0 commercial banks create *deposits* (monetary claims and debts) under the legally required reserve and capital adequacy ratios. The authority to change required reserve ratios is assigned to the monetary policy board of central bank in most nations. Some central banks, however, no longer impose reserve requirements, including the Bank of England and Sveriges Riksbank. The board of federal reserve system recently reduced required reserve ratio to 0% for all depository institutions (effective March 26, 2020). Therefore, legal constraint on deposit creation through the supply constraint of reserves has been eliminated.

The sum of cash and demand deposits is called money stock M_1. Demand deposits created by banks are converted ("saved") into high-yielding fixed-term savings as time deposits. These are temporary leakages from money circulation. Thus, the sum of M_1 and time deposits is the total money stock, which is defined as M_2. BoJ defines M_3 to differentiate time deposits held by different depository institutions such as banks, postal savings, etc. Time deposits will be withdrawn at some point into demand deposit. Some of them may be used to repay debt and eventually disappear from circulation. Figure 3.7 illustrates these life cycles of money, where 99% of money stock exists as debt. This is the bird's-eye view of the money and banking system as currently structured.

Definitions of Monetary Aggregates M_0-M_3

Monetary aggregates classified in Figs. 2.1 and 2.2 are now formalized as follows:
M_0 = Cash + Reserve Deposits
M_1 = Cash + Demand Deposits

[11] It is important to distinguish here that cash legally represents a possessory right of payment objects (bearer money), whereas deposits are claims on currency that are loaned to banks. Under the Japanese legal system, provisions of private law apply to the government's deposits at the Bank of Japan. This means that even the treasury funds are only monetary claims of the government to the central bank. This is why commercial bank's reserves and government's deposits are recorded as the liabilities of the Bank of Japan's balance sheet.

M_T = Time Deposits
$M_3 = M_1 + M_T$
$M_f = M_1 - M_0$
$M_F = M_3 - M_0 = M_1 + M_T - M_0 = M_f + M_T$

The difference between M_1 and M_0 is Functional Money (M_f). By introducing M_f, it becomes possible to identify the fictitious deposits that are not backed by legal tender. Expanded Functional Money (M_F) is further defined as the sum of functional money in the narrower sense (M_f) and time deposits (M_T).

When we define "cash" in M_0, the two concepts must be strictly distinguished; (1) Currency in circulation, which excludes "vault cash" held by deposit-taking institutions, and (2) Currency outstanding, which is a total quantity of currency issued and recorded on the central bank's liability. In monetary theory, the former definition of M_0 is defined as *high-powered money*, while the latter is defined as *base money*. Many textbooks, however, incorrectly define both terms as equivalent. See Yamaguchi (2013, Chap. 5) further for correct definitions.

Confusing Use of the Term "Deposit Currency" by Bank of Japan

Bank of Japan often uses the terms "deposit *currency*" and "quasi *currency*" instead of *deposits*. As discussed above, deposits are not *currency* at all. Why does the central bank call these fake money created by banks as currency? Readers are alarmed not to get confused by such use of the terms, which has kept economists and the general public from understanding the true nature of the debt money system (see Sect. 8.14.2 further). We have also struggled to decipher these confusing terms that appear in the BoJ statistics when we construct ASD macroeconomic models. As a recent example, Modern Money Theory (MMT), which is discussed in Chap. 11, conceal the nature of debt money system by shrouding these monetary concepts in confusion.

3.6 Money Disappears with Debt Repayments

There are two "faucets" that create debt money as shown in Fig. 3.7. While the first faucet is controlled by the central bank, the opening and closing of the second faucet is regulated by the lending behavior of banks. Thus the total quantity of money stock is determined endogenously via the second faucet.

The fact that bank loans create new money was well recognized by economists since the mid-19th century such as MacLeod (1856).[12] In other words, in the history of economic thoughts, the mechanism of deposit creation was analyzed more than half a century prior to the creation of the Federal Reserve System in 1913, or even

[12] Henry D. Macleod [1821–1902], a native of Scotland, became a barrister at the Inner Temple in the City of London, and from 1849 he served as one of directors of the Royal British Bank. Although the bank, which was established under the Joint Stock Banking Act of 1845, was later dissolved in 1856, his experiences in bank management has led him to write books on economic analysis rooted in both theory and practice.

Table 3.1 Money contraction during the great depression

	1926	1929	1933
Money Stock M_1	26	27	20
Cash	4	4	5
Deposits	22	23	15
Currency Ratio $(= \frac{Cash}{Deposits})$	4/22 (= 18.2%)	4/23 (= 17.4%)	5/15 (= 33.3%)

before the establishment of the Bank of Japan in 1882. However, as discussed in Chap. 9, it has became a *taboo* among the mainstream economics profession to point out the direct relationship between business fluctuations and the dishonest scheme of fractional reserve banking.

About 70 years after the publication of Macleod's book on banking, the United States across the Atlantic was in the Roaring 20s. Investors took out leveraged loans and traded on securities, just as investors did before the Lehman Shock in 2008. After the stock market crashed in October 1929, a chain of rumors on bank runs led to a nationwide banking crisis.

Monetary Destruction during the Great Depression of 1930s

The fact that there are two faucets means there are also two channels through which money disappears. The Great Depression was precisely the result of such reductions in deposits via the second faucet, which Fisher (1935) called "the irresponsible creation and destruction of circulating medium by our thousands of commercial banks" as quoted in the epigraph of Chap. 1 (Introduction). When loans get repaid, the corresponding amount of deposits disappear from banks' balance sheets.

Fisher observed the contraction of money stock during the early phase of the Depression as in Table 3.1.[13] First, from 1926 to 1929, M_1 increased by 1 billion dollars, from 26 billion to 27 billion, reflecting the economic boom of the late 1920s. Then, from 1929 to 1933, cash holdings increased by 1 billion dollars, from 4 billion to 5 billion. This was the result of depositors rushing to banks and withdrawing their deposits in cash. This means that depositors increased their currency ratio from 17.4% in 1929 to 33.3%, which reduced the bank's reserves by 1 billion dollars. As a result, demand deposits fell by 8 billion dollars. The reason for such reduction in deposits was the surge in cash due to bank runs and the contraction of deposits caused by debt repayments.

[13] Prepared by authors based on the descriptions by Fisher (1935, pp. 5–6). Numbers in the table are rounded. Therefore, cash-deposit ratios shown in the table do not match precisely with values when they are calculated using numbers in the table.

Taken altogether, cash increased by one billion while demand deposits decreased by eight billion, resulting in a loss of seven billion dollars in M_1 over the four years period. Under the current debt money system, the first faucet is controlled by the central bank but the second faucet is left wide open so that, when a recession hits and private sectors repay their debts, a large amount of money stock gets destroyed. Financial panic at the time became so severe that as many as 10,000 banks were forced to close across the nation.

Fisher likened M_1 to the economic highways essential for businesses and described that 23 billion *miles* (dollars) of highways were suddenly destroyed by 8 billion miles during the first few years of the Depression. Indeed the US economy at the time suffered catastrophic damages comparable to such destructions.

Separating Money Creation from Loans–100% Reserve Plan

The structural defect of the debt money system is this inextricable link between bank loan and money creation. The supply of new purchasing power through bank loans fuels speculative investments and raises asset prices, which in turn raises the value of collateral and attracts more speculative money, causing asset prices to rise even further. This is the formation of economic bubbles.

However, a bubble without substance would eventually become unsustainable. Those "deposits" created out of nothing are destined to return to nothing. Our classification tables of money in Figs. 2.1 and 2.2 distinguish this fundamental difference between public money that are issued without interest and circulates stably, and debt money that are inherently unstable (obverse definition).

In response to the Great Depression, the eight economists at the University of Chicago[14] proposed the "Chicago Plan for Banking Reform" in 1933, which called for a 100% reserve requirement on demand deposits. The 100% reserve requirement closes the second faucet and stops the endogenous creation and destruction of deposits as functional money. Thus, banks become genuine financial intermediaries, which is what most economics textbooks assume.

Fisher, who had also lost his fortunes from the stock market crash, was struggling to find the cause of the Depression (Fisher, 1932, 1933). When he received the Chicago Plan, Fisher soon realized that the root cause of booms and busts lies in the structure of debt money system itself and incorporated the 100% reserve plan into his theory called "*100% Money*" (Fisher 1935, preface):

> The essence of the 100% plan is to make money independent of loans; that is, to divorce the process of creating and destroying money from the business of banking. A purely incidental result would be to make banking safer and more profitable; but by far the most important result would be the prevention of great booms and depressions by ending the chronic inflations and deflations which have ever been the curse of mankind and which have sprung largely from banking.

[14] They are: G.V. Cox, Aaron Director, Paul Douglas, A.G. Hart, F.H. Knight, L.W. Mints, Henry Schulz, and H.C. Simons.

Robert Hemphill, who was a former credit manager at the Federal Reserve Bank of Atlanta, was one of many who held the same observation as Fisher's analysis. He recognized the root cause of monetary instability and fragility of the financial system in the fractional reserve banking system, and wrote down the following foreword to the Fisher's proposal of *100% Money* (Fisher, 1935):

> Neither the banker nor the borrower ordinarily realize that a loan just completed, is putting into circulation that much new money... .
>
> If all bank loans were repaid, no one would have a bank deposit, and there would not be a dollar of currency or coin in circulation.
>
> This is a staggering thought. We are completely dependent on the commercial banks. Someone has to borrow every dollar we have in circulation, cash or credit. If the banks create ample synthetic money, we are prosperous; if not, we starve. We are absolutely without a permanent monetary system.
>
> When one gets a complete grasp upon this picture, the tragic absurdity of our helpless position is almost incredible–but there it is.

Public money system proposed in this book is an adaptation of the 100% reserve system proposed by the *Chicago Plan* and *100% Money* to modern day conditions. The 100% reserve requirement on demand deposits is the second of the three system transition goals explained in Chap. 12.

3.7 Surprising Facts of the Japanese Economy

After the WWII, Japan achieved remarkable growth in the postwar period and was called "Japan as Number One" (Vogel, 1979) by the 1980s. However, since the burst of the bubble in the early 1990s, the economy has undergone decades-long stagnation, despite the bold implementations of all kinds of economic policies suggested by the mainstream economic theories. What went wrong? In order to analyze the Japanese case from the perspective of the debt money relationship obtained in Fig. 3.4, let us continue our analysis by breaking down the debt money relationship.

Decomposition Analysis of $M_3 \simeq$ Total Debts in Japan

We have so far looked at the reason why the relationship "Money Stock $\simeq$ Total Debts" holds in Japan and the United States. Then, the next question naturally arises: whose debts are generating how much debt money?

Figure 3.8 is created by decomposing M_3 and total debts in Fig. 3.4 into time deposits (M_T) and M_1, and private and government debts.

Specifically, we have found from Fig. 3.8 that debt money relationship can be broken down into following macroeconomic relationships:

$$M_3 \text{ (line 1)} = \text{Time Deposit (line 3)} + M_1 \text{ (line 5)} \tag{3.5}$$

$$\text{Total Debts (line 2)} = \text{Private Debts (line 4)} + \text{Government Debts (line 6)} \tag{3.6}$$

By decomposing the debt money relationship this way, we have obtained the following three surprising facts observed in the Japanese economy.

Surprise 1: Economy Stagnates while Money Increase

Figure 3.8 shows that M_3 (line 1) and M_1 (line 5) in Japan have been increasing since 1980. In other words, the economy as a whole has not suffered from money shortage. Historically, however, a close relationship has been observed between money contraction and recessions In fact, Table 3.1 shows that as much as a quarter (25.9%) of M_1 was lost during the Great Depression. This triggered bankruptcies of companies and banks across the nation, resulting in massive unemployment of up to 25% of the workforce. It is therefore easy to imagine that a shortage of money will worsen corporate cash flows, affect consumption and result in recession.

Why, then, did M_1 and M_3 not decline in Japan after the burst of the bubble? Why did the economy, despite steady increases in money stock, suffer long-term stagnation

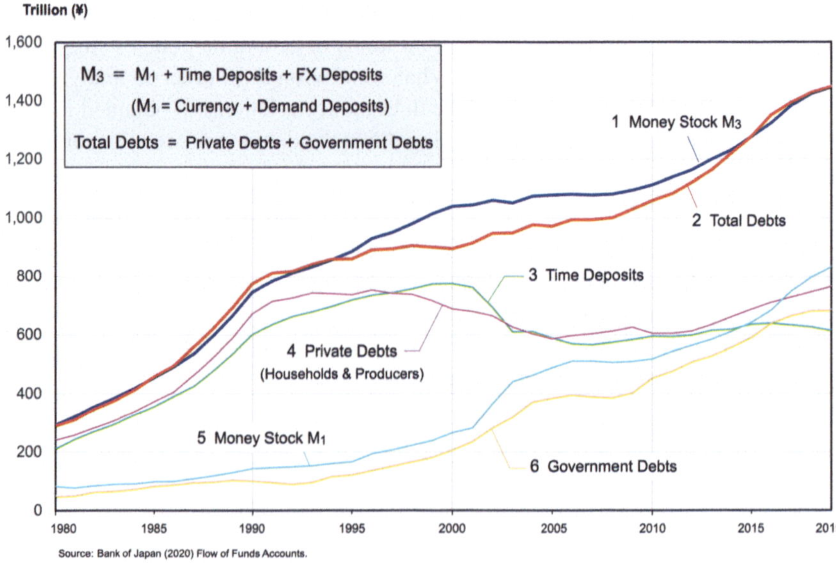

Fig. 3.8 Decomposition analysis of $M_3 \simeq$ total debts in Japan (1980–2019)

with its GDP slumping around 500 trillion yen for almost three decades?[15] The case of Japan is a surprising phenomenon that sharply contradicts the policy lesson learned from the Great Depression.

To understand this, we have reexamined this phenomenon from the side of total debts as shown in Fig. 3.8. Specifically, after the mid-90s, the private debts, especially those of households and producers, began to decline sharply (line 4). This means that the corresponding amount of money stock should have been destroyed as it did in the Great Depression. As if to make up this decline in private debts, government debts (line 6) has been rising since the second half of the 90s due to the fiscal spendings implemented during that period.

As a result, total debts has also been rising steadily, resulting in an overall increase in M_3. Although Japan's M_3 appears to be stable in Fig. 3.4, by looking at the debt money relationship from the side of total debts and their components, we can clearly observe that there has been a reversal, a qualitative change underneath the surface, with a sharp decline in private debts compensated by a sharp increase in government debts.

After the debt repayments among (non-banking) private sectors subsided around the late 2000s, the amount of money created by the increase in government debts exceeded the amount destroyed by the decline in private debts, resulting in the subsequent increase in M_3. Despite this increase in total debt and money stock, the economy fell into the prolonged period of stagnation called *Japan's lost 30 years*. This is a situation that cannot be explained by mainstream economics. Why did this happen?

Surprise 2: Savings Come After Borrowings for Investments

Concerning time deposits and private debts in Fig. 3.8, we have further found the following correlation and obtained a linear regression equation as follows (in billion yen):

$$\text{Time Deposits} \simeq \text{Private Debts (Correlation Coefficient} = 0.9539) \tag{3.7}$$

$$\text{Time Deposits} = 2,935 + 0.9506 * \text{Private Debts} \quad (R^2 = 0.910) \tag{3.8}$$

Why are these surprising results? According to the mainstream monetary theory (discussed in Chap. 9), money is first issued and put into circulation by governments and central banks exogenously. And commercial banks collect some of them from depositors as savings and use them to make loans. In other words, banks are merely intermediaries between depositors such as households, who save a portion of their wages and other incomes, and borrowers such as producers, who need to borrow funds to make investments. Therefore, in order to stimulate investment and economic growth, first, domestic savings must be sufficient as the source of growth. This is what we are taught in macroeconomics.

---

[15] See Fig. 5.3 in Chap. 5 for the relation between money stocks and GDP.

However, the reality of the Japanese economy that we obtained in Fig. 3.8 is the exact opposite. First, producers and households must borrow from banks, and then use those newly created money to invest in production equipments and housings. Those money will become incomes for other households and producers, and some of them will eventually be saved as time deposits as Fig. 3.7 illustrates. Therefore, the correct description of the flow of funds under the present debt money system is that investment and consumption are first made with borrowings (debts) from banks, which will increase the quantity of money.

Conversely, if the private sector debts and investment decline, GDP is also affected and income declines. Since the regression coefficient is 0.95 in Eq. (3.8), savings in Japan as measured in time deposits also decline by 95% according to this simple calculation. Time deposits actually plummeted after the burst of the bubble as depicted in Fig. 3.8. And the economy has completely stalled due to this sharp decline in private debts. This is what we can observe when we apply the debt money analysis and follow the flow of money correctly.

Surprise 3: Government Debts Increase M_1

Next, we found a close correlation between M_1 (line 5) and government debts (line 6), and obtained its linear regression equation as follows (in billion yen):

$$M_1 \simeq \text{Government Debts (Correlation Coefficient} = 0.9934) \qquad (3.9)$$

$$M_1 = 28,781 + 1.1244 * \text{Government Debts} \quad (R^2 = 0.987) \qquad (3.10)$$

The result shows that the majority of Japan's M_1 turned out to be supplied by government debts. When the bubble collapsed in 1990, the government's debt from banks was only 98 trillion yen. Yet it became 693 trillion yen in the fiscal year 2019. Over the past 30 years the government's cumulative debt increased by 595 trillion yen.[16] On average, the annual increase in these money-creating debt newly borrowed from banks was 19.8 trillion yen per year.

Many have criticized that Japan's GDP did not grow due to fiscal austerity by the government to achieve primary balance, *i.e.*, tax revenues–expenditures = 0. However, the data shows the opposite reality to be true. The series of fiscal stimulus implemented by the Japanese government turned out to have been *de facto* anti-austerity. As we will see in more detail in the next chapter, they were implemented in an unprecedented scale both in terms of the size and duration. Starting in 1992, one may further counter argue that there was also no significant delay in the timing of policy implementation. In this sense, fiscal stimulus implemented by the Japanese government was a perfect textbook-style example of counter cyclical policy promoted

[16] In terms of total government bond issuance including FILP (Fiscal Investment and Loan Program) bonds, Japanese government debt was 198 trillion yen in 1990 and 1,208 trillion yen in 2019, that is, a cumulative increase in 1,010 trillion yen over the past 30 years. On average, the budget deficit was 33.7 trillion yen each year, while its nominal GDP stagnated at around 500 trillion yen range during the same period.

by the Keynesian aggregate demand management. This is the another surprising result obtained from our decomposition analysis.

On the other hand, M_1 has increased from 148 trillion yen in 1990 to 879 trillion yen in 2019, that is, an increase of 731 trillion yen over the past 30 years. This comparison suggests that the 595 trillion yen increase in government debt has provided most of the 731 trillion yen increase in M_1. Since the regression coefficient is 1.125, this means that government debts have generated 669 trillion yen ($= 1.125 \times 595$) of M_1 in the above regression equation (3.10).

What would have happened if the government had not taken such aggressive fiscal spendings, then? Japanese economy would have quickly run out of M_1 and stalled completely as the US economy plunged into the Great Depression in the 1930s. Why, then, did the economy fail to emerge from the recession despite the government's fiscal policy that have sustained M_1? And why has there been virtually no economic growth for the past 30 years? From the perspective of mainstream economists, who have long argued for the effectiveness of monetary and fiscal policies as well as structural reform (deregulation and privatization), the case of Japan's Lost 30 Years is indeed far from resolved.

These findings have provided us with clues to the causes of Japan's economic struggle, but also raised new questions. By analyzing the debt money relationship obtained in this chapter, it has now become clear that, in order to explain the puzzling phenomenon that confronted the mainstream economics, we must analyze the Japanese case from the perspective of the debt money system. From the next chapter onward, we will examine why the mainstream economics has completely failed to save the economy by looking at the Japanese case in detail.

Decomposition Analysis of $M_2 \simeq$ Total Debts in the US

Could the same breakdown relationships be observed in the US economy? To our surprise, we found that debt money relationship in the US can be similarly broken down into two macroeconomic relationships as follows:

$$M_1 \simeq \text{Government Debts} \tag{3.11}$$

$$\text{Time Deposits} \simeq \text{Private Debts} \tag{3.12}$$

Similarly, government debts financed by banks approximate M_1 while private debts approximate time deposits as Fig. 3.9 illustrates. Since FAUS data is available since 1945, the two breakdown relationships were found to be established for a much longer period in the US than in Japan.

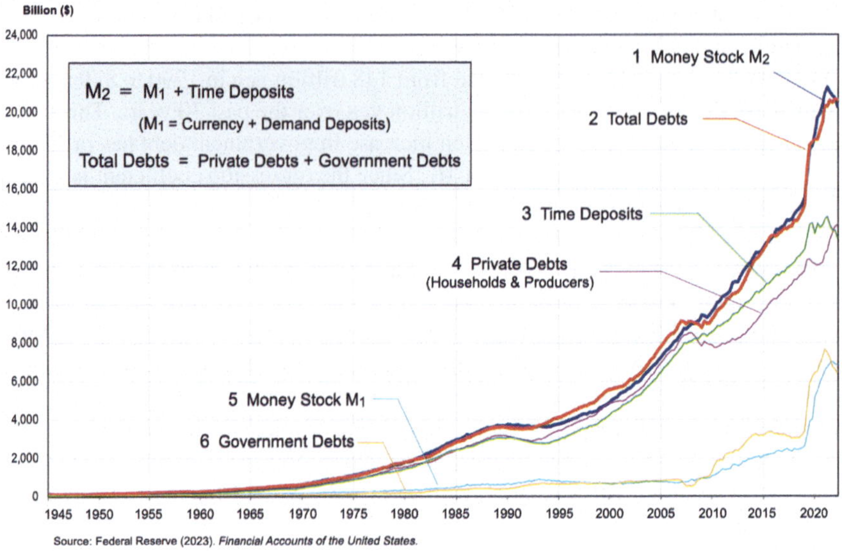

Fig. 3.9 Decomposition analysis of $M_2 \simeq$ total debts in the US (1945–2022)

We have similarly obtained a close correlation between M_1 and government debts and their linear regression equation is determined as follows (in million dollars):[17]

$$M_1 \simeq \text{Government Debts (Correlation Coefficient} = 0.9787) \tag{3.13}$$

$$M_1 = 89,886 + 0.7878 * \text{Government Debts} \quad (R^2 = 0.958) \tag{3.14}$$

Furthermore, a close correlation between time deposits and private debts was found as well as its linear regression determined as follows (in million dollars):

$$\text{Time Deposits} \simeq \text{Private Debts (Correlation Coefficient} = 0.9939) \tag{3.15}$$

$$\text{Time Deposits} = 251,207 + 1.0949 * \text{Private Debts} \quad (R^2 = 0.988) \tag{3.16}$$

The two relationships were disturbed since 2008 when the financial crisis hit the economy. Following the burst of the sub-prime mortgage loan bubble, we can observe a sudden and significant decline in private debts. Under the debt money system, money stock should have contracted in the US as it did in the 1930s. However, we did not see any significant contraction this time. Why? It was because the federal government had stepped in and increased debts on behalf of the private sectors as

[17] Quarterly data becomes fully available for each transaction item in the FAUS from 1951. To obtain more precise results, therefore, the correlation and regression analyses were performed here for the period of 1951–2022.

Fig. 3.9 shows. Deposit contraction was thus avoided by the increase in fiscal expenditures financed by government debts.

By looking at the debt money and their breakdown relationships in Japan and in the US, we can observe the contrasting policy outcomes during the post-bubble period in Japan (1990 onward) and the US (2008 onward). The most noticeable difference is that, in Japan, the growth of private debts (and thus GDP) remained stagnant while M_3 continued to grow as a result of government debts. In the US, there was a significant decline in private debts after the 2008 crisis, just as observed in Japan after the burst of the bubble. Yet it has managed to get back on its pre-2008 growth trend and continued to grow afterwards. However, as a result of government's deficit spendings, the US government is similarly facing with the debt crisis as in Japan. We will analyze the debt problems facing Japan and the United States in Chap. 6.

In terms of monetary and fiscal policy responses, both Japan and the US did much the same thing. Of course, the substance and scale of fiscal policy differed between the two cases, which are important factors that need to be taken into account when analyzing their impacts on the different policy outcome. Figures 3.8 and 3.9 also seem to suggest an interesting hypothesis that there exist common monetary and behavioral mechanisms working at a macroeconomic level in the two economies, but at the same time differing characteristics that have lead to the contrasting policy outcomes. For example, the underlying demographics are contrastingly different between the two economies. While total population of the US continued to grow, the total population of Japan stagnated after the burst of the bubble and began to decline since 2011. As a result, some observers of the Japanese economy have argued that the population decline and resulting aging demographics must have been the major cause of Japan's economic stagnation.

Has the population decline or other supply-side factors really been the decisive factor that divided the subsequent course of the Japanese and the US economies? In order to answer what caused Japan's Lost 30 Years, we must first understand what had enabled Japan's postwar economic success. Accordingly, in the next Chap. 4, let us focus on the Japanese case in more detail to understand why the economy that was once praised as "the Number One" experienced a financial bubble and subsequently fall into the decades of stagnation.

Chapter 4
Debt Money System is Design Failure–Lessons of Japan's Lost 30 Years

What causes economic bubbles? Are they inevitable features of capitalist system? How did a country that was once considered as "Number One" fall into economic stagnation for 30 years? The causes of Japan's Lost 30 Years have been the subjects of many economists. Yet very few, if any, have analyzed the case from the perspective of the debt money analysis obtained in Chap. 3. In order to answer these questions and solve the mystery that confronted the mainstream economics, let us first examine the case of Japan in more detail. In the second half of this chapter, we will then focus on the period leading to the collapse of the bubble and subsequent policies taken by the Government and Bank of Japan.

4.1 Miracle of Japan's Postwar Economic Success

The Postwar Occupation and Reconstruction (1940s & 50s)

Soon after the Iwo Jima island located in the western Pacific Ocean fell in March 1945, the United States (US) forces landed on the main island of Okinawa in April. And full-scale strategic bombings on the mainland Japan began. Of the 66 cities bombed, 59 had been mostly destroyed, leaving only four cities (Hiroshima, Kokura, Niigata and Nagasaki) saved as targets for the experimental atomic bomb. These indiscriminate air raids by the US forces have been reported to kill well over 400,000 civilians alone and the major cities were scorched to their grounds by B-24 and B-29 bombers. On August 6, the uranium bomb was detonated on the city of Hiroshima, and three days later, a plutonium bomb on Nagasaki, which to this day remain as the only usage of nuclear bombs in actual warfare. On September 2, a Japanese delegation of plenipotentiaries signed the Instrument of Surrender aboard the USS Missouri anchored in Tokyo Bay. This formalized the acceptance of the Potsdam Declaration

K. Yamaguchi and Y. Yamaguchi, *Public Money*,
https://doi.org/10.1007/978-981-97-6564-5_4

and Japan was now placed under the occupation of Allied Forces led by the US military.

The postwar Japan began with the dissolution of the *zaibatsu*–large Japanese business conglomerates–ordered by the General Headquarters (GHQ) as one of the measures to democratize the nation and its economy. The objective of the early occupation policies sought by the GHQ was the demilitarization of Japan to prevent the nation from ever going to war again through Article 9 of the new constitution outlined by the GHQ. This meant that its postwar governance required not only the restrictions on economic growth but also the reformation of Japanese politics and the society at large through cultural and educational policies such as the War Guilt Information Program.

The GHQ believed that one of the reasons why Japan acquired industrial strengths to wage the war of attrition, despite the economic sanctions including asset freeze and total ban on oil exports that began in August 1941 (prior to the Pearl Harbor attack) under the Roosevelt administration, was due to the concentration of wealth into the zaibatsu in the course of national arms buildup.

The ownership structure of zaibatsu was vertically linked, from the founder's family members owning the holding company of each zaibatsu, to direct affiliate companies down to other subsidiaries. Thus, shares owned by the zaibatsu families (Mitsubishi, Mitsui, etc.) were taken away. Their holding companies were dismantled. Appointment of family members to directors was prohibited. And the use of their trade names were banned temporarily. To promote healthy market competition, Japan's Antimonopoly Law was promulgated in 1947, which prohibited the establishment of holding companies.

The postwar Japan underwent severe hyperinflation due to shortages of food and energy supplies, destruction of production facilities and currency depreciation. However, the economy began to recover by late 1950s through a variety of measures including fixed exchange rate starting in April 1949, centralized industrial plannings, and increased demand induced by the Korean War.

In October 1949, Mao Zedong established the People's Republic of China. Concerned with the expansion of the communist bloc in the Far East, the Washington decided to position Japan as an anti-communist bulwark and steered its policy toward developing and managing the nation as a free enterprise system. Thus, the Washington's occupation strategy toward the defeated nations shifted from a policy of economically restraining Japan and Germany to one of harnessing their industrial strengths in order to compete with the USSR.

With the Peace Treaty of San Francisco entering into force in April 1952, the allied occupation of Japan ended. It is commonly believed that Japan finally regained its sovereignty and rejoined the international community at this time. However, the postwar occupation continues to this day through the US bases located throughout Japan and policies coordinated through the Japan-US Joint Committee.[1] As a matter

[1] The Japan-US Joint Committee, whose existence was not generally known until recently, is a working-level consultative forum established under the former US-Japan Security Treaty signed on September 1951 and the accompanying Administrative Agreement to discuss the specific operation

of fact, the four of the five major political parties of the postwar Japan, including the Liberal Democratic Party (LDP), the nation's leading political party formed in 1955, were receiving secret political funds from the US and the Soviet Union through CIA and KGB, respectively.[2]

The term "backdoor" got popular to describe a loophole in cyberspace when the whistleblower Edward Snowden exposed the global surveillance programs by the National Security Agency (NSA) in 2013. In Japan there are literally physical backdoors in various parts of the country. Therefore, under such circumstances, it follows that the Constitution of Japan written by the GHQ does not and cannot function as the supreme law of an independent nation contrary to Article 98 of the Constitution that defines as such (see Yabe 2014 further).

As we will see in this chapter, the postwar US-Japan relationship was never one of a reciprocal alliance, but a relationship better described as a suzerainty and a protectorate. Japan's such status as a *vassal state* of the United States would later resurface during trade conflicts that intensified in the 1980s when Japanese companies outpaced American competitors in key technologies, threatening the independence of the US military and national security. This is a political factor that needs to be taken into account but often overlooked despite its significance in the postwar US-Japan relationship and the Japanese politics.

Miracle of Japan's High Economic Growth (1960s & 70s)

The once-devastated economy realized high growths beginning from the late 50s. And the momentum of growth sustained through the next decade. In 1954, the Bank of Japan (BoJ), which had lost its membership to the Bank for International Settlements

---

of the US armed forces stationed in Japan. The committee holds closed-door meetings at least twice a month, once at the New Sanno Hotel (the US Navy controlled facility) located in central Tokyo and once at a location set by the Japan's Ministry of Foreign Affairs. Participants from the US side include the Minister of the US Embassy in Japan and the Deputy Commander of the US Forces Japan Command. Participants on the Japanese side include the Director General of the North American Bureau of the Ministry of Foreign Affairs as well as high-level officials from the Ministry of Finance, Justice, Defense, and Ministry of Agriculture, Forestry and Fisheries. The renewed Japan-US Security Treaty concluded in 1960 has only 10 articles in total. Yet underneath these articles exists the so-called US-Japan Status of Forces Agreement (SOFA), which stipulates court jurisdiction and other legal privileges of the US military in Japan, as well as secret agreements made between the successive Japanese prime ministers and the US government. Although still not commonly recognized even by the Japanese people, the SOFA has left Japan with no borders with the US government and military personnel since the end of WWII. As a result, even 75 years after the war, there are a number of US bases in Japan from north to south, particularly those surrounding the entire Tokyo metropolitan area from Pacific Ocean, such as Yokota (the HQ of US Forces, Japan), Zama (the HQ of US Army, Japan) and Yokosuka (the HQ of US Navy, Japan). Inside these areas are extraterritorial under the SOFA. Thus, Japanese aircrafts cannot fly into the Yokota airspace nor can they identify flying objects without being informed by the US military.

[2] The official documents reveal that Liberal Democratic Party (LDP) accepted financial aids from the US from around 1957 to 1964 (Nagoshi, 2019). Under the pretext of Soviet's financial support for the Japanese Communist and Socialist Parties, the LDP requested the support and accepted secret political funds illegally from the US intelligence agency.

(BIS) due to WWII, was welcomed back again to the BIS Monthly Governors' meetings.[3] In 1955 Japan joined the General Agreement on Tariffs and Trade (GATT), and the Liberal Democratic Party was formed. Based on supports from the CIA and its alignment with the Washington since its inception, the LDP would remain in power for the next 38 years until August 1993 just after the burst of the bubble, and hold a long-term government administration again from the late 90s onward to the present day.

The Japanese government and bureaucrats around this period set a goal of bringing the standard of living on par with that of the advanced Western nations. And the Japanese people joined in a concerted effort to rebuild its economy. Prime Minister Ikeda (LDP), a former finance bureaucrat who took office in July 1960 until November 1964, promoted growth policies under the slogan of National Income Doubling Plan. The policies focused on tax reduction, establishment of social security system and public investment by leveraging foreign capitals and loans from the World Bank. These economic policies were effectively backed by the ambitious entrepreneurs and diligent population.

While the US and Soviet Union was in conflict over the Cuban Missile Crisis, the Tokyo Metropolitan Expressway was partially opened and many routes began operation subsequently. Sony launched micro-TV around this time, and the economy was growing at an accelerating pace in the run-up to the Tokyo Olympics held in October 1964. The Japanese National Railways, now Japan Railways (JR) after its privatization in 1987, began its operation of the nation's first high-speed train known as the *Shinkansen* just before the Tokyo Olympics started, connecting Tokyo and Osaka, which previously took 6.5 hours, in about 3 hours with the maximum speed at 210 km/h–the world's fastest at the time.

Japan joined the OECD in the same year of 1964 and capital liberalization was implemented. Ikeda's economic policies were carried over to the next Cabinet under the Prime Minister Sato (LDP), who took office in November 1964.[4] The Ikeda's initial goal was to double the national income per capita in 10 years. However, the economy recorded faster growth and this goal was achieved as early as in 1967. Japan's nominal GNP measured in US dollars surpassed that of France in 1966 and the UK in 1968 to become the world's second largest economy in just 20 years after the cities were burned to their grounds.

---

[3] The BoJ's formal BIS membership was later granted in 1970 during the term of the 22nd BoJ Governor Sasaki, and the BIS's board membership was finally granted in 1994, just after the burst of the bubble, under the 26th Governor Mieno. After WWII, the practice continued at the BoJ of alternating its governorship between the former bureaucrat from the Ministry of Finance and BoJ's career staff, with the exception of the 21st Governor Usami who came from the Mitsubishi Bank. Both governors Sasaki and Mieno were former BoJ executives.

[4] Sato is the younger brother of former Prime Minister Nobusuke Kishi (LDP) who held the office before Ikeda between 1957–1960. Kishi himself was the Sato's older brother, and one of the 19 people who were originally imprisoned in Sugamo Prison as the Class-A war criminals in the Tokyo Trial but were later released after the indictment was dropped. Kishi is the maternal grandfather of Prime Minister Shinzo Abe (LDP), who held the office for the longest period from 2012 until 2020. During the Abe administration, BoJ introduced the Quantitative Easing (QE) policy in 2013, the effects of which will be analyzed in Chap. 5.

In 1964 the Trans Pacific Cable (TPC-1) was successfully completed as a joint project between the two nations that were once enemies. In the same year IBM introduced the world's first general-purpose computer, the System/360. In Japan, Hayakawa Electric (now SHARP) introduced the world's first desktop-size electronic calculator CS-10A made fully with transistor diodes. In the late 1960s Japan's total population surpassed 100 million for the first time in its history. While the US was still deeply involved in the Vietnam War, Japanese economy continued its growth and overcame the two oil shocks in the 1970s. Specifically, the economy continued to grow for about 20 years from 1956 to 1973, with an average annual growth rate of around 9∼10% in real terms.

With the Nixon Shock in August 1971 and subsequent collapse of the Smithsonian Agreement in 1973, Japan once again found it difficult to maintain the fixed exchange rate. As other developed nations did at the time, Japan also shifted to a floating exchange rate system. As the yen appreciated in tandem with export-led growth, Japan used the foreign currency earned from exports (mainly US dollars) to purchase raw materials from overseas and produced high-quality products on a large scale. Population inflows from rural areas to urban areas also increased, supporting high growth during this period. In May 1972, Okinawa, which had been under US administration since 1954 under the San Francisco Peace Treaty, was finally returned to Japan, except the US bases.

In 1978 Japan followed the lead of the Washington in pursuing a cooperative policy toward the communist government of China. And the Treaty of Peace and Friendship between China was concluded, marking the beginning of economic exchange between the two nations. Deng Xiaoping, the then Vice Premier, visited the Nippon Steel's steelworks and blast furnaces equipped with state-of-the-art facilities. He also visited the Nissan's plant where industrial robots were operating and took a ride on the high-speed bullet train.

Following the Deng's visit, the delegation from China's National Economic Council visited Japan, touring so many places that it was later rumored that they met with everyone but Japanese Communist Party and Self-Defense Forces. Japanese bureaucrats from the Economic Planning Agency gave them lectures on industrial and technology policy. And Japanese industrialists also strongly backed the economic exchange. Petrochemical plants and steel mill construction technology were exported from Japan, and Chinese people learned the Quality Control. These economic exchanges with Japan provided the seeds and grounds for China's subsequent development as the world's factory.

Readers may get the impression that Japan's postwar economic strategy worked perfectly. In reality, this was certainly not the case. In 1960 Japan's energy self-sufficiency rate was around 60% when the country was mainly utilizing domestically produced coal and hydroelectric power. Since the 1970s, however, Japan began to increasingly rely on coal and oil imported from overseas. As a result, it became only 15% in 1970 and by 1980 it had dropped to 12.6%. After experiencing the two oil shocks, the government has been promoting diversification of energy sources and procurement countries. Yet its energy self-sufficiency rate has never recovered since. And the economy's extremely low self-sufficiency rate continues today, with 90% of its crude oil imported from the Middle East.

"Japan As Number One" (From 1980s Onward)

The Japanese economy, which was developing steadily from the mid 1970s, now enters the next decade. Along with growth in its size, technological innovations continued across its industries, especially in automobile, construction, telecommunications and electronics. In 1980 Japan's annual domestic automobiles production exceeded 10 million units, surpassing that of the US as the world's largest producer. In the semiconductor industry, Japan gained international competitiveness and grew rapidly, particularly in the field of dynamic random access memory (DRAM) products, which were used in consumer electronics such as video cassette recorders and computers. Japanese manufactures were constantly striving to improve the yields and manufacturing processes with Japanese-like meticulousness, such as the quality control circle and zero defects movement as bottom-up voluntary activities from the production lines.

Around 1985 Japan overtook the US to become the world's number one producer of semiconductors based on shipment value. Sony introduced a handheld video camera using a high-speed semiconductor (CCD) as the image sensor, and Toshiba launched the world's first mass-market laptop-size personal computer (T1100). In 1989 Toshiba introduced the first-generation Dynabook, an A4-size, 2.7 kg lightweight computer and took the world by surprise.

In the early 1990s, Sony and Asahi Kasei led the world in commercializing lithium-ion batteries, which have become indispensable power sources for our smartphones, hybrid vehicles and so on. The production technology for blue color LEDs, which were also invented by Japanese scientists and engineers, enabled a white light source in electrical appliances and has since contributed to energy conservation in industries worldwide. The QR code, which is used around the world for everything from inventory management to retail payments, was also developed in 1994 by Japanese engineers at Denso Corporation.

In 1997 Toyota brought the world's first mass-produced hybrid vehicles into the market, pioneering and advancing efforts to reduce carbon emission from vehicles. In April 1998, the construction of Akashi Kaikyo Bridge completed and opened to traffic as the world's longest suspension bridge. Of course, Japan also had severe pollutions in the 1950s and 60s. However, urban planning and anti-pollution measures implemented helped to reduce these environmental issues.

From the economic development perspective, Japan's success exemplified the welfare capitalism and its emphasis on public interests as reflected in the *sampo-yoshi* business management principle.[5] And the economy has continuously ranked

---

[5] *Sampo-yoshi* means beneficial (*yoshi*) for the three stakeholders (*sampo*). It is an expression in business management philosophy that a good business is the one in which not only the seller and buyer are satisfied, but the business itself should also contribute to the well beings of the people and their local societies. The significance of social purpose has been highly valued in Japan for a long time. The expression itself originates from merchants based in *Omi*, which is a region around Lake *Biwa* located in east of Kyoto. Omi is known to be the birthplace of many merchants from the late *Edo* to Meiji period who are considered to be the roots of today's leading department stores and general trading companies (*sogo soshas*). Due to their geographical location, their commerce

the highest in the Economic Complexity Index.[6] In many ways, Japan indeed achieved the success that was once praised as the "Number One" (Vogel, 1979).

4.2 Japanese Management and Industrial Structure

Japanese industries and the overall economy were characterized by its (1) business management and working philosophy known as Japanese management, (2) corporate structure through cross-shareholdings called *keiretsu*, and (3) Japanese main banks and decentralized financial system consisting of local banks and credit unions.

From small to medium-sized enterprises (SMEs) to large corporations, Japanese companies have hired people as new "members" of the company (*kaisha*) rather than job-based disposable labor. Once Japanese workers (often new graduates) joined companies, they enjoyed the lifetime employment system with strong family-oriented welfare programs. Japanese companies have also developed a personnel system that fosters generalists and corporate identities by providing new employees with their own housing and dormitories, which in turn provided opportunities to build informal human networks and nurture corporate cultures among employees assigned in different departments. This Japanese-style management and employment culture have not only worked to develop a sense of job security and belonging to the company from the worker's perspective, but also encouraged their teamwork and development of new skills under the long-term (often lifetime) employment prospects.

From managerial and industrial perspectives, this employment practice has enabled Japanese companies to accumulate know-hows, adopt new technologies, and retain skilled workers in the production line while assigning experienced staffs in the administrative departments.

The second characteristics that enabled the sustained growth was the stable business environment as seen in the Japanese corporate groups called keiretsu, each linked by cross-shareholdings among affiliate companies. During the growth period leading up to the mid 1960s, companies from the prewar zaibatsu stream that had still kept their business relationships gathered to form the six major keiretsu: Mitsubishi, Sumitomo, Mitsui, Fuyo, Sanwa and Dai-Ichi Kangyo.

While the prewar zaibatsu segregated their business fields from each other, companies that made up each keiretsu encompassed almost all major industries, from

spanned in two-way directions, bringing goods from Kyoto and Osaka regions, where the Emperor and Daimyos resided until the 17th century, to the countryside, and bringing goods back to more populated areas.

[6] Economic Complexity Index (ECI) published by the Harvard's Growth Lab is "[A] rank of countries based on how diversified and complex their export basket is. Countries that are home to a great diversity of productive know-how, particularly complex specialized know-how, are able to produce a great diversity of sophisticated products." Source: atlas.cid.harvard.edu/rankings [accessed: February 11th, 2023]. According to the ECI, Japan has been observed as the economy with highest index since 1995 when the index starts until the most recent year 2020 in a row. See Hidalgo and Hausmann (2009) for technical aspect.

insurance and other financial services, to general trading companies, food supplies, textiles, mining, construction, and the heavy and chemical industries. Similar to the prewar zaibatsu, each keiretsu had their own *main banks*, from which their keiretsu name came from. However, the biggest difference between zaibatsu and keiretsu lies in their shareholding structures, both of which emerged as methods to form a robust corporate structure and business environment.

Ownership structure of the zaibatsu exhibited a vertically linked top-down hierarchy, while that of the keiretsu was more horizontal mesh-like network structure, where affiliated companies mutually owned a fraction of shares. Japanese companies had anticipated that capital liberalization would allow foreign investors to buy and sell Japanese stocks, increasing the risk of corporate takeovers. In order to defend against potentially hostile takeovers by domestic and foreign entities, cross-shareholdings began to be promoted among affiliated companies, which ultimately strengthened not only their business relationships but also their capital structures. And this was how the Japanese keiretsu were formed in the 1960s.

Japanese Main Banks and Decentralized Financial System

Cross-shareholdings among Japanese companies have not only functioned as a practical means of preventing hostile takeovers, but also enabled stable management while building long-term relationships with other firms in the supply chain, improving logistical efficiency, strengthening marketing efforts, and securing product distribution channels. However, the actual production and commercialization of new products require a great deal of funds for research and development (R&D) and other operational investments. At the foundation of these corporate groups were the Japanese main banks that supported business activities from financial and information domains.

Japanese main banks, as the name implies, refer to the largest of multiple banks with which Japanese companies conduct businesses and maintain close relationships. Main banks played an important role in corporate management by coordinating fund procurement with other banks and dispatching personnel to companies to which they had provided loans. Already established in the 1950s, these main banks not only took the credit risk associated with lending, but also invested in the equities of the companies they lent to. When companies grew, not only did they get back the principal they had loaned, but they also made significant (unrealized) profits on the shares they had invested.

In this way, long-term relationships were established between the main banks and their keiretsu companies. Main banks also gained advantages in understanding the actual business conditions and information of the companies by sending executives. By facilitating and maintaining firm relationships among keiretsu companies and providing them with various advice on corporate finance, the main banks were an integral part of the capitalist system that was unique to Japan, in which banks were incentivized to actively monitor and discipline corporate management through their long-term relationships.

In addition to these major city banks, which were the largest in size, there were well over 4,000 cooperative financial institutions throughout the country, including *shinyo-kinko* (credit banks) and *shinyo-kumiai* (credit unions). Modeled after the German Reiffeisenbank, the eligibility for investment in Japanese credit unions is limited by law to SMEs and individuals in their local areas. For the majority of Japanese SMEs, bank loans have been historically the main source of financing.

While major city banks provide loans to large corporations, these institutions are rooted in the local economies and meet the specific needs of SMEs and individual members of the cooperatives. The geographical area in which they can operate is also limited. Like capillaries of our body, these decentralized cooperative banks and credit institutions enhanced divisions of labor especially in manufacturing industries and have been the backbone of Japan's industrial complexity.

Japanese Technology and Competitive Policies

Shifting our focus from private to public sector, there is no doubt that the industrial and technology policies implemented by the government contributed to the international competitiveness of Japanese companies. Since the mid 1960s, the government, mainly through the Ministry of International Trade and Industry (MITI), implemented policies that were designed to promote non-defense R&D in the private sector. These policies included coordination and strategic funding of cooperative research through national projects, effective use of government subsidies, tax incentives and other public financing schemes, such as conditional loans and the Ministry of Finance's Fiscal Investment and Loan Programs (FILP). Through various channels, the Japanese bureaucrats (MITI in particular) maintained close connections with the industries. This private-public partnership also provided industrial oversight channels for the bureaucrats, whose tasks also involved facilitating information exchange among rival companies through research consortia, promoting competition, while forming industry-wide consensus.

One of the successful national projects around this time was the Very Large Scale Integration (VLSI) technology. In 1975, Nippon Telegraph and Telephone Public Corporation (now NTT Group after its privatization in 1985) started the ultra LSI development project in corporation with Fujitsu, Hitachi, and NEC. The first phase of the project, which lasted three years with total budget of 20 billion yen, succeeded in developing 64K DRAM and 128K ROM. In 1976, a separate four-year joint project was initiated, which had a total budget of around 70 billion yen (of which 30 billion came as government subsidy). This VLSI project, which took the form of technology research association, brought over 100 researchers from five major rival companies in computer manufacturing (Fujitsu, Hitachi, NEC, Mitsubishi and Toshiba) and led to the development of steppers and electron beam lithography equipment.

The later optical steppers were based on developments in this VLSI project, which enabled micro fabrication with significantly high yields, changing the history of semiconductor manufacturing. These projects laid the foundation for the subsequent growths of Japanese semiconductor industry in the 1980s and enabled them to overtake the American manufactures, which were competing in earlier technology of mask aligner. The MITI bureaucrats not only encouraged private companies to conduct their own R&D, but also promoted standardization and technological exchange at the industrial level, successfully creating synergies while balancing competitions.

In this way Japanese companies were able to remain at the forefront of innovation in high tech industries. It was viewed that the Japanese success was simply the result of a state-dominated system as reflected in the popular image at the time, such as "Japan Inc." and "Notorious MITI". However, Japan in the 1980s spent only a slightly higher percentage of its GNP on R&D than the US. For instance, a study on Japan's technology policy by the Council on Competitiveness reported that the Japanese government funded only about 20% of its total R&D in 1989, which was "the lowest percentage of national R&D spending among major industrial nations" (Cheney and Grimes 1991, p.7).

While scholars may point to other factors that led to the Japanese success, such as the mindset, ethos, ethics or other cultural traits, one could thus observe that the Japanese society was organized for the success at all levels; from individuals, families, companies and banks, to government and public-private joint initiatives, all of which were essential elements for the high and sustained growth that Japan achieved in the 1970s and 80s. Competitiveness thus gained, together with highly skilled and diligent workers, led to the overall stability and longevity of Japanese companies.[7] The robust capital structure in turn enabled in-house R&D, process improvement and total quality control, most known to the world by the Toyota's *kaizen* philosophy and lean manufacturing.

4.3 US-Japan Trade Conflicts and Structural Reform Requests

These three institutional pillars, together with industrial policies orchestrated by bureaucrats in the central government, were the overall economic model that characterized Japan's postwar economic system and its welfare capitalism. It was not a "miracle" after all. Japan's economic success was a natural fruit of the joint efforts among private and public sectors, driven by determinations to reconstruct the nation from the ruins of the war and catch up with the West. A secure and cohesive society consisting of a thick middle class has thus been developed. Japan enjoyed a golden

---

[7] Japan is also known to have the world's highest number of "longevity companies" that have more than 100 years of business history. According to the latest survey by Teikoku Databank Ltd. (TDB), the number of longevity companies has exceeded 40,000 in August 2022, with approximately 1,000 to 2,000 new companies celebrating their 100th anniversary each year. According to a 2019 survey conducted by the TDB and Bureau van Dijk, the United States is in the second place with 19,497 companies, Sweden in third with 13,997 companies and Germany in fourth with 4,947 companies. The oldest company in Japan is *Kongo Gumi* founded in 578 by palace carpenters and has been in the business since the construction of Shitennōji Temple in Osaka. By industry, many of these longevity companies are rental offices, breweries, traditional hotels and inns (*ryokan*), clothing retailers and construction.

decade of generally stable growth in real GDP from 1974 to 1984, overcoming its resource scarcity by manufacturing-based high tech industries and export-oriented economy.

Despite being at the mercy of the US's trade policy that demanded voluntary export restraint (VER), the world, including the American consumers, would not stop buying *Made in Japan* products at the time. Japan's exports continued to grow in the 1980s, particularly in steel, machine tools, automobiles, electronics equipments and semiconductor products. As a result, the US under the Reagan administration fell into the twin deficits between the two nations. The US had seen a surge in unemployment already in the mid 1970s, but the trade deficits with Japan continued to expand. And this intensified economic frictions between the two nations.

Growing Frustration over the Trade Deficits and VER

In 1980, the US economy was just in the midst of a recession and the overall demand became sluggish. Yet the sales of Japanese cars increased because small cars got more attractive after the two oil shocks. Especially, the fuel efficiency and reasonable price of Japanese cars were becoming popular. As a result, the Big 3 (GM, Ford, Chrysler) and American Motors all fell into the red.

Chrysler in particular faced with the risk of bankruptcy and needed a $1.5 billion loan guarantee from the federal government. As a result, the American automakers were forced to lay off workers. And there was a growing outcry that "Japan is exporting unemployment." In June of the same year, the United Automobiles Workers filed a complaint with the US International Trade Commission to invoke Section 201 of the Trade Act, claiming that Japanese cars were responsible for the surge in unemployment. Ford followed the same suit and demanded protection of American companies by restricting imports of Japanese cars.

The 1980 was also a year of presidential election. Therefore, the trade friction between Japan was more likely to become political. And the Republican candidate Ronald Reagan promised to "try to convince the Japanese" in his campaign. When he took office in the following year, the key cabinet members called for self-regulation by the Japanese government. Recognizing the need for some kind of trade policy, the United States Trade Representative (USTR) entered negotiations with the Japanese counterpart, the MITI. In the end, demands from the Japanese side were not accepted, and a self-imposed cap of 1.68 million vehicles per year was adopted beginning from 1981, as demanded by the US.

Initially the agreement on VER was limited to three years. However, the American manufacturers were not able to get back on their feet. Hence, the Japanese government under the Prime Minister Nakasone (LDP), who had been under pressure from the US government to eliminate the trade deficit since his inauguration in November 1982, decided to continue the VER on automobiles even after 1984, with the upper limit now increased to 1.85 million units. VER was further extended from 1985 onward, with the maximum limit of 2.3 million vehicles per year. And the cap was finally eliminated at the end of March 1993, with the last year cap set at 1.65 million.

The US's demands for trade restriction on Japan were not limited to the automobile industry. It ranged from steel, machine tools, semiconductors, to supercomputers, construction, and other services. In fact, trade frictions between the two nations had already began from the 1950s to the late 70s, due to rapid increase in Japan's exports of textiles, steel, and other products.

In 1972, Japan and the US signed the textile agreement. In addition, Japan implemented voluntary export controls on steel from 1972 to 1974. And finally, upon the suggestion of the US, the so-called *Market-Oriented Sector-Selective (MOSS) talks* were initiated in 1985 in specific sectors such as electronics, telecommunications, pharmaceuticals, medical devices, and forest products. In the same year Japan further agreed on VER on steels as a way to limit the share of Japanese products to 5.8% of the US consumption. From 1987, Japan implemented export controls on machine tools until 1993. This was how trade between Japan and US entered the era of *managed trade* from 1970s onward.

The US Government's Double Standard on Free Trade

In retrospect, the US's trade policies toward Japan, particularly after the Reagan administration, were full of contradictions, advocating free, open and fairness on the surface, while demanding and strengthening protectionist measures in bilateral agreements. Industry leaders and policy makers in the US viewed the Japan's economic model first with admiration, but gradually with grievance, and then later with resentment and denial, as most exemplified by the 1987 incident where members of the Congress destroyed the Toshiba products with a hammer in front of the Capitol building.

Despite being at the mercy of the US's aggressive stance on its trade policy, the American consumers did not stop buying Toyota, Sony, and other *Made in Japan* products. The US's total trade deficit increased from 25 billion dollars in 1980 to about 160 billion dollars in 1987. Policymakers in the US and lobbyists backing them began to recognize that if Japan were left unchecked, it would not only deprive the US of its economic hegemony, but could undermine the independence of her national security. The US at the time took a firm stand on the issue and claimed that the reason why Japan's trade surplus was not getting reduced as initially expected even amid the strong yen and weak dollar since the Plaza Accord was due to "structural problems" on the Japanese side.

Bilateral talks and trade agreements that took place between Japan and the US in the 70s and early 80s were still focused on sector-specific issues (as in the MOSS talks).[8] However, frustrations among the US policymakers over the trade deficits accumulated toward the end of the 1980s. For them, Japanese companies were now "unfair traders" that were depriving of the US national interest. And the closed nature of Japanese business practices constituted "non-tariff barriers" against the American commercial interests.

[8] Ito and Hoshi (2020, Chap. 13) discuss further details on the US-Japan trade friction.

After all, Japan simply managed its economy in accordance with the principles of capitalism, while adhering to the Constitution outlined by the GHQ after the war and anti-trust law enacted during the occupation period. Yet, somehow, the Japanese domestic laws and regulations as well as its industrial structure began to suddenly appear as "structural impediments" to the US.

Japan-US Structural Impediments Initiative Since 1989

Unfortunately, such views toward Japan was reinforced by the relative decline of the international competitiveness of American companies and unfavorable conditions of the US economy at the time. In 1989, Japanese semiconductor products occupied roughly 50% of the world market share, making Japan truly "Number One". In 1980 Japanese banks had barely ranked in the top tenth in the world ranking by total assets, with Dai-Ichi Kangyo Bank (now part of Mizuho group) ranked in tenth. By 1989, however, Japanese banks dominated the majority of the top 10 positions (Table 4.1).[9]

Table 4.1 Top 10 internationally operating banks in world ranking (1980s)

Rank	1980	1989
1	Citicorp (US)	Daiichi-Kangyo Bank (JP)
2	Bank America Corp. (US)	Sumitomo Bank (JP)
3	Credit Agricole (FR)	Fuji Bank (JP)
4	Banque Nationale de Paris (FR)	Mitsubishi Bank (JP)
5	Credit Lyonnais (FR)	Sanwa Bank (JP)
6	Societe Generale (FR)	Nippon Kogyo Bank (JP)
7	Barclays Group (GB)	Credit Agricole (FR)
8	Deutsche Bank (DE)	Banque Nationale de Paris (FR)
9	National Westminster Bank (GB)	Tokai Bank (JP)
10	Daiichi-Kango Bank (JP)	Citicorp (US)

In response to the increasing pressures from the Congress to deal more aggressively with Japan, the new George H. W. Bush administration proposed to launch the *Structural Impediments Initiative (SII)* in July 1989 to comprehensively remove Japanese domestic regulations that were seen as "barriers" by the American business interests and the Wall Street. Through the joint interagency working groups set up under the SII, negotiators on the US side demanded improvements that went as far as reviewing the Japanese administrative procedures, business practices, corporate governance, banking system and keiretsu.

After July 1993, the SII was renamed as the *US-Japan Framework Talks on Bilateral Trade* under the Clinton administration. And from 1994 onward, various requests by the US government for deregulations and structural reform were put forward on an annual basis. The US government kept close eyes on the implementations by the

[9] Source: Himino (2005, p.23).

Japanese government of the changes submitted and included their evaluation in the annual submission of the following year.

Structural reform demanded by the US covered a wide range of areas and Japan's domestic affairs, including telecommunications, medical equipments, pharmaceuticals, finance, energy, distribution, legal services and competitive policy. These requests were presented ostensibly as "submissions" and "recommendations" to Japan as its economic partner. However, considering the postwar US-Japan relationship, especially the LDP's dependence on and subordination to the Washington, they were policy orders presented by its suzerainty.

Such lists of orders included expanding Japan's public investment by over 400 trillion yen over the course of the next decade in the 1990s; simplifying procedures when foreign companies acquire Japanese companies including triangular mergers; labor market liberalization; lifting the ban on holding companies; introduction of American-style corporate governance as well as various administrative reforms intended to weaken the authority of Japanese bureaucracy.

In the end these requests were steadily implemented in the form of deregulations and legislative amendments under the successive LDP government. In 1997, the Japanese government revised the Antimonopoly Law and liberalized the establishment of pure holding companies, which had been entirely banned under the law since GHQ dismantled the prewar zaibatsu family-owned companies. Japan's antimonopoly law also restricted shareholdings in business holding companies. However, the 1997 amendment lifted the ban on pure holding companies, and the 2002 amendment abolished the total limit on stock ownership by large companies and further removed restrictions on business holding companies. Ironically, this was how the corporate control system that had been banned by the GHQ during the postwar occupation period was lifted again at the request of the US government after the burst of the bubble in the early 1990s.

Semiconductor War between Japan and the US

Economic conflicts between Japan and the US did not abate easily as discussed. Since 1980, the Regan and successive administrations have brought the American industry representatives to Japan and put pressure on trade deals. In particular, Section 301 of the US Trade Act of 1974, ("Super-301 clause") was utilized as a negotiating card to extract concessions from its trade partners. Around February 1986, the Pentagon formed a task force and began discussing the exclusion of Japanese semiconductor products on the basis of its significance to the US national security. Naturally there was a growing concern in the US over the possible decline of its technological competitiveness. How can Japan's market share be reduced? How could its industrial strength be diminished?

The policy strategists in the US, who had been analyzing Japan's economic success model, began by framing that Japanese industries are "closed" and should open up its markets, then pressed for deregulation and structural reform of the economy, starting with the demands for voluntary export controls and dumping complaints as discussed above. Indeed, Japan did protect or subsidize producers of agricultural products (such as rice and beef) and telecommunication equipments. However, the US similarly protected or subsidized domestic producers of textiles, sugar, dairy products, steels, ships, military equipments and so on.

Japanese leaders therefore could have argued at the time that the US economy was as open or as "closed" as the Japanese. Yet Japan, which had been under the rule of the US since the end of WWII and become overly dependent on oil imports from the Middle East since the 1960s, had no choice but to bow to the American pressures. Japanese politicians (mainly LDP) and bureaucrats (mainly MITI) made political concessions with the US counterparts, accepting unfair conditions in the subsequent trade negotiations one after another.

The symbolic result was the Japan-US Semiconductor Agreement concluded in September 1986, which called for the expansion of market share for foreign semiconductor products in Japan as well as measures to prevent "dumping" as often argued by the US at the time. The US side treated the trade conflict over Japanese semiconductors as a national security issue, as their entry into the US market would threaten its advanced technology and defense industries.[10] At that time the market share of foreign semiconductor products in Japan was less than 10%. And the quality of DRAM products made by Japanese manufactures were far superior, as well-recognized by the American businesses executives themselves.

Japanese bureaucrats agreed to try to guarantee the US a specific share in the Japanese semiconductor markets. According to a former US trade negotiator, there was a confidential side letter stating the 20% share goal that accompanied the agreement (Prestowitz, 1988). To achieve the goal, the agreement decided that the Japanese government monitor its domestic market share of foreign-made products, and that Japanese manufacturers must submit their quarterly data for cost and sales to the Japanese government. Based on those data, the US was to decide the "fair market value" and instruct it to each manufacturer.

In August 1991, the earlier agreement expired. Yet a new agreement went into effect as the market share of foreign product did not progress as initially desired. Seeking to expand access to the Japanese market further, the US demanded the 20% share, citing the still low share of American products in Japan compared to that in Europe. With the support by the US, South Korean and Taiwanese products began to catch up by the mid-90s and the market share of Japanese products declined sharply since then. As a result, the goals of the agreement were achieved and the second agreement expired in July 1996.

In retrospect, the US's semiconductor bargaining toward Japan has worked brilliantly. In 1989 Japanese semiconductors occupied roughly 50% of the world market

[10] Note that Japan at the time was developing its own next-generation fighter jet. In 1984 the Japanese Defense Agency decided to introduce a new support fighter (FS-X) due to the aging and obsolescence of the former F-1 fighter. Domestic development was desired as the natural choice of a sovereign nation. However, after many twists and turns, it was decided in 1987 to jointly develop with the US based on F-16 of the General Dynamics (now Lockheed Martin). Not only its domestic development was compelled to be abandoned, but unfair conditions for technology licensing of Japan's proprietary technology to the US was agreed upon. This was another instance where the political reality of the postwar US-Japan alliance has resurfaced.

share, making "Japan as Number One" also in the cutting-edge industry. After the 1990s, however, Japanese manufactures, which had carved out a niche with consumer electronics, were unable to take the *de facto* standard, as the world had already entered the era of personal computers (PC) and mobile phones. The US government and industry leaders seem to have anticipated that Japanese manufactures would eventually be caught up by the South Korean and Taiwanese firms, which were backed by the US.

Therefore, even though the American companies were losing ground to the Japanese in memory devices, it was more important from the US national security standpoint to maintain its dominance in the CPU, which would become more important in the PC market and critical components for combat aircrafts and defense systems. Indeed the Intel had withdrawn from the DRAM business in 1985, and from there, the company shifted its strategy to focus on microprocessors (MPU). In the chip war of the 1980s, the US's strategy of reducing the market share of Japanese firms succeeded. Although the underlying nature of politics and stakeholders are different from that of Japan and the US in the 1980s, the ongoing US-China trade conflicts is reminiscent of the Japanese experience.

4.4 The Bubble and Its Collapse in the 1990s

BoJ's Expansionary Monetary Policy induced the Bubble

In August 1985, in the midst of the US-Japan trade conflicts, a B747 operated by Japan Airlines (JAL) crashed into Mt. Osutaka, killing 520 people. The following September, the G5 finance ministers and central bank governors gathered behind closed doors at the Plaza Hotel in New York City and agreed on the coordinated intervention into foreign exchange markets (the Plaza Accord). Within a year the yen appreciated from 250 to 150 yen per dollar. For an export-oriented economy like that of Japan, a sharp currency appreciation would have lead to a stock price reaction. But the Nikkei average, which was about 12,600 yen in September 1985, remained stable on the back of solid economic fundamentals.

In 1986, the BoJ lowered the interest rate from 5.0% to 3.0% four times in January, March, June, and October. And in February 1987, supposedly as a countermeasure to the strong yen recession, the BoJ further cut its policy rate by 50 basis points from 3.0% to 2.5%, its lowest level ever at that time (see Fig. 4.1).

This low interest rate policy led to unprecedented economic booms as competition among major Japanese city banks escalated. Pursuing for higher market share and profitability, their portfolios began to lean towards mortgage and real estate loans. Their balance sheets expanded rapidly, as reflected in the increase in the slope of total debts as well as private debts shown in Fig. 3.8.

The stock market began to soar from 1986 onward. The shares of NTT, a major telecommunication company just privatized in 1985, got off to a good start in February 1987 with an initial price of 1.6 million yen and soon reached a high of 3.18 million yen on April 22. The interest rate cut by the BoJ in Februrary of 1987 increased the year-on-year growth rate of total bank loans outstanding for another 2%, which had already been hovering at around 11% after the Plaza Accord. As a result of this *super* expansionary credit guidance by the Bank of Japan, prices of condominiums and other real estates in central Tokyo began to sore. And from 1988 onward, prices in Osaka also skyrocketed.

The maintenance of low interest rates during this period clearly caused expansion of the bubble. However, according to a former BoJ executive director at the time, who was interviewed anonymously by the Japan's national TV program (NHK), the New York stock market's crash on October 19, 1987 (the Black Monday) put an end to the discussion of raising interest rates. On December 29, 1989, the Nikkei average reached an all-time high of 38,957 yen and the bubble was at its peak. The BoJ's misjudgment around this time became a turning point. We will analyze what was happening inside the BoJ later in this chapter.

Deposit Creation by Commercial Banks Fueled the Bubble

Non-bank financial institutions were also lending furiously around this time. According to the BoJ statistics, the total increase in non-bank loans was approximately 25 trillion yen per year in the late 1980s. A simple average of such increase in total non-bank loans showed a monthly increase of 2.08 trillion yen, which is equivalent to 65.8 billion yen per day. The total construction cost of the Tokyo Sky Tree project completed in 2012 was estimated to be about 65 billion yen. Given that consumer prices in Japan has not changed much for the last three decades, the increase in non-bank loans during this period was on the scale of the Sky Tree (634m) being built one after another every day.

An another example that was often used to illustrate the scale of the Japanese bubble at the time is that the land price of the Imperial Palace in Tokyo, which is slightly less than 3.4 km^2 or 1.3 mi^2, was almost equal to the land prices of the entire state of California in around 1990. In a similar manner, Cutts (1990) observed "… the calculated cash value of a single ward in downtown Tokyo–Chiyoda-ku–could purchase all of Canada. And another: land in Tokyo's Ginza shopping district is selling for $250,000 a square meter."

Where in the world did these money come from? Non-banks have to borrow money from someone else in order to make loans. Was it the government rolling its printing machines day and night? Or was it the central bank (BoJ) printing so much money and giving out to banks? As discussed in Chap. 3, the incessant lending by commercial banks (called "mother bank") to non-banks in their keiretsu created massive amount of deposits (credits). And asset prices soared as newly created money were channeled to speculative financial transactions.

It was around this period when Japanese investments in iconic real estate properties grabbed the American news headlines. In 1989 Sony acquired the Columbia Pictures and the Mitsubishi Estate bought the Rockefeller Center in Manhattan, although Mitsubishi gave up the building after the bubble collapsed and Sony is no longer the Japanese company, with more than 50% of its shares currently held by foreign investors. Just before the COVID-19 pandemic, the so called "China Money" was said to be buying up companies and properties around the world. Just at the end of 1980s, there was a similar sense of fear that "Japan Money" was buying up America across the board. Kaoru was teaching at the the University of Hawaii at the time and vividly remembers the momentum of Japan money. He was interviewed by a local TV station when the news broke that real estate agents from Japan with bags full of cash were buying up properties and luxury homes in Honolulu at random.

BoJ's Interest Hikes and Collapse of the Bubble (1990s)

In May 1989, the BoJ finally raised the interest rate by 0.75% from 2.5% to 3.25%, and in October, by another 0.5% from 3.25% to 3.75%. On December 17th, Yasushi Mieno from the BoJ was appointed as the next governor, replacing the former Governor Sumita who had previously served as the Administrative Vice Minister of Finance. Since the end of WWII, it has been customary for the BoJ's governor to be appointed alternately from the former Ministry of Finance (MoF) bureaucrats and the proper staff from the staff from the former BoJ executives.

Immediately after taking the office, Governor Mieno further raised the policy rate on Christmas. As a result, the Nikkei plummeted since the beginning of the next year. In the first quarter of 1990, the Nikkei plummeted to the 20,000-yen level; roughly 25% decline. On March 27, 1990, a Director-General of the Bank Supervision Bureau of the MoF issued a ministerial notice regulating the total volume of real estate loans. And this seemed to have signaled that the excessive speculative lending and the real estate bubble must finally come to an end.

The BoJ under Mieno, however, continued to tighten monetary policy in 1990 and raised the policy rate by 1.0% from 4.25% to 5.25% on March 20th. And five months later, in August, BoJ decided on another 0.75% hike from 5.25% to 6.0%. Interest rates were thus raised a total of five times over the course of about a year and a half until July 1991 when the BoJ finally decided to cut rates by 0.5% to 5.5%.

As if to pop a self-inflated balloon with its own needle, these series of interest hikes were later called an outrage, as they took place in the midst of bursting of the bubble that had already began with the stock market crash in Q1 1990. Nevertheless this was the final call to Japan's decades-long prosperity. Stock market crashed further and real estate prices plummeted. And Japan was suddenly left with unprecedented amount of non-performing loans.

4.5 Economic Policies After the Burst of Bubble

As early as in 1993 companies began to cut and suspend new hiring and the effects of the burst of the bubble became evident. In August 1993, a new coalition government led by Prime Minister Hosokawa was formed. This was the first non-LDP government since 1955. However, this government collapsed after just 10 months and the next Hata cabinet resigned in about two months. During this post-bubble phase, tax reform bills were passed, which favored large corporations and became a heavy stumbling block to the subsequent recovery, coupled with cheap labor policy implemented as part of the structural reform.

Debt Deleveraging and Contraction of Money Stock

Figure 4.1 shows the evolution of the BoJ's policy rate and changes in Consumer Price Index (CPI) between 1970–2023. As we can see, bursting of the bubble has coincided with the general decline in prices since 1991, reflecting consumption that had begun to slowdown around this time. In April 1995, the BoJ cut its policy rate from 1.75% to 1.0%. In September, the BoJ further cut rates by 0.5%, bringing the interest rate to near zero. Prior to 1995, the BoJ eased or tightened monetary policy by changing the reserve ratios and the interest rate on its discount loans, along with the window guidance (discussed in Sect. 4.6).

With the completion of interest rate liberalization in 1994, the BoJ began conducting market operations to guide short-term market rates referred to as overnight (O/N) call rates, which is the equivalent of the US federal funds rate. As a result, O/N call rates came in contact with the policy rate for the first time in July 1995 and fell below it afterwards. CPI then turned upward between 1995 and 1998. The mild inflation observed around this period may have been due to the rapid depreciation of yen associated with the Asian currency crisis. Reflecting the subsequent recession, however, the inflation rate declined again. And the economy finally plunged into a deflationary path from 2000 onward.

In the same year when BoJ cut interest rate twice in 1995, the Great Hanshin-Awaji Earthquake occurred in January. In March the Sarin gas attack on the Tokyo subway occurred. These disasters and domestic terrors might have had a fundamental effect on collective mentality of the society, which had just undergone the collapse of the bubble, and might have further increased uncertainty in the people's minds. In August of the same year, Hyogo Bank collapsed, becoming the first bank failure in the postwar Japan. Until then, bailout mergers had been the norm under the support of the Ministry of Finance. As such the bank failure was regarded as the collapse of the Japanese *convoy system*.[11]

---

[11] The convoy system refers to the regulatory arrangements and the overall administrative method implemented by the Ministry of Finance (MoF) since the postwar period up until the late 1990s, when the financial system reform (*aka* Japanese financial Big Bang) began under the Hashimoto cabinet. The convoy system was characterized by (1) strict regulation of bank's business areas, branch establishment, and new entrants, (2) restriction on deposit interest rates, and (3) foreign exchange control. This system ensured the stability of the financial system by placing the highest priority especially on preventing bank failures and aligning them with smaller institutions that were particularly weak in terms of competitiveness. It was so called as it was reminiscent of the way a convoy of ships navigates with the slowest ship when escorting a fleet of vessels. The prewar financial panics had led to a series of bankruptcies of financial institutions, causing shakeouts and social unrests. After the WWII the MoF sought to establish financial order and confidence in the financial system through strict regulations and administrative guidances. In the banking sector, the convoy system meant that deposit interest rates were the same everywhere, as were business hours and transfer fees. In case of bank failures, the MoF strongly encouraged mergers and did not allow financial institutions to go bankrupt. Such administrative methods worked well and the

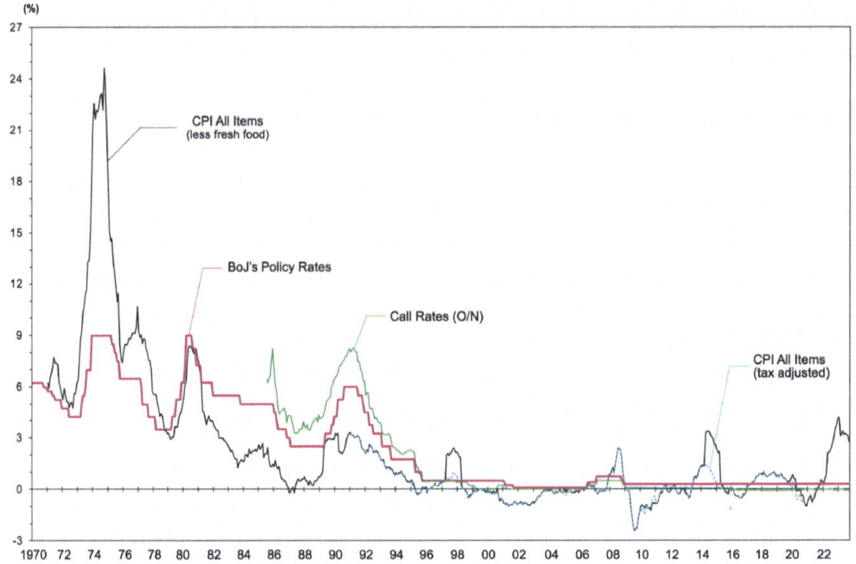

Notes: 1. All figures are monthly data, calendar years.
2. The CPI figures show year-on-year % changes starting from January 1971.
3. Call Rates; Uncollateralized Overnight, Monthly Average; % per annum.
Sources: Ministry of Internal Affairs and Communications; Bank of Japan.

Fig. 4.1 Consumer price index and bank of Japan's policy rates: 1970–2023

This triggered whispers that the conditions of financial institutions were deteriorating rapidly. In fact, ten days after the collapse of the Hyogo Bank, a credit union in Osaka failed. Credit lines began to shrink and call markets became more selective in terms of counterparty's credit risk. In response, the BoJ expanded its market operation from November 1997 and made sure that ample funds were supplied into the market, especially when banks and securities companies (such as Hokkaido Takushoku Bank and Yamaichi Securities) became insolvent.

Bank loans became increasingly nonperforming around this time. The most notable event that determined the subsequent course of the Japanese economy was the massive reduction of private debts that began from that year. These debt repayments would be made on the order of 200 trillion yen over the course of nine years until 2004 as depicted in Fig. 3.8. On average, this represented annual debt reduction of 25 tril-

economy grew through a stable supply of funds to domestic industries. Deposits created by banks became the ample savings of households, which were then reinvested into pensions, insurance, and stocks, and stabilized the financial system. Thus, the convoy system was a practical solution to the problem of how to ensure financial stability while achieving economic growth under the debt money system. However, during the administrative reforms that began in the mid-90s, financial liberalization implemented by the Hashimoto administration ended the convoy system. Interest rates, foreign exchange and other financial services were liberalized. Finally, the Financial Services Agency was newly established to separate supervisory authority over the banking and securities markets from the MoF, and the convoy system was fully dissolved.

lion yen. Coincidentally, this is about the same size of increase in non-bank loans mentioned earlier, which was 25 trillion yen per year.

This stampede to liquidate debt was analogous to a tsunami of monetary expansion during the lending boom since 1986. However, the tsunami after 1995 was moving in the opposite direction–a wave being pulled all the way back to the ocean. As discussed in Chap. 3, repayment of bank loans destroy equal amount of deposits (functional money) under the debt money system. During the Great Depression, Fisher observed that money stock shrank by about 26% over a four-year period (Table 3.1). The collapse of Japanese bubble in the 1990s similarly reduced private sector debts by about 200 trillion yen. This was the most painful phase of the *debt deleveraging*. In other words, a self-reinforcing feedback loop of the bubble, in which bank loans raise the value of collateral and the rise in collateral values draw out more loans, turned into a reverse loop, where money stock decreases as companies rush to repay their debts and banks stripped loans in order to restore their financial health.

These massive debt repayments could have wiped out a quarter of 800 trillion yen of Japan's M_3 outstanding at 1990. Yet it turned not to be the case, because, as we also discussed in Chap. 3, monetary contraction was avoided by the government's counter-borrowings through fiscal policy. Nevertheless, the burst of the bubble hit Japanese banking system hard and triggered bankruptcies of over 200 depository institutions throughout the country. This period coincided with the worsening recession and deflation, aggravating corporate cash flows, and rapid increase in the number of non-regular employees. The number of suicides in Japan exceeded 25,000 in 1983 and 1986, but declined to 21,084 in 1991 and remained in the low 20,000s thereafter. In 1998, however, the number jumped by 8,472 from the previous year to 32,863, and in 2003, the number reached a record high of 34,447 since statistics began in 1978.

It was 1995 when the international financial market was rife with the so-called *Jusen* problem, which was the massive loss on non-performing loans incurred by the Japanese housing loan corporations (non-banks) financed by their "mother banks" in their keiretsu. The fraudulent accounting by the Long-term Credit Bank of Japan led to the arrests of its former managers, followed by the collapse of the bank in 1998. A series of mergers among major banks followed, later forming the three "mega" banks, Mitsubishi UFJ, Sumitomo Mitsui and Mizuho. And finally, Japan's postal savings–the nation's largest banking institution–was privatized in 2007, which was one of the structural reform requests demanded through the US government.

Yen hits Postwar High and then Decline against US Dollar

In April 1997, the government under the Prime Minister Hashimoto (LDP) further raised the consumption tax rate from 3%, at which the tax was introduced in 1989, to 5% (4% for national and 1% for local governments). If the economy is about to stall headlong and prices of daily necessities are raised due to the tax hike, the consumption expenditure would have no choice but to stagnate.

Indeed it was right around this time when the expression *kakaku hakai* (literally, "price destruction") became a buzz word in Japan due to the growth of discount stores and fierce price competition amid strong yen at the time. The term referred to the decline in the price of certain consumer products, which were caused by the households' parsimonious attitude toward consumption and decline in their tolerance for price hikes after the bubble burst. Typical examples included clothing, eyeglasses, fast foods, computer products and services such as private english lessons. Japan's GDP also reached a plateau at 543 trillion yen in 1997 and stagnated thereafter (Fig. 4.4).

The foreign exchange rate was not favorable in the late 1990s either. Figure 4.2 shows monthly changes in USD-JPY spot rate since 1970 and short-term interest rates for both currencies. As we can see, demand for yen remained strong even after the burst of the bubble and the yen continued to appreciate against the dollar for some time, hitting a then postwar high of 79 yen per dollar in April 1995. Following the Asian currency crisis in 1997, Thailand left the dollar peg system in July and Malaysia announced its transition to a floating exchange rate system in August. The yen also depreciated from around 120 to 130 yen in November and December of that year. The Japanese government and BoJ intervened into the foreign exchange market in December, and then April and June of the following year in 1998. However, depreciation of the yen did not stop. And the exchange rate hit 146.75 yen temporarily in June 1998.

Against the backdrop of the Fed's zero-interest rate policy after the Lehman Shock, the yen continued to appreciate even after the massive earthquake and tsunami hit the northern Japan in March 2011. Subsequently, the postwar high recorded in 1995 was renewed when the USD-JPY rate hit 75.52 yen in October. In response the Japanese government conducted its largest-ever dollar-buying (yen-selling) intervention on October 31st, amounting to 8 trillion yen in a single day. The government's tax revenue in FY 2010 was 42.3 trillion yen. That is, the government poured its treasury funds into the market, which was equivalent to one-fifth of the annual tax revenue (for the general account) in just a single day.

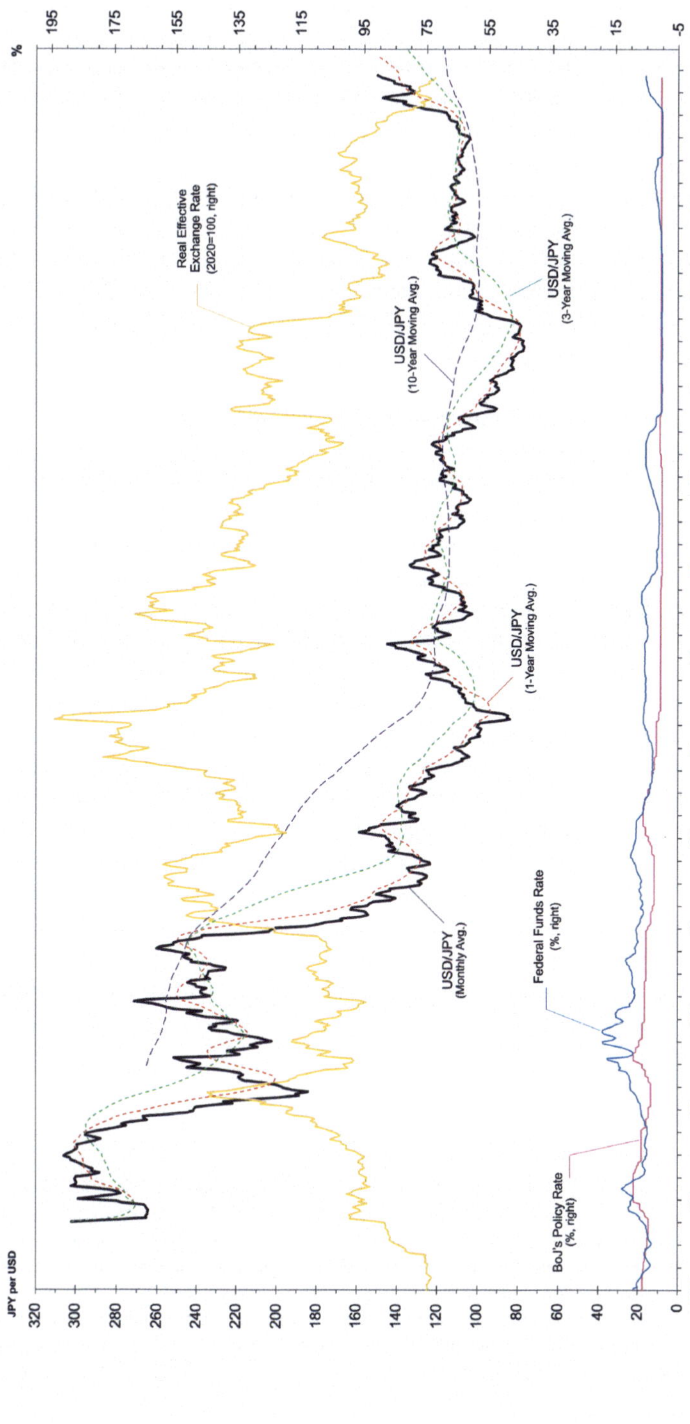

Notes: 1. All figures are monthly data, calendar years.
2. USD/JPY; Spot rate at 17:00 in JST, Average in the Month, Tokyo Market.
3. Real Effective Exchange Rate; As an index with year 2020 as 100.

Sources: Bank of Japan; Federal Reserve; BIS

Fig. 4.2 USD-JPY exchange rates and policy interest rates: 1970–2023

The real effective exchange rate (REER) in Fig. 4.2 reflects the rise and decline of the Japanese economy in terms of the yen's real purchasing power ("strength") relative to foreign currencies of its trade partners.[12] In particular, the Yen's REER reached a 53-year low in 2023, the lowest level since 1970. In general, a decline in the REER essentially means an increase in the export competitiveness of the domestic firms. In the case of Japan, however, this effect has faded as firms had already moved their production overseas in the 2000s.

On the other hand, a decline in the international purchasing power of the yen means an increase in prices of imported goods and services. If the inflation of import prices is passed on to consumers, this may become a factor that diminishes their real wage, which could further restrain their consumption. The post-2021 inflation depicted in Fig. 4.1 accelerated this trend, placing a heavy burden especially on low-income groups and worsening their living standards.

Government Responds with Unprecedented Fiscal Stimulus

During the Great Depression, the Hoover and Roosevelt administrations did not really implement fiscal stimulus as suggested by the Keynesian theory of aggregate demand management and left the economy to recover on its own. On the contrary, the Japanese Government has steadily expanded its expenditure soon after the bubble burst in 1990–91. Figure 4.3 shows year-on-year changes of government expenditures (consumption + investment) along with nominal GDP. In particular, the government expanded public investment by a total of over 400 trillion yen in the 1990s, partly due to the pressure from the US government to increase domestic demand as a way to reduce Japan's trade surplus.

The series of fiscal stimulus were implemented at levels unprecedented in nation's history, both in terms of their magnitudes and annual growth rates. Timing of these fiscal stimulus was also perfect in the sense that public investments were increased immediately after the burst of the bubble along with the interest rate cuts by the BoJ beginning from July 1991. In this sense it was a textbook case of the Keynesian counter-cyclical policy in action. However, as the subsequent trend in GDP growth shows, the series of so-called "deficit spendings" failed to stimulate the economy. At best they have worked to sustain the pre-bubble GDP level of around 520 trillion yen as Fig. 4.4 illustrates.

[12] The effective exchange rate (EER) is the weighted average of the exchange rates of the currencies of foreign nations with which Japan trades, weighted by the ratio of the value of exports to each trading partner to Japan's total exports. The real effective exchange rate (REER) is calculated by taking into account price disparities from the EER, and thus represents the yen's real purchasing power ("strength") relative to currencies of the trade partners. Therefore, the REER is often used as an indicator of the price competitiveness of a country's exports. Bank of Japan uses the Broad-based EER (covering 65 countries and regions) published by the BIS since 1993. Pre-1993 data shows the BoJ's estimation.

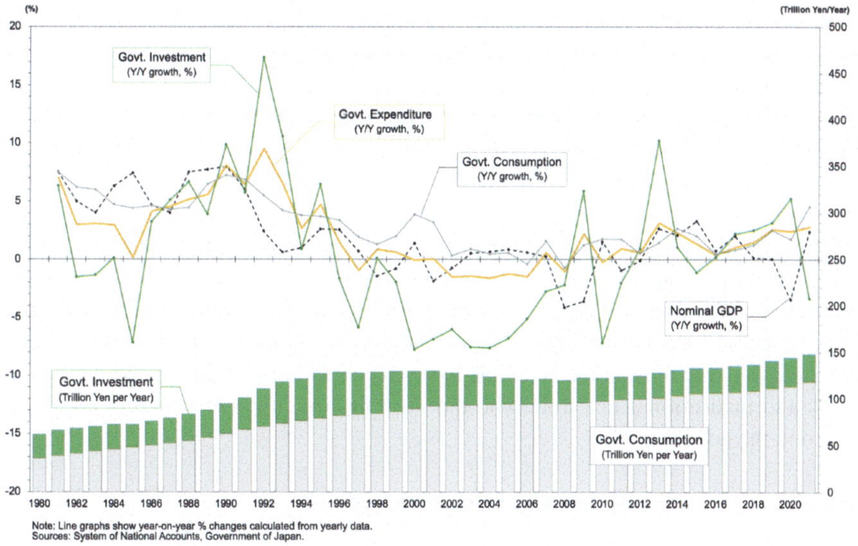

Fig. 4.3 Japanese government expanding fiscal expenditures since 1990s

Under the debt money system, the government raises money either by taxes or borrowing money by issuing treasury securities. As shown in Fig. 3.8, bank loans to the private sector (private debts) began to decline from 1996 onward. This debt reduction could have led to a massive deposit contraction over the next decade and a quarter of Japan's M_3 could have been destroyed as a result. However, at the same time, Japanese banks dramatically changed their portfolio during this period from corporate loans to treasury securities, underwriting newly issued Japanese Government Bonds (JGB) year after another.[13] Declines in private debts were therefore offset by the increase in government debt, thus narrowly avoiding the kind of monetary destruction that wrecked the US economy during the Great Depression.

For banks, underwriting JGB was a good investment from the standpoints of both credit risk exposure and funding cost, as government spendings would eventually return their reserves back to them. Stable interest revenues from JGBs soon became attractive deals that they could not miss, especially when they were struggling with non-performing loans and the BoJ's extremely low interest rate policy. In addition, the Basel I, which was fully applied in Japan since the end of 1992, required banks with international operations to achieve a capital ratio of at least 8%. In particular, it set a zero risk weight on treasuries.

---

[13] Figure 11.3 in Chap. 11 shows the historical change in the Japanese government debt during the same period including from the overseas, which clearly shows how the banking sector's investment in JGBs helped to absorb much of the government's deficit in the 1990s and 2000s. The next Fig. 11.4 depicts changes in the amount of borrowing by the top five sectors in Fig. 11.3 as a percentage of total government debts, most of which are JGB.

When the Basel Accord was finally formulated in July 1988, the fierce lending boom among Japanese city banks had been going on for years. And the bubble had already bloated as much as it could sustain. For Japanese banks that were suffering from bad debts after the burst of the bubble, this risk asset-based capital requirement conversely became a systemic constraint that made them more reluctant to increase loans to businesses, further hindering the economic recovery from the post-bubble recession.[14]

This was the reason why the Japanese banks' portfolio shifted from private to public debts around this time, and the underlying mechanism that has driven the qualitative change in the composition of Japan's total debts in Fig. 3.8. Around this time, Japanese banks also began to divest their equity holdings and Japanese stocks were released into the market. Needless to say, it was foreign investment banks, hedge funds and institutional investors who did not miss this unprecedented opportunity and took the advantage.[15]

Stagnation of Consumption and Capital Investment

Despite the continuous fiscal stimulus by the government, the large scale fiscal spending policies implemented in the 1990s did not help the economy to recover. How exactly did the Japanese economy perform at that time? Figure 4.4 shows Japan's nominal GDP and Aggregate Demand since 1980 as a stacked line graph. Note that aggregate demand excludes Net Export and Change in Inventory, which are negligible.[16] First, Japan's GDP hits the ceil in 1997 and hovers around at 520–540 trillion yen range, reflecting the overall stagnation of the last 30 years. GDP indicates how production (supply) side of the economy has been able to adjust to its demand. Therefore, in order to see why Japan's GDP stagnated, we need to look at the economy from the expenditure (demand) side.

Historically, increase in private consumption has been accompanied by the increase in private sector's investment such as capital investment (I_K) and housing investment (I_H). However, this self-reinforcing feedback loop suddenly came to an end with the collapse of the bubble in 1991. Specifically, the consumption expenditure (C) stagnated, and capital investment in particular declined. This sudden and

---

[14] The Basel Accord's capital requirement has pro-cyclical nature of constraining excessive expansion of loans for undercapitalized banks, thereby preventing the rapid explosion of the bubble. However, the capital adequacy framework based on portfolio approach is not designed to prevent the bubble itself, and it never can, as it was proven by the subsequent sub-prime mortgage crisis in the 2000s. The root cause of the bubble is deposit creation by banks. Hence, formations of speculative bubble cannot be prevented unless the deposit creation is regulated. Moreover, the capital adequacy requirement for banks becomes counterproductive in the face of recession as evidenced by the Japanese case. Under the present debt money system, where banks expand their balance sheets through loans themselves, the Basel Accord is just another "patchwork, leaving the basic structure still unsound." (Douglas et al. 1939, preface).

[15] See also Fig. 11.5 that shows changes in foreign sector's ownership of Japanese equities.

[16] Therefore, nominal GDP becomes less than Aggregate Demand (AD) in Fig. 4.4 when net export becomes negative, that is, trade deficits. Theoretically, however, GDP (production side) and AD (expenditure side) must match, except some statistical discrepancies.

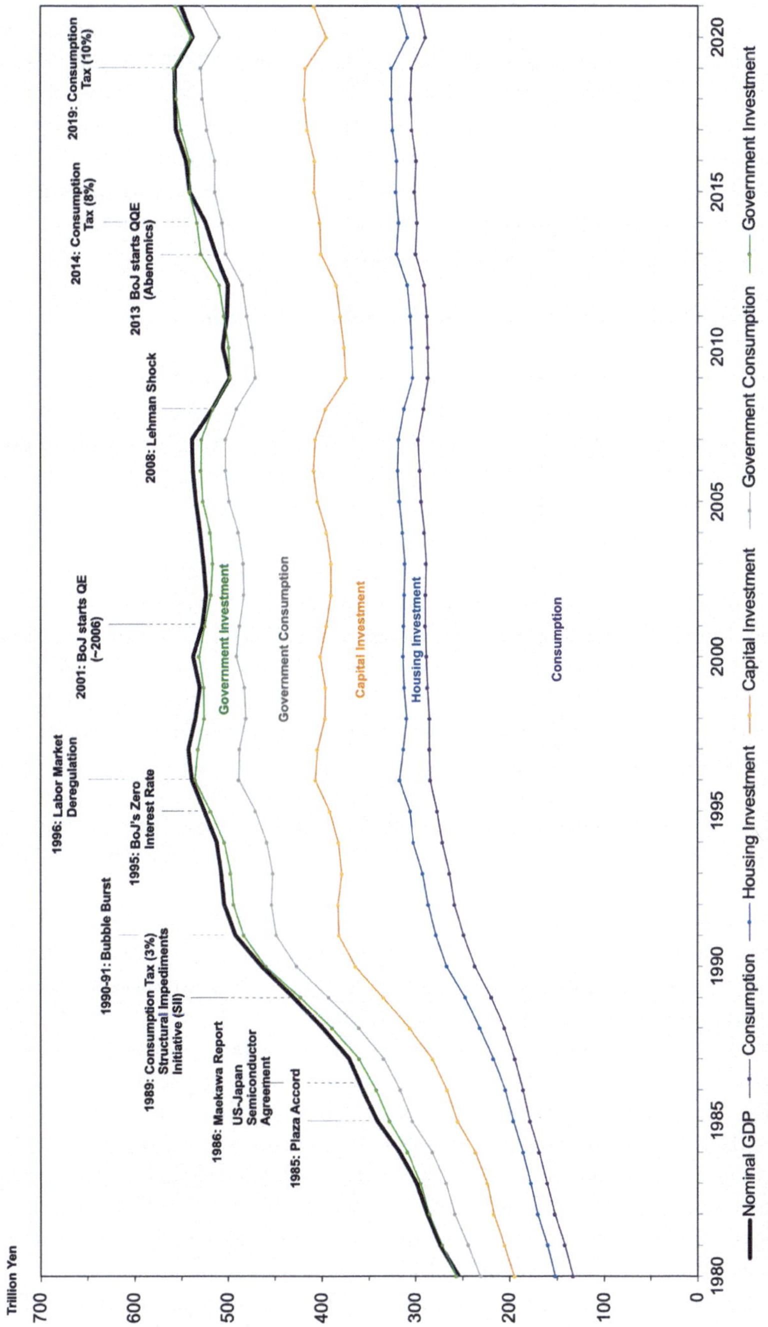

Note: All figures are annual data; excluding Inventory Investment and Net Exports from expenditures.
Source: System of National Accounts, Cabinet, Government of Japan.

Fig. 4.4 Japan's nominal GDP and aggregate demand components: 1980–2021 significant decline in private investments ($I = I_K + I_H$) is also observed as negative growth rates recorded from 1992 to 1994 in Fig. 4.5.

When we compare these expenditure data with our debt-money analysis in Fig. 3.8, it now becomes clear as to why private sector debt, which had been increasing until 1991, suddenly stagnated and peaked in 1993, and then began to decline all the way untill 2010. In other words, private debts for capital and housing investments began to decline. As a result, the private sector's aggregate demand ($C + I$), which had been the main driver of Japan's economic growth, stagnated and came to a complete halt. As if to fill these gaps in private demand, the government in turn has been increasing its expenditure through debt.

BoJ introduced QE Policy Yet Demand Remained Sluggish

In March 2000, the NASDAQ hit an all time high of $5,048. In anticipation of the Dot-com (IT) bubble, the BoJ decided in August to lift its zero interest rate policy initiated in February 1999. As Fig. 4.1 depicts, deflation in Japan got worsened around this period. As the criticism for the prolonged stagnation began to be directed toward the central bank, the BoJ was searching for something different from the conventional policy of interest rate manipulation.

In March 2001, under the 28th Governor Hayami, the BoJ introduced the Quantitative Easing (QE). Under this policy, BoJ changed its primary target of market operations from the short-term money market rate (call rate) to the BoJ's current account balance (reserve deposits). Figure 4.5 shows year-on-year percent changes in nominal GDP, private investments ($I_K + I_H$), and bank loans outstanding, together with the BoJ's policy rate and components of base money, consisting of Government Coins, the BoJ Notes and BoJ reserve deposits.

The QE policy has brought the call rate down below 0.01% level, and interest rates remained at virtually zero. However, this base money expansion did not prove to be particularly effective and was abolished in 2006 under the 29th governor Fukui. The Lehman Shock hit the Japanese economy under the next Governor Shirakawa, who took office in April 2008. As we can see from Fig. 4.5, the private investment also dropped in Japan. The Fed lowered its rate to zero lower bound and so did the BoJ (Fig. 4.2). The policy rate was once again lowered to the zero lower bound, but the BoJ was running out of policy tools by this time.

In 2010, the BoJ introduced "comprehensive monetary policy", which expanded the types and size of assets to be purchased. Under this policy, the BoJ also began purchasing Exchange Traded Funds (ETFs) and Japanese Real Estate Investment Trusts (J-REITs), which became instruments to support stock market in the next Abe administration. The Democratic Party of Japan (DPJ), which had pledged not to raise the consumption tax for four years, came to power in 2009, but collapsed in three years due to persistent criticism by the media, the US military base relocation issue, and the Fukushima nuclear accident in 2011.

The LDP won the next general election in 2012 and regained its power. The new Abe administration called for "overcoming deflation" and proceeded with the Abenomics supported by the BoJ's large-scale JGB purchases implemented under the

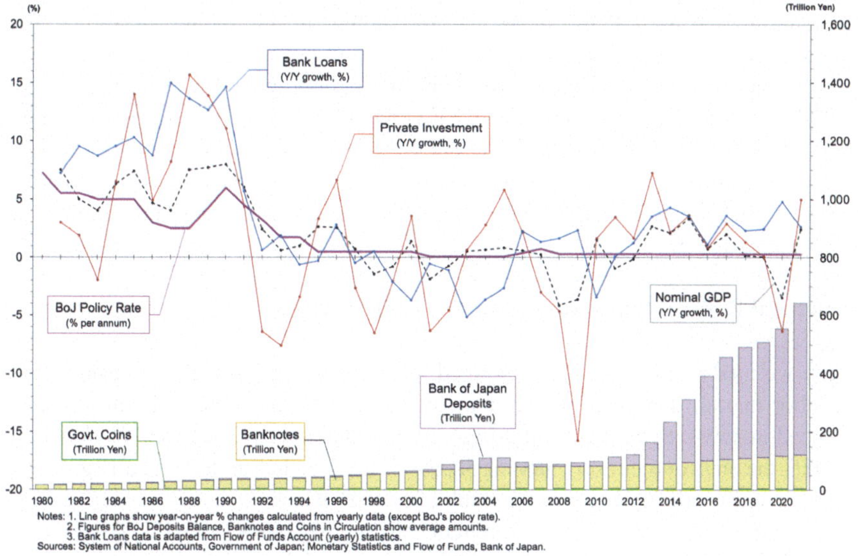

Fig. 4.5 Bank of Japan's zero interest rate and QE policies

next (31st) governor Haruhiko Kuroda, the former MoF bureaucrat. When Kuroda was summoned to the National Diet for a hearing, he stated that "the reason why Japan could not break out of deflation was that the BoJ had not done enough monetary easing" and criticized the BoJ's passive stance, while advocating a reflation theory.

Ironically, this reflationary policy was originally proposed by Fisher as a policy to get out of the Great Depression in his *Debt-Deflation Theory* (Fisher, 1932) (discussed in detail in Chap. 5 and from Chap. 7 onward). As Fig. 4.5 depicts, the BoJ once again shifted its policy from 2013 to further expanding base money.

In April 2013, soon after Kuroda took office, the BoJ decided to introduce Quantitative and Qualitative Easing (QQE) policy. Specifically, the BoJ announced that it would conduct market operation so as to increase the base money at a pace equivalent to about 60–70 trillion yen per year. Due to its size and intensity of asset purchases, this QQE policy was called "Kuroda bazooka". It was an expanded version of QE implemented under Fukui and Shirakawa.

The series of QE policies have indeed lowered the cost of government debt. In effect, the BoJ's massive buy-up of JGBs since 2013 served as a way to compensate for the sharp decline in the bond market's ability to absorb the increasing amount of new JGB issuance required by the Abenomics. However, even if the government and central bank collude together, such fiscal finance could not continue indefinitely. That is, it is impossible to contain the exponential growth in public debt without causing systemic crisis in the end. We will examine the government debt sustainability in Japan, the US, and OECD countries in the next Chap. 6.

From Figs. 4.1 and 4.4 we can observe that neither the government's fiscal expansion nor the BoJ's zero interest rate policy succeeded in bringing back the economic momentum. It was as if the more the government injects money into the economy and the more BoJ lowered interest rates, the more the economy cooled down. These policies were supposed to stimulate the economy by lowering the cost of capital investment and consumption. That is what all mainstream macroeconomics textbooks teach us. However, they did not work out that way in reality. What went wrong, then? What exactly was happening in the economy around this time? In order to answer these questions, therefore, we need to analyze what caused the stagnation of private demand.

Structural Reform that Caused Japan's Lost 30 Years

When we analyze the Japan's prolonged stagnation, it is critical to consider how the labor market deregulations implemented in the 1990s coincided with the economic slowdown. Specifically, starting with the enactment of Agency Worker Law in 1986, the environment surrounding Japanese workers has undergone a 180-degree turnaround after the collapse of the bubble in 1990–91.

As part of the structural reform requests in the 1990s, the US government demanded deregulation of the Japanese labor market, claiming that Japanese employment practices have been a major structural impediment for American companies wanting to hire workers at lower costs. In 1996, the law was amended, expanding the scope of dispatch labor service to 26 industries from the initial 13 types. And in 1999, dispatch labor business was liberalized in principle.

Deregulation continued. In 2002, the Council for Regulatory Reform, established under the Cabinet Office in April of 2001 as part of the government administrative reform initiated by Prime Minister Hashimoto (LDP) in the late 1990s, has reported to the Cabinet on the expansion of dispatch labor, including lifting the ban on worker dispatching business in the manufacturing industry. In March 2004, the law was further amended to allow the dispatch labor indefinitely in 26 industries. And three years later, in 2007, the maximum dispatch period was extended in the manufacturing industry from one to three years.

Figure 4.6 shows the number of Japanese labor force since 1984 and their employment status; regular, non-regular, self-employed, executives and unemployed workers. First, the number of regular employees increased slightly by 680,000 people from 34.88 million in 1990 to 35.56 million in 2020. On the other hand, the number of non-regular employees increased by 12.2 million from 8.81 million in 1990 to 21 million in 2020, while the number of self-employed workers has been decreasing year after year. To put this into perspective, the increase in employed workers were all non-regular (dispatched) workers during the last 30 years, roughly equivalent to Tokyo's population of 13.49 million as of 2015.

As a result, the non-regular employment rate, calculated as the ratio of non-regular employees to total employees (regular + non-regular employees), has nearly doubled from 20.2% in 1990 to 37.1% in 2020. As we can see, the rate of its increase has accelerated especially since 1996. It is now estimated that the non-regular employment rate in the service industry has already exceeded 70%, and one out of three non-agricultural and forestry workers is said to be employed on a non-regular basis.

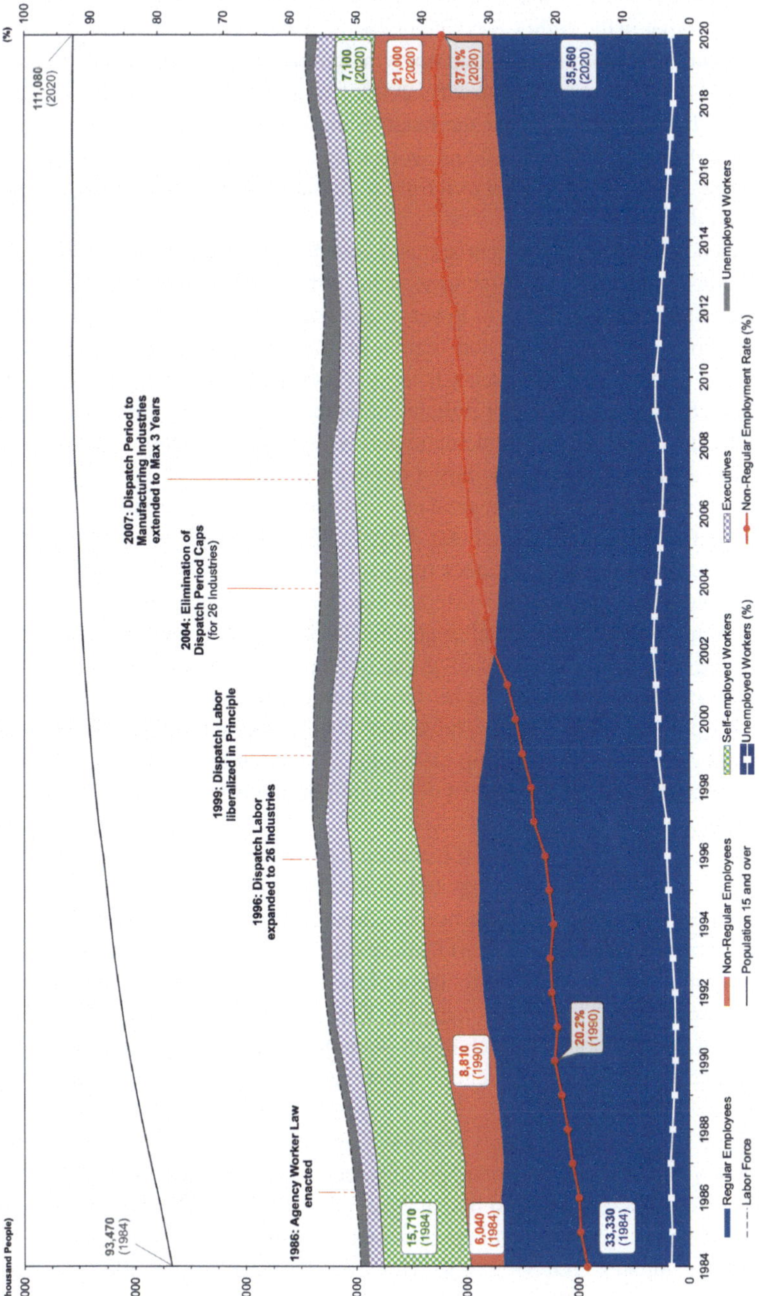

Note: Line graphs with markers show year-on-year % changes calculated from annual data.
Sources: Ministry of Health, Labour and Welfare, Government of Japan.

Fig. 4.6 Labor market deregulations and destruction of Japanese management by structural reform

The number of unemployed workers also rose from 1.34 million in 1990 to 1.66 million in 1993. In 1998, the unemployed workers rose to approximately 2.8 million, doubling its number in the eight years since 1990. The number of unemployed peaked in 2002 at about 3.59 million when unemployment rate hit 5.6%. These data indicate that the period from the late 1990s to early 2000s was a turning point for the Japanese labor market. In other words, after the burst of the bubble, businesses were forced to cut costs in the face of downturn and worsening deflation. And many companies actively relied on non-regular labor as a form of human resource outsourcing, which had just been deregulated.

Under such unstable employment status, households consumption is unlikely to expand. If consumption does not increase, sales will not increase either. If sales do not increase, firms are compelled to lower prices with discounts, causing consumer prices to decline. As the shift to non-regular employment progressed, wages also stagnated. The parsimonious households tighten their purse strings, creating a self-fulfilling deflationary spiral. Labor policies implemented to bring the economy out of recession conversely depressed demand and brought the economy to a standstill. This was how Japan fell into the deflation in the early 2000s.

The victory of DPJ in the 2009 general election symbolized the economic situation around this period. It was estimated that roughly 220,000 people were cut off from the manufacturing industry as a direct result of the financial crisis in 2008. After the ban on holding companies was lifted, a number of holding companies of giant corporate groups were created one after another. In the name of "shareholder profit", sell-offs, mergers and acquisitions of group subsidiaries became rampant. Many subcontractors and affiliated companies have been cut off, and workers have been forced to move to the split company, have their wages lowered or converted to non-regular employment. When recession hits again, no one knows when his or her job will be terminated next. And a fear of corporate restructuring became no longer a matter of someone else's concern.

In this way, Japanese management has been destroyed from its foundation. And the increasing number of workers has been forced to shift from life-time employment to the mercy of American-style human resource management. Since 2012, the regulatory emphasis has finally shifted from deregulation to worker protection, such as the abolition of day worker dispatching and the requirement for staffing agencies to disclose information on dispatch margins. However, the regulatory environment that allowed dispatch labor has not changed since the liberalization in the late 1990s. As a result, the percentage of non-regular employees has remained high in the upper 30% range since 2012.

Amid these fundamental changes in worker's psychology due to the shift to non-regular employment, the newly formed government under Prime Minister Abe (LDP) raised the consumption tax rate to 8% in 2014 and to 10% in October 2019. Consumption is the starting point of all other demands in the economy and amounts to roughly 60% of Japan's GDP (Fig. 4.4). However, the series of tax hikes, together with the decline in job security, have shifted the spending attitude of households, especially among low-to-middle income groups, from not just "saving" but "defending our lives" type of attitude as indicated by the sudden decline in consumption expenditure depicted in Fig. 4.4.

The result has been zero economic growth for the past 30 years, the case that only Japan has experienced among industrialized nations. The shift to non-regular employment has brought about the decline in job security and deep anxiety among Japanese workers. Anxiety destabilizes mental health and has given rise to various health and social problems, increasing cancer patients, *hikikomori* (extreme avoidance of social contacts by adults) and poverty among single-parent families. It is unimaginable from the days of "Japan as Number One". Yet this is the reality after 30 years of economic struggle and the result of failed policies suggested by the mainstream economics.

4.6 Root Cause of the Bubble and Its Lessons

As we have seen so far, Japan's Lost 30 Years was a period of stagnant demand brought on by the decline of employment stability and growth prospect. Therefore, economic policies the government should have adopted were the ones that stimulate private sector's demand and restore the self-reinforcing feedback loop that made "Japan as Number One". From economic management perspective, it is the government's task to design and implement policies that would break the cycle of debt-deflation that the private sector alone has become unable to cope with. Thus, the prescription economists must provide now is how to stimulate private demand and restore such growth engine loop of Consumption ⇔ Investment.[17]

However, policies pursued by the successive (mostly LDP) governments included the series of labor market deregulations, preferential tax reform for large corporations, administrative and government organization reforms, strengthening the central bank independence and privatization of the Postal Savings Bank. These structural reforms implemented at the behest of Structural Impediments Initiative (SII) have not only destroyed Japan's industrial and economic model, but lifted the ban on holding companies and introduced triangular mergers that have made foreign banks and financial capitals easier to acquire Japanese companies.

The result has been the increasing foreign shares and incorporation of Japanese "blue-chip" companies into the Network of Global Corporate Control, which we will discuss in Chap. 10. It is clear that the promotion of cheap labor policy will not lead to the revival of the economy suffering from lack in demand. Pursuit of the US-style shareholder capitalism will only strengthen the concentration of wealth into the hands of international bankers (owner class) while aggravating income inequality at the expense of the working class.

---

[17] In Chap. 14 we will present our causal loop analysis of Japan's lost 30 years and propose a set of policies called "Public Money Initiative" to revitalize the Japanese economy.

Bubble is Always and Everywhere A Central Bank Failure

After all is said and done, Japan would not have fallen into the decades-long stagnation and suffered hardships had the bubble not burst in the first place. Therefore, the question is why did the BoJ maintain such expansionary monetary policy all the way up to 1989, which caused the unprecedented booms of the late 1980s? Did the central bank simply overlook the bubble and let it go unnoticed?

In fact, the BoJ, through window guidance implemented by the Banking Department (*eigyōkyoku*), not only kept track of the volume of loans on a daily basis for major city banks, but subdivided those loans by industry and even kept track of the names of significant borrowers (Ishii and Werner 2003; Werner 2003).[18] The BoJ implemented window guidance until July 1991 when the bubble collapsed. Therefore, there is no question as to who recognized the bubble earlier than anybody and anticipated that bad debts would pose problems.[19]

As the bubble got heated up and total loans (debt) increased rapidly from the mid-80s, did policy makers at the BoJ feel the same way as Fisher and Hemphill did in the 1930s? Specifically, the Banking Department, especially the first section of the planning and coordination division, was in charge of monitoring cash flows of large city banks. What was the head of the division, the Director-General as well as the executive director in charge of the Banking department doing when the bubble was exploding in front of their eyes?

Below is an excerpt from the obituary recently appeared in July 2019 issue of the BoJ's in-house bulletin contributed by a former BoJ executive director Yoshio Suzuki titled "In Memory of Ryōji Tsukuda-Kun" (Suzuki, 2019)[20]:

---

[18] Under the credit guidance policy, commercial banks were required to submit a monthly loan plan to the BoJ. Along with interest rate manipulation, window guidance has been the BoJ's primary policy tool (albeit unofficial) to control total volume of loans by instructing banks on their cash management and lending policies 'over-the-counter', thus its name "window guidance". When Japan was undergoing high growth and demand for loans were enormous, this system of centralized credit control functioned as the effective means to suppress excessive expansion of purchasing power by directly controlling deposit creation by banks. By providing direct guidance on how much funds are to be supplied to which companies in which industry, the BoJ was in effect manipulating the flight control stick of the entire economy. Ishii and Werner (2003) discussed that this window guidance was originally learned by Hisato Ichimada [1893–1984] when he was stationed at the Reichsbank in the 1920s, and was something that every proper BoJ governors ("Princes") learned during their career paths. Ichimada was the central figure during the postwar period, who served as the BoJ governor between 1946-1954 and Finance Minister between 1954-1956. Due to his immense authority in the Japanese financial affairs, Ichimada was called "Pope". He was also one of the plenipotentiaries to the San Francisco Peace Treaty and the Japan-US Security Treaty, along with Shigeru Yoshida (prime minister 1946–47, 1948–54; LDP), and Hayato Ikeda (prime minister between 1960–64; LDP).

[19] Indeed the first thing the BoJ did before the bubble collapsed was to set up a new department in 1990 that focused on assessing the risks of financial system (macro prudential policy) and overseeing the disposition of non-performing loans of problematic banks.

[20] The original text is in Japanese, upon which translation was made by the authors of this book. Emphasis were added to preserve the nuance and authenticity of the original text. For instance,

> The two men loved to drink and often exchanged information about each other's departments over drinks. One day, Tsukuda-kun told me that there was a legend within the *eigyōkyoku* that even if the official discount rate was raised and window guidance was strengthened, monetary tightening would not become effective unless the call rate was induced to rise. To rephrase that in the terminology of the Research and Statistics Department, the call rate is the key variable of bank behavior, and at the same time, an important policy variable. ... I measured the call rate and used it in a paper in the *Chōsa Geppō* [BoJ's Monthly Financial Statistics Report], a special lecture at the University of Tokyo's Faculty of Economics, and in my dissertation, all thanks to Tsukuda-kun. ... After returning to the head office, the two were assigned to the Banking Department and the Research and Statistics Department, but continued to communicate even after we were assigned to the general managers of the Niigata and Matsumoto branches, which were next to each other. After that, Tsukuda-kun became the Deputy General Manager of the Osaka Branch, Deputy General Manager of the Personnel Department, General Manager of the Nagoya Branch, and then Director-General of the Banking Department. In September 1986, he was promoted to the board of executive directors, ahead of his peers.
>
> Looking back on those days, Tsukuda-kun, in his later years, would mutter every time he got drunk and said "We are the war criminals of the bubble." This was because in 1988, when the West Germany raised interest rates, the two of us had discussed that Japan should also raise interest rates, but we did not insist on it at *marutaku* [executive board meeting] even if we were to risk our jobs.

Marutaku, which literally means a round table in Japanese, is the BoJ's executive board's meeting attended by the governor, two deputy governors and executive directors. It is the BoJ's highest decision-making body on the technicalities of monetary policy implementation, separate from the policy board. Before the central bank independence was strengthened in 1998, the BoJ's monetary policy board, which decides and votes on the next policy such as interest rate (but not on window guidance controlled by the senior BoJ staffs in the Banking department), consisted of seven members including one representative each from the Ministry of Finance and the Economic Planning Agency.[21]

On the other hand, the executive directors attending the *marutaku* were chosen from the proper BoJ staff, who all happen to be the graduates from University of Tokyo, maintaining close relationships as seniors and juniors.[22] At that time, the

---

"–kun" is a Japanese honorific used to express positive friendliness to a close male friend of the similar age and status, similar to "Mr.".

[21] After the Bank of Japan Act was amended in 1997, the monetary policy committee now consists of nine members, including the governor and two deputy governors. The other six members are selected from private financial institutions and academia, more akin to the member composition and the governance structure of the Federal Reserve System.

[22] Ishii (1996, 2001) was the first to sound the alarm about the stereotyped career system within the BoJ, in which graduates of the University of Tokyo always rise to the top. As the former senior staff at BoJ who had also worked in the Banking department, Ishii detailed on how the central bankers had exercised its tremendous power over financial institutions as the lender of last resort, while at the same time taking high salaries and extravagant benefits. Ishii also describes how the former BoJ executives find positions after their retirements as the directors of financial institutions as well as top corporations and expanded its sphere of influence. In particular, Ishii highlights how the central bankers utilized its position of authority with its own sources of information on financial markets to control the flow of information and reputation of the central bank by controlling what type of information is allowed to appear in the public domain.

governor was Satoshi Sumita from the Ministry of Finance and deputy governor was Yasushi Mieno from the BoJ. The Director-General of the Banking Department was Toshihiko Fukui and the executive director in charge of the Banking department was Ryōji Tsukuda. Note that Fukui succeeded Tsukuda to serve as the Director-General of Banking Department from September 1986 to May 1989, and later went on to lead the central bank as the governor from 2003.

Central Banker's Blueprint for Transformation of Japan

Therefore, our last remaining question is why did Mieno (as a deputy governor) leave the bubble untouched? Was Fukui in a similar position as his ultimate superior Mieno? The meticulous analysis by Richard Werner on this subject, "Princes of the Yen" (Werner, 2003), has established the indisputable case for intentionality behind the BoJ's expansionary window guidance maintained in the late 1980s to induce the bubble and create the unavoidable crisis. Through interviews and empirical analyses, Werner (2003) concluded that the reason why the key central bankers at the BoJ ("Princes of the Yen") kept interest rate low and maintained such expansionary credit policy was to create a much needed impetus to further their structural reform agenda, which was called the "ten-year plan" among the BoJ senior staffs.

Indeed, it was none other than the former BoJ governors who initially promoted the structural reform even before the bubble exploded and consistently spearheaded after the bubble collapsed on the side of Japan. Specifically, Maekawa report issued in April 1986 served as a guide for the subsequent structural reform. This report, named after the 24th Governor Haruo Maekawa who chaired the study group, was compiled by the Study Group on Economic Structural Adjustment for International Cooperation, a private advisory body to the then Prime Minister Yasuhiro Nakasone (LDP), who had been under pressure by the US government (under Reagan administration) to improve trade deficits and eliminate "non-tariff barriers".

Kaoru was teaching economics at the Business school of University of Hawai'i at Manoa that summer when the report had just been published. One of his students asked him after the lecture, "As indicated in the Maekawa Report, I think the Bank of Japan will lead structural reforms, and trade from the US will increase. What do you think?" Kaoru was somehow intrigued by the Report, partly because he had not heard of such a report that would 'outline' the Japan's future, and partly because he was more into the futures studies at that time, leaving economics behind out of dissatisfaction with the field (see Chap. 9).

The "Princes of the Yen" (Maekawa, Mieno and Fukui) seemed to have followed the blueprints laid out in this report all along. In fact, at the time of the second interest rate cut in September 1995, the central bank was touting structural reforms, saying, "The Bank of Japan believes that these monetary easing measures will be fully effective only if accompanied by structural reforms."

What was recommended in the Maekawa Report, then? It outlined four points; (1) expansion of Japan's domestic demand, (2) transformation to an internationally harmonized industrial structure, (3) further improvement of market access and promotion of product imports, and (4) stabilization of the value of international currencies and liberalization and internationalization of finance.

Expansion of domestic demand means further tightening of restrictions on Japanese exports (VER). Needless to say, Japan's postwar growth has been supported by the expansion of domestic demand, and any economic growth is due to increased domestic demand. Hence, there was no need to loudly promote that domestic demand should be expanded. Therefore, this might have been an excuse to justify the on-going low interest rate policy that had been introduced by the BoJ as a counter measure to the Plaza Accord and was necessary to induce a bubble.

On the other hand, transformation of industrial structure and improving market access meant eliminating the cross-shareholdings among keiretsu, the main bank system and Japanese employment practices, which have been the source of the strength and international competitiveness of Japanese companies. Financial liberalization and internationalization should go without saying. As discussed in Sect. 4.3 the top policy priority for the major US and European banks was how to prevent Japanese banks from expanding their international market share (Table 4.1). In other words the "liberalization and internationalization of finance" as advocated by the Maekawa report was a message to Japanese banks to align themselves according to the rules of the US and European banks. The aforementioned Basel I regulation was formulated in this context. Most importantly, when we look back at the path taken by the Japanese economy since then, all four of these proposals have been steadily implemented.

For instance, the intense lending boom since 1986 and the SII proposal in July 1989. The subsequent crash of the stock market beginning in 1990 and further interest rate hikes by the governor Mieno, which caused the entire economy to stagnate. At every turn, the BoJ took the position that the economy would not grow, let alone recover, unless structural reforms were implemented in a timely manner. Were all these events just a series of coincidence? It was as if everything was proceeding according to some kind of a plot that was carefully orchestrated by special interests group.

Thirty-five years have passed since the day when Kaoru first heard of the Maekawa report at the University of Hawaii. Now we are left with a grim hindsight that the bubble, the subsequent recession and structural reforms may have all been a part of the central banker's plan to transform the Japanese economy from the beginning. In fact the very first "unofficial" meeting for the Structural Impediments Initiative was held nowhere other than at the Federal Reserve Bank of New York on July 2nd, 1989, which is a private bank established as an independent body from the US government.

Thus, a half century after the Great Depression, the structural flaw of the debt money system became evident once again. This time across the Pacific. And this was how a land of the rising sun was plunged into the Lost 30 Years.

Booms and Busts are System Design Failures of Debt Money

Are economic bubbles inevitable features of capitalist system? The above memoir by the former BoJ executives attests to the conclusion reached by Werner (2003) and puts an end to the meaningless discussion that whether it was the central bankers who made the initial failure. At the same time, their recount is also suggesting that there was a psychological factor that prevented the two BoJ executives (Tsukuda and Suzuki) from expressing their opinion to their superior (Mieno), perhaps due to a particular hierarchy that existed within the institution. This is in contrast to the Fed's policy failure during the period leading to the Great Depression where the governor of Federal Reserve Bank of New York, George L. Harrison (1928-1940), repeatedly requested the Board of Governors to raise the discount lending rate in 1929, which was delayed by the Federal Reserve Board until August of that year.[23]

In the case of the BoJ's failure in the late 1980s, the executive directors at the time were too defensive and hesitant to request the interest rate hike, which in turn implicates the deputy governor Mieno's commitment (and perhaps his insistence) on the expansionary policy stance. However, we cannot conclude from these facts that the Japanese bubble and its burst was solely due to the central bank policy failure. That would be the same mistake as concluding that a plane crash was caused by pilots (human error). In other words, there is a deeper systemic cause: the debt money system. No matter how skillled the pilots are at flying the airplane, the present system has a design failure and doomed to generate economic instabilities and eventually crash. As Fisher and Hemphil had warned us more than half a century prior, booms and busts are inevitable features of the debt money system.

Accordingly, the lessons we learned from the Great Depression in the 1930s and the case of Japan's Lost 30 Years can be summarized in two points:

1. Debt money system is structurally unstable and causes booms and busts (system design failure).
2. Central banks have historically caused financial crises either by overlooking them or acting in self-interests, and cannot prevent the next crisis (human error).

The first lesson points to the structural defect of the present debt money system where money creation is tied to bank loans. The second lesson indicates that, because of the system design failure, human errors cannot be contained, leading to the policy failure. Policymakers are humans with bounded rationality. Therefore, institutions made up of people are also bound by their collective cognitive (in)abilities. This is why it is critical to design our financial system (and institutions that make up the system) on the premise that mistakes are bound to occur so that, even if the person in charge of a specific domain overlooks signs of a potential accident, the system itself stops the chain of errors.

Herbert W. Heinrich, who had investigated industrial accidents with regard to human error, advanced his observation in the "Industrial Accident Prevention: A

---

[23] See Chandler (1971); Richardson et al. (2013). However, it would have been impossible for the already inflated bubble to have had a soft landing even if interest rates had been raised as fast as Harrison had demanded. The Dow Jones was already in a bubble by the second half of 1927. Note that the timeline is very similar to the Japanese case. However, one must take into account that, under the international gold standard system of the time, an increase in US interest rates would naturally force other countries to raise their interest rates, and using monetary policy to restrain asset price bubbles could have broad, unintended, and undesirable consequences.

Scientific Approach" (Heinrich, 1931) that there were 29 minor accidents behind every major *accident*, and behind every minor accident, there were 300 near misses or *incidents* that could have led to an accident. The Heinrich's rule of thumb formed the basis of accident prevention in various industries since. It is precisely in our monetary system, which is the foundation of our globalized economy, that we need to install systems that place the highest priorities on stability and resiliency in the face of potential human error. This is one of the main purposes of the monetary reform.

Yet, despite these lessons, no reform was implemented during the structural reforms in Japan or in the US since the Great Depression, leaving the basic structure of our financial system still unsound. More fundamentally, this was an error of the mainstream economics itself, which must have identified the root cause of the bubble and provided a prescription. What was the error in mainstream economics, then? Let's dive into this question in the next chapter.

Part II
Analysis

Chapter 5
Collapse of the Mainstream Economics

After the burst of bubble in 1990, Japan's GDP stagnated in 500 trillion yen range. Japan is the only country among industrialized nations that has experienced such a prolonged period of stagnation. During this period the government and Bank of Japan tried all kinds of policies suggested by the mainstream economics, but to no avail. Therefore, it can be argued that Japan's *Lost 30 Years* is the result of misguided prescriptions written by wrong economics. In medicine, a patient did not recover as a result of bad treatments with wrong diagnosis.

What is mainstream economics, then? Which prescription went wrong and why? It would be futile to ask foreign economists for the answer. It has to be a job of Japanese researchers, who have had to live through the difficult days, to elucidate the causes of the *Lost 30 Years*. In a nutshell, it has to be a theoretical elucidation that the two mainstream monetary theories on which mainstream economic policies are based were wrong. We then need to establish the alternative theory of public money. In this chapter let us analyze the policy failures of mainstream economics as revealed by the Japanese case. After that, a detailed analysis of the monetary theories will be presented in Chap. 9.

5.1 Neoclassical Economics is A Big Fiction

What are Mainstream Economics?

The two major schools of mainstream economic thoughts that continue to exert influence on our society are Neoclassical and Keynesian economics. Neoclassical economics has evolved from the classical school of economics, which was based on the *laissez-faire* principle advocated by Adam Smith in his book *The Wealth of Nations* (1776). However, classical economics, which asserts that the economy functions well only under competitive conditions in the private sector with minimal government interference, lost its credibility after the Great Depression.

K. Yamaguchi and Y. Yamaguchi, *Public Money*,
https://doi.org/10.1007/978-981-97-6564-5_5

Nevertheless, with the existence proof of general equilibrium by Arrow and Debreu (1954),[1] the classical economics once again came back to life as neoclassical economics. The DSGE (Dynamic Stochastic General Equilibrium) model, based on the general equilibrium theory, is now at the core of neoclassical economics. For this general equilibrium model to be effective, one must make a number of assumptions; that is, markets are competitive, prices are elastic and free to adjust, information is perfect and complete, and consumers and producers are taking rational behaviors towards maximizing utility and profit under the free markets. The neoclassical theory claims that, under such strict but unrealistic assumptions, general equilibrium will be naturally attained in all markets.

Another branch of mainstream economics is the Keynesian economics. Faced with the failure of *laissez-faire* classical economics in the 1930s, the two leading economists at the time simultaneously proposed novel theories independently that would provide a way out of the Depression. They were Irving Fisher's *100% Money* (Fisher, 1935) and John M. Keynes's *General Theory* (Keynes, 1936). Along with the subsequent developments in national income and flow of funds accounts, Keynes's *General Theory* has evolved as macroeconomics that is featured in all standard economics textbooks used around the world.[2]

The main tenet of Keynes' theory is that a market economy is not self-corrective and thus cannot achieve equilibrium by laissez-faire policies. Keynes advanced that the equilibrium can be achieved if the government implements appropriate policies. Here, the Keynesian policies specifically refer to the aggregate demand management through fiscal and monetary policies. Fisher's *100% Money* theory, on the other hand, was made a taboo subject by the economics establishment and gradually forgotten as we will discuss in Chap. 8. Yet we have inherited it as *Public Money* on the basis of Accounting System Dynamics (ASD) modeling method (Yamaguchi, 2013) as illustrated in Fig. 1.3.

Illusions of Neoclassical Market Fundamentalism Policies

Broadly speaking, these two streams of economic thoughts currently form the mainstream economics. Let's start with the neoclassical economics. Then, the prescriptions of Keynesian economics (fiscal and monetary policies, and reflationary theory as its extension) will be examined in the following sections.

At the core of neoclassical economics is the DSGE model mentioned above. Neoclassical policies derived from this theory are aimed to bring the distorted, non-

[1] See Sect. 9.2 for further details of the Arrow-Debreu model.

[2] Smith was apparently the one who first made use of a business income statement in defining aggregate production and in inventing circular flow of income (Dawson 1996, p. 96). Dawson also named Irving Fisher (along with Smith) as one of the two precedents of which Copeland was "well aware" as pioneers who had showed the indispensability of accounting foundation in economics when Copeland began his famous studies on the "moneyflows" (social accounting) at NBER, which later became the flow of funds accounts after the Fed took it on.

competitive market structures of the real world into conformity with the model's assumptions (price elasticity, perfect competition, perfect information, rational behavior, etc.) as much as possible. Based on such deductive approach, its *a priori* policy goal is to destroy all supply-side structures that impede free competition and reform our societies according to the assumptions of the model. This is the *market fundamentalism* policy that neoclassical economics suggests. In this sense, structural reforms by the neoclassical economics can be regarded as a *religious doctrine*, as it tries to reform the structure of the real economy to conform to the unrealistic assumptions of the general equilibrium model rather than deriving (inducing) appropriate polices based on empirical observation.

With the advent of stagflation in the 1970s, Keynesian economics was discredited and this neoclassical market fundamentalism began to regain its momentum. This market fundamentalism becomes the policy that has been favored and advocated by the international bankers, who intend to control the financial markets and industries through monopolistic power over the supply of money, and let the weak and strong compete each other as if the free market is always the best solution, while they themselves remain aloof from the competition and clamor of the market and snatch the fruits whenever and as much as possible.

The bankers' plan for financial liberalization was a prime example of this market fundamentalism policy including the repeal of the Glass-Steagall Act, which had been the bone in their throats since it was passed in 1933.[3] The Glass-Steagall Act had, to a certain degree, stabilized the US financial system and averted a systemic crisis like that of the 1930s. However, the act was finally repealed in 1999 under the Clinton administration.

The repeal of the Glass-Steagall Act have broken down the barriers between banking and securities investment, allowing big banks in particular to use their greater leverage to turn their hands to high-risk mortgage-backed securities (MBS) and other financial derivative products. Many have attributed the repeal of the Glass-Steagall act to be the major factor that triggered the subprime mortgage loan bubble and the Lehman Shock in 2008. This repeal of the act by the President Clinton also meant that the Chicago Plan proposed by the eight economists in 1933 to then President Roosevelt, was completely choked to death. The illusion of market fundamentalism was once again brought to light by the global financial crisis, or what we call "the Second Great Depression".

Japan was also mercilessly hit by this wave of globalization spearheaded by this market fundamentalism. As outlined in Chap. 4, the structural reform implemented in Japan included various deregulations, privatizations and government administrative and organization reforms. As part of the financial system reform that began in the late 1990s, the Japanese *convoy system* collapsed, the Bank of Japan's independence was strengthened, and sweeping deregulations in the banking, insurance, and

---

[3] The Banking Act of 1933, which was passed in the midst of the Great Depression, was an alternative bill prepared as a concession of the Wall Street international bankers to water down the Chicago Plan, which would have ended deposit creation by commercial banks by requiring 100% reserve ratio on demand deposits. The act instead created the Federal Deposit Insurance Corporation (FDIC) and separated banking from securities investment operations.

securities businesses were implemented. In this way, the structural reform of the Japanese financial sector was carried out all at once. These market fundamentalism policies implemented in Japan after the collapse of the bubble have been perfectly in line with the so-called "Washington Consensus", which is a set of policy prescriptions promoted by the International Monetary Fund (IMF), World Bank and the US Department of the Treasury for 'crisis-wracked' nations including preferential tax reforms that favor the multinational enterprises, trade liberalization, and property rights protection.

Japan As the Victim of Neoclassical Economics Ideology

The lesson we have learned from the case of Japan is that there was virtually no supply-side problem that hindered the economy from growing. Japan's decades-long stagnation was caused by the stagnation of demand (Fig. 4.4). Then, the question is why did households reduce consumption and firms did not expand investment. Since consumer prices have remained virtually unchanged over the past 30 years, the fact that consumption has remained stagnant while the total population of Japan (or its labor force) have risen over the same period suggests that consumption per capita (or per worker) has declined both in nominal and real terms. As already discussed in Chap. 4, it was nothing but the structural reform itself that has encouraged cheap labor policy and increased the number of non-regular employment, which has led to the stagnation in consumption.

Let us assume for the sake of argument that there were supply-side factors impeding growth in the Japanese economy after the collapse of the bubble. Then, why were Japanese companies able to become the most competitive in the world in many fields and achieve phenomenal growth in the 1970s and 80s when there must have been supply-side structural issues? The burst of the bubble and subsequent recession occurred long before its total population began to decline in 2011 (see Fig. 14.1 for total population data). Moreover, there has been no apparent supply constraint when we observe the population over 15 or labor force (Fig. 4.6).[4] By observing these macroeconomic data comprehensively, it should be clear to anyone that demographics were not the main culprit of Japan's low growth.

Nevertheless, we still often see it argued that Japan's weak economic performance has been due largely to declining productivity and potential growth due to its shrinking and aging population. If one relies on this view, the Japanese labor market is "illiquid". Thus, allowing firms to freely shed workers through more deregulations would increase job mobility, therefore bringing labor force to growing industries, while encouraging competition, productivity and corporate metabolism among

[4] The fact that the number of unemployed persons doubled in the late 1990s can only be attributed to the post-bubble decline in production demand relative to labor supply. Moreover, it is out of the question that Japanese firms, which had achieved growth based on abundant investment and research and development (R&D), were constrained by capital productivity.

Japanese firms, that is, letting inefficient businesses ("zombie companies") go out of market. Only then can Japan grow, they repeat.[5]

This is the typical example of attributing the cause of Japan's Lost 30 Years as a supply-side problem, which led to the prescription of neoclassical economics. As also discussed in Chap. 4, Japanese government, seduced by the illusion of this market fundamentalism and catchy political slogans such as "No growth without structural reform", introduced a series of labor market deregulations and privatizations, which have fundamentally destroyed the Japanese economic model that had enabled its postwar success. Did workers' wages rise and the economy improve as they had promised? Did the economy grow as a result of these market fundamentalist policies? The results were quite the opposite.

As a result of the globalization, the situation of global economy seemed to have been brought back to the *laissez-faire* state of free competition prior to the Great Depression of 1930s. Alas, as if history repeats itself, the Lehman Shock triggered a financial crisis again on September 15, 2008. At this point, the neoclassical market fundamentalism policies had failed irrefutably and must have been dead. In spite of these historical facts, however, mainstream economists who are deeply indoctrinated in neoclassical economics ideology of general equilibrium theory refuse to acknowledge its debacle and beginning to wriggle again, as if market failure is nothing but a transient nightmare.

5.2 Keynesian Economics that Assumes Exogenous Debt Money

Let us next examine macroeconomic policies derived from the Keynes's general theory. Keynesian economics is built on the assumption that money is exogenously supplied by the central bank. This is called the *exogenous money*. On the contrary, we have demonstrated in Chap. 3 the exact opposite theory of debt money is true; money is endogenously created by someone's debts. That "someone" is households, producers (firms), and government. Why do they need to borrow money, then? Because any kind of transaction require money, and under the current debt money system, money cannot be supplied into the economy unless the non-banking sectors borrow money from commercial banks.

Why do households borrow money? Because their wage incomes and savings cannot cover the cost of large expenditures such as durable consumer goods (*e.g.*,

[5] See Shirakawa (2019) and Harding (2019), for example. The former BoJ governors, executive directors, and policy board members never seem to stop promoting these "supply-side" arguments. Since the central bank has no direct policy tool nor mandate to address the country's population decline, it has been not only convenient but necessary for them to frame that the cause of Japan's stagnation lies in supply-side in order to rationalize their structural reform agenda. In any case, the rationale for central bank independence proclaimed in the 1997 revision of the Bank of Japan Act has proven itself to be completely self-contradictory, as it failed to coordinate with the government's economic policy, which in turn caused the lost 30 years.

cars and refrigerators), educational loans for children and other expenses for purchasing condominiums and houses. Why do firms borrow money? Under the capitalist system, corporations are owned by their shareholders, and all profits from corporate activities are distributed to shareholders. In general, firms (producers) are not allowed to keep retained earnings out of profits. Therefore, in order to continue their business activities, firms are always obliged to raise investment funds from outside sources. Their main financing methods include borrowing from banks and issuing corporate bonds and new shares.

Why does the government borrow money, then? Because it always needs additional funding for public services (education, diplomacy, defense, etc.), unexpected expenditures (natural disasters, pandemics, etc.) and infrastructure development that cannot be fully covered by tax revenues. In addition, social security and welfare expenses will increase year by year with the aging of society.

If money is created as someone's debts, how are they related with economic activity? Here, let's consider economic activity as represented by GDP, which is nothing but the total value-added of goods and services produced in a country during one year. Then, the question becomes more specific: what is the relationship between GDP and debts of these macroeconomic sectors? According to the Keynesian theory, GDP (as income) is determined by the following income determination formula (also known as the principle of effective demand)[6] :

$$\text{GDP} = \text{Consumption} + \text{Investment} + \text{Govt. Expenditure} + \text{Net Exports} \tag{5.1}$$

$$\text{Govt. Expenditure} = \text{Tax Revenue} + \text{Govt. Deficits (Govt. Bond Issuance)} \tag{5.2}$$

By defining "Savings = GDP−Tax Revenue−Consumption", the above formula can be simplified as follows (omitting Net Exports hereafter for simplicity):

$$\text{Savings} = \text{Investment} + \text{Govt. Deficits (Govt. Bond Issuance)} \tag{5.3}$$

If we define the difference between Savings and Investment (or *IS* Balance) as "GDP gap",[7] the above income determination formula becomes "GDP gap = Government Deficits". Keynesian economics of exogenous money is built on the assumption that production yields income, and the distributed amount of income that leaks out money circulation (flow of funds) becomes the total savings in the economy. Accordingly, if the investment falls below the savings (savings > investment), a recession will occur due to the lack of demand. Goods that have been produced remain unsold, inventories build up, and firms adjust their level of production, cutting jobs and thus causing unemployment.

---

[6] The standard Keynesian IS-LM model, which will be discussed in Chap. 8, usually assumes a closed economy without trade, and hence, income and GDP are treated as the same, *i.e.*, national income accounting identity. Strictly speaking, the two macroeconomic concepts must be distinguished. We will address this theoretical issue in Sect. 8.10.

[7] This is different from "output gap" defined as the difference between potential and actual GDP (output).

This approach to defining disequilibrium in Keynesian economics is fundamentally flawed and incompatible with the reality of endogenous money (debt money system), which we will pointe out below. Until that point, however, let us hold this Keynesian concept of disequilibrium as *tentatively* acceptable, and further define "GDP gap" as the difference between savings and investment. Then, the income determination formula in equation (5.3) holds as follows:

$$\text{GDP Gap} = \text{Government Deficits} = 0 \text{ (in Equilibrium)} \tag{5.4}$$

$$= \text{Government Deficits} > 0 \text{ (in Disequilibrium)} \tag{5.5}$$

In terms of GDP gap, a recession is thus a situation in which the gap occurs, and Keynesian state of income equilibrium is attained when "GDP Gap = 0", in which balanced budget of the government is also attained. In this case, the equilibrium state of "savings = investment" holds with balanced budget.

Keynesian equilibrium could also be attained under "GDP Gap > 0" so long as government's budget deficits can fill in the gap. In such case, the disequilibrium state of "Savings > Investment" holds, yet this gap is filled in by the budget deficits. In both cases, Keynesian income equilibrium is attained such that aggregate supply = aggregate demand as formulated in equation (5.1).

In order to attain this income equilibrium, Keynesian theory proposes the following three policies: monetary policy, fiscal policy and reflation policy (quantitative easing). Let us now examine, one by one, how these Keynesian policies have been applied to save the Japan's lost 30 years of economic stagnation.

5.3 Monetary Policy to Reduce GDP Gap Failed

First, let's consider the case of a recession: Savings > Investment. Suppose the economy is not in equilibrium so that GDP gap > 0, that is, the case of equation (5.5). In this case, in order to get out of the recession and achieve macroeconomic equilibrium, producers and households must increase investment to reduce the GDP gap to zero. What can be done to increase their investments? Policy makers can lower interest rates to make it easier for them to borrow funds.

How can interest rates be lowered, then? If the central bank could increase M_1, then, the increased money stock will eventually decrease interest rates. This is the so-called Keynesian monetary policy. Most undergraduate-level textbooks use the so-called IS-LM analysis to explain the effects of this policy, as we will discuss in detail in the next Chap. 7. And through this IS-LM analysis we are gradually brainwashed into believing that macroeconomic phenomena such as inflation, recession, and unemployment can be controlled ("fine-tuned"). Brainwashed in this way, the BoJ policymakers applied the wrong prescriptions to the Japanese economy. So, let us examine their monetary policy next.

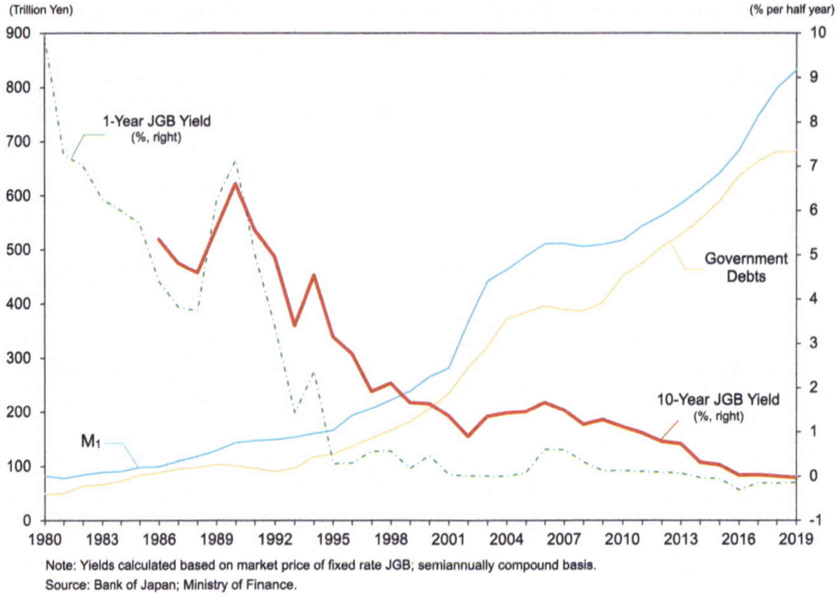

Fig. 5.1 Japan's falling interest rates goes against crowding out theory

Mystery of Falling Interest Rates Under Crowding Out

Strictly speaking, this monetary policy was not applied alone during the Japan's lost 30 years. Instead, a mix of monetary and fiscal policies has been applied. As we have already seen in "Surprise 3" in Sect. 3.7, the Japanese government increased 595 trillion yen of bonds (money-creating debts) and mobilized the largest fiscal stimulus in nation's history. As a result, on average, the government borrowed about 20 trillion yen each year. Nevertheless, interest rate of 10-year JGB (Japanese Government Bond) peaked at 8.1% on September 28, 1990 and began to decline, falling below the 1% level on October 31, 2002.

Figure 5.1 plots the decline of JGB yields against increasing government debts.

Note that the graph is plotted on annual basis at the end of each calendar year. Therefore, it does not depict the September 1990 peak in JGB yields. Subsequently, 10-Year JGB yields (secondary market) temporarily recorded a negative rate of -0.02% for the first time on February 9, 2016, and again on February 24 at -0.046%. This negative interest rate continued until November of that year. Negative rates meant that investors were willing to pay interest back to the government to buy and hold treasury securities. It is an unusual level that would have never occurred without deflation and rising money values.

According to mainstream economic (monetary) theory, if the government raises funds by issuing bonds, interest rates will rise and the bond prices will fall as the supply-demand balance in the money market becomes tight. This is because it is assumed that the total amount of money is exogenously supplied by the BoJ (central bank). This is the so-called *crowding out* effect theory. Why, then, did interest rates not rise despite the fact that the government issued 595 trillion yen of JGBs (as money-creating debt) over the past 30 years? As discussed in Chap. 3, this amounts to new borrowings of 19.8 trillion yen per year. The money market must have tightened as a result. Why didn't the price of government bonds plummet and interest rates jump? On the contrary, yields continued to decline until they became negative. This became a mystery that cannot be solved by the crowding out theory of mainstream economics.

We have solved this mystery based on debt money theory. As already analyzed in Sect. 3.7, there is a close positive correlation between government debts and M_1. The regression analysis of this causal relationship revealed a regression coefficient of 1.125, indicating that government debt increases M_1 by a factor of 1.125. Since the actual government debts during the lost 30 years increased by 595 trillion yen, the increase in M_1 due to government debt becomes 669 trillion yen ($= 1.125 \times 595$), even by a simple calculation with the regression equation (3.10). The actual increase in M_1 during this period was 731 trillion yen. Therefore, it can be interpreted that 91.5% ($= 669/731$) of the increase in M_1 was supplied by the government debts. In this way, money stock M_1 continued to grow with the increases in government debts.

This was made possible by the BoJ's massive purchases of JGBs. The BoJ's quantitative easing (QE) policy injected huge amount of reserves into the banking system. As a result, interest rates continued to fall due to the supply-demand relationship in the money market, and interest rates on JGBs continued to fall in tandem with the decline in money market rates, or overnight (O/N) call rates in Japan. That is, the following relations took place: fiscal stimulus $\rightarrow$ JGB purchases by the BoJ $\rightarrow$ increase in M_1 $\rightarrow$ fall in interest rates.

Observing this way, the increase in government debts and the decline in interest rates are not mysteries, but the result of economic rationality under the debt money system where money is endogenous. Conversely, if the BoJ were to stop purchasing government bonds, interest rates would rise, government bond and stock prices would plummet. And the *financial meltdown*, which will be discussed in Chap. 6, would ensue. In other words, the very construction of the crowding out theory under the exogenous money assumption was wrong in the first place.

In the midst of such continuous declines in interest rates, the Japanese economy fell into what Keynesian economists called a "liquidity trap". And interest rates were stuck at near zero. Therefore, the BoJ was forced to adopt zero-interest rate policy from February 1999 to August 2000, during which the O/N call rate reached zero lower bound (Fig. 4.1). However, even under such low interest rate environment, investment and consumption were not stimulated as Keynesian monetary policy would have predicted.

Specifically, Japanese firms prioritized debt repayments to clean up their balance sheets, and households, who had became anxious about their future, cut back on consumption and housing investment. In other words, Japanese (non-banking) private sector did not respond to the zero interest rate and have been virtually insensitive to the decrease in the cost of borrowings. Hence, the decline in nominal GDP growth associated with the fall in nominal interest rates observed in Japan (Fig. 4.5) was not a mystery when one takes into account the mechanism of endogenous debt money. However, these were economic situations that could not be imagined from the traditional theory of investment. And the BoJ itself had to abandon this traditional monetary policy of influencing demand through interest rate cut and replaced it with the next reflation policy.

5.4 Reflation Policy to Reduce GDP Gap Failed

What is Reflation Policy?

Faced with this situation, the BoJ adopted the QE policy, in which the BoJ purchased large amounts of financial assets (mainly JGBs) from commercial banks and injected additional reserves. This was a desperate measure taken by the BoJ in response to the collapse of traditional monetary policy, in which the interest rate had been used as the policy instrument. The underlying logic here is that, if the BoJ sets the inflation target at, say, 2% and increases money stock M_1 accordingly, the value of money will eventually begin to decline and the real interest rate will begin to fall if households and producers expect inflation to occur, even when nominal interest rates remain stuck around zero.

Behind this reasoning is the so-called *Fisher equation* that defines the relationship between the nominal and real interest rates, and expected inflation rate. For now, let us leave the theoretical detail in Chap. 8. If expected inflation rate rises and real interest rates fall as the central bank announces, then, household and corporate debts will be substantially reduced in real terms, and households will further accelerate their consumption in anticipation of inflation, while producers will activate their investment activities. In other words, the essence of reflation theory is how much the central bank can work to shape people and firm's expectations.

This reflation theory and its policy prescription were originally proposed by Fisher (1932, 1933) as a way to escape from the Great Depression. Behind this logic, Fisher also based his thinking on the quantity theory of money, which he had previously developed (Fisher, 1911). However, shortly after this proposal, he was handed *the Chicago Plan for Banking Reform* and immediately realized the error in his reflation theory and buried it with his own hands (the historical background will also be explained in Chap. 8). Specifically, Fisher realized that, under the debt money system, central bank had no control over M_1, and instead proposed the monetary reform by the *100% Money* (Fisher, 1935).

Knowing Fisher's theoretical conflict or not, the BoJ jumped on this reflation theory and has implemented QE three times and piled up massive amount of M_0 (Fig. 4.5). The first series of QE was introduced under Governor Fukui (2001–2006), the second QE under Governor Shirakawa (2010–2013), and the third QQE under

Governor Kuroda (2013–2023).[8] The BoJ must have been so driven into a corner by the collapse of mainstream economics and failure of its monetary policy.

Premise of Reflation Theory 1: Constant Money Multiplier

As we have seen in Chap. 3 (Fig. 3.7), central banks can only control base money M_0 under the debt money system. According to the money multiplier (m) theory, M_1 can be controlled by M_0 as the following equation indicates:[9]

$$M_1 = m * M_0 \quad \Longrightarrow \quad \hat{M}_1 = \hat{M}_0 \tag{5.6}$$

where $\hat{M}$ implies a growth rate of the variable M such that $\hat{M} = \frac{dM/dt}{M}$.

This relationship holds only when the money multiplier m is constant, in which case the BoJ can control money stock M_1 by controlling base money M_0. Only under this environment monetary policy may become effective by using money stock as the policy instrument, as assumed in textbooks. As Fig. 5.2 shows, the money multiplier in Japan remained stable until 1998, when it reached 3.89. However, after that, it has fluctuated up and down, reaching a peak of 5.55 in 2006. It then began to decline rapidly from 2011, reaching 1.72 in 2019. In other words, no matter how much the BoJ increased base money M_0, money stock M_1 did not increase as expected due to the decline in the money multiplier. That is, the premise of reflation theory has broken down.

---

8 Policymakers at the BoJ also believed that as banks accumulate excess reserves, they will rebalance their portfolios to private-sector loans in search of investments offering better returns rather than leaving those funds lying dormant in their reserves accounts. If the central bank purchases JGB persistently and bank lending starts to increase, capital investment and other activities will be promoted. By calling such monetary policy transmission as "portfolio rebalancing effect," the BoJ under the governor Kuroda desperately tried to convince the public that QE was justified. However, all of these assumptions ended up in wishful thinking.

9 When currency ratio (α), required reserve ratio (β_r) and the excess reserve ratio (β_e) are used, money multiplier (m) is more accurately obtained as

$$m = \frac{\alpha + 1}{\alpha + \beta_r + \beta_e}$$

Here, the currency ratio is a value determined by the liquidity preference of households and producers over their deposits, and the excess reserve ratio is a value determined by bank deposits and loans. If the currency ratio or excess reserve ratio rises due to some external factors, the money multiplier must fall because the central bank can only control the required reserve ratio. Accordingly, the central bank also loses control over M_1. For detailed discussions, see Yamaguchi (2013, Chap. 5).

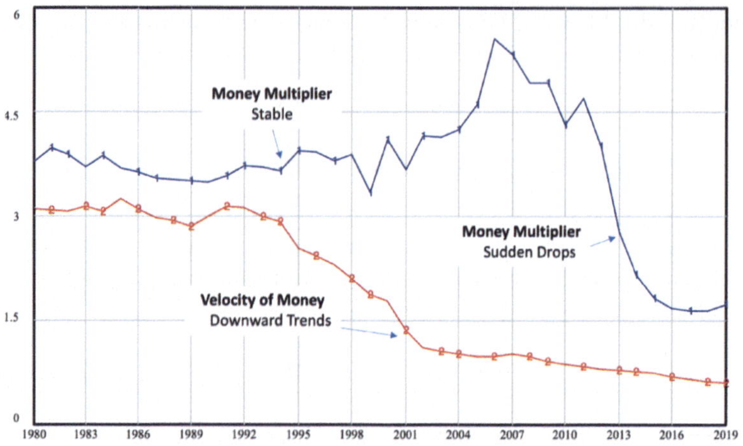

Fig. 5.2 Money multiplier and velocity of money: 1980–2019

Premise of Reflation Theory 2: Constant Velocity of Money

For this reflation theory to be effective, stability of the money multiplier is not enough; stability of the velocity of money circulation must also be necessary. To understand this, it is necessary to elucidate the quantity theory of money proposed by Irving Fisher, which is formulated as follows:

$$M\ v = P\ T \tag{5.7}$$

where v is a velocity of money stock, P is a price level and T is transaction volume.

If the velocity v is constant, an increase in M will eventually lead to an increase in price P or volume of transactions T such that $\hat{M} = \hat{P} + \hat{T}$. This is the quantity theory of money. If we regard M as M_1, PT as nominal GDP, and further assume that the money multiplier and velocity of money are both constant, the following relationships hold:

$$\hat{M}_0 = \hat{M}_1 = \text{G}\hat{\text{D}}\text{P}\ (\equiv \hat{P} + \text{Real}\hat{\ }\text{GDP}) \tag{5.8}$$

Accordingly, if the BoJ sets an inflation target of $\hat{P} = 2\%$ and increases M_0 (mainly reserves) to, say, 5% by purchasing government bonds through asset purchase programs, M_1 will also increase by 5%. As a result, the actual rate of inflation gradually begins to approach the expected inflation rate of 2%, which will stimulate consumption and investment. Eventually, nominal economic growth rate of 5% (of which real economic growth rate constitutes 3%) will be achieved as indicated by the equation (5.9) below, and the economy will be out of recession.

$$\hat{M}_0\ (5\%) = \hat{M}_1\ (5\%) = \text{G}\hat{\text{D}}\text{P}\ (5\%)\ (\equiv \hat{P}\ (2\%) + \text{Real}\hat{\ }\text{GDP}\ (3\%)) \tag{5.9}$$

However, this reflation policy has also turned out to be a fiasco. The reason is clear. As mentioned already, the two premises of the reflation theory, *i.e.*, constant money multiplier m and velocity of money v, have both collapsed.

The velocity of money in Fig. 5.2 was calculated from the data on M_1 and nominal GDP. According to this figure, the velocity of money began to decline from 3.14 in 1991 after the burst of the bubble and has dropped to less than 1 as of 2019. During this period, M_1 continued to increase due to the increase in government debts. However, the decline in the velocity of money absorbed the effect of the increase in M_1.[10] As a result, money stock almost ceased to circulate, and nominal GDP growth rate did not increase. This is why Japan entered its "lost 30 years" from the perspective of reflation theory.

Relationship between GDP and Money Stocks

What has been the relationship between GDP, base money M_0, and money stock M_1 during the lost 30 years (1990–2019)? It turned out that the correlation coefficient between GDP and M_0 was 0.5886 during this period, and that of GDP and M_1 was 0.4576. In other words, there has been no close correlation between GDP and M_0 or M_1. In Chap. 3, we have already demonstrated that the amount of total debts affects economic activities and results in the endogenous creation of money stock. In direct opposition to this debt money theory is the mainstream theory, which assumes that money stock is exogenously supplied. Combining this exogenous money theory with the quantity theory of money would imply that the money stock affects real economic activities such as GDP.

Let us assume for a while that this mainstream monetary theory is correct, and perform the following regression analysis to find out how the money stocks (independent variables) have affected the determination of GDP (dependent variable) during the lost 30 years. The results were as follows (in billion yen):

$$\text{GDP} = 511,177 + 0.0887 * M_0 \quad (R^2 = 0.3464) \tag{5.10}$$

$$\text{GDP} = 504,521 + 0.0456 * M_1 \quad (R^2 = 0.2094) \tag{5.11}$$

---

[10] It has been historically shown that the velocity of circulation related to transactions for the *real* economy (as opposed to financial transactions) has remained nearly constant. For example, Werner (2005) showed that, while the traditional measure of velocity in terms of the broad money aggregates ('V_M') declined in Japan, real velocity of credits for GDP-related transactions ('V_R') remained stable during 1979–2001 by replacing the monetary aggregates (such as money stock) traditionally used in the quantity equation with bank credits ('C'). This empirical finding was indeed consistent with what Fisher (1932) had anticipated, and in fact initially relied on, when he proposed the reflation policy as the proponent of the quantity equation (see Chap. 8 further). It is also consistent with the observation of relatively stable money velocity later advanced by Friedman and Schwartz (1963) based on the United States data between 1869–1960 (using the traditional measure of money aggregates M). Mahmud et al. (2017, p. 52) observed that (Friedman, 1987) had made a similar suggestion on the usefulness of dividing the money flows into "sub-categories".

Our calculation indicates that the increase in base money M_0 contributes only 8.9% of that to GDP, and the increase in money stock M_1 contributes only half that amount, 4.6%, to GDP.[11] This regression analysis reaffirmed our earlier analysis that the declines in the money multiplier and velocity of money absorbed the increase in M_0 and M_1, respectively, and prevented GDP growth.

Why did the reflation theory that has applied the quantity theory of money (monetarism) fail, then? From above discussions, one could reason that it was due to the wrong assumption that money multiplier and velocity of money are both constant. Indeed, they did fall and turn out to be not constant. Nevertheless, such an argument is also false because it is putting the cart before the horse. The correct answer is that money stock is not exogenously supplied (by central bank), as mainstream economics argues, but is created and destroyed endogenously. That is, the volume of transactions itself determines the quantity of money. Consequently, the above quantity theory of money is not an equation, but merely an identity that always holds. Fisher originally proposed the quantity theory as an identity. However, this identity was at some point transformed by monetarists into an equation, as if to indicate that policymakers can directly influence the quantity of money, which determines prices and real economic transactions.

Hence, in order to reflect the economic reality of endogenous debt money, the quantity theory of money as an identity must be precisely expressed as a function of transaction volumes as follows.

$$M(T)\, v \equiv P\ T : \text{Identity} \tag{5.13}$$

This way, it becomes obvious that the above inference that the money stock affects prices and real economy does not hold. Rather, the essence of debt money becomes clear such that money stock is endogenously generated from economic activities, which involve bank loans. What do the BoJ policymakers, who reconstructed and implemented the Fisher's reflation theory based on the false premise and interpre-

---

[11] We have decomposed and analyzed the total amount of money (M_3 in Japan) as follows:

$$M_3 = M_0 + M_f + M_T$$

where M_f denotes Functional Money, and M_T denotes Time Deposits (see Sect. 3.5 further for the definition of monetary aggregates). Then, we have further extended the mainstream exogenous money theory and performed multivariate analysis to obtain the following results:

$$\text{GDP} = 126,489 + 0.0935 * M_0 + 0.2086 * M_f + 0.4502 * M_T \quad (R^2 = 0.96497) \tag{5.12}$$

As expected, the regression coefficient of base money M_0 is the smallest at 0.0935, a level that has virtually no effect on GDP. However, it is not reasonable to derive the causality from the regression analysis that assumes an exogenously supplied money stock, because in this analysis time deposits are treated as the cause and GDP as the effect. As discussed in Chap. 3, the correct causality derived from the debt money theory is that private debts determine investment, which then determines GDP, and the money stock created by those investments becomes time deposits. Therefore, from this correct relationship, it can be concluded that the regression equation that is based on exogenous money stock assumption does not hold.

tation of the constant money multiplier and the velocity, think about their policy failure? Japanese people are still suffering from their mistakes.

5.5 Fiscal Policy to Fill in Nonexistent GDP Gap

So far, we have examined how the monetary policy and reflation theory suggested by the mainstream economics failed to achieve the equilibrium with "GDP Gap = 0" and rescue Japan's lost 30 years. If these policies cannot reduce the GDP gap to zero, what should be done, then? The second formula for achieving equilibrium is "GDP Gap = Government Deficits" as indicated in equation (5.5). In other words, it is now the government's turn to fill in the GDP gap by issuing bonds and finance the fiscal deficit. This is the essence of fiscal policy suggested by the Keynesian economics. The "anti-austerity policy" and political movement also rely on this Keynesian fiscal policy framework.

Keynes's *General Theory* was published in 1936. This was the time when the world economy was still suffering from the fallout of the Great Depression. After the WWII, Keynesian economics spread around the world thanks to the popularity of the IS-LM analysis, combined with its *apparent* explanatory power and applicability to the real world phenomenon such as short-run business cycles (to be detailed in Chaps. 7 and 8). Fiscal policies based on this Keynesian theory began to be implemented among OECD countries. Since these periods coincided with the period of high economic growth that began in the 1960s, this gave policymakers and economists the impression that fiscal policies had been reasonably effective. And a number of economists began to boast that they can now control and "fine-tune" the macroeconomy like engineers. As a result, the mobilization of fiscal policy for attaining "GDP Gap = Govt. Deficits" has become the trump card to counteract with recessions.

Nevertheless, the United States economy experienced stagflation in the 1970s. Kindled by the Lucas critique of the Keynesian econometric models (Lucas, 1976), neoclassical economics with general equilibrium theory at its core came back to life as the mainstream economics (Fig. 1.3). Meanwhile, the bubble burst in Japan. To get out of the recession, fiscal policy was actively implemented as a matter of course. Yet, the economy has failed to recover from the post-bubble recession and suffering from stagnant demand as analyzed in Chap. 4 (Fig. 4.4).

GDP Gap Does Not Exists!

Why didn't Keynesian fiscal policy work, then? The fundamental mistake of Keynesian economics is that it is built on the exogenous money. Consequently, if investment falls below savings (as leakages from money circulation), a GDP gap occurs and policies are needed to fill that gap. Keynes argued that the root cause of the Depression was the lack of effective demand (consumption + investment) so that the depression and recession could be overcome if the government increases its expenditure so as to fill the GDP gap by fiscal policy.

On the other hand, Fisher analyzed that the root cause of the Depression was the debt money system itself where money is endogenously created or destroyed, and called for *100% Money* in which all money would be issued at interest-free (public money) and its total quantity is controlled exogenously by an independent currency commission established under the government. However, his proposal was subsequently considered a taboo subject in economics, and was completely eliminated from textbooks and university lectures.

So, what would happen if investment determines GDP, and savings are derived *ex post* to match the investment such that Investment = Savings? There will be no such thing as "GDP gap" to begin with. As discussed in Sect. 3.7 as "Surprise 2", we found that money circulates from Private Debts → Investment → Savings → Time Deposits under the present debt money system. In other words, GDP is determined first of all by investment, and then, savings corresponding to that investment are generated endogenously and *ex post*.

Accordingly, there is no such thing as GDP gap that assumes savings as the precondition of investment. If it doesn't exist, it would not be possible to calculate it in the first place! If this were the case, it would be also impossible to use fiscal policy that would make up the difference between savings and investment.[12] Therefore, even if fiscal policy is available as a policy tool, it should be limited to support investment activities in the private sector, and can never play a leading role as countermeasures against recession, especially against post-bubble stagnation like that of Japan. As verified as "Surprise 3" in Sect. 3.7 fiscal policy financed by government debts did increase M_1. However, this increase in M_1 did not necessarily contribute to an increase in GDP, as the failure of the reflation theory discussed above also makes clear.

---

[12] If full employment is not achieved even at that GDP level, then, employment policies should be naturally proposed that would raise the level of private investment and revitalize economic activity, so that full employment will be attained. It should be noted here that GDP is not necessarily directly related with the level of employment as mainstream theory assumes. Standard macroeconomic theories, be it neoclassical or Keynesian, assume (as if it is a matter of course) that firms can hire labor whenever they wish and shed workers whenever they can. As researchers who are familiar with the success of Japanese management, we feel a strong sense of discomfort with (Western) economic theories and business management that treat workers as if they were disposable commodities that can be freely traded on labor market like slaves. Alternatively, we propose an employment policy that revives the strength of Japanese management practices by encouraging firms to shift their non-regular employees to regular employees irrespective of GDP levels under the Public Money Initiative in Chap. 14.

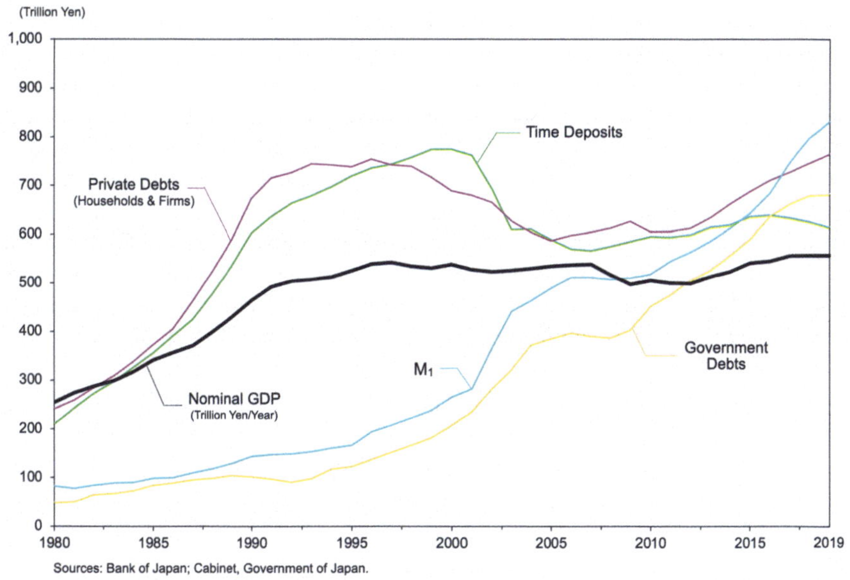

Fig. 5.3 GDP and private and government debts: 1980–2019

Relationship between GDP, Private and Government Debts

How did private and government debts actually contribute to GDP, then? To examine this, we have created Fig. 5.3 by removing M_3 and total debts from Fig. 3.8 and adding GDP.

As already discussed as "Surprises 2 and 3", there are close positive correlations between time deposits and private debts, and M_1 and government debts. That is, if private debts increase or decrease, investments increase or decrease, and time deposits also increase or decrease. Moreover, the more the government borrows, the more the M_1 increases.

Therefore, let's examine the impact of those borrowings (debts) on GDP based on data in Fig. 5.3. When households and producers borrow money, consumption and investment will increase, and when the government borrows money, government spending will increase. In either case, borrowing will stimulate the economy and boost GDP according to the Keynesian income determination formula in equation (5.1). Most macroeconomic textbooks teach these relations as if they are facts. But are they really so?

Let us first consider the relationship between private debts and GDP. If corporate and household debts increase capital and housing investment, the aggregate investment will increase, resulting in an increase in employment, wage income, and consumption. Conversely, if investment declines due to a recession, wages fall and consumption would also stagnate or fall. In this way, it is easy to infer that there is a positive correlation between corporate and household debts and GDP. From Fig. 5.3, it can be observed that both corporate and household debts and GDP were growing concurrently until 1990.

After the collapse of the bubble, however, corporate and household debts declined sharply. As a result, GDP has also stagnated. Accordingly, the correlation coefficient between the two turned out to be 0.9389 during 1980–2019, indicating that private debts and GDP are strongly correlated. Since private debts declined rapidly after the burst of the bubble, this close positive correlation suggests that the decline in private debt was almost certainly a factor behind the Japan's stagnant GDP. On the contrary, the correlation coefficient between government debts and GDP turned out to be 0.6159; that is, they were not much correlated. We have similarly performed simple linear regressions and obtained the results as follows (in billion yen):

$$\text{GDP} = 139,485 + 0.5576 * \text{Private Debts} \quad (R^2 = 0.8815) \tag{5.14}$$

$$\text{GDP} = 401,345 + 0.266 * \text{Government Debts} \quad (R^2 = 0.3793) \tag{5.15}$$

Government Debt is Inefficient for Increasing Production

In addition to these correlations, we have performed a multivariate analysis of the causal relationships to further examine the impact of private and government debts on GDP, and obtained the following result (in billion yen):

$$\text{GDP} = 148,537 + 0.4917 * \text{Private Debts} + 0.10934 * \text{Govt. Debts} \ (R^2 = 0.93333) \tag{5.16}$$

It turns out that an increase or decrease in private debts increase or decrease GDP by 49% of its amount during the period between 1980–2019. The above linear regression equation also indicates that no matter how much the government increases its debt, it only contributes 11% of that amount to the increase in GDP. That is, the same amount of government borrowing contributes only about one-fifth as much to GDP as it does in the case of private debts.

In macroeconomics textbooks, the effect of investment on GDP is indicated by an *investment multiplier*, and the effect of government debts (fiscal expenditure) on GDP is indicated by a *fiscal multiplier*. It is then explained that private investment and government debts both increase GDP by the same multiplier times. For example, if the marginal propensity to consume is 0.6 and the tax rate is 0.16, both the investment and fiscal multipliers will be 2.976 according to the income determination formula.[13] That is, GDP will increase by about three times the amount of investment and government debts.

---

[13] Let us denote macroeconomic variable as follows: GDP (Y), consumption (C), government expenditure (G), tax revenue (T), investment (I), change in government debts (ΔD), marginal propensity to consume (c), and tax rate (t). Then, macroeconomic equations of income determination are formulated as follows (net export is ignored here for simplicity):

However, when we reexamined the relationships between private sector and government debts and GDP from the perspective of debt money theory, a surprising reality emerged that goes against the efficacy of fiscal policy argued by the Keynesian theory. In other words, government debts become far less effective to stimulate and revitalize the economy. We have already discussed that M_1 and GDP have no significant correlation (correlation coefficient $= 0.458$). Combining these evidences, our statistical analyses show that government debts increase M_1, but increase GDP only by 11% or about one-fifth of private debts. We have also verified already that no matter how much the BoJ increases base money M_0, GDP will increase by only 8.9%. In other words, just as monetary (reflation) policy have failed, Keynesian fiscal policy with government debts proved to be equally ineffective.

Why did fiscal policy fail so miserably? Let's take a look at Fig. 5.3 again. Private debts begin to decline from 1995 onward. Using the above regression equation (5.16), a simple calculation shows that, while private debts decreased by 125 trillion yen between 1995 and 2012, GDP has decreased by 61 trillion yen ($= 125 \times 0.49$). On the other hand, government debts have increased by 383 trillion yen, and GDP has increased by 42 trillion yen ($= 383 \times 0.11$). Thus, the total change in GDP due to these two factors is a decrease of 19 trillion yen ($= -61 + 42$). The actual data shows GDP decreased by 26 trillion yen during this period, which is close to the value calculated from the regression equation.

Between 1995 to 2012, Japan's total debt increased by 258 trillion yen ($= 383 - 125$) and M_3 also increased by 277 trillion yen ($M_3 \simeq$ total debts). Moreover, while M_1 had increased by 397 trillion yen, GDP decreased by 26 trillion yen. What would have happened if the private sector (instead of the government) had made all of the increase in total debts during this period? That is, the net increase of the entire 258 trillion yen in debt had been invested by the private sector, and that the government had switched to a policy of compensating private sectors for their debt repayment costs, rather than borrowing money from banks and spending on its expenditure such as public investment.

Had the government been wise enough to implement such policies, Japan's GDP would have increased by 126 trillion yen ($= 258 \times 0.49$) according to the above

---

$$
\begin{aligned}
&Y = C + I + G &&: \text{Income determination formula} \\
&C = c(Y - T) &&: \text{Consumption function} \\
&T = tY &&: \text{Tax function} \\
&G = T + \Delta D &&: \text{Government budget equation}
\end{aligned}
$$

Then, GDP can be obtained as follows.

$$
Y = \frac{1}{(1-c)(1-t)}(I + \Delta D)
$$

Here, both the investment and the fiscal multipliers become $1/(1-c)(1-t)$, and if c = 0.6 and t = 0.16, these multipliers become the same 2.976. If all investments were made by private debts, GDP is determined to be about three times the total annual debts of private sector. According to this formula, government debts would similarly increase GDP by the same factor. In Chap. 8 we will introduce a system dynamics macroeconomic model and analyze the Japanese case.

regression equation. As a result, Japan's lost 30 years would have disappeared and the days of "Japan as Number One" would have returned by now. Even from these simple calculations, it is clear that Keynesian fiscal policy and anti-austerity "deficit spendings" have failed and its rationale has collapsed.

The Myth of Fiscal Multiplier and Its Collapse

Why has Japan made such mistake for 30 years? As discussed in Chap. 4, one may assert that politically Japan was forced to implement fiscal policies as part of the US government's demand for structural reforms. However, that is not the whole story. As economists, we need to analyze the causes of policy failures from the standpoint of macroeconomic theory. Specifically, it is the myth of fiscal multiplier that has obscured the failure of the fiscal policy.

Macroeconomic textbooks explain that increasing government expenditure (G) increases GDP by a factor of the multiplier. It is formally described as follows:

$$\Delta GDP = \text{Fiscal multiplier} \times \Delta G$$

However, there is usually no explanation as to whether this multiplier effect will occur after one year or several years later. This is because it is merely a comparative analysis of two equilibria based on the so-called *comparative static analysis*. However, students who learn this multiplier effect are led to a shortsighted understanding that an one-time fiscal stimulus of, say, 10 trillion yen, would immediately increase GDP by 30 trillion yen ($= 3 \times 10$) as if by magic. We have pointed out this erroneous reasoning by constructing a simple ASD macroeconomic model (see Yamaguchi 2013, Chap. 8).

The correct understanding of the multiplier effect is that an one-time fiscal stimulus temporarily increases GDP, yet it will immediately return to its original level unless those increases in G induce further demand (such as private capital investment). For example, consider the recent case in which the Japanese government paid out 100,000 yen per citizen as an emergency measure against the COVID-19 economic shock. If all of these subsidies are spent on meals or travel expenses, GDP will temporarily increase by 12.6 trillion yen ($=$ 126 million people $\times$ 100,000 yen per person). Yet GDP will return to its original level in the following year, resulting in only 12.6 trillion yen of government debt accumulation.

For this fiscal multiplier to be effective, the government must continue to mobilize the same amount of fiscal stimulus year after year until GDP increases by a factor of multiplier and sustains at that level. Indeed the Japanese government continued to mobilize an average of about 20 trillion yen per year on fiscal stimulus during the lost 30 years. Assuming that a new equilibrium has been achieved after 30 years of continuous deficit spending, Japan's GDP would have increased by 60 trillion yen ($= 3 \times 20$) by applying the fiscal multiplier of 3. Meanwhile, government debts have accumulated to 600 trillion yen ($=$ 20 trillion yen per year $\times$ 30 years). In other words, despite the fact that the government has borrowed about 600 trillion yen, which exceeds the annual GDP, the level of GDP increased only by 60 trillion yen. Applying this amount to the above regression equation, the increase in GDP during this period is 66 trillion yen (= 600 × 0.11). This is consistent with the increase in GDP of 60 trillion yen calculated with the fiscal multiplier of 3.

However, the regression equation above shows that the annual increase in GDP resulting from government debts has been only 2.2 trillion yen (= 0.11 × 20). On the other hand, from 1995 to 2012, private debts decreased by 125 trillion yen, reducing GDP by 61 trillion yen (= 125 × 0.49). This means that the 61 trillion yen decrease in GDP resulting from the decline in private debts was only compensated for by the 66 trillion increase in GDP resulting from 600 trillion in government debt. This has resulted in a net increase in GDP only by 5 trillion yen (= 66 − 61).

Even with these simple calculations, it is impossible for Japan to come out from the prolonged stagnation by following the traditional Keynesian aggregate demand management policy. Yet the Japanese policymakers, the media, and academics seemed to have all been brainwashed by this myth and expected that the economy would eventually escape from the decades-long stagnation, until they found that their government has accumulated over 1,000 trillion yen of national debt and their economy is plunging into the abyss of debt hell. What's worse is that these problems are not unique to Japan. As the side effects of continued fiscal deficits, the US government is now facing debt crises, while other economies are also facing similar issues as those of Japan, such as declining birth rates, anemic growth and growing inequality.

What Should the World Learn from Japan's Lost 30 Years?

In this chapter we have analyzed why neoclassical as well as Keynesian policies all failed to revitalize the Japanese economy. For the past three decades, the government and the bank of Japan have diligently implemented these mainstream economic prescriptions. If they were students of mainstream economics, they would certainly be graded as honors. Yet, the patient was not saved as a result of the wrong prescriptions. In other words, the case of Japan's Lost 30 Years was the final testament to the failure of mainstream economics, which we, the Japanese people, sacrificed our lives to prove to the world. This collapse of mainstream economics will also become clear from the failures of their underlying monetary theories, which we will examine in detail in Chap. 10.

How can Japan overcome this situation, then? What should the world learn from the case of Japan's Lost 30 years? The conclusion that has been verified from our analyses is that we must now free ourselves from the brainwashing of mainstream economics, and establish the alternative economics based on public money theory to pay off national debts and implement the Public Money Initiative proposed in Chap. 14. This book will serve as a guide for the bright future, and show us the way.

In the next chapter, let us focus on the national debt problems, and analyze why transitioning to the public money system will be the fundamental solution to overcome the systemic problem.

Chapter 6
Debt Money System is Debt End!

6.1 Debt Crisis of Japan

According to the Ministry of Finance's data on long-term public debts, the Japanese government's debt outstanding has ballooned to a total of 1,106 trillion yen as of 2019. This includes both the central and local governments' debts, of which the central government debts are 914 trillion yen. Given that Japan's total population of the same year was around 126 million, the per capita debt outstanding was 8.78 million yen. As a reference, the Japanese average annual income was 4.36 million yen in the same year, according to the National Tax Administration Agency. In other words, the national debt per capita has accumulated to twice the average annual income of Japanese working people.

Of the government revenues in Fiscal Year (FY) 2019, tax revenues were 62.5 trillion yen. Of the expenditures, government bond costs were 23.5 trillion yen, of which interest payments were 7.8 trillion yen. In other words, 37.6% of tax revenues were spent on debt payments. Accordingly, the amount of principal and interest payments per person is 187,000 yen per year, which is about 85% of average monthly salary of Japanese workers in the early 20s (225,000 yen per month). The one-time subsidy provided by the Japanese government during COVID-19 in 2020 was 100,000 yen per person. Yet the government as a whole collects about twice as much money as taxes every year from people and businesses for debt-related payments. Yes, that's right. Every year!

The government decided that it was still not enough, so it borrowed 32.7 trillion in FY 2019. It was 9.2 trillion yen (= 32.7 − 23.5) of net increase in debt, which was the primary balance deficit. This simple fact alone shows the Japanese government is by no means in austerity. It is rather being forced to increase its spending each year in order to pay off its debts! In addition to these debt repayments that appear in the "general account", the government has been issuing a huge amount of refunding bonds every year under the "special account" for many years. The amount of refinancing bonds issued in FY 2019 was a whopping 127.6 trillion yen, far more

K. Yamaguchi and Y. Yamaguchi, *Public Money*,
https://doi.org/10.1007/978-981-97-6564-5_6

than the 101 trillion yen of the general account's total annual budget. Indeed, the government is in an endless *debt hell*.

Government Debt Continues to Increase Exponentially

Faced with this budgetary hardship, the government raised the consumption tax rate to 10% in October 2019. However, it is clear from the above simple analysis that the government will not be able to repay 100% of its debts, even if it will enforce consumption tax hikes by another 20~30% in the future, or achieve the primary balance through fiscal austerity. In other words, there is no realistic policy to stop the accumulation of government debts.

By accepting this harsh reality of the government's debt hell, we must ask: "What will happen if it continues to accumulate debt?" In fact this was the question Kaoru had raised in his previous book published almost 10 years ago (Yamaguchi, 2015). To answer this question, Chap. 6 of the book presented "Fig. 6.2: Changes in Government Debt of Japan and Debt-to-GDP Ratio: 1970–2014" and analyzed the Japanese debt problem as follows:

> What can be observed from these two lines of GDP and Debts is that, first of all, the long-term debts exceeded GDP in 1998, and secondly, the growth of nominal GDP has stopped during "the lost 20 years" since the mid-1990s, yet the long-term debts continued to increase regardless of the zero growth of GDP. Why did this happen? As already mentioned in Chap. 5 "Fear of the Debt Hell", once the government borrows money, its debt will grow exponentially due to compound interest calculations (Yamaguchi 2015, p.124).

Figure 6.1 presents the same diagram where we updated our previous simulation of government debt. Based on newly updated data up to 2019, the growth rates of debt obtained this time by the optimization method were as follows: 32.7% between 1970–1979, 8.3% between 1980–1999, 3.07% between 2000–2019. These results are used to simulate the government debts growth until the year 2050.

According to this simulation, the situation has not changed in any way as it was almost ten years ago. In fact, it appears to be getting worse. Therefore, we have extended the simulation period to 2050 this time from the previous 2014. As a result, the outstanding debt will reach 1,674 trillion yen in 2036, 12 years from 2024. And Japan's debt-to-GDP ratio will exceed 300%, or more precisely, 3 years worth of its GDP. Furthermore, Japan's outstanding national debt will be 2,193 trillion yen in 2050, and its debt-to-GDP ratio will be about 400%.

What this result is indicating is that, sooner or later, the Japanese economy would end up with the three devastating scenarios (S) as described in Chap. 6 of Yamaguchi (2015): (S1) financial meltdown, (S2) hyperinflation, and (S3) government default. And the economy seems to be currently heading straight toward them. What exactly will happen if Japan continues to accumulate its national debt? Let's take a closer look at three scenarios in more detail below.

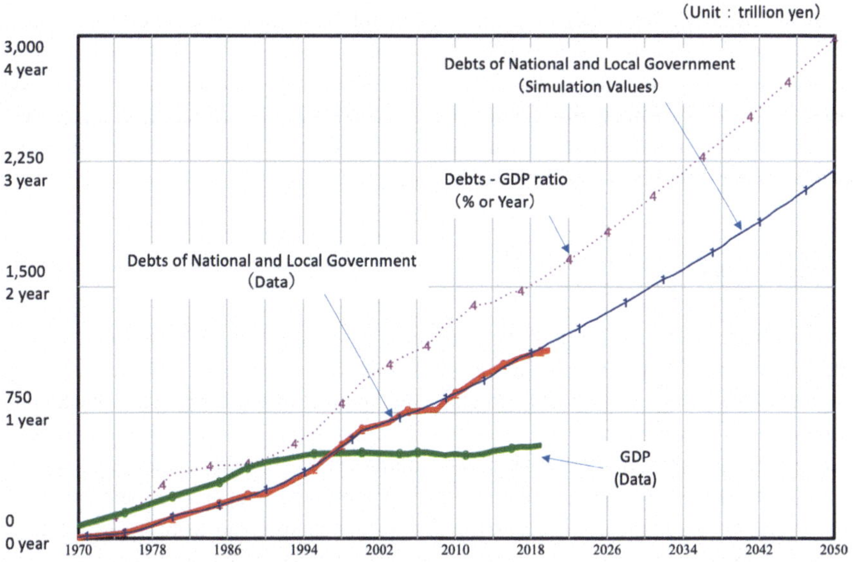

Fig. 6.1 Japanese government debts and Debt-to-GDP ratio: 1970–2050

Three Catastrophic Scenarios Awaiting Japanese Economy

S1. Financial Meltdown

The first scenario is a financial meltdown. If the government continues to borrow money at the current rate, doubts arise among bond market participants about the prospects for repayment of government bonds. Interest rates would rise at some point and the bond prices will plummet, which in turn may trigger stock market crash. As a result of such market crash, banks and security companies will experience a sharp decline in their financial assets (mark-to-market accounting) and their balance sheets become insolvent. Eventually, a number of weak financial institutions will begin to go bankrupt one after another.

Of course, Japan is not in such a critical situation yet. This is because since 2013, the BoJ has been buying up Japanese Government Bonds (JGB) and stocks through Exchange Traded Funds (ETF) under the guise of Quantitative Easing (QE) policy, and trying desperately to contain the plunge in bond prices. In fact, JGB rates have already risen many times, but in each such occasion, the BoJ has conducted fixed-rate purchase operations of JGB and ETF to kept the markets from crushing. As we saw in Sect. 4.4, non-bank lending during the bubble period amounted to 65.8 billion yen per day. However, since the introduction of the QE policy, the BoJ has been purchasing 70 billion yen of ETF and Real Estate Investment Trusts (J-REIT) almost on a daily basis, and has been flooding the market with its newly issued reserves (BoJ deposits).

Since the BoJ is another private institution independent of the government, there is no guarantee that it can or will continue this money-printing spree for another decades to come. And if the BoJ once faces the risk of its own balance sheet becoming insolvent, it will be forced to stop purchasing bonds and stocks immediately to protect itself. At that point, interest rates will skyrocket while bond and stock prices plummet. And a financial meltdown will quickly ensue.

S2. Hyperinflation

The second scenario is a state of rapid inflation or hyperinflation. If we use the well-cited definition of hyperinflation as "monthly inflation of 50% or more" suggested by Cagan (1956), prices may be 129.7 times higher or more a year later; that is, the annual inflation rate becomes 12,970% or more.[1] Alternatively, the International Financial Reporting Standards (IFRS) defines hyperinflation as "a cumulative increase in prices of at least 100% (26% per annum or 9.9% per month) over a three-year period". According to this standard, the postwar Japan indeed suffered from hyperinflation, since her inflation rate in 1946 (Tokyo Retail Price Index) was about 500% per annum (monthly inflation rate of about 14.4%). The Japanese government's debt to GNP ratio reached 204% at the end of the WWII, but it only survived by forcibly withdrawing banknotes, blocking deposits, and introducing the fixed exchange rate system against the US dollar.

There are two possible routes to hyperinflation. First, as the possibility of a financial meltdown emerges, the government and BoJ will be forced into additional monetary easing, resulting in a surge in base money M_0. And as our analyses in previous chapters reveal, M_1 begins to flood the market as government debt increases. Eventually, a typical inflationary situation will occur, in which the surplus of money chases after the shortage of goods and services.

Once prices begin to rise, banks and security companies will use the money that has been poured into their BoJ current accounts to create more credits in speculative lending, which will then flow into financial markets such as equities and real estate. This bullish market attract more easy money and could trigger another financial bubble. This self-reinforcing feedback loop repeats itself and fuels the asset prices further, and hyperinflation could be the final phase. That will be a typical case of demand-driven or demand-pull inflation. Indeed, as we finalize the editing of this chapter, the Nikkei average reached the record high of 40,109 yen in March 4th, 2024 while GDP continues to be stagnant.

Secondly, the rapid increase in outstanding government debts and the accompanying surge in M_0 could rapidly erode confidence in the currency. Selling pressure on the yen builds up in the foreign exchange (FX) markets. This will cause a gradual or even sudden depreciation of the yen and a surge in the price of imports, leading to hyperinflation. This will be a typical case of cost-push inflation. Due to its heavy

[1] Calculation here is based on the Euler method. If the Runge-Kutta method is used, prices will be about 403 times higher.

energy dependence on foreign imports, the yen depreciation will have further effect on Japanese economy through various price channels. Hyperinflation through either demand-pull or cost-push route (or a combination of both) would first hits the low-income earners and pensioners, and then the middle class, spurring social disorder and the economic collapse.

S3. Government Default

The third scenario of default erupts when the government becomes unable to pay its debts and eventually goes bankrupt. It is the situation in which the government accumulates its debts to the point where it will become unable to cover its fiscal needs by rolling over its debt through refinancing bonds as no one including the primary dealers and the Bank of Japan become willing to purchase treasury bonds. Under such a situation, tax revenues will no longer be sufficient to cover the principal and interest payments associated with rising interest rates. In this way, the government is finally forced into default.

The main example of a government default is the suspension of payment on external debts held by foreign creditors. For example, the financial crises of Mexico (1982), Brazil (1987), Russia (1998), Argentina (2008, 2014, 2020), Greece (2015), Lebanon (2020) all resulted from governments' failure to continue and repay the money they borrowed from abroad. There is a widespread belief that Japanese government will not default since Japan has no 'net' external debt in contrast to those historical cases. They say Japan is the world's largest net creditor nation. However, the "default" we are referring to here is the default of the government as a macroeconomic sector, not the default of the entire nation.

As we will discuss in detail in Chap. 11, we must separate the "nation" as the sum of all economic sectors from the "government", which is just one of sectors within the nation. Although Japan has long been and still is the world's largest net creditor nation with 364 trillion yen in external net assets as of 2019, the majority of those net assets are foreign assets of private companies and individuals. Here we are discussing a default scenario in which the government itself as a macroeconomic sector falls into the debt hell and becomes unable to service its debts, while private-sector's capital flees from Japan to overseas, resulting in the self-destruction of the government.

The default and shutdown of government would cause various social security systems and public infrastructures to cease functioning, which in turn could cause the FX and other financial markets to enter a state of crisis. As a result, the Japanese economy will undergo a major turmoil. The on-going life extension measure implemented as QE by the BoJ can only last until the central bank is financially solvent and public's confidence in the Japanese Yen is maintained.

As Fig. 6.1 indicates, the Japanese economy will begin to encounter one of these catastrophic scenarios as the debt-GDP ratio approaches the psychological level of 300% in around 2036. During the WWII, the Japanese government debt exceeded 200%. If things continue as they are, however, the debt-to-GDP ratio will reach

300%, a level that Japan has never experienced. Moreover, no one can stop this trend, because it is caused by the design failures of the debt money system itself. Japan is indeed driven into the "helpless position" as Hemphil expressed, which we quoted in Chap. 4 as follows: "When we get a complete grasp upon this picture, the tragic absurdity of our helpless position is incredible–but there it is".

Optimistically, Japan seems to have only 12 years left before such scenarios are likely to unfold. But, will the JGB credit ratings remain the same for another decade? Will the Japanese yen keep its status as a safe asset 12 years from now?

6.2 Debt Crisis of the United States

So far, we have analyzed the three catastrophic scenarios the Japanese economy will have to face in the near future. Is this really a problem that is unique to Japan? The following observation of the current state of the US national debt suggests that the answer is no. In fact, the US seems to be in an even more serious *debt hell* than Japan. Let's now focus on the case of the US's debt crisis.

Milton Friedman, a well-known monetarist, was awarded the Nobel Memorial Prize in Economics in 1976. In the fall of 1977, immediately after Friedman received the prize, Kaoru went to UC Berkeley to study economics. The Friedman's book "A Program For Monetary Stability" (Friedman, 1960) was one of the textbooks in the macroeconomics course at Berkeley, perhaps influenced by his Prize reception. In 1992, its tenth edition was reprinted, and Friedman added a foreword with the following recount on the international monetary system:

> The collapse of the Bretton Woods system was the final step in the abandonment of any link, however indirect, between money and a commodity. ... The current monetary system of the world has no historical precedent. For the first time, every major country has a pure fiat currency, not as a temporary expedient, but as a permanent system. The quantity of money is determined entirely by the discretion of a monetary authority that does not pay even lip service to a link with a commodity. The initial result of embarking on this uncharted sea was understandably much uncertainty and experiment ... [the wide spread inflation and simultaneous adoption of flexible exchange rates] (Friedman 1960, page viii).

As Friedman pointed out, albeit ironically, the recession, inflation, and government debt crisis that we are currently facing all seem to stem from the gold-dollar suspension in 1971 and discretionary monetary policy conducted by central banks under the debt money system. The Club of Rome, who defends the present system as we will discuss in Chap. 9, commissioned a book titled "Money and Sustainability" (Lietaer et al., 2012). According to the book, the global economy has experienced, on average, more than 10 currency, banking, and sovereign debt crises per year over the past 40 years (*ibid.*, p.51).

As discussed in Chap. 4, Japan was viewed with wonder and respected as "Japan as Number One". However, the nation soon underwent severe bubble and its collapse. During this period, the Western economies seemed to have managed to navigate the uncharted sea, with the exception of Japan and other Asian and Latin American countries that were hit by the financial crisis. However, 16 years after Friedman's 1992 warning, the global economic Titanic finally ran aground and was wrecked by the Lehman Shock of 2008.

With that shipwreck, the neoclassical economic prescriptions that had become dominant since 1980s were once again knocked down following the Great Depression, reconfirming that the current debt money system does not work. Nevertheless, the only economic prescriptions left to us to escape the shipwreck were traditional fiscal and monetary policies based on Keynesian economics. As we have seen in Chap. 5, Japan was quick to seek relief from Keynesian policies in order to avoid the post-bubble depression and regain the dream of "Japan as Number One". Yet, interest rates fell and the monetary policy lost its effectiveness. Therefore, the government turned to fiscal stimulus measures. But these policies also failed miserably and in turn have created the debt hell.

After the Lehman Shock, Western countries were forced into a similar situation as that of Japan. They had mobilized fiscal stimulus, but the effects were not as great as initially expected, and they were hit by government debt crises. Therefore, they were forced to adopt QE policy as the last forbidden measure. But this too had little effect on the real economy. Then, in 2020, the COVID-19 pandemic broke out, and the US government under the Biden administration implemented unprecedented fiscal stimulus, issuing huge amounts of treasury bonds, which resulted in a further increase in the federal government debt.

So, what is the situation of the US national debt? To answer this question, Chap. 6 of our previous book (Yamaguchi, 2015) also presented "Fig. 6.5: Changes in the US Government Debts and Debt-to-GDP Ratio: 1970–2025" (adapted as Fig. 6.2 in this book) and observed its growth speed as follows:

> Line 2 (in red) in Fig. 6.5 shows the actual evolution of the US debt from 1970 to 2014. A simulation analysis of this data using optimization method reveals that the debt has increased as follows. From 1970, the year before the Nixon shock, to 1988, the debt increased rapidly with an annual growth rate of 10%. The doubling time is about 7 years. In other words, every seven years, the US debt surged by a factor of two, and four. From 1989 to 2014, however, the speed of debt growth slowed down slightly. Still, the debt increased at a rate of 7.7%. The doubling time is about 9 years.
>
> Line 1 (in blue) shows the projected debt growth through 2025 at that 7.7% growth rate. According to this line, the US debt outstanding in 2014 was $17.6 trillion, which will double to about $35 trillion in 2023, about nine years later. Assuming that the US's GDP at that time is $21 trillion, the debt-to-GDP ratio will be 129%, which will certainly exceed 100% (Yamaguchi 2015, p.135).

Figure 6.2 was a prediction made about 10 years ago based on simple simulation. How does the situation of the US national debt look like today? The most recent data published by the US Department of Treasury shows the outstanding national debt was at 31.4 trillion dollars at the end of 2022. The GDP in 2022 was roughly at 26.1 trillion. So, the debt-to-GDP ratio was already at 120%.

Although there have been several unpredictable shocks in the real economy, such as the COVID-19 pandemic, we can see that the US government debt has developed almost exactly as the simulation had assumed. As the convertibility with gold

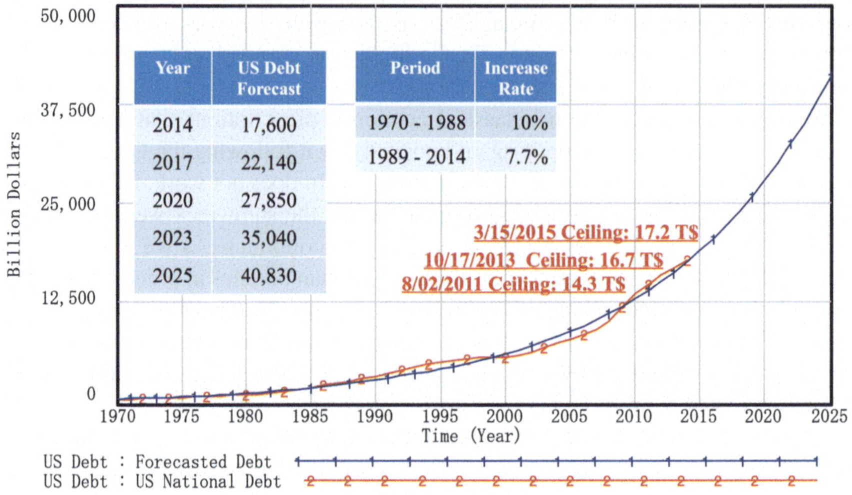

Fig. 6.2 The US government debt and Debt-to-GDP ratio: 1970–2025

was suspended in 1971 and fiscal stimulus has been repeatedly used to support the economy, the US government debt has been increasing at a rapid pace, just as in the case of Japan. In fact, since Japan's annual debt growth rate from 2000 to 2020 was 3.07%, the US debt growth rate of 7.7% between 1989–2014 turned out to be more than twice that of Japan. From these observations, we can conclude that the US is in a more serious "debt hell" than Japan. To make the situation worse and more unsettling, the Japanese government is also the world's largest holder of the US Treasuries. In other words, the US and Japan, which are the first and third largest economies as of 2020, are carrying the world's biggest economic *time bombs* in the form of national debts.

Debt Money System is Debt End!

At the invitation of the Congressman Dennis Kucinich, a former two-time Democratic presidential candidate from Ohio, Kaoru was visiting Washington, D.C. on July 26, 2011. The purpose of the visit was to report at a congressional briefing the latest results of his macroeconomic simulation showing that the government debts could be paid off immediately by transitioning to the public money system. The deadline for capping the federal budget at $14.3 trillion was approaching in one week on August 2 of that year. And the Capitol Hill was extremely tense because the US federal government would be forced into default if the Congress did not approve further increases to the debt ceiling.

It was the first time the researcher experienced the harsh reality of the US debt problem at firsthand. In the end, however, the Democrats and Republicans reached a settlement, and the federal debt ceiling was raised to $16.7 trillion.

Two years later, on October 1, 2013, the big news came from the US: the partial closure of federal agencies began on October 1 because the provisional budget for the new fiscal year starting in October was not passed due to a congressional conflict between the Democratic and Republican parties. It was indeed a surprise to hear that the US government's default had finally become a reality. And if the Congress could not approve the new debt ceiling by then, the US government will default. However, this chicken race between Democrats and Republicans was again settled just in time, with the House of Representatives approving a bill to raise the debt ceiling at 8 p.m. and the Senate at 10 p.m. on October 16, two hours before the date changed. And the default was avoided.

The next limit approved was $17.2 trillion, with a deadline of February 2014. However, as the deadline approached, a rescheduling of the deadline to March 15, 2015 was easily approved. Observing these US debt ceiling issues at the time, Kaoru became increasingly puzzled. Is this a game of chicken between the two political parties to deceive the US electorate? Or is this really a serious "fiscal cliff" game facing the US federal government?

Subsequently, it became clear to us that these chicken races between the Democrats and the Republicans were largely political ceremonies. The latest race of lifting the $31.4 trillion ceiling was performed on June 3, 2023. However, if the debts continue to grow at this rate, sooner or later, the Congress will have to face a 'real' default crisis. If the exponential growth rate of 7.7% continues at the current rate, the return of the default crisis will come even sooner. This is obvious to anyone who looks at this problem as the perpetual debt growth system. This game of chicken will inevitably lead to a real crash in the not-too-distant future and cause a catastrophe for the US economy.

There is a phrase "dead-end" in English. When Kaoru presented his simulation at the congressional briefing and expresssed that "the current debt money system is a dead-end", the Congressman Dennis Kucinich quickly commented on him, saying "It's not a dead-end. It's a *Debt-End*." Kaoru quickly replied, "Yes, that's right! It is indeed DEBT END, as you correctly pointed out." The current system is debt end. We still cannot think of a better way to put it. Since then, we have been using the phrase "Debt money system is debt end!"

6.3 Debt Crisis of the OECD Countries

Japan and the United States are not the only nations facing debt crisis. The so-called PIIGS countries (Portugal, Italy, Ireland, Greece, and Spain) in the EU and other OECD countries are similarly facing debt crises. Figure 6.3 shows the Debt-to-GDP ratios of 25 OECD countries that are above 50% as of 2019, with Mexico (50.7%) being the last country crossing the 50% border line. Numbers in parentheses ([ ])

Country	Debt-to-GDP (%)	Country	Debt-to-GDP (%)
1. Japan	234.8 [204.4]	15. Australia	77.0 [41.3]
2. Greece	200.8 [130.4]	16. Finland	75.2 [58.0]
3. Italy	154.2 [124.3]	17. Israel	74.1 [79.8]
4. United States	136.1 [125.3]	18. Ireland	68.8 [83.4]
5. Portugal	135.6 [105.7]	19. Germany	67.6 [87.3]
6. France	123.1 [101.0]	20. Poland	63.6 [62.2]
7. Spain	120.4 [67.4]	21. Slovak Republic	63.0 [48.3]
8. Belgium	119.6 [108.7]	22. Netherlands	62.3 [69.3]
9. United Kingdom	118.8 [89.2]	23. Sweden	56.2 [53.4]
10. Canada	111.9 [107.4]	24. Korea	52.7 [42.4]
11. Austria	89.3 [90.5]	25. Mexico	50.7 [41.0]
12. Hungary	83.9 [86.1]	26. Denmark	48.4 [53.4]
13. Columbia	82.9 [n/a]	OECD Average (**Worst 10**)	145.5 [120.8]
14. Slovenia	81.5 [47.9]	OECD Average	80.0 [70.0]

Fig. 6.3 Debt-to-GDP ratios of 26 OECD countries as of 2019

are those from 2010, when the total number of OECD countries became 30 in 2010 when Estonia, Israel, Chile, and Slovenia joined.

According to this OECD data, Japan has the highest debt ratio of 234.8%, followed by Greece (200.8%), Italy (154.2%), and the United States (136.1%).[2] Japan was the only country exceeding 200% until 2019 when the Greece exceeded 200% for the first time. Apart from Japan and Greece, the only country that exceeds 200% as of 2021 is Sudan, which is not the OECD member countries. As we can also see from the data, all PIIGS countries, except Ireland, are on the list of the 10 worst countries in boldface. According to the Maastricht Treaty, the debt-to-GDP ratio must not exceed 60% if a nation wants to join the EU. Therefore, none of these countries meets this requirement. And all other EU countries including Germany, France, Italy and Spain would be rejected if they had to reapply for the EU membership.

The average debt-to-GDP ratio of the OECD countries was 80% in 2019. Since the average debt-to-GDP ratio for OECD countries was at 70.0% as of 2010, the average debt-to-GDP ratio increased by 10% in 9 years. The largest percentage increase by country was that of Greece, +70.4%.[3] On the other hand, looking at the average for

---

[2] Source: OECD (2019). Note that OECD defines general government debt as the sum of the following liability items (as applicable): currency and deposits; debt securities, loans; insurance, pensions and standardized guarantee schemes, and other accounts payable. Differences in debt-to-GDP ratios in Japan and the US from our simulation in Figs. 6.1 and 6.2 are due to the differences in underlying data as well as the definition of Government Debt.

[3] According to the same OECD data, the ten worst OECD member countries in debt-to-GDP ratios as of 2010 were as follows: 1. Japan (204.4%), 2. Greece (130.4%), 3. United States (125.3%), 4. Italy (124.3%), 5. Iceland (110.3%), 6. Belgium (108.7%), 7. Canada (107.4%), 8. Portugal (105.7%), 9. France (101.0%), and 10. Austria (90.5%).

the top ten worst OECD countries as of 2019 shows 24.7% increase from 120.8% in 2010 to 145.5% in 2019.

These debt-to-GDP ratios do not necessarily reflect the whole picture as economic conditions vary from country to country. However, even from this simple observation, we can discern that developed nations seem to be all heading towards debt crises. In other words, we can conclude that many OECD countries are in the same "debt hell" as in the US and Japan. This clearly indicates that the current system is on the verge of collapse, and it is a global phenomenon. The situation becomes clearer when we apply systems thinking on this problem.

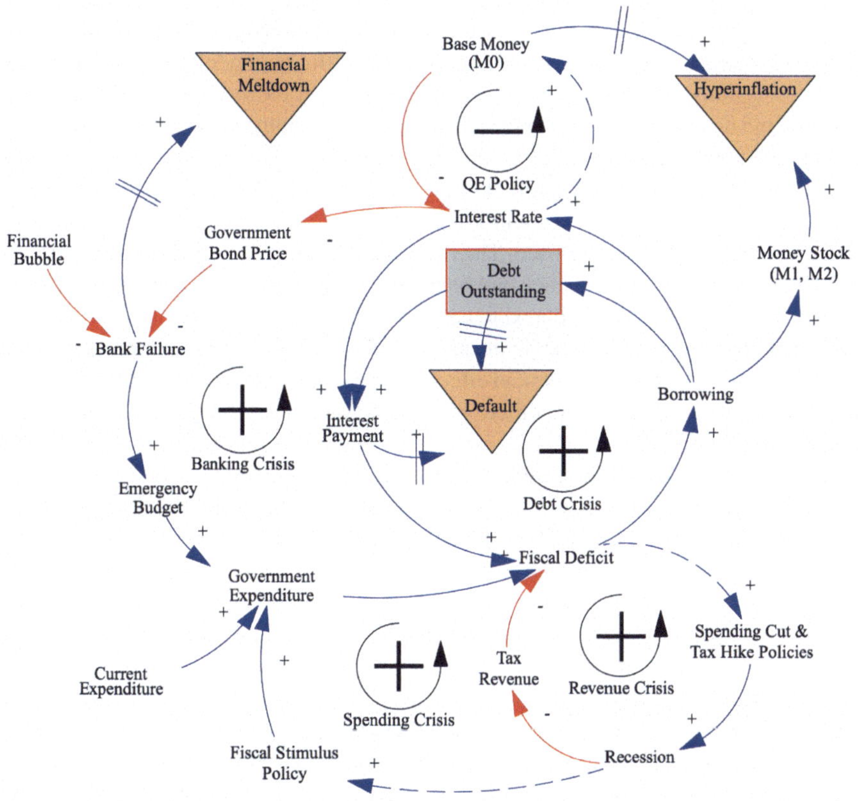

Fig. 6.4 Systems thinking of three catastrophic scenarios

6.4 Systems Thinking of "Debt End" Scenarios

The current debt money system is moving headlong toward systemic collapse. How well do we really understand the seriousness of this situation? What kind of catastrophe is our economy heading toward? As we analyzed in the Japanese case above, there are three possible devastating scenarios. Figure 6.4 depicts the process that leads to the three economic catastrophe by applying the systems thinking, also known as the causal loop diagram (CLD) analysis.

As the diagram shows, our economy is a complex and self-organizing (self-fulfilling) system comprising of various actors transacting with each other; from individuals, families, small and medium-sized enterprises (SMEs), to large transnational corporations (TNCs) and sovereign entities such as governments and international organizations. Systems thinking is a scientific methodology that elucidates complex system structure and analyzes the behavior of the system in order to come up with and design policies that will be effective. Especially, CLD is a powerful tool to map the feedback structure of complex systems.

To perform systems thinking, first of all, we start with identifying possible causal relations by connecting causes and effects with arrows, and continue the process until the feedback loops are closed. The resulting loops have two different properties: reinforcing (or positive) feedback and balancing (or negative) feedback. Blue arrows with positive sign (+) attached next to each arrowhead indicate that changes in cause and effect increase (or decrease) in the same direction. Red arrows with negative sign (–) denotes that changes in cause and effect are in the opposite direction. Double cross lines on the arrow indicates that there is a certain time delay for the cause to induce change in the effect.[4]

A positive feedback loop refers to a state in which the loop starts from a cause, and when it comes a full circle, it returns a change in the initial cause in the same direction. This loop, also called "self-reinforcing" feedback loop, acts like a growth engine that magnifies (amplifies) the behavior of the system. A negative feedback loop, on the other hand, refers to a state in which a loop starts from a cause and when it comes a full circle, it returns a change in the initial cause in the opposite direction. This loop plays the role of keeping the behavior of the system stable toward an equilibrium (stability).

A positive feedback loop appears when there are *even number* of negative causations so that its original cause changes in the same direction when its loop is closed. A negative feedback loop appears when there are *odd number* of negative causations so that its original cause changes in the opposite direction when its loop is closed. A positive (+) or negative (−) sign surrounded by a round arrow inside the loop is a *loop identifier* indicating whether the loop is a reinforcing or balancing feedback loop.

In this way, all systems consist of these positive and negative feedback loops. This is how we approach complex problems and analyze their underlying system

[4] See Sterman (2000), a textbook used in System Dynamics course at the MIT Sloan School of Management, for an introduction to systems thinking and causal loop analysis.

structures. When reinforcing loops dominate, the system grows exponentially. When balancing loops dominate, the system stagnates and eventually stabilizes toward an equilibrium. Let us follow the loops depicted in Fig. 6.4 and analyze each scenario; financial meltdown, hyperinflation, and government default.

S1. Financial Meltdown

First, as the government continues to borrow money, supply and demand for funds (liquidity) will eventually tighten. And interest rates will surely rise at some point. This is indicated by Borrowing → Interest Rate (+) in the diagram. As a result, government bond and stock prices will plummet, and financial assets of banks and securities companies will plummet, and eventually a string of bankruptcies will begin to emerge among financially weak institutions. Similarly, this chain of events is indicated by Government Bond Price → Bank Failure (–). The most recent example is the Silicon Valley Bank (SVB) that went bankrupt in March 2023, which was caused by bond price declines and accompanying fear, which in turn caused deposit withdrawals and liquidity shortages. A systemic crisis similar to the Lehman Shock reappears.

The psychology of trying to avoid further losses leads to divestment and further selling of financial assets. The counterclockwise loop of the "Banking Crisis" in Fig. 6.4 goes round and round. Collective fear among investors grow and panic erupts in the banking system. As the situation gets worse and worse, it will eventually be pulled into "Financial Meltdown". The positive sign in the "Banking Crisis" loop indicates that this causal loop has the characteristics of self-reinforcing or positive feedback. Just like an active volcano, the pressure builds until it cannot contain the energy inside and releases all the pressure.

The final phase of financial meltdown is displayed in Fig. 6.4 as follows:

Banking Crisis Loop Borrowing → Interest Rate (+) → Government Bond Price (–) → Bank Failure (–) → <u>Financial Meltdown</u>

S2. Hyperinflation

Next, to avoid such a financial meltdown, the government intervenes and bails out banks and other financial institutions, saying, "We cannot simply let them go bust because they are *too big to fail*." The most recent example is the Credit Suisse bankruptcy in March 2023 and its 'timely' bailout. As a result, government spending increases, fiscal deficit expands, and public debts accumulate further, leading to more government borrowing. As a result, interest rates will rise and the possibility of the financial meltdown analyzed above will emerge.

To avoid this situation, governments will implement emergency lending along with QE by central banks as a last resort to quell such market turbulence and suppress sudden rise in interest rates. This will in turn create "QE Policy" loop shown at the top of the figure. Banks and securities firms will use the money they have obtained to earn gains and flood the financial markets with liquidity, including stocks and real estate, which in turn draws out more speculative money from domestic and foreign investors, triggering another financial bubble.

Moreover, as we have demonstrated in Chap. 3, an increase in government spending (debt) increases money stock (Debt $\simeq$ Money Stock). The new supply of purchasing power thus causes the typical type of demand-pull inflation where more demand chases fewer supply. A global inflation the world has been seeing since the COVID-19 pandemic attests to the likeliness of this trend to occur more frequently. Finally, these money-printing spree leads to a loss of confidence in certain currencies and induce sell-offs in the FX market, while pushing up prices of commodities such as gold. The combination of these factors brings about the final phase of "Hyperinflation". Under the Weimar-type of hyperinflation, income inequality will widen and social riots will eventually erupt. Amid such chaos, another war may be instigated to reset the whole situation (debt jubilee).

Again, the "Banking Crisis" loop goes round and round. In due course, this loop is pulled into "QE Policy" loop and eventually heads for the hyperinflation. QE may work to buy sometime, but makes the eventual collapse all the more severe. The final phase of Banking Crisis and QE loops is displayed as follows:

Banking Crisis and QE Policy Loops Bank Failure → Emergency Budget & Fiscal Stimulus Package (+) → Government Expenditure (+) → Fiscal Deficit (+) → Borrowing (+) → Interest Rate (+) → Base Money (+) & Money Stock (+) → Hyperinflation

A Prelude to Government Default

Tax Revenue and Spending Crises Loops

Figure 6.4 also shows that fiscal austerity measures (spending cuts and tax hikes) to reduce the deficit may conversely reduce tax revenues, exacerbating the situation. In other words, if spending cuts are implemented to prevent the government debt from increasing, economies that are already stagnant will be kicked into a recession. As a result, tax revenues will decrease, leading to an increase in fiscal deficit and debt.[5] Policies to reduce the increase in government debt will in turn increase the debt. Policies to improve fiscal soundness in turn worsen fiscal revenues and make public financing unsound. Policies intended to stabilize the inflation actually brings about inflation. These are indeed counter-intuitive behaviors often observed in complex

[5] This is not just our intuition, but is actually confirmed by our simulation analysis. Readers who are interested in more details are referred to Yamaguchi (2013).

systems, and can be hidden "traps" for macro stabilization policies under the debt money system.

Using the causal loop diagram in Fig. 6.4, we can indentify the existence of two positive feedback loops in which fiscal deficit-reducing policies actually increase the fiscal deficit. One is the "Revenue Crisis" loop and the other is the "Spending Crisis" loop shown at the bottom of the diagram. This means that the effects of spending cuts (fiscal austerity) will be cancelled out as follows:

Revenue Crisis Loop Fiscal Deficit → Spending Cut & Tax Hike (+) → Recession (+) → Tax Revenue (–) → Fiscal Deficit (–)

Spending Crisis Loop Fiscal Deficit → Spending Cut & Tax Hike (+) → Recession (+) → Fiscal Stimulus Package (+) → Government Expenditure (+) → Fiscal Deficit (+)

S3. Government Default

The worsening fiscal deficit analyzed above serve as a prelude to the third scenario. As the government increases borrowing to cover its deficit, the debt grows exponentially. Furthermore, as interest rates rise and tax revenues become insufficient to cover the principal and the interests, the government is finally forced to default on its debt. Similarly, the self-reinforcing feedback loop of the "Debt Crisis" in Fig. 6.4 goes round and round, which is the typical exponential growth that we've seen in Japan (Fig. 6.1) and the US (Fig. 6.2). This will eventually lead to the catastrophe of "Default" shown at the center.[6]

The final phase of government default will emerge in two ways as follows:

Debt Crisis Loop Fiscal Deficit → Borrowing (+) → Debt (+) → Default
Borrowing (+) → Interest Rate (+) → Interest Payment (+) → Default

6.5 Fiscal and Monetary Policy Lock-In

Due to the counter-intuitive effects analyzed above, policy makers become more and more limited with what they can do as they go deeper and deeper into specific policy actions. This kind of situation in which certain policies implemented in the past limit the future policy possibility set is also known as *policy lock-in* (see Palley 2017a, for example). As analyzed so far, the Japanese economy is precisely in a state of *fiscal policy lock-in* under the on-going debt crisis. To be worse, the economy has also fallen into a state of *monetary policy lock-in*.

[6] Readers may also take a look at the section of "Wonder and Horror of Compound Interest" in Chap. 10, where we discuss the mechanism behind the exponential growth.

Suppose, for example, that some exogenous factor causes energy prices to rise or the yen depreciates against the US dollar. Since the economy is highly dependent on energy imports, rise in energy prices and currency depreciation cause domestic inflation. The BoJ will need to raise interest rates in order to curb such runaway inflation. However, if the BoJ tries to raise interest rates, the price of its treasury securities (JGB) holdings will in turn decline, damaging the market value of assets it holds on its balance sheet. The deterioration of the BoJ's financial condition will inevitably erode confidence in the currency it issues, which will eventually spill over to the exchange rate. Therefore, the BoJ itself cannot easily tolerate a rise in interest rates at this point.

At the same time, raising interest rates would mean a change in the BoJ's policy stance and an admission of the failure of its QE, which we have discussed in Chap. 5. A fall in the price of government bonds risks further short-selling, which would literally be a "debt end". So far, central banks have been able to bail out banks when the Lehman Brothers collapsed in 2008. But if central banks themselves collapse in the next crisis, who will be the "lender of last resort" to save our economy?

One can also picture a scenario in which interest hikes further worsen the already stagnant economy. Should another recession occur, that will cause stock markets reaction and invite short-selling, which then affects the balance sheet of the BoJ that have been purchasing ETF. In other words, the BoJ has run out of policy options and thus can do nothing but maintain the current low interest rates. The policy initiated to stimulate the economy has in turn narrowed down its exit strategy, making cost-push inflation and currency depreciation getting out of control and worsening the economy. This state of monetary policy lock-in is analogous to a terminally ill patient who has been given a very powerful drug (QE) with deadly side effects, and now unable to break free from its addiction.

As we have analyzed in this chapter, this situation is not limited to Japan or the US. Sooner or later, other economies will have to fall into this trap. That is, as long as our economy operates under the current debt money system, it will irrevocably drive us into one of three catastrophic scenarios. Therefore, we cannot afford to spend our time predicting which of these scenarios will come first and when. Any prescription by economists that does not address this *system design failure* cannot be a fundamental solution for solving the imminent crisis. This is the conclusion we have reached in this chapter.

Accordingly, what we must do is to show that there is a prescription to prevent these scenarios. To do so, we need to first free ourselves from the old paradigm of mainstream economics now. We will begin to do that from the next chapter.

Chapter 7
Paradigm Shift in Macroeconomics

Immediately following the publication of the *General Theory* (Keynes, 1936), Hicks (1937) devised a simple model based on his interpretation of the *General Theory*. This model, now well known as the Keynesian short-run IS-LM analysis, has been widely used in macroeconomic textbooks since the 1950s, and played a central role in the postwar history of economic thoughts. Even today, when undergraduate students take a macroeconomics course, what they'll learn first is the Keynesian theory of income determination using IS-LM curves. Therefore, the collapse of mainstream economics discussed in Chap. 5 must also be the failure of the IS-LM model itself. Nevertheless, skeptical readers may think that our discussions provide only one example based on the case of Japan's Lost 30 Years. Therefore, while neoclassical economics must be discarded, the other branch of mainstream economics cannot be said to have collapsed in general, and Keynesian fiscal and monetary policies are still effective in other economies, they may argue. In this chapter we will advance against such skepticism and further demonstrate that Keynesian economics has generally collapsed by examining the IS-LM theory.

7.1 IS-LM Analysis of The Great Depression

The IS-LM theory, which stands for Investment, Saving, demand for Liquidity and supply of Money, is an analytical method to find a combination of interest rate and the level of national income that simultaneously equilibrates the market for goods and services and the money market. The original model was developed by Hicks (1937) based on his interpretation of the Keynes' *General Theory*, and later refined by the Harvard Professor Alvin H. Hansen as the IS-LM diagram (Hansen, 1949). As such, the IS-LM theory is also known as the Hicks-Hansen Synthesis. Hansen, who was initially skeptical of the Keynes' proposal on the need for government intervention in counteracting with recession, soon embraced the idea and began

K. Yamaguchi and Y. Yamaguchi, *Public Money*,
https://doi.org/10.1007/978-981-97-6564-5_7

inspiring his students such as Paul Samuelson, who later went on to further popularize it as "Neoclassical-Keynesian synthesis".

Due to its simplicity and (alleged) versatility of explaining real-world phenomena such as business cycles, the IS-LM analysis became the standard pedagogical device in economics curricula by the 1960s, and is still widely used to analyze the effects of monetary and fiscal policies in undergraduate textbooks.[1]

Interest rate and national income are taken on the vertical and horizontal axes, and the intersection of the *IS* curve and *LM* curve is obtained in order to analyze the macroeconomic effects of fiscal and monetary policies. The rigorous analysis of IS-LM model is presented in Chap. 8 for readers who need further mathematical details. In this chapter let us refer to the simplified graphical model introduced in one of the most popular textbooks "Macroeconomics" ((Mankiw, 2016), ninth edition) written by Professor Nicholas Gregory Mankiw at Harvard University. This undergraduate-level textbook is widely used in many universities around the world. In fact, it is also used in the Turkish university where Kaoru had been teaching until June, 2022.

The *IS* curve is based on the formula that balances income and aggregate demand (= consumption + investment + government expenditure) in the goods and services market. As shown in Fig. 7.1, *IS* curve is drawn as a downward-sloping curve in the GDP-interest rate plain.[2] On the other hand, *LM* curve, which is drawn as an upward-sloping curve in the same diagram, is based on the formula that balances the supply and demand for money stock (called "liquidity preference") in the money market. The point at which the two curves intersect is the equilibrium point of the economy, where GDP and interest rate are determined. Equilibria are shown as points A and B in Fig. 7.1.

Can the IS-LM model be used to investigate the causes of the Great Depression of 1930s and recessions in general? If the causes cannot be determined, no countermeasures can be taken. Keynes analyzed in his *General Theory* that the cause of the Depression was a lack of effective demand such as consumption and investment.

---

[1] While much has been discussed about the origin and conformity of the IS-LM model to the Keynes's conceptualizations discussed in his *General Theory* and its lasting influence on the subsequent course of the evolution of macroeconomics teachings and thinking (see Young and Zilberfarb 2001; Backhouse and Laidler 2004b; Brady 2017, for example), the pedagogical tool, which will turn 100 years old in about a decade, still features in popular textbooks including Mankiw (2016). Although Hicks himself became gradually dissatisfied with it (Hicks, 1980), and the model has been the target of criticisms (both theoretically and methodologically) and attempted revisions have been made over the years especially in the "Post-Keynesian" literatures (see Keen 2014; Kriesler and Nevile 2016; Palley 2017b; Rochon and Rossi 2017, for example), few have presented an alternative simulation model that fully integrate their claims and overcome the limitations. In this sense, the IS-LM model still underlies the dominant 'mainstream' thinking of the economics profession and continues to influence generations of future economists as if there is a rationale behind monetary and fiscal polices implemented by governments and central banks under the present debt money system.

[2] In the IS-LM model, which usually assumes a closed economy without trade, Income and GDP as the total value-added (output) are treated as the same, *i.e.*, national income accounting identity. Strictly speaking, the two macroeconomic concepts must be distinguished in simulation models that are stock-flow consistent. See Sect. 8.10 for further details.

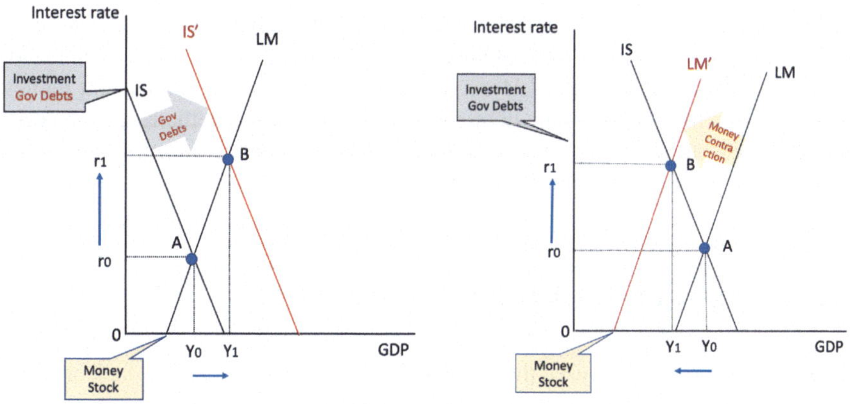

Fig. 7.1 IS-LM analysis of the great depression: Deficiency of effective demand (left) and monetary contraction (right)

Such decline in demand is equivalent to the *IS* curve moving to the left. Now, suppose that the economy was at point B before the depression occurred on the left-hand diagram. Then, if the *IS* curve shifts to the left, the equilibrium point moves from B to A, and GDP decreases from Y_1 to Y_0. If a recession or the Great Depression is a decline in GDP, which results in massive unemployment, this leftward shift of the *IS* curve can be analyzed as the cause of the Depression.

On the other hand, Irving Fisher, who was handed the *Chicago Plan for Banking Reform* in 1933, analyzed that the contraction of debt money was the root cause of the Depression in his *100% Money* (Fisher, 1935). If we hold this IS-LM model as tentatively acceptable and apply his thinking, such decrease in money stock would be described by the *LM* curve moving to the left. In other words, if the *LM* curve shifts to the left on the right-hand diagram of Fig. 7.1, the equilibrium point moves from A to B and the GDP will decrease from Y_0 to Y_1. Accordingly, Fisher analyzed that the Depression was caused by this contraction of money stock. Later, Milton Friedman, who won the Nobel Memorial Prize in Economics in 1979, followed Fisher's analysis and verified that the contraction of debt money was the primary cause of the Great Depression.

Chapter 12 of Professor Mankiw's textbook, however, rejects the hypothesis that the debt money contraction (leftward shift of the *LM* curve) caused the Great Depression. Professor Mankiw (the title will be omitted hereafter) pointed out two reasons why such is the case. First, for the *LM* curve to shift to the left, the real money stock would have to decline, but it rose only slightly from 1929 to 1931. Furthermore, if the *LM* curve shifted to the left, the interest rate would have to rise from r_0 to r_1. However, during the Depression, nominal interest rate began to decline from 5.9% in 1929 to below 1% in 1935 and hovered near zero thereafter (see Table 8.5 for data). Mankiw then concluded that "[T]hese two reasons appear sufficient to reject the view that the Depression was instigated by a contractionary shift in the *LM* curve" (Mankiw, 2016, p.354).

Accordingly, the causes of the Great Depression analyzed by Keynesian economics must be the leftward shift of the *IS* curve due to the lack of effective demand. Since the leftward shift of the *LM* curve caused by the contraction of debt money cannot explain the decline in the nominal interest rate observed, the Keynesian economics based on the IS-LM theory concludes that the contraction of money stock cannot be the real cause of the Depression.

7.2 Keynesian Policies Using IS-LM Model

Keynesian economics analyzed the cause of the Great Depression as the lack of effective demand. Then, what kind of prescription did it propose to get out of recessions? The solution was to shift the *IS* curve to the right and restore its original (equilibrium) state. However, it is nearly impossible to increase private consumption and investment during recessions, not to mention in a sever downturn as that of the Depression in the 1930s. This is where the Keynesian fiscal policy comes in. From the left-hand diagram of Fig. 7.1, if the government increases its spending through fiscal stimulus (financed by issuing treasury bonds), the *IS* curve will shift to the right this time, and the original equilibrium point B will be achieved. In other words, GDP (or Income) increases from Y_0 to Y_1. This is a typical example of the Keynesian counter-cyclical policy through fiscal expenditure.

However, as is clear from the left-hand diagram, this fiscal policy will increase GDP, but at the same time, the interest rate will also rise from r_0 to r_1. This is because the government and the private sector would be competing for limited amount of funds available under a given supply of money stock. This is called *crowding out* effect as we have discussed in Sect. 5.3.

The IS-LM theory and mainstream economics in general warn us that such use of fiscal stimulus should be limited in order to avoid government defaults, because rising interest rates will cause government bond prices to plummet, and could diminish private investment as the result of interest rate rise. In other words, the government's finances must be sound and in good health to achieve the *primary balance*. The Japanese government, guided or 'misled' by such a warning, has implemented fiscal stimulus in a bid to escape from the Lost 30 Years, while emphasizing the principal importance of primary balance target. However, as we have also discussed in Chap. 5, the *crowding out effect* that the mainstream economics has warned of did not occur in Japan. That is, the IS-LM analysis and the crowding out theory on which it is based were wrong.

Keynesian monetary policy seeks to increase GDP while avoiding this crowding out effect. The IS-LM model, which assumes exogenous money, cannot explain the endogenous contraction of money stock. However, it does not reject the controllability of money stock by the monetary authority. If we follow this logic and assume that either the government or central bank could increase money stock as shown on the right-hand diagram of Fig. 7.1, the *LM* curve would shift to the right. The interest rate goes down and firms would expand investment. As a result, GDP increase from

Y_1 to Y_0. Since the interest rate would also fall from r_1 to r_0, *crowding out* can thus be avoided at the same time.

However, this Keynesian monetary policy was also not effective in Japan. Then came the "unconventional" monetary policy of Quantitative Easing (QE). Interest rates fell due to this QE policy, but consumption and investment did not increase, and GDP remained stagnant. The Japanese economy was eventually got caught in a so-called *liquidity trap* in which interest rate became almost zero. As a result, the traditional monetary policy based on interest rate manipulation became no longer workable. In other words, the IS-LM model failed to rescue the Japan's lost 30 years and has collapsed both theoretically and empirically.

7.3 IS-LM Model of Endogenous Debt Money

Paradigm Shift by Endogenous Money IS-LM Model

The IS-LM model, developed as the Hicks-Hansen Synthesis of the Keynes's *General Theory* based on the general equilibrium framework, became the postwar paradigm of economics as it began to be used in textbooks in the late 1940s. Since then, it has reigned as the standard income determination theory in macroeconomics for over 80 years. However, this paradigm is now collapsing because it cannot explain the real economic phenomenon such as the declines of interest rate against crowding out situation and debt money contraction.

The reason of these failures of IS-LM model is that it assumes that the money stock is exogenously given and can be controlled only by the central bank. In Chap. 3 we have shown that money stock is endogenously created and destroyed along with economic activities, and discussed in Chap. 5 that it must be expressed as a function of transactions in the framework of the quantity theory of money; that is, $M = M$ (Transactions). In the IS-LM model, the volume of transactions is narrowly defined as the volume of GDP-related transactions, so the money stock should be a function of GDP: that is, $M = M(\text{GDP})$.

GDP (as income) is in turn determined by effective demand such as consumption, investment, and government spending. In order for investment and government spending to occur, however, borrowings by private sector and government must precede them. That is, households and producers must first borrow money to make investments, and government must borrow money by issuing treasury bonds before it can spend them. Therefore, money stock must increase endogenously under the debt money system. That is, money stock in the *LM* curve must be a function of investment and government debt such that

$$M = M(\text{Investment, Government Debt}) \tag{7.1}$$

If effective demand is determined by investment and government spending, and the *IS* curve is drawn, money stock also changes simultaneously. And the *LM* curve must be drawn in tandem with it as Fig. 7.2 illustrates. This is the paradigm shift we have incorporated into the IS-LM model based on the insight of endogenous debt money. To distinguish it from the conventional (traditional) IS-LM model, it is alternatively called the *Endogenous Money IS-LM* model.

7.4 Endogenous Money IS-LM Analysis of the Japan's Lost 30 Years

Endogenous Money IS-LM Model can Explain Japan's Case

Can we explain the case of Japan's lost 30 years with this paradigm shift, then? In Fig. 7.2, let point A be the state of recession right after the collapse of the bubble in the early 1990s. The Japanese government introduced fiscal policy to shift the *IS* curve to the right. As a result, the model would predict that point A now moves to point B, and GDP increases from Y_0 to Y_1. If we focus on the period from 1995 to 2012 (as we have done in Chap. 5), investment decreased due to the reduction in private debts by 125 trillion yen. As a result, GDP declined by 61 trillion yen (point B → A). However, the deficit spendings and cumulative increase in government debt of 600 trillion yen somehow made up for this loss by increasing GDP by 66 trillion yen (point A → B).

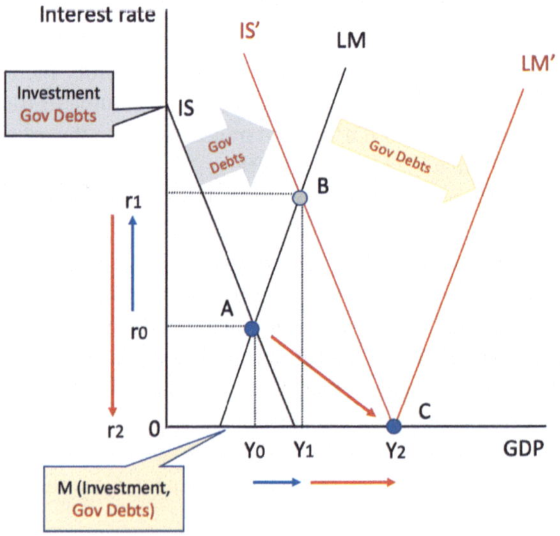

Fig. 7.2 Endogenous money IS-LM analysis of Japan's lost 30 years

In conjunction with the shift of the *IS* curve induced by this aggressive fiscal policy, the 600 trillion yen increase in government debts has in turn increased money stock and simultaneously shifted the *LM* curve to the right. And the Japanese economy found itself caught in a liquidity trap and moved to point C, where the interest rate became zero. In other words, the expected effect of the traditional fiscal policy (point A $\rightarrow$ B) did not occur, and the economy moved from the original point A to point C instead. GDP recovered slightly from the initial decline in investment ($Y_1 \rightarrow Y_0$) and rose slightly to Y_2. Consequently, the outcome of Japan's lost 30 years is the stagnant GDP level indicated at Y_2.

Now, if the *IS* and *LM* curves were linked in this way under the *endogenous debt money*, there would be no crowding out as claimed by mainstream economics, nor would there be a crash in government bond prices due to rise in the interest rate. And the government would not be bound by the mainstream's alarming that fiscal policy should be constrained by the balanced budget. Nor did it have to waste its time on pointless policy debates in the National Diet.

A Scenario of Escaping from Japan's Lost 30 Years

Is it possible, based on this paradigm shift IS-LM model, to draw a scenario for escaping from the lost 30 years? Yes, it is possible. However, we must first transition to the public money system where the total money stock is controlled (as explained in Chap. 12), and cut off this interlocking shifts in IS-LM curves. This will keep the *LM* curve and fix it at the location of *LM'* in Fig. 7.2.

Next, the public money spending policy must be implemented to promote private investment (such as capital and housing investment) rather than expanding fiscal expenditures through government debts. The IS-LM model presumes any increase in investment or government debts will shift the *IS* curve to the right. However, as we have analyzed in Chap. 5, government debts may end up with a foolish policy of drinking beer or digging holes and piling up further debts. Accordingly, an increase in government debts contributes only about one-fifth of an increase in GDP compared with an increase in private investment.

On the other hand, if private investment is increased, firms will increase employment and capital will accumulate, thus increasing the economy's productive capacity (potential GDP growth) from the next year. Even if the *IS* curve is shifted to the right by the same amount, the effect of private investment in stimulating GDP will be about five times larger than that of government debts.

This is the "Public Money Initiative" we propose in Chap. 14 to revitalize the Japanese economy and escape from the lost 30 years on the basis of this paradigm shift IS-LM model. Now we invite readers to try their own thought experiments by further shifting the *IS* curve, for instance, from IS' to IS" in Fig. 7.2. Then we can see how quickly Japan can escape from decades-long stagnation. Public money policies to make such shift, such as investment promotion subsidies, are proposed in Chap. 14 based on causal loop diagrams. The limitation of the conventional IS-LM model is that it cannot capture this kind of GDP growth dynamically. Such limitation becomes clear in the next Chap. 8 where we develop a simulation model of the endogenous money IS-LM based on Accounting System Dynamics (ASD) method.

To summarize our discussion so far, the paradigm shift of the endogenous money IS-LM model has enabled us to identify the way to save Japan by

- transforming the debt money system to the public money system, and
- implementing public money policies to encourage private demand (investment and consumption), not the government expenditure through debts.

7.5 Endogenous Money IS-LM Analysis of the Great Depression

Using this endogenous money IS-LM model, we can now explain the decline in GDP without causing an increase in interest rates, even if the leftward shift in *LM* curve occurs due to a contraction in money stock. In other words, the Great Depression caused by the contraction of debt money, which Mankiw rejected as implausible, can be readily explained in accordance with historical facts.

Let's consider point A in Fig. 7.3 as the point when the bubble bursts and money stock contracts. As a result of the decrease in money, the *LM* curve shifts to the left (LM $\rightarrow$ LM'), moving the equilibrium point from A to B, and GDP also decreases from Y_0 to Y_1. This is the outbreak of the Great Depression or the occurrence of a recession in general under the debt money system. However, the interest rate also rises from r_0 to r_1, so the decline in nominal interest rates observed during the Depression cannot be explained, as Mankiw pointed out. Because of this, he rejected the hypothesis of debt money contraction.

On the contrary, we have analyzed that a paradigm shift occurs here, and that the *IS* curve simultaneously shifts to the left in conjunction with the leftward shift in the *LM* curve. This is because the collapse of the bubble reduces effective demand such as investment. Thus, the *IS* curve also shifts left in tandem, the equilibrium point shifts from point B to point C, and GDP declines further from Y_1 to Y_2. On the other hand, while a contraction in money may cause a shortage of funds, decline in investment will further reduce the demand for funds, resulting in excess supply in the money market. And the interest rate will simultaneously fall from r_1 to r_2. These series of movements (of equilibrium points) brought about by the simultaneous shifts in IS-LM curves reproduce the behaviors of the Great Depression in a manner consistent with data.

Keynes attributed the Great Depression to the leftward shift of the *IS* curve. Fisher, on the other hand, correctly attributed the decline in investment, consumption, and accompanying contraction of money as the causes of the Depression. However, Fisher's original analysis and monetary reform program based on the *100% Money* theory was subsequently made a taboo subject, and even the standard textbooks by

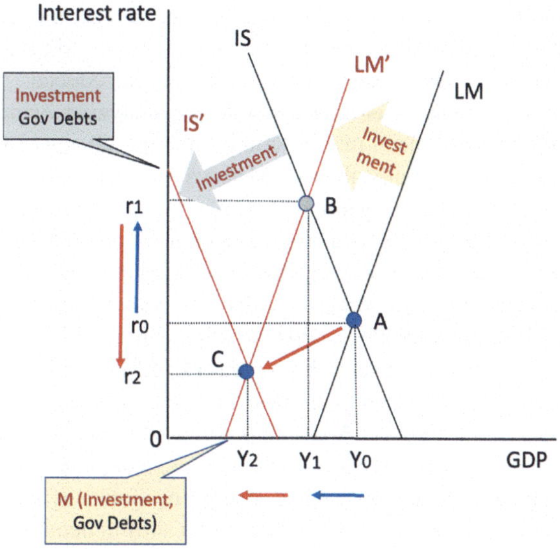

Fig. 7.3 Endogenous money IS-LM analysis of the great depression

Mankiw and others have dismissed the debt money contraction as a false hypothesis that could not be validated by the IS-LM theory.[3]

We have struggled to find out if we could integrate the Keynes's hypothesis of deficient effective demand and the Fisher's debt money contraction hypothesis, both of which were proposed in 1935. And we have succeeded in unifying the two theories with the ASD macroeconomic modeling approach (Yamaguchi, 2013) as Fig. 1.3 illustrates. In this chapter, we were also able to unify these two theories within the framework of the conventional IS-LM model.

Under the debt money system, recessions and depressions occur as a result of the shift from point A to point C, which is caused by the inextricable link between bank loans and deposit creation. We hope that readers have come to share the understanding that the root cause of recessions is the contraction of debt money, and why our government is destined to accumulate more and more debts just to sustain the economy. Therefore, unless we make a transition to the public money system and fix this system design failure, we will never escape the imminent systemic crisis as the next "Great Depression".

In this chapter we have discussed how the endogenous money IS-LM model can explain the Great Depression and Japan's Lost 30 Years in a manner consistent with data. This paradigm shift allows the *IS* and *LM* curves to move in tandem to any point on the two-dimensional plane of GDP-Interest Rate. However, it is

[3] For Fisher, the decline in demand was only one of the causes that precipitated the Great Depression, if not the main culprit (see Sect. 8.5 further). Mankiw (2016) cites Friedman as the proponent of this "money hypothesis," yet he does not emphasize Fisher as its original proponent. In this way, Fisher's novel analysis advanced in *100% Money* has been completely removed from the standard macroeconomics textbooks and teachings.

important to note that the conventional IS-LM model (or any variation of it) is a static model that compares two different equilibrium points before and after the changes in macroeconomic variables are introduced.

Such analysis is only possible for analyzing *ex post* changes in the economy, and does not mean that we can predict the effects of fiscal and monetary policy in advance. Originally, the IS-LM curve has been used to illustrate Keynes' principle of effective demand (income determination formula) and likely effects of these policies *a priori*. However, with the endogenous money IS-LM analysis, the two curves are now linked, making it impossible to predict in which direction the equilibrium point will move and in what way. This is another limitation of the conventional IS-LM analysis revealed due to this paradigm shift.

With the collapse of the standard IS-LM model, the old paradigm that had dominated macroeconomics textbooks has also collapsed and forced to shift to the endogenous money theory. And this *theoretical* paradigm shift to the endogenous money IS-LM theory must also be a *methodological* paradigm shift from comparative statics to dynamic analysis based on accounting system dynamics (ASD) method. In the next chapter, let us examine this paradigm shift in detail using the ASD macroeconomic model of the endogenous money IS-LM.

Chapter 8
Mathematical Analysis of the Paradigm Shift

The IS-LM analysis, first devised by Hicks (1937) based on his interpretation of the *General Theory* (Keynes, 1936), is arguably the most popular model taught in undergraduate macroeconomics courses as a comparative statics method. In order to analyze the causes of the Great Depression, Mankiw (2016) presented (1) spending hypothesis–shocks to *IS* curve–as proposed by Keynes and (2) money hypothesis–shocks to *LM* curve–as proposed by Friedman and Schwartz (1963), and then rejects the latter by applying them in the IS-LM model. In this chapter we will first introduce a system dynamics model of the Keynesian short-run IS-LM and examine if one of the two seemingly contrasting hypotheses should be dismissed in favor of the other. We will then revise the model into the *Endogenous Money IS-LM* discussed in Chap. 7 based on Accounting System Dynamics (ASD) modeling method. This chapter discusses advanced topics for readers who require more rigorous analysis of the *paradigm shift* model discussed in the previous chapter.[1] Accordingly, general readers may skip this chapter, except Sects. 8.5 (endogenous money spending hypothesis) and 8.14 (chapter summary), and continue to the next Chap. 9 on monetary theories.

8.1 Keynesian Short-Run IS-LM Model

Immediately following the publication of Keynes's *General Theory*, Hicks (1937) expanded the Keynesian model to include the money market. This model is now well known as the Keynesian short-run IS-LM analysis, and has been widely used as a standard Keynesian model in many macroeconomic textbooks. IS-LM stands for Investment, Saving, demand for Liquidity and supply of Money.

---

[1] This chapter is mostly an adaptation from our recent working papers (Yamaguchi and Yamaguchi, 2022a, b, 2023, 2024) to the extent suitable for the purpose of this book. Readers are encouraged to refer to the original papers for further details.

K. Yamaguchi and Y. Yamaguchi, *Public Money*,
https://doi.org/10.1007/978-981-97-6564-5_8

8.1.1 Model Equations

Let us begin by overviewing the IS-LM model. This short-run IS-LM model consists of the following 9 unknowns or equations;
$Y, AD, C, I, G, Y_d, T, i, L^d$ (L^d stands for liquidity demand)

with 13 exogenously determined parameters

$$C_0, c, T_0, t, T_r, I_0, \bar{G}, M^s, P, V, \alpha, a, b.$$

The Keynesian short-run model are thus described as the following 9 equations:

$$Y = AD \quad \text{(Aggregate Demand Equilibrium)} \tag{8.1}$$
$$AD = C + I + G \quad \text{(Aggregate Demand)} \tag{8.2}$$
$$C = C_0 + cY_d \quad \text{(Consumption Decisions)} \tag{8.3}$$
$$Y_d = Y - T \quad \text{(Disposable Income)} \tag{8.4}$$
$$T = T_0 + tY - T_r \quad \text{(Tax Revenues)} \tag{8.5}$$
$$I = \frac{I_0}{i} - \alpha i \quad \text{(Investment Decisions)} \tag{8.6}$$
$$G = \bar{G} \quad \text{(Government Expenditures)} \tag{8.7}$$
$$\frac{M^s}{P} V = L^d \quad \text{(Equilibrium of Money)} \tag{8.8}$$
$$L^d = aY - bi \quad \text{(Demand for Money)} \tag{8.9}$$

According to the IS-LM theory, income Y (as production)[2] is determined by the aggregate demand as defined in Eq. (8.1). This is the standard formulation of Keynesian income determination, also known as the principle of effective demand. Equation (8.2) defines aggregate demand and Eq. (8.3) determines consumption in which c is a marginal propensity to consume. Equation (8.4) defines disposable income. Note that capital accumulation ($\frac{dK}{dt}$) is not considered and excluded from this short-run IS-LM model. Accordingly, the capital depreciation (δK) is not included in Eq. (8.4).

Government revenues defined in Eq. (8.5) are assumed to be consisting of three parts; that is, lump-sum taxes such as property tax (T_0), income taxes (tY) that are proportionately determined by the income (Y) times income tax rate (t), and government transfers such as subsidies (T_r). Investment is assumed to be determined by an interest rate i in Eq. (8.6) in which α is an interest sensitivity of investment.

[2] Since the IS-LM model disregards the dynamics around production, which is the major source of income, into the background, it is assumed that supply is always met in response to changes in demand. Hence, real income has to be interpreted as real production (GDP) or vice versa under the IS-LM framework. This over simplification of macroeconomic dynamics made in the standard IS-LM model will be addressed in Sect. 8.10.1 where we define Income, Aggregate Demand and GDP more precisely in a system dynamics simulation model.

Government expenditures are exogenously determined by a constant amount $\bar{G}$ in Eq. (8.7). Equations (8.1)–(8.7) complete the *IS* side of the short-run IS-LM model.

Next, Eq. (8.8) is an equilibrium condition in the money market such that real money stock used in, say, a year, is equal to the demand for money L^d in which M^s denotes money stock, V is a velocity of money having a unit 1/year, and P is a general price level. It should be noted here that P is an exogenously given parameter at this point.

Finally, the demand for money defined in Eq. (8.9) consists of two parts: transactional demand for money (aY) where a is a fraction of income, and speculative demand for money (bi) where b is an interest sensitivity of demand for money. Behind this formulation of the demand for money is the standard textbook interpretation of the Keynes's theory of liquidity preference. Equations (8.8) and (8.9) complete the *LM* side of the short-run IS-LM model.

Both *IS* and *LM* sides of equations constitute the standard Keynesian macroeconomic model, which we call *Keynesian short-run IS-LM* here.[3] Note that all variables in this IS-LM model are expressed in terms of *real* units (e.g. DollarReal) except for money stock M^s, which has a *nominal* unit (Dollar).

8.1.2 Simple IS-LM Equilibrium as Comparative Statics

To perform manual analysis of the short-run IS-LM model described above, the investment decisions in Eq. (8.6) is simplified in many textbooks (including the most recent MMT texts such as Mitchell et al. 2019, pp.467–468) as follows:

$$I = I_0 - \alpha i \qquad \text{(Simple Investment Decisions)} \qquad (8.10)$$

Then, from the equilibrium condition in goods market, a relation between income and interest rate, which is called *IS* curve, is derived as follows:

$$Y = \frac{C_0 + I_0 + G + c(T_r - T_0)}{1 - c(1-t)} - \frac{\alpha}{1 - c(1-t)} i \qquad (8.11)$$

[3] As briefly mentioned in Footnote 1, there has been a long debate as to whether the IS-LM formulation of the Keynes' conceptualization should be labeled as "Keynesian". Such critical stance against the IS-LM framework is most summed up by the Robinson's famous insult "bastard Keynesianism" (Robinson, 1973) as being the neoclassical synthesis interpretation of the Keynes's *General Theory*. Many commentators have observed that the important elements of the *General Theory* had been already lost with the IS-LM. Here, it is only intended to emphasize that the IS-LM model (as the "Hicks-Hansen Synthesis") did embody the central ideas as well as theoretical formalizations expounded in the *General Theory* (income determination, consumption propensity, liquidity preference, etc.), and policy implications that are widely believed to be characteristically "Keynesian" and not others (as formally discussed below). See Backhouse and Laidler (2004a) for a general discussion of the elements of the *General Theory* that were (not) incorporated into the IS-LM framework.

On the other hand, from the equilibrium condition in the money market, a relation between income and interest rate, called *LM* curve, is derived as follows:

$$Y = \frac{1}{a}\frac{M^s}{P}V + \frac{b}{a}i \tag{8.12}$$

Equilibrium income and interest rate (Y^*, i^*) are now completely determined by the *IS* and *LM* curves. For instance, the aggregate demand equilibrium of income or GDP is obtained as

$$Y^* = \frac{C_0 + I_0 + G + c(T_r - T_0)}{1 - c(1-t) + \alpha(a/b)} + \frac{\alpha/b}{1 - c(1-t) + \alpha(a/b)}\frac{M^s}{P}V \tag{8.13}$$

This is a standard Keynesian process of determining an aggregate demand equilibrium of income in the short run where price is assumed to be fixed. Figure 8.1 illustrates how *IS* and *LM* curves determine the equilibrium income and interest rate (Y^*, i^*). The interest rate and income are taken on the vertical and horizontal axes, respectively, and the equilibrium point is determined at the intersection of the *IS* and *LM* curves.

The effect of Keynesian fiscal and monetary policies are then analyzed on the basis on this theoretical framework. When C_0, I_0, G increase or decrease, the *IS* curve shifts to the right or left, while *LM* curve shifts towards the right or left when money stock M^s or real money stock $\frac{M^s}{P}$ increases or decreases. As a result, we can easily predict a movement of new equilibrium income and interest rate (Y^*, i^*). This analytical method has been dominant in introductory and intermediate macroeconomic textbooks as the comparative statics.

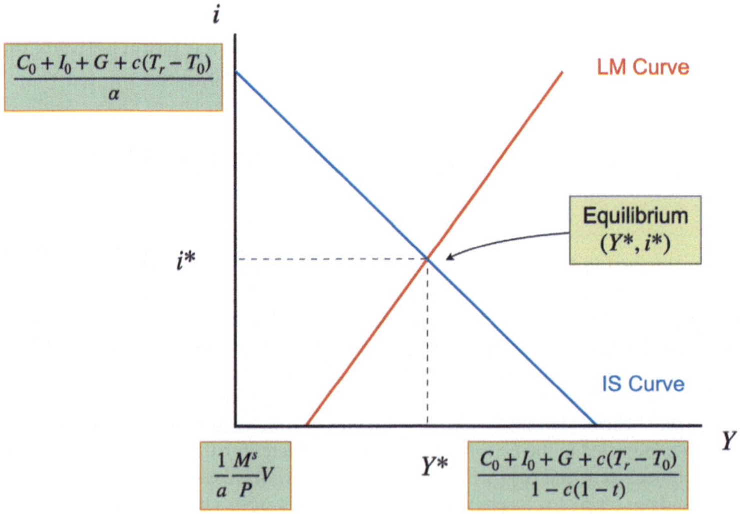

Fig. 8.1 IS-LM determination of income and interest rate

As discussed in most textbooks, income or GDP thus determined needs not to be equal to the full capacity output, Y_{full}. The Keynesian model only specifies income as determined by the level of aggregate demand. This is why it is called *aggregate demand* equilibrium of income. To realize a *full capacity* equilibrium, that is $Y^* = Y_{full}$, price needs to be flexibly changed. However, the Keynesian model presented above lacks this type of price flexibility.[4]

8.2 System Dynamics Model of Keynesian IS-LM

Whenever the investment decisions in Eq. (8.6) is restored, we can no longer apply the above simple income determination by comparative statics method. To fully analyze the short-run IS-LM model, therefore, we need to construct a dynamic model of aggregate demand equilibria based on the IS-LM curves.

8.2.1 Dynamic IS Sub-Model

Major limitations of the conventional IS-LM analysis is that it is static (atemporal analysis) and grounded on the general equilibrium framework. Therefore, it not only fails to capture how production is adjusted in response to changes in demand, but also how income affects and gets affected by various other factors. To make it a dynamic adjustment process, the introduction of inventory stock becomes essential. Specifically, the aggregate demand equilibrium Eq. (8.1) must be replaced with *disequilibrium* equation (of course this does not mean the model cannot handle equilibrium cases as we will see later).

Accordingly, our System Dynamics (SD) modeling of Keynesian macroeconomic system begins with introducing an inventory stock I_{nv}. This production adjustment process is already constructed as the dynamic *IS* sub-model of the "Keynesian Adjust-

---

[4] Note that we employ the term "short-run vs. long-run" not to indicate a specific time horizon, but to indicate whether the model lacks a dynamics around capital formation. When capital accumulation is considered, the Keynesian model presented here needs to be revised as follows (where δ denotes a depreciation rate):

$$Y_d = Y - T - \delta K$$
$$\frac{dK}{dt} = I - \delta K$$

Most textbooks explain that economists use the term 'short-run' when P is assumed to be fixed, and 'long-run' when price is flexible. See Mankiw (2016), for instance. Such dichotomic reasoning is redundant and inappropriate in system dynamics (SD) modeling as we integrate price rigidity as varying degrees of assumption on the price elasticity within a single model. This is one of examples of the modeling flexibility in SD-based approaches. In Sect. 8.4.3 we will extend the model to allow price to be flexible in response to changes in inventory. Yet, the flexible price model is still called the *short-run* IS-LM model under our terminology.

ment SD Model with Inventory" presented in Yamaguchi (2013, Chap. 9). Specifically, we have introduced the following three equations in place of the equilibrium Eq. (8.1):

$$\frac{dI_{nv}}{dt} = Y - AD \qquad \text{(Inventory Stock)} \qquad (8.14)$$

$$\frac{dAD_f}{dt} = \frac{AD - AD_f}{AT_f} \qquad \text{(AD Forecasting)} \qquad (8.15)$$

$$Y = AD_f + \frac{I^* - I_{nv}}{AT_{inv}} \qquad \text{(Production Decision)} \qquad (8.16)$$

Equation (8.14) describes how a discrepancy between production and shipment (or aggregate demand) is adjusted as a change in inventory stock. This is a more realistic inventory adjustment process under the disequilibrium, and allows the model to reflect how firms (producers) adjust their production based on aggregate demand forecasting (AD_f). Equation (8.15) assumes how producers update their aggregate demand forecasts for the next period against the current aggregate demand that has been shipped this year (note that unit of time is 'year' in our model). Accordingly, producers make production decisions for the next year based on two factors as presented in Eq. (8.16); that is, they adjust the level of production based on the aggregate demand forecasts for the next period and the amount of inventory that they think is optimal to hold, which is called the desired inventory (I^*).

Our *IS* sub-model has now introduced two new Eqs. (8.14) and (8.15) for two unknowns: I_{nv} and AD_f with three parameters: desired amount of inventory I^*, and adjustment times for aggregate demand forecasting AT_f and for inventory AT_{inv}. This is our System Dynamics (SD) approach to model the Keynesian macroeconomic system, which always begins with the introduction of inventory stock. In addition, we have also introduced human psychological factor such as aggregate demand forecasting to incorporate expectation formation concerning production decision, all without changing the basic framework of the standard Keynesian short-run IS-LM model.

Figure 8.2 illustrates the *IS* sub-model of our Keynesian short-run IS-LM thus constructed, and reflects the investment and production decision-making processes described above. In SD modeling software, a box indicates a stock variable whereas double-line arrows pointing into and out from stocks indicate inflow and outflows. On the other hand, single line arrows indicate instantaneous causal relationships between variables and parameters.[5]

[5] In causal loop diagrams (CLD), arrows are often represented in different colors to indicate the type of causation (e.g. blue and red as in Figs. 6.4 and 8.12) so that the polarity of feedback loops can be easily identified. In stock flow diagrams (SFD) such as Fig. 8.2, no particular meaning is assigned to the color of arrows indicating instantaneous relationships.

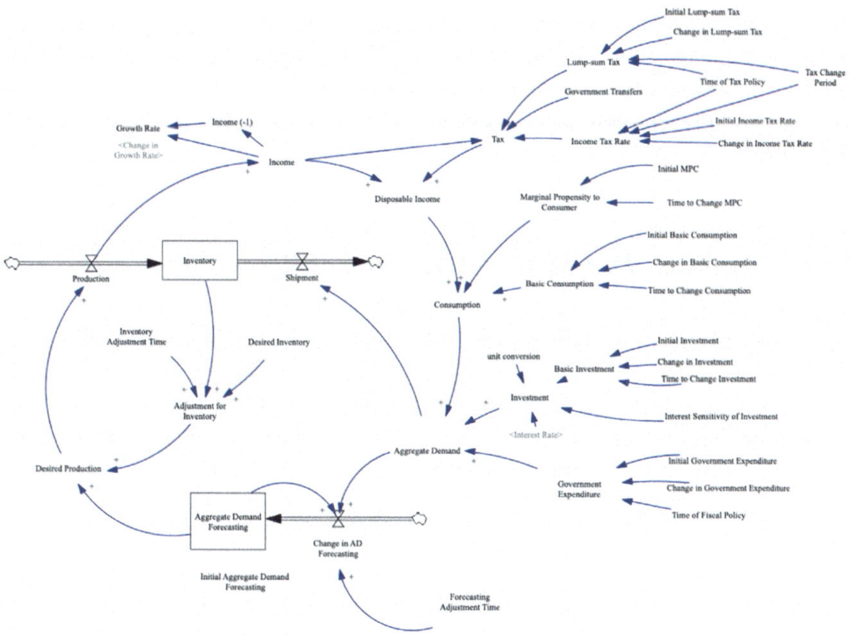

Fig. 8.2 IS sub-model: aggregate demand adjustment with inventory

8.2.2 *Dynamic LM Sub-Model*

Interest Rate Adjustment Process

Next, we need to build the *LM* sub-model of the SD version of the short-run IS-LM model. For this purpose, the equilibrium money market in Eq. (8.8) needs to be replaced with a disequilibrium dynamic adjustment process of interest rate as a function of excess demand for money such that:

$$\frac{d\,i}{dt} = \Phi\left((aY - bi) - \frac{M^s}{P}V\right) \tag{8.17}$$

Applying the general formulation of adjustment processes described in Yamaguchi (2013, Chap. 2), the interest rate adjustment process is further specified as

$$\frac{d\,i}{dt} = \frac{i^* - i}{\text{Delay Time}} \tag{8.18}$$

where i^* denotes desired interest rate. Desired interest rate i^* is obtained as

$$i^* = \frac{i}{\left(\frac{M^s}{P}V/(aY - bi)\right)^e} \tag{8.19}$$

where *e* denotes a money ratio elasticity of desired interest rate. Figure 8.3 illustrates the *LM* sub-model of the adjustment process of interest rate. Note that Fig. 8.3 also illustrates price and expected inflation rate adjustment processes for later use (from Sect. 8.4 onward). For now, price is assumed to be fixed as in the standard short-run IS-LM model.

8.2.3 Keynesian IS-LM Model Analysis of Recessions

Let us next see how the short-run IS-LM model thus developed can demonstrate the Keynesian monetary and fiscal policies as described in textbooks. Economic recessions can be described as the decrease in income or GDP. One of the benefits of using the IS-LM framework in macroeconomic analysis is that we can visualize recessions as the shifts in *IS* and *LM* curves. In other words, if we can identify the

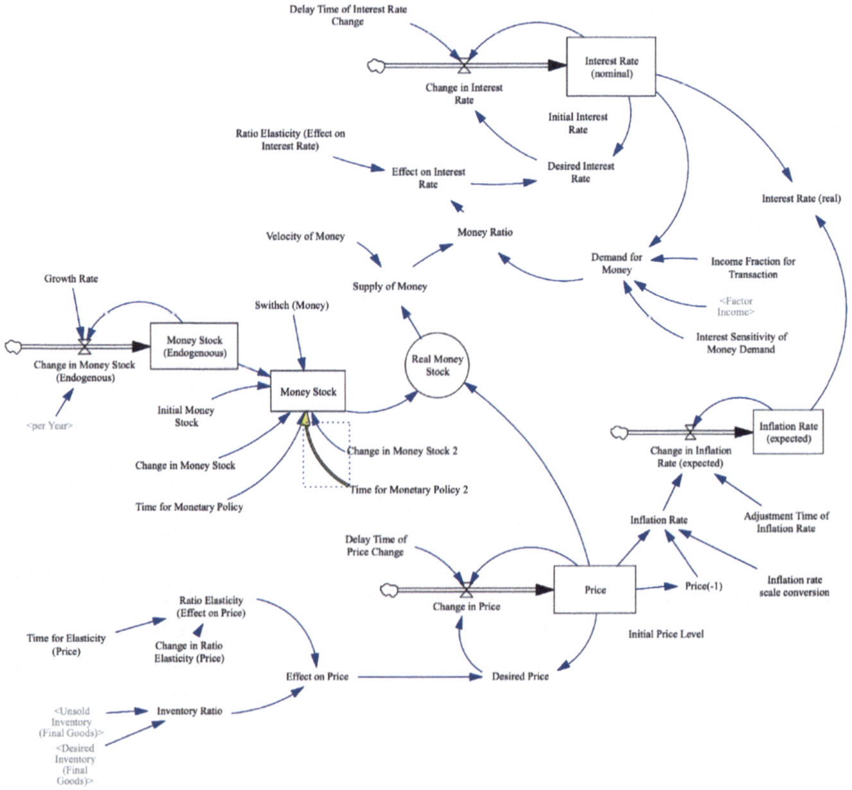

Fig. 8.3 LM sub-model: interest rate and price adjustment processes

causes of recessions in this way, we can then apply fiscal and monetary policies in a reverse way to recover from recessions.

Recessions Caused by the Shifts in *IS* Curve

Let us first analyze recessions caused by the shifts in *IS* curve on the left phase diagram in Fig. 8.4. The simulation starts with the equilibrium at point A. Then, recessions caused by decreases in aggregate demand can be observed as the leftward shift in the *IS* curve indicated by dotted black lines. First, the decline in investment by $\Delta I = -20$ at time t = 8 causes the original equilibrium point A to move to a new equilibrium at point B. This is implemented by decreasing the basic investment (I_0) using a STEP function. That is, the level of investment decline by 20 from t = 8 until the end of the simulation. In our dynamic IS-LM model, this movement (point A → B) caused by the leftward shift in the *IS* curve is captured by a red trajectory on the phase diagram of income taken on the horizontal axis and interest rate on the vertical axis.

Now let us further assume that consumption has declined by $\Delta C = -20$ at t = 24 by similarly decreasing the basic consumption (C_0). Then, the *IS* curve is moved further towards left. As a result, the second equilibrium point B moves to a new point C as captured by the green trajectory line (point B → C) . In this way, both the equilibrium level of income as well as interest rate decline.

If the economy experiences these types of recessions caused by decreases in aggregate demand, the IS-LM model tells us that we can not only restore the equilibrium, but also grow the economy further to point F by increasing the government expenditure by $\Delta G = 40$ at t = 35. The effects of such government spendings are shown by the gray trajectory from point C → F. Notice how these shifts occur along the gentle hyperbolic *LM* curve (a thick black line drawn manually) since changes in aggregate demand do not affect the *LM* curve. This is the fiscal policy suggested by the IS-LM framework.

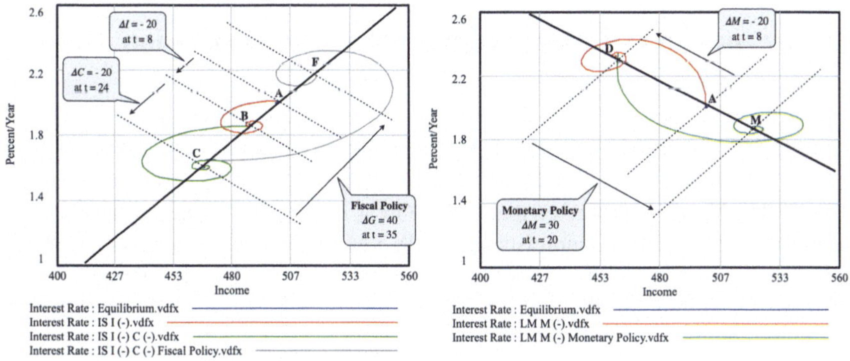

Fig. 8.4 Dynamic IS-LM analyses of fiscal (left) and monetary (right) policies

Recessions Caused by the Shifts in *LM* Curve

Recessions caused by the decrease in money stock can be illustrated by leftward shifts of *LM* curve on the right diagram of Fig. 8.4. For our purposes, we do not question how such reductions in money stock are brought about at this stage. We can observe how the original equilibrium point A now moves to a new point at D as the decline in money stock causes the *LM* curve to shift towards the left. In our dynamic IS-LM model, this movement (point A $\rightarrow$ D) caused by the decrease in money stock by $\Delta M^s = -20$ at t = 8 is captured by the red trajectory. Similarly, it can be observed that equilibrium level of income declines and interest rate rises as a result.

If recessions are caused by reductions of money stock, the IS-LM model teaches us we can not only restore the equilibrium easily, but also grow the economy further to the new point M by increasing money stock by $\Delta M^s = 30$ at t = 20 as shown by the green trajectory line (point D $\rightarrow$ M). Notice how these shifts occur along the gentle hyperbolic *IS* curve (a thick black line drawn manually), which is produced by investment decisions in Eq. (8.6). This is the monetary policy suggested by the IS-LM framework in standard textbooks.

With the introduction of the IS-LM model, recessions are analyzed as the leftward shifts in the *IS* and *LM* curvest, while recoveries are analyzed as the rightward shifts in the *IS* and *LM* curves. Figure 8.4 illustrates these standard textbook explanations of IS-LM analysis as a phase diagram of income and interest rate in the SD model. By combining outside shocks to aggregate demand and money stock, we can describe many different possible scenarios of recessions. Furthermore the model indicates that we can attain recoveries from wherever the previous recessions end by mixing fiscal and monetary policies (policy mix). Macroeconomics textbooks are full of these exercises and we have been taught in classes, for over 80 years since Hicks (1937) first introduced the framework, that economies are now under the control of policy makers. Indeed, our simulations using this short-run IS-LM model so far seems to support the effectiveness of such macroeconomic 'fine-tunings'.

8.3 Keynesian IS-LM Analysis of the Great Depression

Convinced by the analytical capabilities of the IS-LM model, Mankiw (2016, p. 351) attempted to explain the causes of the Great Depression in his popular macroeconomics textbook used worldwide, as briefly discussed in the previous chapter. Specifically, Mankiw expresses that "[t]he Great Depression provides an extended case study to show how economists use the IS-LM model to analyze economic fluctuations". Let us now examine how the Keynesian IS-LM analysis is applied to study the case of the Great Depression.

8.3.1 Spending Hypothesis Versus Money Hypothesis

As discussed above, there are only two causes that trigger recessions in the IS-LM model; decreases in the aggregate demand causing leftwards shift of the *IS* curve, and decreases in the money stock causing leftwards shift of the *LM* curve. Mankiw (2016, Chap. 12) called the former *spending hypothesis* and the latter *money hypothesis*. The original proponent of the spending hypothesis was John M. Keynes. In essence Keynes (1936) analyzed that under-capacity (investment) and under-consumption in real sectors are the main causes of the Great Depression, and suggested the management of aggregate demand through fiscal and monetary policies as a way to counteract and get way from the depression (recession). In the context of the IS-LM framework, the policies should be aimed at economic stimulus through government expenditures and restoring investments by lowering the costs of borrowing, i.e., interest rates.

On the other hand, Mankiw (2016) argues that *money hypothesis* "places primary blame for the Depression on the Fed for allowing the money supply to fall by such a large amount (p. 353)". He then continues to explain as follows:

> The best-known advocates of this interpretation are Milton Friedman and Anna Schwartz, who defended it in their treatise on U.S. monetary history. Friedman and Schwartz argue that contractions in the money supply have caused most economic downturns and that the Great Depression is a dramatic example (p. 353).

In order to examine which of the two seemingly contrasting hypotheses is the plausible causes of the Depression using the IS-LM model, Mankiw arranged time-series data of key macroeconomic variables starting from 1929 until 1940. Figure 8.5 reproduces all data presented in the original Table 12-1 from Mankiw (2016, pp. 352–353). Here, we can easily observe that the IS-related variables such as real GNP, consumption and investment all fell during the initial period between 1929–1933, while the LM-related variables such as nominal interest rate, money supply and price level also fell during the same period except real money balances (stock), which rose slightly and then fluctuated.

Table 12-1: What Happened During The Great Depression?

Year	Unemployment Rate	Real GNP	Consumption	Investment	Government Purchases	Nominal Interest Rate	Money Supply	Price Level	Inflation	Real Money Balances
1929	3.2	203.6	139.6	40.4	22.0	5.9	26.6	50.6	—	52.6
1930	8.9	183.5	130.4	27.4	24.3	3.6	25.8	49.3	-2.6	52.3
1931	16.3	169.5	126.1	16.8	25.4	2.6	24.1	44.8	-10.1	54.5
1932	24.1	144.2	114.8	4.7	24.2	2.7	21.1	40.2	-9.3	52.5
1933	25.2	141.5	112.8	5.3	23.3	1.7	19.9	39.3	-2.2	50.7
1934	22.0	154.3	118.1	9.4	26.6	1.0	21.9	42.2	7.4	51.8
1935	20.3	169.5	125.5	18.0	27.0	0.8	25.9	42.6	0.9	60.8
1936	17.0	193.2	138.4	24.0	31.8	0.8	29.6	42.7	0.2	62.9
1937	14.3	203.2	143.1	29.9	30.8	0.9	30.9	44.5	4.2	69.5
1938	19.1	192.9	140.2	17.0	33.9	0.8	30.5	43.9	-1.3	69.5
1939	17.2	209.4	148.2	24.7	35.2	0.6	34.2	43.2	-1.6	79.1
1940	14.6	227.2	155.7	33.0	36.4	0.6	39.7	43.9	1.6	90.3

Fig. 8.5 The great depression data presented by Mankiw (2016)

Mankiw then examined both spending and money hypotheses by shifting the *IS* and *LM* curves to the left, and then rejects the money hypothesis as the cause of the Depression as follows:

> Using the IS-LM model, we might interpret the money hypothesis as explaining the Depression by a contractionary shift in the *LM* curve. Seen in this way, however, the money hypothesis runs into two problems.
>
> The first problem is the behavior of *real* money balances. Monetary policy leads to a contractionary shift in the *LM* curve only if real money balances fall. Yet from 1929 to 1931 **real money balances rose slightly** because the fall in the money supply was accompanied by an even greater fall in the price level. Although the monetary contraction may have been responsible for the rise in unemployment from 1931 to 1933, when real money balances did fall, it cannot easily explain the initial downturn from 1929 to 1931.
>
> The second problem for the money hypothesis is the behavior of interest rates. If a contractionary shift in the *LM* curve triggered the Depression, we should have observed higher interest rates. Yet **nominal interest rates fell continuously** from 1929 to 1933.
>
> These two reasons appear sufficient to reject the view that the Depression was instigated by a contractionary shift in the *LM* curve. (Mankiw 2016, p. 354; Italics in original. Bold emphases added by the authors of this book.)

8.3.2 Which Hypotheses Explain the Great Depression?

Let us now turn to our short-run IS-LM model and examine if the Mankiw's above assertions are justified. In the phase diagrams of Fig. 8.4, shocks to the *IS* curve (spending hypothesis) is represented as a movement from point A to points B and C on the left diagram, and shocks to the *LM* curve (money hypothesis) is illustrated from point A to point D on the right diagram. In order to study the spending and money hypotheses more in line with that of the Great Depression, let us run simulations by decreasing investment and consumption at the same time. Unit of time is "year". For spending hypothesis, let us suppose that consumption decreases by $\Delta C = -20$ at t = 1930 once, and then investment decreases by $\Delta I = -20$ at t = 1930 and 1931 (for two consecutive periods) and at t = 1935, respectively. For money hypothesis, let us assume that money stock M^s is now decreased by $\Delta M^s = -10$ at t = 1930. In our dynamic IS-LM model, these scenarios are implemented using a PULSE function. These scenarios are more realistic than simply decreasing *C* and *I* separately in time using STEP function as was done in the previous case shown in Fig. 8.4.

The left diagram of Fig. 8.6 shows the behaviors of income over time under the two hypotheses. Note the simulation time (1928–1940) displayed on the horizontal axis is a supplemental label.[6] The right diagram shows the behavior for nominal interest rate instead of real interest rate. Under the fixed price assumption, however,

[6] The SD simulation software that we used (*Vensim*®) has a functionality that allows users to display an arbitrary time range for graphs. Here, simulation is run for 50 years (1920–1970), but we are only showing the period between 1928–1940 when pulse function is implemented using this custom graph functionality. It does not mean, however, that model parameters and initial values have been calibrated nor optimized using the actual historical reference data.

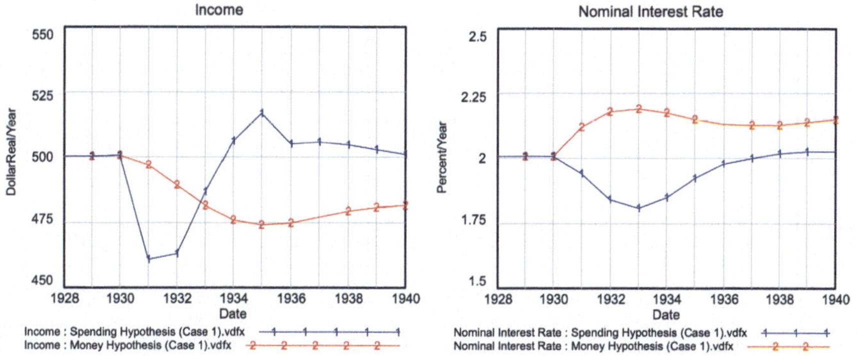

Fig. 8.6 Income and interest rate under spending and money hypotheses (Case 1)

there is no difference between nominal and real interest rates, and behaviors of the two exactly match in our simulation. Specifically line 1 (blue) in both diagrams show behaviors under the spending hypothesis whereas line 2 (red) shows that of the money hypothesis.

On both diagrams the spending hypothesis indicates falls in both income and interest rate, while income falls but interest rate rises under the money hypothesis. Indeed the rise in interest rate under the money hypothesis fails to explain the fall in nominal interest rate observed from the data in Fig. 8.5. Mankiw pointed out this contradictory behavior in the nominal interest rate as "[T]he second problem for the money hypothesis". Our simulation also confirms that each hypothesis has different effects on income. Note that "Case 1" in the caption of Fig. 8.6 means that the simulations are run under the "fixed price" and "exogenous money" assumptions. Table 8.6 presented in Sect. 8.14 classifies simulation models that will be discussed in this chapter step-by-step and their underlying assumptions.

How about the the behavior of *real* money balances, then? Fig. 8.7 shows both money stock and real money balance fell under the money hypothesis. Recall that price is fixed under both hypothesis in case 1, which reflects the assumption of the standard Keynesian IS-LM model featured in many textbooks. Therefore, as Fig. 8.7 indicates, both spending and money hypotheses fail to explain that prices fell while real money balances rose during the Depression.

In fact, this problem, which Mankiw called "the first problem" of the money hypothesis, occurs under both hypotheses. Accordingly, both hypotheses should have been rejected as the causes of the Great Depression. In other words, the IS-LM model itself should have been rejected at this point of analysis as it cannot explain the behaviors of key macroeconomic variables. However, Mankiw somehow rejected only the money hypothesis fallaciously without examining the applicability of the short-run IS-LM model itself grounded on flawed exogenous money and fixed price assumptions. Rational economists should question the validity of the IS-LM model itself, rather than applying each hypothesis separately and rejecting only one of them in favor of the other.

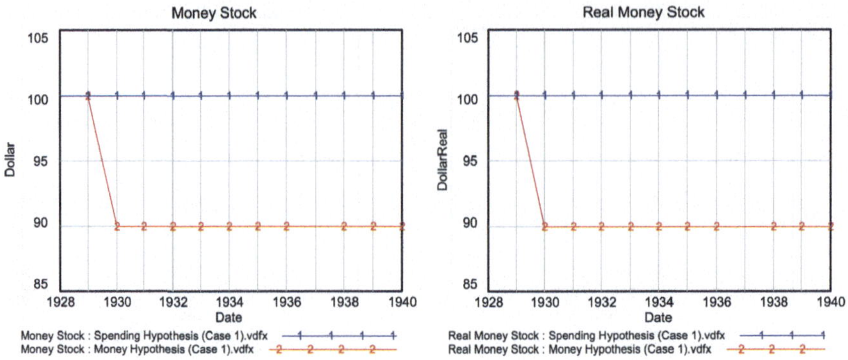

Fig. 8.7 Money stock and real money stock under spending and money hypotheses (Case 1)

8.4 SD Model of Flexible Price IS-LM

8.4.1 Mankiw's Extended IS-LM Model

In an attempt to explain the effects of deflation on income under the spending hypothesis, Mankiw (2016, p. 355) then presents an extended version of the IS-LM analysis in a section titled "The Money Hypothesis Again: The Effects of Falling Prices". Referring to the debt-deflation theory proposed by Irving Fisher in 1933, Mankiw introduces a new variable: expected future inflation ($E\pi$). His extended IS-LM analysis is then presented as follows:

$$Y = C(Y - T) + I(i - E\pi) + G \qquad \text{(Extended } IS\text{)} \qquad (8.20)$$

$$\frac{M}{P} = L(i, Y) \qquad \text{(Extended } LM\text{)} \qquad (8.21)$$

where the difference between nominal interest rate (i) and expected future inflation ($E\pi$) is defined as *ex ante* real interest rate (r) from the Fisher equation. With the introduction of expected future inflation, nominal and real interest rates are now distinguished. For reference, the original *Fig. 12-8* of his Extended IS-LM analysis presented in Mankiw (2016, p. 356) is adapted here as Fig. 8.8.

Mankiw then goes on to explain that the spending hypothesis in his extended version of the IS-LM analysis shown above can explain how the destabilizing effects of deflation affect income without a need to rely on the money hypothesis as follows:

> Now suppose that everyone suddenly expects that the price level will fall in the future, so that $E\pi$ becomes negative. The real interest rate is now higher at any given nominal interest rate. This increase in the real interest rate depresses planned investment spending, shifting the *IS* curve from IS_1 to IS_2. (The vertical distance of the downward shift exactly equals the expected deflation.) Thus, an expected deflation leads to a reduction in income from Y_1 to Y_2. The nominal interest rate falls from i_1 to i_2, while the real interest rate rises from r_1 to r_2.

Fig. 8.8 Mankiw's extended IS-LM model

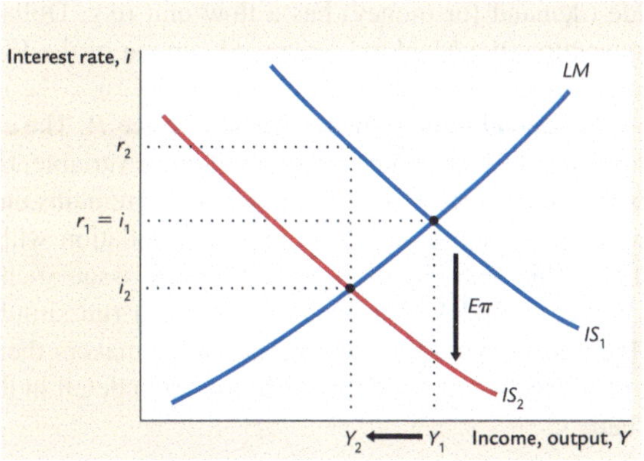

Image Source: Mankiw (2016, p.356).

> Here is the story behind this figure. When firms come to expect deflation, they become reluctant to borrow to buy investment goods because they believe they will have to repay these loans later in more valuable dollars. The fall in investment depresses planned expenditure, which in turn depresses income. The fall in income reduces the demand for money, and this reduces the nominal interest rate that equilibrates the money market. The nominal interest rate falls by less than the expected deflation, so the real interest rate rises.
>
> Note that there is a common thread in these two stories of destabilizing deflation. In both, falling prices depress income by causing a contractionary shift in the *IS* curve. Because a deflation of the size observed from 1929 to 1933 is unlikely except in the presence of a major contraction in the money supply, these two explanations assign some of the responsibility for the Depression—especially its severity—to the Fed. In other words, if falling prices are destabilizing, then a contraction in the money supply can lead to a fall in income, even without a decrease in real money balances or a rise in nominal interest rates. (*ibid.*, pp. 355–356)

The first one of the "two stories of destabilizing deflation" refers to the debt-deflation theory proposed by Fisher (1932, 1933), which, according to Mankiw, analyzed that the wealth redistribution effects of deflation between debtors and creditors reduce the spending of debtors more than raise those of the creditors, thus giving rise to a net reduction in spending and causing contractionary shift in the *IS* curve. The second story is the role that expected inflation plays in the rise of real interest rate as explained in the quotation above.

Before we examine the Mankiw's above assertions under the extended IS-LM model, it should be pointed out that there are two problems in his formulation when applying this extended analysis to the case of the Great Depression. The first issue is unit inconsistency in the *LM* equation (8.21). From system dynamics modeling perspective, the supply of money $\frac{M}{P}$ (or real money balance) on the left side of Eq. (8.21) has a stock unit expressed in real term (e.g. DollarReal) whereas the right side (demand for money) has a flow unit (e.g. DollarReal/Year). In SD modeling convention, the Mankiw's extended version of the IS-LM model does not pass the basic unit consistency test.[7]

The second issue is the treatment of price P. The extended model introduced the expected inflation, which is a psychological variable. However, P itself remains to be fixed in the short-run IS-LM. Therefore, it remains unclear as to how the Mankiw's extended model describes an expected deflation without flexible price in the first place. This leads us to a methodological issue such that he also fails to present a dynamic model with which readers can run simulations and verify his claims. Model-less arguments can mislead policymakers themselves and lead to mistaken policy conclusions as we have discussed in detail in the context of Japanese case in Chap. 5.

8.4.2 *Flexible Price IS-LM Model Equations*

With these issues in mind, let us now incorporate the Mankiw's idea of extending the short-run model towards flexible price. The introduction of expected inflation allows us to distinguish nominal and real interest rates within the IS-LM model presented in Sect. 8.1.1. Based on the Fisher equation, an *ex ante* real interest rate r can be approximated as the difference between nominal interest rate i and expected inflation rate π^e such that $r = i - \pi^e$.[8] With the introduction of expected inflation and real interest rate, our extended version of the IS-LM model is now described as follows:

$$Y = AD \quad \text{(Aggregate Demand Equilibrium)} \tag{8.22}$$

$$AD = C + I + G \quad \text{(Aggregate Demand)} \tag{8.23}$$

$$C = C_0 + cY_d \quad \text{(Consumption Decisions)} \tag{8.24}$$

$$Y_d = Y - T \quad \text{(Disposable Income)} \tag{8.25}$$

$$T = T_0 + tY - T_r \quad \text{(Tax Revenues)} \tag{8.26}$$

$$I = \frac{I_0}{r} - \alpha r \quad \text{(Investment Decisions)} \tag{8.27}$$

$$G = \bar{G} \quad \text{(Government Expenditures)} \tag{8.28}$$

$$\frac{M^s}{P}V = L^d \quad \text{(Equilibrium of Money)} \tag{8.29}$$

[7] Refer to the Eq. (8.8) of our IS-LM model where Real Money Balance (DollarReal) is multiplied by Velocity (1/Year). Our short-run IS-LM model thus clears both the unit and model structure checks built into the simulation software. However, the velocity V itself is in fact only an "observable variable" in terms of other economic variables, and should not be used as a variable to determine the behavior of the model (*LM* sub-model in this case). This theoretical issue will be addressed in the ASD model discussed in Sect. 8.10.2 where we expand the model to incorporate sectoral balance sheets and transaction items.

[8] Notice the different symbols used for expected inflation in Mankiw's textbook ($E\pi$) and our model (π^e).

$$L^d = aY - bi \qquad \text{(Demand for Money)} \tag{8.30}$$

$$r = i - \pi^e \qquad \text{(Fisher Equation)} \tag{8.31}$$

With the addition of a new Eq. (8.31) to the previous Keynesian short-run IS-LM model presented in Sect. 8.1.1, our extended IS-LM model now consists of 10 equations with 10 unknowns;

$$Y, AD, C, I, G, Y_d, T, i, r, L^d$$

with 14 exogenously determined parameters

$$C_0, c, T_0, t, T_r, I_0, \bar{G}, M^s, P, V, \alpha, a, b, \pi^e.$$

Equations (8.22) through (8.26) are the same formulation as in Eqs. (8.1) through (8.5) of the previous model under fixed price. The extended model above distinguishes nominal (i) and *ex ante* real interest rate (r) as in Eq. (8.31). Accordingly, investment decisions in Eq. (8.27) is now a function of *ex ante* real interest rate r, whereas the liquidity demand is a function of *nominal* interest rate i. Furthermore, we can also define the *ex post* real interest rate (r_{post}) based on nominal interest rate and inflation rate, which is explained below.

8.4.3 SD Model of the Flexible Price IS-LM

To examine whether the Mankiw's assertions on the validity of spending hypothesis under the flexible price assumption are justified, let us introduce the expected inflation into our system dynamics model. To do so, we first need to incorporate price dynamics.

Price Adjustment Process

Price level in the short-run IS-LM model is assumed to be exogenously determined, by reflecting the Keynesian view that price tends to be rigid in the short run.[9] Hence, price has been assumed to be fixed also in our SD model so far. Introduction of inventory stock (discussed in Sect. 8.2.1) allows us to model price dynamics even in the short run, because fluctuations of inventory are always reflected as a change in price in the real economy such that

[9] Yamaguchi (2013, Chap. 9) discusses the contrasting views on the role of price adjustment in the Neoclassical long-run equilibrium and Keynesian aggregate demand equilibrium of GDP based on a causal loop diagram.

$$\frac{dP}{dt} = \Psi\left(I_{nv}^{*} - I_{nv}\right) \tag{8.32}$$

where I_{nv}^{*} denotes desired inventory, which represents the amount of inventory stock that the economy as a whole desires to hold at any moment in time. This price adjustment process can be further specified as follows

$$\frac{dP}{dt} = \frac{P^{*} - P}{\text{Adjustment Time}} \tag{8.33}$$

where the desired price P^{*} is obtained as

$$P^{*} = \frac{P}{\left(I_{nv}/I_{nv}^{*}\right)^{e}} \tag{8.34}$$

where e is an inventory ratio elasticity of desired price. This elasticity is a parameter (constant) in our SD model so that its value can be changed according to different assumptions on the degree of price rigidity that we wish to run simulations with. The default value is set to be 0, which assumes fixed price. We have set the price adjustment time to 4 (years) in our subsequent simulations. The stock-flow diagram in Fig. 8.3 already illustrates this price adjustment process.

Expected Inflation Formation Process

With the introduction of price adjustment process above, the model can be further extended to incorporate the formation of expected inflation as a psychological variable. Specifically, the expected inflation rate can be modeled as

$$\frac{d\pi^{e}}{dt} = \frac{\pi - \pi^{e}}{\text{Adjustment Time}} \tag{8.35}$$

in which the inflation rate is obtained as follows:

$$\pi = \frac{d(lnP(t))}{dt} \tag{8.36}$$

where $lnP(t)$ is a natural logarithm of price $P(t)$. The adjustment process of expected inflation defined in Eq. (8.35) above reflects the *adaptive expectation*. With the inclusion of the price adjustment and expected inflation rate, our extended IS-LM model with flexible price assumption is now completed.

8.4.4 Spending and Money Hypotheses Under Flexible Price

Let us now run simulations and test the spending and money hypotheses under this extended IS-LM model. Specifically, we allow the price to move flexibly by setting its elasticity to 0.2 at t = 0 from its default value of 0 (fixed price). The inflation expectation adjustment time is set to 10 (years).

Figure 8.9 shows the behaviors of income (left) and price level (right). "Case 2" in the caption means that the simulation is now run under flexible price assumption. Declines in consumption, investment (spending hypothesis) and money stock (money hypothesis) are implemented in the same way as was done in Case 1. Both hypotheses cause income to fall similar to Case 1 simulations.

Left diagram in Fig. 8.10 shows nominal interest rate (line 1 in blue), *ex ante* real interest rate (line 2 in red) and *ex post* real interest rate (line 3 in green) under the spending hypotheses. Right diagram shows those interest rates under the money hypothesis. Spending hypothesis under flexible price (Case 2) captures what Mankiw called the *destabilizing effects of deflation* on income, the fall in nominal interest rate

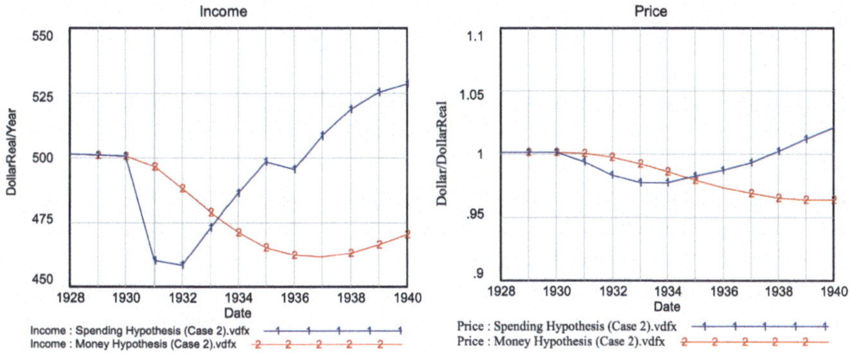

Fig. 8.9 Income and price under spending and money hypotheses (Case 2)

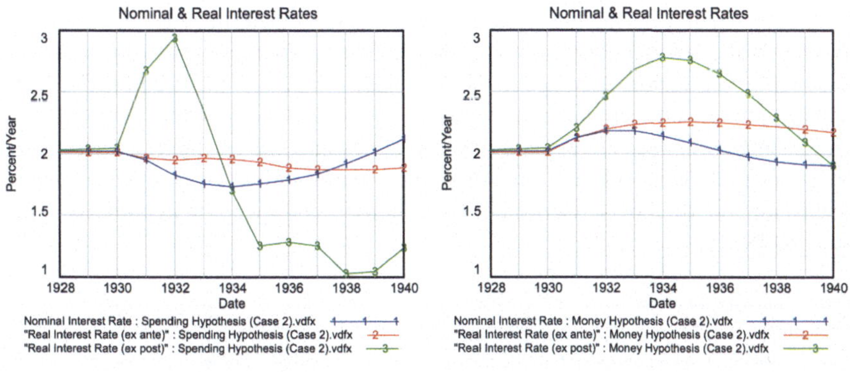

Fig. 8.10 Nominal and real interest rates under spending and money hypotheses (Case 2)

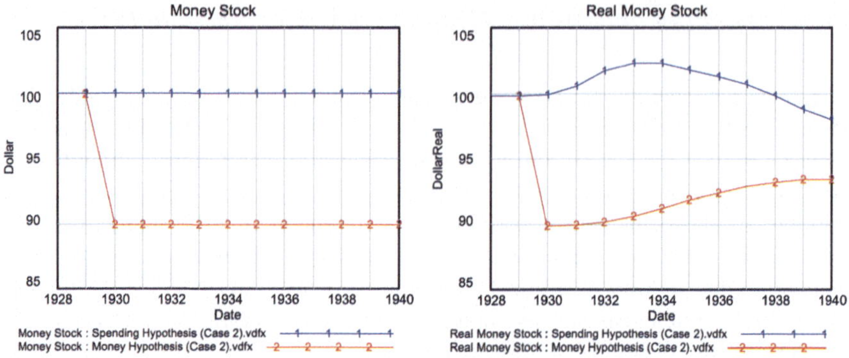

Fig. 8.11 Money stock and real money balance under spending and money hypotheses (Case 2)

as well as the rise in real interest rate. Though the magnitude of rise in *ex ante* real interest rate (line 2) under the spending hypothesis is not significant when viewed as an absolute value, the decline in nominal interest rate causes the *ex ante* real interest rate to appear relatively higher. Moreover the spending hypothesis captures the sudden rise in *ex post* real interest rate (line 3 in green), which is consistent with data in Fig. 8.5.

Case 2 analysis is what Mankiw's extended model of the IS-LM has attempted to implement, yet he did not present a corresponding simulation model. Our simulation results indeed confirms the validity of Mankiw's claim, and this is one of the contributions of our SD model. However, the problem of spending hypothesis in Case 2 is that it still treats money stock M^s as exogenously given, thus failing to explain the contraction of money as was discussed in Case 1.

To see this visually, Fig. 8.11 compares the behaviors of money stock (left) and real money balance (right) under the two hypotheses. From the right diagram we can observe that real money stock under the spending hypothesis (line 1 in blue) increases whereas that of money hypothesis (line 2 in red) decreases initially and then rise thereafter. This seems to suggest that spending hypothesis explains the behavior of real money balance during the Great Depression better than the money hypothesis. Looking at the left diagram, however, the spending hypothesis does not take into account the contraction of money in the first place. Therefore, the rise in real money balance without contractions in money stock shows that the spending hypothesis in Case 2 simulation does not explain the real money balance for the right reason. As far as our simulation results indicate, therefore, we did not find a theoretical evidence which supports Mankiw's assertion of the validity of the spending hypothesis in his extended IS-LM analysis.[10]

[10] Recall also how Mankiw (2016, p. 356) maintained in the quotation above that "if falling prices are destabilizing, then a contraction in the money supply can lead to a fall in income, even without a decrease in real money balances or a rise in nominal interest rates". One can see here that he presupposes money contraction under the spending hypothesis in his extended IS-LM analysis.

Money hypothesis under the Case 2 simulation, on the other hand, captures the money contraction, deflation, and the rise in real money balance for the right reason. Also, the rise in *ex post* real interest rate is consistent with the data. However, the nominal interest rate also rises under the money hypothesis, which is inconsistent with what was observed during the Great Depression.

Problems of Spending Hypothesis Under the Flexible Price Model

In summary the spending hypothesis in the extended model still fails to explain the contraction of money, and thus the behavior of real money balance for the right reason. It does not also take into account the fact that money stock contracted significantly during the Depression. This anomaly alone should have prompted economists to question the validity of IS-LM model itself, rather than rejecting only the money hypothesis in favor of the spending hypothesis twice; that is, first in the Keynesian IS-LM model and, again, in the extended model.

Our simulations imply that the conventional IS-LM model, which is built upon the fixed price and exogenous money assumptions, fails to explain the causes of the Great Depression under both spending and money hypotheses. Should we abandon the IS-LM model, then? If so, the cause of the Great Depression becomes unexplainable again even in the undergraduate-level textbooks, which is a serious issue for the field and for the economics profession.

8.5 Endogenous Money Spending Hypothesis

What is wrong with the IS-LM analysis, then? As discussed so far, the problem lies in the assumption that money stock M^s is exogenously given and prices are fixed. Since the introduction of the model by Hicks (1937), it has been a norm among economists to assume that money is exogenously determined; that is, money stock has been assumed to be put into circulation and can be controlled by the government and (or) central bank.[11] However, evidences are conclusive. As discussed in Chap. 3, the majority of money stock is created endogenously by banks as interest-bearing debts under the fractional reserve banking system.

This presumption, however, contradicts with his own definition of the spending hypothesis or the exogenous money assumed in his extended version of the IS-LM model.

[11] Hicks (1937) simply assumed "[L]et M be the given quantity of money" (p. 148). Modigliani (1944) followed Hicks (1937) and treated M as given. We do not know whether Hicks himself or others who followed the IS-LM framework made such an assumption for the sake of mathematical simplicity, or by the unfamiliarity with the fractional reserve banking.

8.5.1 Fisher's Debt-Deflation Theory and Reflation Policy

Have economists been ignorant for such a long time so as to disregard the role of money and debts? No, they have not. Indeed, just around the same time when Keynes published the *General Theory* in 1936, Irving Fisher, who had served as president of the AEA in 1918 and just became the first president (1931–1934) of the Econometric Society that he had founded with Ragnar Frisch,[12] proposed that the main cause of the Depression was the fractional reserve banking system itself where money is created and destroyed by banks. However, when he first received the Chicago Plan in 1933, he showed little interest in the proposal. In fact, when he met with President Roosevelt in August 1933, two months after the passage of the Glass-Steagall Act, Fisher did not propose the 100% reserve system. His main interest at the time was to elucidate the causes of business cycles in general and how to stabilize prices, i.e., the value of the dollar. And, just like Keynes, Fisher was struggling in search for the remedy.

(a) Debt-Deflation Theory—Fisher's Diagnosis of the Great Depression

Fisher's solution was the paper published in the first volume of Econometrica titled "The Debt-Deflation Theory of Great Depressions" (Fisher, 1933), which was essentially a summary of his book published a year before titled *Booms and Depressions* (Fisher, 1932). Fisher analyzed that the crux of the Depression was the *over-indebtedness*, which triggered financial crisis at the initial phase, and then *deflation* that worsened the burden of debtors. In other words, he had a conviction that the central factors that precipitated unprecedented downturn were "debt disease" (excess bank loans) and "dollar disease" (increasing value of the dollar) rather than real factors such as over- or under-production, consumption, saving or investment, as many economists believed at the time.

Let's briefly revisit the debt-deflation theory based on his original article. Fisher (1933) focused on nine macroeconomic variables and described them as the "chain of consequences" that characterized the overall dynamics of the Great Depression as follows:

> (1) *Debt liquidation* leads to *distress selling* and to (2) *Contraction of deposit currency*, as bank loans are paid off, and to a slowing down of velocity of circulation. This contraction of deposits and of their velocity, precipitated by distress selling, causes (3) *A fall in the level of prices*, in other words, a swelling of the value of the dollar. Assuming, as above stated, that this fall of prices is not interfered with by reflation or otherwise, there must be (4) *A still greater fall in the net worths of business*, precipitating bankruptcies and (5) *A like fall*

[12] Ragnar Frisch was a visiting scholar at Yale at the time, and they founded the Econometric Society together with Charles F. Roos, Joseph Schumpeter, Henry Schultz, and others in the late 1930s. Frisch received a fellowship from the Rockefeller Foundation to visit the US in 1927 during which he associated himself with Fisher, Wesley Clair Mitchell, Henry Schultz and others. After becoming a full professor at University of Oslo in 1931, Frisch founded the Institute of Economics at University of Oslo in 1932 and became its Director of Research.

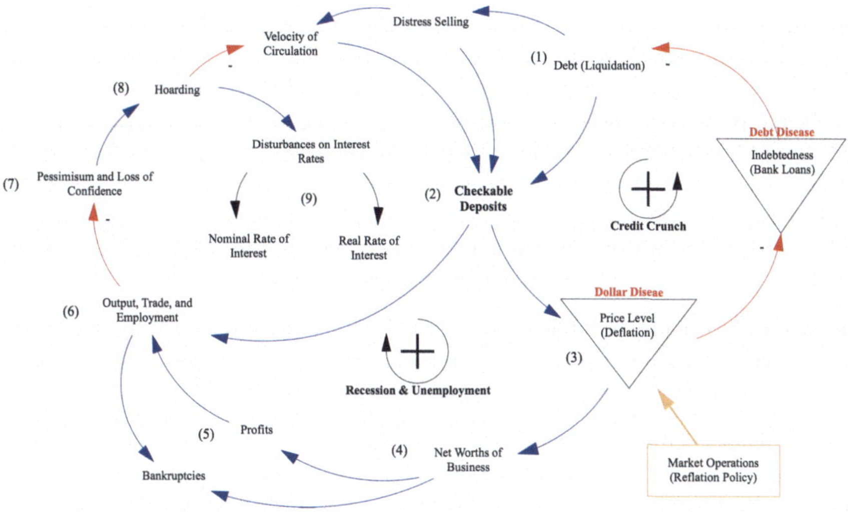

Fig. 8.12 Fisher's debt-deflation theory in causal loop diagram

> *in profits*, which, in a "capitalistic," that is, a private-profit society, leads the concerns which are running at a loss to make (6) *A reduction in output, in trade, and in employment* of labor. These losses, bankruptcies, and unemployment, lead to (7) *Pessimism and loss of confidence*, which in turn lead to (8) *Hoarding and slowing down still more the velocity of circulation*. The above eight changes cause (9) *Complicated disturbances in the rate of interest*, in particular, a fall in the nominal, or money, rates and a rise in the real, or commodity, rates of interest. (p. 342; emphasis original)

Here, Fisher evidently pointed out the contraction of money stock and the fall in nominal or a rise in real interest rates. We can also notice that his line of thought is inherently a causal loop analysis in systems thinking. For example, Fisher uses the term "logical order" as opposed to "chronological order" in the debt-deflation theory. The former is generally called the "causal (loop) analysis" and the latter "behavior over time analysis" in the SD nomenclature.

Figure 8.12 illustrates a causal loop diagram of the debt-deflation theory.[13] Blue arrows indicate that the causal relationship changes in the same direction. Red arrows indicate the opposite. Numbers in parenthesis follow the original sequence in the Fisher's exposition above. The starting point of his analysis is the occurrence of over-indebtedness and insolvency upon the burst of financial bubble. Firms and individuals repay bank loans in order to retain financial health and reduce their debts (1). Demand deposits decrease as a result (2). Distress selling (fire sales) causes business activities to shrink and sales become sluggish. As corporate managers become defensive and backward-looking, their spendings and thus the velocity of money slows down. As a result of declines in investment and consumption, price levels will fall (3). Then, net assets of businesses begin to decrease further (4), and bankruptcies increase. At the

[13] Adapted from Yamaguchi (2015, Fig. 8.1, p. 177) with minor modifications.

same time, profits will decline (5) and corporate losses increase. Production declines in this way (6), which in turn decreases employment. In addition, the recession makes managers pessimistic and reduce confidence in their businesses as losses and bankruptcies become more evident (7). They then cut expenditures and stop spending. Money begins to be hoarded and its velocity of circulation slows down further (8). As a result, recession deepens as prices decline further (3). All of the above turmoils affect interest rates, lowering nominal interest rates as demand for money and bank loans plunge, while raising real interest rates (9). This causal loop is called "Recession and Unemployment" loop in Fig. 8.12.

Recession and Unemployment Loop Price Level → Net Worth of Business (+) → Profits (+) → Output, Trade and Employment (+) → Pessimism and Loss of Confidence (–) → Hoarding (+) → Velocity of Circulation (–) → Checkable Deposits (+) → Price Level (+)

Fisher called this effect (symptom) of excess debts and insolvency the "debt disease", and effects of deflation the "dollar disease". He then analyzed that debt disease results in the contraction of money stock, lower prices, and bring about the dollar disease. Compounding effects of debt and dollar diseases bring about the so-called fallacy of composition; "*the very effort of individuals to lessen their burden of debts increases it, because of the mass effect of the stampede to liquidate in swelling each dollar owed ... the more the debtors pay, the more they owe.*" (Fisher 1933, p. 344; emphasis in original). This feedback loop is referred to as "Credit Crunch" loop and follow the causal path as follows:

Credit Crunch Loop Over-Indebtedness as "Debt Disease" → Debts (–) → Checkable Deposits (+) → Price Level as "Dollar Disease" (+) → Indebtedness (–)

If we focus on the macroeconomic dynamics around the falling prices, the economy is in a deflationary spiral. As is now clear, money and debt (bank loan) always occupy indispensable roles in the Fisher's theory.

(b) Reflation Policy—Fisher's Initial Prescription for the Depression

How do we get out of the Depression, then? In system dynamics, the question becomes: which dominant feedback loops to break? Fisher's answer was straightforward. He came to a conclusion that price level should be stabilized and the economy will be "reflated". Specifically, he considered prices P would naturally rise if the Federal Reserve conducts open market operations and increases the quantity of money M. Using the causal loop diagram in Fig. 8.12, this policy can be thought of as breaking the Credit Crunch loop through monetary policy. On the other hand, Keynes's analysis put more emphasis on the real economic variables such as aggregate demand and employment. Thus, Keynesian policies can be thought of as breaking the Recession and Unemployment loop.

Behind this logic Fisher had the quantity theory of money (Fisher, 1911) in mind, which we presented as Eq. (5.7) in Chap. 5 as follows:

$$M\ v = P\ T \quad \text{(same as Eq. (5.7))}.$$

where T denotes trade or transaction volumes (not to be confused with the notation for Tax Revenues in Eq. (8.5)). Notice how the quantity theory is embedded in the causal analysis of Fig. 8.12. Based on this equation of exchange, Fisher argued that the increase in money M will eventually lead to increases in prices P or transaction volumes T (or income Y), if the money velocity v remains constant (or increases). Specifically, he contended that, as long as the velocity v keeps its pace with T, which had already been observed statistically by Dr. Carl Snyder (a statistician at the Federal Reserve Bank of New York), the price level P can be kept steady along with the steady progress of M in the long-run. This was the *reflation policy* discussed in Chap. 5.

Fisher (1932, Chap. X) believed that this reflation policy would cause prices to rise moderately, and the economy would eventually recover from the dollar disease as illustrated at the bottom right corner of Fig. 8.12. For this reflation policy to be effective, he stated "[w]e need only to assume that an increase in the quantity of the circulating medium has *some* tendency to raise the price level, and *vice versa*" (Fisher, 1932, p. 124; emphasis in original).

Fisher himself seemed very pleased at the time that his theory was highly regarded by experts as "both new and important" (Fisher, 1933, p. 337). As a matter of fact, he was convinced that the reflation policy, while acknowledging that it was not a "panacea", could have escaped the Depression as follows:

> In fact, in my opinion, this [prevention of the Depression] would have been done had governor Strong of the Federal Reserve Bank of New York lived, or had his policies been embraced by other banks and the federal reserve board and pursued consistently after his death. (Fisher, 1933, p. 347)

The reflation policy continued to have influences on economists and became the rationale of asset purchase programs called the Quantitative Easing (QE).

8.5.2 Fisher's Conversion to the 100% Money Theory

In March of 1933, the same year as he published the debt-deflation paper, Fisher received a six-page memorandum that would later be called "The Chicago Plan for Banking Reform" jointly proposed and signed by the eight economists at the University of Chicago.[14] With his debt-deflation theory published in October, Fisher had still full hopes for reflation policy by the Federal Reserve as explained above. In fact, as if to reflect his expectation and confidence in his theory, Fisher (1935)

[14] They were Garfield V. Cox, Aaron Director, Paul H. Douglas, Albert G. Hart, Frank H. Knight, Lloyd W. Mints, Henry Schultz, and Henry C. Simons. This memorandum along with the letter sent to Secretary Henry A. Wallace is reproduced in the Appendix of Phillips (1995). See Sect. 9.5 in Chap. 9 further for historical background of the Chicago Plan.

confessed that he "had not at the time of stating them [conclusions of the Booms and Depressions] given attention to the 100% system" (p. 119).

However, from around 1934, Fisher began to devote himself with the monetary reform envisioned by the Chicago Plan to the extent he abandoned his own reflation theory. Undoubtedly, Fisher must have been in a hurry to publish *100% Money* at the time. Perhaps due to the demanding publication schedule, he simply reproduced the original section in the *Econometrica* article titled "THE ROLES OF DEBT AND DEFLATION" into Chap. 7 of his new book with the section titled "BOOMS and DEPRESSIONS". In doing so, he took the insight he gained after the publication of the debt-deflation theory and slipped the following sentence into his book published two years later in March of 1935:

> It should be noted that practically *all the events listed occur through a contraction of check-book money.* (Fisher, 1935, p. 123; emphasis in original)

"*All the events listed*" are the nine events he listed in the original debt-deflation paper (as illustrated in Fig. 8.12), and "*check-book money*" are demand deposits. In other words, Fisher realized, upon receiving the Chicago plan, that money stock was not an exogenous policy variable. Instead he realized bank loans create deposits under the fractional reserve banking system or "the 10% system" *à la* Fisher (1935) as already discussed in Sect. 3.6 of Chap. 3. This contraction in money stock can also be confirmed in Fig. 8.5.

As a result, money stock is endogenously determined and becomes a function of transactions T. Therefore, the quantity equation presented in Eq. (5.7) is no longer an equation, but must be accurately expressed as identity, as already defined in Eq. (5.13) in Chap. 5, such that:

$$M(T)\,v \equiv P\,T \quad \text{(same as (5.13))}.$$

Expressed in this way, the causal inference that money stock M affects price P and the real economy T is no longer convincing.[15] On the contrary, the relationship between money and economic activities becomes clear. Changes in money stock occur endogenously and M should not be treated as an exogenous policy variable. Thus the reflation policy initially envisioned by Fisher himself is only effective up to the stage where base money (M_0) can be increased by central banks. The asset purchase programs, however, do not increase money stock $M_{1,2,3}$ per se. This means that another premise of the reflation policy, as described in Eq. (5.6) in Chap. 5, will not be guaranteed under the fractional reserve banking system:

$$M_1 = m M_0 \Longrightarrow \text{(if } m \text{ is stable)} \Longrightarrow \hat{M}_1 = \hat{M}_0 \quad \text{(same as (5.6))}$$

15 Fisher proposed the quantity theory as an identity. However it was somehow transformed later into an equation that determines price P and income-related variables by the monetarists. This is also noticeable from Mankiw's explanation of the Friedman's money hypothesis, even though it was originally put forward by Fisher.

where m is the money multiplier. In other words, Fisher realized further that the money multiplier m cannot be assumed to be stable. This means that two major premises of reflation policy, i.e., the stable velocity v and money multiplier m, do not hold simply because m cannot be controlled by the central bank nor by the government under the fractional reserve banking system. This was the reason why he emphasized in italics that all the events in the Great Depression "*occur through a contraction of deposits*".

Upon receiving the Chicago plan, he was convinced that the root cause of the Depression lies in the structure of fractional reserve banking system itself. Under this system, money is created through bank loans, driving speculative investments and financial bubbles. When the bubble bursts, the 8 billion dollars of "check-book money" disappeared during the financial turmoil. He then continued the analysis and concluded as follows:

> Booms and depressions can doubtless, to some extent, be cured and prevented without recourse to the 100% system, but, if my analysis is correct, not so surely, quickly, and easily as under 100% system; for an underlying cause (or precondition) of great booms and depressions is the 10% system itself (Fisher, 1935, p. 120)

In this way Fisher buried his own reflation theory with his own hands and replaced it with 100% money theory that contends the effectiveness of stabilization policy and other socio-economic benefits.[16] Under the 100% reserve system, demand deposits will not disappear from circulation even if debts (bank loans) are repaid. Additionally the money velocity will not be affected. That is, two causal arrows pointing from "Debt Liquidation" towards "Checkable Deposits" in Fig. 8.12 disappear, and the credit crunch loop is eliminated. As a result, there will be no debt disease or dollar disease that caused the Depression. The reflation policy may eliminate the effects of dollar disease as Fisher initially hoped, but it could not eliminate the effects of debt disease. He was theoretically convinced that, even if these illnesses were to occur, they would not cause economic fluctuations to be as severe as the Great Depression under the *100% money system*.

After the WWII and until his death in 1947, Fisher continued to advocate the monetary reform, collaborating with other economists, informing members of the American Economic Association (AEA) where he had served as the past president in 1918, and engaging with members of the Congress to enact a bill that would establish the *100% Money system* in the United States and at international level (Phillips, 1995). However, the Fisher's analysis of the Great Depression was gradually forgotten, due to a systematic distortion and undervaluation of his theory by the economics establishment as if it were a *taboo*, and the endogenous money theory itself disappeared completely from the mainstream economic schools of thoughts and their textbooks. We will discuss briefly how such retrogression occurred in economic science at the end of this chapter.

---

[16] See Fisher (1935, pp. 10–14) for all eight advantages that he claimed his plan would achieve. All of them still apply even today since the basic structure of the debt money system remains the same as was in the 1930s, except the gold standard was abolished in 1971.

8.5.3 Endogenous Money Spending Hypothesis

In Chap. 3 we have shown that the majority of money stock is created by bank loans. That is, money stock exists as interest-bearing debts of non-banking sectors. Accordingly, money stock must be incorporated as an endogenous variable into the IS-LM model under the current *debt money system*. Yet the conventional Keynesian IS-LM model assumes that money stock is exogenously given and controlled by the monetary authority. How can it be revised, then, into a model in which money is endogenously created and destroyed? More specifically, how can we integrate the spending hypothesis by Keynes and money hypothesis by Fisher within the IS-LM framework?

In terms of Fisher's quantity theory, money stock M must be a function of transactions as shown in Eq. (5.13) such that

$$M = M(T) \tag{8.37}$$

Since the IS-LM model analyzes this transaction volume in a narrower sense as those related to income Y, money stock must be a function of income, $M = M(Y)$. Income in turn is determined by effective demand such as consumption, investment and government expenditure within the IS-LM framework. Under the debt money system, debts by private sector and government precede investment and spending, since money stock is only put into circulation when banks grant loans and create deposits. Only when private sector increases investments or the government issues debt securities, the quantity of money in the economy increases. That is, money stock M^s in the *LM* curve must be a function of investment (I) and government debt (D_G) such that

$$M^s = M^s(I, D_G) \tag{8.38}$$

If effective demand is determined by investment and government spending and the *IS* curve is drawn, then, money stock would also change simultaneously. Therefore, *LM* curve also has to be redrawn in conjunction with *IS* curve.

Based on this insight of endogenous debt money, we propose an alternative hypothesis for the causes of the Great Depression; that is, *Endogenous Money Spending Hypothesis*. Specifically, we have assumed that economic recessions under the present debt money system are generally caused by a combination of spending and money hypotheses as follows:

(a) Aggregate demand falls (real sector is assumed to trigger recessions here).
(b) Declines in demand for loans follow (including forced debt repayments and credit crunch).
(c) Money stock contracts as a result, followed by deflation, which increases debt burdens of borrowers and real interest rate. This brings the causality back to (a).

Left diagram of Fig. 8.13 illustrates the above three events as a positive feedback loop of our endogenous money spending hypothesis. It can cover the case of recessions as well as economic booms. One can visualize the case of booms by simply

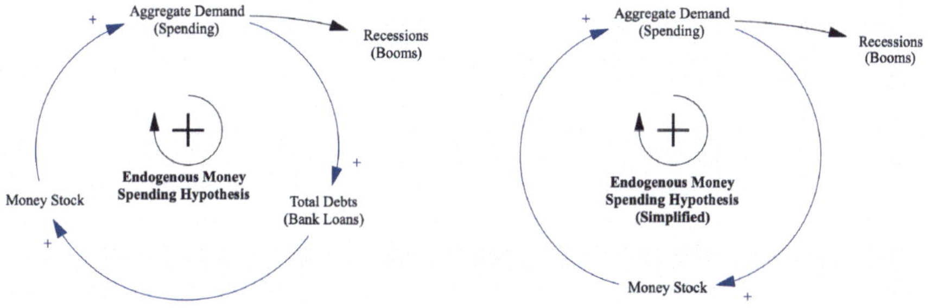

Fig. 8.13 Endogenous money spending hypothesis (positive feedback loop)

reversing the causal direction in events (a), (b) and (c) in the same feedback loop. This causal loop diagram can compactly capture how economic booms and recessions are triggered and intensified under the debt money system. This is our revised model of *Endogenous Money IS-LM* where money and debts play a central role in the overall macroeconomic dynamics.

Note that Fisher's causal analysis stops at the interest rates (9) as illustrated in Fig. 8.12. However, under our endogenous money spending hypothesis applied to the flexible price IS-LM model, the *ex ante* real interest rate affects the level of investment I as described in Eq. (8.27). Accordingly, we can draw another negative causation in Fig. 8.12 by drawing a red arrow from Real Rate of Interest (9) to Output, Trade and Employment (6). As a result, another feedback loop will be closed under the Case 4 model with flexible price and endogenous money assumptions (see Table 8.6 for classification of models).

8.6 SD Model of Endogenous Money IS-LM

To fully incorporate this endogenous money spending hypothesis into the SD model, however, we need to bring the analyses of budget equations and expand the model structure to incorporate lending and borrowing of money among macroeconomic sectors. To avoid such complexity arising from the introduction of budget equations, let us proceed with a simplified version the endogenous money spending hypothesis, which is presented in the right diagram of Fig. 8.13.

8.6.1 Model Equations and SD Model

The flexible price IS-LM model under the endogenous money is hereafter called "Endogenous Money IS-LM Model". It is formally presented as follows:

Same Equations as the Flexible Price IS-LM Model: (8.22)–(8.31), and

$$\frac{dM^s}{dt} = F(\hat{Y}, M^s) \tag{8.39}$$

where $\hat{Y}$ is a growth rate of income. That is, money M^s is endogenously increased or decreased as a function of income growth rate $\hat{Y}$. This is more straightforward approach to incorporate endogenous money without modeling complex inter-sector transactions and their balance sheets (which will be undertaken in Sect. 8.8 onward), and without losing the essential feature of the debt money system.

With the addition of a new Eq. (8.39) to the previous flexible price IS-LM model of 10 equations in Sect. 8.4.2, the endogenous money IS-LM model consists of 11 equations and unknowns, including a new endogenous variable of M^s:

$$Y, AD, C, I, G, Y_d, T, i, r, L^d, M^s$$

with 13 exogenously determined parameters

$$C_0, c, T_0, t, T_r, I_0, \bar{G}, P, V, \alpha, a, b, \pi^e.$$

SD modeling of the above simple endogenous money mechanism is already included in the stock-flow diagram of *LM* sub-model in Fig. 8.3 as a stock variable of "Money Stock (Endogenous)". The model will switch between exogenous and endogenous money mode by turning on/off the "Switch (Money)". In our subsequent simulations we assume that money stock increases or decreases endogenously by 70% of the income growth rate, which is defined by the parameter called "Endogenous Money Fraction". The default value is set to 0.7. By setting this endogenous money fraction = 0, the growth rate of money stock becomes zero and the model will run under the exogenous money mode. Thus, users can test different assumptions on the degree of money endogeneity by changing this ratio. Similarly, as explained in Sect. 8.4.3, by setting the value of price ratio elasticity to 0, the model will run simulations under a fixed price assumption.

Figure 8.14 displays a simulation panel of the endogenous money IS-LM model where users can implement customized scenarios by moving sliders. On the left hand side of the figure are sliders for changing parameters related to the *IS* sub-model. Sliders for changing parameters related to the *LM* sub-model are located on the right hand side. In this way, by setting the price ratio elasticity, endogenous money fraction and other variables available in the model to different values and combinations, simulation analysis can be performed under various assumptions within a single model, such as the Keynesian short-run IS-LM model (Case 1), flexible price IS-LM model (Case 2), Endogenous Money IS-LM under the fixed price (Case 3) and flexible price (case 4) assumptions. This is the versatility of SD modeling that can accommodate and test theoretical controversies among different schools of thoughts in a integrative manner.

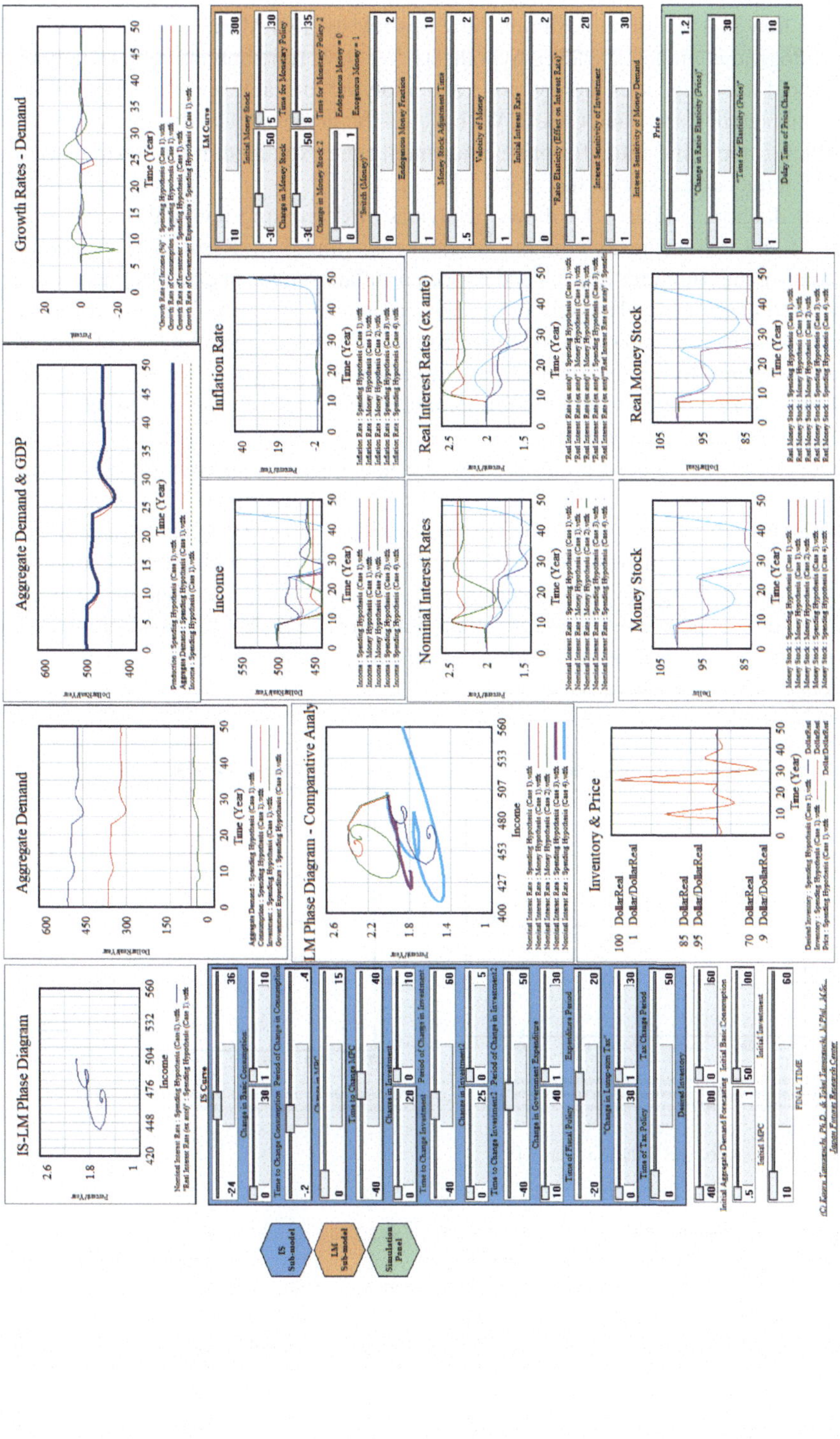

Fig. 8.14 Simulation panel view of the SD model of endogenous money IS-LM

8.6.2 *Endogenous Money Analysis of the Great Depression*

We are now in a position to examine how this revised IS-LM model behaves under the endogenous money spending hypothesis. We have run simulation by switching the model to endogenous money mode and applying the same spending hypothesis implemented in Case 1 and Case 2. We have set the money stock adjustment time to 4, which is the same value for price adjustment time explained in the flexible price IS-LM model discussed in Sect. 8.4.3.

Left diagram of Fig. 8.15 shows behaviors of decreasing nominal interest rate (line 1) and increasing *ex post* real interest rate (line 3).[17] Right diagram shows decreasing inflation rate (line 1) and expected inflation rate (line 2). As we can see on the left diagram, the behavior of *ex ante* real interest rate (line 2) shows complex effect of the Depression on the real interest rate. Though its magnitude of change is small compared to nominal and *ex post* interest rates, we can observe that *ex ante* real interest rate declines along with nominal interest rate during the initial phase and then moves slightly upward.

Our simulation indeed confirms how the real interest rate rises or falls when the price is assumed to be flexible, exactly as Fisher described "(9) *Complicated disturbances in the rate of interest*" (Fisher, 1933, p. 342). Since the impact of the Depression on real interest rates varies depending on the combination of nominal interest rate and expected inflation rate, it is not possible to determine their causal relationship. This is why our causal loop diagram in Fig. 8.12 uses black arrows to indicate both causalities to interest rates, instead of blue or red arrow indicating either positive or negative causation.

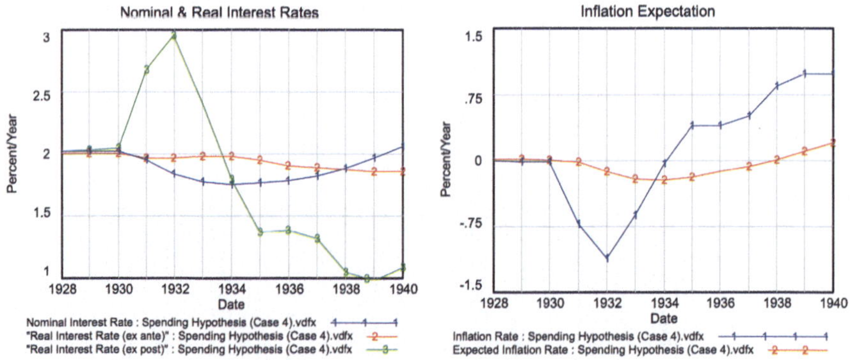

Fig. 8.15 Interests and inflation (Case 4)

[17] Although graph legend shown below the diagrams only says "Spending Hypothesis (Case 4)", note that "Case 4" in the caption indicates this simulation is run under the flexible price and endogenous money assumptions. Therefore, the spending hypothesis applied in Cases 1 and 2 now becomes the endogenous money spending hypothesis under Case 4 simulation.

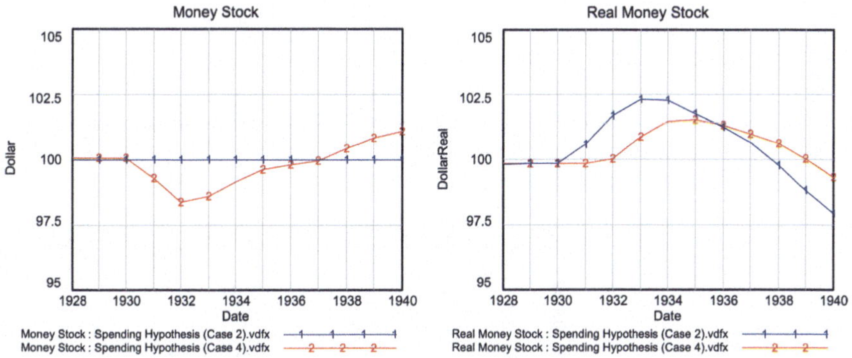

Fig. 8.16 Money stock and real money stock (Cases 2 and 4)

Figure 8.16 compares behaviors of money stock (left) and real money stock (right) under the spending hypothesis in Case 2 (line 1 in blue) and the endogenous money spending hypothesis in Case 4 (line 2 in red). Our simulation results shows that the endogenous money spending hypothesis (Case 4), which was the Fisher's original analysis on the causes of the Depression, can successfully capture the behaviors of nominal and real interest rates already explained under the spending hypothesis in Case 2 model, as well as the contraction of money stock, which was unexplained in the previous Case 2 model. Accordingly, the rise in real money balance is now explained for the right reason.[18] In conclusion, the endogenous money IS-LM model can successfully explain the behaviors of the Great Depression as depicted in Fig. 8.5 under the endogenous money spending hypothesis (Case 4).

8.6.3 Evaluation of the Depression Hypotheses

Figure 8.17 summarizes our qualitative evaluations of the spending, money, and endogenous money spending hypothesis applied to the case of the Great Depression. Directions of arrows indicate implied directions of the change in each macroeconomic variable. Arrows pointing upward or downward imply increases or decreases in those variables. Similarly, arrows pointing rightward imply no change or 'fixed'. Arrows are blue if the simulations explain the data, and black if they do not. For example, a blue arrow pointing upward indicates that the simulation under a certain hypothesis is consistent with the increase in the same variable observed during the initial phase of the Great Depression.

[18] As explained already, the current model is not calibrated against the reference data. Consequently, the initial rise in real money balance observed in data is not replicated precisely.

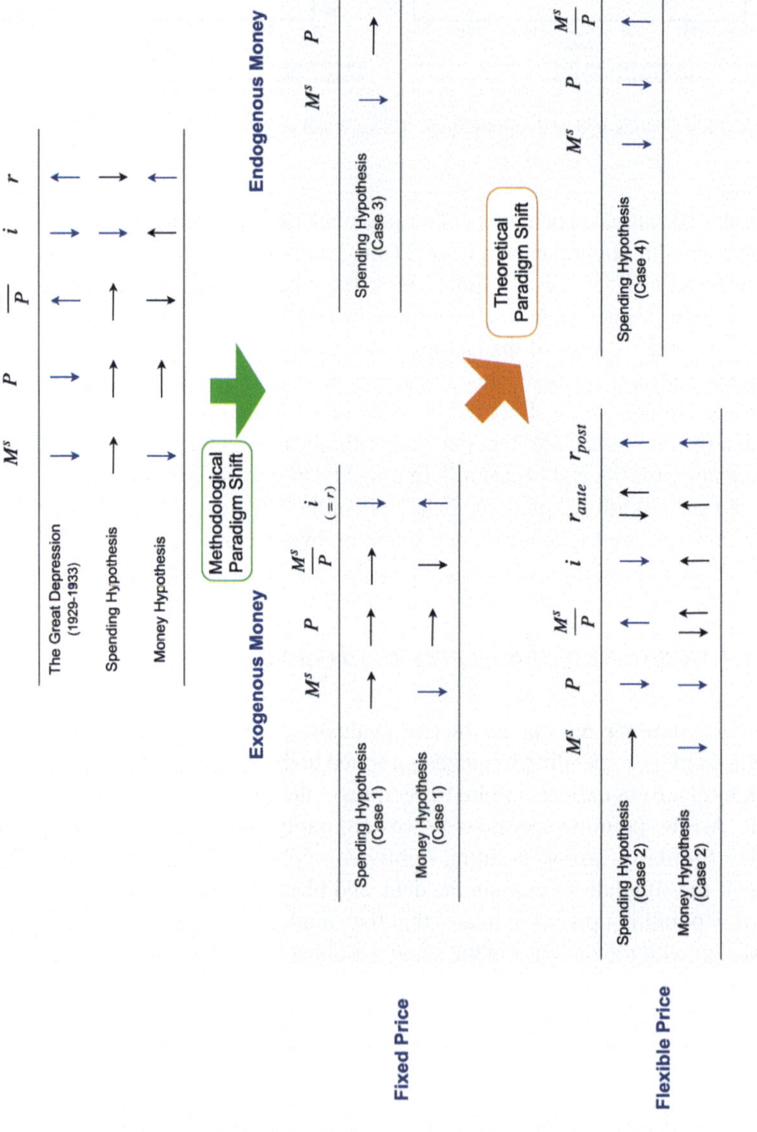

Fig. 8.17 Evaluations of depression hypotheses and paradigm shift by endogenous money spending hypotheses

Depression Hypotheses under the Conventional IS-LM Analysis

Let's start with the table at the top of the figure. Arrows in the second row show the directions of changes observed from the data during 1929–1933. Arrows in the third row are obtained by applying the spending hypothesis to the conventional (comparative static) IS-LM model, and those in the fourth row are similarly obtained under the money hypothesis. As discussed in Sect. 8.3.2, Mankiw pointed out that money hypothesis cannot explain the rise in real money balances $\frac{M^s}{P}$ ("the first problem") and decline in nominal interest rate i ("the second problem") observed in the data. He then argued that these problems are "sufficient to reject" the money hypothesis.

However, we discussed that the spending hypothesis does not explain the contraction of money in the first place. We further pointed out that, when i and P declined during the Great Depression, the real interest rate r must have risen, which is what money hypothesis correctly implies. Accordingly, we may similarly counter-argue that money hypothesis performs better than spending hypothesis when it comes to explaining the behavior of (*ex post*) real interest rate, though its data is absent in the original Table 12-1 in Mankiw (2016). The fundamental problem here is that as long as price level P is fixed, there can be no theoretical distinction between nominal and real interest rates, or between *ex ante* and *ex post* real interest rates. This means that we cannot evaluate the behavior of interest rate by applying the Keynesian IS-LM model against the real world data. Accordingly, we cannot test nor reject either one of hypotheses.

Hypotheses Evaluation Under the Case 1 Through Case 4 Models

Methodological limitation of the traditional comparative static IS-LM analysis has now become clear, which has led us to the introduction of system dynamics method to convert it into dynamic simulation model. What follows are our qualitative evaluations obtained from the behaviors of SD models.

Case 1 SD model (fixed price, exogenous money) discussed in Sect. 8.3.2 corresponds to the Keynesian short-run IS-LM analysis in standard textbooks. It can be alternatively interpreted as what Mankiw's extended IS-LM model has actually analyzed because his model only introduced the expected inflation rate, but not the flexible price itself. Spending hypothesis applied under Case 1 model only captures the reduction in nominal interest rate i. Since M^s and P are assumed to be fixed, real money balance $\frac{M^s}{P}$ is also fixed. Hence, we concluded that the spending hypothesis should be rejected. On the other hand, money hypothesis in Case 1 accounts for the contraction of M^s, but not for the decline in i. As discussed already, Mankiw interpreted the interest rate in the standard IS-LM model as the nominal interest rate i and compares it with data to falsely reject the money hypothesis. Since P is fixed and $\frac{M^s}{P}$ drops against the data, we claim that money hypothesis should also be rejected here.

Case 2 SD model (flexible price, exogenous money) is the model discussed in Sect. 8.4.4. Spending hypothesis in Case 2 captures what Mankiw called the destabilizing effects of deflation on income, the fall in nominal interest rate i as well as the sudden rise in *ex post* real interest rate in the data. Case 2 analysis is what the extended analysis discussed in Mankiw (2016) has attempted to show but without a working model. Our simulation results corroborate Mankiw's claim. However, the problem of spending hypothesis in Case 2 model is that it still treats M^s as an exogenous policy variable, thus failing to explain its contraction during the Depression. This meant that behavior of real money balance is not explained under the spending hypothesis for the right reason.

For the behavior of *ex ante* real interest rate, our simulation suggests that it rises relative to nominal interest rate and then fluctuate, as it is affected by multiple factors including inflation and the change in nominal interest rate, which in turn is affected by various factors even in our simple model. From these reasons we claim that the spending hypothesis should be rejected in Case 2.[19]

Money hypothesis in Case 2, on the other hand, captures the money contraction, deflation, and rise in real money balance for the right reason. Furthermore, the rise in *ex post* real interest rate is consistent with the data. However, the nominal interest rate i rises, which is not consistent with the Great Depression data. Accordingly, we claim that the money hypothesis in Case 2 should be rejected as well.

Case 3 SD model (fixed price, endogenous money spending) captures the endogenous contraction of M^s. However, the decrease in real money balance $\frac{M^s}{P}$ accompanying the decline in aggregate expenditure contradicts with the data. Accordingly, we claim that the endogenous money spending hypothesis under the fixed price assumption should also be rejected. As a reminder, this contradicted behavior under the spending hypothesis in Case 3 is not mentioned at all in Mankiw's analysis. Recall that the decrease in real money balance under the money hypothesis was the main reason why Mankiw rejected it in the standard Keynesian IS-LM analysis (Case 1 model). As for the behavior of interest rates, we cannot fully evaluate it for the same reason as discussed in Case 1. That is, there is no theoretical distinction between nominal and real interest rates under the fixed price assumption.

Case 4 SD model (flexible price, endogenous money spending) discussed in Sect. 8.6.2 captures the data already explained under Case 2 model as well as the endogenous contraction of money stock M^s, which was unexplained in Case 2. Accordingly, the rise in real money balance is explained for the right reason under the endogenous money spending hypothesis applied under the flexible price assumption. As a result, all arrows are in blue, indicating that direction of changes in variables are consistent with data. Hence, we claim that the endogenous money spending hypothesis under flexible price can not be rejected.

---

[19] Note that the *ex ante* real interest rate is indicated in black arrows because we have no data to compare against in Fig. 8.5. The same applies for the evaluation of Case 4.

Methodological and Theoretical Paradigm Shifts

Figure 8.17 also illustrates how the behaviors of the Great Depression that were unexplained by the conventional Keynesian IS-LM analysis as well as the flexible price IS-LM model can now be explained by our SD model of the endogenous money IS-LM. A wide green arrow represents a *methodological* paradigm shift from comparative statics to disequilibrium analysis based on system dynamics simulation method. A wide orange arrow represents a *theoretical* paradigm shift from exogenous money to endogenous money theory.

8.7 Paradigm Shift of the IS-LM Model

The endogenous money spending hypothesis is shown to be able to explain the causes of the Great Depression. In this section let us explore this hypothesis further to see if it can explain other types of recession such as the on-going case of Japan's lost 30 years.

8.7.1 The Depression Hypotheses and Recessions

Figure 8.18 compares simulations under the three hypotheses on the phase diagram of nominal interest rate (vertical axis) and income (horizontal axis) as a more general case of economic recessions. Behaviors of spending hypothesis (points B and C) and money hypothesis (point D) under the exogenous money are the same as those shown in Fig. 8.4. On the other hand, behaviors around points B' and C' under the endogenous money spending hypothesis are newly added in order to illustrate the difference between exogenous and endogenous money. Specifically, the rise in nominal interest rate at point D, which Mankiw attributed as the second problem of the money hypothesis, does not occur under the endogenous money spending hypothesis. Yet, these points no longer move along the *LM* curve in contrast to the spending hypothesis applied under the exogenous money assumption (Case 1) discussed in Sect. 8.2.3. Consequently, the endogenous money spending hypothesis can be said to be a better prospect for the analysis of recessions in general. Not only that, it also provides a unified view of Fisher's and Keynes's analyses on the causes of the Great Depression.

8.7.2 Joint Shifts of IS-LM Curves Under Endogenous Money

Following our discussion in Sect. 8.6.3, the endogenous money IS-LM model further provides us with another insight about the joint shifts of IS-LM curves. As Fig. 8.19 illustrates, point C' attained under the endogenous money spending hypoth-

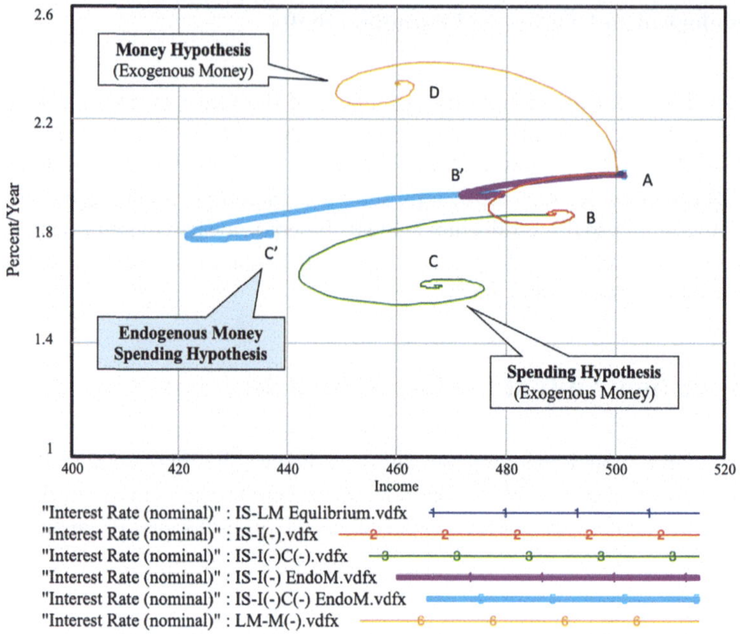

Fig. 8.18 Joint shifts of IS-LM curves under endogenous money spending hypothesis

esis is the combination of independent shifts in both *IS* and *LM* curves, which have been applied separately under the exogenous money assumption. Line 6 (orange) in Fig. 8.19 illustrates how the point C' can be attained as a combination of independent shifts in the *IS* curve caused by the spending hypothesis (point A → B by $\Delta I = -20$ at t = 8; and point B → C by $\Delta C = -20$ at t = 24) first, and then in the *LM* curve caused by the money hypothesis (point C → C' by $\Delta M = -14$ at t = 8). Moreover, the point C' can be attained irrespective of the order of shocks among ΔI, ΔC and ΔM. Yet the exogenous and endogenous money models show different paths to point C'.

The important point here is that the endogenous money spending hypothesis is not the same as moving both curves simultaneously using the conventional IS-LM analysis simply because the two models with different assumption on money endogeneity will eventually settle at the same equilibrium point. In the real economy, a state of imbalance is followed by a shock that causes a transition to the next state of imbalance. In other words, it is important to analyze the complex behavior caused by the interaction of various economic variables, which are constantly changing over time. As Fisher stressed, "[It] is as absurd to assume that, for any long period of time, the variables in the economic organization, or any part of them, will "stay put," in perfect equilibrium, as to assume that the Atlantic Ocean can ever be without a wave" (Fisher, 1933, p. 339).

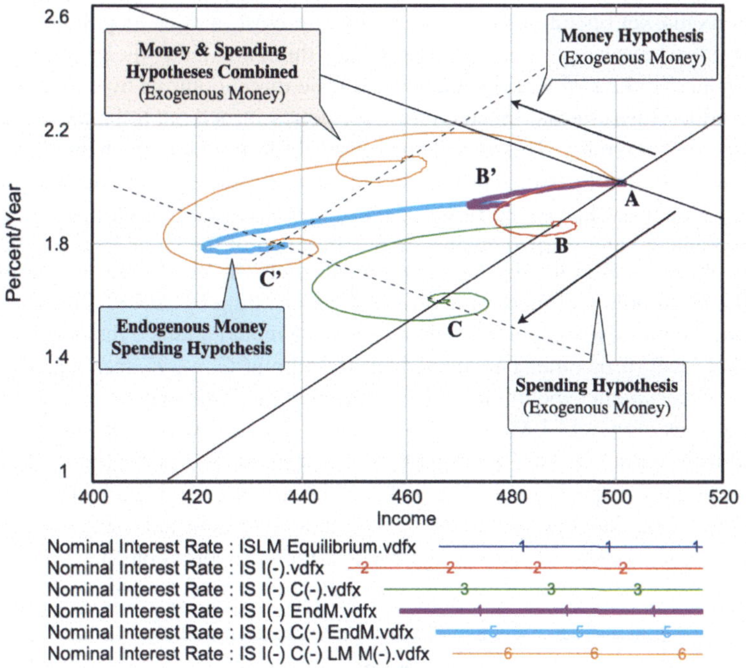

Fig. 8.19 Analysis of joint shifts of IS-LM curves under endogenous money spending hypothesis

This implies that the traditional comparative static analysis of shifting either *IS* or *LM* curve separately and observing its impact on the economy, as we have been thoroughly taught in macroeconomic textbooks, is no longer applicable to the analysis of recessions under the current debt money system. For the analysis of recessions, both *IS* and *LM* curves must be jointly shifted all the time. Economists must now abandon the traditional IS-LM analysis from their textbooks and undergraduate courses or incorporate dynamic analysis along the endogenous money IS-LM model presented here. This is the paradigm shift in macroeconomics we have discussed in Chap. 7. This chapter formally presented its mathematical analysis.

8.7.3 Japan's Lost 30 Years as Unpredictable IS-LM Shifts

Monetary policy explained in the Keynesian exogenous money IS-LM model, which is to directly control money stock M^s as discussed in Sect. 8.2.3, is no longer available in the endogenous money IS-LM model, simply because the central bank cannot control a variable that is ultimately determined by commercial banks' lending behavior. Furthermore, it cannot control real interest rate either, because money stock and price are not under its direct t control. Central bank can only change base money M_0

through its market operations to guide nominal interest rates as its policy target. In this sense, we have been indoctrinated to falsely think that either the governments or central banks in the real world somehow exercise direct controls over money stock as their policy instruments. Indeed, monetary policy turned out to be far less effective in the real economy. This is why the series of QE policy implemented in Japan turned out to be ineffective. As discussed in Sect. 8.5.1, they were destined to fail at its theoretical level as Irving Fisher, the original advocate of reflation policy, had already predicted and warned against in the aftermath of the Great Depression.

How about fiscal policy by the government, then? In Fig. 8.20 we have implemented a fiscal policy of increasing government spending by $\Delta G = 40$ at $t = 35$ to get out of the recession at point C'. As a result, the model attained the point F' with the higher level of income. This movement from point $C' \rightarrow F'$ seems predictable since the government expenditure G is increased in the same manner as was done in the exogenous money IS-LM model. In the latter case, a new equilibrium point was attained from point C toward F (point C → F) along the LM curve (dotted line).

Driven by this expectation on the power of fiscal policy stylized by the standard IS-LM model, the Japanese government has increased its debt and spent a total of 595 trillion yen over the last 30 years to avoid a post-bubble depression and stimulate the

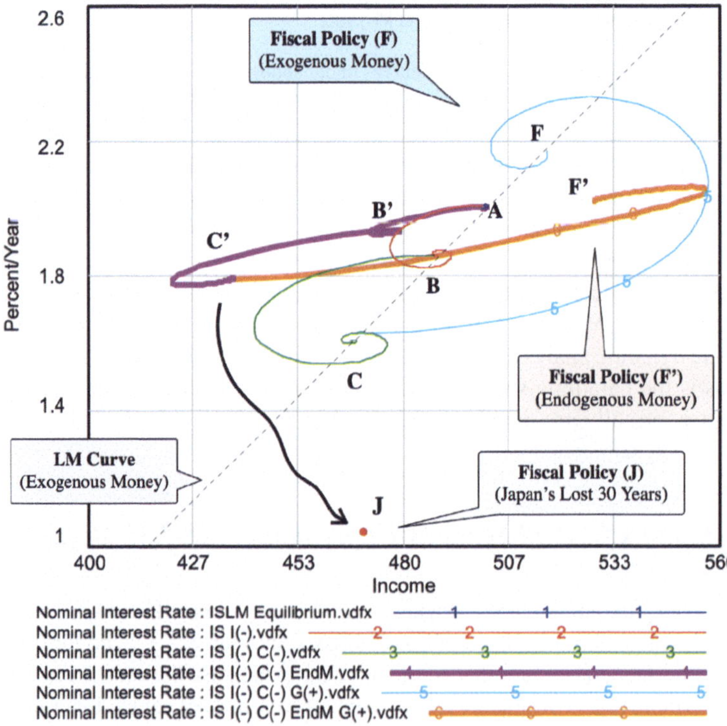

Fig. 8.20 Fiscal policy under the endogenous money IS-LM model & illustration of Japan's lost 30 years as point J

economy; that is, its cumulative amount of government debt became larger than its annual GDP. On average, it implemented roughly 20 trillion yen of deficit spending per yer. Yet, her GDP only increased by a total of about 60 trillion yen during the same period, that is, an average increase of 2 trillion yen per year. This expansionary fiscal expenditure of 20 trillion yen only ended with an increase in GDP by 2 trillion yen per year.

This poor performance is in stark contrast with the textbook explanation of fiscal multiplier effect implied by the Keynesian theory. By substituting the parameter values ($c = 0.76, t = 0.1, \alpha = 8, a = 0.3, b = 25$)[20] into the simple IS-LM equilibrium in Eq. (8.13), the fiscal multiplier is obtained as follows:

$$\frac{\Delta Y}{\Delta G} = \frac{1}{1 - c(1-t) + \alpha(a/b)} = 2.427 \tag{8.40}$$

If we use this multiplier for the calculation purpose only, then Japan's nominal GDP should have increased by 48.5 trillion yen ($= 2.427 \times 20$) every year instead of the 2 trillion yen that was actually realized. The Japanese policy makers seemed to have been mislead by this illusion of fiscal multiplier taught by the standard textbooks.[21] They might have expected that the economy would move, say, from the point C to point F in Fig. 8.20. This is another example of the flawed interpretation and application of comparative static analysis.

The Keynesian IS-LM analysis gives an impression that one-time government spending brings the economy into a new equilibrium with higher level of income. However, if we examine the effects of fiscal policy in a dynamic model, we could easily learn that such is not the case.[22] Hence, the correct interpretation and application of fiscal multiplier should be that the government needs to continue spending by either raising taxes or borrowing money by issuing treasury bonds all the way until a new (comparative static) equilibrium is attained and sustained at such points.

Based on the empirical data, the actual effect of fiscal policy in Japan must be shown in Fig. 8.20 to have moved its equilibrium point from point C' to, say, a point J, which is manually drawn. (Its real scales of income and interest rate are neglected here). This was how fiscal policy failed to stimulate the economy contrary to what the Keynesian IS-LM analysis would have predicted. However, so long as we apply fiscal policy under the revised endogenous money IS-LM model, we are still led to expect that the economy will move toward the upper right direction such as the point F'. In other words, there is no way to end up with the point J as long as government expenditure is increased even in the revised IS-LM model. Accordingly, the point J such as observed in the Japanese case becomes entirely unpredictable even under the revised model. This seems to be the limitation of our SD model developed so far

---

20 These are the same values used in all simulations presented throughout this chapter.

21 In Japan this type of calculation exercise using the IS-LM analysis has been one of compulsory subjects in the recruitment test for government officials.

22 See Chap. 9 of Yamaguchi (2013) further for simulation analyses.

based on the IS-LM framework. Can we still analyze the point J with the endogenous money spending hypothesis, then? We'll challenge this issue in the next section.

8.8 Loanable Funds Model with Budgets

All SD models of IS-LM presented so far lack the analysis of budget equations; the borrowing and lending of money and debts. As a result, the endogenous money spending hypothesis has to be incorporated in a mechanistic way such that money stock changes along with the growth rate of income as in Eq. (8.39). Consequently, the endogenous money IS-LM model is shown to have limitations; it failed to present endogenous money creation by the government spending and the case of Japan's lost 30 years as a point J in Fig. 8.20.

With these analytical limitations in mind, we now start with the construction of a complete IS-LM model with budget equations of macroeconomic sectors. Yet, in this section, we hold the mainstream Keynesian assumption again that money is *exogenously* given, and that banks merely play a role as pure financial intermediaries of existing funds between savers and borrowers. Let us call this model *Loanable Funds Model* and examine its working analytically in this section first. Then, we will construct the *Endogenous Money Model* in the next Sect. 8.9. After we discuss the paradigm shift by endogenous money model, we will translate them into simulation models based on Accounting System Dynamics (ASD) method in Sect. 8.10 and compare their behaviors in Sect. 8.11.

8.8.1 Model Equations

To overcome such analytical limitations, we must consider budget equations in the following flexible price IS-LM model, which was presented in Sect. 8.4.2.

Flexible Price IS-LM Model: Same as Eqs. (8.22)–(8.31)

$$Y = AD \quad \text{(Aggregate Demand Equilibrium)} \tag{8.41}$$

$$AD = C + I + G \quad \text{(Aggregate Demand)} \tag{8.42}$$

$$C = C_0 + cY_d \quad \text{(Consumption Decisions)} \tag{8.43}$$

$$Y_d = Y - T \quad \text{(Disposable Income)} \tag{8.44}$$

$$T = T_0 + tY - T_r \quad \text{(Tax Revenues)} \tag{8.45}$$

$$I = \frac{I_0}{r} - \alpha r \quad \text{(Investment Decisions)} \tag{8.46}$$

$$G = \bar{G} \quad \text{(Government Expenditures)} \tag{8.47}$$

$$\frac{M^s}{P}V = L^d \quad \text{(Equilibrium of Money)} \tag{8.48}$$

$$L^d = aY - bi \quad \text{(Demand for Money)} \tag{8.49}$$

$$r = i - \pi^e \quad \text{(Fisher Equation)} \tag{8.50}$$

Budget Equation of Households

Let us begin with the budget equation of households. Their income consists of incomes at factor cost such as wages and dividends $(W + \Pi)$ paid by producers, in nominal unit, and borrowings from banks (ΔD_H) for housing investments. With these income revenues, households spend on consumption, pay taxes to the government, and purchase houses (I_H). The remaining income after these expenditures are saved with banks as savings (S). Hence, their budget equation becomes as follows:

$$PC + PT + PI_H + S = W + \Pi + \Delta D_H \quad \text{(Households Budget)} \tag{8.51}$$

$$W + \Pi = PY \quad \text{(Distributed Income)} \tag{8.52}$$

$$PI_H = \Delta D_H \quad \text{(Housing Budgets)} \tag{8.53}$$

$$I_H = \bar{I}_H \quad \text{(Housing Investment)} \tag{8.54}$$

where housing investment is assumed to be made by the given amount of $\bar{I}_H$ for simplicity, and paid with the borrowings from banks.

Budget Equation of Producers

Producers' revenue comes from the sales of output from production (Y), which is assumed to be fully distributed among workers as wages (W) and their owners (shareholders) as dividends (Π). In other words, producers retain no profits. Accordingly they are obliged to raise funds to make new investment (I_P). For simplicity we assume that they borrow all funds required for their investment from bank loans (ΔD_P). Hence, their budget equation becomes as follows:

$$W + \Pi + PI_P = PY + \Delta D_P \quad \text{(Producers Budget)} \tag{8.55}$$

$$I_H + I_P = I \quad \text{(Total Private Investment)} \tag{8.56}$$

where total private investment in the economy (I) consists of housing investment (I_H) and corporate investment made by producers (I_P).

Budget Equation of the Government

Government's revenues consist of taxes (T) and borrowings by issuing bonds (ΔD_G) in case government expenditures (G) exceeds tax revenues. For simplicity, we assume that government borrows directly from banks, instead of issuing and selling bonds to the banks. Hence, the budget equation of the government becomes as follows:

$$PG = PT + \Delta D_G \qquad \text{(Government Budget)} \qquad (8.57)$$

Budget Equation of Banks

The *exogenous money theory* posits that it is the monetary authority (central bank) that issues currency, and bank are just financial intermediaries who accept deposits in cash and lend a portion of those savings to borrowers. Therefore, banks accept savings from households and make loans out of those savings (time deposits) received from households (called loanable funds ΔLF). That is to say, savings are considered as the source of loanable funds for banks to extend loans. Hence, the budget equation of banks becomes as follows:

$$\Delta LF = S \qquad \text{(Banks Budget : Loanable Funds)} \qquad (8.58)$$

Loanable Funds Model with Budgets

The construction of the flexible price IS-LM model with budget equations is now complete. Let us call this model of financial intermediaries *Loanable Funds Model with Budgets*, or simply Loanable Funds (LF) model. In addition to the flexible price IS-LM model consisting of 10 Eqs. (8.41) through (8.50), 8 Eqs. (8.51) through (8.58) have been added. Accordingly, 8 additional unknown variables corresponding to these 8 equations are identified as follows:

$$S, I_H, W + \Pi, I_P, \Delta D_H, \Delta D_P, \Delta D_G, \Delta LF^{23}$$

with one additional exogenous parameter: $\bar{I}_H$

More comprehensively, Keynesian loanable funds ASD model consists of 18 equations in total; (8.41) through (8.58) with 18 unknown variables, and 15 parameters (consisting of the previous 14 parameters and the additional parameter $\bar{I}_H$). Money stock M^s is assumed to be exogenously determined and price level is fixed

[23] Income at factor cost such as wages and dividends ($W + \Pi$) is to be determined by producers' output (PY) and treated as an unknown variable.

by default.[24] Hence, the loanable funds model with budget equations does not change the core analytical framework of the flexible price IS-LM model presented in Sect. 8.4.2.

8.8.2 Equilibrium Analysis

To analyze the workings of this LF model, let's obtain the so-called Walras Law, which is calculated from the budget equations (8.51) through (8.58) as follows:

$$P(C+I+G-Y)+\Delta LF-(\Delta D_H+\Delta D_P+\Delta D_G)\equiv 0 \quad \text{(Walras Law)} \tag{8.59}$$

This Walras law holds true under any situations, and that is why it is presented as identity (≡). Since the Keynesian aggregate demand equilibrium of real economic sector is assumed as the Eq. (8.41), the equilibrium of the following *loanable funds* is simultaneously attained:

$$\Delta D_H+\Delta D_P+\Delta D_G=\Delta LF \qquad \text{(Loanable Funds Equilibrium)} \tag{8.60}$$

This indicates that banks must make loans to households, producers and the government out of their loanable funds deposited or 'saved' by the households. Since the total quantity of money M^s is given by the central bank as an exogenous parameter under the LF model, banks' lending behavior is always constrained by the available amount of loanable funds. In other words, there is no extra room for deposit creation under this loanable funds model. This has been the doctrine of exogenous money that has dominated the Keynesian economics for over 80 years (see Chap. 9 further for classification of monetary theories).

From the above Walras law, if the equilibrium of the loanable funds (8.60) is assumed first, the aggregate demand equilibrium in Eq. (8.41) is also simultaneously attained. Which assumption of the equilibrium should be made as the appropriate model of loanable funds theory, then? Aggregate demand equilibrium? Or loanable funds equilibrium?

Since households, producers and the government cannot start their economic activities without sufficient funds at hand, their borrowings must come first. This means that the equation of the loanable funds by banks (8.60) must be met first. Then, the aggregate demand equilibrium is simultaneously attained to be equal to GDP. In this way, from a macroeconomic point of view, it would be more appropriate to assume the loanable funds equilibrium in the LF model first such that

$$(\Delta D_H+\Delta D_P+\Delta D_G=\Delta LF)\Longrightarrow(C+I+G=Y) \tag{8.61}$$

[24] Note that price can be similarly made flexible in the simulation model as we have already described in Eq. (8.33) in the flexible price IS-LM model.

Hence, the loanable funds model must be formally presented by replacing the aggregate demand equilibrium (8.41) in the Keynesian IS-LM model with the loanable funds equilibrium (8.60). That is, the loanable funds IS-LM model now consists of 18 equations, from (8.42) through (8.50), (8.51) through (8.58) and (8.60), with the same 18 unknowns and 15 parameters.

Savings in the loanable funds model are fully utilized as follows:

$$S \Rightarrow \Delta LF \Rightarrow PI_H + PI_P + \Delta D_G = PI + \Delta D_G \tag{8.62}$$

That is, savings made by households become the sources of investment by households and producers, and government debts, with banks acting as intermediaries.

8.8.3 *Model Anatomy with* Ex Ante *and* Ex Post *Incomes*

At its analytical framework, the loanable funds model developed here is the same as the Keynesian IS-LM model presented in Sect. 8.1. We have already shown that the Keynesian IS-LM model, even under the flexible price assumption (which is called the Flexible Price IS-LM model in Table 8.6) failed to explain economic behaviors such as the Great Depression and Japan's lost 30 years, and discussed the reason why. The Keynesian IS-LM analysis incorrectly assumed the exogenous money under the current debt money system. Can we similarly argue that the loanable funds model is flawed, then?

To answer this question, let us examine the validity of the model by introducing the concepts of *ex ante* and *ex post* discussed by Keen (2014). The term *ex ante* is used here as a previous period in which income is distributed as wages and profits such as last month, last quarter or last year, while *ex post* is used as its next period such as this month, this quarter or this year.[25] In order to integrate the endogenous money into macroeconomic theory consistently with the Keynes' principle of effective demand, Keen (2014) discussed that it "requires replacing the accounting truism that *ex post* expenditure equals *ex post* income with the endogenous money insight that *ex post* expenditure equals *ex ante* income plus the *ex post* turnover of new debt." However, the loanable funds model based on exogenous money assumption leads us to the opposite result; that is, *ex ante* income determines *ex post* aggregate demand.

To examine this logic, let us now interpret aggregate demand $AD = I + C + G$ as *ex post* demand, and income Y as *ex ante* income $\underline{\mathrm{Y}}$ in the model. This makes sense because *ex ante* income realized by producers is assumed to be distributed as wages and profits. For the economy to grow, then, we need to assume that

$$C + I + G > \underline{\mathrm{Y}} \qquad (Ex\ post\ AD\ >\ Ex\ ante\ \underline{\mathrm{Y}}) \tag{8.63}$$

[25] To avoid confusion, it should be noted that the terms *ex ante* and *ex post* here are used in a different way as we did in the previous sections (Cases 1–4) to distinguish the *ex ante* and *ex post* real interest rates.

From the Walras law in Eq. (8.59), we have

$$C + I + G > \underline{\mathrm{Y}} \iff \Delta\underline{\mathrm{LF}} < \Delta D_H + \Delta D_P + \Delta D_G \tag{8.64}$$

where $\Delta\underline{\mathrm{LF}}$ implies *ex ante* loanable funds saved by households with banks (as time deposits). This is because loanable funds of banks are constrained by the *ex ante* savings from their own budget constraint (8.58). Hence, *ex ante* loanable funds equilibrium (8.60) must always be applied under the exogenous debt money. Accordingly, from the Walras law, we must have

$$C + I + G = \underline{\mathrm{Y}} \qquad (Ex\ post\ AD = Ex\ ante\ \underline{\mathrm{Y}}). \tag{8.65}$$

In this way, under the loanable funds model, *ex post* aggregate demand (or income) is always determined or constrained by the *ex ante* income.

In order for the *ex post* aggregate demand to determine the *ex post* income Y, as the Keynesian theory asserts under the exogenous debt money, the additional amount of money ΔM^E must be put into circulation *exogenously* such that

$$\Delta M^E = \Delta D_H + \Delta D_P + \Delta D_G - \Delta\underline{\mathrm{LF}} \tag{8.66}$$

Then, in order for the Walras law to hold, we must have

$$C + I + G = \underline{\mathrm{Y}} + \Delta M^E \iff \Delta\underline{\mathrm{LF}} + \Delta M^E = \Delta D_H + \Delta D_P + \Delta D_G \tag{8.67}$$

Keen (2014, p. 284) attained a similar assertion such that "*ex post* expenditure equal *ex ante* income, plus the velocity of money multiplied by the *ex post* change in debt", which is equal to ΔM^E defined in Eq. (8.66) above.

In order to claim that *ex post* aggregate demand determines *ex post* income, therefore, the loanable funds model must have a built-in mechanism to put ΔM^E into circulation automatically (unless accompanied by a corresponding increases in the velocity of money). Only under such circumstance, we have:

$$C + I + G\ (= ex\ post\ \mathrm{AD}) \Longrightarrow \underline{\mathrm{Y}} + \Delta M^E = Y\ (= ex\ post\ \mathrm{Income}) \tag{8.68}$$

Yet the loanable funds model lacks this mechanism of additional money injection, or endogenous destruction of money stock (deposits). This is why the flexible price IS-LM model failed to explain the Great Depression. That is, the flawed assumption of exogenous money discussed in Sect. 8.6.2 is the same as that of the loanable funds discussed here. This failure can only be fixed when the flawed assumption of loanable funds model is replaced with the endogenous debt money. We will now address this in the next section.

Remarks: The loanable funds model itself is not flawed under certain conditions. For instance, under the 100% reserve banking system money stock is exogenously adjusted by the monetary authority. Hence, the balance between *ex post* and *ex ante* incomes are constantly adjusted through public money policy to sustain a stable economic growth under price stability.[26] Accordingly, aggregate demand can be said to determine *ex post* income even in the loanable funds model under the public money system. Application of the loanable funds model is claimed to be flawed only under the present *debt money* system, but not under the exogenous *public money* system. This is an important distinction when we analyze the behavior of LF model in Sect. 8.11.1.

8.9 Endogenous Money Model with Budgets

The loanable funds model presented above is destined to fail, in a similar way as the Keynesian IS-LM model did, to explain the Great Depression and Japan's lost 30 years due to the flawed assumption that money stock is exogenously given. Now we are in a position to formally present a paradigm shift of the IS-LM model with endogenous debt money. Our target is to change the *exogenous* money stock into the *endogenous* money stock with budget equations.

8.9.1 *Budget Equation of Banks*

So far, banks are assumed to act as pure intermediaries, accepting savings deposits from households and making loans out of those savings (called loanable funds ΔLF). However, loanable funds of banks are not constrained by preexisting savings as banks can create new deposits to finance loans under the fractional reserve banking system. Deposits thus created can be interpreted as the increment of money stock (ΔM^s), because they are used for payments as *functional money*. Here, let us continue to use the same terminology of the loanable funds (ΔLF), to describe the sources of loans made by banks. Then, the budget equation of banks in Eq. (8.58) is now replaced with the following:

$$\Delta LF = \Delta M^s \qquad \text{(Banks Budget : Deposits Creation)} \qquad (8.69)$$

In other words, the total amount of deposit creation constitutes, at a macro-level, the overarching budget constraint on the domestic sector's demand for loans (excluding any incoming cross-border loans denominated in foreign currencies).

[26] For separation of powers, Yamaguchi (2012, 2014, 2015) proposed that monetary policy should be implemented by the Public Money Administration (PMA), established as an independent committee under the direct supervision of the legislature such as the Congress in the US, the parliament in UK, and the National Diet in Japan. This governance mechanism ensures the PMA is isolated from political pressures by other branches of government in fulfilling the price stability objective and other functions as the sole issuer of money as interest-free currency. See Yamaguchi (2010, 2011, 2013) for ASD-based simulation studies on the topic.

Consequently, money stock M^s is now endogenously obtained by the following equation:

$$M^s = \int \Delta M^s dt \qquad \text{(Endogenous Money Stock)} \tag{8.70}$$

We have now added two more unknowns to the loanable funds model: ΔM^s and M^s, with two additional equations: (8.69) and (8.70) in place of the budget equation of banks (8.58). Hence, we need one more equation to complete the model. For this purpose, we may bring back the aggregate demand equilibrium (8.41), which has been removed in the loanable funds model as a redundant equation from the Walras law. Under the endogenous debt money system, it is no longer redundant because the revised Walras law now becomes

$$P(C + I + G - Y) + \Delta LF - (\Delta D_H + \Delta D_F + \Delta D_G) + S - \Delta M^s \equiv 0 \text{ (WalrasLaw)} \tag{8.71}$$

Due to the additional equation of savings and increment of money stock ($S - \Delta M^s$), the aggregate demand equilibrium (8.41) and loanable funds equilibrium (8.60) can now coexist. Under the loanable funds model, this additional equation of savings and money stock was missing. As a result, either the aggregate demand equilibrium or loanable funds equilibrium had to be made redundant.

Endogenous Money Model with Budgets

The endogenous money model with budgets is now complete, in which money stock M^s is created endogenously. Let us call this revised model *Endogenous Money Model with Budgets*, or simply Endogenous Money (EM) model. The endogenous money model consists of the following 20 equations; (8.41) through (8.50), (8.51) through (8.57), (8.60), (8.69) and (8.70) with 20 unknowns:

$$Y, AD, C, I, G, Y_d, T, r, i, L^d, S, I_H, W + \Pi, I_P, \Delta D_H, \Delta D_P, \Delta D_G, \Delta LF, \Delta M^s, M^s$$

and 14 exogenously determined parameters:

$$C_0,\ c,\ T_0,\ t,\ T_r,\ I_0,\ \bar{G},\ P,\ V,\ \alpha,\ a,\ b,\ \pi^e,\ \bar{I}_H.$$

Note that the endogenous money model thus constructed can successfully integrate our endogenous money spending hypothesis discussed in Fig. 8.13.

8.9.2 Features of Endogenous Money Model

Model Feature 1: Money Stock = Total Debts

We have analyzed, both theoretically and empirically, in Chap. 3 that total money stock is approximated by total debts from banks held by non-banking private sectors (households and producers) and the government. Let us denote these debts by D_H, D_P, D_G, respectively. Then, these debts (stocks) can be obtained by integrating their flow amounts of $\Delta D_H, \Delta D_P, \Delta D_G$ such that

$$D_H = \int \Delta D_H dt \qquad \text{(Debts of Households)} \tag{8.72}$$

$$D_P = \int \Delta D_P dt \qquad \text{(Debts of Producers)} \tag{8.73}$$

$$D_G = \int \Delta D_G dt \qquad \text{(Debts of Government)} \tag{8.74}$$

Thus, from Eqs. (8.60), (8.69) and (8.70), we obtain the following:

$$M^s = \int \Delta LF = \int (\Delta D_H + \Delta D_P + \Delta D_G) dt = D_H + D_P + D_G \tag{8.75}$$

Accordingly, we have shown that money stock M^s is to be endogenously determined, and equals to the total debts held by households, producers and the government under the endogenous money model.[27] In the case of discrete formula, Eqs. (8.72)–(8.74) can be replaced with

$$D_{H_t} = D_{H_{t-1}} + \Delta D_{H_t} \tag{8.76}$$

$$D_{F_t} = D_{F_{t-1}} + \Delta D_{F_t} \tag{8.77}$$

$$D_{G_t} = D_{G_{t-1}} + \Delta D_{G_t} \tag{8.78}$$

where initial stock amounts are given as follows:

$$D_{H_{t-1}} = \bar{D}_H, \; D_{F_{t-1}} = \bar{D}_F, \; D_{G_{t-1}} = \bar{D}_G.$$

Hence, these equations support formal statement of the paradigm shift discussed in Sect. 8.7; *LM* curve is no longer independent of *IS* curve. Both *IS* and *LM* curves are closely linked with one another and must move jointly. Flow amounts of money stock such as $\Delta D_H, \Delta D_P, \Delta D_G$ have to be borrowed from banks. Hence, we now need to consider their budget equations more precisely.

---

[27] Public money such as coins issued by the government only constitutes 0.3% of M_3 in Japan and negligible in terms of the circulating amount as discussed in Chap. 2. Thus they are omitted from our analysis here.

Model Feature 2: Increased Money Stock Ends up with Savings

Let us continue to examine the endogenous money model in more detail. At the equilibrium, we have, from the revised Walras law (8.71):

$$S = \Delta M^s \qquad \text{(Savings as Monetary Increase)} \tag{8.79}$$

That is, savings are equal to the increased amount of money stock. How should we interpret this relation? When aggregate demand determines (*ex post*) GDP as the Keynesian theory presumes, loanable funds by banks must be first made available to meet the demand for the total flow amounts of debts ($\Delta D_H + \Delta D_P + \Delta D_G$), which in turn increase money stock ΔM^s. In this way, loanable funds under the endogenous money are indeed created endogenously by banks as follows:

$$\Delta D_H + \Delta D_P + \Delta D_G \Rightarrow \Delta LF \Rightarrow \Delta M^s \tag{8.80}$$

On the other hand, at the equilibrium, aggregate demand determines (*ex post*) GDP such that

$$C + I_H + I_P + G \Rightarrow Y \tag{8.81}$$

Accordingly, from the Walras law (8.71) we must have:

$$\Delta M^s \Rightarrow S \tag{8.82}$$

What does this mean? In the loanable funds and endogenous money models, we have assumed that households receive all distributed income of wages and profits $(W + \Pi)$ as income at factor cost. Hence, savings S are defined in Eq. (8.51) as the balance between income and expenditure by households and include all kinds of savings made by them as their demand deposits. They are then transferred into time deposits as a leakage from monetary circulation or withdrawn back to demand deposits to be used for other payments as Fig. 3.7 in Chap. 3 illustrates.

Additionally, we have found that time deposits are approximated by total debts held by non-banking private sectors, while M_1 is approximated by the government debts in Japan and the US (Figs. 3.8 and 3.9). Using these decomposition relations, we could advance our analyses from Eqs. (8.80) and (8.82) that debts by households and producers ($\Delta D_H + \Delta D_P$) end up with time deposits, and debts incurred by the government ΔD_G end up with demand deposits as follows:

$$\Delta M^s \Rightarrow S \Rightarrow \begin{cases} \Delta D_H + \Delta D_P \Rightarrow \text{Time Deposits} \\ \Delta D_G \qquad\qquad\; \Rightarrow \text{Demand Deposits} \end{cases} \tag{8.83}$$

This implies that deposits newly created by banks under the debt money system ends up with savings, which are further broken down into demand and time deposits.

In the loanable funds model, savings become the source of loans and investments. In the endogenous money model, savings are the final leakages which will accumulate as demand and time deposits. This provides a theoretical foundation of our empirical findings on the debt-money decomposition analyses presented in Chap. 3.

Can the endogenous money model as well as the loanable funds model we have developed here produce these decompositions? To examine them, we have to convert the models into the ASD model first, which will be challenged in the next section. Before doing so, let us make one more remark on savings.

Paradigm Shift on Savings

Against the mainstream macroeconomic theory, which asserts that savings determine investments, we have observed completely opposite facts; debts determines investment, which then ends up as savings. Therefore, when aggregate demand (AD) exceeds *ex ante* income $\underline{\mathrm{Y}}$, two different macroeconomic behaviors take place under the two different assumptions of exogenous money (loanable funds) and endogenous *debt money* systems:

$$AD > \underline{\mathrm{Y}} \Rightarrow \Delta LF = \underline{\mathrm{S}} \quad \Rightarrow AD = \underline{\mathrm{Y}} \quad \text{(Loanable Funds)} \tag{8.84}$$

$$\Rightarrow \Delta LF = \Delta M^s \Rightarrow AD = Y \Rightarrow S \text{(Endogenous Money)} \tag{8.85}$$

where $\underline{\mathrm{S}}$ implies *ex ante* savings, and Y and S imply *ex post* income and savings.

As discussed in Eq. (8.65), (*ex post*) aggregate demand is always constrained by *ex ante* income under the loanable funds model. In other words it ends up with the Say's law ("Supply creates its own demand"). Ironically, the loanable funds model, which falsely assumes exogenous money, has played a role of supporting the Say's law, even though the Keynes's *General Theory* was intended to departure from it as being the 'Classical' economics. In the endogenous money model, on the other hand, it holds as a truism that (*ex post*) aggregate demand determines *ex post* income as claimed by the Keynesian theory. That is, "Demand creates its own supply". Thus, Keynesian theory must be presented under the endogenous money model, which reveals the following:

- Debt money are endogenously created and destroyed against loans so that central bank has no direct control over money stock (Negation of "exogenous money").
- Investment is not constrained by the loanable funds, but followed by the *ex post* savings (Negation of "Banks as financial intermediaries").

Paradigm shift discussed in Sect. 8.7 is now completed based on mathematical models with budget equations.

8.10 ASD Model of Loanable Funds and Endogenous Money

To confirm the paradigm shift in macroeconomic theory, we need to construct simulation models for loanable funds and endogenous money models for comparative analysis. The Accounting System Dynamics (ASD) modeling method (Yamaguchi, 2003) turns out to be effective for integrating budget equations and various inter-sector transactions into a simulation model, including lending and borrowing of money and debts. Once an integrated ASD model that covers both the endogenous money (EM) and loanable funds (LF) is built, we can run simulations in a single ASD model by turning on and off the switch between the EM and LF mode, just as we did with the endogenous money IS-LM model discussed in Sect. 8.6. In this way the theoretical controversies, such as described above, can be comparatively analyzed to find out which of the model assumption, i.e., loanable funds or endogenous money, is better suited for macroeconomic analyses under the current debt money system.

8.10.1 GDP, Aggregate Demand and Distributed Income

To construct such an integrated ASD model, the above equilibrium loanable funds and endogenous models need to be changed into a dynamic disequilibrium model as was done for the Keynesian IS-LM model in Sect. 8.2. Macroeconomics textbooks often discuss the IS-LM by assuming the equivalence of macroeconomic aggregates such as production (GDP), distribution (Income) and expenditure (Aggregate Demand) as national income accounting identity. However, these relations only hold at the equilibrium under very strong assumptions. In other words, they do not hold at off-equilibrium. Accordingly, to construct the dynamic ASD model with budget equations, we need to redefine the concepts of these macroeconomic aggregates more rigorously.

As was done in the SD model of the Keynesian IS-LM model (Sect. 8.2.1), let us start by rewriting the equation of inventory stock (8.14) as follows:

$$Y = AD + Y_{unsold} \tag{8.86}$$

which implies that real production Y is now separated into aggregate demand and unsold products.

With the introduction of budgets by producers, we also need to apply accounting rules to properly evaluate them on their balance sheet. Specifically, Cost of Goods Sold (CGS) needs to be evaluated by unit cost of inventory that is different from market sales price P as follows:

$$\text{Unit Cost of Inventory } (P_{uc}) = \text{Price } (P) - \text{Gross Margin} \tag{8.87}$$

Hence, there are two ways to evaluate Unsold Products (as inflows to Inventory stock) such that

$$Y_{unsold}\ (\text{at}\ P) = P * Y_{unsold} \tag{8.88}$$

$$Y_{unsold}\ (\text{at}\ P_{uc}) = P_{uc} * Y_{unsold} \tag{8.89}$$

That is, Unsold Products evaluated at current market price P becomes different from Unsold Products evaluated at Unit Cost P_{uc}. The general rule for recording non-monetary asset is to evaluate them at unit cost. Producers thus need to evaluate their inventory asset at unit cost on their balance sheets. Hence, we have

$$Y_{unsold}\ (\text{at}\ P) > Y_{unsold}\ (\text{at}\ P_{uc})\ (\text{for Gross Margin} > 0) \tag{8.90}$$

On the other hand, production defined as the total value-added amount of all domestic sectors or GDP is generally evaluated at the market sales price P such that

$$\begin{aligned} \text{Production (GDP)} &= P * Y \\ &= P * (AD + Y_{unsold}) \\ &= \text{Aggregate Demand} + Y_{unsold}\ (\text{at}\ P) \end{aligned} \tag{8.91}$$

where Aggregate Demand is the nominal purchased amount of real aggregate demand (AD) sold at market prices $(= P * AD)$, consisting of Consumption, Investment by Producers and Households and Government Expenditure

Corresponding to the evaluation of inventory asset at unit cost, the monetary value of production (real) may also be evaluated at unit cost basis such that

$$\text{Production (Unit Cost Basis)} = \text{Aggregate Demand} + Y_{unsold}\ (\text{at}\ P_{uc}) \tag{8.92}$$

Therefore, for positive Gross Margin > 0 and Unsold Products > 0, we have

$$\text{Production (GDP)} > \text{Production (Unit Cost Basis)} > \text{Aggregate Demand} \tag{8.93}$$

In our Loanable Funds model with budgets (Sect. 8.8) as well as the Endogenous Money model with budgets (Sect. 8.9), we have assumed that producer's revenues are fully distributed to households as wages (W) and dividends (Π), that is, Eq. (8.55). Similarly, let us assume here that producers pay wages for the production (Y), which are denoted as Wages (Y), while the actual labor cost incurred for sales realized during the same period are called Wages ($Cost$). Producers must compensate for labor employed in the production in the current period regardless of whether the products are sold in the current period. So long as $Y_{unsold} > 0$, the amount of Wage (Y) becomes greater than Wages (Cost) that were put into the production sold (demanded) in the current period. Therefore, income distributed to households as workers and shareholders becomes the following:

$$\begin{aligned} \text{Income at Factor Cost} &= \text{Wages } (Y) + \text{Dividends} \\ &> \text{Wages } (Cost) + \text{Dividends} \\ &= \text{Aggregate Demand - Depreciation (Cost)} \end{aligned} \quad (8.94)$$

Since producer's sale revenue realized from Aggregate Demand are distributed at factor cost, we have

$$\begin{aligned} \text{Aggregate Demand} &= \text{Cost of Goods Sold} + \text{Profits} \\ &= \text{Wages } (Cost) + \text{Depreciation } (Cost) + \text{Dividends} \end{aligned} \quad (8.95)$$

where "Dividends = Profits" is assumed for the sake of simplicity, i.e., producers retain no profits.

We have now introduced four macroeconomic aggregates: Production (GDP), Production (Unit Cost Basis), Income at Factor Cost and Aggregate Demand. Distinguishing these aggregates is essential to construct off-equilibrium dynamic adjustment process for the integrated ASD model of Loanable Funds and Endogenous Money. In other words, any macroeconomic model that lacks these four aggregates is disqualified as dynamic macroeconomic model.

8.10.2 Transactions of Macroeconomic Sectors

Producers

Let us begin with transactions of producers. In the macroeconomic system, producers face two important decisions all the time: production for this period and investment for the futures. Hence, their behaviors are briefly summarized as follows.

- Producers make production decisions according to the equation of production decision (8.16) as the sum of the forecasting amount of the next year's aggregate demand and adjustment of the current level of inventory against the desired inventory (I^*) as already assumed in the *IS* sub-model of the Keynesian IS-LM model. Investment decision is assumed to be made by the standard macroeconomic investment function as Eq. (8.46).
- Producers pay wages for the desired production: Wages (Y). Out of sales revenue, producers recover Cost of Goods Sold as Wages ($Cost$) and Depreciation ($Cost$). The remaining becomes profits before tax. Various taxes imposed on producers are not considered under the current model. Then, producers distribute dividends out of profits to their shareholders, and remaining profits are booked as retained profits (which is assumed to be zero here).
- Producers are constantly in a state of cash flow deficits as analyzed by Yamaguchi (2013, Chap. 4). To make new investment, therefore, they have to raise funds. Under the loanable funds, they can borrow from banks out of savings. Under the

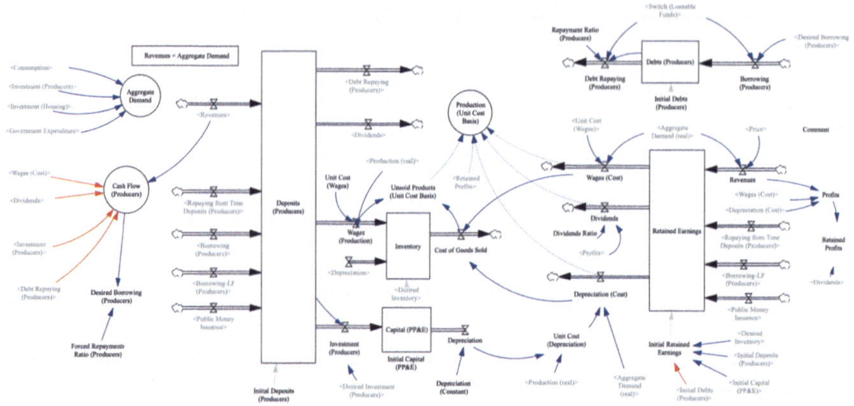

Fig. 8.21 Transactions and balance sheet of producers

endogenous money, banks finance loans by creating "deposits" out of nothing. Interest payments between non-banking sectors and banks are not considered here for simplicity.[28]

Figure 8.21 illustrates transactions of producers as a balance sheet.

Households

Households as consumers have to make two decisions: firstly, how much to consume and how much to save, and secondly, how much to borrow for housing investment. Consumption decision is assumed to be made according to the standard consumption function as Eq. (8.43). Some of the transactions by households are summarized as follows.

- Households receive income at factor cost (wages and dividends) from producers.
- Out of the total income received including government transfer, they pay income taxes, and the remaining becomes their disposable income. Interest payments between banks are not considered here.
- Out of their disposable income, they spend on consumption. The remaining is thus saved as time deposits.
- Households borrow funds needed to purchase houses from banks (housing investment).

As explained in the loanable funds model, we have assumed that households receive all income at factor cost as wages and profits (didivends) $(W + \Pi)$. Hence, savings

[28] See Yamaguchi and Yamaguchi (2024) further for a more comprehensive model with various interest rates and simulation-based analysis of their macroeconomic impacts on income distribution and inequality.

S are defined in Eq. (8.51) as the balance between income and expenditure of households and include all kinds of savings made by the households sector. Those savings are first made as demand deposits, which are then converted into time deposits as a leakage from monetary circulation, or withdrawn back to demand deposits according to the needs for debt repayment. The current model is set up so that households mechanistically convert time deposits to demand deposits based on the parameter called "desired deposit ratio", which acts like a portfolio balance ratio. It is possible in the future research to allow the interest rate, for instance, to endogenously determine how much of the demand deposits are converted into time deposits with higher yields. Figure 8.22 illustrates transactions and balance sheet of households.

Government

Government must decide how much taxes to levy as revenues and how much to spend as expenditures. Tax revenues are assumed to be collected according to the standard formula in Eq. (8.45), while expenditures are determined by the revenue-dependent tax and primary balance ratio. Primary balance ratio is assumed to be "1" by default so that the government budget is in equilibrium at the beginning. In the current model government consumption and investment are not distinguished. Some of the transactions by the government are summarized as follows.

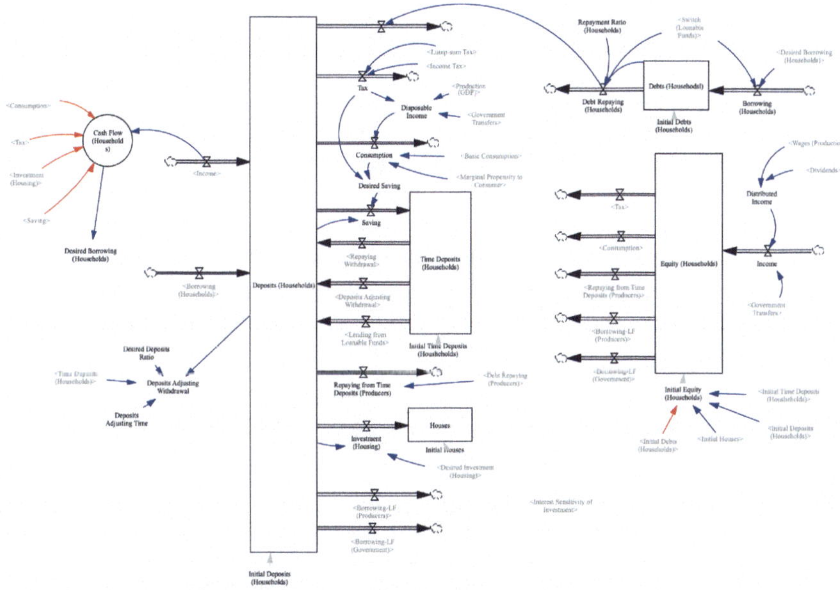

Fig. 8.22 Transactions and balance sheet of households

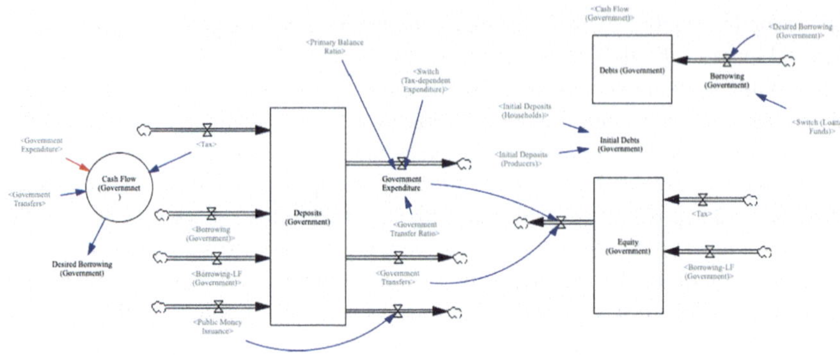

Fig. 8.23 Transactions and balance sheet of government

- Government receives income taxes from households as tax revenues.
- Government spending consists of government expenditures and transfers.
- Government expenditures are assumed to be endogenously determined by tax revenue-dependent expenditures.
- If spending exceeds tax revenues, government has to attract and utilize household's time deposits through banks as intermediaries under the loanable funds, or borrow directly from the central bank (for simplicity) in the case of endogenous money.

Figure 8.23 illustrates transactions of government as a balance sheet.

Banks

Under the loanable funds model, banks are assumed to act as intermediaries of time deposits (savings) between savers (households) and investors (producers). Under the endogenous money model, banks are assumed to play a passive role; that is, they only make loans for the amount asked by producers and households.[29] Furthermore, they do not purchase government bonds, which are assumed to be directly purchased by the central bank here for simplicity. They are also assumed to make no portfolio decisions among loans and other financial assets. Some of the transactions of banks are summarized as follows.

- Banks accept demand deposits from households and producers, and time deposits from households (interests payments are neglected for a simplicity here).

[29] Of course, under the current debt money system, central and commercial banks exercise tremendous power over various aspects of the economy based on their controlling position as monopolistic issuers of money. For example, Yamaguchi and Yamaguchi (2016) conducted simulation analyses of the money stock instability created by bank's lending behavior or changes in the household's cash-deposit preference. However, the ideal modeling step is to start with the simplest structure and then incorporate various behavioral hypotheses that would emerge during the course of research and analyze them step-by-step. In the future, our current simple model can be revised further to reflect more realistic institutional settings.

- In the case of loanable funds, banks make loans out of the savings of time deposits. Under the endogenous money, banks make loans by creating deposits of as much as the desired amount of borrowings demanded by producers and households. Interests on these loans are not considered likewise for simplicity.

Figure 8.24 illustrates transactions of banks as a balance sheet.

Central Bank

The central bank accept deposits from banks as reserves and the government. In our macroeconomic model, its primary role is to transfer money (reserves) between banks and the government on behalf of the treasury as well as to make loans directly to the government in the case of endogenous money. Transactions are made simple enough to avoid complexity and summarized as follows.

- Whenever government borrows, the central bank transfers funds to the government through reserves of the banks in the loanable funds model, while in the case of endogenous money, it is assumed that the central bank make loans directly to the government for simplicity.
- As explained in "Remarks" of Sect. 8.8.3, the workings of loanable funds model are fundamentally the same as (thus applicable to) that of the public money system where PMA (public money administration) regulates the total supply of money in place of the central bank. Accordingly, it is also assumed that the central bank issues public money on behalf of the PMA.

Figure 8.25 illustrates transactions of central bank as a balance sheet.

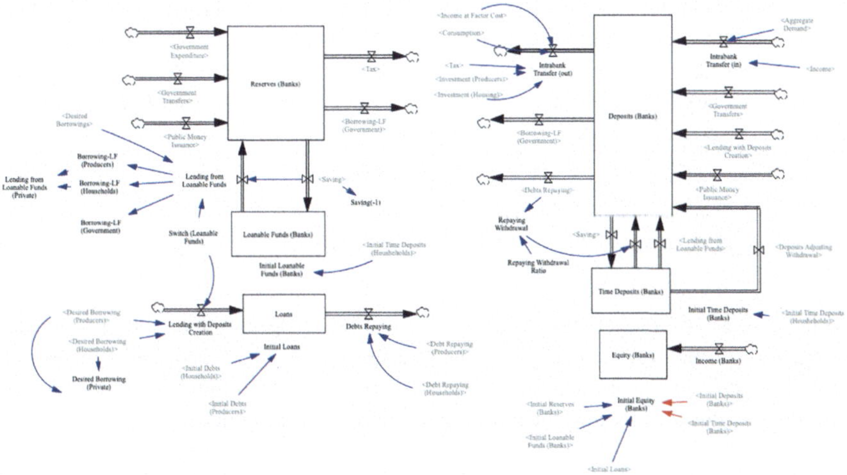

Fig. 8.24 Transactions and balance sheet of banks

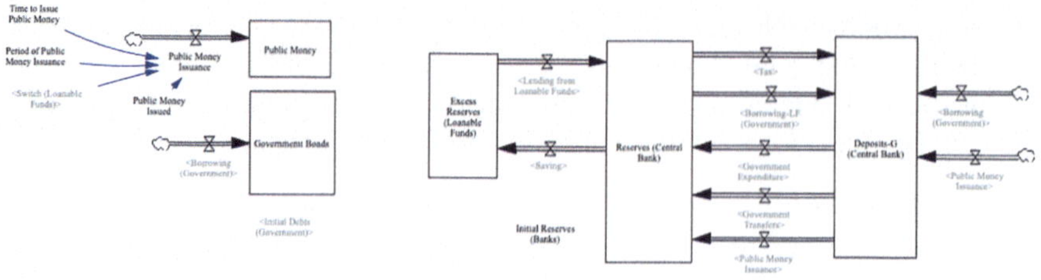

Fig. 8.25 Transactions and balance sheet of central bank

Revised LM Sub-Model

With the introduction of budget equations, total amount of money stock is now obtained endogenously within the model as follows:

$$\text{Money Stock } (M^s) = M_1 + M_T \text{ (Time Deposits)} \tag{8.96}$$

where M_1 is the sum of demand deposits held by households, producers and government as shown at the left middle part of Fig. 8.26. Demand for money are obtained as the sum of outflows from Deposits held by each sector. In Chap. 5 we discussed that the quantity Eq. $(Mv = PT)$ must be an identity (5.13) that holds at any time. This means that the velocity v is only an observed variable that is estimated *a posteriori* and should not be used as a determinant in macroeconomic analysis. However, in the traditional IS-LM model discussed in this chapter, V is used in the definition of the supply of money, and such criticism apply to our SD model discussed so far as well.

Since M^s is now obtained within the model, we no longer need to rely on the parameter V and we can redefine interest rate dynamics in Eq. (8.19) based on endogenous variables. Specifically, Money Ratio previously shown in the *LM* sub-model (Fig. 8.3) is now modified in the ASD model here as a moving average ratio of real money stock and demand for money. Figure 8.26 presents this newly revised version of Money Ratio (Moving Average). This becomes the revised *LM* sub-model of the integrated ASD model.

8.10.3 Validations of the ASD Macroeconomic Model

We have now completed our ASD modeling that integrates loanable funds and endogenous money mathematical models presented in Sects. 8.8 and 8.9. As model validations, we have examined the following four tests as the minimum requirements that must be met for any macroeconomic model to be a reliable tool.

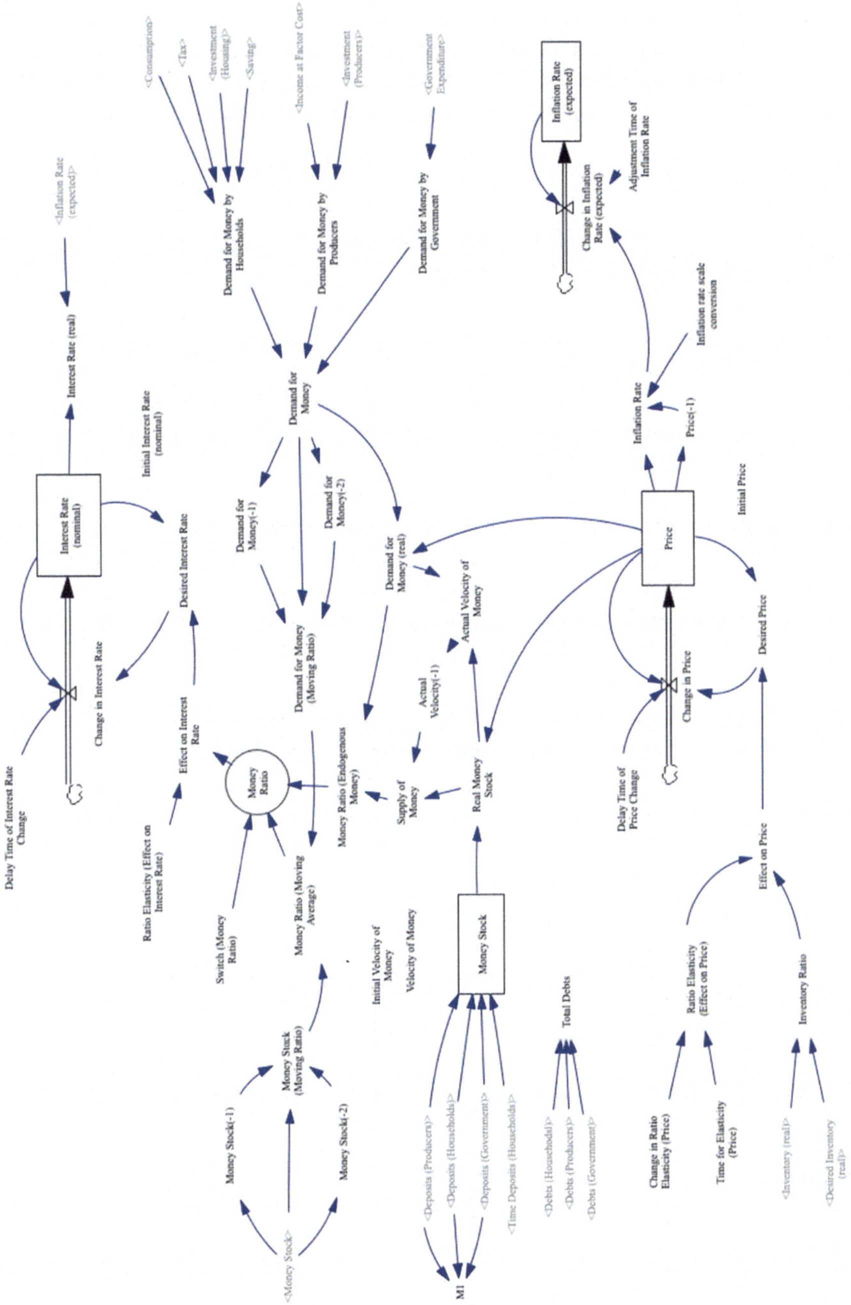

Fig. 8.26 Revised *LM* sub-model for the ASD model

(1) Validation as SD Model: Model and Units Check

First validation test that must be cleared is built-in model test performed by the SD simulation software (Vensim) such as "Check Model" and "Units Check". Our model have passed these tests. Recall that we have pointed out in Sect. 8.4.1 that the Mankiw's extended IS-LM model with expected inflation rate failed to pass the unit check.

(2) Validation as ASD Model: Balance Sheets and Flow-of-Funds Consistency Checks

Accounting system requires that balance sheets of all sectors must be in balance. This test is called balance sheets (B/S) check. Furthermore, the flow-of-funds framework requires that all assets and liabilities (equity or net asset) of all transaction items in the model must be in balance across all sectors involved. This test is called the flow of funds (F/F) check.

The left diagram of Fig. 8.27 illustrates that, for the Endogenous Money (EM) model, the balance of each sector's balance sheets are almost zero, indicating that the model passes the B/S check for all macroeconomic sectors. The right diagram illustrates that the Flow of Funds are all in balance (almost zero) among transaction items such as deposits, time deposits, reserves, and loans (debts). B/S and F/F checks on Loanable Fund (LF) model are also confirmed.

(3) Validation as Macroeconomic Model: Debt Money Check

We have mathematically shown in the Eq. (8.75) that money stock is equal to total debts under the debt money system. As discussed in Chap. 3, we have found that the following relations hold in Japan and the United States.

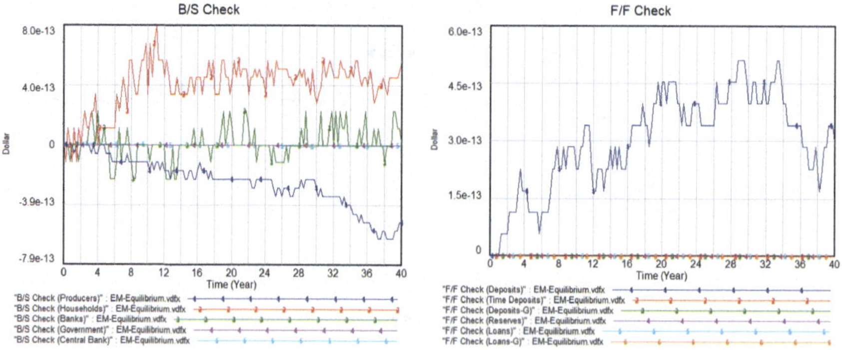

Fig. 8.27 Validation test (2)—balance sheets (B/S) and flow of funds (F/F) checks

1. Money Stock ($M_{2\sim3}$) = Total Debts
   (corresponding to lines 1 = lines 2 in Fig. 8.28)
2. Time Deposits (M_T) $\simeq$ Private Debts (by Producers and Households)
   (corresponding to lines 3 $\simeq$ lines 4 in Fig. 8.28)
3. M_1 (= Currency + Demand Deposits) $\simeq$ Government Debts
   (corresponding to lines 5 $\simeq$ lines 6 in Fig. 8.28)

Our empirical findings and mathematical analysis presented in Eq. (8.83) suggest that the second and third relations could be similarly observed in other currency areas. Depending on the specific case under study, the second and third breakdown relationships may be tested additionally. Certainly, our empirical findings indicate that the first relation, at least, must hold in any economy operating under the debt money system. Hence, we have introduced this additional validation test for macroeconomic models as *Debt Money* check.

Left diagram of Fig. 8.28 shows all three relations of Debt Money check hold at the equilibrium under our Endogenous Money model. Right diagram also shows that the first relation similarly holds (line 1 = line 2) under a different scenario where Investment is increased by \$50 at t = 10 (this case simulation is done in the following section). Moreover, the second and third relations are shown to hold under the parameter value of Repaying Withdrawal Ratio = 0.4; that is, line 3 $\simeq$ line 4, and line 5 $\simeq$ line 6 toward the end of simulation period. Changes in this parameter value only affect the amount between demand and time deposits, but do not affect other behaviors of the model. These relations similarly hold under the Loanable Funds model.

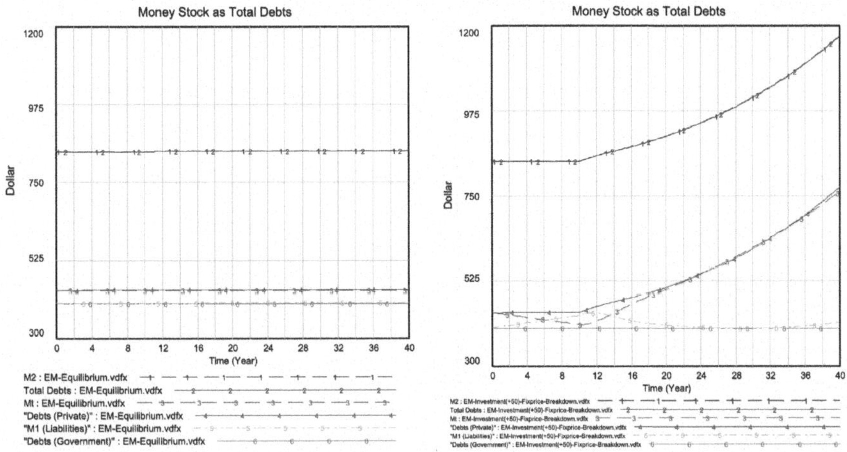

Fig. 8.28 Validation test (3)—debt money check: money stock $\simeq$ total debts

(4) Production, Expenditure and Distribution: Non-Equivalence Checks

Our fourth validation test compares the four macroeconomic aggregates such as Production (GDP), Production (Unit Cost Basis), Aggregate Demand (Expenditure) and Income at Factor Cost (Distributed Income). They are in general not equivalent in values. As illustrated by the left diagram of Fig. 8.29, only at the equilibrium in which Unsold Products = 0, we observe the following equivalence relations (numbers within parentheses correspond to line numbers in the figure):

$$
\begin{aligned}
\text{Production (GDP) (1)} &= \text{Production (Unit Cost Basis) (2)} \\
&= \text{Aggregate Demand (3)} \\
&= \text{Income at Factor Cost (4)} + \text{Depreciation (Cost) (6)} \\
&\geq \text{Income at Factor Cost (4)} \qquad (8.97) \\
&\quad \text{(for Depreciation (Cost)} \geq 0)
\end{aligned}
$$

Only when Depreciation (Cost) is zero, equivalence relations holds: that is, GDP = Income at Factor Cost = Aggregate Demand. These relations are called "national income-product account identity" or "three-sided equivalence principle". To be precise, for these equivalence relations to hold, there must be another strong assumption that all value-added products are distributed during each period such that producers fully distribute profits and thus retain no earnings (which is the current assumption made in our model).

Right diagram of Fig. 8.29 is a simulation in which investment is increased by \$50 at t = 10. Around the time t = 14 when Unsold Products (at Price) is positive, the following relations are observed:

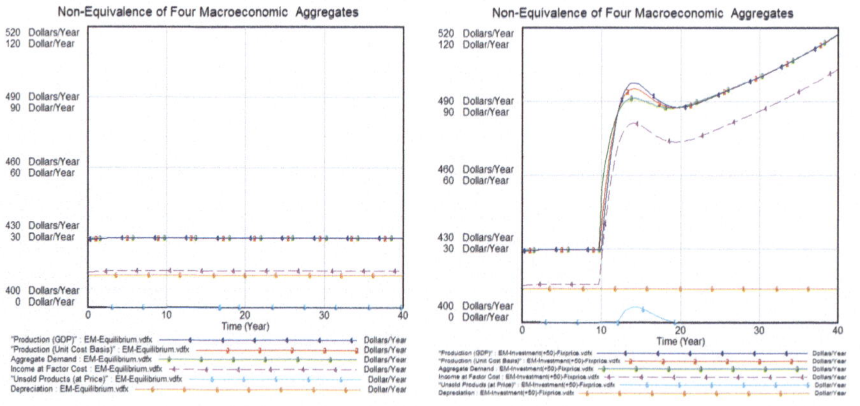

Fig. 8.29 Validation (4)—non-equivalence of four macroeconomic aggregates

$$\begin{aligned}\text{Production (GDP) (1)} &> \text{Production (Unit Cost Basis) (2)}\\ &> \text{Aggregate Demand (3)}\\ &> \text{Income at Factor Cost (4)}\end{aligned} \tag{8.98}$$

These relations indicate that macroeconomic models that presume only the equivalence relation in Eq. (8.97) cannot differentiate important concepts such as GDP, distributed income and profits, and are thus too simplistic from our viewpoint of the ASD modeling approach to dynamic off-equilibrium analysis.

8.11 Behaviors of ASD Model: Loanable Funds Versus Endogenous Money

Our integrated ASD model of Loanable Funds (LF) and Endogenous Money (EM) is now validated. Let us call the ASD model simulated under the loanable funds mode as the LF model, and the endogenous money mode of the ASD model the EM model. To run the model under LF assumption, we simply set the value of "Money (switch)" to 1. The default value is set to be 0 for the EM model.

To compare the model behaviors under the EM and LF mode, the model assumes a growing economy by default as our base run scenario. Specifically, it assumes that Producer's Investment increases exponentially over time. Then, we have run two cases of simulations: the equilibrium case and a case of outside shock caused by investment increase in $50 at $t = 10$. Table 8.1 summarizes legend names of simulations used in Figs. 8.30 and 8.31, in which line 1 (in blue) and line 2 (in red) show behaviors of the EM model, while lines 3 (in green) and and 4 (in pink) are those of the LF model (except the lines in the left diagram of Fig. 8.30).

Left diagram of Fig. 8.30 shows desired amount of borrowing by producers under the EM model (line 1) and LF model (line 4). When investment increases, producers need to raise funds irrespective of their investment environments. It is interesting to observe how the outside shock of such investment increase affects macroeconomic behaviors differently due to different lending behaviors of banks under the EM and LF models. In the EM model, Desired Borrowing (line 1) is shown to be always met with Lending with Deposits Creation (line 2) without being constrained by the amount of Saving (line 3). Money is indeed endogenously created to meet the desired investment as indicated by Eq. (8.69). In the EM model, thus, saving takes place only

Table 8.1 Loanable funds (LF) versus endogenous money (EM) simulations

Endogenous Money ASD (Case 6)	Loanable Funds ASD (Case 5)
Line 1: EM-Equilibrium	Line 3: LF-Equilibrium
Line 2: EM-Investment(+50)-Fixprice	Line 4: LF-Investment(+50)-Fixprice

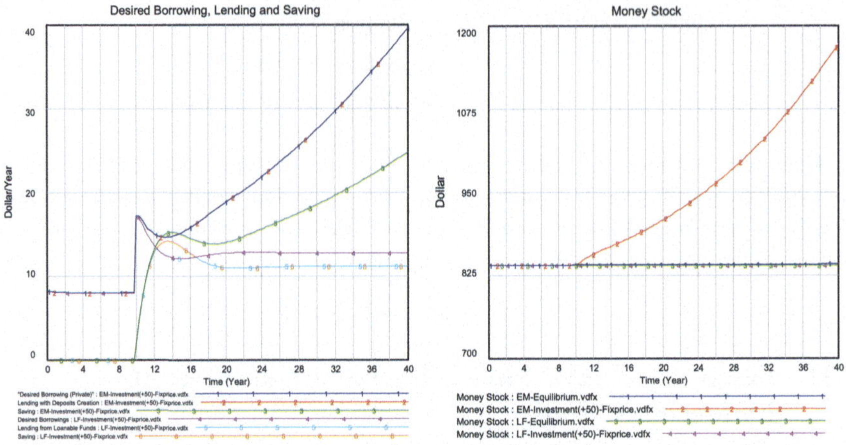

Fig. 8.30 Loanable funds versus endogenous money: how money is created?

after these investment decisions are made and money is created by banks as indicated by Eq. (8.82).

In the LF model, on the other hand, Desired Borrowing (line 4) failed to be met, because Lending from Loanable Funds (line 5) is shown to be constrained at maximum by the minimum amount of Desired Borrowing (line 4) and Saving (line 6); that is,

$$\text{Lending from Loanable Funds} = \text{Min(Desired Borrowing, Saving)} \tag{8.99}$$

This lending behavior confirms our mathematical analysis in Sect. 8.8. That is, savings in the LF model become the only sources of desired investment as analyzed by Eqs. (8.58) and (8.62).

Right diagram of Fig. 8.30 presents comparative behaviors of money stock. At equilibrium under fixed price assumption, money stocks in EM model (line 1) and LF model (line 3) do not change. However, when investment increases, money is created by banks for lending under EM model, and money stock keeps increasing (line 2). Meanwhile, in the LF model money stock (line 4) does not increase, because lending is done out of saving.

Let us next observe how interest and production (GDP) are affected by the investment increase. Left diagram of Fig. 8.31 shows that, after the investment increase at t = 10, nominal interest rate (line 2) first jumps but then continues to decrease due to the increase in money stock under EM model. Meanwhile, interest rate in the LF model (line 4) jumps but eventually converges to a constant level under constant amount of money stock. Right diagram indicates how these different behaviors of interest rate affect production (GDP). Production (GDP) (line 2) continues to grow under the EM model due to the endogenous creation of money, followed by the decrease in interest rate, while it get stagnated at constant level under the LF model

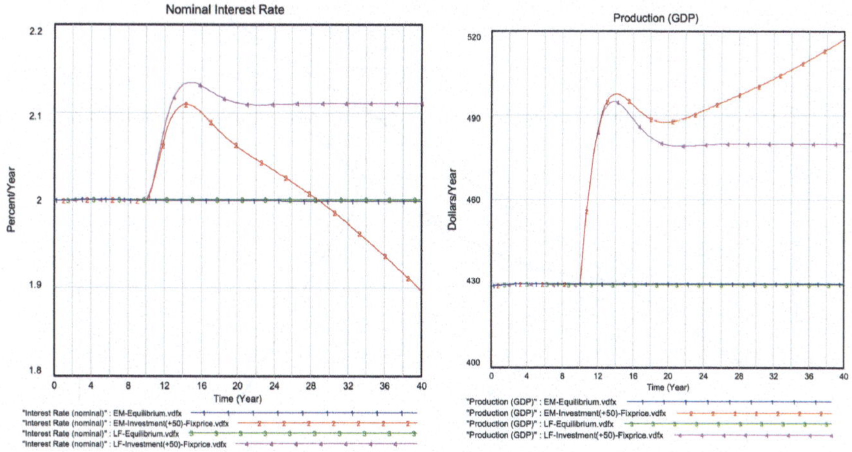

Fig. 8.31 Loanable funds versus endogenous money: nominal interest interest and production (GDP)

(line 4) due to the exogenously fixed amount of money, followed by the constant interest rate.

Let us now compare the above different behaviors of EM and LF models in terms of phase diagram as done in Sect. 8.2.3. Figure 8.32 illustrates behaviors of production (GDP) and interest rate as IS-LM phase diagram. By drawing imaginary IS and LM curves, equilibrium points under EM and LF models are illustrated at the intersection point of IS and LM curves. LM curve is basically the same as the Keynesian IS-LM model in Sect. 8.2.3. Therefore, when investment increases by $50 at t = 10, new equilibrium point moves along with the same LM curve (line 2) since money stock does not change.

On the other hand, as discussed in Sect. 8.7.2, under Endogenous Money, joint shift of IS and LM curves must take place to capture new endogenous money dynamic equilibrium (line 1). It is illustrated in the diagram as if both IS and LM curves move jointly to capture new equilibrium point. In other words, it's impossible to capture this dynamic macroeconomic behavior in terms of comparative static method of IS-LM curves. We need paradigm shift for the analysis of endogenous money macroeconomic behaviors.

Having analyzed the behaviors of both LF and EM models, we now have to decide which model is appropriate for macroeconomic analysis under the current debt money system. In the EM model, interest rate is shown to decrease and production (GDP) is shown to grow as illustrated by lines 2 in Fig. 8.31. On the other hand, money stock in the LF model does not increase, and growth of production (GDP) is constrained. This is a fatal flaw as a macroeconomic model.

We have rejected the exogenous money IS-LM model in Sect. 8.3.2, because it failed to produce the contraction of money stock during the Great Depression. Our simulation analysis demonstrates that loanable funds ASD model suffers from the

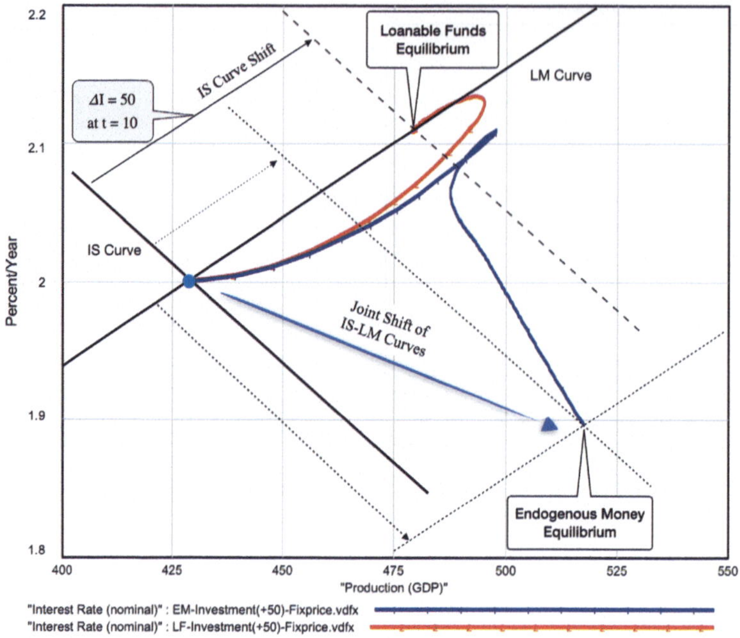

Fig. 8.32 Loanable funds versus endogenous money: joint shift of IS-LM curves

same flaw as the one in the exogenous money Keynesian IS-LM model discussed earlier in this chapter. Consequently, the LF model has to be similarly rejected here as a reliable model for the macroeconomic analysis of the debt money system in which money is endogenously created and destructed against bank loans. There is no built-in mechanism of endogenously creating money in the LF model. Central bankcan only control the amount of base money M_0, but cannot control M_1, M_2, etc., through its monetary policy.

Therefore, the Keynesian *exogenous money theory*–the orthodox view that money stock is given exogenously by the monetary authority and that savings (collected prior to bank lending) become the source of "loanable funds" for future investment–can no longer be applied in a legitimate macroeconomic model. Now we have a conclusive theoretical substantiation from our simulation results. This is the reason why we have argued in Sect. 8.7 that there is a need for a paradigm shift toward the endogenous money ASD macroeconomic model.

8.11.1 Public Money System as Loanable Funds Case

Our rejection of the Keynesian loanable funds model does not mean that it is of no use as a macroeconomic model. We are simply claiming that it is not relevant as a macroeconomic model of the current debt money system. Convinced by the visions of monetary reform and Fisher's *100% Money* theory, we have developed public money system Yamaguchi (2013) and Yamaguchi and Yamaguchi (2016). Under this new macroeconomic system, total supply of money is constantly monitored and adjusted by the Public Money Administration in place of a central bank (as detailed in Part III), and banks become genuine intermediaries of public money that are already in circulation. Accordingly, the Keynesian loanable funds model that we have developed so far will become suitable for the analysis of economic system under public money.

In this sense, the LF model is a candidate of the macroeconomic model under the public money system, but not for the present debt money system. For this reason, let us assume, as a hypothetical case, that the Public Money Administration has newly injected public money of \$11 at t = 10 for 30 consecutive years; that is, \$330 in total. As a result, money stock shown by a bold line 5 (in sky blue) in Fig. 8.33 increased from \$840 to \$1,170 for 30 years. Voila! This amount of money can be issued at interest-free and becomes readily available under the public money system, without causing government debts! Due to the injection of public money, production (GDP) depicted by bold line 5 in the right diagram now increases from the constant level of production (line 4 in pink) under the LF model, and above the production level (line 2 in red) under the EM model (debt money system). This is the essence of monetary policy under the public money system.

In summary, the loanable funds ASD model could serve as a macroeconomic model of the public money system. However, it cannot serve as a model of the debt money system where money is endogenous to the banking system.

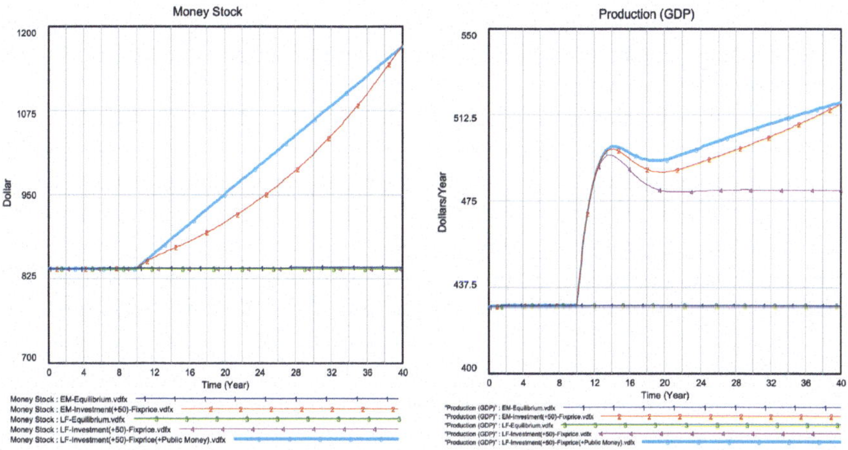

Fig. 8.33 Behaviors of public money as if loanable funds

Table 8.2 Parameter values for the great depression simulation

Great Depression (Fixprice)	(1) Repayment Ratio (Households) = 0.04 ($\leftarrow$ 0.018) (2) $\Delta C_0 = \Delta I_0 = \Delta \bar{I}_H = -20$ at t=1929, 1930, 1931 (Δ implies a change)
Great Depression (Flexprice)	(3) Change in Ratio Elasticity (Price) = 0.06 ($\leftarrow$ 0)

8.12 The Great Depression Case Revisited

In Sect. 8.6, we has successfully reproduced behaviors of the Great Depression by introducing the *endogenous money spending hypothesis*. Let us now examine if the ASD model constructed here can similarly reproduce the behaviors of Great Depression. We have run simulations under EM and LF models for the cases of fixprice and flexprice for detailed comparison. This time instead of PULSE function applied previously, we have used STEP function as one-time changes. Simulations for the Great Depression are run for 20 years starting from 1925 through 1945.[30] Parameter values used for the simulations are summarized in Table 8.2.

Simulation behaviors thus obtained for the Great Depression are shown in Fig. 8.34 through 8.35. Table 8.3 lists corresponding names of diagram legends throughout simulation results.

Flexprice simulation behaviors of the EM model (bold lines 3 in green) are what we want to examine as the behaviors for the Great Depression. They turned out to reproduce similar model behaviors successfully as in Sect. 8.6, and qualitatively capture the behaviors of the Great depression Data as presented in Fig. 8.17. Specifically, they have captured the behaviors such as the decrease in price, destabilizing effects of deflation, fall in nominal interest rate, and rise in real interest rate (Fig. 8.34), and decrease in money stock and rise in real money balance (Fig. 8.35).

On the other hand, flexprice simulation behaviors of the LF model (dotted line 6 in orange) failed to capture the contraction of money stock (Fig. 8.35), though the other behaviors are successfully captured. Hence it is concluded that LF model has to be rejected as a legitimate macroeconomic model for analyzing economic recessions such as the Great Depression, confirming our conclusion in Sect. 8.6.

Figure 8.36 is a summary evaluation of the simulation behaviors of EM and LF ASD models for the case of the Great Depression obtained above, which presents similar results as Fig. 8.17. Specifically, behaviors of the EM model here are similar to those of Spending Hypothesis (Case 4) of the IS-LM model in Sect. 8.6. Behaviors of the LF model are similarly presented except that of money stock M^s. This is because when economy is driven into recessions in general, its behaviors need not be constrained by the existing loanable funds anymore, since producers may not demand for further borrowings of funds. Hence, economic behaviors of the LF model

[30] Technically speaking, initial time = 0 is specified as t = 1925. The SD software that we used in this book (Vensim) allows users to overlay a custom time frame (1925–1945 in our case here) on top of the original time frame used by the model (0–20) for simulation.

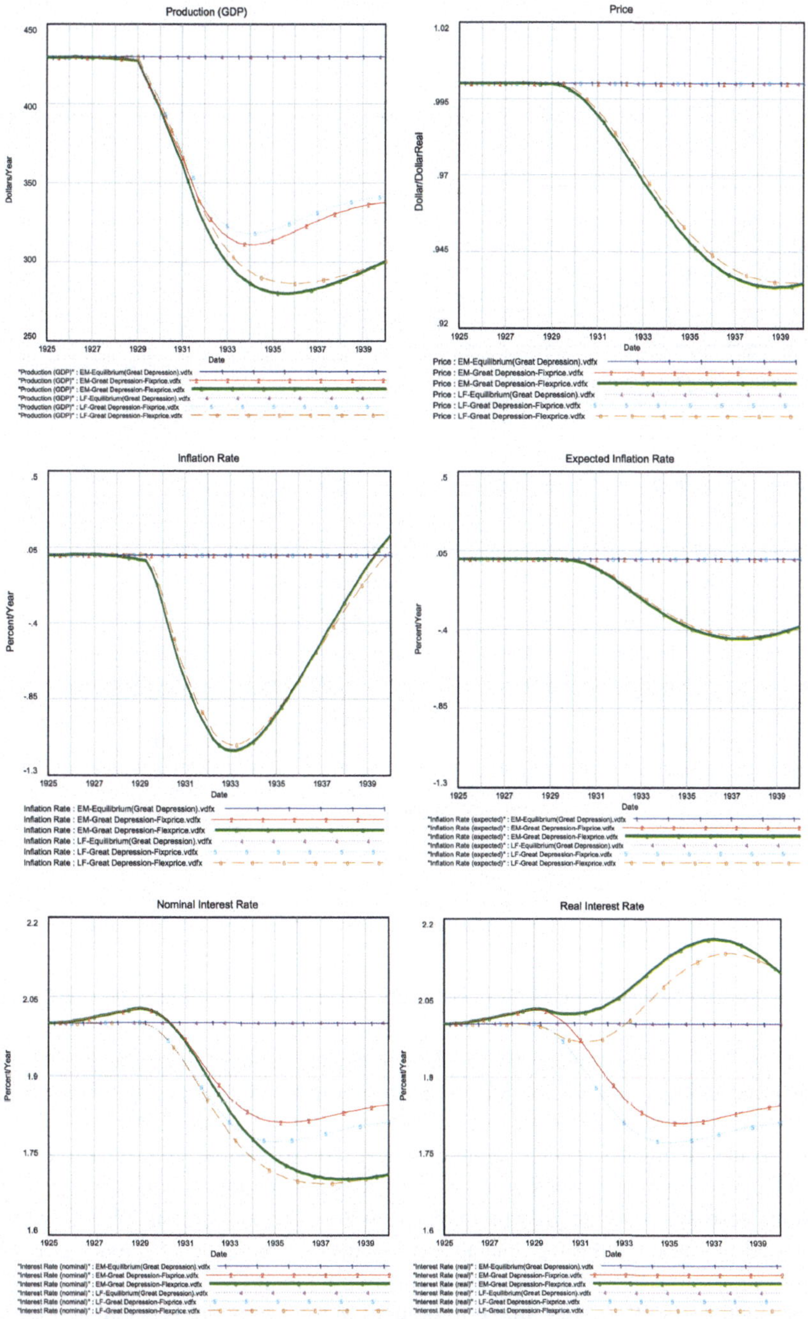

Fig. 8.34 The great depression revisited—production, price, inflation and interest rates

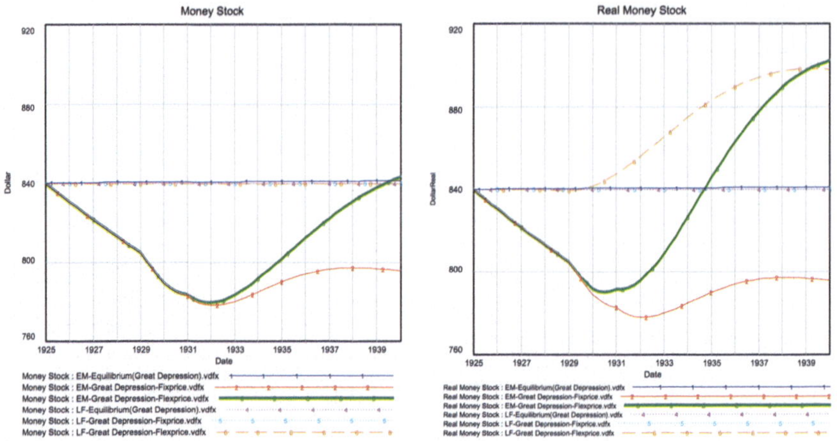

Fig. 8.35 The great depression revisited—money and real money stocks

Table 8.3 Legend names for simulations under the great depression revisited

Endogenous Money ASD	Loanable Funds ASD
Line 1: EM-Equilibrium	Line 4: LF-Equilibrium
Line 2: EM-Great Depression-Fixprice	Line 5: LF-Great Depression-Fixprice
LIne 3: EM-Great Depression-Flexprice	Line 6: LF-Great Depression-Flexprice

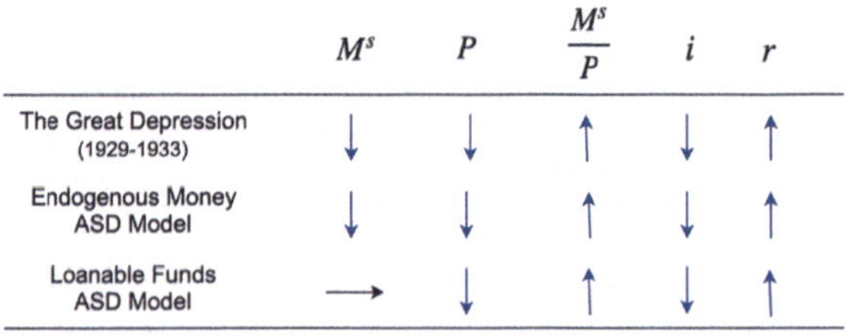

Fig. 8.36 Qualitative evaluation of endogenous money (EM) and loanable funds (LF) ASD models

become similar to those of EM models except money stock as already pointed out in Sect. 8.6.

Figure 8.37 shows comparative IS-LM analyses of phase diagram: production (GDP) and interest rate. In the left diagram, nominal interest rate is taken on the vertical axis whereas real interest rate is taken in the right diagram. EM model (lines 3 in green) and LF model (lines 6 in orange) seem to behave similarly, because under the Great Depression money stock contracts and does not become behavioral constraint as in the case of economic growth analyzed in the previous section. We should not be misled by these similarities, because as discussed above the LF model failed to capture the contraction of money stock during the Great Depression. Accordingly, the production (GDP) (dotted line 6 in orange) in the LF model is calculated larger than that of EM model (line 3 in green) in the above left diagram of Production (GDP) in Fig. 8.34. That is, recessions and financial instability tend to be under-estimated

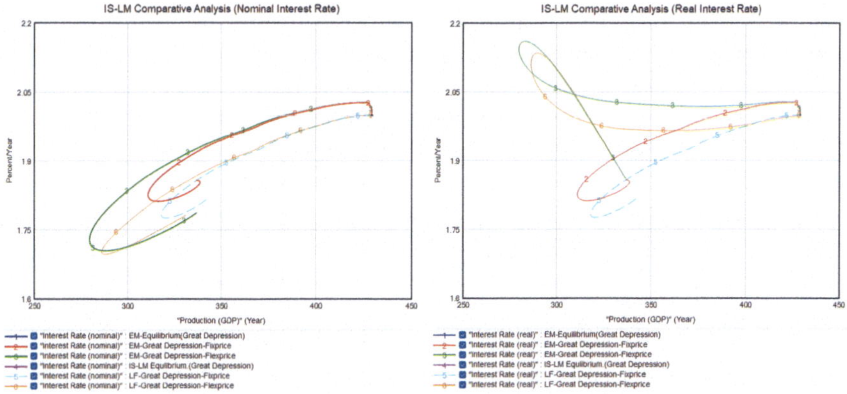

Fig. 8.37 The great depression revisited—IS-LM phase diagrams

as long as we use the LF model. This is another reason why the LF model must be rejected as a macroeconomic model of debt money system.

8.13 Japan's Lost 30 Years as Another Case

8.13.1 Can the ASD Model Capture Japan's Lost 30 Years?

In order for the endogenous money ASD model developed here to be claimed as a generic macroeconomic model of debt money system, it has to be able to capture another big economic recession in history; that is, Japan's lost 30 years, starting in 1991. Though simulation here is run for 40 years from 1980 through 2020,[31] it should be reminded that this is not a quantitative data-fitting simulation against real economic data of the corresponding period in Japan. Instead, it is regarded as a qualitative simulation to investigate if our ASD model can capture the observed behaviors of the Japan's lost 30 years qualitatively, using the one-time changes of parameter values as if they were outside shocks. Parameter values used for the simulation are summarized in the following Table 8.4.

Table 8.5 lists corresponding names of diagram legends throughout simulation results shown in Figs. 8.38 and 8.39. EM-Equilibrium (Japan) (lines 1 in blue) shows a base run as a growth path as usual as if "Japan as Number One". EM-Japan's Great Depression (lines 2 in red) indicates "what if" behaviors without active fiscal spending policies of the Japanese government during the lost 30 years. In other words, behaviors presented by lines 2 could be interpreted as the prolonged behaviors of the Great Depression spread over 30 years in Japan. Indeed, if they were compressed to

[31] Initial simulation time t = 0 in the model is specified as t = 1980. Accordingly, simulation time t = 11 implies 1991 and t = 13 implies 1993.

Table 8.4 Parameter values for the simulation of Japan's lost 30 years

Equilibrium (Japan) (a growth path as usual as if "Japan as No. 1")	(1) Repayment Ratio (Households) = 0 (← 0.018) (2) Change in Ratio Elasticity (Price) = 0.06 (← 0) (3) Primary Balance Ratio = 1.1 (← 1) (4) Initial Deposits (Households) = 50 (← 360) (5) Initial Time Deposits (Households) = 550 (← 440)
Japan's Great Depression (without gov. spending)	(6) $\Delta C_0 = -20$ at t = 1991, $\Delta I_0 = -50$ at t = 1991 $\Delta \bar{I}_H = -30$ at t = 1991
Japan's Lost 30 Years	(7) $\Delta \bar{G} = 15$ at t = 1993 (Fiscal Policy)

Table 8.5 Legend names for the simulations of Japan's lost 30 years

Endogenous Money ASD	Loanable Funds ASD
Line 1: EM-Equilibrium (Japan)	
Line 2: EM-Japan's Great Depression	(With Fiscal Policy)
Line 3: EM-Japan's Lost 30 Years	Line 4: LF-Japan's Lost 30 Years

those of 10 years, they exhibit similar behaviors as those of the Great Depression (1929–1939) revisited above. Indeed, we can observe that behaviors of the Japan's lost 30 years are similar to those of the Great Depression in terms of the underlying behavioral patterns in key macroeconomic variables. Therefore, we may conclude that under the debt money system, economic recessions, whether the Great Depression, the Japan's lost 30 years, or any other recessions in general, could exhibit similar behaviors observed under the endogenous money spending hypothesis.

EM-Japan's Lost 30 Years (lines 3 in green) shows simulation behaviors, under the endogenous money spending hypothesis, when fiscal spending policy is applied. Accordingly, lines 2 and 3 provide comparative behaviors of the Japan's recession cases without or with fiscal policy. For instance, production (GDP) shown at the top left of Fig. 8.38 indicates that Japan's GDP would have been reduced significantly (line 2), compared with line 3, if the government did not apply the active spending policy. LF-Japan's Lost 30 Years (dotted lines 4 in pink) is additionally included to see how Japan's lost 30 years could have been described under the mainstream LF model.

Similarly, top right diagram indicates that deflation would have been more severe without fiscal policy (line 2) than the case with spending policy (line 3). The remaining diagrams present another comparative behaviors of Japan's lost 30 years such as inflation rate, expected inflation rate, nominal and real interest rates. These variables produce similar behaviors as those obtained in the above section of the Great Depression case revisited.

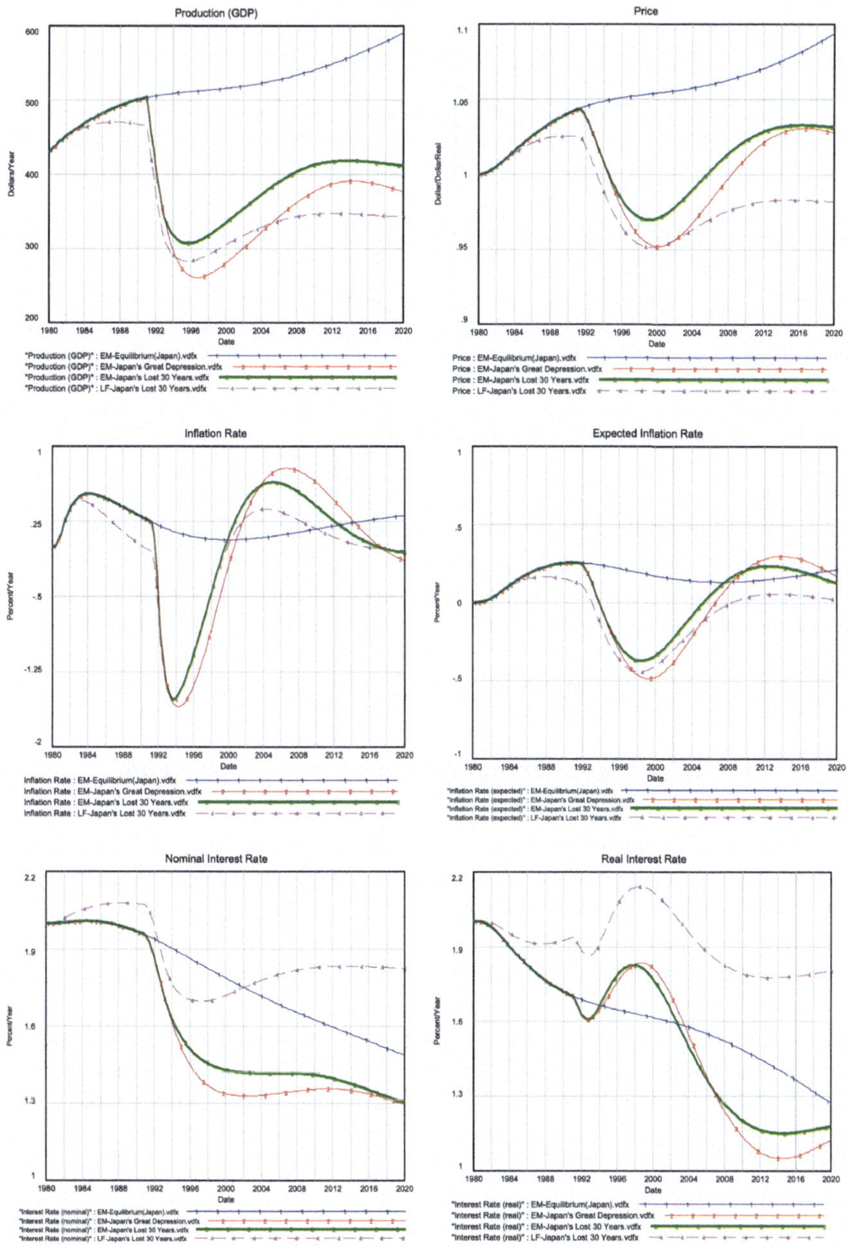

Fig. 8.38 Japan's lost 30 years—GDP, price inflation and interest rates

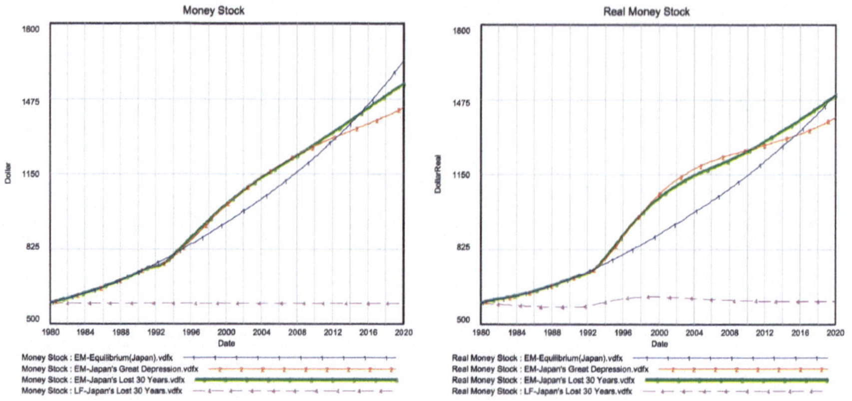

Fig. 8.39 Japan's lost 30 years—money and real money stocks

Figure 8.39 illustrate the behaviors of money stock and real money stock. Both money stock and real money stock continue to increase in Japan against the observed contraction of money stock during the Great Depression in the US. These odd behaviors of the increase in money stock are related with a crowding out effect to be discussed below.

8.13.2 A Myth of Mainstream Economic's Crowding Out

One of the claims made by the mainstream economics was that if the government continues to accumulate its debt the economy would sooner or later faces with rising interest rate and the so-called "crowing out" effect, which reduces private investment and cancels out the effects of fiscal policy. Yet, such rises in interest rates did not occur in Japan. To examine this mainstream claim, we have run simulations under the loanable funds ASD model, which are illustrated by the dotted lines 4 (in pink) in Figs. 8.38 and 8.39. Indeed, line 4 in the bottom left diagram of Fig. 8.38 shows that nominal interest rate is increasing as the government continues to increase its debts under fiscal policy during the lost 30 years. That is to say, crowing out effect suggested by mainstream economists seem to have been supported under the flawed LF model.

On the contrary, nominal interest rates continued to decline during the lost 30 years in Japan. Line 3 (in green) of endogenous money ASD model shown in the same diagram illustrates this continued decline in nominal interest rate. This declining nominal interest rate has been a puzzle (anomaly) among the mainstream economists whose mindsets are occupied by the loanable funds (exogenous money) model. Our EM model indicates that money stock (line 3) shown in the left diagram of Fig. 8.39 continues to increase due to the government's debt accumulation, which pushes down the nominal interest rate. This is another example that demonstrates how the mainstream theory of loanable funds model is flawed.

Interestingly, real interest rate temporarily rises and then continues to decline, even under the loanable funds model as shown by line 4 in bottom right diagram of Fig. 8.38. Mainstream theory of exogenous money failed to show this cyclical behavior of real interest rate, which reflects the complexity of economic dynamics.

8.13.3 Debt-Money Relations and Their Decomposition

Let us continue our analysis, using only the endogenous money ASD model. We have observed three surprising monetary relations in Japan as illustrated in the top left diagram of Fig. 8.40 (Yamaguchi and Yamaguchi, 2021b). Specifically, we have found the following correlations as presented in Chap. 3:

- Money Stock (M_3) $\simeq$ Total Debts (corr.coef = 0.987)
  (line 1 $\simeq$ line 2 in the top left diagram of Fig. 8.40)
- Time Deposits (M_T) $\simeq$ Private Debts (by Producers and Households)
  (corr.coef = 0.928) (line 3 $\simeq$ line 4 in the same diagram)
- M_1 (= Currency + Demand Deposits) $\simeq$ Government Debts
  (corr.coef = 0.992) (line 5 $\simeq$ line 6 in the same diagram)

The diagram on top right in Fig. 8.40 shows that our EM model can successfully produce money-debt breakdown relations as observed in Japan. Specifically, money stock (line 1 in blue) is shown to be always equal to total debts (line 2 in red) in the model. This confirms that the Eq. (8.75) we presented above holds true in the EM model of the debt money system. Under the present system, money is created only when producers, households and the government come to borrow from banks at interest. Bankers receive interests against those loans that are created as borrowers' deposits out of nothing.

Our endogenous money ASD model can successfully reproduce these macroeconomic relations of money stock such as M_1, M_T, M_2, M_3 and debts by producers, households, and the government. Hence, the EM model would also help analyze and identify system structures underlying the macroeconomic behaviors of debt money by manipulating the model parameter values.

Bottom diagrams in Fig. 8.40 are the same as the top ones except that money stocks (lines 1 in blue) in the top are replaced with GDP (lines 1 in blue) in the bottom in order to compare the behaviors of GDP and monetary breakdowns directly. They demonstrate that GDP gets stagnated due to the decrease in the private debts as analyzed in Chap. 4. To sum up, the endogenous money ASD model developed here can be used as a standard macroeconomic model for explaining the Japan's lost 30 years as well as the Great Depression. In this sense, it could be the model of paradigm shift in macroeconomics we have emphasized in this book.

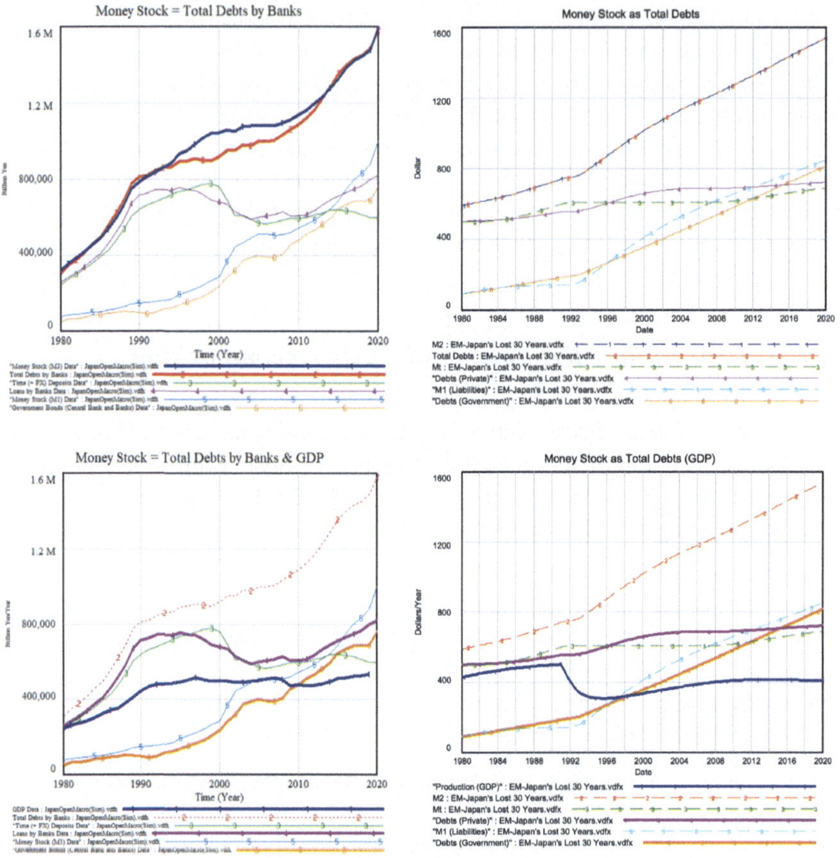

Fig. 8.40 Money-debt relationship in Japan and its decomposition analyses

8.13.4 *Japan's Lost 30 Years as Joint Shifts of IS-LM Curves*

For our EM model to be a standard ASD model in macroeconomics, however, it has to be further able to solve the limitation of the short-run IS-LM model discussed in the Introduction. Specifically, we have to be able to produce "point J" indicated in Fig. 8.20.

Figure 8.41 presents the phase diagrams of production (GDP) and nominal interest rate by the behaviors of Japan's lost 30 years produced in the EM model (lines 1, 2 and 3) and LF model (dotted line 4). Line 1 indicates a base run behaviors of Japanese economy as if "Japan as Number One". Line 2 indicates how production (GDP) and nominal interest rate would have been more extremely worsened if no fiscal policy were applied in Japan. Bold line 3 indicates that production (GDP) continued to decline in the beginning and failed to recover the point of "Japan as Number One" in spite of the aggressive fiscal policy by the Japanese government, while interest rate

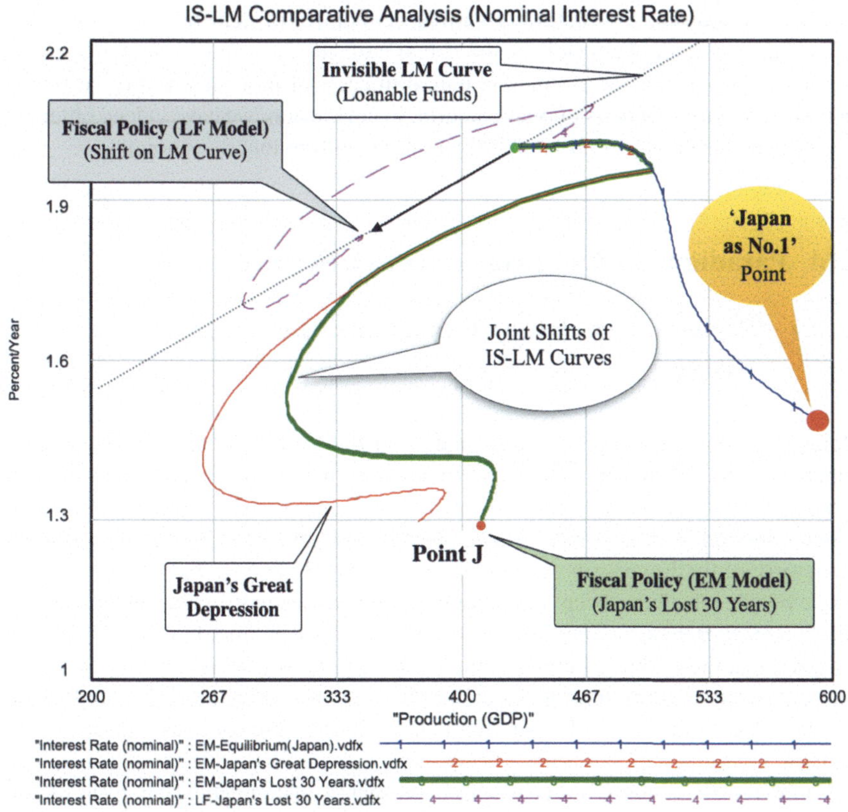

Fig. 8.41 Simulation of Japan's lost 30 years as point J

continued to decline against the mainstream claim of the crowding out effect. These joint shift behaviors ended at "point J", which looks like a point actually observed during the lost 30 years in Japan. In this way we have successfully captured the behaviors of Japan's lost 30 years in the phase diagram by the endogenous money ASD model developed here.

On the contrary, if we are obliged to apply macroeconomic model of exogenous money such as the LF model, its economic behaviors are always constrained as if they are moving only along the LM curve which is, though, hidden or made invisible in the above phase diagram. We can easily confirms these behaviors on the invisible LM curve by changing the level of consumption, investment and government spending, whatever amounts we apply. In other words, we could not have explained the move to the "point J" as long as we stick to the old paradigm of loanable funds or exogenous money system.

Our simulation results here seem to demonstrate that macroeconomic behaviors of recessions in general could be similarly captured by the EM model as long as they are running under structurally similar economies of debt money system. By calibrating the model behaviors to the actual case studies, the EM model could be used by policy-makers to examine potential impacts of monetary and fiscal policy on their economy before its implementation. In conclusion, we have indeed obtained the endogenous money ASD model of paradigm shift in macroeconomics.

8.14 Paradigm Shift in Economics as a Science

8.14.1 *Keynesian Models of* Exogenous Money *are All Wrong*

Mainstream macroeconomics, originated from the Keynes's General Theory and popularized by the IS-LM analysis, is founded on the premise that money stock is controlled by the monetary authority such as the central bank. Monetary and fiscal policies applied by policy makers have been deeply influenced by this conventional framework of the Keynesian economics. As discussed in Chap. 5, virtually all economic policies that have been implemented in Japan during the post-1990 recession failed to recover the economy from its decades-long stagnation. In Chap. 7 we have analyzed that these policy failures stem from the failures of mainstream macroeconomic analysis built on the flawed assumption of exogenous money rooted in the IS-LM model, and proposed a paradigm shift based on endogenous money IS-LM analysis.

Following these discussions we have presented mathematical analysis of the paradigm shift model in this chapter and presented the corresponding System Dynamics (SD) and Accounting System Dynamics (ASD) macroeconomic models step-by-step. Since our analyses have become complex at this stage, let us summarize the paradigm shift obtained in this chapter along with the bird's-eye view of Table 8.6 classifying the SD and ASD models developed so far.

1. We have started this chapter with the Keynesian Short-Run IS-LM Model, which is built on the assumptions of fixed price under exogenous money. By applying this standard IS-LM model, Mankiw rejected the Money Hypothesis and only accepted the Spending Hypothesis as the plausible cause of the Great Depression. Since it is a comparative statics, we have converted it into a dynamic model with SD modeling approach in Sect. 8.2. Base on the dynamic IS-LM model, we have demonstrated in Sect. 8.3 that the behaviors of the Great Depression cannot be explained under both Spending and Money Hypotheses (Case 1 simulation).
2. Following the Mankiw's extended version of the Keynesian IS-LM model, we have built the corresponding SD model of Flexible Price IS-LM in Sect. 8.4 in which price is made flexible under *exogenous money* assumption. Yet, again, both Spending and Money Hypotheses failed to explain the behaviors of the Great Depression (Case 2 simulation).

Table 8.6 Classification of SD and ASD macroeconomic models

(Main Features)	Exogenous Debt Money (flawed)	Endogenous Debt Money (valid)
Fixed Price	Case 1 Keynesian IS-LM (SD)	Case 3 Endogenous Money IS-LM (SD)
Flexible Price	Case 2 Flexible Price IS-LM (SD)	Case 4 Endogenous Money IS-LM (SD)
Budget Equations & Transactions	Case 5 Loanable Funds (ASD)	Case 6 Endogenous Money (ASD)
Capital Accumulation	Case 7: Long-run Loanable Funds (ASD)	Case 8: Long-run Endogenous Money (ASD)
Unfair Income Distribution & Built-in Inflation	Case 9: Long-run Loanable Funds at Interest (ASD)	Case 10: Long-run Endogenous Money (ASD) at Interests (ASD)
MuRatopia Economy	Public Money (Exogenous) MuRatopia Economy Model (→ Chap. 15)	

3. Failures of these Keynesian models are caused by the assumption of exogenous money stock. By hypothesizing in this way, we have reviewed the *Debt-Deflation* and *100% Money* theories (Fisher, 1932, 1933, 1935) in Sect. 8.5, which has led us to formulate the Endogenous Money Spending Hypothesis (EMSH) in place of the Spending and Money Hypotheses.
4. Based on this hypothesis we have built the SD model of Endogenous Money IS-LM in Sect. 8.6. Yet, under the fixed price assumption, this model also failed to explain the behaviors of the Great Depression (Case 3 simulation). However, when price is assumed to be flexible, the Endogenous Money Spending Hypothesis was able to explain the behaviors of the Great Depression in a manner consistent with data (Case 4 simulation).
5. Accordingly, the Endogenous Money IS-LM is our paradigm shift model, we thought initially, because, as discussed in Chap. 7, under the present debt money system, the *IS* and *LM* curves must move jointly on the phase diagram of income and interest rate, and this model can demonstrate such dynamics of joint shifts in *IS* and *LM* curves. These findings further led us to identify the methodological and theoretical problems of the standard Keynesian IS-LM model, in which the two curves are shifted separately for macroeconomic policy analysis. Therefore, we have concluded at this stage of our analyses that the standard IS-LM model is no longer valid as a reliable model of the economy operating under the fractional reserve banking system.
6. The Endogenous Money IS-LM model, however, failed to explain the on-going case of Japan's lost 30 years, which was represented symbolically as a "Point J" in the IS-LM phase diagram of Fig. 8.20 discussed in Sect. 8.7. Specifically, we have identified that its explanatory limitation is due to the mechanistic application of

the EMSH where money stock is assumed to fluctuate endogenously according to the growth rate of income.

7. To overcome this limitation, we have further expanded the above IS-LM models by incorporating the budget equations of domestic sectors such as producers, households, the government and banks. Specifically, we first presented a mathematical analysis of the Loanable Funds Model with Budgets and discussed its validity by introducing the concepts of *ex ante* and *ex post* in Sect. 8.8. Next, we have presented a mathematical analysis of the Endogenous Money model with Budgets in Sect. 8.9 and shown that it can capture the fundamental macroeconomic relationships observed under the debt money system such as "Money Stock $\simeq$ Total Debts" and its breakdown relationships discussed in Chap. 3.
8. To examine behaviors of these two models, we have converted them into ASD macroeconomic models by incorporating transactions among macroeconomic sectors including the central bank. They are called Loanable Funds and Endogenous Money models, respectively. As minimum requirements for a coherent simulation-based economic analysis, these two models were further tested against four validations in Sect. 8.10; (1) unit checks as SD models, (2) balance sheets and flow of funds consistency checks as ASD models, (3) debt money checks as macroeconomic models, and (4) non-equivalence check of macroeconomic aggregates (production, income and expenditure).
9. The Loanable Funds ASD model thus constructed failed to explain the behaviors of the Great Depression due to the exogenous money assumption (Case 5 simulation). At this stage we were convinced that the Keynesian theory built on exogenous money is flawed and can no longer hold as a valid macroeconomic theory under the current debt money system, as demonstrated by Case 1, 2 and 5 simulations. The model could be effective, however, under the public money system where total money stock is controlled by the monetary authority as discussed in Sect. 8.11.1.
10. On the other hand, the Endogenous Money ASD model (Case 6) is shown to produce behaviors that are consistent with data of the Great Depression, albeit qualitatively. As discussed in Sect. 8.12, initial values and parameters are not fitted to the reference data. Therefore, the simulation is presented as a preliminary study to explore the possibility of whether the newly constructed model can capture the behaviors of key macroeconomic variables during the Great Depression.
11. To further examine the validity of the Endogenous Money ASD model as the paradigm shift in economics, we have arranged parameter values in Sect. 8.13 such that it captures the Japan's lost 30 years at least qualitatively (Case 6). Indeed, the model is able to (i) produce the point J on the phase diagram successfully, (ii) revealed the myth of crowing out effect, and (iii) reproduced the debt money relationships, all of which were discussed in Chaps. 3 and 5.
12. In this way, the Endogenous Money ASD model (Case 6) is shown to explain the two major events that have taken place in modern economic history and remained unexplained. Therefore, it could be the benchmark model that can be used to study complex macroeconomic dynamics under the present debt money systems.

> All textbooks that still apply the conventional (static) and flawed (exogenous money) IS-LM analysis must be rewritten based on this integrated framework.

This finishes the summary of our paradigm shift in economics. Table 8.6 also presents our latest research; that is, Long-run Loanable Funds and Endogenous Money ASD models with capital accumulation and production function newly incorporated (Cases 7 and 8). Similar behaviors observed under Case 5 and 6 simulations were obtained even in these long-run models where capital accumulation takes place. Furthermore, in Case 10 simulation, we have analyzed how the debt money creation causes unfair income distribution by way of interests, while systematizing inflation of total income and causing wage share to diminish. These built-in unfair features of the debt money system have been largely neglected even in Post-Keynesian literature that stress endogenous money. These model expansions allow us to analyze functional income distribution explicitly in relation to neoclassical long-run growth dynamics. However, these advanced topics are beyond the scope of this book. For more details, readers are referred to our latest working papers (Yamaguchi and Yamaguchi, 2023, 2024).

In conclusion, the long-run endogenous money ASD model thus developed as Case 10 embodies the paradigm shift in economics as a science and provides a flexible framework for the development of an integrated theory that help us understand the major economic problems facing the world.

8.14.2 The Lost Century of Economics

Should economics be grounded on the exogenous money or endogenous money? The answer is clear as we have discussed so far in this book. However, the question remains as to why did economics profession lose sight of its scholarly duty and promulgate the opposite view of banks as intermediaries of pre-existing money (loanable funds)? When did economics textbooks begin to fail to clarify that it is private banks that create 99% of money and charge interests?

To investigate when and how such *retrogression* in economics occurred, Black (2021) recently conducted a survey of 218 titles from American economics textbooks catalogue from 1877 to 2017, including the popular textbook by Mankiw (2016) discussed in this chapter. By categorizing the literature reviewed into four groups as (1) loans create deposits (LCD), (2) deposits create loans (DCL), (3) both are true under certain situations (BOTH), and (4) the author abstains from discussing bank credit creation (ABSTAIN), Black (2021) found that deposit creation theory (LCD) was the only predominant view of banking with virtually 100% share until Samuelson (1948) effectively broke away from the economist's consensus[32] and set

[32] That the deposit creation theory was the "consensus" among economists up to the 1940s was well recognized at that time. Lloyd W. Mints, one of the eight economists who signed the Chicago Plan memorandum, acknowledged the central part played by Phillips and wrote:

> The fact that the banks "create" money when they acquire earning assets has been conceded almost, but not quite, unanimously in recent years. There is nearly as close an approach to

the stage for popularizing the financial intermediation theory (DCL) in his influential textbook that dominated the American textbook market in the 1950s and 60s. Black (2021) explains:

> The findings reveal there are two distinct phases of intellectual change which occur after the 1876 to 1947 period when the view that individual banks create new money when granting loans was unchallenged. The initial change occurs from 1948 to 1971 when Samuelson's *Economics* (1948) breaks with tradition and popularizes the unit bank versus monopoly bank framework; and then from 1971 to the present when the first textbook presents a "deposits create loans" model and the monopoly bank model is dropped from *Economics* in 1985 to join[s] other textbooks where only the unit bank model describes the representative banking system and endogenous loan creation is removed from the story. ...
>
> Finally, this approach to money supply determination was integrated into macroeconomic models in the post-war period which marginalized the role of money. These models deliberately simplified the inherent complexity of bank credit creation and from the IS-LM framework to Real Business Cycle and Dynamic Stochastic General Equilibrium models, money was always represented as a fixed quantity controlled by the monetary authorities. When Samuelson's twelfth edition in 1985 dropped the reference to the monopoly bank–the model he had first introduced in 1948–the mythology was complete and a century of orthodox "banking view" of money creation no longer fit into this new paradigm. (Black, 2021, pp. 86–88)

The "monopoly bank" was a unique phrasing Chester A. Phillips–who originally came up with the novel theory of deposit multiplication in his doctoral dissertation completed in 1919 under the supervision of Fisher–used to draw a distinction between a small country ("unit") bank and monopoly bank system where cash drains (such as deposit withdrawals) limit each individual bank's ability to expand credits.[33]

What was striking among other findings discussed by Black (2021) is the Samuelson's suspicious role in further confusing how banks actually operate.

> Samuelson also revived the banker-goldsmith analogy that Macleod had appealed to generations of authors to avoid and was the first to popularize the term "fractional reserve banking" as well as the Federal Reserve's unit banking model. (Black, 2021, p. 70)

The Fed's unit banking model is the standard description of how the fractional reserve banking works where the initial amount of cash deposited into a bank gets loaned

---

> unanimity in regard to the manner in which the system operates to expand or contract the money supply and as to the extent to which expansion may be carried. For this state of affairs much credit is due Phillips (1920). While it is true, as we have seen, that the essentials of the process were accurately and clearly depicted by a number of writers before Phillips, it is nevertheless also true that it has been the latter who has brought about substantial agreement in regard to this matter. (Mints, 1945, pp. 257–258)

See also Footnote 4 in Chap. 3 where Fisher himself credits the Phillips' findings in *100% Money*.

[33] See Black (2021) on the original contribution of the Phillip's formulation of the mechanics of deposit multiplication process and how Phillips' model influenced the subsequent literatures on money and banking in the context of American economics textbooks. Based on ASD macroeconomic models, Yamaguchi and Yamaguchi (2016) showed how such deposit withdrawals in cash precipitated by the change in household's liquidity preference can destabilize money stock under the debt money system in addition to bank's capricious lending behavior.

out and redeposited into another bank, and the same process repeats until the summation of individual bank's deposits results in multiplication of the initial amount of cash supplied exogenously by the central bank. According to Black (2021) the view that banks are financial intermediaries originated from a publication by the Federal Reserve Bulletin of May 1939 titled "The Federal Reserve System: Its Purposes and Functions."[34]

Such obscurantism–overturning endogenous money and replacing it with exogenous money view–initiated by the monetary authority itself is quite revealing. However, it is consistent with prior observations by economists who have seen the Fed's role as downplaying the role of banks and the endogenous money. For instance, Cohen (1972), who performed a review of Copeland's 'moneyflow' analyses since 1947, asserted that "the breadth of Copeland's money-flows has been substantially narrowed in the hands of the Federal Reserve and foreign account-makers." Dawson (1996) similarly observed that the Copeland's original flow of funds analysis was compromised by removal of his money circuit calculations after it was carried on to the Federal Reserve as part of its integration into the National Income and Product Accounts System.

Based on the catalogue of over two hundred titles, Black (2021) concluded that the share of loans create deposits (LCD) rapidly declined in the 1970s, falling to about one-third of the textbook market. On the other hand, both are true (BOTH) position quickly rose to 40% such as the Mankiw's textbook (9th edition) discussed above.[35] In the 1980s, the share of LCD approach declined further to an all-time low of 8%, while the share of deposits create loans (DCL) approach or the exogenous money view continued to rise after the 1970s, and remained stable at more than one-third from the 1980s to 2000s. Then, the share of both are true (BOTH) approach rapidly declines after the 2000s from about 30 to 10%, while the share of ABSTAIN approach rose to nearly 40%. In addition, the share of LCD has recovered above the 20% level since 2010, leaving the LCD and DCL approaches close together at around 30% each.

Concerning the economists' conflicting views on banking, Werner (2016, p. 365) had already pointed out how Samuelson's influential textbook from its first edition rejected the credit creation theory as "false explanations still in wide circulation" (Samuelson, 1948, p. 324) and how he continued to adhere to the financial intermediation theory in subsequent editions. Thus, Black's extensive literature survey and

---

[34] Black (2021) observed that the Federal Reserve's Monthly Bulletin, which were sent to member banks free of charge, "was a key source of data for economists writing about money and banking" (p. 68), and that the May 1939 issue, which was reproduced again in February 1940, was the instance where the "Lilliputian model of deposit expansion was first introduced to a wide audience of economists and subsequently repeated through textbooks–first in Peterson's *Money and Banking* (1941) and then in Samuelson's *Economics* (1947)" (p. 12).

[35] Note that Black (2021) referenced the Mankiw's textbook (2005, 5th edition) into (2) DCL approach while this chapter referenced 9th edition published in 2016 and classified it as being in the confusing group, or (3) BOTH approach *à la* Black (2021). On the other hand, when it comes to IS-LM case analysis of the Great Depression, Mankiw (2016) accepted the exogenous money view as discussed in this chapter.

analysis corroborated the prior knowledge advanced by Werner (2016) and provided us with the last piece needed to get us a more detailed picture of how "the economics profession has failed over most of the past century to make any progress concerning knowledge of the monetary system, and why it instead moved ever further away from the truth as already recognised by the credit creation theory well over a century ago" (Werner, 2016, p. 361).

Why Did Samuelson Overturn the Endogenous Money?

As to why this retrogression in economic science has occurred, Black (2021) submitted the following five "most likely" explanations (pp. 74–76). First, the growing popularity of Samuelson's *Economics* effectively (re)shaped the dominant thinking of the next generation of economists, who followed the Samuelson's middle-of-the-road approach to banking and then went on to write new textbooks in the 1970s and 1980s when the major shift in paradigm occurred. Second, the rise of the neoclassical-Keynesian synthesis (such as IS-LM model) from the 1950s to 70s popularized the exogenous money view and became mainstream.

Third, in addition to the market share transition described above, a growing number of authors, especially those of the specialized textbooks on monetary and financial economics, began to "abstain" from discussing the fractional reserve banking as either an endogenous or exogenous money approach, which constituted the fourth group (ABSTAIN) in the Black's literature analysis.

Fourth, since 1970s, most authors that took the "both are true" position have stopped referring to bank money creation process. Hence, the degree of ambiguity has deepened. And fifth, as the American economics textbook market began consolidating in the 1980s, the lineup of textbooks has been reduced to a small number of best-selling authors under the big five publishers. And those textbooks that took the exogenous money (DCL) position, while they were limited in numbers (less than 20 titles in total since 1980s), eventually became the most-assigned textbooks in American universities' curriculum. And these few lineups, Black (2021) observed, might have conveyed "the impression of consensus among economists" (p. 76).

These five factors indeed provide a chronological analysis of *how* the false view of banking–first introduced by the Fed and popularized by Samuelson–has gradually shifted the perception of subsequent generations and morphed into a dominant paradigm. There still remains, however, a fundamental question as to *why* Samuelson went to the trouble of overturning the deposit creation theory and continued to propagate the false view of "fractional reserve banking" in subsequent editions. The question gets even deeper when we are reminded that his economics teachers at Chicago and Harvard included some of the Chicago Plan economists who criticized the debt money system, and Joseph A. Schumpeter who was working on a new business cycle theory based on credit creation by banks (Schumpeter, 1934). It is unlikely that Samuelson was unaware of their critical position on fractional reserve banking and the nature of endogenous debt money.

One may argue that the reason why Samuelson did so was simply to avoid mathematical complexity and make models numerically solvable, just as Keynes said "technical monetary detail falls into the background" in the *General Theory* (as we will see in the next Chap. 9). Or did he simply follow the original formulation of money supply function by Hicks (1937) when he introduced the IS-LM framework (see Footnote 11 of this chapter)? Indeed, personal computers were not yet widely available in the 1980s. However, it would be a fatal mistake, particularly as a young rising scholar at MIT's economics department, to categorically deny the deposit creation theory as "false explanations" with no empirical basis.

In the next Chap. 9, we will discuss Samuelson's political motive that was likely behind his risky attempt to break away from the economist's consensus and overturn the predominant deposit creation theory. If economics is to be saved from a century-old confusion and obscurantism, a next generation of economists must incorporate the paradigm shift by endogenous debt money analysis presented in this chapter.

Chapter 9
There Exist Only Four Monetary Theories

Economy can be viewed as a whole of various transactions conducted with money. Therefore, economics as a branch of social science must include money at the center of its theoretical framework. How has economics dealt with money, then? Why has economics failed to incorporate banks as they are operating in the real world? Monetary theories underlying each school of economic thoughts seem to be complicated and diverse at first glance. On the contrary it turned out there are only four monetary theories as listed in Fig. 9.1, which is created based on the classification of money in Fig. 2.1. This finding was our grateful harvest from writing this book. Let us examine them one by one in this chapter.

9.1 Classification of Monetary Theories

Our classification starts with (1) public money theory. Then, two mainstream monetary theories follow: (2) moneyless price and commodity money theory as mainstream neoclassical theory, and (3) exogenous debt money theory (flow approach) as mainstream Keynesian theory. Finally, the last group of economists distinguishes themselves as the proponents of (4) endogenous debt money theory (stock approach), which has been the basis of 100% reserve banking proposals in the 1930s–40s including the Chicago Plan and Fisher's 100% Money.

The following authors are referenced in Fig. 9.1. (1) Public Money Theory: Aristotle (1934 [350]), Soddy (1926), Knight et al. (1933), Fisher (1935), Douglas et al. (1939), Zarlenga (2002), Yamaguchi (2010, 2011, 2013), Yamaguchi and Yamaguchi (2016, 2017a). (2) Moneyless Price and Commodity Money Theory: Smith (1776), Marx (1867), Arrow and Debreu (1954), Lucas (1972). (3) Exogenous Debt Money Theory: von Mises (1912), Phillips (1920), von Hayek (1929), Keynes (1936), Hicks (1937), Modigliani (1944), Samuelson (1948), Hansen (1949), Tobin (1963), Bernanke and Blinder (1988), Stiglitz (1997), Koo (2009), Krugman (2015), Mankiw (2016). (4) Endogenous Debt Money Theory: MacLeod (1856), Fisher (1932, 1933),

K. Yamaguchi and Y. Yamaguchi, *Public Money*,
https://doi.org/10.1007/978-981-97-6564-5_9

Classification of Monetary Theory				
	Monetary Theory	Overview	Models	Representative Economists
Public Money	Public Money Theory	Interest-free money is issued by the legislature as equity of the Public (under 100% reserve banking). This will prevent booms and busts, and realize price stability, sustainable growth, full employment and social welfare. EPM (Electronic Public Money) is proposed to protect privacy and freedom against control by retail CBDC (Central Bank Digital Currency).	ASD (Accounting System Dynamics) macroeconomic models, which integrate flow and stock approches of modeling bank lending as the Heads and Tails of the same endogenous debt money. Banks are both intermediaries and creators of debt money under the current fractional reserve banking system.	Aristotle, Soddy, the Chicago Plan economists, Irving Fisher, and other proponents of 100% reserve banking, Stephen Zarlenga (AMI), Kaoru Yamaguchi, Yokei Yamaguchi, and more economsits to follow.
Commodity	Mainstream Neoclassical: Moneyless Price and Commodity Money Theory	Relative prices are determined by general equilibrium of markets. Its numeraire commodity becomes money and determines absolute price levels. Money is thus neutral and only a veil of economic activities.	Neoclassical models such as Dynamic Stochastic General Equilibrium (DSGE) models and Real Business Cycle (RBC) models, etc.	Adam Smith, Karl Marx, Arrow, Debreu, Lucas, and other Classical and Neoclassical economists.
Debt Money	Mainstream Keynesian: Exogenous Debt Money Theory (Flow Approach)	Central bank supplies base money (M0), and money stock (M1, M2) is determined by the money multiplier. Banks are financial intermediaries of exogenously supplied money that collect deposits (loanable funds) from savers and lend to borrowers (flow approach of modeling bank lending).	Keynesian macroeconomic models such as the IS-LM analysis featured in standard macroeconomics textbooks, applied macroeconometric models, and Austrian Business Cycle theory, etc.	Mises, Phillips, Hayek, Keynes, Hicks, Modigliani, Samuelson, Hansen, Tobin, Bernanke, Blinder, Stiglitz, Koo, Krugman, Mankiw, and other (New) Keynesian economists, etc.
	Endogenous Debt Money Theory (Stock Approach)	Central bank supplies base money, with which banks create "deposits" out of nothing and destroy them when loans are repaid (stock approach of modeling bank lending). MMT defines "money is IOU (debt)" and falsely equates treasury bond issuance as issuance of sovereign government currency.	Proposals of 100% reserve banking in 1930s such as the Chicago Plan are based on this endogenous debt money theory. Monetary reform groups of the American Monetary Institute (AMI) and MMT are in a fruitless debate without models.	Macleod, the Chicago Plan economists, Irving Fisher, Schumpeter, Friedman, Minsky, Werner, Keen, and other Post Keynesian and MMT economits (such as Wray), etc.

Fig. 9.1 Classification of monetary theories and their proponents

Schumpeter (1934, 1954), Friedman (1960), Minsky (1982), Werner (2005, 2016), Wray (1990, 2012), Keen (2014).

Historically, two classes of monetary theory have evolved along with the emergence of capitalism and classical economics since 18th century, and eventually became the mainstream monetary theories underlying each school of thoughts. However, as discussed in Sect. 8.14.2, as far as economists' view on banking is concerned, (4) endogenous debt money theory, i.e., "loans create deposits" view *à la* Black (2021), was the academic consensus from at least the late 19th century until 1960s in the American textbook market.[1]

To avoid a lengthy bibliography, priority was given here to references that appear in other parts of this book as well as contemporary scholars in each school of thoughts. Some economists (e.g. von Mises, 1912; Mankiw, 2016) take the (3) exogenous money position in some passages where banks are assumed to be financial intermediaries, while in other passages their explanations or arguments assume the endogenous money where banks finance loans by creating new deposits *ex nihilo*. Strictly speaking, such authors should be categorized into both (3) and (4) in Fig. 9.1, just as Irving Fisher are classified into both (1) and (4) as the leading proponent of 100% reserve banking. Another issue that arises when classifying literatures of money and banking in general is that economists often use ambiguous terms, or they later change their views, which makes it not an easy task to categorically judge their types. However, we do not show such confusing cases in every detail here.

Werner (2016) conducted an extensive literature survey on banking theories and classified them into three types: (1) financial intermediation theory, (2) fractional reserve theory, and (3) credit creation theory. According to the taxonomy employed by Werner (2016), the first theory says that banks collect deposits and lend them out just as other non-bank financial intermediaries do, while the second class of literatures assumes that each individual bank is a financial intermediary without the power to create money, yet the banking system as a whole can collectively create money through the process of deposit expansion.

For the purpose of literature classification, the three theories are indeed "distinct and mutually exclusive theories of banking" (Werner, 2016, p. 361). From legal, operational and accounting perspectives, commercial banks are acting as both financial intermediaries for the deposits they accept and creators of new "deposits" for the loans they make under the fractional reserve requirement (as we have seen in Sect. 3.4 through Fisher's analogy). Therefore, whether it is an individual bank or the banking system as a whole that can create money or not, which Samuelson (1948) began to emphasize and was reiterated in its fifteenth edition (see Sect. 8.14.2), is an irrelevant question in terms of the monetary theories. It only obfuscates the fact that private banks are the creators of 99% of money stock and allocators of new purchasing power. Hence, under our taxonomy in Fig. 9.1, all literatures assuming

---

[1] In this regard Black (2021) adopts a same taxonomy to our classification. However, note that Black (2021) did not use "endogenous vs. exogenous money" categorization in his literature survey and instead categorized them into four groups as discussed in Sect. 8.14.2.

banks as financial intermediaries are classified into (3) exogenous debt money camp altogether.

The decisive difference between the first and fourth groups of economists is whether or not they identify fractional reserve banking system as the root cause of booms and busts and other major economic problems and propose to eliminate them by imposing a 100% reserve requirement. The contemporary economists classified into (1) Public Money Theory explicitly call for the 100% reserve banking in their writings, both in terms of their economic theories and political as well as moral causes. Economists in this category espouse that the power of issuing currency is the sole prerogative of the government that is publicly elected, controlled, and held accountable by the people.

Similar to the first group, the fourth group of economists distinguish themselves from the two mainstream theories (neoclassical and Keynesian) by their recognitions of the role of banks as creators of money. However, they do not necessarily identify the debt money system as structurally problematic, thereby either accepting it as the inevitable feature of the modern capitalist societies or simply avoiding to challenge it for political reasons (which will become clear later in this chapter).[2]

---

[2] One of the few exceptions among the contemporary economists listed in Fig. 9.1 is Prof. Richard A. Werner, who is a long-time critique of central bank monetary policy centered on interest rate manipulation (Werner, 1995, 2005; Lee and Werner, 2018) and increasing concentration of power into the hands of central planners (Werner, 2003). Concerning the Japanese case, he originally took the position that the Bank of Japan should conduct open market purchase operations to stimulate bank credit creation and redirect the supply of new purchasing power to GDP-related transactions (Werner, 1995). He also rightly warned at the time that Keynesian fiscal policy would be doomed unless banks' credit creation is channeled into the real sector. Werner (2005) also referred to the idea of the government issuing interest-free notes (such as the US Notes) as "the most desirable, efficient, and equitable method" (pp. 258–259) to fund fiscal expenditure, and later recommended full reserve banking in a joint submission to UK's Independent Commission on Banking (Dyson et al., 2010).

Prof. Joseph Stiglitz, while referring to the Fisher's debt-deflation theory and the fact that monetary authorities have no direct control over the provision of private credit, similarly made a proposal on the issuance of government notes as a way to tackle Japan's deflation and stimulate the economy in his speech given at the Ministry of Finance on April 16th, 2003, titled "Deflation, Globalization and The New Paradigm of Monetary Economics" (Stiglitz, 2003). While acknowledging that such a proposal may be a cardinal sin for an economist who holds a PhD in economics from MIT, Stiglitz expressed strong confidence in the effectiveness of his policy proposal, saying he would be fine to have his trump card (his MIT PhD) taken away if it triggered inflation. Interestingly, Mr. Kuroda, the former Governor of the Bank of Japan, was also present in this meeting as a senior adviser to the Minister of Finance and made a comment that he "basically agree with Professor Stiglitz's theory and policy recommendations." It should be noted here that proponents of "government-issued money" do not necessarily call for abolition of money creation by private banks. If governments increase cash (M_0) without closing the tap of bank deposit creation (i.e., without raising the legal reserve ratio to 100%), banks will use them to further expand credit creation (M_F). Hence, there is a risk of losing control over the total supply of money (purchasing power). That is why the Public Money System imposes a 100% reserve ratio as one of three conditions during transition. See Chap. 12 for details on the implementation of public money policy and governance system designed to achieve price stability and responsible management of currency.

9.2 The Battle of Economic Ideologies

The Arrow-Debreu Model of General Equilibrium Theory

In the history of modern economics, the first monetary theory that laid the foundation was the mainstream neolassical theory. When Kaoru began to study economics at the University of California, Berkeley, he was most impressed by a law called *Walras Law*, which, according to the general equilibrium theory, holds in any capitalist market economy consisting of goods and services, labor, financial and money markets. This law states that the sum of all budget constraints involved in these market transactions will yield an equation of identity.

Although it was Léon Walras [1834–1910] who first found this law, he could not prove whether there is a general equilibrium in which prices of goods and services, labor, financial and money markets are all in equilibrium at the same time. That is, Walras succeeded in formulating a mathematical model to the extent of matching the number of equations with the number of variables. However, he could not prove the existence of the general equilibrium.

The existence proof of the general equilibrium has remained a difficult problem in theoretical economics nearly for a century. It was finally answered by the two economists, Kenneth J. Arrow [1921–2017] of Stanford University and Gérard Debreu [1921–2004] of the University of California, Berkeley. At Berkeley, Kaoru attended Professor Debreu's seminar on mathematical economics every week. In this seminar, Professor Arrow always sat at the front of the room and asked a lot of questions, while Debreu sat in the back and rarely spoke. They were very contrasting in their characters. There was always a sense of nervousness among the graduate students, wondering what would happen if they were interrupted by Professor Arrow when presenting their researches.

It was in 1954 that these two economists proved the existence of general equilibrium in a competitive market economy (Arrow and Debreu, 1954). Since then, the neoclassical general equilibrium theory, known as the *Arrow-Debreu model* named after these two professors, has dominated economics and revolutionized the world of theoretical economics in particular. The neoclassical theory, which envisioned that the market economy is harmonic and works perfectly, took over the world of economics. Whenever Kaoru was stuck in his study, he used to go to the Professor Debreu's office and beg for his help, so much so that he can still hear Debreu's French accent whenever he closes his eyes.

Arrow won the Nobel Memorial Prize in Economics earlier in 1972. And 11 years later, Debreu won the same prize in 1983. One morning, Kaoru happened to hear "Berkeley professor won the Nobel prize in economics" on the radio news and immediately rushed to the campus on his bicycle. Other graduate students had already gathered, opened a bottle of wine, and held a small party to celebrate Professor Debreu. Kaoru still vividly remembers that during the press conference that followed, when Debreu was asked how his theory would be useful for the current situation of the U.S. economy, he replied flatly, "My general equilibrium theory is not useful at all for day-to-day economic activities." Such was how the Berkley's mathematical economics shone in the 1980s.

Essence of Neoclassical Economics

Although Debreu himself acknowledged that their general equilibrium model is completely "useless" for day-to-day economic activities, it was of a paradoxical expression. In fact, the theory played a central role in the subsequent market fundamentalist policies and continues to have a strong influence on international economic policy making. The so-called neoclassical economics is based on this general equilibrium theory, and the essence derived from this theory is twofold:

- There is always an equilibrium price (relative price) in the market that leads to general equilibrium, and under that equilibrium price, consumers maximize their utility, producers maximize their profit, and resources are allocated most efficiently in this process.
- From Walras law, the money market, as a last remaining market, is always put into equilibrium at the general equilibrium, so that money only serves to set the *absolute* price level and thus becomes like a veil that has no effect on the real economy.

Adam Smith, the father of economics, is often quoted as saying, "Markets are always brought to equilibrium by the God's Invisible Hand." According to this view, the market is a whirlpool of desires, with consumers trying to maximize their satisfaction (utility) by purchasing goods as cheaply as possible, and producers trying to produce and sell goods to maximize their profits. Although, at first glance, a market in which each economic agent pursues his or her own economic interest may appear chaotic, this pursuit of self-interest results in a state of general equilibrium in which all market participants are satisfied. This is Adam Smith's concept of the God's invisible hand achieving market equilibrium. If this were true, market harmony would be achieved without government intervention into the market. The proof of the existence of general equilibrium prices is thus a theoretical pillar of strong economic thought that defends the harmonious functioning of free markets and is commonly referred to as market fundamentalism as we discussed in Chap. 5.

It was a time when Kaoru was a teaching assistant for "Economics 1" course at Berkeley. In front of more than 200 undergraduate students gathered in the main auditorium, the lecturer asked the following question: "Ladies and Gentlemen, there is a more influential person in the West than Jesus Christ. Do you know who he is?" Of course, the students were astonished at such an abrupt question. "It is Adam Smith, the father of economics," the lecturer replied with a confident smile. Kaoru was strangely impressed, as he was listening to the lecture, that the father of economics, which formed the intellectual basis of capitalism, had more influence on the Western societies than Christianity. Come to think of it, the Great Depression in the 1930s, financial crisis of 2008 and subsequent global financial crisis were also caused by Adam Smith's market fundamentalist worldview.

That was a bit of a digression, but what is determined in this way is the general equilibrium price, which is in fact a *relative* price. For example, if we consider coffee as a standard unit, cheesecake is equivalent to 1.5 cups of coffee, and so on. In this way, all prices are determined by the number of cups of coffee (commodity), which is the relative price. So, if one cup of coffee is priced at 2 dollars, the cheesecake would be priced at 3 dollars. And if one cup of coffee is priced at 4 dollars, the cheesecake would be priced at 6 dollars. And what determines these absolute prices is the total quantity of money circulating in the market at that point in time. In other words, the quantity of money determines the absolute price level, but relative prices are determined in the market as general equilibrium prices. Hence money becomes like a veil and has no significant effect on the real economy.

Anyhow, the above two essences became the tenet of neoclassical economics, founded on the Arrow-Debreu model. And it continues to exercise a great influence on our society and livelihoods, whether we realize it or not. Looking back, Kaoru was truly lucky to have been able to study directly under the tutelage of Professors Arrow and Debreu during his years at Berkeley.

Heyday of Berkeley's Economics and Kaoru's Challenge

In addition to Debreu's recipient of the economics prize, the Nobel Memorial Prize was awarded to John C. Harsayi [1920–2000] in 1994 for his work in game theory, and also to George A. Akerlof in 2001. As an aside, when Kaoru first visited the Berkeley campus in the summer of 1977, Dr. Akerlof and his youthful wife, Janet Yellen, then Assistant Professor at the Haas School of Business, welcomed him as the host of foreign students and treated him with a sandwich.

Akerlof was kind enough to arrange a study room for Kaoru, saying he couldn't wait until the new semester starts in September. The work of Akerlof, who won the Nobel Memorial Prize for his contribution to the analysis of markets with asymmetric information, was in a field that seemed to be the opposite of Berkeley's mathematical economics research. And the mixing of these opposing fields was another example of broad-mindedness in economics research at Berkeley and what made it a unique place to do research at the time. Yellen later went on to serve as the 15th Chair of the Federal Reserve Board before serving as the Treasury Secretary under the Biden administration since 2021.

There was also a mathematician at Berkeley named Stephen Smale at that time, who was awarded the Fields Medal in mathematics. In his special lecture course on the theory of dynamical systems, Professor Smale would arrive at the classroom five minutes before the lecture time, sit still in his chair as if thinking about something. And when the chime ringed, he would suddenly say, "I will think about this problem today" and start writing mathematical equations on the blackboard. Of course, there were no lecture notes at all. For Kaoru, as a student from Japan, Professor Smale looked very much like a samurai confronting a math problem in front of a big blackboard, not with a Japanese sword, but with a piece of chalk. Professor Smale occasionally got a shove from graduate students but boldly moved on to the next problem.

There were so many world-class researchers at UC Berkeley at that time. Perhaps because he was surrounded by such researchers, Kaoru was tormented by a sense of inferiority at all times. However, being in such an atmosphere on the campus, he sometimes felt challenged and overly ambitious, as if one day he may win a "Nobel Prize in Economics" if he could beat the theories of these brilliant professors. Of course it was an illusion (in many ways!) But other graduate students at Berkeley must have felt the same way. In this sense, it is very important to create and provide an excellent research environment.

Kaoru's research in mathematical economics at Berkeley was a series of hardships. He spent most of his research hours on studying mathematics such as probability and measure theory, linear algebra, calculus, ordinary differential equations, stochastic differential equations, topology and theory of dynamical system, and occasionally attending some of these lectures. Through such intellectually arduous path, he gradually began to have doubts about the methodology of mathematical economics, especially in the direction of unrealistic abstraction and axiomatization of neoclassical economics, which had strayed into the world of pure abstraction away from real economic activities. Specifically, even though he was in the midst of such heyday of Berkeley's mathematical economics, he gradually began to question Debreu's thinking. Of course, Arrow-Debreu's general equilibrium theory is mathematically brilliant in its use of the fixed point theorem, for instance. However, in the light of economic reality, he began to think that the framework of general equilibrium theory itself was built on a complete fiction.

A Critique of Professor Debreu's Theory of Value

Kaoru summarized his thoughts in his doctoral dissertation in 1986 titled: *Beyond Walras, Keynes and Marx–One Synthesized Paradigm Toward A New Social Design.* It was subsequently published as a book under the same title but slightly different subtitle, "Synthesis in Economic Theory Toward A New Social Design"(Yamaguchi, 1988). As a critique of the Walrasian paradigm, he appended the section in the book titled "*A Critique of Prof. Debreu's 'Theory of Value'*" and pointed out its five theoretical fictions (Sect. 2.2, pp. 36–48):

Fiction 1 It is timeless and static. That is, production takes no time and all raw materials are spontaneously produced.

Fiction 2 Capital and land (services) are given as initial endowments.

Fiction 3 There are no classes such as workers and managers.

Fiction 4 Rental and rent are uniformly used as prices of capital and land services.

Fiction 5 There is no money. As Debreu (1959) himself acknowledged, "[N]o theory of money is offered here, and it is assumed that the economy works without the help of a good serving as medium of exchange" (p. 28).

Based on these fictions, Kaoru concluded that, while Debreu's *Theory of Value* (general equilibrium theory) is a mathematically elaborate and beautiful analysis from an axiomatic point of view, if we try to understand our real economic activities using these axioms, it would lead to some serious logical inconsistencies (Yamaguchi, 1988, p. 41). Specifically, he criticized Debreu's theoretical fictions and presented seven criticisms of the Walrasian paradigm by constructing mathematical formulas (*ibid.*, pp. 42–48).

If there are readers who still believe in the general equilibrium theory, we would like them to critically examine these criticisms. We hold that these criticisms can still withstand counter-criticisms by neoclassical economists. As an example, Debreu's static theory is once claimed to be made dynamic by formulating future economic activity as a contract of uncertainty within the static framework of general equilibrium theory, which has led to the subsequent stream of DSGE (Dynamic Stochastic General Equilibrium) models. The above criticisms can still be applied to them, and we could assert that these family of general equilibrium models are also inconsistent with economic activities of the real world.

Keynesian Revolution and Friedman's Counter-Revolution

If we take a step back from the world of mathematical economics at Berkeley, we realize that neoclassical thinking is just one branch of economics. Marxian economics was still influential at the time also in Japan. And Keynesian economics was still alive and well in the world, although it was beginning to fade in the face of stagflation and the "counter-revolution" led by Milton Friedman.

Speaking of Marxian economics in Japan, there was Nobuo Okishio who developed Marx's labor theory of value from a mathematical economics perspective. Okishio was known worldwide for his bold introduction of mathematical methods into Marxian economics and the establishment of a unique system, which was called "Okishio theory." Before coming to Berkeley, Kaoru happened to have an opportunity to receive a rigorous training in the basic theory of Marxian mathematical economics directly from Professor Okishio.

Monetarism, on the other hand, is a policy position that criticized Keynesian economics, which insists on the effectiveness of fiscal and monetary policies at the discretion of the government. Based on the quantity theory of money as developed primarily by Fisher (1911), monetarists advocated fixing the (growth rate of) money supply by placing more trust in the workings of market mechanisms than the government's ability to conduct proactive or counteractive policies. Although Friedman himself did not favor the term "monetarism," by the 1970, he became a firm believer in his own thinking, so much so that he boasted "if Keynes were alive today he would no doubt be at the forefront of the counter-revolution" (Friedman, 1970, p. 171).

The reflation policy turned out to be fundamentally flawed in that Fisher's prescription, on which Friedman's monetarist thinking was also based, had assumed the flawed assumption of *exogenous money* (as analyzed in Chaps. 5 and 8). When Fisher received the Chicago Plan in 1933, he immediately realized the mistake in his own thinking about controllability of money stock, and began to advocate the 100% reserve banking system to make his reflation policy truly work. Friedman, who had studied under the original Chicago school founders, was also aware of this fundamental issue and agreed with the principles of the Chicago Plan (Friedman, 1960).[3]

Yet Friedman's proposition and policy stance were later misrepresented by none other than the "Keynesians" and a distorted interpretation of Friedman's original argument (that would later be called "Monetarism") began to be promulgated. This has been the root cause of the confusion surrounding the Friedman-Keynesian controversy in the 1960s and 70s and the debates about the validity of monetarism under the debt money system. Such confusion is still prevalent in popular undergraduate textbooks. As we discussed in Chap. 8, Mankiw (2016) explained that it was Friedman and Schwartz (1963) who had asserted that the Fed's actions caused the monetary contraction and were responsible for the 1929–33 catastrophe. In doing so, Professor Mankiw merely refers Friedman and Schwartz (1963) as the advocate of such money hypothesis, but does not explicitly refer to the debt-deflation theory in its entirety nor the *100% Money* as the original version of the money hypothesis, leaving the most essential part of the Fisher's conclusion on the causes of the Great Depression (and boom-bust cycles in general) away from the attention of his readers.[4]

Thus, attributing the Fed's policy mismanagement as the the root cause of booms and busts is the classic example of misleading the students of economics about the important lesson the economists learned from the Great Depression. Contrary to such misrepresentation of Fisher's debt deflation theory popularized by the influential textbook writers, this was not the conclusion drawn by Irving Fisher whom Friedman admired as "by far the greatest American economist" (Friedman, 1970, p. 172). As

---

[3] As a matter of fact, Friedman later confessed himself to be a persistent advocate of the 100% reserve plan (Friedman, 1960, pp. 65–66). He recommended, in addition to the original Chicago Plan, that interests should be paid on those 100% reserves so as to "improve the economic results . . . , and also render the system less subject to the difficulties of avoidance that were the bug-a-boo of the earlier proposals" (*ibid.*).

[4] Professor Mankiw explains his personal views in one of his essays on the practice of writing textbooks, which he reproduced in his blog post titled "On Textbook Writing" (Mankiw, 2007). A paragraph is excerpted below from his blog post to highlight our assertion on his conscious "choice" on how to present the subject of money and banking in his textbooks:

> Of course, the most immediate benefit of classroom teaching and textbook writing is that they allow you to mold the minds of students. Economics is not a straightforward discipline like Newtonian mechanics or Euclidean geometry. Whenever you teach economics, you have wide latitude in choosing what material to include and how to present it. In making these choices, you give your own "spin" to the subject and help determine the views of your students. Although classroom teachers and textbook writers share this responsibility, textbook writers reach a larger audience. For those who want to bequeath their view of economics to the next generation, textbooks are the most efficient medium. Indeed, because textbooks are so important in shaping the field, many of the most prolific writers in academic journals are also textbook authors: Samuelson, Baumol, Blinder, Stiglitz, Barro, Dornbusch, Fischer, and on and on.

discussed throughout this book, the Chicago school economists, Fisher, and many others who supported monetary reform in the 1930s criticized that the very structure of fractional reserve banking system was the primary cause of the Depression, that is, *system design failure*.

For some reason (which should become clear by the end of this chapter), this part of analysis was later dropped from the popular version of Fisher's debt-deflation theory. And Friedman was presented as if he concluded that the Depression was caused by the Fed's policy failure alone, which was later echoed and acknowledged by the incumbent chairman of the Federal Reserve Ben Bernanke. If economics could establish the wrong lesson learned from the Great Depression episode–that there was simply a monetary policy failure by the Fed and thus there is no need to reform the debt money system, then, that is very convenient for bankers who profit from this system.

Since around this time, economist's discussion of macroeconomic stability has gradually shifted and confined into a question of appropriate (a) policy targets and objectives of monetary policy conducted by central banks, such as money stock, GDP growth, inflation and unemployment rates, (b) policy instruments, such as interest rate (price) vs. quantity of money, and (c) operating principles in light of the rational expectations and neutrality of money as prevalent in the "rule vs. discretion" literatures (Lucas, 1972; Barro, 1976; Kydland and Prescott, 1977; Fischer, 1977; Taylor, 1993). Discussions in the subsequent economic policy evaluation research implicitly assumed that money is either neutral, or money stock is a policy control variable (i.e., exogenous money), while the instability caused by the debt money system was hardly questioned.

Unfortunately most economists still do not doubt this debt money system, and continues to debate night and day how they can recover the economy from recessions and reduce unemployment. What if the system itself is flawed? The alternative approach is inevitable. That is, we must *redesign* the system structure so that it could function properly and be controlled. This is how economics must also approach to complex problems as both a science and engineering.

Three Branches of Economics and the Battle of Ideas

The 1980s was a time of conflict in economic thoughts and the battle of ideas. As such, Berkeley also had a mix of opposing economics, such as Keynesian economics by Professor Akerlof and others, and (mathematical) Marxian economics by Professor John E. Roemer (later professor of political science and economics at Yale University) and others, in addition to neoclassical mathematical economics centered on Professor Debreu. This conflict in economics transcended academic disciplines and was reflected in international politics, creating ideological tensions between the East and West as Communist vs. Capitalist system.

As his study of economics deepened, Kaoru began to wonder why there were three different schools of thought in economics. Ever since he began studying it in his first

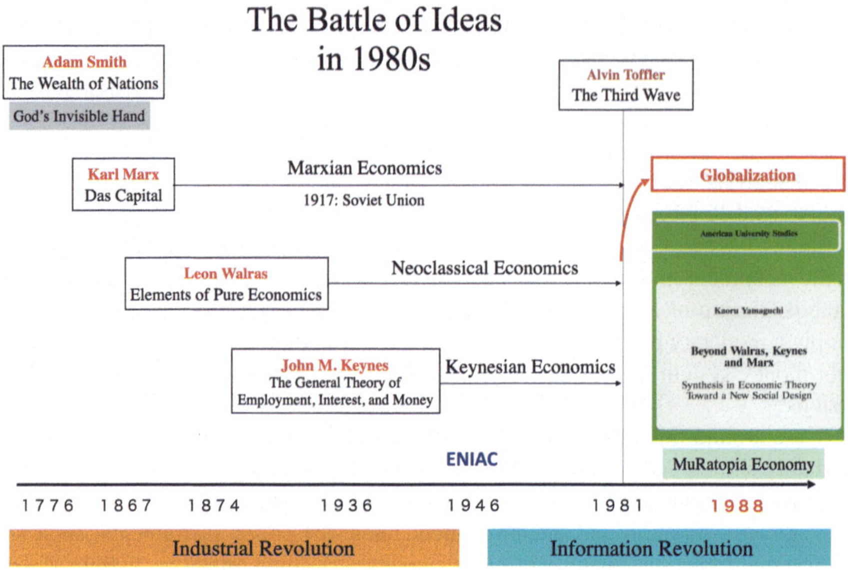

Fig. 9.2 Battle of ideas in theoretical economics in the 1980s

year of undergraduate (1965), he had held the belief that economics should "save the people and cure the society's diseases." If there were three different prescriptions, people would only be confused, he thought. And he gradually became inclined toward the faint feeling that a new peaceful world could be created by unifying these three branches of economics. Then, perhaps out of youthful enthusiasm, Kaoru began to immerse himself in research during his time at Berkeley with the determination to unify the three schools in economics. While identifying the methodologies of these three economics, he began to seriously consider whether economics could create something like an attempt at a unified theory that would unify the four forces in physics (gravity, weak force, electromagnetism, and strong force).

Figure 9.2 illustrates the overview of these genealogy of economics as the battle of ideas, which culminated in the 1980s. To recap our discussion so far using this Fig. 9.2, first, in 1776, Adam Smith published *The Wealth of Nations*, in which he famously proposed the idea that the market is regulated by the God's invisible hand. Karl Marx wrote his *Das Kapital* in 1867. And seven years later, in 1874, Walras elaborated Smith's ideas once more in mathematical equations in his *Elements of Pure Economics*, which became the starting point of neoclassical economics. Later, after experiencing the Great Depression in the early 1930s, Keynes' *General Theory* emerged, and Keynesian macroeconomics spread rapidly after the WWII as the Keynesian revolution. By the 1960s, it became so dominant in the world as mainstream theory that policy makers were told and believed that the economy could be controlled by fine-tuning fiscal and monetary policies based on Keynesian theory.

However, from around 1970s, Keynesian economics began to stall rapidly in an era of stagflation.

Figure 9.2 was prepared for Kaoru's graduate school lecture notes in 2005. As you can see here, there is no *Chicago Plan* or Fisher's *100% Money* yet. Kaoru did not learn anything about the history of monetary reform movements in the 1930s and 40s when he was studying at Berkeley. And until about 15 years ago, his research was conducted within this framework of economics.

Post-Industrial Revolution and the Birth of MuRatopia

While these three economics were battling it out, Alvin Toffler [1928–2016] published *The Third Wave* in 1980, which became an international bestseller. His thesis was that each wave have pushed the older societies and cultures aside and that mankind was now covered by a third wave of information revolution.

The first wave was the agricultural revolution that began in the Neolithic Age about 15,000 years ago. And the second wave was the industrial revolution that took place in the 18th century. Then, in 1946, the vacuum tube computer called ENIAC (Electronic Numerical Integrator And Computer) was introduced, and Toffler described that the world was about to enter the third wave of the information age. He also argued that the three previous economic theories, whether neoclassical, Keynesian, or Marxian, were all merely products of the Industrial Revolution, and that the coming information age would be different.

During his graduate studies, Kaoru faced with logical difficulties as he attempted to understand the Walrasian paradigm–an area particularly strong in Berkeley– in terms of the Marxian and Keynesian paradigms. So when he came across with Toffler's book at Berkeley he was shocked and pondered, "What, then, is the new frame of economics that will emerge in the information age?" Unfortunately, Toffler did not provide an answer. He was not an economist.

This was how the research for a unified theory of economics began to take off. Kaoru started to work on his research with the idea of creating a new economics for the information age that replaces the three previous economics. Specifically, he began to explore a new system of the post-industrial society that was neither capitalist nor socialist. In the course of his research, he found out that the new economic system he was proposing did not have a name. So he took a hint from the term "Global Village" advocated by Herbert M. McLuhan [1911–1980] and coined the name *MuRatopia Economy* on his own.[5]

Mu stands for "nothingness" or "emptiness" in Japanese. *Ra* means "nakedness" or a state of "no possession." The Greek word *Topia* means "place" as in *Utopia*. In

[5] McLuhan coined the term global village in 1964 as a futuristic vision where the electronic network covers the globe, making information easily accessible everywhere, and the world becomes like a single village where all human beings have become like neighbors. With the proliferation of smartphones and social networking services, the conditions for the global village McLuhan advocated more than half a century ago are, so to speak, now in place.

Japanese the word *MuRa* has a meaning of "village." The reason why he came up with such a name is that, as we mentioned in Chap. 4, the 1980s was a time when Japan was shining and Kaoru saw Japanese management was being touted everywhere he went on the West Coast, including Silicon Valley. He thought that behind the brilliance of Japan's economic success was the good aspect of the Japanese village society that values harmony with neighbors and nature. Therefore, he decided that if he was going to create a concept to express the alternative to capitalist society, he should use the Japanese word *mura*. This was how he gave it a name *MuRatopia* as the ideal economic system of the information age.

Through these twists and turns, Kaoru finally completed his doctoral dissertation titled *Beyond Walras, Keynes and Marx–Synthesis in Economic Theory Toward a New Social Design* in 1985 (420 pages, 870 equations). The title included the names of three economists and was intended to suggest that beyond these three schools of economics, a unified economic theory had been developed for a new social design. Later, a partially rewritten version of his dissertation was published under the same title (Yamaguchi, 1988), with Chap. 8 titled "Marx's Theory in the Light of General Systems Theory" omitted. We will discuss MuRatopia economy in more detail in the last Chap. 15.

Meanwhile, the Soviet Union collapsed in 1991. Socialism, one of the products of the Industrial Revolution, which Toffler described as the second wave, collapsed amid the information revolution. Kaoru thought intuitively at that time that the theory of MuRatopia Economy was correct, partly because his book was enthusiastically received by some researchers in the Soviet Union and China. However, it did not receive much attention from mainstream economists in the West.

The book was introduced in Russian and he was invited twice by the Russian Academy of Sciences. Taking advantage of these opportunities, he repeatedly suggested to the researchers of the Russian Academy of Sciences that after the collapse of the Soviet Union, the Russian economy should be revitalized based on the theory of the MuRatopia economy. He also suggested to Chinese economists that they do the same, saying, "Even if you were to abandon Chinese-style socialism, do not go back to capitalism!" Unfortunately, Harvard economists and others went to Russia and transplanted US-style capitalism. And economic revival based on the MuRatopia theory stopped at the proposal stage.

In the midst of these upheaval, a new idea emerged: the Globalism. And Kaoru realized that it was too early to put the MuRatopia theory into practice. Moreover, he had still no idea what was missing from the MuRatopia theory at the time. It took a detour of another decade in his life, breaking away from traditional economics research, to finally realize after the Lehman Shock that the missing part was monetary reform (Fisher's *100% Money*). During this detour he happened to encounter the computer simulation method called System Dynamics (SD). He fervently felt the need to learn SD directly from Prof. Jay Forrester and visited MIT twice as a visiting scholar.[6]

[6] There is this episode in the preface of *Money and Macroeconomic Dynamics* (Yamaguchi, 2013). Readers who are interested may refer to the textbook for further details.

9.3 Mainstream Neoclassical Monetary Theory

Stimulated by Toffler's *The Third Wave*, Kaoru believed that the world would be guided from the industrial revolution into the new age of information revolution, in which a new economic system that he called MuRatopia would provide a new social design that goes beyond the battle of ideas illustrated in Fig. 9.2. The battle, however, turned out to be the victory of globalism based on the neoclassical worldview; that is, moneyless economy or money *as a veil*. With hindsight, we can see that the economic science was already going in a wrong direction around this time. Let us now look at how these three main branches in economics have dealt with money based on the analyses and insights gained so far.

Public Money Theory turned Upside Down!

If we look back the history of money, our ancestors have been using money to conduct economic activities for thousands of years before the birth of western economics. Historically, public money such as metallic coins has been the only type of money widely used and circulated. In fact, as the classification table of money in Chap. 2 (Fig. 2.1) shows, Lydian coins in Asian Minor—the present day Turkey—are known to be the world's oldest coin (around 610-600 BC) made of electrum, which is an alloy of gold (55%), silver (43%) and copper (2%). The Lydian king, Alyattes, is said to have declared that only the coin with his roaring lion mark must be used for trades. The world's oldest coin was thus issued as interest-free public money. In this way, the systematic coinage first began to develop in the city states of Sardis, Ephesus and Miletus in Lydia in the 7th century BC (Zarlenga, 2002, p. 33). This culture and technology of coinage was later inherited in the Greek civilization. And the city states situated in what is now the southern part of Balkans peninsula issued their own coins.

Having observed how money had been created and put into circulation, the Greek philosopher Aristotle [384-322 BC] articulated about the money's legal nature of existence in *Nicomachean Ethics* as follows:

> and this is why it has the name *nomisma* - because **it exists not by nature, but by law (*nomos*)** and it is in our power to change it and make it useless (Zarlenga, 2002, p. 34; bold emphasis added).

In this way the introduction of public money as legal tender had developed in Asian Minor and ancient Greece and gradually began to spread worldwide.

Yet, the public money theory had been gradually taken over by the commodity money theory since the early days of modern economics, which began to dominate as a mainstream monetary theory in 18th century. In fact, Adam Smith [1723–1790], the father of economics, reversed the Aristotle's definition of money as follows:

> By the money price of goods it is to be observed, I understand always, *the quantity of pure gold and silver* for which they are sold, without any regard to denomination of the coin (Zarlenga, 2002, p. 313; emphasis added).

Smith thus defined gold and silver as money because of their intrinsic value associated with metallic nature. This view had been once put into practice as gold standard system in his time. This was perhaps the reason why he observed money in a such way and proclaimed commodity money theory, even though commodities do not function as money by nature as pointed out by Aristotle. As the neoclassical economic theory advances as the general equilibrium theory, this view of commodity money is further abstracted to the moneyless price theory. Accordingly, we have classified both commodity money and moneyless price theories uniformly as the mainstream neoclassical monetary theory here.

Moneyless Price Theory

This theory comes out of the general equilibrium theory, which is originated from Walras's *Elements of Pure Economics* (1874). It can be further traced back to Adam Smith's *Wealth of Nations* (1776) as quoted above. The basic framework of general equilibrium theory can be best understood by considering a pure exchange game in the markets in which producers bring N goods and services to maximize profits, and consumers want to maximize utility by purchasing these goods and services. If there is a common value scale at the time of this exchange game, the exchange will take place smoother.

Accordingly, this exchange game is better played by selecting a value scale commodity called *numeraire*. That is, it becomes a market exchange game consisting of $(N - 1)$ goods and services and one *numeraire* commodity as money. To make this moneyless price theory workable, there must exist relative prices that match supply and demand in all markets. If gold or silver is chosen for value scale commodity, their units of weight are the relative prices. This is the existence problem of general equilibrium. As explained above, this problem has become the most difficult question in economics since Walras mathematically formalized the framework. Nearly a century later, the proof of existence was provided by Arrow and Debreu (1954). According to this general equilibrium theory, if equilibrium is achieved in $(N - 1)$ markets, supply and demand in the remaining commodity money market must always be in equilibrium. This is what is known as the Walras' law. In this exchange game, money is thus supplied supplementarily as an exogenously given commodity.

In this general equilibrium framework, producers and consumers are shown to be able to achieve equilibria in all markets. Only when the equilibria are attained, they are allowed to start trading goods and services according to the transaction contracts made at the relative equilibrium prices. In other words, economic transactions in neoclassical theory can take place at the equilibrium prices attained through adjustment mechanism in the logical world of mathematical computations. Apparently, no money is needed for such market transactions, and all exchanges are completed in all markets of N goods and services, including the commodity money itself. All what is needed for these transactions to occur are information of relative prices at the equilibrium. In such a logical world, money is completely useless. This is the essence of moneyless price theory in neoclassical economics.

Who would believe in such an unrealistic moneyless economic theory based on pure mathematical logic? In the real world, money is always required for transactions, and it must exist as a means of exchange. Kaoru was fortunate to have participated in Debreu's seminar on mathematical economics as a graduate student at UC Berkeley and learned this general equilibrium theory directly from him. Debreu won the Nobel Memorial Prize in Economics with his contribution to the existence proof of the general equilibrium theory in 1983 when Kaoru used to attend his seminar.

As time goes on, however, he became skeptical about Debreu's approach to the market economy and pointed out seven flaws underlining his general equilibrium theory as a static, classless, and moneyless economic fiction (Yamaguchi, 1988, pp. 42–48) as discussed above. Although some of these assumptions have been relaxed in subsequent DSGE literatures, they still suffer from drawbacks such as their reliance on exogenous shocks to simulate non-linearities and over-simplifications of the banking system (Mahmud et al., 2020; Yamaguchi and Yamaguchi, 2021a).

Commodity Money Theory: Money as a Veil

Eventually a classical interpretation of the commodity money theory began to revive and replaced the abstract moneyless price theory of general equilibrium. Theoretically speaking, any commodity could be selected as *numeraire* money in the process of attaining general equilibrium. Yet, it has been argued, according to the commodity money theory such as the one by Adam Smith, that gold and silver had been historically selected as money, and became the *numeraire* for the remaining $(N - 1)$ goods and services. In other words, to explain the monetary market economy of the real world, neoclassical economics had no choice but to construct a fictitious commodity money theory such that precious metals like gold and silver had been extracted as money out of a primitive barter economy.

Indeed, in the exchange game discussed above, it is possible to assume that gold is chosen as *numeraire* out of the barter economy, and its weight of 1 pound = 16 ounces (= 453.6 grams) becomes a unit of commodity money as the unit of value scale for other goods and services. Karl Marx's classical theory of *Das Kapital* (1867–1894) also started with this fiction. In this way, this revived framework of neoclassical general equilibrium theory finally seemed to be integrated with a period in actual monetary history when gold was used as the chief means of exchange without any logical contradiction, as it has been claimed since Adam Smith. This is the essence of commodity money theory.

This theory, however, has been criticized in recent years as a fantasy fabricated in the heads of neoclassical economists since there is no such evidence that money has evolved from a primitive barter economy into a modern monetary market economy. As quoted above, Adam Smith, the father of economics, once asserted that the metallic (physical) nature of gold, such as durable, divisible, portable, easy to forge but difficult to counterfeit, provided the intrinsic value of gold as money and argued that gold thus began to circulate as money. Theoretically speaking, gold standard system could be explained along with this commodity money theory. For example, suppose that the price of gold as commodity is set at 1 ounce = 20 dollars. Then the dollar-denominated absolute price of commodity is determined, and dollar-denominated paper money such as dollar notes begins to be put in circulation so long as its convertibility into gold is guaranteed. Hence, the gold standard system could be understood to have originated historically in this way.

In this line of thinking, price of gold as *numeraire* again determines the absolute price of goods and services. Yet it remains neutral from the relative prices determined by the general equilibrium. For instance, as gold production increases, as in the Gold Rush in California in the 1850s, the relative price of gold as commodity rises and the monetary value of gold decreases. Yet the absolute price of 1 ounce = 20 dollars does not change. In other words, the dollar-denominated money remains neutral to the real economy so long as its convertibility is sustained. Hence, dollar-denominated gold money becomes a veil and cannot affect the real variables of the economy, the neoclassical theory argues.

In this way, arguments were made that no matter what kind of commodity it is, money becomes neutral and has no effect on the real economy. Since the gold standard continued for few hundred years when many of the influential economic thinkers and political philosophers lived, there are still many economists and politicians who are brainwashed by this commodity money theory.

Collapse of Gold Standard as Commodity Money System

In the course of considering the commodity money theory, the question arose among authors as to which type of money in the classification table in Fig. 2.1 should this commodity money be classified as. Since *numeraire* will be chosen as the commodity money in the general equilibrium theory, it must fist be *legal tender* for it to become money according to the reverse side definition. Furthermore, since this commodity money is minted using materials such as gold and silver as media of money, it can no longer be one of N goods. Rather it must be $(N+1)$st money at this point. In other words, if the Nth commodity is gold, then the $(N+1)$st gold coin made of the Nth commodity as its media must be born as *legal tender*. Then a newly-minted gold coin weighing 1 ounce is stamped with value information (face value) of, say, \$20. Commodity money must be analyzed in this way based on our definition and classification table.

However, most neoclassical economists since Adam Smith have considered the Nth gold material (commodity) itself to be the money. If they try to complete their logic of general equilibrium, they have no choice but to regard so. However, the birth of gold as legal tender must imply a creation of new market economy consisting of N goods and services and $(N+1)$st money using gold, silver, or copper as its media. In the logical world of general equilibrium, transactions are completed with N goods and services. Yet it cannot be completed in the real market economy consisting of $(N + 1)$ dimensions. Money as the $(N + 1)$st object must be required all the time.[7]

Considering this way, the methodology of general equilibrium theory itself becomes fictional, because it assumes that if $(N - 1)$ markets of goods and services are in equilibrium, then the Nth money market must also be in equilibrium due to the Walras Law. Does a new general equilibrium exist, then, in the real monetary market economy consisting of N goods and services and $(N + 1)$st money as legal tender?

History has proven that there exist no such general equilibrium in this $(N + 1)$ market economy with money. This was the collapse of the gold standard that used gold as commodity money. Under the gold standard, gold coins have been used as *legal tender* separately from gold as commodity. This gold standard system, however, did not last longer either. There was a shortage of gold material as the Nth commodity, and it became practically infeasible to cast gold coins as the $(N + 1)$st commodity money. In fact, the President Nixon provided a historical proof with the suspension of the gold-dollar convertibility in August 1971 that a commodity money economy based on the general equilibrium theory could not be sustained.

To examine this proof, let's take a brief look at the history leading up to the collapse of the gold standard. In Britain, the *de facto* gold standard started when a quarter ounce of gold was declared to be 21 shillings in 1717 by Sir Isaac Newton [1642–1727], then Master of the Royal Mint, who established classical mechanics and calculus. A century later, in 1819, it became the *official* gold standard. In the U.S. the gold price was set at \$20.67 per ounce in 1834 under the President Andrew Jackson, effectively setting the gold standard in the nation. This gold price was used for a century until 1933. In order to quell the bank runs after the Great Depression, President Roosevelt raised gold prices to 1 ounce = \$35 under the Gold Reserve Act of 1934. Yet the gold standard already began to collapse worldwide around this period.

In order to maintain the gold standard, the Bretton Woods System of 1944 established the direct convertibility of the USD to gold which maintained the existing standard of \$35/ounce and allowed gold to be exchanged only for US dollars. However, gold production could not keep up with the growth of the international economy and volume of trade, and the price of gold began to rise due to the increase in demand for gold. Consequently, gold began to outflow from the United States to Europe until its gold reserves got depleted.

To maintain the international monetary system based on the Bretton Woods regime of fixed-rate gold-exchange standards, a group of seven European central banks and the Federal Reserve established the London Gold Pool and General Agreements to Borrow (GAB) to defend a gold price of 35 USD per ounce via market intervention. By 1965, however, the pool was increasingly unable to balance the outflow of gold reserves and the US's payment deficit had grown substantially. The gold-USD con-

---

[7] Yamaguchi (2009, 2013, Chap. 2) constructed market exchange models by strictly distinguishing the time into *logical* time presumed in the general equilibrium theory (neoclassical economics) and *historical* time of actual economies.

vertibility became increasingly suspicious and France finally decided to withdraw from the pool in 1967.

Under such situations, the US President Nixon was finally forced to cancel the gold-dollar convertibility in 1971. This was the "Nixon shock" and the gold standard was thus ended. Since then, the world's monetary system has transitioned to a so-called "managed currency system" with the US Dollar as the reserve currency, no longer backed directly by gold or any particular type of commodity. From these historical events, commodity money theory is no longer the analytical subject of monetary theory in economics.

Summary: Moneyless Price and Commodity Money Theory

To summarize the above, the moneyless price and commodity money theory of neoclassical economics has the following characteristics:

- Relative prices are determined by general equilibrium, out of which a *numeraire* commodity becomes money, and money is supplied exogenously.
- The absolute price of money is neutral to the determination of relative prices, and is merely a veil of real economic activity (money neutrality).
- The gold standard collapsed in 1930s as the production and supply of gold (as commodity money) was constrained, and nations failed to cooperate.
- The gold-dollar system of 1944 also collapsed in 1971 and has since been replaced by a managed currency system with no ties to specific commodity.

9.4 Mainstream Keynesian Monetary Theory

Exogenous Debt Money Theory (Flow Approach)

Upon the collapse of neoclassical theory, this exogenous debt money theory is widely disseminated through standard economics textbooks as the only mainstream monetary theory. As we have discussed in Chap. 8, the theory holds that it is the central bank that issues currency, and bank deposits are multiplied many times in the process of banks lending cash from left to right. The reason why it is called "flow approach" is that banks under this theory are viewed as pure financial intermediaries who collect deposits in cash and lend a portion of those savings to borrowers. Thus, as we analyzed in Sect. 8.8, the budget of a bank or the banking sector as a whole is constrained by the amount of savings in the economy, which is a "flow" variable, thus its name. The theory is also called the financial intermediation theory, or loanable funds theory.

What is (4) endogenous debt money theory (stock approach) as opposed to (3) exogenous debt money theory (flow approach), then? As the name "debt money theory" indicates, both are theories that incorporate banks operating under the fractional reserve requirement. However, they differ in the following points. Exogenous debt money theory (flow approach) starts with "savings" first, which are then lent out by banks to firms and households. On the other hand, the endogenous debt money theory (stock approach) takes the base money (M_0) issued by the central bank as "stock" of reserves, and then assumes that banks finance new loans by creating new "deposits" out of nothing, even if they do not possess the corresponding cash at hand prior to lending. As a result, the role of banks in the latter theory (stock approach) is assumed to be far more than pure financial intermediaries of existing money. That is, banks are creators and allocators of new purchasing power.

It is said that modern banking began in the medieval Europe when goldsmiths took custody of gold and issued deposit certificates in exchange, and those deposit certificates eventually began to circulate as gold convertible bills of exchange. In the U.K. many private banks were goldsmiths who were able to issue banknotes until the Peel Banking Act was enacted in 1844. The situations were similar in the U.S. during the Gold Rush of the 1850s. Bankers soon found by experience that there was not much demand for conversion to the gold deposited. Hence, they began to lend more banknotes at interest than the convertible notes they could have originally issued if they were abided by 100% reserve requirement. This was the beginning of the fractional reserve banking.

If bankers did not have enough gold in storage to meet the demand for return of the original gold deposits, they got together to lend excess amount of gold to each other. This was the idea behind the central bank and beginning of the debt money system. Under the Peel Banking Act of 1844, the Bank of England, which was established in 1694 as a joint stock company, finally acquired the status as the bank with monopoly over note issuance. Other private banks were then able to create deposits (credits) out of nothing at interest using the Bank of England notes as the base money, and began to devour unearned income and profits from interests on those loans. This was how the modern banking system developed, in which the central bank's note issuance were separated from the deposit creation (lending) business run by private commercial banks.

Historically, the rush to establish central banks began in Europe in the 1800s: Bank of France in 1800, Bank of Finland in 1811, Central Bank of the Netherlands (DNB) in 1814, National Bank of Austria and Bank of Norway in 1816, National Bank of Denmark and Bank of Portugal in 1818, National Bank of Belgium in 1850, on which Bank of Japan (est.1882) was modeled after, Bank of Spain in 1874, the German Reichsbank in 1876, Bank of Italy in 1893, and finally the Swiss National Bank in 1907, followed by the Federal Reserve System in 1914. In this way, a network of central banks was established on top of the private banking system largely operating on the fractional reserve principle. As the final finishing touch, the Bank for International Settlements (BIS), known as the central bank of central banks, was founded in 1930 in Basel, Switzerland.[8] Furthermore, the International Monetary Fund (IMF) was established in 1947 out of the Bretton Woods system.

---

[8] The role of the Bank for International Settlements, which is an extraterritorial jurisdiction situated inside Switzerland, has broadened since it was formed in 1930 to handle reparation payments imposed on Germany after World War I. In the 1970s it became the center of discussions on bank capital rules, which culminated in the Basel Accord in the late 1980s as we briefly mentioned in

In 1969 the IMF set up the Special Drawing Rights (SDR) and began allocating them to its member states in proportion to the amount of the member state's investment quotas. SDR is used specifically for settlements among its member states and is the right to withdraw foreign currency from other IMF member states that have excess foreign currency in the event of a deterioration in the balance of payments or a shortage of international liquidity (reserves for external payments). Finally, after the gold standard collapsed, central banks began to issue deposits (and banknotes) on a discretionary basis. This is the architecture of the current international monetary system.

Fisher and Keynes on *Endogenous Money*

Our paradigm shift analyses of the Great Depression and Japan's Lost 30 Years are made possible by the presentation of the Endogenous Money Spending Hypothesis in Sect. 8.5, where we discussed how Fisher, upon realizing the significance of endogenous money, incorporated it into his debt-deflation theory. As the original proponent of reflation policy, Fisher immediately came to the conclusion that the debt money system itself was preventing the US economy from not only recovering as quickly as possible, but has been the root cause of the Great Depression, which led him to propose the *100% Money*. On the other hand, as the proponent of spending hypothesis, what was the Keynes position on the endogenous money, then?

To reconsider the foundation of our paradigm shift in economics from the perspective of the history of economic thoughts, this is a good place to revisit how the two leading economists at the time incorporated the endogenous money into their economic theories and policy proposals.[9]

Keynes began his research on monetary theory from his *Treatise on Money* (Keynes, 1930). The subject of money and banking must have been a confusing topic even for Keynes. Schumpeter (1954) was especially curious as to why Keynes, who initially recognized banks as "creators" of deposits in the *Treatise*, failed to incorporate the role of banks in the *General Theory* and expressed his suspicion as follows:

> The deposit-creating bank loan and its role in the financing of investment *without any previous saving up of the sums thus lent* have practically disappeared in the analytic schema of the General Theory, where it is again the saving public that holds the scene. Orthodox Keynesianism has in fact reverted to the old view according to which the central facts about the money market are analytically rendered by means of the public's propensity to save coupled with its liquidity preference. I cannot do more than advert to this fact. Whether this spells progress or retrogression, every economist must decide for himself. (Schumpeter, 1954, p. 1081; Italics in original)

Chap. 4. In the 1990s, the Bank became the meeting place for central bankers to discuss about global economy. See Lebor (2013) further on the history of the BIS.

[9] This section owes largely to Sect. 8.4.2 of Yamaguchi (2015, pp. 204–206) titled "Keynes and the Chicago Plan".

Why did Keynes change his position? Since he was based in the UK, it might be possible that he was simply not aware of the Chicago plan nor Fisher's *100% Money* at the time of writing the General Theory, and did not consider the role of money creation to be as important as his American counterparts did. Or, perhaps, he thought the *General Theory* would not complete unless he assumed investment comes from savings and that the supply of money was determined exogenously. In fact, readers of the *General Theory* immediately find in the preface of his book his own reflection regarding his change of the view:

> The relation between this book and my *Treatise on Money*, which I published five years ago, is probably clearer to myself than it will be to others; and what in my own mind is a natural evolution in a line of thought which I have been pursuing for several years, may sometimes strike the reader as a confusing change of view.... This book, on the other hand, has evolved into what is primarily a study of the forces which determine changes in the scale of output and employment as a whole; and, whilst it is found that money enters into the economic scheme in an essential and peculiar manner, technical monetary detail falls into the background. ... The difficulty lies, not in the new ideas, but in escaping from the old ones, which ramify, for those brought up as most of us have been, into every corner of our minds. (Keynes, 1936, preface; emphasis in original)

Contrary to what Keynes wrote in the book, however, the reason why he changed his view (at least in his General Theory) was not just for simplification. There was a political necessity. In fact Keynes was one of the 40 people that Henry C. Simons and other Chicago economists had selected to privately send the memorandum that laid out the money and banking system reform. Keynes replied to Simons on March 31st of 1933, stating "Much interested by the memorandum which you kindly send me" (as quoted in Phillips, 1995, p. 51).

Eleven years later, in July 1944, delegates from forty-four nations gathered in Bretton Woods, New Hampshire to discuss the post-war international monetary system. Keynes, then adviser to the British Treasury, participated in the Bretton Woods negotiations and proposed the establishment of Clearing Union and a new supranational currency called Bancor to facilitate clearing of imbalances in international settlements. The US delegate Harry Dexter White, then chief international economist at the Treasury Department, proposed a Stabilization Fund plan such as the establishment of the International Monetary Fund (IMF) and what later became the World Bank Group.

Meanwhile, Fisher sent a letter to Keynes on July 4th, asking him to take up the 100% reserve plan in the Bretton Woods negotiations as follows:

> I think it's quite possible it could, after the war, be put over for Americans and other countries, as the best *national* plan to interlock with the *international* plan you are now trying to put over. We could then avoid great inflation and deflation in future over a wide area. (as quoted in Allen, 1993, p. 715; emphasis in original)

This was the Fisher's proposal to integrate the 100% reserve banking system with Keynes's international monetary stabilization scheme. Three days later, on July 7th, Keynes replied to Fisher that he was "one of my earliest teachers on these matters," but expressed his "considerable reservations" about "the 100 per cent money" and declined being "an advocate" (*ibid.*). Keynes then continued:

> In my judgment deflation is in the near future a much more dangerous risk than inflation. I am afraid of your formula because I think it would, certainly in England, have a highly deflationary suggestion to a great many people. Apart from that, I am satisfied that in British conditions anyhow . . . we can obtain complete control over the quantity of money by means much less capable of exciting unfavorable comment and opposition. (Allen, 1993, p. 715)

As is now clear from his reply to Fisher, Keynes was well aware that the 100% reserve plan excited "unfavorable comment and opposition" in the US. Here we can also notice that Keynes had still maintained that money stock could be controlled so as to prevent inflation and deflation. On the other hand, when Fisher received the Chicago plan, he immediately noticed a flaw in his reflation theory and converted to be a leading proponent of 100% reserve banking so as to obtain a complete control over the quantity of money. These misconceptions on money and banking at the core of the Keynesian economics have led to the current government debt crises as discussed in Chap. 6, and are the reason why mainstream neoclassical models (such as DSGE models) and Keynesian models (including the standard IS-LM analysis) are all flawed as discussed so far in this book. This is why the paradigm shift in economics must be a paradigm shift in the underlying monetary theory.

Summary: Exogenous Debt Money Theory (Flow Approach)

Exogenous debt money theory (flow approach) as the mainstream Keynesian monetary theory was advanced to camouflage and justify the international banking network and operations of central and private banks established historically. Of course, it does not question the fraudulent business scheme of fractional reserve banking. The characteristics of this mainstream Keynesian monetary theory still prevalent in standard textbooks can be summarized as follows:

- Central bank is a government's bank as in "National Bank of ..." or "Federal Reserve Bank of ...") and the issuer of banknotes as legal tender as debt money.
- The government issues only small amounts of coins (legal tender, public money) as supplementary money to central bank money.
- The central bank has direct control over base money and can indirectly control money stock by assuming a stable money multiplier.
- Private banks, as with other non-bank financial institutions, are genuine intermediaries of money that collect savings from depositors (such as households) and allocate those funds to borrowers (such as firms) for their investment.
- The government can only raise funds through either tax or issuing treasury bonds to borrow from banks and other financial institutions.
- When government debt accumulates, crowding out occurs. Consequently, interest rates rise and public finance collapses. Therefore, the government must maintain a balanced budget called "primary balance" and constantly aim for fiscal soundness through tax increases and fiscal austerity.

9.5 Endogenous Debt Money Theory

The Chicago Plan and Fisher's 100% Money Proposal

Until the Great Depression of the 1930s, commodity money theory in neoclassical economics was the dominant theory. Joseph A. Schumpeter [1883–1950], known for his concept of "creative destruction," was also working on the endogenous money theory of business cycles (Schumpeter, 1934). Unfortunately, his theory was never completed. However, it is important to note that it was the endogenous debt money theory that was competing with the neoclassical theory of commodity money and the Keynesian exogenous money theory at the time.

The Great Depression shocked neoclassical economists who had believed in the harmonious equilibrium of the market economy through price mechanism. Among them were the eight economists at the University of Chicago. They came to conclude that the root cause of the Depression was the endogenous creation and destruction of bank deposits and proposed 100% reserve banking. This was the essence of the Chicago Plan. Politically, however, this was a move that would go against the business model of the international bankers.

The University of Chicago founded by the oil magnate and banker John D. Rockefeller [1839–1937] was a stronghold of liberalism and market fundamentalism that defends and advances the banker's interest. The proposal of the Chicago Plan, which would have challenged the intent of its founder, must have put unimaginable pressure on the eight Chicago economists. In fact, Professor Henry C. Simons [1899–1946], one of the central proponents of the banking reform, died tragically of unknown cause at the young age.[10] However, these founders of the Chicago School maintained their morale and conviction as economists and held that the banking reform is logically consistent with the principles of liberalism and market fundamentalism conceived by these scholars.

Concerning the role of government in monetary system, Knight (1933, p. 244) criticized the Alvin Hansen's 1933 article for accepting the fractional reserve banking as the inevitable feature of capitalist system and stressed as follows:

> No violation of the basic principles of extreme laissez faire theory would be involved in separating the monetary system from the vicissitudes of speculative private business as quoted in (as quoted in Phillips, 1995, p. 45).

The Chicago economists secretly handed over the plan to President Franklin D. Roosevelt (FDR) in 1933 during the midst of banking crisis. However, FDR, who feared the bankers around him, ignored such proposals by economists. Instead, he enacted the Glass-Steagall Act, a watered-down version of the banking regulation called by the Chicago plan. In the wave of financial liberalization in the 1990s, this act was also repealed by President Clinton in 1999.

---

[10] The cause of Simon's death, whether from an overdose of sleeping pills or suicide, is still debated. See Horn (2014), for example. Speaking of Frank H. Knight, David Rockefeller [1915–2017], a grandson of John D. Rockefeller, completed his doctoral dissertation in 1940 titled "Unused Resources and Economic Waste" under the advisory of Knight, Jacob Viner, and Oskar Lange.

Irving Fisher, after receiving the Chicago Plan, understood the correctness and validity of the proposal and included his debt-deflation theory in the *100% Money* as discussed already in Sect. 8.5. In this sense, it could be said that Fisher completed, albeit qualitatively, Schumpeter's unfinished theory of business cycle based on endogenous money.

Furthermore, in 1939, Fisher co-authored *A Program for Monetary Reform* with five economists (Douglas et al., 1939) to inform his fellow economists across the nation on the significance of monetary reform. However, through a carefully orchestrated plan to push America and Japan into a direct military confrontation,[11] the American public, which had been largely non-interventionist, quickly shifted to entering into a war under the FDR's agitation. With the US's involvement into WWII, monetary reform became a matter of less priority. And the importance of monetary reform was gradually forgotten by postwar generation of economists (for the reasons discussed later in Sect. 8.14.2).

Nevertheless, the war did not stop Fisher's campaign towards the 100% Money. He responded to criticisms one by one while developing a political momentum. In 1944, Fisher again approached FDR to remind him of the importance of the issue and wrote a letter to the President as follows:

> The most helpful at this juncture would, I think, be my "100% money." (Your advisor, Lauchlin Currie–first recommended by me, as you may remember–made this 100% proposal earlier than I.) Four hundred other economists have endorsed the idea including Professor Angell of Columbia who has added improvements to my first version. Jerry Voorhis in the House is for it and has the following of many other Congressman. Mr. Eccles [7th Chairman of Federal Reserve] is, I believe, at heart for it; but would, I think, not to touch it politically until assured of your backing. ... You–and I think you alone–could make it politically feasible and would thereby make good on your "bombshell" telegram to the London Economic Conference for which you have been unjustly abused ever since. (Fisher to Roosevelt, November 22, 1944, *President's Personal File 431*, as quoted in Phillips, 1995, p. 162)

On July 2 of the next year, Congressman Horace Jeremiah ("Jerry") Voorhis from California introduced a bill (H.R. 3648) that would create a Monetary Authority of the United States as the sole issuer of currency. In October of the same year, Fisher published the new third edition of *100% Money*. The following year, in 1946, Fisher sent a mass mailing to the members of the American Economic Association (AEA), pleading for approval of the 100% reserve plan. Of the 4,662 AEA members at the time, Fisher claimed to have received responses of approval from over 1,100 members. He also sent a letter to Simons to confirm that if he had signed on it or not. It must have been a tragedy that Simons, 33 years younger than Fisher, died a month later on June 19 at the age of 46.

[11] According to researches conducted by independent historians, the Pearl Harbor attack was ultimately a result of the failure, contrary to the official stance of the U.S. government, on the part of the FDR and his surroundings who had withheld critical information about the potential sign of the attack. Stinnett (1999), for instance, drawing on his decades of original research and access to scores of previously classified documents, presented evidences that led him as the US veteran (with ten battle stars and a Presidential Unit Citation) to conclude that a plan to push Japan into war was initiated at the highest levels of the U.S. government.

Fisher's misfortunes continued. As Phillips (1995, p. 164) observed, the "end of the political possibilities for the 100 percent reserve plan came in the elections of 1946 when Congressman Jerry Voorhis was defeated in his reelection bid by a young, up and coming politician, Richard, M. Nixon." Despite these circumstances, Fisher never lost his hope and worked on monetary reform until his death at the age of 80. On March 27, 1947, about a month before his death, he sent a lengthy letter to President Truman from the hospital on the need for a legislation that would cut the ties between bank loans and money stock.

About a week before his death, Fisher, with all his might, revised his last manuscript, "Our Inflation and Deflation–How Come? How Stop?" In it Fisher restated that the 100% reserve system must be set in place in conjunction with the legal condition stipulating a new injection of money when there is a threat of deflation and their withdrawal upon inflation.

The American Monetary Act and The NEED Act

In *The Lost Science of Money* published in 2002, Stephen A. Zarlenga [1941–2017], an independent economic historian, resuscitated the Chicago Plan and Fisher's 100% Money in Chap. 24 titled "Proposals for U.S. Monetary Reform" (Zarlenga, 2002, pp. 651–686). Zarlenga had also founded the American Monetary Institute (AMI) in 1996 and has annually held the international conference on monetary reform in Chicago since 2005. Centered around this conference, the AMI drafted the modern version of the Chicago Plan and Fisher's 100% Money as the American Monetary Act (AMA). The essence of the AMA proposed by Zarlenga and his monetary reform group are as follows:

- Reclaim the government control over issuance of money through consolidation of the Federal Reserve System with the Department of Treasury.
- Abolish money creation by private banks with 100% reserve ratio.
- The government supplies money for economic growth and social welfare.

The first two are the gists of the Chicago Plan, and the third point is a new condition explicitly added by the AMA. At the time of the first Great Depression, government debt was not as serious as it is today. Of course, the advocates of monetary reform in the 1930s well understood that their programs could also mitigate the adverse effects of increased public debt. Yet, the main focus of their proposals was how to overcome and prevent the primary adverse effects of the Depression. However, after the Lehman Shock and the second Great Depression since 2008, the government debt crisis became a major problem both in Japan and the US. It was around this time when Kaoru first learned about the AMA on the Internet by chance. Until he first saw the proposal, however, he had no idea about the Chicago Plan, let alone that it had its origins in the monetary reform movements culminated in the 1930s. But, just like Fisher did, he immediately understood its correctness intuitively.

Then, using his Accounting System Dynamics (ASD) method (Yamaguchi, 2003), which he had already developed by that time, Kaoru has started building a macroeconomic model of the American Monetary Act. As a first step, a relatively simple model with no cross-border transactions was developed. He has successfully performed simulations and obtained results, which were surprising. His simulations showed that the US government debt can be reduced to zero if the above three conditions of American Monetary Act were implemented. Furthermore, even if a deflationary recession generates GDP gap, it can be easily overcome by direct monetary policy.[12] These results were reported at the 28th International System Dynamics Conference held in July 2010 in Seoul (Yamaguchi, 2010), and the 6th International Monetary Reform Conference held in September in Chicago. It was a great honor that he received the Advancement of Monetary Science and Reform Award from the AMI for his contribution to the analysis of the effects of government debt redemption.

Subsequently, the simulation analysis was extended to an open macroeconomic model with foreign trade. The simulation showed that the government debt can be paid off without raising taxes and causing unemployment, inflation, and contagious recessions abroad. The results were presented at the 29th International System Dynamics Conference held in Washington DC on July 25th, 2011 under the title "Workings of A Public Money System in Open Macroeconomies–Modeling the American Monetary Act Completed" (Yamaguchi, 2011).[13] Since then, these results quickly became known to researchers interested in monetary reform. Kaoru has participated in the monetary reform conferences in Chicago every year ever since until COVID-19 erupted in 2020.

Zarlenga immediately recognized Kaoru's simulation results presented at the AMI conference in 2010 and invited him to present his findings at the Congressional Briefing organized by the Congressman Dennis Kucinich (Ohio 10th) on July 26, 2011. Congressman Kucinich, Democratic nomination candidate for the US President in 2004 and 2008, took a historic initiative to introduce a bill H.R. 6550 (111th Congress) on December 17, 2010, named the National Emergency Employment Defense Act of 2010 or the *NEED Act*. The bill, though it did not received a vote, called for the (1) introduction of the United States Notes–public money–in place of the Federal Reserve Note–debt money, (2) reconstitution of the Federal Reserve System and establishment of National Monetary Authority consisting of 9 public members appointed by the President with the advice and consent of the Senate, and (3) improvement of the public infrastructure. The bill, if it had been passed, would have paid off most of national debts by now.

Following the Kaoru's congressional briefing in July 2011, Congressman Kucinich re-introduced a slightly modified bill H.R. 2990 (112th congress) named the National Emergency Employment Defense Act of 2011 on September 21 with a co-sponsor John Conyers (Michigan 14th), which failed to receive a vote unfortunately. More importantly, however, the bill read as follows:

---

[12] Recall that the concept of GDP gap discussed in Sect. 5.5 in Chap. 5 becomes valid under the public money system where money stock is exogenously supplied and fully controlled.

[13] On the following day, July 26, 2011, the paper was presented at the US Congressional Briefing, Cannon 402, sponsored by the Congressman Dennis Kucinich as mentioned in Chap. 6. See Yamaguchi (2013) for details on these series of simulation studies.

> To create a full employment economy as a matter of national economic defense; to provide for public investment in capital infrastructure; to provide for reducing the cost of public investment; to retire public debt; to stabilize the Social Security retirement system; to restore the authority of Congress to create and regulate money, modernize and provide stability for the monetary system of the United States, retire public debt and reduce the cost of public investment, and for other public purposes (A Bill, H.R. 2990)

Summary: Endogenous Debt Money Theory (Stock Approach)

Therefore, the endogenous debt money theory (stock approach) captures the main characteristics of debt money system as historically developed as follows:

- Central bank is a private bank and has usurped the prerogative of the government to issue money granted by the Constitution.
- Private banks are not just financial intermediaries; they create deposits out of nothing through fractional reserve banking and lend them to the (non-banking) private sector and governments at interest.
- The central bank can control base money, but not money stock ($M_{1\sim3}$), which is endogenously created and destroyed against bank loans.
- The government not only has the power to issue coins as legal tender, but can also issue all kinds of money in form as deemed necessary. Therefore, it does not need to borrow funds by issuing treasury bonds at interest.

Why has the endogenous debt money theory (stock approach) that correctly analyzes the debt money system in this way been regarded as an enemy by the international bankers and eliminated from economics? Why do many textbooks only deal with the exogenous debt money theory (flow approach) as mainstream Keynesian theory? This may be obvious to readers who have read this chapter so far. It is because the flow approach can conceal the truth that they do not want the general public to realize; that is, (1) the central bank is not a government's bank, but a private bank independent of the government, that lends money to the state and earns interest, and (2) most of the money they issue are created endogenously as debt at interest.

There are several groups that have been critical of the exogenous debt money theory (flow approach) and aiming for such monetary reform. The two main groups are the AMI's Monetary Reform group and the MMT (Modern Money Theory) group. At the AMI's annual conference on Monetary Reform held in Chicago, many researchers, financial professionals, monetary reform promoters, and interested citizens participated from the US and Europe. Positive Money group from UK and the German Monetary Reform group were also present.

Participants gathered every year and expanded their activities toward the common goal of ending the economic injustice under the debt money system. They were passionate about the need to uncover the lies of mainstream monetary theories and free economics from the *taboo* based on endogenous debt money theory (stock approach). And thanks to these efforts by monetary reformers all over the world, we have now come to a point where central banks unanimously reject the exogenous money view as a popular misconception (see Mcleay et al., 2014; Bundesbank, 2017 for example).[14]

Farewell to the MMT Group

At the 2012 AMI Conference on Monetary Reform, the MMT group exhibited a book published that year titled *Modern Money Theory* (Wray, 2012) and sold it at the venue. With the publication of this book, the definition of money espoused by the group of MMT researchers became clear to the general public. In a nutshell, MMT defines that "*money cannot be a commodity; rather, it must be an IOU*" (p. xi, *ibid.*). Hence, according to our classification of money in Fig. 2.1, all money must be *debt money* for MMT. That is, money is not commodity money, but rather debt certificates such as banknotes and government bonds.

MMT argues that money is just liability on the balance sheets of the central bank and government. Furthermore, by citing Hyman Minsky as one of the forerunners of MMT, Wray (2012) argues that "anyone can create money by issuing an IOU denominated in the social unit of account" (p. 272).

While the AMI's Monetary Reform group shared the same view with MMT that money is not commodity money, it was Stephen Zarlenga, director of the AMI, who vehemently disagreed with the MMT's definition that "money is IOU and can be created by anyone". In Chap. 24 of his aforementioned book, Zarlenga (2002) bitterly criticized this definition of MMT under the heading THE "ALL MONEY IS DEBT" FACTION as follows:

> This group confuses the nature of money, through their observation of one perverted form of it. They say that since most of the money in circulation is in the form of credits issued by banks (which are also debts to those being credited), that therefore the nature of money is that it is always debt, and some of them define money as "assignable debt"! ... But these credits are only one form that money has taken, as recognized both in Del Mar's and in Knapp's definitions. Those who argue that it is the only form of money should realize that they are actually defining "money" out of existence, and substituting "credit" for it. Money and credit denote two different things. That's one of the reasons we give them separate names. (Zarlenga, 2002, p. 661)

[14] It is worthwhile to recognize here that the reality of the debt money system has gradually come to be known for what it is thanks to the works of and courage shown by many over the years; including the US congressman Henry Gonzalez, chairman of the house banking and currency committee until 1994, who regularly introduced legislation to repeal the Federal Reserve Act; John William Wright Patman, Chairman of the banking and currency committee from 1963 to 1975, who alerted Americans to the dangers of the Federal Reserve System; Eustace C. Mullins, who was one of the early writers exposing the shadowy history and origin of the Federal Reserve (Mullins, 1983), and Bill Still, who has opened up the eyes of many on this subject with his 3 hours-long documentary titled "The Money Masters" (1996). Mullins (1983) in particular wrote in the foreword of his own book that it was none other than Ezra Pound, who commissioned and supported his private research on the political history of the federal reserve. Less well known is the fact that Pound was among dozens of influential figures to whom Fisher had sent the manuscript of *100% Money* that were listed in the Preface to its first edition. Had Fisher not given Pound his manuscript at that time, and if Pound had not assisted Mullins in writing his book "Secrets of the Federal Reserve", this monetary issue might not be as well recognized today as many people are at present.

Given the long history of public money over at least the past several thousand years, the erroneous definition that "only IOUs are money" was simply unacceptable to Zarlenga as the monetary historian and the founding director of AMI. Thus, for Zarlenga, the MMT group was nothing but a "FACTION" within a larger group of economists that recognize endogenous debt money.

One day at the AMI's conference floor, the MMT researchers and Zarlenga began to engage in fierce debate, spitting criticism on each other. Kaoru stood up quickly and tried to clarify their point of disputes by remarking as follows:

> The difference between the two can be explained by applying the principle of double-entry bookkeeping in accounting. MMT interprets money as debts (IOU and bonds) and record them as liabilities, while public money is booked as equity or net assets of the issuer. If we create macroeconomic models and compare how these different journal entries as liability or equity create different economic behaviors, a common understanding would naturally emerge.

Unfortunately, their disputes were too harsh to pay attention to his remarks. Kaoru felt a certain emptiness in the unproductiveness of such arguments without the support of macroeconomic simulation models. To him, they were merely fighting a battle in the air. And fighting each other within the common group of endogenous debt money theory (stock approach) would only benefit the vested interests that profit from the current debt-based monetary system. Since then, the MMT group has stopped attending the AMI's Conference in Chicago. Kaoru has also started to take his own research path. In retrospect, this controversy has led to the birth of public money theory based on the simulation analysis of ASD macroeconomic models published in his textbook (Yamaguchi, 2013).

The Precursor of "Money is Debt" Faction

When did such a fallacy that "all money is an IOU" begin? Zarlenga (2002) points out clearly in Chap. 19 titled "TRIUMPH OF THE BANKERS – THE FEDERAL RESERVE SYSTEM" that it was Alfred Mitchel-Innes [1864–1950] who first promoted the definition of money as debt. Indeed, proponents of MMT seems to have been influenced by Innes's biased definition, as evidenced by their writings on the Innes's view on money (see Wray, 2004, for instance). Is it a coincidence, then, that Innes began to promote such view at the beginning of the 20th century when bankers were conspiring to establish a central bank in the US, which they initially called "United Reserve Bank" (Warburg, 1930)?

Of course Zarlenga knew very well about the political intent of such falsification. In his book published a decade before the above debate with MMT group took place, Zarlenga (2002) adverted to the origin of "Money is debt" faction as follows:

> Thus the Federal Reserve System appeared to be based on gold as money, but the Fed had the potential to substitute bank credit for money. Just around the time of its inception, two articles appeared in the *Bankers Law Journal* (in May 1913, and in February 1914), written by A. Mitchell Innes, then Consul of the British Embassy in Washingotn, DC.... Innes attempted

> to substitute the idea of credit for the idea of money. To do this he first had to disavow Adam Smith's erroneous metallic position of money being gold and silver by weight. That was well and good. The best and easiest way to attack Smith was to promote a historical analysis of money–so far so good.
>
> But then in order to promote the notion that all money is credit, Innes had to ignore the historical examples of government money, especially the American examples such as the Greenbacks and the colonial currencies. He presented a fictional history substituting credit for money, erroneously claiming that even coins were credit. In effect Innes attempted to define money out of existence. He was yet another English expert befuddling American minds.
>
> This is the general direction 20th century establishment economists followed: they made inappropriate and false distinctions between "high powered money" (actually money) and lower powered money (actually credit). Instead of doing their jobs as economists, and clarifying the crucial distinctions between money and credit, they confused and obfuscated the concepts. (Zarlenga, 2002, p. 530)

As we will discuss in Chap. 11 where we debunk MMT, there is no more convenient theory than that which defines money as IOU for the bankers who control the system. Such theory obscures the reality of debt money system and thus serve to protect their vested interests from monetary reform movements.

The Club of Rome's Attack on the Chicago Plan

As mentioned briefly, Kaoru was invited to a congressional briefing on July 26, 2011, to report on his latest research findings of the ASD macroeconomic modeling on US national debts (Yamaguchi, 2011). In a nutshell, the simulation results showed that if the American Monetary Act was introduced and monetary reform (the Chicago Plan) was carried out, the US government debt would be reduced to zero, and enable us to achieve a more stable economy. Two months later, on September 21, Congressman Kucinich introduced the NEED Act (H.R. 2990), which was based on the American Monetary Act. This was the first time in 66 years that Congressman Jerry Voorhis had introduced a landmark bill (H.R. 3648) embodying the Chicago Plan and Fisher's 100% Money on July 2, 1945. However, the bill, despite being such an important piece of legislation, did not receive enough support and was not enacted.

In the fall semester of 2011, Kaoru began lecturing on the macroeconomic model of the Chicago Plan in his macroeconomics course at the Graduate School of Business at Doshisha University in Kyoto. To his surprise, that same fall he was suddenly contacted by the Japan's former Minister of Internal Affairs and Communications, who said he was eager to receive a lecture on the macroeconomic model of the Chicago Plan. It seemed the content of the briefing was conveyed to the former minister via the London School of Economics. Kaoru arranged the schedule on February 26 of the following year and the former Minister accompanied by two secretaries visited Kaoru's office at Doshisha University. They spent about three hours learning the public money model from him.

In the summer of 2012, a student whispered the following information into Kaoru's ear after a lecture, saying, "Your research is critically presented in the recently published report by the Club of Rome-EU Chapter." The report was included as Chap. VI of the 200-page book titled *Money and Sustainability–The Missing Link* (Lietaer et al., 2012). Kaoru was intrigued by the book's content, partly because the preface was written by Dennis Meadows, who is a well-known System Dynamics researcher famous for his involvements in the *Limits to Growth* and the World Model projects (Meadows et al., 1972, 1992, 2004). Kaoru promptly purchased the book by Lietaer et al. (2012) in September of the same year and read through the relevant sections as quoted below:

> Congressman Dennis Kucinich is proposing the American Monetary Act, an equivalent of the Chicago Plan. On 26 July 2011, Kucinich invited Professor Kaoru Yamaguchi from the University of California at Berkeley and Doshisha University in Japan, to give a congressional monetary briefing on this idea. Yamaguchi's paper uses a systems approach to show that the liquidation of debts under the current monetary regime will trigger multiple recessions and massive unemployment in the USA with contagion to other economies. In contrast, under the American Monetary Act, debt reduction and even debt liquidation can be put into effect without causing recessions, unemployment and inflation, either in the USA and abroad (p. 129, Sect. 7. 'Chicago Plan', Chap. VI)

One of the Club of Rome's main purpose of publishing the book appeared to be to thoroughly crush the Chicago Plan with the following five "Reasons for Not Recommending the Chicago Plan" (Lietaer et al., 2012, p. 130) as follows:

1. Replacing a monoculture of debt money with another monoculture of public money (through 100% reserve banking) merely replaces a private monopoly with a public one, and does not eliminate structural instability.
2. While it is true that the Chicago Plan reform would eliminate the risk of widespread banking crashes and of sovereign debt crisis, it will not necessarily solve the monetary (currency) crisis.
3. If the government issues money, the risk of inflation will be greater as recently demonstrated in the Zimbabwean Dollar case in 2009 after the president instructed the central bank to print its currency by the trillions.
4. The Chicago Plan is politically unfeasible.
5. Implementation of the Chicago Plan at the national and EU levels poses greater risks.

What do readers think of these criticisms? Are they convincing or legitimate reasons to reject the Chicago Plan or 100% reserve banking? Let us consider the first point. What makes the private monopoly of money better than the responsible administration by a publicly accountable institution? When the money creation by profit-driven irresponsible banks is the cause of financial instability, why does disciplining it make the system structurally more unstable?

As to the second point, the authors argue that monetary crashes "would not necessarily have been avoided" even if the Chicago Plan had been implemented. First of all, what they failed to mention was the fact that all of "the 208 monetary crashes that occurred during the 1970–2010 period" were caused under the debt money system. It is simply misguided to dismiss the effectiveness of a solution proposed to address certain problems on the basis of problems that occur in systems where the solution has not yet been implemented. Their second argument is a typical example of misrepresenting the issue to deny the advantages and positive effects of money reform by applying facts that are out of the context.

Secondly, Lietaer et al. (2012) defines a monetary crisis as the situation where "the currency of a country suddenly suffers a substantial drop in value in relation to other currencies" (p. 50). The cause of such an exchange rate collapse and hyperinflation is always and everywhere the result of failures in domestic economic policy (as in the Zimbabwe's case), which attracts short selling by currency speculators and hedge funds. When currency is issued in a disciplined manner by the monetary authority, as was envisioned by the Chicago Plan and Fisher's 100% Money, the risk of monetary policy failure will be reduced. Therefore, the risk of monetary crashes will also be reduced greatly. As we have analyzed in Chap. 6, monetary, banking, and sovereign debt crises are closely interrelated phenomena (Fig. 6.4). Thus, eliminating their root cause, i.e., fixing the design failure of debt money system, will also reduce a potential risk of inflation, contrary to what Lietaer et al. (2012) argued.

Under the public money system, there is a legal protection for the independence of the monetary authority from the Treasury, lobbyists, or any other branches of government (including the legislature). This governance mechanism ensures that the issuer of public money is more independent of the administration or the government of the day. Thus, the risk of inflation and the risk of contagion effect at the international level would be reduced under the public money system (Yamaguchi, 2011). Accordingly, the third and fifth points pointed out by Lietaer et al. (2012) do not apply either.

Rather than these common misunderstandings of the 100% reserve banking plan, Kaoru's eyes were particularly drawn to the fourth point; that "the Chicago Plan is *politically* unfeasible." The authors of the report wrote as follows:

> Any version of the Chicago Plan will be fought to the death by the banking system because it threatens both its power base and its business model. (Lietaer et al., 2012, p. 130)

It sent chills down his spine when Kaoru read this section, as it seemed like a threatening letter from the international banking network that if he did any more research in this field, he would lose his life. Why would a modest presentation of research findings in Washington, D.C. become Kaoru's office visit by a former Japanese minister a few months later? Why was his research named by the Club of Rome report within a year and threatened in this way? Kaoru wondered and was impressed at the same time by the breadth of their network and the unusual thoroughness of their attack. The answer was described on the same page.

> Even after the excesses triggering the 2007–2008 collapse, or in the middle of the Great Depression of the 1930s, the banking lobby managed to deflect the implementation of any significant changes. Recall that in 2010, for every elected official in Washington, there were three high-level lobbyists working full-time for the banking system.... What are the chances of something as radical as the Chicago Plan being implemented when legislators themselves are part of an army of bank lobbyists? (Lietaer et al., 2012, pp. 130–131)

Although Lietaer mentioned that there is "an army of bank lobbyists," the 99% of employees who work for the big banks are ordinary working people. And it should be a handful of stakeholders that may oppose the abolition of fractional reserve banking. Looking back, it only makes sense to assume that, on that day of the congressional briefing, the venue was packed with these "full-time" lobbyists from the industry to gather information about the macroeconomic model of the Chicago Plan and the news was spread to their relevant networks around the world.

In any case, the authors of the Club of Rome's report mentioned that they work day and night to keep abreast of any information and alternative proposals that challenge the current financial system. Until then, Kaoru was a naive researcher of system dynamics, completely ignorant of such a political reality. Then, in December 2012, just a few months after picking up the Club of Rome report, Kaoru was abruptly fired from his full professorship at the graduate school of Doshisha University. This unprecedented ouster took place despite the presence of his graduate students who were in the midst of their doctoral dissertations under his supervision. Exactly as the above Club of Rome's report had foretold, Kaoru was academically assassinated and "fought to the death" !

Economic Science and the Lost Academic Freedom

Apparently, this news quickly became known to System Dynamics and monetary researchers around the world. The president of the SD Society and other prominent researchers in the field kindly sent letters to the president of Doshisha University, pleading with him to observe academic freedom, especially freedom of the SD education and research. Congressman Kucinich, who invited Kaoru to the briefing, also sent a petition to the president of the university to become a "sanctuary of academic freedom." Below is the full text of his letter:

> February 19, 2013
> Washington, DC
>
> Dear Dr. Hatta,
>
> It is with sincere appreciation and respect that I approach you humbly for your consideration of my plea on behalf of one of your esteemed faculty members whose work has made a powerful impression upon government officials in the United States. It has come to my attention that the appointment of Professor Kaoru Yamaguchi to the faculty of Doshisha University may in fact be in jeopardy and that his position teaching system dynamics in Business Economics is being eliminated. If this is true then I am urging you to use the good graces of your office to protect the world-relevant work of a man who is one of the most important economists on the topic of monetary reform, of great relevance to Japan and the United States as well as the rest of the world.
>
> As a 16 year member of Congress and a two-time Democratic Presidential candidate, I am deeply involved in issues relating to monetary science, I sponsored a special congressional briefing at which Dr. Yamaguchi shared his visionary system dynamics approach. Here in the United States, where money can be created by only borrowing it into existence, the work of Dr. Yamaguchi has achieved great importance as we search for ways to make our financial systems economically viable and socially just. As someone who has worked the last seven years on the system dynamics involved in monetary policy I can well understand

> the difficulty in approaching such a subject. It requires a new way of thinking, a new way of looking at money, which informs a new way of looking at the world, which, of course, is consistent with the deeper mission of a university and all of education.
>
> Herein is the relevance of Dr. Yamaguchi's work and his vision: It is only by being able to unchain ourselves from the wheel of endless debt that society can aspire to higher levels of social evolution. Professor Yamaguchi may someday win the Nobel Prize for economics, given his extraordinary insight into system dynamics. It would be a tragedy as he strives to continue to make world-wide contributions to monetary science if his own university would turn its back on him and his work. Let Doshisha University be known as a world-renowned sanctuary of academic freedom for a visionary man, not a graveyard where great ideas have come to die. Thank you for your careful consideration of my humble plea on behalf of a great man.
>
> Submitted with the greatest respect,
>
> Dennis J. Kucinich
> Member of the United States Congress, 1997–2013.

The University and its president have continued to ignore these sincere pleas and have not responded them since. As a Japanese researcher, Kaoru felt deeply disappointed by this lack of international manners on the part of a higher education and research institution. He appealed to the Supreme Court, arguing that such unilateral dismissal was an illegal act in violation of Article 23 of the Japanese Constitution, which stipulates that "*Academic freedom is guaranteed*." However, the Supreme Court dismissed the appeal on the grounds that the case was not amenable to the constitutional decision.

"Never Touch The Money System"

On May 17, 2017, four years later after Kaoru was dismissed from his professorship, an international symposium titled "Greece, Out of The Crisis: Debt-End or Dead-End" was convened at Webster University in Vienna. Monetary reform experts and government and media officials were invited to the event. Kaoru gave a presentation titled "Electronic Public Money (EPM) is a Savior for Debt-Economies: An On-going Experiment in Japan." His presentation was based on our joint paper published in February of the same year (Yamaguchi and Yamaguchi, 2017b). Coincidentally, Bernard Lietaer, the lead author of the above Club of Rome report, was also invited to this symposium.

Kaoru took advantage of the breakfast time to talk to him. He informed Lietaer that the criticism of the Chicago Plan that he had developed in his report was nothing more than an empty criticism that had no academic or theoretical basis. After a heated debate, the two were able to agree that the current debt money system is structurally flawed.

Lietaer's argument, however, was that the systemic flaws could be compensated for by issuing "complementary currencies" in local economies. He reiterated that the

Chicago Plan, like the present debt money system, would be structurally unstable, and politically risky and unrealistic to be implemented. Unfortunately, Lietaer did not seem to understand that public money will be the white knight that will also save banks from government debt and banking crises, as the Chicago economists and Fisher emphasized. After nearly two hours of heated debate, Lietaer could not argue against Kaoru's critique that Lietaer's local complementary currencies themselves do not solve the problems of debt money system and that EPM is the money of futures. Kaoru presented his macroeconomic simulation results and thoroughly debunked Lietaer's counterarguments.[15]

Later, it became evident that Lietaer was close to the members of the Economics Establishment, consisting mainly of MIT PhDs, and that he was strongly brainwashed by their politics. Some time after the Vienna conference, Kaoru happened to stumble across one of Lietaer's presentation, which he gave at the European Journalism Center (ECJ) conference held in Brussels on November 9–10, 2009. There, Lietaer told the audience the following startling anecdote:

> Paul Krugman told me personally that I was totally crazy to talk about the money issue. He said "HAVE YOU NOT". We were both from MIT, okay? . . . We got the same professors, right? And what he told me [was] "Didn't they tell you? NEVER TOUCH THE MONEY SYSTEM. NEVER TOUCH THE MONEY SYSTEM." You can touch everything else. Never touch the money system. The reason is there. [Lietaer pointing to one of participants who had correctly pointed to the political nature of Nobel Prize in Economics] You will not be invited to right places and you can kiss goodbye. Or the Nobel on anything else. That is worthwhile getting. You're killing yourself academically if you touch the money system.[16]

Surprisingly, Lietaer confessed that the professors at MIT told their students to "never touch the money system." The question is who reminded him of that advice? It was the winner of 2008 Nobel Memorial Prize in Economics himself, whose textbooks still remain as one of the top-10 most assigned textbooks on university syllabi along with Mankiw's textbooks in the US as well as in Japan.[17]

---

[15] Lietaer was later involved in a crypto asset project called Bancor. Crypto assets created by private entities or Central Bank Digital Currencies (CBDC) will not provide a solution to the problems caused by the underlying debt money system. How do crypto assets (including Bitcoin) and CBDC differ from EPM? We will discuss these issues in Chap. 13.

[16] Source: Bernard Lietaer's presentation titled "The New Paradigm of Money–Monetary blind spots and structural solutions" given at the European Journalism Center (ECJ) Interface conference on the role of media in financial crisis. The recording of his entire speech is available at YouTube: www.youtube.com/watch?v=Q7uJIjSO-a4 [Accessed: February 21st, 2024].

[17] The Open Syllabus Project, which collects titles from over 18 million English-language syllabi from 140 countries, ranks the following textbooks for the top-10 most-assigned titles in "Economics" field in the US (total 81,735 syllabi searched): 1. *Principles of Microeconomics* by N. Gregory Mankiw, 2. *Principles of Economics* by N. Gregory Mankiw, 3. *Principles of Macroeconomics* by N. Gregory Mankiw, 4. *Introductory Econometrics: A Modern Approach* by Jeffrey M. Wooldridge, 5. *Macroeconomics* by N. Gregory Mankiw, 6. *International Economics: Theory and Policy* by Paul R. Krugman, 7. *Microeconomics* by Robert S. Pindyck, 8. *An Inquiry Into the Nature and Causes of the Wealth of Nations* by Adam Smith, 9. *Intermediate Microeconomics: A Modern Approach* by Hal R. Varian, 10. *Macroeconomics* by Paul R. Krugman.

A situation in Japan is similar. The Open Syllabus ranks the following textbooks for the top-10

Why did Lietaer attack the Chicago plan so viciously without theoretical basis? The revelation by himself finally connected all the dots. That is, he was not against the Chicago Plan from an economic standpoint. In fact just before the above quoted passage, Lietaer emphasized that "chartalism" has never been refuted academically, meaning that public money theory is also correct. This also explains why he came up with such nonsensical logic that public money is not a solution because it only changes the monopoly of money from private banks to the government. He knew that it was simply a *taboo* to propose it politically. Lietaer reconfirmed the above episode to Kaoru in person in Vienna.

The Network of Economics Establishment

Why, then, did Prof. Mankiw trivialize the Fisher's debt-deflation theory in such a way as we have discussed in Chap. 8? Is it just a coincidence that he is also an MIT PhD (1984)? Why does Dr. Ben Bernanke (MIT PhD 1979), who is well-known for his study of the Great Depression for which the 2022 Nobel Memorial Prize was awarded, or other members of the so-called "economics establishment" all come to misrepresent Fisher's debt-deflation theory and promulgate that "Fisher's idea was less influential in academic circles" (Bernanke, 1994, p. 23), while making no reference to his *100% Money* theory?[18]

As we have discussed in Sect. 8.14.2, there seems to have been a systematic obfuscation by the authors of popular textbooks and "authorities" in the field to minimize the significant role of banks as creators and allocators of new money into financial intermediaries by trivializing the major theoretical contributions made by the leading economists in the 1930s, who were all critical of the fractional reserve banking system. In view of these politics, there was no surprise when the 2022 Sveriges Riksbank Prize (aka Nobel Memorial Prize in Economics) was awarded to the former chairman of the Federal Reserve.[19]

---

most assigned titles in Economics in Japanese universities (total 2,534 syllabi searched): 1. *International Economics: Theory and Policy* by Paul R. Krugman, 2. *Economic Development* by Michael P. Todaro, 3. *Intermediate Microeconomics: A Modern Approach* by Hal R. Varian, 4. *Introductory Econometrics: A Modern Approach* by Jeffrey M. Wooldridge, 5. *Development Economics* by Debraj Ray, 6. *Macroeconomics* by N. Gregory Mankiw, 7. *Economic Growth* by Robert J. Barro, 8. *The East Asian Miracle* by World Bank, 9. *Economics of the Public Sector* by Joseph E. Stiglitz, 10. *Determinants of Economic Growth: A Cross-Country Empirical Study* by Robert J. Barro. Both rankings in the US and Japan were retrieved from the project website (www.opensyllabus.org) on December 21st, 2023.

[18] The trivialization of Fisher's debt-deflation theory is not confined to the academic community as discussed already in Sect. 8.14. Koo (2009) is the prime example.

[19] Recall also that, as with other MIT PhDs who were awarded the Sveriges Riksbank prize (Klein, Akerlof, Stiglitz, Krugman, etc.), the 2018 Prize was awarded to William D. Nordhaus (MIT PhD 1967), who dropped the 1948 reference to "monopoly bank" in the twelfth edition of Samuelson's textbook published in 1985, which, according to Black (2021, p. 61, Footnote 51), "cut any remaining ties with Phillips's presentation of bank credit theory and reflected a new era of textbooks teaching that banks are mere intermediaries of preexisting deposits".

Zarlenga (2002, p. 445) had already reminded us many years ago that

> the Nobel Prize in Economics is not part of Alfred Nobel's legacy, but is awarded by the Swedish Riksbank, and demonstrates the propagandistic and deceptive practices of the economics Establishment. Nobel's heirs have been trying to force the Riksbank to stop pretending it gives a "Nobel Prize" in economics: "The economics prize runs counter to the idealism in Alfred's declaration that the prizes should be awarded each year to those 'who have conferred the greatest benefit on mankind … The vast majority of economics prizes have gone to people who reflect the dominating western view of the world. It's doubtful whether this really is of benefit to all man kind,' says Peter Nobel." Financial Times, 11/24/01.

Whether it was Samuelson, who was instrumental in turning the MIT's economics department into a world-renowned institution, or other MIT PhDs who followed Samuelson and few other key advisers there, it seems as if they all naturally knew the risk of "touching" the debt money system. Indeed, if we follow the network of influential economists in this way, there is no coincidence as to why many of the world's leading central bankers and economic policy makers share a common root that all traces back to the MIT's economics department and a handful of key advisers there, who were in turn mostly trained at MIT.

In the academic world, they go on to occupy various key positions, including tenures, editors of major journals and learned societies, forming a small yet highly connected and influential network of mostly Jewish scholars.[20] Considering the larger network of economists who are not MIT PhDs but later joined MIT as faculty members (Kindleberger, Modigliani, Solow, Fisher, Dornbusch), and MIT PhDs who went on to hold positions at MIT and other elite universities (Akerlof, Stiglitz, Rothschild, Fischer, Blinder, Blanchard, Mishkin, Krugman, Bernanke, Mankiw, etc.), it comes as no surprise that their writings shaped the currently dominant thinking in the American economics textbooks market.

[20] In addition to Samuelson's scholarly influences, Weintraub (2014) discussed that MIT's openness to hiring the Jewish scholars was another reason why MIT economics department's rise to prominence coincided with the postwar transformation of American economics. Caution should be taken here, however, as to what the term "Jewish" denotes. It can mean more than one definition depending on the context and from author to author. Since it is one of the most complex identities, unless the word is used with a clear distinction of (1) genetically/biologically/racially-defined Jews and (2) culturally/ethnically/religiously-defined Jews, any claim asserting something to be related with "Jewish" becomes spurious and academically irrelevant. In fact, it has been pointed out by researchers both in Japan and from abroad that ancient Jewish cultural influences remain strong also in Japan in shrines and festivals throughout the country. According to them, there are also not a few Japanese words with pronunciations corresponding to ancient Hebrew words that are still intact in modern Japanese language. Genetically, recent DNA and nuclear genome researches indicate that we, as a collective human race, have undergone various admixtures throughout history, and that it is scientifically nonsense to assume a specific ethnic group that corresponds to a certain single genetically-defined population. On the current debate on the origins of Ashkenazi Jews, for instance, see Das et al. (2017). Discriminations based on prejudice, social class or ethnicity that encourage hate towards any racial identities are inconsistent with our values.

Of course it should be clarified here that simply because a person is associated with a certain institution(s) does not always mean he or she is a part of the economics establishment that serves the international banking interests.[21] Nevertheless, the most recent appointment of Dr. Kazuo Ueda (MIT PhD 1980) as the BoJ governor in 2023 further strengthened the validity of our observation about the existence of such network of economists and seemed to be highlighting their increasing influence over international economic policy affairs.[22] Every two months these members of the "MIT Club" gather at the *Tower of Basel* as the heads of central banks of the leading nations to discuss issues related to the global economy over the Sunday dinner table, which is a part of two-day meetings held bimonthly at the Bank for International Settlements.

By connecting all these facts one may now conclude why the existing mainstream theories (and economists who profess them) do not or *cannot* analyze the debt money system, let alone propose the alternative. Of course, resorting to threats (such as those Kaoru received) is itself a serious problem that goes against the principles of science and academic freedom. More importantly, however, the authors of this book are concerned about the future of economics, if it continues to be a field where researchers cannot address the economic reality and such scientific undertakings are actively suppressed by politics.[23]

Looking back, it was a fortunate opportunity for Kaoru to have an intensive discussion with Lietaer in Vienna. Despite being close to such a network of economics establishment, Lietaer was an open minded thinker who could admit that the present system is structurally flawed and above all "*debt-end*." Through the discussion with him, Kaoru became convinced that proponents of the debt money theory cannot refute the public money theory, which is examined below.

---

[21] We may further remind readers that one of the professors mentioned above includes one of distinguished economics researchers who kindly sat on the advisory committee for Kaoru's doctoral dissertation at UC Berkeley. Therefore, our observations presented here, which are purely for academic purposes, should in no way be taken as personal attacks. Furthermore, this section should not be cut off, reproduced or presented to imply hate toward particular individuals.

[22] This is especially true when we consider the fact that Ueda was the first academic to be appointed as the Governor in the BoJ's history of the traditionally tucked-in appointments with the former Finance bureaucrats.

[23] In view of these circumstances, it is also concerning from the diversity perspective that American economics textbook market has followed a steady path towards consolidation since the 1980s into the best-selling authors under the "big five" publishers (as Black, 2021 also documented in his survey), which are now owned mostly by the Wall Street private equities.

9.6 Public Money Theory

Heads and Tails of the Same Coin

In order to analyze the debt money system as currently structured, why do we have two different theories such as the exogenous debt money theory (flow approach) and endogenous debt money theory (stock approach)? We have been caught by this question since the publication of our previous book (Yamaguchi, 2015). As discussed already, the only monetary theory that confronted the commodity money theory was the endogenous debt money theory until the 1940s. However, with the emergence of the Chicago Plan and Fisher's 100% Money, the endogenous debt money theory had been buried as a politically *taboo* subject by the banking interests as it would expose their means of devouring profits and controlling industries. Since then, only the exogenous debt money theory has been treated in standard textbooks as the mainstream Keynesian theory.

To scientifically examine these two approaches, we have constructed two ASD macroeconomic models that apply the flow and stock approaches of bank lending transaction and compared the behaviors of monetary aggregates in these two models. Our simulations showed that these two theories describe almost identical behaviors of money stocks, as if they were the "heads and tails" of the same coin (Yamaguchi and Yamaguchi, 2016). These results were immediately reported at the 34th International System Dynamics Conference held in Delft, the Netherlands, in July 2016. Although our analysis is based on simple ASD models that assume aggregate banking sector, the study clarified why the two seemingly contrasting theories of banking have coexisted in the literature.

In light of this new insight on these two monetary theories, the interpretation of exogenous debt money theory (flow approach) that has dominated textbooks since 1940s has been proven to be incorrect. That is, in a world where private banks (are allowed to) operate on a fractional reserve basis, they are acting as intermediaries for the deposits they receive and creators of new deposits for the loans they make. Thus, any Keynesian theories and macroeconomic models that rests on the exogenous money assumption (including the standard IS-LM model discussed in Chap. 7) is wrong and must be refuted entirely.

Therefore, it is a natural consequence that monetary and fiscal policies as well as quantitative easing (QE) policies are all destined to fail as we have examined in Chap. 5. Economic disasters such as the Great Depression and the failures of QE policy by the Bank of Japan cannot be explained as long as we conform to the wrong monetary theory. In other words, the endogenous debt money theory (stock approach) that has been made a *taboo* was simply correct.

Public Money Fixes System Design Failures of Debt Money

Through a series of studies using ASD macroeconomic models (Yamaguchi, 2013, Part II: Debt Money System), it became increasingly clear that the present debt money system has system design failures. "System design failures" mean that no matter how wise a government is, and no matter how sensible its policies are, we cannot escape from system failures. Imagine a poorly designed airplane. Even the most skilled pilot with longest flight hours cannot safely fly the airplane.

Following is a list of six design failures of the debt money system:

1. Booms and depressions, inflation and deflation, and financial instabilities are caused by the fractional reserve banking system, in which money is created only when non-banking sectors (households, firms and the government) borrow from banks at interest; Total Money Stock $\simeq$ Total Debts.
2. Since 99% of money is issued as someone's debt at compound interest, national debts will continue to increase exponentially.
3. This debt money system causes constant transfers of equity from borrowers to lenders of new money, and becomes an unfair *zero sum game* in favor of bankers who receive dividends as shareholders of banks.
4. Income inequality between bankers and non-bankers (the gap between "1% vs. 99%") stems from this unfair banking practices that create fictitious "deposits" out of nothing and lend them at compound interest rate.
5. This built in unfair income distribution inflates total income of households beyond income realized by production. Consequently the economy gets inflationary as long as the government is obliged to keep borrowing at interests. Inflated income in turn diminishes wage share, causing workers relatively poor against bankers as unearned income earners (interclass inequality).
6. Furthermore, this built-in unfair income distribution and inflation cannot be controlled by the central bank nor the government, and devalues currency and life savings of pensioners (intergenerational inequality).

As a natural consequence, these socioeconomic problems arising from the debt money system can be overcome by transitioning to public money system. This is the essence of public money theory. Its outline is summarized as follows:

- In a modern constitutional state based on the separation of powers, the authority to issue currency as public money belongs to the legislature. The Congress in the US, the Parliament in the UK, and the Diet in Japan.
- The executive branch has the right to collect taxes, appropriate public funds, and execute the budget. However, it cannot issue public money.
- The legislature that issues its own public money and the executive branch of the government that uses it for public finance do not default.
- Additional public money is put into circulation only when the growing economy needs it. The government is provided with such money as equity, not as interest-bearing debts. The appropriate supply of money that does not cause inflation or

deflation can be adjusted through the government's budget process (fiscal expenditure, tax increases or tax cuts). Accordingly, price and purchasing power of currency is stabilized.

- Under this public money system, interest income is generated only when the economy grows so that the increased amount of GDP is fairly distributed among wage earners and bankers who reinvest savings (S). Built-in equitable distribution of interest income and its positive-sum game among investment stakeholders will be achieved.

For separation of powers, public money are issued by an independent policy committee established under the direct supervision of the legislature called Public Money Administration (PMA). This governance mechanism ensures the commission is isolated from political pressures by other branches of government in fulfilling its price stability objective. The macroeconomic system that meets these institutional conditions is called the public money system.

Banks Become Genuine Intermediaries of Public Money

How would the existing debt money system be reformed, then, if these conditions were incorporated? Table 9.1 compares the system structures of public money versus debt money.

The crucial difference is that, by requiring all banks (depository institutions) to keep 100% reserve ratio on demand deposits under the public money system, banks will no longer be the creators of money stock and become genuine intermediaries between savers and borrowers. This will separate money creation from private banks's lending business.

Loanable funds of banks come from three sources: (1) their own funds (managed separately from customer's deposits), (2) time deposits, and (3) loans that get

Table 9.1 Public money versus debt money—system structure comparison

	Public Money System	Debt Money System
Money Issuer	Public Money Administration	Central Bank & Private Banks
Its Owner	Legislature (the Public)	Bankers and Financiers
Reserve Ratio	100% for Demand Deposits	Fractional Reserve (0~99%)
Role of Banks	Intermediaries of Money	Creators of Money (Deposits)
Money Stock	Public Money directly put into circulation as economy grows (Banking business unaffected)	Base Money: by Central Bank Deposits: by Private Bank Loans (Governments issue coins only)
Interest	Interest-free Money	Money as Interest-bearing Debt
Economic Policies	Monetary Policy: PMA Fiscal Policy: Government	Monetary Policy: Central Bank Fiscal Policy: Government

Table 9.2 Public money versus debt money—system behavior comparison

	Public Money System	Debt Money System
Monetary Stability	Stable Money Stock Stable Price Level	Bubbles, Credit Crunches Inflation & Deflation
Financial Stability	No Bank Runs Robust Financial System	Business Cycles, Financial Crises, Booms & Depressions
Employment Stability	Lifetime Employment	Involuntary Unemployment
Government Debt (Fiscal Stability)	No Debt is necessary under the Balanced Budget	Built-in Debt Accumulation → Recession & Unemployment
Inequality (Social Stability)	Income Inequality between Workers and Capitalists	Income Inequality between Financiers and Non-financiers
Sustainability & Environmental Conservation	Sustainable Development becomes attainable with Public Money (see Part III)	Debt Accumulation → Forced Growth → Environmental Destruction

repaid. Especially, time deposits are savings of the economy and become the main source of loanable funds for the banking sector under the public money system. As a result, bank's main source of income consists of (a) interests earned from lending business and (b) service fees accrued from providing various financial services (including foreign exchange). In this way, a robust foundation of financial system will be established. This business model of banks as genuine intermediaries of public money, which is what most economics textbooks have assumed to be, provides them with incentives to seek for investments in real productive purposes rather than on zero-sum financial speculations.

Consequently, interest rates under the public money system will be determined in the market, making the whole financial sector more competitive, fair, and efficient from resource allocation standpoint. In this respect, the Public Money Administration (PMA) will be free from conventional monetary policy of manipulating interest rates as presently done by the central bank. No further explanation of Table 9.1 would be necessary for readers who have traveled this far. Only the basic element related to money and banking is reformed, i.e., the money issuer and legally required reserve ratio. There is no need for changes in other parts of the economy or how we conduct our daily businesses.

System structure determines behaviors (outcomes) of the system. This is the system dynamics view of how our society and economy develops over time. How would these small changes in the debt money system change the behavior of our economy, then? Table 9.2 compares the different behaviors that will emerge under the public money system against those of the debt money system.[24]

---

[24] Tables 9.1 and 9.2 are adapted from Yamaguchi (2013), Chap. 19 titled "Public Money and Sustainability".

Table 9.3 Public money versus debt money: which one do you support?

Public Money Theory	Money is issued by the legislative branch of government as equity without interest. Its total supply is *exogenously* regulated by an independent monetary authority towards price stability.
Debt Money Theory	Money is *endogenously* created by private banks as debt at compound interest and destroyed when loans are liquidated. Its total supply is not directly regulated by the monetary authority and thus inherently unstable.

Especially, elimination of income inequality and sustainability are behaviors that become attainable under the public money system. Specifically, the Public Money Initiative presented in Chap. 14 describes policy programs designed to achieve economic prosperity and sustainability in the context of Japan.

9.7 Only Two Theories Have Survived

We have examined four monetary theories as summarized in Fig. 9.1. Mainstream neoclassical (moneyless price and commodity money) theory is detached from the reality of our monetary economy, and no longer applicable to the current economic analysis because gold and silver are no longer in circulation as commodity money. On the other hand, the mainstream Keynesian (exogenous debt money) theory is shown to be flawed not only because it is inconsistent with how money has been issued under the present system, but also Keynesian models based on the exogenous money (flow approach) failed to explain the historical cases such as the Great Depression and Japan's lost 30 years as demonstrated in Chap. 8. Moreover, commercial banks are acting as intermediaries for the deposits they accept and as creators of money for the loans they make under the fractional reserve requirement. In this sense, exogenous debt money theory (flow approach) and endogenous debt money theory (stock approach) are the heads and tails of the same coin. Accordingly, the two monetary theories shall be renamed collectively as "Debt Money Theory" hereafter.

Which Path: Public Money or Debt Money?

In this way there are two theories that have survived our examination as summarized in Table 9.3. Notice how the two theories match the obverse definition in our classification of money in Fig. 2.1. Which monetary theory do you support? We hope the readers will follow the right path. Because that is what the paradigm shift in economics is confronting us all.

Chapter 10
Debt Money as a Means of Control

In Chap. 9 we have discussed what kind of monetary theories existed in economics and which of them can correctly capture the real world economies. To fully understand the role of money and its importance in society, we need to analyze the function of money. In this chapter we will discuss how money functions as a means of control, in addition to the three well-recognized functions. Let us first review how standard economics explains the functions of money.

10.1 Fourth Function of Money

Three Economic Functions of Money

Most textbooks begin by explaining transactions through barter. They analyze that the market is restrictive and does not function well under the barter economy, as no exchange can take place unless both parties can find an exchange partner who needs each other's goods simultaneously. In order to compensate for this defect of barter system, commodities that everyone is willing to accept are selected from the market. And these will eventually become *commodity money*. The question is then asked as to what kind of commodity will serve as money. It is often explained that a commodity that satisfies the following three functions will eventually become money; (1) unit of value or account, (2) means of exchange, (3) store of value. That is, economics textbooks define money as satisfying these three conditions in an axiomatic manner.

Let us called these conditions here as three *economic* functions of money. As discussed in Chap. 9, Adam Smith defined gold and silver as money because of their metallic nature (physical properties) that meets three economic conditions. However, the idea that gold and silver are gradually extracted from barter as commodity money is a fiction invented by those economists who refuse to learn about the legal nature of money from the history. Specifically, the commodity money theory is a fiction

K. Yamaguchi and Y. Yamaguchi, *Public Money*,
https://doi.org/10.1007/978-981-97-6564-5_10

invented by neoclassical economists who tend to pursue logical and mathematical beauty based on deductive reasoning. Instead, we have analyzed that money has to be, first of all, created and established as legal tender, which then, begins to exhibit (perform) the three economic functions. In other words, the definition of money has been turned upside down!

Why, then, has the definition of money undergone a 180-degree turn? The reason is rather simple. If gold and silver serve as money, which was once true, the owners who possess those precious metals can monopolize their wealth, gain control, and exert power through it. Since the advent of Adam Smith's perverted definition of money, the fourth function of money as a *means of control* has been obscured and cleverly hidden from textbooks. And, together with the general equilibrium theory, the fourth function of money was replaced with the axiomatic logic of monetary functions in the mainstream economics.

Debt Money as a Means of Control

What do we exactly mean when we say "money function as a means of control"? Let's think about this step by step. Money has been functioning as a store of value. With money, we can not only buy and sell goods and services for our daily needs, but also acquire non-economic things that cannot be produced by production activities. In the extreme case, money can buy virtually everything. So, what exactly can we buy with money? There are similar proverbs on money in Japanese, Chinese as well as in English such as follows:

- The end of money is the end of love.
- Everything can be settled with money even in hell.
- It's money that talks.

As long as we have enough money, we can make business relationships and earn social status. Moreover, money can be used to subjugate people, or religious salvation may be obtained with it. You can even settle disputes in hell! You can virtually control everything in this world. Regardless of whether you believe in these things or not, the existence of these proverbs shows that people have been trying to understand the magical power and danger of money for a long time. For instance, we read in the sacred writings of Christianity as follows:

> For the love of money is the root of all kinds of evil, for which some have strayed from the faith in their greediness, and pierced themselves through with many sorrows (Timothy 6:10; New King James Version).

Still, the readers might argue that money cannot buy things like personal emotion, national secrets or eternal love. However, these can be done by using the power of money to create a system in which even these things can be bought and sold indirectly. The doctrine of Original Sin, which holds that people are born with sins inherited from Adam and Eve, has been used to systematically extort money from people. To be specific, the Church of Rome before the Reformation of Martin Luther imposed mind control on the people by telling them that the punishment for their sins would be atoned if they tell all their secrets in front of religious figures such as the Pope, bishops and priests, and pay money for the indulgences. Religious people, then, wittingly utilized the secrets of kings and other powerful figures thus obtained for their political goals. In other words, by taking advantage of people's insecurities, fear or sadness, and acquiring money and building magnificent churches such as Basilica of Saint Peter in the Vatican, they were able to indirectly control the human mind and spirit of love, people's benevolence, and so on. The unrestricted sale of indulgences by pardoners had been a widespread abuse in the late Middle Ages.

In this way, a social structure has been created in which such a system of money as a store of value is built up and used to exercise power and control over the people. At this point money has gone beyond being a means of exchange and become a means of control. Furthermore, the people who are ruled by money begin to think and view money itself as their enemy, as if the existence of money is the reason why they have suffered such a terrible fate. However, it is the love for money that is the root of evil as the Timothy describes. What is to be abhorred is the cunning of those who abuse the function of money.

From a short examination of proverbs about money from the East and West, the essence of the current financial system emerges. Indeed, proverbs are the wisdom of the people. Summing up the above, the fourth function of money becomes explicit as shown in Fig. 10.1. This figure illustrates the relationship among these four monetary functions. First, money is located at the opposite end of economic activity and facilitates the exchange and distribution of goods and services. It is important to note that the fourth function, means of control, is what encompasses these three economic functions. It is this fourth function of money that mainstream economists fail to analyze in their textbooks, causing wrong prescription and suffering to the people. Let's find out how this has been the case in more detail.

10.2 Outer Loop of Control: Compound Interest

The Wrath of Jesus Christ

The fractional reserve banking system is truly the modern "magical money tree". Like the alchemy Isaac Newton studied in his later years, or the goose that lays the golden egg, private banks can create money in the form of 'deposits' with a stroke of a pen or entry into computer database in our time. As we discussed in Chap. 9, bankers have perfected and monopolized this money tree. And they have succeeded in legitimizing this fraudulent financial system by establishing central banks and maintained their vested interests to dominate economic and political spheres. Not only that, they have reconfigured this money tree as a means of domination into a self-propagating system as the adage describes, "the rich get richer". It is a financial

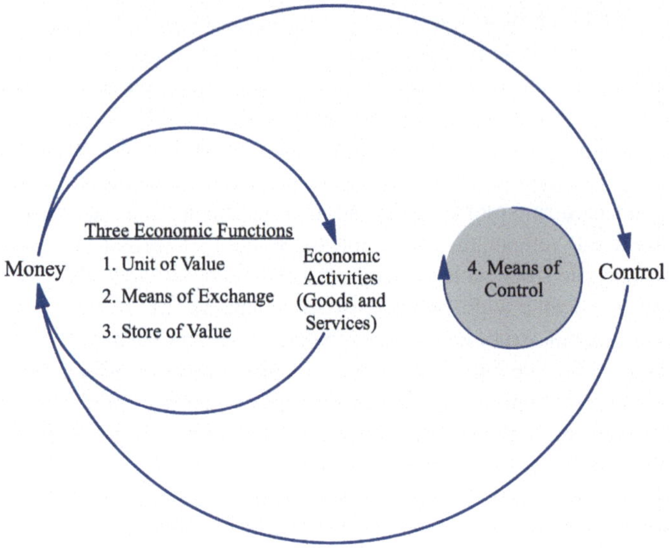

Fig. 10.1 The forth function of money as means of control

system in which interest is paid on the basis of compound interest calculation where "money makes more money".

So what is interest and why should it be paid? Readers may take it for granted that whenever they borrow money from their banks, they must pay interest on them. It is said the only incident that infuriated Jesus Christ in his life was the greedy act of bankers and money changers who collected high interest in the sacred temple. Known as the cleansing of the temple, Jesus Christ, when entering the temple court, overturned the table and drove those bankers out (Fig. 10.2).[1]

> So he made a whip out of cords, and drove all from the temple courts, both sheep and cattle; he scattered the coins of the money changers and overturned their tables. (John 2:15, NIV)

Even today, Islamic finance in Muslim nations avoid charging nominal interest (although investors do receive a substantial amount in the form of a *gratuity*).

Forbidden Act of Usury in World Religions

The sacred scripts of the world's major religions emphasize usury as an act of evil. For instance let us quote from the religious scriptures of the three leading religions as follows:

[1] National Galleries of Scotland—Accession number: NG 32. https://www.nationalgalleries.org/art-and-artists/4939

Fig. 10.2 Christ driving the money changers from the temple, painting around 1540–1550 by the Italian painter Benvenuto Tisi da Garofalo

Buddhism

One discerns wrong livelihood as wrong livelihood, and right livelihood as right livelihood. And what is wrong livelihood? Scheming, persuading, hinting, belittling, and charging *interest*. This is wrong livelihood (Siddharta Gautama Buddha in his sermon on the Eightfold Path; Majjhima Nikaya Suttra 117).

Christianity

36 Do not take *interest* or any profit from them, but fear your God,
so that they may continue to live among you.
37 You must not lend them money at *interest* or sell them food
at a profit (Leviticus 25:36 37, Old Testament).

Islam

And (for) their taking of *usury* while they had been forbidden from it, and their consuming of the people's wealth unjustly. And we have prepared for the disbelievers among them a painful punishment (Quran, Chapter 4: verse 161).

In light of these moral principles, the present system of debt money and compound interests is the most fundamental issue the world must end first and foremost. Money reform is a preliminary to all other social reforms.

The Origin of Interest

The origin of interest may be traced back to the time when farmers who borrowed seeds due to a bad harvest gave back extra crop as "seeds+α" to the farmers who initially gave them seeds. In modern terms, interest was originally paid back only when the farmer had borrowed money to finance a successful business venture, as a thank-you for the seed money. The practice of paying back the borrowed money with an extra amount of interest was eventually replaced by the practice of paying back the borrowed money with interest even if a person borrowed something other than agricultural products that did not yield extra harvests by themselves. At some point in our history, banks began to charge interest on any amount of money they loaned, regardless of whether the borrower's business was productive or not.

In macroeconomics terms, if GDP increases by, say, 3% as a result of new investment (i.e. capital formation), the producer and the bank can share the 3% increment in interest as income. That was the original form of interest. However, even in zero-growth economy, such as today's Japan, banks demand interests and force foreclosures. As a result, the income gap between bankers (0.1%) and borrowers (99.9%) grows wider. Even worse, on top of this anomaly, these lenders demand *compound interest* from the debtors for the 99% of debt money created out of nothing, irrespective of economic circumstances. Such system is more absurd and inequitable than what we would expect in the famous board-game *Monopoly*. But this is the reality as explained in Chap. 3. To replace this debt money system and return the compound interest to its original form, we are proposing the public money system. Before we discuss the solution in Part III, let us take a further look at the mechanism of how "money makes money" under compound interest calculation.

Wonder and Horror of Compound Interest

Figure 10.3 illustrates how debt increases debt through compound interest as a stock-flow diagram of system dynamics modeling method. As interest is added to the debt, the debt increases (debt → interest → debt). The same interest rate is then applied to the increased debt. Accordingly the interest on the debt increases further, which in turn continues to augment debt as a self-reinforcing positive feedback loop. It is this mechanism of compound interest calculations that drives the debt hell in the US, Japan, and OECD countries as analyzed in Sect. 6.1.

If we replace this stock of "Debts" with "Bank Deposits", money makes money (deposits → interest → deposits). In other words, it is a financial system where the rich gets richer. In System Dynamics, this system of growth is generalized as an exponential growth model. This self-growing exponential growth model is observed not only in the financial system, but also in various aspects of human society and nature, such as population growth models and reproduction models of animal species in our ecosystem. Although this model appears at first glance to be a simple growth model,

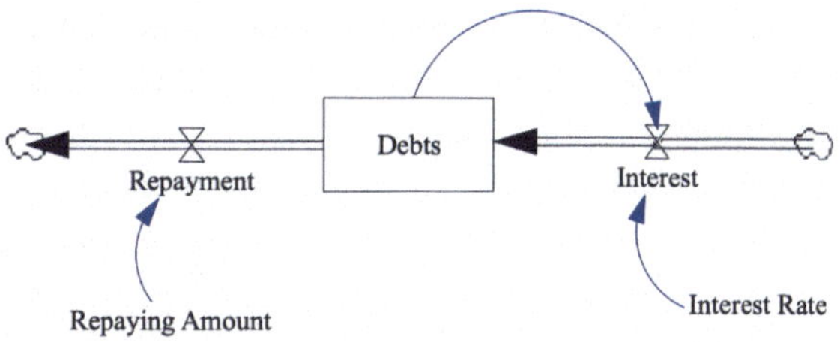

Fig. 10.3 Money makes money: compound interest

it actually behaves in a surprisingly rapid manner that goes beyond our common sense and intuition.

After getting disappointed with the methodology of mathematical economics. Kaoru gave up his economic research and made a "transition" to the field of system dynamics (as explained in Chap. 9). He strongly felt in those days that in order to make such a transition successfully, he needed to learn directly from the founders and top researchers in the field, including Professor Emeritus Jay W. Forrester, the founder of systems dynamics, and Professor John D. Sterman, the world's leading researcher and practitioner in the field, at MIT's Sloan School of Management. His desire to learn directly from such world-class researchers was fulfilled when he visited MIT as a visiting scholar twice in the falls of 1999 and 2000. Sterman's lecture on System Dynamics was one of the most popular courses at the Sloan School, and Kaoru attended his lectures during his visits.

In one of his lectures, Professor Sterman asked his graduate students: "How tall would a sheet of paper be if it were folded over 42 times? Although they were at one of the top business schools in the world, their answers were surprisingly mixed: "about the height of a person", "about the height of a three-story building", "no, about the height of the Eiffel Tower in Paris". Another student said, "it would be even higher, maybe the Himalayas". While listening to the exchanges of these replies, Kaoru intuitively thought, "it would be about the size of Tokyo Tower". What do you think the answer would be?

Folding a sheet of paper 42 times makes it $2^{42} = 4.398 * 10^{12}$ thick. Assuming the thickness of a sheet of paper to be 0.1 mm and converting it to kilometers, the thickness is $1 * 10^{-7}$ km. Therefore, if we convert the total thickness of the folded paper into kilometers, we get

$$4.398 * 10^{12} * 10^{-7} = 4.398 * 10^{5} = 439,800 \text{ km}.$$

This length far exceeds the distance to the moon, which is about 380,000 km. No wonder how few of his graduate students attained the correct answer. This is a good example of how human cerebrum makes a quick judgment. And this would also be the reactions of the majority of general public to the counter-intuitive behavior of exponential growth.

Professor Sterman continued similar questions that seemed to challenge the students' conventional wisdom about exponential growth[2]:

Lily Pond There is a lily that doubles in growth every day and covers the pond in 30 days. On what day does the lily grow to about 1% of the pond's area? And on what day does its presence begin to become noticeable?

Iranian folktale A courtier presented the king with a wonderful chessboard (64 squares) and was told that he could have anything he liked as a reward. A courtier replied that he would be happy to start with a grain of rice and receive double that amount for each square moved on the chessboard. The king agreed immediately, wondering if such a reward was enough. Now, by the time he reached the 64th square, how large would the grain of rice be?

The exponential growth model is a basic model for capturing dynamic movements, but the behavior of the increase is far beyond our common sense. If we apply such an exponential growth model to the financial system, we will see the emergence of an financial situation, in which deposits (and wealth) of the rich increase tremendously and debts of the poor swell in the blink of an eye. Many people, their companies and governments around the world fail to understand this part of the story when they go into debts, so it does not make sense when they are told how fast "the rich will get richer and the poor will get poorer". And they easily fall into the trap of loan sharking at interest rates as high as 20%.

Exponential Growth and Doubling Time

While exponential growths exhibit a very scary (powerful) property in our world and has very real effect on our society, this exponential growth model has a very beautiful property. That is, the doubling time of deposits and debts in the above example is always constant and can be obtained by the simple formula below:

$$\text{Doubling (halving) time} = 69 \text{ years} / \text{Rate of increase (decrease)}$$

For instance, the doubling time at 20% of interest rate is 69 years divided by 20, which is about 3.5 years. If you borrow 150,000 dollars from a loan shark at 20% of interest rate, your debt will double to 300,000 dollars in about 3.5 years, quadruple to 600,000 dollars in about 7 years, and eightfold to 1.2 million dollars in about 10.5 years. The Greek government's debt, whose interest rate on bonds exceeded 20% at one point, also increased rapidly in a similar way.

Table 10.1 shows examples of more moderate growth rate of 3% per annum, and decrease rate of −2.3%. Applying the above formula, the doubling time of the growth is 69 years/3 = about 23 years, and the debt will double in about 23 years, quadruple in about 46 years, and increase eightfold in about 69 years.

---

[2] These exercises can also be found in the Professor Sterman's textbook *Business Dynamics* (Sterman, 2000).

Table 10.1 Doubling (halving) time of exponential growth (decay)

Exponential Growth (Decay) Table

Formula: Doubling (halving) time = 69 /Growth (decrease) rate (%)

Doubling time at growth rate = +3%		Halving time at decrease rate = −2.3%	
After about 23 years	2 times	After about 30 years	50 %
After about 46 years	4 times	After about 60 years	25 %
After about 69 years	8 times	After about 90 years	12.5 %
After about 92 years	16 times	After about 120 years	6.25 %
After about 115 years	32 times	After about 150 years	3.13 %
After about 138 years	64 times	After about 180 years	1.56 %
...		After about 200 years	1%

As a simple application, let us recall the good old days of the 1960s in Japan when the economy grew at more than 7% per year. The Prime Minister Ikeda proclaimed in 1960 that he will double the Japanese income in 10 years. Kaoru still remember when he was in a junior high school that how such newspaper headlines excited him with the expectation that an era of affluence was coming. Using the above formula, the time required for income to double is 69 years/7 = approximately 10 years, which means that income will indeed double in 10 years as we discussed in Chap. 4.

Furthermore, with that rate of growth, income will quadruple in 20 years, 8 times more in 30 years, 16 times more in 40 years, and 32 times more in 50 years, that is, in 2010. Since Japan's GDP in 1960 was 13.6 trillion yen, 32 times that amount would be 435.2 trillion yen. The nominal GDP of Japan in 2010 was 482 trillion yen. This means that the GDP growth of the economy exceeded the simple calculation of the doubling time. In other words, even though Japan had lost the last 20 years of that 50-year period due to the collapse of the bubble since 1990, the economy has grown by more than 7% on average over the past 50 years until 2010.

Using the constant doubling time property of the exponential growth model, we can quickly do the calculation by rote and constantly check the fuzzy common sense of our cerebrum. If we continue with the calculations, GDP will increase 64 times more in 60 years, that is, in 2020. In other words, Japan's GDP will be 64 times the 13.6 trillion yen of GDP in 1960, or 870.4 trillion yen. Is such economic growth really possible? The answer will be a resounding yes, if Japan were to shift to the public money system and implement growth strategies proposed under "Public Money Initiative" in Chap. 14. Such reasoning should be applicable not just in Japan but also in other countries, if we could elect national leaders who will implement right economic policies under the public money system.

Exponential Decay and Halving Time

Despite these hopes, the earthquake and tsunami that hit the eastern Japan in March 2011 caused major damages to the Fukushima Daiichi Nuclear Power Plant operated by TEPCO (Tokyo Electric Power Company) and has left deep scars on the people and local economies in that region. High levels of radioactive waste such as strontium-90 and cesium-137 were spread in large quantities. It has been reported that large amounts of cesium-137 were released and contaminated the fertile land in the northeastern region. The question is how long it will remain in the environment. Its halving time can be calculated in the same way as using the above formula of exponential growth model. In other words, exponential growth and exponential decay have the same properties.

The halving time of cesium-137 is said to be about 30 years. Therefore, using the formula in reverse, the rate of decrease of cesium-137 is 69 years/30 years = 2.3%. In other words, cesium-137 decreases only slowly, at 2.3% per year. From Table 10.1, it takes 60 years for cesium-137 to decrease to 25%, 90 years to decrease to 12.5%, etc. Some people claim that we'll be safe if the cesium-137 level is reduced to 1%. From the table, it takes about 200 years for the cesium-137 level to be reduced to 1%. Moreover, this is only the rate of decrease, not the actual amount of cesium-137 remaining. If 100 times as much cesium-137 had been released as in the Hiroshima atomic bomb, then even after about 200 years, the same amount of cesium-137 would remain as in the Hiroshima bomb.

Outer Loop of Control via Compound Interests

Money lenders have fully utilized compound interest and cleverly planted the "magical money tree" as the current debt money system. They then have exploited this mechanism of compound interest to control our industries, government, and economy. Figure 10.4 illustrates *outer loop of control* by compound interest through deposit creation enabled under the fractional reserve banking system as well as *inner loop of control* exercised through equity ownership.

Consequently, whenever we speak of interest rates nowadays, it always means *compound* interest, not *simple* interest. Borrowing at simple interest rate is rarely put on the table of negotiation. This simple fact tells us that the whole society has been shaped under the logic of money lenders. Even worse, most economists, religious leaders or artists nowadays do not talk about this issue. Students of economics learn how to calculate compound interest but not necessarily its social repercussion. As a result, they come to believe that they deserve to pay interest on money they borrowed, which were created by banks out of nothing. In this sense, we have been fundamentally brainwashed by the bankers.

10.3 Inner Loop of Control: Equity Ownership

Whenever we discuss the current socioeconomic problems caused by the debt money system, it is important to be aware of this control mechanism exercised through compound interest. Based on this system of control, bankers continue to accumulate more wealth as if to further grow the money tree and control the global economy as we shall analyze in the next section. However, the outer loop of control by compound interest turned out to be not sufficient to control industries and the economy as Fig. 10.4 illustrates. In macroeconomics term, interest is only a part of unearned income of a nation. There are also dividends, rents and other parts of unearned income. In order to exploit as much profits as possible, establishing a scheme for creating money and putting companies and governments into debt was not enough. To extract more gains, bankers and financiers have sought to establish another scheme to exert control over the business entities (corporations).

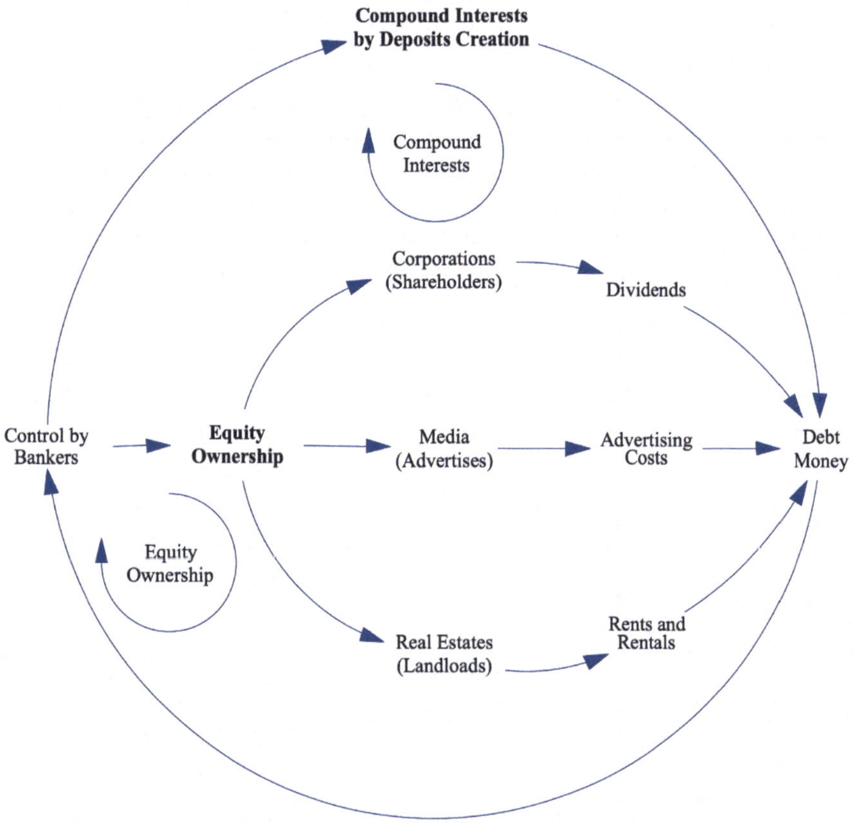

Fig. 10.4 Mechanism of control by compound interest and equity ownership

Inner Loop of Control via Equity Ownership System

The system of private joint stock company has been utilized for this purpose, in which these institutions are legally "owned" by those who have purchased their stocks and shares. That is, ownership of corporations per se is made exchangeable in the markets, just like goods and services are traded. In this way, with the money accumulated, bankers begin to control business organizations as their rightful shareholders. Furthermore, under private ownership of capitalism, lands and real estates are also made possible to be owned by the landlords.

Bankers have thus succeeded to establish a system of control where they can exert their influences on the entire social fabric as we know it. They now control entire sectors of businesses as shareholders and landlords, and collect dividends and rentals. To further strengthen the grip of their control, they simultaneously own media and control public opinions in favor of their policies. Here, this entire money-collection system embedded into capitalism is called *Equity Ownership System*. Notice how this system of control complements to the debt money system, through which additional money is extracted as interests, dividends, advertising fees, rents as well as taxes on public debt.

In this way, the inner and outer loops of control have evolved historically.[3] A means of control as the fourth function of money has now evolved into an overarching means of domination. The outer loop of control is governed by the debt money system, a main theme of this book, and the inner loop of control is dictated by the equity ownership system. In this way, the current capitalist economy has become an ultimate system of control in which these two dominant control loops are intertwined. These two systems are collectively referred to as the *Debt Money and Equity Ownership System*.

Hence, in order to be freed from the control of capitalism, it is not enough to transform debt money system into public money system. We also need to transform equity ownership system into *Equity Possession System*, which will be discussed in the last Chap. 15.

10.4 Network of Global Corporate Control

Top 50 Control-Holders

Our analysis of control exercised by bankers and financiers may sound like a conspiracy theory. Yet it is a reality of the global economy that has been revealed by scientific research. In 2011 three researchers at ETH Zurich published a paper titled

[3] As Fig. 10.4 illustrates, the inner loop of control further splits into three sub-loops; control loop by shareholding, land-holding, and media advertisement. Since information control through media is achieved by corporate shareholding control, these three loops can be summarized into two. However, they are depicted separately to emphasize the importance of controlling information in establishing this system of control.

"The Network of Global Corporate Control" (Vitali et al., 2011). According to the paper, the analysis of 37 million companies data from 194 countries, taken from the Bureau van Dijk's Orbis 2007 commercial database, has revealed an "architecture of the international ownership network" (equity ownership structure) of 13 million companies worldwide. In their study, the concept of "control" was proxied by the potential control over the operating revenue of transnational corporations (TNCs). Of the 13 million companies, 43,060 TNCS located in a total of 116 countries were identified according to the OECD definition of multinational enterprises. Of these, 5,675 TNCs were quoted in stock markets. The corporate network thus constructed consists of 600,508 economic entities (natural persons, families, foundations, government agencies, listed and unlisted companies, etc.) as nodes and 1,006,987 corporate ownership relations. Then, these network relations were subjected to simulation analysis. Their findings are shown as bow-tie network topology as illustrated in Fig. 10.5, which is adapted from Fig. 2 (B) in Vitali et al. (2011, p. 4).

Here, the 43,060 TNCs are classified into five corporate groups: in-section (IN), strongly connected component or core (SCC), tubes and tendrils (T&T), out-section (OUT), and other connected components (OCC). IN is a top layer of equity ownership control revealed by their computer simulation. SCC becomes a core group of directors and managers who intermingle and control.

According to the bow-tie network topology discussed in the paper, ownership control flows from the top group IN to other network positions as follows:
(a) IN → SCC → OUT → T (tendrils): network control through SCC

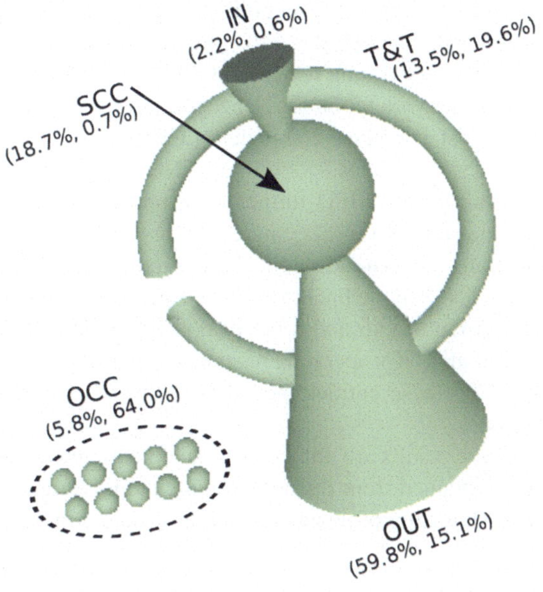

Fig. 10.5 Bow-tie network topology

Source: Vitali et.al. (2011); Figure 2 (B).

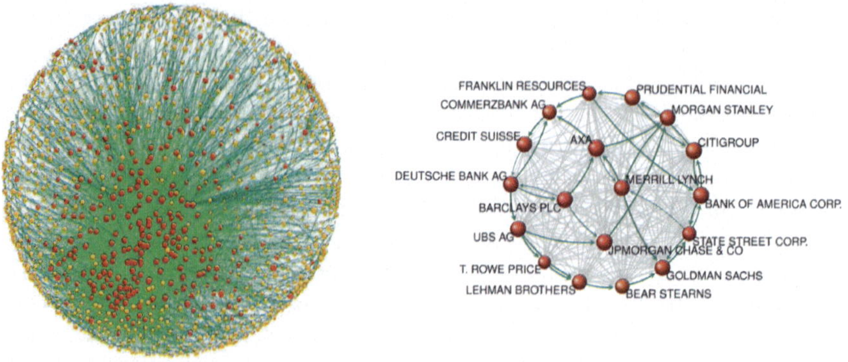

Source: Vitali et.al. (2011); Figure 2 (C) and (D).

Fig. 10.6 Network topology: SCC (1,318 nodes) layout (left) and some major TNCs in financial sector zoom-in (right)

(b) IN → T (tubes) → OUT → T (tendrils): network control through T&T
(c) IN → T (tendrils): network control through T.

Values inside parenthesis imply percentage of operating revenues and numbers of TNCs. For instance, IN (2.2%, 0.6%) implies 2.2% of total TNC operating revenues, realized by 0.6% of 282 TNCs out of total 43,060 TNCs. Similarly, the strongly connected core SCC (18.7%, 0.7%) implies 18.7% of total TNC revenues by 0.7% of 295 TNCs out of total 43,060 TNCs. This indicates that less than 1% of core group SCC dominates roughly one-fifth of total TNCs operating revenues. On the other hand, OCC (5.8%, 64%) implies that 64% (27,569 TNCs) takes up less than 6% of total operating revenues. OCC is not connected to the control network in the bow-tie network topology. Hence, the analysis of this network topology revealed that the largest connected component LCC (=IN+SCC+T&T+OUT), consisting of 36% of TNCs, dominates 94.2% of all TNC operating revenues.[4]

Vitali et al. (2011) further analyzed the network structure of control in terms of nodes through (cross) shareholdings as illustrated in Fig. 10.6. The left diagram illustrates 1,318 nodes of SCC core group (295 TNCs), and right diagram focuses on major TNCs in the financial sector. Specifically, their analysis indicated the top SCC core group of 146 nodes out of 600,508 economic entities (only 0.024%) controls 40% of all TNCs operating revenues. When expanded to the top 737 nodes (still only 0.123%), these entities indeed collectively controlled 80% of all TNC operating revenues.

These results are not a conspiracy theory, the researchers of the paper claim, but those obtained from scientific research to investigate who are the key actors, what is the architecture of ownership and how their controls are distributed globally. These

[4] Total TNCs are decomposed in number and percentage as follows:
- 43,060 TNCs = IN(282) + SCC(295) + T&T(8,426) + OUT(6,488) + OCC(27,569).
- 100% TNCs = IN(0.6%) + SCC(0.7%) + T&T(19.6%) + OUT(15.1%) + OCC(64.0%).

are all highly relevant academic questions in terms of measuring connectedness and resiliency of our financial system and the global economy. Notably, the paper also presented a list of top 50 control-holders (shareholders) that are ranked by their network control ownership according to the threshold model (see Vitali et al., 2011, Sect. 3, pp. 16–24). Figure 10.7 replicates the top 25 control-holders shown on Table S1 in page 33 of the original paper. Columns indicate country, NACE industrial sector code, actor's network position and cumulative network control. Note that NACE code starting with 65, 66, 67 belong to the financial sectors.

According to this list, the top 25 control-holders are all dominated by financial institutions. At the top of this list was Barclays that controlled 4% of network control. Then, the top three control-holders controlled about 9% and the top 10 control-holders controlled almost 20% of total ownership network. As we can see, the top 25 control-holder do not include any of the world's well-known companies, such as automobile makers (GM, Toyota, etc.), oil majors (ExxonMobil, Royal Dutch Shell, BP, etc.), or chemical and pharmaceutical companies (Dupont, Pfizer, Bayer, etc.). In fact, multinational manufacturing companies are not even among the top 50 control-holders that dominate the global network of ownership control. Most of them are international banks and wealth management funds. And they all are in the network position of IN, SCC and T&T.

The study was conducted on the database before the Lehman Shock in 2008. Since then, the global economy has undergone number of shocks including the COVID-19 lockdowns in 2020. These events have prompted failures and mergers of financial institutions ranked top in the list of control-holders as well as those in the non-banking sectors that are out of the list. Hence, the network of control may have

Rank	Economic actor name	Country	NACE code	Network position	Cumul. network control (TM, %)
1	BARCLAYS PLC	GB	6512	SCC	4.05
2	CAPITAL GROUP COMPANIES INC, THE	US	6713	IN	6.66
3	FMR CORP	US	6713	IN	8.94
4	AXA	FR	6712	SCC	11.21
5	STATE STREET CORPORATION	US	6713	SCC	13.02
6	JPMORGAN CHASE & CO.	US	6512	SCC	14.55
7	LEGAL & GENERAL GROUP PLC	GB	6603	SCC	16.02
8	VANGUARD GROUP, INC., THE	US	7415	IN	17.25
9	UBS AG	CH	6512	SCC	18.46
10	MERRILL LYNCH & CO., INC.	US	6712	SCC	19.45
11	WELLINGTON MANAGEMENT CO. L.L.P.	US	6713	IN	20.33
12	DEUTSCHE BANK AG	DE	6512	SCC	21.17
13	FRANKLIN RESOURCES, INC.	US	6512	SCC	21.99
14	CREDIT SUISSE GROUP	CH	6512	SCC	22.81
15	WALTON ENTERPRISES LLC	US	2923	T&T	23.56
16	BANK OF NEW YORK MELLON CORP.	US	6512	IN	24.28
17	NATIXIS	FR	6512	SCC	24.98
18	GOLDMAN SACHS GROUP, INC., THE	US	6712	SCC	25.64
19	T. ROWE PRICE GROUP, INC.	US	6713	SCC	26.29
20	LEGG MASON, INC.	US	6712	SCC	26.92
21	MORGAN STANLEY	US	6712	SCC	27.56
22	MITSUBISHI UFJ FINANCIAL GROUP, INC.	JP	6512	SCC	28.16
23	NORTHERN TRUST CORPORATION	US	6512	SCC	28.72
24	SOCIÉTÉ GÉNÉRALE	FR	6512	SCC	29.26
25	BANK OF AMERICA CORPORATION	US	6512	SCC	29.79

Fig. 10.7 Top 25 control-holders in the Global Corporate Control Network

increased its degree of concentration even more. Is this highly centralized system resilient enough to overcome the next financial crisis? A follow-up study is awaited as more and more nations are facing debt crises.

List of International Banks Bailed Out by the Fed during 2007–2010

The U.S. Government Accountability Office (GAO) submitted a historic report to Congress in July 2011 (GAO, 2011). The GAO report was the first report of an audit conducted under the one-time condition imposed by the Federal Reserve Transparency Act, which was first introduced in 2009 and passed in 2011 at the urging of Congressman Ronald E. Paul. The subject of audit was directed at the Federal Reserve System, which has stubbornly refused inspections throughout its 100-year history by citing the independence of the central bank. Kaoru happened to be invited to Washington D.C. for the Congressional Briefing held on July 26 of that year and was handed the copy of this report in person by the Democratic Congressman Dennis J. Kucinich (Ohio 10th).

Table 8: Institutions with Largest Total Transaction Amounts (Not Term-Adjusted) across Broad-Based Emergency Programs (Borrowing Aggregated by Parent Company and Includes Sponsored ABCP Conduits), December 1, 2007 through July 21, 2010

Dollar in billions

Borrowing Parent Company	TAF	PDCF	TSLF	CPFF	Subtotal	AMLF	TALF	Total loans
Citigroup Inc.	$110	$2,020	$348	$33	$2,511	$1	-	**$ 2,513**
Morgan Stanley	-	1,913	115	4	2,032	-	9	**2,041**
Merrill Lynch & Co.	0	1,775	166	8	1,949	-	-	**1,949**
Bank of America Corporation	280	947	101	15	1,342	2	-	**1,344**
Barclays PLC (United Kingdom)	232	410	187	39	868	-	-	**868**
Bear Stearns Companies, Inc.	-	851	2	-	853	-	-	**853**
Goldman Sachs Group Inc.	-	589	225	0	814	-	-	**814**
Royal Bank of Scotland Group PLC (United Kingdom)	212	-	291	39	541	-	-	**541**
Deutsche Bank AG (Germany)	77	1	277	-	354	-	-	**354**
UBS AG (Switzerland)	56	35	122	75	287	-	-	**287**
JP Morgan Chase & Co.	99	112	68	-	279	111	-	**391**
Credit Suisse Group AG (Switzerland)	0	2	261	-	262	0	-	**262**
Lehman Brothers Holdings Inc.	-	83	99	-	183	-	-	**183**
Bank of Scotland PLC (United Kingdom)	181	-	-	-	181	-	-	**181**
BNP Paribas SA (France)	64	66	41	3	175	-	-	**175**
Wells Fargo & Co.	159	-	-	-	159	-	-	**159**
Dexia SA (Belgium)	105	-	-	53	159	-	-	**159**
Wachovia Corporation	142	-	-	-	142	-	-	**142**
Dresdner Bank AG (Germany)	123	0	1	10	135	-	-	**135**
Societe Generale SA (France)	124	-	-	-	124	-	-	**124**
All other borrowers	1,854	146	14	460	2,475	103	62	**2,639**
Total	**$3,818**	**$8,951**	**$2,319**	**$738**	**$15,826**	**$217**	**$71**	**$16,115**

Source: GAO analysis of Federal Reserve System data.

Fig. 10.8 List of international banks assisted by the FED's emergency loans during December 2007–July 2010 (The 2011 GAO report)

On page 131 of the report, there was a list of banks as shown in Fig. 10.8. This was a list of 20 banking institutions that the Federal Reserve secretly made loans to and supported under the *Too Big To Fail* policy before and after the collapse of Lehman Brothers in September 2008. Specifically, between December 2007 and July 2010, the Fed made a whopping $16 trillion in loans in less than three years. Yes, you read it correct. That is TRILLION Dollars!

The total amount of $16 trillion was astonishing, not to mention each amount given to these banks, because on August 2, 2011, the U.S. government debt reached the $14.3 trillion upper-limit approved by the Congress. At that time Washington D.C. were on the verge of default if the Congress would not raise the debt ceiling further. Yet, in less than three years, more money larger than the total U.S. government debt was secretly created by the Federal Reserve and handed over to these big banks, who in turn held shares of the Federal Reserve Banks. The last column in the figure lists the amount of loans (in billion dollars) bailed out by the Fed. Readers are encouraged to check each figure in the list.

Had the inspection by the GAO not been made, this unpleasant fact might have remained in the dark and the American people would have remained unknown about these unprecedented amounts of loans given to these financial institutions forever. Conversely, if the Fed's bailout could have been done so easily, then the US government's debts could have been similarly bailed out by issuing public money as we will discuss in Chap. 12.

Eleven Top-50 Control Holders Bailed Out by the Fed

While taking a closer look at the list of these big banks in Fig. 10.8, we realized (to our surprise) that the 11 financial institutions bailed out by the Fed also appeared in the list of top 50 control-holders presented by Vitali et al. (2011). Specifically these 11 banks are shown in Table 10.2. Each ranking number in Table 10.2 indicate their rank in the top 50 control-holders (top-25 institutions are listed in Fig. 10.7). Notice that they all hold network positions of SCC core group (0.7% of all TNCs) in the bow-tie network control topology.

Further astonishing fact was that the Fed, the central bank of the US, bailed out not only domestic banks but also those of Europe. In fact it turned out that, out of the 11 international banks in Table 10.2, six banks are non-U.S. banks. Why is such bailout even allowed to happen? Isn't it because these banks are themselves shareholders of the Fed?[5]

[5] Typically, these large Federal Reserve loans are made by the Federal Reserve Bank of New York (FRB-NY), the main unit of monetary policy decided by the FOMC. The shareholder list of FRB-NY has not been publicly disclosed for a long time. However, a recent FOIA request filed by Institutional Investor in 2019 revealed its major shareholders dating back to 2007 (Teitelbaum, 2020). According to a report disclosed by the FRB-NY (called Capital Stock Master Report), of the bank's total outstanding shares of approximately 205.4 million shares as of the end of 2018, the top two banks in order of number of shares were (1) Citibank (87.9 million; 42.8%) and (2) JPMorgan Chase Bank (60.6 million; 29.5%), which together accounted for 72.3% of the bank's total shares.

Table 10.2 Eleven international banks and financial groups (control-holders)

Rank	Economic actor name	Country	Network position
1	Barclays PLC	BG	SCC
6	JP Morgan Chase & Co.	US	SCC
9	UBS AG	CH	SCC
10	Merrill Lynch & Co., Inc.	US	SCC
12	Deutsche Bank AG	DE	SCC
14	Credit Suisse Group	CH	SCC
18	Goldman Sachs, Inc.	US	SCC
21	Morgan Stanley	US	SCC
24	Société Générale	FR	SCC
25	Bank of America Corporation	US	SCC
46	BNP Paribas	FR	SCC

Moreover, all of the 11 banks turn out to be the control-holders in the SCC core group in the network of global corporate control. This means that they are certainly controlling the world economy by sending their directors and managers to each other and forming the international banking cartel as SCC core corporations. Even so, they could not have survived the Lehman Shock and other subsequent crises without the massive loans by the Fed and its counterparts in Europe. This indicated the magnitude of the crisis of the Lehman Shock, so it deserves to be called the Second Great Depression.

Fox guarding the Hen House

The GAO report mentioned above has revealed their secret and corrupt deals for the first time to the public. The deals are seemed to be made such that financial institutions in the SCC group would never be allowed to simply go bust unless they are intended like controlled demolition of buildings. Is this free competition? It is as if the athletes are playing the role of referees themselves. Fox guarding the hen house! Contrary to the teachings of microeconomics textbooks, our economy built on the debt money system has never been fair to all players by design. It is fundamentally distorted in favor of SCC core group in the bow-tie network control topology.

The authors of the paper "Network of Global Corporate Control" described the SCC core group that forms the international banking cartel as an economic "super-entity" that has no territory but acts like a state. An example of such an entity is the Sovereign Entity, a virtual state recognized by the United Nations. A well-known example is the Sovereign Military Order of Malta (SMOM), also known as Knights of

---

Others included HSBC Bank USA (12.6 million; 6.1%), Goldman Sachs Banks USA (8.3 million; 4%), Bank of New York Mellon (7.2 million; 3.5%), Morgan Stanley Bank (4.8 million; 2.3%), its affiliate Morgan Stanley Private Bank (2.8 million; 1.4%), and Deutsche Bank Trust Co. Americas (1.7 million; 0.83%). These major shareholders revealed by the FOIA request match with the list of international banks bailed out by the Fed as listed in Fig. 10.8.

Malta. SMOM is an organization that has no territory but has established diplomatic relations with about 100 countries around the world, issues its own passport, and participates as an observer in the UN. It has been pointed out on the Internet that some bankers are in fact high-level members of the Knights of Malta. Since this is an online information, we do not know how much to believe it. However, Dr. Karen Hudes, a former senior legal counsel of the World Bank at its legal department for 21 years (1986–2007), happened to attend the Public Money Forum held at the National Diet Members' Office Building in Tokyo in May 2014 and confirmed the same thing to Kaoru.

10.5 Tactics of a Means of Control

President John F. Kennedy's Speech: Spheres of Influence

Are those who control these international banks the ultimate rulers of the world? If so, did they create the magical money tree (fractional reserve banking system) for their own economic interests only? On April 27, 1961, President John F. Kennedy delivered a historic speech titled "The President and the Press" before the American Newspaper Publishers Association at the Waldorf Astoria Hotel in Manhattan. While emphasizing the critical role of media to a well functioning of government and healthy democratic society (with an anecdote of Karl Marx as a former foreign correspondent in London for the New York Herald Tribune), the incumbent President warned the American public that a secret society had infiltrated the branches of the U.S. government "without a declaration of war" and been expanding its "Sphere of Influence" secretly around the world.[6]

> The very word secrecy is repugnant in a free and open society. And we are as a people inherently and historically opposed to secret societies, to secret oaths and to secret proceedings. We decided long ago that the dangers of excessive and unwarranted concealment of pertinent facts far outweighed the dangers which are cited to justify.
>
> Even today there is little value in opposing the threat of a closed society by imitating its arbitrary restrictions. Even today there is little value in insuring the survival of our nation if our traditions do not survive with it. And there is very grave danger that an announced need for increased security will be seized upon by those anxious to expand its meaning to the very limits of official censorship and concealment.
>
> That I do not intend to permit to the extent that it's in my control. And no official of my administration, whether his rank is high or low, civilian or military, should interpret my words here tonight as an excuse to censor the news, to stifle dissent, to cover up our mistakes or to withhold from the press and the public the facts they deserve to know. . . .
>
> For we are opposed around the world by a monolithic and ruthless conspiracy that relies primarily on covert means for expanding its sphere of influence, on infiltration instead of

[6] The full speech delivered by President JFK is easily accessible on the Internet. Whatever the message he intended to convey, his words are timeless and sound more relevant today than ever before. Our readers should take the time to listen to his entire 20-minute speech.

> invasion, on subversion instead of Elections, on intimidation instead of free choice, on guerrillas by night, instead of armies by day.
>
> It is a system which has conscripted vast human and material resources into the building of a tightly knit highly efficient machine that combines military, diplomatic, intelligence, economic, scientific and political operations.
>
> Its preparations are concealed, not published. Its mistakes are buried, not headlined. Its dissenters are silenced, not praised. No expenditure is questioned. No rumor is printed. No secret is revealed. It conducts the Cold War in short with a wartime discipline no democracy would ever hope or wish to match.

Kaoru happened to come across with his speech on the Internet. Since then he has been wondering who are those that are anxious to expand its "sphere of influence" that President Kennedy risked his life to warn the world about.

Half a century after the JFK's speech, a book titled "Who Really Owns Your Gold" (Garner, 2010) was published. The author is William Dean A. Garner. According to one of his interviews, he has edited the international bestseller *the Da Vinci Code* by Dan Brown and has a unique background as a marine biology researcher and the former US Army Airborne Ranger with the 1st Ranger Battalion. Surprisingly, in his book he used the same phrase of "a dark and sinister *sphere of influence* (*ibid.* p. 4)" as President Kennedy used in his speech 50 years ago. Then, a secret society or a cabal is referred to as "the Jesuits, plus their accountants, the House of Rothschild, and their extensive network of sycophants and minions" (*ibid.* p. 4). In the same book they were also suspected to have been deeply involved in the assassination of President Lincoln who issued the greenbacks dollar during the Civil War,[7] and more recently, the assassination of President Kennedy who issued the Executive Order 11110 on June 4, 1963 and issued the United States Notes (Fig. 1.2).[8]

---

[7] Several books shall be referred for the assassination of 16th President Abraham Lincoln, such as McCarty (1922), and Hughes (2002). The latter author states:

> And after twenty years of constant and most difficult researches, I come fearlessly today before the American people, to say and prove that the president, Abraham Lincoln, was assassinated by the priests and the Jesuits of Rome (Hughes, 2002, p. 48).

[8] The Society of Jesus or Jesuits is the Roman Catholic order founded by Ignatius of Loyola and his six companions in 1534 to become a spearhead of counter-reformation against the progression of Protestantism. The order was granted a formal authorization by the papal bull issued by Alessandro Farnese (then Paulus III) on September 27th 1540. Led by Loyola as its first Superior General, members of this new military order scattered to South America, India, China, etc., with a grand mission to establish papal authority and expand its territories around the globe. One of the founding members Francis Xavier reached southern Japan in 1549. In addition to proselytization of Catholicism, their activities involved raising operational funds through trades and intelligence for the Vatican. Jesuit scholars also played crucial roles in the exchange of knowledge between the East and West through their translations of historically important texts. Today the society has become one of the largest religious order and engaged in evangelization and apostolic ministry in 112 nations. There are Jesuit educational institutions around the globe and its policy think tanks such as CSIS are highly influential especially in the U.S. foreign policy circles. The alumni of Jesuit schools and colleges have held and currently hold highest levels of positions in all branches of governments as well as in private sectors, especially in international banks and law firms. On the other hand, the Rothschild banking family is well known for the series of major loans they arranged

However, Mr. Garner points out carefully that the existence of such secret society is not a conspiracy theory, but only his *working hypothesis*. In one of his interviews, he says if a curious person follow their footprints marked everywhere throughout the history and connect those events as individual dots, then certain behavioral patterns emerge and the existence of such conspiracies can be explained in a scientifically consistent manner.[9]

If that is the case, it would no longer be a major issue whether there is such a secret society on top of the super entity that controls international banking and finance. The existence of such a cartel is not our interest as researchers either. If the debt money system is eliminated, the control structure analyzed above will have to collapse simultaneously. This is the methodology for solving complex problems through systems approach. Let's move on.

"Divide and Rule" Tactics

Over the past 250 years, the instruments of control and power have evolved more sophisticatedly under the debt money system. Bankers and money lenders have created a world in which ordinary people are incited into fighting each other, while they finance both sides of the conflict and siphon off profits. As the Japanese proverb tells, "rich people do not fight each other". The richer a person gets, the less likely he or she is to get involved in fights, as he or she knows that fighting will result in a net loss and being expelled from the circle. Rather, they cooperate in undertaking investments and maintain their status quo.

Such tactics has been well recognized as *divide and rule* strategy. Specifically, debt money has been used to nurture and dispatch agents (*controlled opposition*) to a peaceful society to first create opposing groups, and then finance these groups in order to further aggravate conflicts towards the pre-existing goal. Such tactics may seem difficult for the average person to imagine, yet it is a lucrative business model. Even if one group loses, the creditors who have also invested in the opposing groups are much less likely to lose. And they continue to sow the seeds of conflict one after another and incite confrontation through the media they control.

There are too many examples of such governance by "divide and rule" throughout history. To list a few, the East vs. West conflict, racial discriminations, religious

---

for the Holy See in the 19th century (Posner, 2015; Felisini, 2017) and has held the title of Sacred Military Constantinian Order of Saint George (SMOCG). As the religious order bearing the name of Jesus Christ, we believe the Jesuits are the ones who will drive the money lenders out of the sacred Temple as the Jesus of Nazareth has done over 2,000 years ago (Fig. 10.2).

[9] The term "conspiracy theory," which became increasingly popular in major news networks and newspapers nowadays, should be properly called "conspiracy hypothesis" in conformity with scientific research and methodology. A hypothesis only becomes a theory after passing rigorous testing against data and observational facts. If we start to label and dismiss social science research (or even any investigative process) simply as a "conspiracy theory," it will only lead to cessation of critical thinkings and inevitable suppression of the freedom of speech.

wars, political and military conflicts, conflicts between management, labor classes and shareholders and so on. As a historical example that illustrates the case, take the case of Capitalism vs. Communism and the Cold War. Although Karl Marx would be classified as the proponent of moneyless price and commodity money theory in the classification table of Fig. 9.1, the fact that he was the proponent of debt money system is hardly recognized.

In the *Communist Manifesto*, for instance, Marx and Engels (1848) described the system design of debt money with central banks installed at the top (disguised as 'national' bank) in order to centralize the supply of credit. Specifically, in the final part of the "II. Proletarians and Communists" where they list ten items to describe the general course of development under which the communist revolution changes the mode of production in "most advanced countries", Marx and Engels (1848) proposed "5. Centralization of credit in the hands of the state, by means of a national bank with State capital and an exclusive monopoly." The two political philosophers also called for "2. A heavy progressive or graduated income tax." This way the confiscation of national wealth through compound interests on public debt is cleverly embedded also in the Communist regime.[10]

In the world of such constant opposing conflicts, it is always the international banking cartel that has reigned and made profits. In this way, they have dominated the world economy by establishing "the network of global corporate control" and succeeded in advancing their agenda, until now.

System of Control is the Root of World Problems

We have now identified two control systems, (1) outer loop of debt money system and (2) inner loop of equity ownership system, under which bankers have exercised their means of control through "divide and rule" tactics. Figure 10.9 illustrates how the outer and inner loops of control system have spun out as the opposing economic, social, environmental, and political issues.

These issues are symptoms of the underlying system design failure and can be briefly described as follows.

Economic Issues such as booms and depressions, unemployment, inflation and deflation, debt crisis, income inequality are caused by the current debt money system.

[10] This is the underlying system structure driving today's income inequality and wealth concentration globally. In capitalist regimes, the ruling class is the individuals that ultimately own major international banks. In communist regimes, it is a handful of privileged class (elites) sitting in the central standing committee of the politburo. From a standpoint of international bankers and financiers who have historically financed both sides of the conflict (Sutton, 1974, 1976), the differences between capitalist and communist regimes are of little practical importance as long as the underlying systems of control is in tact. Readers may then wonder if the well-known connection of Karl Marx with the Rothschild banking family (through their common Barent-Cohen ancestor of Amsterdam) is just a coincidence of history.

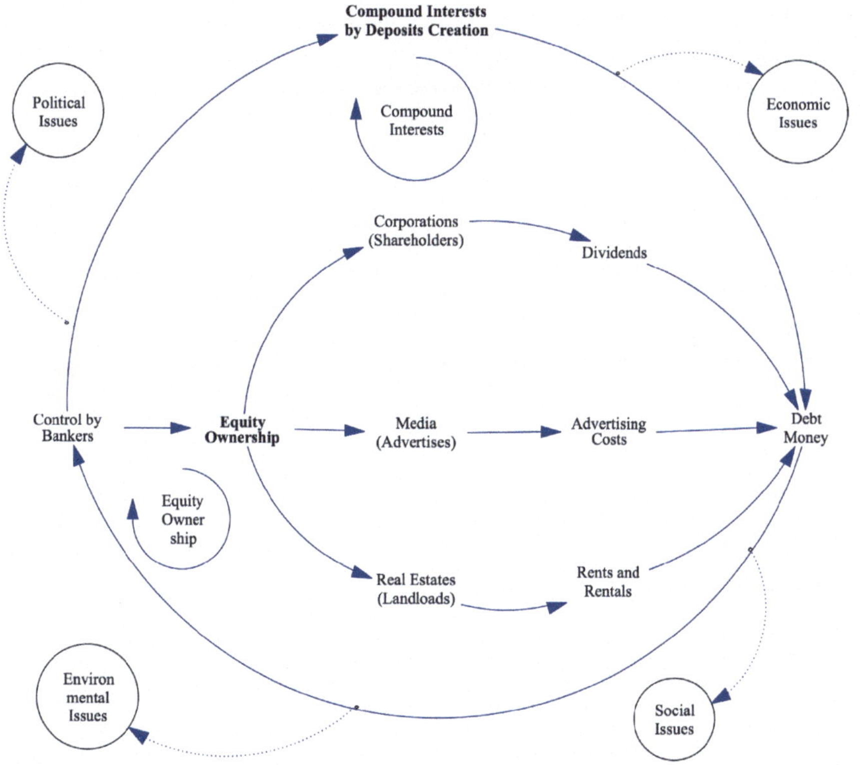

Fig. 10.9 Opposing issues caused by the systems of debt money and equity ownership

Social Issues such as racism, gender discrimination, illegal immigrants, religious conflicts, COVID-19, etc. are caused by the current equity ownership system through the tactics of "divide and rule".

Environmental Issues such as climate change, genetic modification, destruction of agriculture are complex by nature, but have been largely caused by the current debt money and equity ownership systems.

Political Issues such as wars, terrorism, nuclear conflicts etc. are caused by the current equity ownership system through "divide and rule" tactics.

These opposing issues are nothing but patterns of system behaviors (symptoms) caused by the underlying system structures. Therefore, we must focus on how the debt money and equity ownership systems are generating these opposing issues repeatedly. Complex problems do no exist in isolation. They are inter-connected. That is why we cannot solve them comprehensively without reforming these underlying systems. A fundamental solution to economic issues will also become the solutions to social, environmental, and political problems. Thus, in order to create an economically stable, peaceful, discrimination-free, and globally sustainable society, we must focus all our energy in reforming the two systems of control that lie underneath these issues.

That is the solution of MuRatopia economy discussed in Part III. Before we move to the solution, let us continue our analysis in one more chapter and debunk Modern Money Theory, which tries to hide the system design failures of debt money.

Chapter 11
MMT Hides System Design Failures of Debt Money

In Part II of this book we have analyzed from the standpoint of public money theory that the present debt money system is headed toward a collapse. A monetary theory that is in direct opposition to our analysis has been spreading in the US, Japan and other countries in Europe. It is called Modern Money Theory (MMT). According to MMT, governments issuing their own sovereign currencies *cannot* default and even if rapid inflation does occur, it can be controlled by raising taxes. Economists who advocate MMT say it is simply a theory that explains the monetary system and fiscal arrangements as they are. Are these claims valid? In this chapter we will reveal the falsity of MMT and expose that it is another propaganda created to serve the international banking interests.

11.1 MMT Is a False Theory

First it is important to distinguish here that what MMT refers to as "government issuance of its own currency" is government borrowing (debt). If we carefully consider the "wonder and horror" of exponential growth by compound interest rate discussed in Chap. 10 there is no way one would be fooled by such a blanket statement. Kaoru became aware of this sophistry in 2012 when he attended the 8th International Conference on Monetary Reform in Chicago hosted by the American Monetary Institute (AMI). As explained in Chap. 9, the MMT's definition that "money is IOU" became clear to the public by the book published by Wray (2012) in that year. Such definition of money was simply incompatible with the public money theory and the vision of our monetary reform group. Accordingly, the two groups started arguing at the conference floor. Since then, MMT group has stopped participating in the monetary reform conference and broke away from the AMI monetary reform group.

Kaoru, who knew little about MMT until then, realized from the heated discussion at the conference venue that MMT was a false theory that does not understand the

K. Yamaguchi and Y. Yamaguchi, *Public Money*,
https://doi.org/10.1007/978-981-97-6564-5_11

legal nature of money, thus failing to take into account the obverse definition in our money classification tables (Figs. 2.1 and 2.2). Since then, he has paid little attention to it. However, to our surprise, MMT has recently been picked up by the media even in Japan and begun to spread all of sudden. There are more than 10 introductory books on MMT lined up on bookstore shelves throughout the country as of writing the original book (Yamaguchi and Yamaguchi, 2021b) from which this chapter is adapted. These MMT books are spreading a rosy illusion that aggressive fiscal stimulus will improve the Japanese economy, prevent the government from going bankrupt, and, of course, can control inflation.

Based on ASD macroeconomic simulation models, we have proposed public money initiative that will bring back vitality of the economy, which we will present in Chap. 14. On the other hand, MMT failed to build its own macroeconomic models that support their claims. Without a macroeconomic model, MMT appears to be nothing more than a convenient defense for international bankers to cover up the system design failures of debt money. In other words, MMT is in direct conflict with our analysis discussed in Chap. 6 that the government debt accumulation under the present debt money system will eventually lead to three catastrophes. The aggressive fiscal spending that MMT advocates is an attempt to hasten the inevitable crash of a falling airplane by violently reviving up its jet engines. No matter how skilled the pilots are, they cannot avoid the crash, as it is a *system design failure*.

So, what is MMT in the first place? We have two original books on MMT at hand. The first book, titled "Modern Money Theory" (Wray, 2012, 312 pages), was translated into Japanese in 2019 as "Introduction to Modern Monetary Theory". As the Japanese title indicates, this book is a jumble of essay-type articles, not a theoretical economics textbook. The other one is "Macroeconomics" written by three MMT researchers (Mitchell et al., 2019, 573 pages). To our disappointment, this book has no MMT macroeconomic model either, and seems to be a partial commentary book, compared with our research book on public money (Yamaguchi, 2013) published 6 years earlier. Thus, MMT does not have its systematic macroeconomic model to begin with. In this sense it is fatally defect and inappropriate to call it a theory in the first place.

Therefore, in writing this chapter, we have additionally gathered online information on MMT and summarized its main points in our own manner. Especially we have referred to "Modern Money Theory 101: A Reply to Critics" (Tymoigne and Wray, 2013). It turned out that there are seven elements in the resulting MMT framework. In the following sections, we will briefly explain them one by one and point out their falsehoods.

Falsehood 1: Money is IOU (Certificate of Debt)

There are public money and debt money in circulation as our classification of money in Figs. 2.1 and 2.2 show. However, MMT defines that "money must be an IOU" (Wray, 2012, p. xi). Therefore, money as defined by MMT must always be debt money according to the obverse definition. Let's take the Japanese money for instance. Currently, 99.7% of money in circulation is debt money, and as our recent study revealed in Chap. 3, these debt money are issued as debts of households, firms, the government, etc. Since 99.7% of Japanese Yen is currently debt money, there seems to be no problem in analyzing "modern money" based on such definition by MMT.

However, according to this MMT's definition, public money, which has been around for at least more than 1,300 years since the introduction of Wado-kaichin (one of the oldest coins in Japan) in 708, would disqualify as money and is no longer money. In this sense, the MMT's definition of money is not only inconsistent with the history of money, but also grossly prejudiced, considering only debt money issued by the Bank of Japan, which was established only recently in 1882, and those "deposits" created by commercial banks at interest.

Outside Japan, public money has been around for at least another thousand years since the Lydian electrum circulated in 7th century BC as the world's oldest coin. As a scientific definition of money, MMT is already disqualified at this point. In other words, it is merely defending debt money issued by banks at interest as the only type of money that is legitimate. Why does MMT need to go to the trouble of defining debt money created by banks as the only legitimate money, when our governments (can) issue public money without interest?

As we take a look at the classification table from the reverse side, money consists of legal tender (currency) and functional money. In this reverse definition, we have inherited the observation of Aristotle that "money exists not by nature, but by law" Zarlenga (2002, p. 34). Therefore, functional money that is not legal tender becomes fake money or *counterfeit* money that is created out of nothing based on legal tender. Under the MMT's definition, however, legal tender and functional money are indistinguishable, and functional money created by banks also becomes genuine money (as IOU) by definition. No monetary theory is more convenient for international bankers than such sophistry.

MMT further discusses that the government's right to collect taxes is the basis for the establishment of debt money. In order for this argument to be valid, the establishment of legal tender (fiat) must first precede the establishment of money. It is logically impossible to discuss money as being the IOU while ignoring this point. Since MMT is discussing on the premise of currency as a unit of account, it should start its discussion with the definition of money as legal tender. This would make the MMT's peculiar logic that links the value of money and the government's right to collect taxes redundant, and eliminate the need for such an erroneous argument that conflates the existence of money (monetary system) and the government's tax system, which relies on money.[1]

---

[1] Whether or not the government decides to oblige itself to receive taxes as a means of giving effect to its fiat currency to be accepted in commerce, and whether money so issued must be debts of the issuer (which are not), are arguments of different dimensions. As explained in Chap. 3, it is critical to distinguish between (1) legal concepts, such as claims and debts, (2) debt securities or instruments, such as bonds and IOUs, and (3) money, which is a means of settlement to resolve creditor-debtor relationships in legal contracts. Since MMT proponents conflates these concepts altogether, they are unable to distinguish the basic difference between public money and debt money. As such,

Among the debt money so defined by MMT, functional money accounts for about 65% in Japan as of 2018. The right to issue money as legal tender, which was granted only to the legislature, was seized by central banks that began to be established in these nations since 1800s, and commercial banks operating under the fractional reserve basis. When MMT talks about the possibility of controlling money stock through taxation, it fails to take into account the deposit creation by these banks. Since the government has no direct control over the creation of functional money by private banks, it is impossible for the government to control the quantity of money (purchasing power) through taxation. Once a financial bubble emerges, the government cannot control the quantity of money by all means. It is this biased definition of money by MMT that gives rise to false illusion such as controlling the quantity of money through taxation.

MMT's definition of money, which ignores public money and only refers to debt money (obverse definition), and does not distinguish between legal tender and functional money (reverse definition), is nothing more than a consideration for vested banking interests. Irving Fisher also proposed monetary reform repeatedly to the President Roosevelt, yet the president, who was deeply acquainted with the bankers continued to ignore it. In a letter to his son, Fisher once scathingly criticized the FDR, saying "[while Congress is ready] the President is afraid of the bankers" (Allen, 1993, p. 710). If Fisher were to write a similar letter to his son today, he would no doubt write "the group of MMT researchers is afraid of the bankers".

To summarize the above, under the debt money system, 99.7% of "money is IOU" as MMT claims. Under the public money system, however,

Money is Public Money issued at interest-free.

Falsehood 2: MMT Can Be Explained More Simply by Assuming the Consolidated Government with Central Bank

At the 39th Eastern Economic Association's conference held in New York, on May 10th, 2013, Kaoru reported his simulation results of public money system obtained from the ASD macroeconomic model in the Monetary Reform session chaired by Stephen Zarlenga, the director of AMI. Since the MMT group happened to hold its session at the same conference venue, Kaoru also attended the meeting and asked the presenter, "Why are some private banks shareholders of the Federal Reserve, which is believed to be the central bank of the U.S. government?" "Well, they happened to be so historically", the presenter mumbled and refused to mention further. At that moment, Kaoru immediately realized the true identity of MMT.

At the same time, he couldn't help but feel a certain sympathy for the MMT researchers who were trying hard to survive academically at the regional universities

---

in order to justify their erroneous definition of "money as IOU," some MMT proponents even argue that money and debt are inherently inseparable since payment in commerce are also made by promissory notes, which is a form of IOU. However, bills of exchange are merely substitutes for deferred payment that presuppose the existence of money as means of final settlement.

in the U.S. As already mentioned in Sect. 9.5, Kaoru sensed they were well aware that they could also be expelled from their positions immediately if they publicly discuss such a politically taboo topic at academic conferences.

However, MMT's refusal to acknowledge the fact that the central bank is a private bank is clearly a cover-up. Partly influenced by the MMT, the false argument that "the Bank of Japan (BoJ) is a subsidiary of the government because the government owns 55% of its stocks" has become widespread in Japan. How can a debtor be more powerful than a creditor? It is deceptive to assert that the government (debtor) has a superior political power to the creditor (BoJ). Such a superficial argument would be blown away instantly when one learns of the immense power exercised by the BoJ's Banking Department through its window guidance and lending facility discussed in Chap. 4.

MMT proudly claims that it has simplified the monetary theory and analyzed the function of "modern money" by assuming that the central bank and the government are a consolidated government.[2] In this way, MMT assumes a consolidated balance sheet of the central bank and the Government (Treasury Department), and attempts to analyze the amount of money in circulation between the consolidated government and the rest of the private sector. If the financial statements of both entities are consolidated, then, the government debt (treasury bonds) owned by the central bank will be written off. Furthermore, it is argued that issuance of government debts (debt money) increases private sector's asset (deposits) as explained in Falsehood 6 discussed below. Even so, the MMT's assumption of the "consolidated government" is false in terms of factual recognition and methodology of flow of funds (financial accounts) analysis.

First of all, let us consider the case of Japan-US trade friction that became a major issue in the 1980s as discussed in Chap. 4. Considering that Japan is a *de facto* vassal state of the US, the trade friction problem between the two nations would be quickly resolved if we consider trade statistics with Japan as the 51st state of the US. What will happen if we then argue that Japan-US trade friction is not an issue because we can assume consolidated accounting?

You will be slammed by the media for professing such an irresponsible statement as economists. The sophistry of such argument is obvious to anyone. Yet MMT researchers continue to deceive students and general public by using a similar sophistry. In other words, MMT claims that if we assume a consolidated government and consider the issuance and circulation of money under the consolidated balance sheet, government debt (fiscal deficits) is no longer a problem. It is only necessary for the government, proponents of MMT say, to control amount of money circulating among private sectors in order not to cause inflation, which the government cannot under the present debt money system.

---

[2] The concept of "integrated government" is frequently (yet incorrectly) used in Japanese translations of MMT books. When a balance sheet of the parent company and its subsidiary are integrated, it is called Consolidated Accounting or Consolidated Balance Sheet. Therefore, the integrated government as often used in Japanese translation has to mean the consolidated balance sheet and financial statement of the Ministry of Finance (as government) and the Bank of Japan. In this sense, it is appropriate to translate it as "consolidated government".

Next, let us discuss the issue from the perspective of flow of funds analysis. We are also proposing the nationalization of central bank and resulting consolidated government under the public money system. Therefore, if the discussion is about how to realize such a consolidated government, rather than simply assuming it with consolidated accounting, the direction of analysis is correct and we can agree with it. Nevertheless, the biggest difference between MMT and public money system is that all money issued under the public money system is interest-free stable currency, while the debt money assumed by MMT are issued by central bank and commercial banks at interest. How many US presidents and economic researchers have sacrificed their lives and careers in order to realize the consolidated government? MMT, which avoids this harsh reality and easily assumes the "consolidated government," is nothing but a delusion. First of all, the MMT group should show us the path to achieve a real consolidated government.

Let us take the discussion one step further and assume that MMT's "consolidated government" has become a reality under the public money system. Even in that case, would it still be necessary and theoretically correct to integrate the central bank and the government through consolidated accounting as MMT claims? Even if we transition to the public money system, balance sheets of the currency issuer (Public Money Administration under the legislature) and the government that implements fiscal policy (the Treasury under the executive branch) can never be consolidated in practice. From the theoretical perspective, the two should never be consolidated under the flow of funds analysis and in our ASD macroeconomic simulation models.

Thus, the legitimacy of MMT's argument based on the assumption of "consolidated government" is nowhere to be found, either in terms of fact recognition, in terms of monetary theory, or macroeconomic statistical framework. MMT should abandon the false methodology (misconception) of assuming the consolidated government and face up to the adverse effects and difficulties of capitalism caused by the design failures of debt money system. We hope that followers of MMT will wake up from the rosy illusion and join in our discussion on how to realize the integrated government under public money system that eliminates such system design failures.

Accordingly, in any economic analysis, whether it is under the debt money system or the public money system,

The assumption of a consolidated government is theoretically and practically impossible.

In summary the two logical falsehoods of MMT were discussed as follows.

1. By ignoring the public money, MMT defines only debt money as money.
2. By using debt money thus defined, MMT assumes the "consolidated government" and attempts to explain the behavior of money.

These are the two fundamental logical contradictions of MMT. In the following, let us focus on five specific points that illustrate various MMT falsehoods derived from these logical contradictions.

Falsehood 3: Government Can Issue Its Own Currency

MMT claims that the government can issue its own currency. This statement is causing a great confusion in the first place. Therefore, let us first consider what "government-issued currency" is based on the Japanese case. Since monetary system in most nations is similarly structured, the following discussion also applies to other countries. According to the Classification Table of Money (Fig. 2.1), we have

$$\text{Cash} = \text{Government Coins} + \text{Bank of Japan Notes.}$$

Assuming that part of cash is deposited with the central bank by the commercial banks, we can define currency as follows:

$$\text{Currency} = \text{Government Coins} + \text{Bank of Japan Notes} + \text{Reserve Deposits.}$$

MMT defines money is IOU (debt money). Therefore, since government coins are not IOUs, they are not money, and only BoJ notes plus reserve deposits are currency, according to the MMT. These currencies are issued by the BoJ and recorded in the liabilities account on its balance sheet. On the other hand, the BoJ's assets mainly consist of Japanese government bonds (JGBs) as the corresponding liability items. In other words, the BoJ issues its currency mainly against these JGBs (government debts). Hence, it is mistaken and unreasonable to assume that "the government issues its own currency" based on this fact.

Furthermore, government debt is only a part of the total debt that creates M_3 in Japan. As analyzed in Chap. 2, total amount of debt money in Japan (1,420.9 trillion yen) is roughly equal to the sum of private debt by firms and households (748 trillion yen) and the government debt (681 trillion yen). And most of the debt money issued against government debts (bonds) is not legal tender, but functional money created by private banks as Fig. 2.1 shows. Therefore, when examined in light of the reality of the debt money system, what MMT claims "the government can issue its own currency" is synonymous with "government can issue its bonds (debts) in its own monetary unit", which accounts for only 48% of total debt money in circulation as of 2018. Yet, MMT seldom asserts that "firms and households can issue their own currency". Why does it not mention the issuance of debt money by private sectors, which accounts for 52% of the total debt money outstanding? Herein lies the confusion and stench of the MMT. In any case, we will proceed the discussion below by understanding that "government issue (48% of) debt money by borrowing from banks" whenever MMT claims that "government can issue its own currency".

We have been proposing that "governments can issue public money". Public money here means coins, notes, and electronic public money (digital currency) issued directly by the government. In the MMT's analysis, government coins are completely ignored (otherwise its framework collapses as discussed in Falsehood 1). Of course, under the present debt money system, only 0.3% of public money is in circulation as coins. Hence, ignoring it for the analysis of current system may not have a significant impact, although coins still play a substantial role in Japan. As a monetary theory, however, the existence of public money cannot be ignored. It is also impossible to ignore it in commercial bookkeeping.

How, then, is the 4.8 trillion yen of public money (government-issued coins) recorded on the balance sheets of Japanese government and the BoJ? How are they put into circulation? All government coins in Japan are minted at the National Mint located in Osaka and delivered to the Bank of Japan. At that point, government coins become assets of the national treasury (managed by Ministry of Finance). How does the BoJ account for these public money on its balance sheet? In short the BoJ first receives government coins in a separate account temporarily, and then convert them to the government deposit account whenever they are put into circulation through commercial banks. All of these bookkeepings and account transfers take place within the BoJ's liability items.

How, then, does the BoJ record government coins on its asset side and in the Flow of Funds Account statistics? We have solved this accounting mystery of handling public money by the BoJ by following the above process with our ASD macroeconomic model. The BoJ treats coins in the asset accounts of its balance sheet in the Flow of Funds statistics as if they were equivalent to BoJ notes (even though the BoJ is an independent institution and not part of the government) and treats them as a joint account with the government, which is an account manipulation technically speaking. Even under the current law and in practice, this indicates how the BoJ and the Japanese government are separate entities like water and oil. Assuming the "consolidated government" in analyzing the current debt-based economy is nothing more than a deception to hide the existence of interest-free currency and the fact that government can issue its own public money.

In summary, what MMT refers to as the government's issuance of its own currency is the 48% of debt money created by government borrowing (debt) from banks, excluding public money (coins). The remaining 52% of debt money is created by private sector's borrowing (debt) from banks. In this sense, MMT is a significantly distorted monetary theory. On the contrary, the only money the government can issue under both debt money and public money systems is not *debt money*, but *public money*. Therefore, the correct statement is

The government can issue its own public money.

Falsehood 4: Government Issuing Its Currency Does Not Default (Monetarily Sovereign Government Cannot Go Broke)

According to MMT, the governments in EU, such as Greece, cannot avoid default because they cannot issue their own currency and have to borrow in Euros, while governments like Japan and the US that borrow in yen and dollars will not default. Japan has been the world's largest net creditor nation over the last three decades. Therefore, according to MMT, there is no such thing as a default by its government. MMT also uses a phrase such as "a monetarily sovereign country with debts denominated in its own currency and a floating exchange rate cannot go broke." There are many such obscure and roundabout assertions in MMT, due to their ambiguous classification of money and use of terminology. As such, the MMT's above notion is interpreted like a dream story by some. And there are now widespread arguments that seem to support this claim by MMT, as if governments can rely on a "magical money tree" without worrying about any possibility of defaults and depreciation of their currencies.

So what is wrong with this argument? As our analysis so far has shown, whenever MMT says "the government issues its own currency" or "monetarily sovereign government with debts denominated in its own currency", they are synonymous as saying "the government borrows money by issuing bonds (to banks)". The word "default" literally implies that debts cannot be repaid. Repayment of debts implies the repayment of principal and interest. If the principal payments can be financed by rolling over its debts, or through refinancing by perpetual debts, then, the default can be avoided by paying only interest portion of debts as a minimum annual payment. For banks that lend to the government, it is more efficient and preferable to keep borrowers in debt for a long time and receive only interest payments every year, rather than getting the principal repaid and then reinvest. Therefore, the meaning of "the government that issues its own currency does not default" implies that "no matter how much debt the government owes, it will never default on its debt so long as it can use refinancing bonds to defer principal repayment and pays only interest."

However, from the perspective of debt money (obverse definition of money in Fig. 2.1), government is not the only entity issuing debt money. First of all, debts by firms and households are necessary for them to make transaction and any economic activities to take place under the debt money system. On the other hand, government debt is secondary. And even if government debt were zero, the market economy would continue and grow (such was the success of postwar Japan).

Only when corporate and household debts decline due to a burst of bubble or recession, and economic activity stagnates due to a decrease in total quantity of debt money, the government must borrow on behalf of the private sector only to sustain their economic activities but cannot induce growth. This is the fiscal policy of Keynesian economics as we analyzed in Chap. 5. MMT does not understand this true nature of economic activities under the debt money system. It instead makes the government out to be the protagonist or an economic savior, arguing that the government will not default even if it aggressively pulls the economy like a locomotive with its aggressive fiscal policy. This one-sided emphasis on government debt is clearly a misdirection.[3]

[3] Remember that Japan began issuing government bonds in 1965. By that time, the economy had already achieved remarkable growth as discussed in Chap. 4. Even referring to this historical fact as an example, MMT's view that the government should pull the economy like a locomotive through fiscal spending is a fiction that ignores the basic working mechanism of the capitalist system. It is also a biased policy recommendation that does not analyze the causes of why Japan's private sector demand became stagnant, despite series of fiscal spendings through massive increase in government debt.

As we have analyzed so far, the debt money defined by MMT is equal to the sum of firm's and household's debt (52%) and government debt (48%). Therefore, if we were to simplify the economy by dividing it into two macroeconomic sectors (as proponents of MMT like to "consolidate" macroeconomic sectors), it is more accurate and fairer to consider the issuance of debt money as follows:

(A) Firms and households that issue their own currencies (debt money) do not default.
(B) The government that issues its own currency (debt money) does not default.

Now, are these claims by the MMT expressed in line with the reality under the debt money system really correct? Let us consider an opposite case in which these macroeconomic sectors (or their components) do default; that is, a case in which these sectors borrow money from abroad and default on the repayment of total principal and interest. In the case of the government (B), the country goes bankrupt and becomes a colony of the creditor country. In the case of a producer (A), it becomes a subcontractor of the creditor country, and in the case of a household, it becomes a slave of the creditor country. However, such cases are exceptions in the current debt money system.

Therefore, except these extreme cases, as long as economic activity is conducted in its own currency, it can be said that not only the government but also firms and households will never default. This is because, considering producers, households, and governments as one integrated macroeconomic sector, and if these sectors did not borrow money, no debt money will ever be issued and hence no economic activity would take place. Conversely, if all the debts of these sectors were repaid, the circulation of debt money would be zero and all economic activities would stop. Thinking in this way, it is obvious that firms, households, and governments will not default as long as their economic activities continue. However, if MMT is claiming that they do not default in this sense, it is a pointless argument, as if to say, "Because you are eating without dying (because you are borrowing to finance your economic activities), you will not die (you can continue to borrow)." This is an empty tautology. In fact it does not analyze the possibility of default in any way.

Will firms, households, and governments that issue their own currency (i.e., borrow in their own currency) never default, then? As mentioned above, they must at least pay annual interest to avoid defaults. Therefore, let us first consider the case (A) in which firms or households borrow money (issue debt money) and repay the interest. If their economic growth rate is higher than interest rate, their sales and wage income will rise every year. Accordingly, interests on capital investment and housing investment (and in some cases, the principals) can be repaid with a margin. The problem is when economic growth halts such as in the case of Japan's lost 30 years. Even in this case, interest repayments are inevitably forced, and the net assets (equities) of producers and households will eventually begin to decline. Sooner or later, they will be forced into insolvency. At this point, producers and households must default first.

Next, consider the case (B) in which the government issues its bonds, spends debt money into circulation, and pays interest on it. Again, as long as the economic growth rate is higher than interest rate, tax revenues will increase and the government will be able to repay the interest on the bonds with a surplus. The problem is when the economic growth stops as in the Japanese case. Even in such a case, the government will be forced to pay interests by increasing taxes on the private sector. In this way, the government can barely avoid its default. However, as a result, the net assets (equity) of the private sectors who are now forced to pay higher taxes, will continue to decline, and eventually become insolvent and forced into defaults. No matter how much MMT claims that the government will not default, firms and households (private sector) will be cornered to default behind the back of such a reckless government. In other words, the MMT's argument is equivalent to saying that even if private sectors default and their economic activities cease, only the government will not default until the end. Herein lies the deception of MMT's sloppy logic and the concealment of the system design failures of the debt money.

In order to avoid such defaults in private sector, let us assume that the government will avoid further tax hikes and borrows more to cover interest repayments by issuing more bonds. In this case, the principal amount of debt outstanding will continue to accumulate. As a result, interest repayments will increase further and the government falls into the "debt crisis" loop in Fig. 6.4. As we have analyzed in Sect. 6.1, it is clear that this self-reinforcing loop (debt hell) will eventually lead not only to government default but also to catastrophe for Japan, the US and so on (also see the exponential horror of compound interest in Chap. 10 once again). Before discussing hyperinflation, MMT should show how it can avoid default due to this hell of debts.

So where will the interest payments go? Under the current debt money system, unless firms, households, and the government borrow money from banks, there will be not enough supply of money needed. As a result of this debt-based economic system, a huge amount of interest on these astronomical debts are transferred to the shareholders of private banks as unearned income and will be born by the generation of taxpayers yet unborn. This is the root cause of growing income disparity we have been seeing everywhere. If we compare those international bankers to the 1%, the income gap of "1% vs. 99%" in the *Occupy the Wall-street* movement is exposed as a system design failure of debt money. In reality, it would be less than 0.1% as suggested by the analysis on the Network of Global Corporate Control in Chap. 10. Even so, MMT claims that "the government that issues its own currency does not default, so let the government borrow more through aggressive fiscal spendings".

In the end, MMT will only benefit the 0.1%. Promoting MMT is essentially same as promoting to make income inequality even worse. We should not be fooled by these sweet words promulgated under the guise of "Modern Money Theory". Before assuming the unrealistic consolidated government with the central bank, MMT should calculate the consolidated net assets of the "consolidated private banks" including the central bank (1%) and compare it with the combined net assets of non-banking sectors such as firms, households and government (99%). This would reveal the reality of the massive deprivation of income by banking interests and the harsh reality of firms and households as well as our governments.

In summary, our discussion so far has lead us to the opposite conclusion from MMT's claim under the current debt money system as follows:

> **Producers, households, and governments that issue their own currency as *debt money* will eventually default.**

If readers are further interested in the analysis of income distribution by way of interests, they are encouraged to run simulations of "Monetary Goodwin model" in Yamaguchi (2013, Chap. 5) developed with ASD modeling method.

Analysis from the Reverse Definition of Money

Our discussion so far has been based on the obverse definition of money. From now on, we will discuss along with the reverse definition of money, which MMT tends to ignore. According to the reverse definition, "modern money" consists of legal tender and functional money. Using this definition, let us further discuss the possibility that "the government that issues its own currency" will default.

According to the 2018 data, legal tender in Japan was 506.3 trillion yen (35.5%), functional money was 324.9 trillion yen (22.8%), and time deposit was 594.5 trillion yen (41.7%). Total amount of functional money called "Expanded Functional Money (M_F)" in Fig. 2.1 was 919.4 trillion yen (64.5%), which is the sum of time deposits and a portion of demand deposits that are not backed by legal tender. Whenever bubble bursts and recession hits, bank failures are rumored. Depositors rush to withdraw their demand deposits and cancel their time deposits to secure safer cash (legal tender). This is the classic type of bank run. As a result, during the Great Depression, the US banks were forced to close (bank holidays). At that point, functional money ceased to function as money. From depositors' point of view, their functional money disappeared instantly.

As of 2018, only 35.5% of Japan's M_3 is backed by legal tender, which commercial banks can use to meet withdrawals in such an emergency. In other words, if another financial crisis occurs, there will be a possibility that bank holidays need to be implemented. In that case, 919.4 trillion yen (64.5%) of functional money may be destroyed and disappear from circulation. This is precisely the financial instability of the debt money system. The aforementioned defaults of firms and households as well as bank failures will occur first before the government finally defaults.

Therefore, what we must aim for is to avoid the disappearance of these functional money. And to do so, we must make all debt money legal tender. That way, defaults caused by the suspension of deposits (bank holidays) can be avoided. Such monetary reform proposals were the Chicago Plan in 1933, Fisher's 100% Money in 1935, and Public Money proposed in this book. The only way to achieve this is to raise the legally required reserve ratio to 100%.

However, MMT is in direct opposition to the full-reserve banking system by arbitrarily interpreting it as follows:

> Someone else has to do the lending since the banks are not allowed to do it, so it isolates "narrow banks" from lending risk, but others will do the lending and create IOUs that are not backed by 100 percent reserves. It is not clear that the proposal would in any way reduce the creation of "money", defined as IOUs denominated in the money of account. (Wray, 2012, p. 80).

With 100% reserve requirement, all money is issued exogenously by the government (as explained throughout this book), which would theoretically make it impossible for any depository institutions to create "IOUs" endogenously. Furthermore, new loans by banks will be financed by pre-existing savings without problems, contrary to what MMT purports to be. It came as a rather surprise to us that MMT cannot understand the basic logic of the 100% reserve proposals. Are MMT scholars really researchers of money? It is no wonder that they cannot develop a macroeconomic simulation model that supports their ideas. On the other hand, we have presented a macroeconomic model of public money system that can avoid financial instability, while ensuring stability of the value of currency (see Yamaguchi, 2013, Chap. 18, "Monetary and Financial Stability").

In summary, if MMT is practiced and debt money is issued, producers and households (private sectors) will default first, and then the government will default, which eventually destroys our nation. On the contrary,

Government issuing its own *public money* does not default.

And the economy and society where public money circulates will prosper. This is the correct conclusion from the standpoint of public money theory.

Falsehood 5: Ballooning Government Debt Won't Cause Hyperinflation

According to MMT, there is no such thing as hyperinflation because inflation, if it does occur, can be controlled by pulling money out of circulation through tax hikes. It also argues that there is nothing wrong with budget deficits or public debt as long as the money that the state pours into the economy does not cause inflation. MMT researchers like to point out to the fact that interest rates have fallen to zero in Japan despite the nation's ballooning government debts and proudly claim that Japan's case alone proves the correctness of MMT.

Why, then, has the Japanese economy not grown despite the fact that the government has accumulated approximately 600 trillion yen in debt through "deficit spendings" over the past 30 years? Does not the case of Japan's lost 30 years demonstrate the fallacy of MMT? For those who have suffered from the economic hardship during the last decades, such an irresponsible discussion by MMT must be intolerable. Moreover, government spending in response to the COVID-19 shock resulted in further increases in debt and accelerated inflation, particularly in the US. Such irresponsible arguments must be no longer of interest to the general public.

What's wrong with these arguments, then? First of all, according to the mainstream Keynesian monetary theory, when government debts increase, the interest rates rise and the crowding out occurs (as already discussed in Chap. 5). MMT also criticizes this mainstream monetary theory and argues that it does not occur because money is endogenously created. Since debt money (as defined by MMT) is endogenously supplied when someone borrows money, an increase in government debt also means an increase in the supply of debt money. Therefore, interest rates cannot rise. It rather must fall. As discussed in the classification of monetary theories in Chap. 9, MMT as a branch of endogenous debt money theory (stock approach) also analyses the economy operating under debt money system in this way.

Indeed, the behavior of the Japanese economy observed during the lost 30 years, in which rising government debt and falling interest rates have coexisted, appears to exemplify the legitimacy of MMT insofar as it refutes this mainstream crowing out effect theory. However, in light of our classification of monetary theory in Chap. 9, the truth was that mainstream Keynesian monetary theory, i.e., exogenous debt money theory (flow approach), was simply wrong. Hence, Japan's case does not prove the validity of MMT nor is there any need for its proponents to emphasize it. In terms of the history of economic theory, the endogenous debt money theory (stock approach) was simply correct. Nothing more.

Can higher taxes stop the increase in debt money and control inflation as MMT argues, then? As our analyses in Chap. 3 has demonstrated, the more the government borrows, the more M_1 increases by the equivalent amount in Japan as well as in the US. Especially, Japan's money stock, which has lost its destination for spending, has been piling up in corporate checking accounts (which is part of M_1) as retained earnings. As of 2018, they are about 446 trillion yen. As a result, once inflation kicks in, these excess funds begin to overflow into financial assets and real estate investments. In addition, Japanese banks have stacked up a huge amount of base money M_0 (506.3 trillion yen) that has inflated due to the Quantitative Easing (QE) by the BoJ. Once inflation trends, further demand for funds (mainly financial and real estate investment) from firms and households will increase, and banks will overflow huge amount of credit into the market based on their increased base money.

If the faucets of credit creation by banks are not closed, no matter how much the government turns off the faucet of its own debt money (48%) by raising taxes, the faucet of private-sector's debt money (52%) will remain open and uncontrollable (see Fig. 3.7). Therefore, the overall increase in debt money ($M_1 \sim M_3$) will also be uncontrollable. Foreign investors and hedge funds who have lost confidence in the BoJ's monetary policy management will sell off the yen and the exchange rate will plummet. At this point, inflation runs out of control and explodes into hyperinflation. That is, MMT cannot prevent hyperinflation.

Can such a hyperinflation be controlled then? To do so, the government has to invoke the last forbidden measure. That is, a suspension of deposit withdrawals, thereby forcibly stopping the circulation of debt money. A similar situation occurred in Japan during the postwar hyperinflation. On February 16, 1946, Minister of Finance announced emergency measures, forcing people to deposit the BoJ notes, blocked their deposits and banned the old BOJ notes out of circulation. Property taxes were raised and their savings forcibly confiscated to pay back holders of government bonds and absorb the losses of financial institutions (bail-ins). Yet it was too late. Violent inflation had eliminated the value of currency and people lost their pensions and life savings. In other words, rapid inflation and hyperinflation, once they ensue, cannot be controlled by raising taxes under the present debt money system.

Although MMT has rightly criticized the mainstream monetary theory as the flawed exogenous debt money theory, governments fooled by the MMT will have to face sever counterattacks of the debt money system against themselves because of MMT's inability to understand its own endogenous debt money theory.

Cost-Push Inflation and Currency Depreciation

Up to this point, we have examined inflation caused by demand-pull. From now on, we will discuss cost-push inflation. In Chap. 6 we have discussed that Japan's government debt-to-GDP ratio will exceed 300% in 2036. As the economy approaches this point, one of three catastrophic scenarios becomes more realistic: a financial meltdown, hyperinflation, or default. When the credit rating agencies downgrade treasury bonds ratings and the crash of bond prices becomes a reality, the following may take place.

(1) Private banks will stop underwriting government bonds for fear of insolvency, and interest rates will begin to rise. The question then becomes, "how much can the Bank of Japan absorb declines in the treasury bonds?"
(2) The yen will gradually lose its value, first in the foreign exchange market. Soon a collapse of the yen becomes inevitable, and import prices begin to soar. For example, price of oil and gasoline begins to skyrocket from the current one hundred yen per liter to two hundred and three hundred yen.

In this way, cost-push inflation becomes uncontrollable and eventually leads to hyperinflation. In the postwar hyperinflation mentioned above, attempts were made to forcibly control purchasing power through emergency measures. However, since inflation did not stop even after property taxes were raised, GHQ finally fixed the exchange rate at 360 yen per US dollar in 1949. It was too late by then. As stated earlier, the value of financial assets held by households and companies had already evaporated. Japan has relied on imports for most of its energy demand for 75 years after the war. This is the terminal station of the debt money catastrophe to which MMT's policy will lead. Has MMT economists forgotten or do not know the Japan's postwar experience?

From the above, it can be concluded that the MMT's claim that inflation and hyperinflation can be controlled by raising taxes is a false argument, because it does not understand the system design failures of debt money. No matter how smart and timely government's policies are (which is itself a big assumption), MMT's claim that money stock can be controllable becomes impossible under this debt money system. Therefore, inflation and subsequent hyperinflation also become uncontrollable. On the contrary, under the public money system, the government does not need to borrow money in the first place. And even if the total amount of public money in circulation turn out to be excessive, inflation can be promptly controlled by adjusting the total quantity of money (purchasing power) in circulation through taxes.

In other words, under the public money system we are proposing,

> **Inflation can be controlled by raising taxes. Therefore, hyperinflation will not occur and price stability is achieved.**

The issuance of Electronic Public Money (EPM) and Uniform Tax System proposed in Chap. 13 will provide a more direct and agile policy tool to control inflation.

Falsehood 6: Government Borrowing Increases Private Sector's Assets (Deposits)

According to this MMT's claim, government borrowing increases the financial assets (deposits) of the private sector so that private sector is enriched and no one loses money. Too many people tend to view the term 'public debt' negatively, because we have been imprinted with the explanation that the public debt is "our debt" and we will eventually have to pay them back either through tax increases or spending cuts. In order to wake the world up from such brainwashing, proponents of MMT like to chant "Their debts are our assets". In this way, MMT treats the government as if it were a complete stranger and claims that if they (the government) borrow more, we (the people) will be richer. Is such an irresponsible logic really correct? Since this argument is the crux of MMT, we will evaluate it carefully using macroeconomic balance sheets.

Figure 11.1 illustrates the simple balance sheets of government, private sector (households and producers), banks, and the central bank (BoJ). All of these four sectors are affected by the issuance of government bonds. The following discussion is based on the Japanese case but it certainly applies to other countries. For example, read "BoJ" as "the Fed" for readers in the United States.

Deposits (Credits) Creation by Government Debts

Step (1): All transactions with account number (1). The government borrows, say, 80 billion yen from banks as COVID-19 emergency relief aid (paid out to households as subsidy) by issuing treasury bonds. As a result, government's deposits (asset) and bonds (liability) increase by 80 billion yen both at the same time.[4] This is the double-entry bookkeeping. The same applies hereafter.

Next, bonds (asset) of banks increase by 80 billion yen, which banks pay out of their reserve deposits at the BoJ. On the BoJ's balance sheet, the bank's reserve deposits (liability) decrease by 80 billion yen, and at the same time 80 billion yen is

[4] Note that unit in Fig. 11.1 is shown in terms of 0.1 billion yen. Thus, 80 billion yen is shown as "800" in the balance sheets in Fig. 11.1.

Government B/S

Assets		Liabilities	
(1) Gov.Deposits	800	800	(1) Bonds Issuance
(2) Gov.Expenditure	-800		
(3) Taxes	100		
(4) Interests	-100		
		Net Assets	
		-800	(2) Gov.Expenditure
		100	(3) Taxes
		-100	(4) Interests

Bank of Japan B/S

Assets		Liabilities	
		(Reserves Deposits)	
		-800	(1) Reserves
		800	(2) Gov.Expenditure
		(Gov. Deposits)	
		800	(1) Gov.Deposits
		-800	(2) Gov.Expenditure
		Net Assets	

Private (Households & Producers) B/S

Assets		Liabilities	
(2) Deposits	800		
(3) Taxes	-100		
		Net Assets	
		800	(2) Deposits
		-100	(3) Taxes

Banks B/S

Assets		Liabilities	
(1) Reserves	-800		
(2) Gov.Expenditure	800	800	(2) Deposits
		-100	(3) Taxes
		Net Assets	
(1) Bonds	800	100	(4) Interests

(Unit: 0.1 billion yen)

Non-Financial Net Assets (-100)	
-800	Government
700	Private Sector
Financial Net Assets (100)	
100	Banks

(Remarks)
Bonds Purchases by Banks with Reserves do not increase Money Stock.
(Reserves Increase/Decrease --> Money Stock Increase/Decrease)
Bonds Purchases with Excess Reserves increase Money Stock.

Fig. 11.1 Changes in balance sheets of four macroeconomic sectors after issuance of government bonds and interest payments

credited to the government deposit account (liability). This completes all transactions with account number (1).

Step (2): All transactions with account number (2). In order to transfer 80 billion yen to households account through its fiscal stimulus, the government first transfers 80 billion yen from its BoJ's deposit account to the bank's reserve deposit account. As a result, the changes in the BoJ's government and bank reserve deposit balances become zero at this point.

Next, 80 billion yen in government deposits disappear from its balance sheet as a result of the government expenditure, and at the same time, the government's net assets are now 80 billion yen in red. On the other hand, the banks' balance sheet shows an increase in deposits as a result of government spending. Banks then transfer the same amount to the deposit accounts of the private sector (households and producers). At this point, the bank's balance sheet will have 80 billion yen in government bonds (assets) and 80 billion yen in deposits from the private sector (liabilities). In other words, from the perspective of banks that purchased treasury bonds, the government debt (bond issuance) are essentially a loan of 80 billion yen to the government in the form of debt securities (bonds), which in turn create new "deposits" of 80 billion yen on the private-sector's demand deposits account.

In this sense, the result is not different from a loan to the private sector, where banks tap their keyboards and enter numbers into their customer's deposit account. In other words, the essence of government bond issuance is the creation of new "debt money" out of nothing by the government debt on the bank's balance sheets. On the other hand, the balance sheet of private sector will show an increase of 80 billion yen in deposit assets and 80 billion yen in net assets due to the transfer of government expenditures.[5]

Based on the discussion so far, let us now examine whether "government debts increase private sector's assets (deposits)" as MMT claims. Certainly, the issuance of government bonds has resulted in a 80 billion yen deficit while private-sector's deposits and financial assets (bonds) have increased by the same amount. In this sense, the MMT's claim appears to be correct. However, from a macroeconomic perspective, both the government and private sectors are non-bank (or non-financial) sectors. If we look at the net assets of the non-banking (non-financial) sector, we find that the government's net assets = −80 billion yen and the private sector's net assets = +80 billion yen. If the government is a complete "stranger" as MMT purports it to be, we certainly need not worry about "their" (the government's) negative net assets, and we can be genuinely happy with the increase in "our" (the private sector's) net assets.

However, if the government is seen as a member of the non-banking sector, representing "us" in the private sector, the story is different. That is, the increase in households' (net) assets is offset by the decrease in the government's net assets, so that the net assets of the non-banking sector becomes 0 (= −80 + 80). As a result, the net assets of the non-banking sector has not increased at all from the macroeconomic perspective. Nevertheless, if the government's borrowing cost (interest) were zero, there would be no overall loss of net assets for the non-banking sectors, and the private sector's assets (deposits) and net assets would increase. However, would banks extend loans, i.e., purchase bonds as primary dealers, without demanding anything in return?

There is not such sweet deal in reality. MMT is promoting this illusion by either assuming this zero borrowing cost or ignoring (hiding) the government's negative net assets of −80 billion yen. Surprisingly, there are many MMT followers in Japan and elsewhere who are completely fooled by this story. Such an idealistic story is possible only under the public money system where government issues its own currency without interest and records them as its net assets. What happens, then, when the government's cost of borrowing (interest) is positive?

---

[5] Here it may appear that money stock M_1 will always increase because government debts increase private sector's deposits, but that is not true. If banks' reserve deposits are equal to legally required reserves, money stock does not increase. Only when the banks' reserve deposits are in excess of their required reserves, money stock will increase by the same amount if banks use those funds to purchase government bonds. If there are no excess reserves, the central bank must supply additional funds needed before the bond purchase by banks can take place. Therefore, the increase in money stock resulting from the purchase of government bonds by banks is limited to cases where there is little demand for loans to the private sector and thus reserve deposits are in surplus. That is, money stock increases only when the government borrows from banks to compensate the decline in lending to the private sector. When the cash ratio of M_0 changes, M_1 also fluctuates. Only when there is a surplus of M_0, M_1 can be increased by the government debts.

The Government's Debt Hell Is the Hell of "We the People"

Step (3): All transactions with account number (3). From here onwards, a horrifying story of government's debt hell begins. Let us assume that interest payments on the government bonds is 1.25% per annum or 1 billion yen per year. Since the government will not be able to repay this debt anyway, it has no choice but to continue to borrow every year by refinancing bonds. However, bond holders still ruthlessly insist on interest payments every year.

Let us consider the balance sheet after 10 years have passed. The government's cumulative interest payments will be 10 billion yen. The government will be forced to collect taxes from the private sector in order to pay the banks this 10 billion yen in interests. As a result, the government's balance sheet will show an increase of 10 billion yen in taxes and the corresponding 10 billion yen in net assets. On the other hand, on the private sector's balance sheet, these tax payments will reduce their assets and net assets by 10 billion yen.

On the bank's balance sheet, private-sector's deposits are reduced by 10 billion in order to transfer tax payments from the private sector to the government deposit account at the BoJ. To do so, banks reduce their own reserve deposits by the same amount, and transfers the reserves to the government deposit account on the BoJ's balance sheet. Note that all these transactions happen as account transfers among liabilities of the BoJ. Also note that the bookkeeping involved in this series of settlements is the same process as in the case of bond purchases. It is therefore omitted from the BoJ and banks' balance sheets in Fig. 11.1 to avoid further complexity.

Step (4): All transactions with account number (4)–Interest payments and the Hell of Debts. The government immediately transfers the money received as tax payments to the bank's reserve deposit account for interest payments. The bank then records this transfer from the government as its own interest income (net assets).

Looking at the changes in the balance sheets of the government and the BoJ in Steps 3 and 4 above, there is no change in their balance sheets. From the balance sheet of the private sector, however, taxes for interest payments are collected every year, which reduces the assets and net assets of the private sector. On the other hand, on the banks' balance sheet, this interest payments are transferred from the private sector's deposit account to their net assets every year.

In conclusion, MMT is wrong in its assertion that government debt is an increase in private sector's asset (deposits). While the government's net worth remains unchanged at -80 billion yen, the private sector's net asset has declined cumulatively from 80 billion to 70 billion yen. As a result, the net assets of the non-banking sectors as a whole will now be a deficit of -10 billion yen ($= -80 + 70$). On the other hand, the banks' net assets have increased by the same amount of these cumulative interest payments. Comparing the net assets of the banking sectors ("the 1%") and the non-financial sectors ("the 99%" sector), the net assets of banking sector (1%) will increase by 10 billion yen, while those of the non-banking sectors (99%) will decrease by 10 billion yen. In other words, government borrowing (issuance of debt money as defined by the MMT) transfers net assets from the private sector to the banking sector every year. Furthermore, even if the government debts were to be refinanced by perpetual bonds (such as the British consols), private sector's deposits must be taxed every year until it eventually reduces private sector's net asset to zero.[6]

This is the system of control through compound interests discussed in Chap. 10, where the private sector's interest payments become net assets of the banks year after another. Where do these interests go? They will be ultimately paid out to the bankers as their bonuses and their dividends as shareholders of banks. In this way, the debt money system is designed to enrich "the 1%". Income inequality is embedded into the money system. Thus, the income gap between "1% and 99%" widens. If we read the numerical example of 80 billion yen here as Japan's current outstanding government debt of 800 trillion yen (as of 2018), it reveals the harsh reality and future of Japan, where roughly 10 trillion yen of our assets (about 80,000 yen per capita) are being siphoned off by bankers every year. Herein lies the essence of debt money theory being advocated by MMT. Does this still leave readers to support the debt money theory of MMT?

Our analysis leads to the following conclusion under the debt money system:

Government debts do not increase private sector assets (deposits) but ultimately increase banks' net assets, which increase income inequality between the bankers and the rest.

Falsehood 7: Government Spending Comes First!

Listening to online introductory videos by MMT researchers such as William F. Mitchell, Warren Mosler, Larry R. Wray, Stephanie A. Kelton, we often hear them explain that "since the government can issue its own currency, money is first spent into circulation by fiscal spending to stimulate economic activity, and then, after serving its purpose, they are collected and recovered as taxes". MMT proponents in Japan are also spreading this claim. Is this really the case?

In order for the government to be able to make the initial expenditure, whether by bank transfer or check, those money must be in the government's deposit account before it can "spend first". To raise that money, even the government must "borrow first" by issuing treasury bonds (IOUs) and short-term treasury bills. In the case of payments by promissory notes, if the deposit is not ready by the settlement date, they become empty bills, which immediately results in a bankruptcy. A typical example of this is a company making profits but financially becomes insolvent due to liquidity shortages. This is true whether a debtor is a company, a bank or a government. However, since MMT defines "money as IOU", government's debts become the issuance of the government's own money. Therefore, according to the MMT's definition, "government spending must come first."

No matter how much sophistry is used, the claim that "government spending comes first" is false and impossible in practice. In order for the government to be

[6] We have analyzed this behavior as the *built-in unfair income distribution* in favor of bankers under the debt money system. See Yamaguchi and Yamaguchi (2024) in detail.

able to spend first, it must first borrow money and have money in its deposit account at the central bank. In the above example of Fig. 11.1, the government begins by issuing 80 billion yen in JGBs in order to avoid going bankrupt with empty bills. In other words, under the current debt money system, even if we assume that the government can increase an unlimited amount of money stock as a result of issuing bonds, "Borrowing Comes First!" It is unclear whether MMT is ignoring this point or intentionally hiding this transaction step since they do not discuss using balance sheets like Fig. 11.1. In any case, the government cannot "spend first" without having the money to spend with.

The question then becomes, "Can the government always 'borrow first'?" In other words, will private banks underwrite government bonds at any time and under any conditions, even if they perceive the risk of default? As already mentioned, there is no guarantee that for-profit private banks, including central bank, will go along with such government charity. "Spending Comes First!" is only possible under the public money system, where the government issues its own interest-free money as legal tender. Thus, MMT is either confusing debt money with public money, or intentionally misleading the public by using the two different types of money interchangeably depending on the context.

Public Money Spending Comes First!

Therefore, in order to clarify the difference between debt money and public money, let us consider the case in which 80 billion yen is issued as public money. What would happen if the 80 billion yen in COVID-19 emergency relief fund were financed by public money instead of issuing government bonds? Figure 11.2 shows the balance sheet of the four macroeconomic sectors associated with the issuance of public money. Here the BoJ is assumed to be reorganized into the Public Money Vault (PMV) after completing the transition to public money system, which will be detailed in the next Chap. 12.

Step (1): All transactions with account number (1). Suppose that the Public Money Administration (PMA)–monetary policy committee that manages the PMV– independently reviews the budget requests submitted by the Ministry of Finance and approves a new issuance of 80 billion yen. Then, 80 billion yen of public money is recorded to the assets and net assets of the balance sheet of the Public Money Vault. In response to this, the PMV immediately transfers 80 billion yen to the government's deposits account. As a result, the net assets of 80 billion yen is transferred to government deposits (liability) on the PMV's balance sheet. Public money assets of 80 billion yen remain unchanged. On the other hand, on the government's balance sheet, both assets and net assets increase by 80 billion yen as government deposits. At this point the government is ready to "spend first" without borrowing money.

Step (2): All transactions with account number (2). The government wants to transfer 80 billion yen to households. First, it transfers 80 billion yen to the banks' reserves account at the PMV. The 80 billion yen in deposits disappear from the government's balance sheet as fiscal expenditures, and at the same time, the government's

Government B/S

Assets		Liabilities	
(1) Gov.Deposits	800		
(2) Gov.Expenditu	-800		
		Net Assets	
		800	(1) Gov.Deposits
		-800	(2) Gov.Expenditure

Public Money Vault B/S

Assets		Liabilities	
(1) Public Money	800	(Reserves Deposits)	
		800	(2) Gov.Expenditure
		(Gov. Deposits)	
		800	(1) Gov.Deposits
		-800	(2) Gov.Expenditure
		Net Assets	
		800	(1) Public Money Issue
		-800	(1) to Gov.Deposits

Private (Households & Producers) B/S

Assets		Liabilities	
(2) Deposits	800		
		Net Assets	
		800	(2) Deposits

Banks B/S

Assets		Liabilities	
(Reserves Deposists)		800	(2) Deposits
(2) Gov.Expenditure	800		
		Net Assets	

(Unit: 0.1 billion yen)

Non-Financial Net Assets (800)	
0	Government
800	Private Sector
Financial Net Assets (0)	
0	Banks

(Remarks)
Public Money increases Money Stock and Private Net Assets.
Bank Reserves increase, yet no credit creation by 100% requirements.

Fig. 11.2 Changes in balance sheets of four macroeconomic sectors after issuance of public money

net assets will also decrease by 80 billion yen to zero. On the other hand, the bank's balance sheet will see an increase in deposits as a result of government expenditure, and the same amount will be transferred to the deposit accounts of the households (private sector). At this point, the banks' balance sheet will have 80 billion yen in reserve deposit (asset) and 80 billion yen in private sector's deposit (liability). On the other hand, the balance sheet of the private sector increases by 80 billion yen in deposits assets and net assets.

As a result of these government expenditures through the issuance of public money, the PMV's net assets will move to the net assets of the government (Ministry of Finance), and then to the net assets of the private sector. Corresponding to these net assets of the private sector are the public money assets of 80 billion yen on the PMV's balance sheet. That is, the issuance of public money immediately translates into an equal amount of private sector's net assets (and deposit assets) through fiscal expenditure. Once they are put into circulation in this way, they start to circulate and support private-sector's economic activity. The issuance of public money does not cause the private sector's net assets to be gradually taxed as interest payments, as was the case with expenditures through issuance of government bonds. In other words, the forced transfer of (net) assets from the private sector to banks (Steps 3 and 4 in the previous example of MMT) do not occur under the public money system. As a result, income inequalities such as 1% vs. 99% do not occur either.

In this way, even if the government were to spend the same 80 billion yen in government money as subsidies, MMT would treat it as debts (liability), while public money would treat it as net assets (equity) of the public. Our numerical example clearly shows which system would result in a more efficient, neutral, and equitable distribution of assets and national wealth. At the 2012 International Conference on Monetary Reform in Chicago, Kaoru pointed out this difference between the two monetary theories (see Sect. 9.5). Yet in the midst of heated debates between the AMI's Director Zarlenga and the MMT presenter, his remarks unfortunately did not reach the MMT proponent. This is why we decided to summarize the fundamental differences between public money and debt money in this Chapter. Let's not be fooled by the MMT anymore.

In summary, "government spending comes first" is impossible even under the debt money system, whereas under the public money system, it is certain that

Public money spending comes first.

11.2 MMT will Destroy Our Nation

We have just examined the falsity of MMT by arranging it into seven false claims. Nevertheless, why has MMT gained much attention in recent years? Why have so many MMT-related books (many of which are full of false explanations) been published? The answer is simple: the exogenous debt monetary theory (flow approach) explained in Chap. 9 has been gradually exposed as a false theory. And MMT has begun to be recognized as a better explanation of the reality. Since 99.7% of the money in circulation is debt money, MMT, which defines "money as IOU," was deemed to explain the reality of the debt money system more realistically than the mainstream Keynesian monetary theory. As a result, economists and commentators who were educated in the monetary theory of mainstream economics either realized its errors and became silent, or they were forced to accept MMT as the next likely alternative.

In Chap. 9 we have advanced that the alternative to the mainstream Keynesian monetary theory is not MMT, but the public money theory. MMT can never be a valid theory, as evidenced by the above seven falsehoods. Nevertheless, anti-austerity and aggressive fiscal policies fueled by MMT gained some traction at national level in Japan. This was especially true around 2019 when the original Japanese version of this book was being written. Ironically, however, MMT's credibility and popularity seems to have declined rapidly due to subsequent global inflation. In any case, what would happen to Japan if MMT followers were to take charge of national policy and put their ignorance into practice? As our last criticism of MMT from the perspective of public money theory, let us examine this issue here in depth.

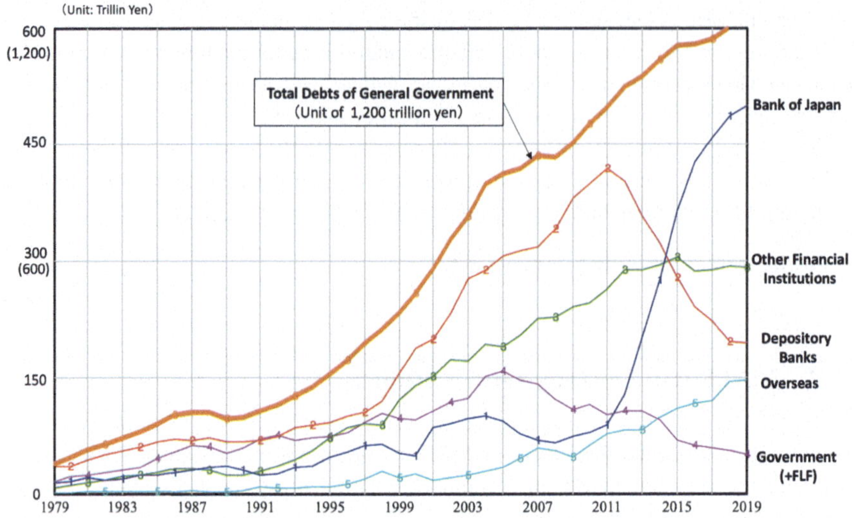

Fig. 11.3 Total debts of general government and its top five lenders

From Who Has the Japanese Government Borrowed Money?

As discussed in Falsehood 6, MMT is spreading the delusion: "their (the government's) debts are our assets". In order for this delusion to be persuasive, the government must be able to borrow as much money as it needs and when it wants. However, under the present system, no matter how hard the government tries, it cannot borrow money without creditors who are willing to make loans. From who, then, has the government of Japan borrowed money so far? Using the latest Flow of Funds Accounts data as of 2019, we have analyzed from "which sector" the Japanese government has borrowed over the past 40 years.[7]

Figure 11.3 shows total amount of general government debts, including the FILP (Fiscal Investment and Loan Program) bonds and municipal bonds, and its top five lenders to the government from 1979 to 2019. According to this, the general government has already fallen into a debt hell with the total debts of 1,207 trillion yen (thick orange line 6). As analyzed in Chap. 4, there are three final outcomes of this debt hell: financial meltdown, hyperinflation, or government default. As we have concluded there, we have 12 years left before its debt-to-GDP ratio reaches about 300% in around 2036 (optimistically speaking).

[7] Specifically, we have classified the macroeconomic sectors into eight sectors as top-layers of the flow of funds analysis as follows: 1. the Bank of Japan, 2. depository institutions (banks, etc.) 3. financial institutions such as securities investment, insurance, and pensions, 4. producers (non-financial business corporations), 5. general government (including fiscal loan fund), 6. households, 7. nonprofit organizations, and 8. overseas (the rest of the world).

Here, we would like to add another possible fourth scenario to the above three scenarios of debt hell. This scenario emerges by analyzing from whom (from which sector) the government will have to borrow in the future. To do this, we begin by considering the sectors from which the government has been borrowing heavily in the past. As illustrated in Fig. 11.3, until the Lehman Shock in 2008 and subsequent global financial crisis, the government borrowed mainly from the following five sectors: 1st—Banks (line 2), 2nd—Other Financial Institutions (line 3), 3rd—Government (mainly public pension funds GPIF) (line 4), 4th—Bank of Japan (line 1), and 5th—Overseas (line 5). The other three sectors (Producers, Households, and Non-profit Organizations) represent only about 6% of total government debt in 2019, and are therefore omitted from the graph here.

This ranking of government borrowing sources began to change dramatically in 2014, the year following the introduction of Quantitative Easing (QE) Policy as part of the Abenomics. Specifically, the ranking changed significantly as follows. 1st—Bank of Japan, 2nd—Other Financial Institutions, 3rd—Banks, 4th—Overseas, and 5th - Government. The other three sectors have shrunk to about 2% of the total. More specifically, the ranking reversed significantly in two places: from Banks to the Bank of Japan, and from the Government (public pension funds GPIF) to Overseas.

Let us first look at the reversal of the ranking from the Banks to the Bank of Japan. To achieve the inflation target of 2%, the BoJ introduced the last trump card to get out of the recession and began purchasing a large amount of Japanese Government Bonds (JGBs) held by the banks through QE, thereby increasing the base money. As a result, JGBs held by the BoJ jumped 2.5-fold from 201 trillion yen in 2013 to 499 trillion yen in 2019. On the other hand, JGBs held by the Banks fell sharply by about 46% from 358 trillion yen to 194 trillion yen. Thus, the huge amount of JGBs held mainly by domestic banks was monetized and converted into BoJ reserve deposits through QE, sharply reducing the banks' credit risk exposure to JGBs.

Next is the reversal of the ranking from the Government's public pension funds to Overseas. The amount held by the government's public pension funds plummeted by about 52%, from 107 trillion yen to 51 trillion yen. On the other hand, foreign holdings of JGBs surged 1.8 times from 82 trillion yen in 2013 to 147 trillion yen in 2019. During just seven years of the Abenomics, the government's borrowing sources have dramatically shifted to reliance on the Bank of Japan for fiscal finance, and on the overseas sector.

Shift of the Japanese Government's Borrowing Sources

What kind of economic rationality was at work, then, behind this reversal in the order of lenders to the Japanese Government? To answer this question, let us consider the economic effects of government debts by macroeconomic sectors. The sectors from which the government borrow its money can be broadly classified into three types: (a) Banks and the Bank of Japan, (b) Domestic Lenders other than Banks, and (c) Overseas Lenders. First, if the government borrows money from (a) Banks and the

Bank of Japan, the money stock will increase accordingly. Then it is expected that the inflation target of 2% will eventually be achieved (according to the reflation theory). In particular, if the government can borrow from the Bank of Japan, this would be the so-called fiscal finance. However, Article 5 of the Fiscal Law prohibits the government from directly financing from the BoJ. This would also be the case in other countries. Therefore, when the government issues new bonds, it must first borrow from the banks. But this didn't cause an increase in interest rates; that is, the crowding out effect didn't take place as claimed by the mainstream monetary theories. This is because, as the endogenous debt money theory correctly analyzes, government's borrowing from banks did not lead to a competition for exogenously given amount of funds, but rather increased the money stock. At the same time, as discussed in MMT's Falsehood 6, borrowing from banks ultimately increased banks' net assets and widened income inequality.

If the government borrows money from (b) Domestic Lenders other than Banks, such as securities investment, insurance companies, private and government's public pension funds, money stock will not increase and the inflation target becomes unattainable. Thus this policy cannot be used to combat recessions. On the contrary, as the mainstream theory points out, the crowding out effect will cause the government to compete with the private sector for funds, causing interest rates to rise, which in turn will cause government bond prices to plummet. Rising interest rates will eventually lead to financial collapse and accelerate government defaults. Mainstream monetary theory becomes indeed valid when the government borrows from domestic sectors other than banks. In this sense, not all mainstream theories are wrong, as MMT criticizes, but there are some aspect that are valid.

Considering these different economic effects of government debts by sectors, the rational policy for the Japanese government is to reduce borrowing from (b) Domestic Lenders other than Banks and increase borrowing from (a) Banks, while relying on the QE by the BoJ as a side support for this policy. Has the government, then, actually been borrowing money on the basis of this economic rationality? In order to analyze the changes in this government's borrowing sources, the top five lenders in Fig. 11.3 were reconstructed into a 100% composition chart as shown in Fig. 11.4.

It shows that the share of government borrowing from (b) Domestic Lenders other than Banks has declined substantially, as expected, by 20% from 48% just after the bubble burst in 1991 to 28% in 2019 (thick red line 2). Thick red line 2 is the sum of debts from financial institutions (securities investment, insurance, pensions) shown by the dotted line 3, and the government's public pension shown by the dotted line 4. Looking at the breakdown of this decline, we see that debts from financial institutions other than banks has remained stable at 15% to 25% (dotted line 3), while the government has drastically reduced its debts from its own public pensions (dotted line 4). That is, the government's debt from public pensions has plummeted by a factor of eight, from 33% just after the bubble burst in 1991 to 4% in 2019. In actual terms, the amount of government debt has plummeted by 107 trillion yen, from the peak of 158 trillion yen in 2005 to 51 trillion yen in 2019 as depicted by the line 4 in Fig. 11.3. In this way, it can be said that the Japanese government, knowingly or unknowingly, reduced its borrowing from the government sector (mainly public

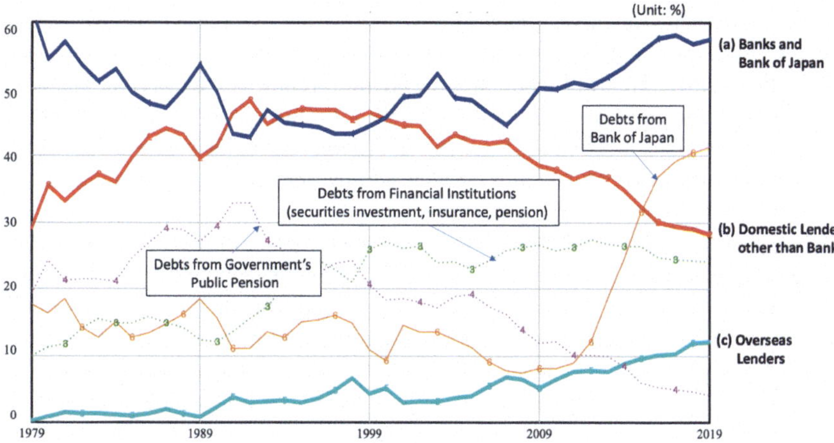

Fig. 11.4 Top five lenders to the government (100% ratio composition) top five lenders to the government (100% ratio composition)

pensions) in order to avoid the default caused by rising interest rates. If this had not been done, rising government debts would have raised interest rates and plunged government bond prices. The crowding-out effect by the mainstream (Keynesian) monetary theory would have also occurred in Japan, and MMT theorists could not have pointed out that "the Japanese economy demonstrates the correctness of MMT."

In any case, the government, while making rational decisions at the time, has been forced to shift its policy of borrowing from the banks to a policy of borrowing from the BoJ that adopted the quantitative easing as a last possible measure. The thick blue line 1 represents the combined ratio composition of (a) Banks and the BoJ. As already observed from Fig. 11.3, debts from banks have dropped sharply, but those from the BoJ rose sharply due to the QE policy. Looking at both sectors, the total debts have increased since the Lehman shock in 2008. In fact, from 2013 to 2019, the sum of the two have increased from 559 trillion yen to 693 trillion yen. However, as far as the composition ratio of government debts is concerned, the sum of the two has remained almost stable between 45% and 60% for the past 40 years.

What does this mean? These data show that, since the BoJ is also a private bank independent of the government, no matter how much the government forces it to buy its bonds through QE, the banking sector as a whole, including the BoJ and Depository Banks, cannot lend more than 60% of the total government debt outstanding, given the various risks associated with government bonds. This composition ratio data clearly show there is an upper limit to the risk these economic agents can bear based on their past investment behaviors. In other words, the unlimited borrowing through fiscal finance that MMT advocates cannot be expected from the rational economic behavior of private banks.

Therefore, the government is forced to rely on borrowings from (c) Overseas Lenders as the lender of last resort for government debt. Thick line 5 shows how rapidly government borrowing (debts) from overseas have increased over the last 40 years. In 1980, foreign debt was almost zero, but by 2019, the ratio has sharply risen to 12%. In nominal terms, this amounts to 147 trillion yen, which means that Japanese per capita debts from overseas is approximately 1.17 million yen. In other words, if the government wants to continue to increase its debts, it will have to rely heavily on overseas borrowings (debts). Can the Japanese government borrow infinitely from overseas lenders, then? The answer is "No".

Even if we optimistically assume that the government can borrow money from abroad in its own currency and that it can repay the principal amount with refinancing bonds, overseas lenders will not wait for interest repayment. Interest repayments could be covered by issuing new bonds, which the government has already been doing for the last decades. As discussed in MMT' Falsehood 4, however, that would plunge the Japanese government into debt hell, from which it would never be able to escape. Of course, Japan does not have the military power to overturn its debt obligations by force. Therefore, payment of interest to these overseas lenders will ultimately have to be financed from the income of Japanese people through taxation. In other words, the more the government borrows from abroad, the more Japanese assets are siphoned off by foreign lenders (international bankers), and the poorer the Japanese people become. Like developing countries that have defaulted in the past, Japan will eventually default on its debts. If the government defaults, the nation itself goes broke and its economy will also be devasted. This is the fourth scenario of the government's debt hell as mentioned at the beginning of this section.

11.3 Money as a Means of Controlling the Nations

In Chap. 10 we focused on the eleven international banks and financial groups that were bailed out by the Federal Reserve after the Lehman shock. These banks are listed among the top 50 financial institutions that control the global economy through the network of corporate stock ownership revealed by Vitali et al. (2011). How have they continued their domination of the global commerce and world economy since then?

The Japan's Ministry of Finance designates special participants in the treasury bond market called "primary dealers" as main purchasers of newly issued bonds (JGBs). Since 2016, 21 companies have been listed as the prime dealers of JGBs. According to the list, there are nine Japanese primary dealers: SMBC Nikko Securities, Okasan Securities, Daiwa Securities, Tokai Tokyo Securities, Nomura Securities, Mizuho Bank, Mizuho Securities, Sumitomo Mitsui Banking Corporation, and Mitsubishi UFJ Morgan Stanley Securities. On the other hand, there are 12 foreign primary dealers, more than the number of the Japanese primary dealers. Specifically, they are as follows: Crédit Agricole Securities, Crédit Suisse Securities, Goldman Sachs Securities, JP Morgan Securities, Citigroup Securities, Société Générale Securities, Deutsche Securities, Barclays Securities, BNP Paribas Securities, Merrill Lynch Japan Securities, Morgan Stanley MUFG Securities, and UBS Securities. Not very surprisingly, 10 out of these twelve foreign primary dealers (excluding

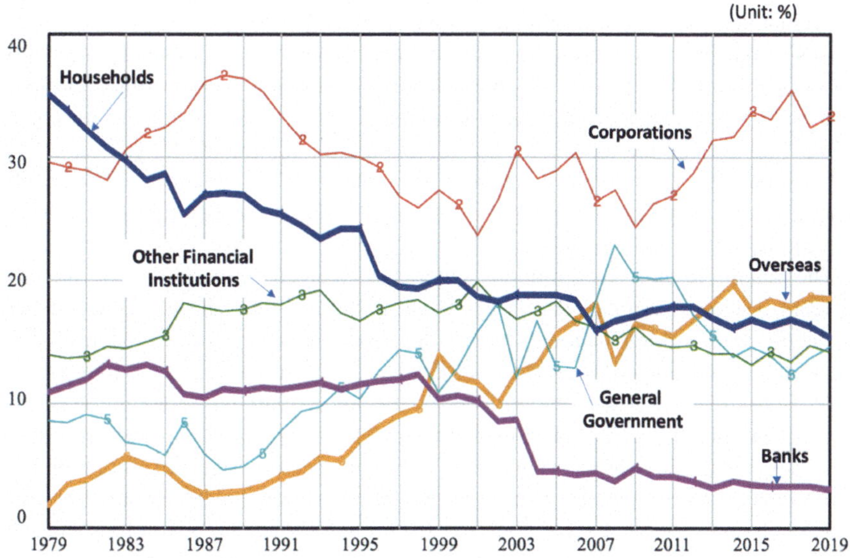

Fig. 11.5 Top 6 shareholders of Japanese equity stocks by sectors (%)

Crédit Agricole and Citigroup Securities) coincide with 10 out of the eleven international banks and financial groups listed in Table 10.2 (excluding Bank of America Corporation) as the top 50 control-holders dominating the global economy.[8]

What will happen if the government increases debts indiscriminately through anti-austerity policy, following the MMT's claim that "their (government's) debts are our assets"? As analyzed above, the government will be forced to borrow large amounts of money from these foreign lenders that have already exceeded 12%. As a result, the more the government practices MMT, the more the Japanese government will be controlled by international bankers. Eventually, it begins to suffer from the hell of debts, just like developing countries have fallen into debt traps of the Chinese Communist Party.

Speaking of foreign controls of domestic companies, almost 20% of Japanese private companies are already controlled by foreign shareholders during the lost 30 years. For example, many of the top-tier companies that once represented the industries of Japan such as Sharp, Nissan, Toshiba, Sony, Fujitsu, etc., are already controlled more than 50% by foreign shareholders. While these are micro-level observations, our macro-level analysis reveals the reality of rapid domination over Japanese economy by foreign shareholders.

Figure 11.5 shows the equity ownership ratio of top 6 sectors among eight macroeconomic sectors (including shares listed in the Stock Exchange, unlisted, and other).

---

[8] Note that, although Citigroup Inc. is not in the list of the eleven control holders, it is listed at the top of major banks that were bailed out by the Fed in Fig. 10.8 during the FED's Emergency Loans between December 2007–July 2010.

The remaining two macroeconomic sectors, such as the BoJ and private non-profit sectors (producers and households), are omitted because their combined ownership ratio is less than 1%. In 1980, when the Japanese economy was growing at a rapid pace as "Japan as No. 1", the shareholders ranking was as follows (the line numbers in Fig. 11.5 corresponds to these ranking as of 1980): 1st households (33.7%), 2nd corporations (29%), 3rd other financial institutions (13.7%), 4th banks (11.5%), 5th general government (including local governments, social security funds, and fiscal loan funds, 8.5%), and 6th overseas (3.5%).

The ranking of these shareholding sectors has changed dramatically over the last 40 years. The most dramatic declines in the shareholding ratios have occurred in the household and banking sectors. That is, the shareholding ratio of the Households (thick line 1) plummeted from 33.7% in 1980 to 15.4% in 2019, and fell to the third place. Banks (thick line 4), which ranked in the 4th in 1980, has fallen to the sixth-lowest position, with a sharp decline from 11.5% in 1980 to 3.1% in 2019, less than one-third of what it used to be in 1980. These two sectors together accounted for 26.4% decline. In comparison, Corporations (line 2), which ranked 2nd in 1980 with 29%, went up to 1st place with 33.4% in 2019. Other Financial Institutions (line 3) have fallen from 3rd to 5th place, but the ratio remained relatively stable, from 13.7 to 14.2%.

What fluctuated substantially was the General Government's (mainly public pension fund) shareholding ratio (line 5). Its shareholdings ratio rose from 8.5% in 1980 and peaked at 22.9% in 2008, just before the Lehman shock. After the collapse of Lehman Brothers, however, it decreased rapidly, and in 2019 it decreased to 14.7%, which is on par with Other Financial Institutions (line 3). Taking a closer look at this chart, the government's ownership ratio rapidly decreased after the Lehman shock. Just around 2013, when Abenomics was launched, the General Government's ratio declined to 17%, and the shareholdings ratio of Overseas finally reversed that of the General Government and Households. In other words, these data indicate that while these domestic non-banking sectors have been decreasing their shareholdings, the overseas sector has been increasing its shareholdings in Japan.

Thus, the Overseas (thick line 6), which was ranked at the lowest place in 1980, has jumped from 3.5% in 1980 to 18.6% in 2019, moving into second place. Its shareholding ratio has actually increased by 15.1%. About 20% or one-fifth of Japanese stocks are now held by the Overseas. Looking at the past 40 years as a major trend, we can see that stocks held by households and the banks began to be rapidly purchased by foreign investors. Furthermore, it can be seen that after the Lehman shock government-owned stocks also began to be purchased by the Overseas. These foreign shareholders are mainly the international banks and financial institutions mentioned above.[9]

---

[9] Figure 11.3 shows the sharp increase in banks' holdings of government bonds just after the bubble burst in the early 90s, while in Fig. 11.5 the sharp decline in banks' stockholdings ratio is observed. Although the two phenomena seem unrelated at first glance, both can be reasonably explained by considering that the Basel capital adequacy rule, which set the risk weight of treasury bonds against equity assets at zero, changed the behavior of Japanese main banks as discussed in Chap. 4. Decline in bank's shareholding ratio reflects the collapse of cross-shareholding structure

What does this mean? Almost one-fifth of the dividends to shareholders of Japanese companies are siphoned off each year by the foreign shareholders. Shareholders demand higher dividends as a matter of course. The quickest way to increase profits is to cut wage costs. Specifically, by demanding Japanese companies to switch their workers from regular to non-regular (part-time) employments. In this way, dividends have been quietly siphoned off into the pockets of international bankers and financiers, which in turn has impoverished Japanese households year after year. The fact that Japanese companies are now controlled by foreign shareholders by about 20% also indicates that Japan has been incorporated successfully into the network of global corporate control discussed in Chap. 10 after the burst of the bubble in the 1990s.[10]

In addition, the government has been forced to rely on borrowings from the Overseas Lenders for 12% of its debts as of 2019 (Fig. 11.4). In this way, Japan's private sector as well as the government are slowly getting controlled by international bankers and financiers through debt money system. This is the current situation of Japan in her lost 30 years. The more debts the government increases through MMT's anti-austerity and aggressive fiscal policies, the more it will be stuck in the hell of debts caused by the international bankers, who will wield more influence over the political process and public policy.

In this way, the Japanese economy will be largely controlled by the foreign capitals, and eventually Japan as a nation may also be destroyed. This is because the ultimate goal of the international bankers seems to be to put national governments under a global government with a single currency.[11] In this way, the more MMT is practiced, the more the economy will be dominated by the international money lenders, and the more our nations will be controlled. Isn't MMT exactly the "minion" of the globalists? To those who have unknowingly supported the MMT in Japan and elsewhere, wake up Now!

---

of Japanese keiretsu. It was foreign financial institutions who bought up Japanese stocks that these domestic sectors had unloaded after the burst of the bubble.

[10] Here we do not discuss the control of overseas shareholdings by the six macroeconomic sectors such as Japanese banks, securities companies, and corporations. Japan's foreign direct investment for the purpose of control is 183 trillion yen as of 2019, which is almost the same amount as the overseas sector's Japanese shareholdings of 189 trillion yen. With this fact, it could be argued that the shareholders of Japan's six macroeconomic sectors may have equal control over the overseas sector. However, that is a superficial argument that does not take into account the control structure of the global economy through stock ownership. For reference, Japanese foreign securities investment for the purpose of asset holding is 611 trillion yen.

[11] The notion of a single currency under the global government is not as far-fetched as one might think, given that many heads of the international banks and key organizations, including the IMF, have been publicly discussing the future for a single currency issued independently from national currencies for many years (Marshall, 2010; Chossudovsky and Marshall, 2010). According to them, such a fundamental change in the global monetary architecture, however, requires a "global financial crisis" as the pretext for more centralization of the current international financial system.

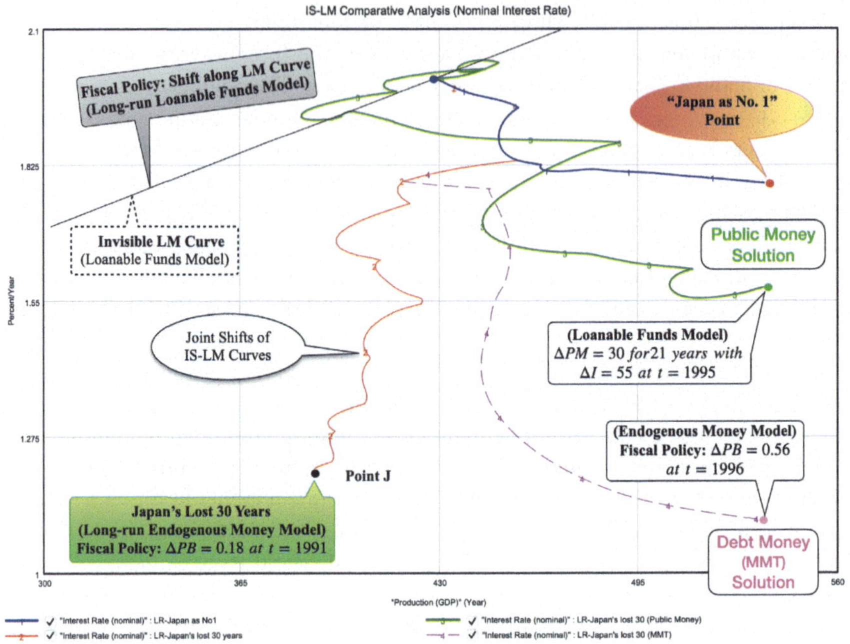

Fig. 11.6 Two solutions out of the point J (Japan's lost 30 years)

11.4 Which Is the Solution: Public Money or Debt Money (MMT)?

So far we have revealed seven false claims of MMT and concluded that Japan will be destroyed if MMT is practiced. That is, MMT cannot be the solution for Japan to get out of her lost 30 years. On the other hand, we have contended that public money can remove system design failures of debt money on which MMT is based; that is, public money must be the solution. In fact, since the publication of the Japanese books Yamaguchi (2015) and Yamaguchi and Yamaguchi (2021b), we have been posing the question: which is the solution to get out of the Japan's lost 30 years: MMT or Public Money?

In Chap. 8, we have completed the foundation model of paradigm shift in macroeconomics: the endogenous money ASD model. Let us try to answer this question by applying its latest version of the model: Long-Run Endogenous Money ASD model (Yamaguchi and Yamaguchi, 2023). Figure 11.6 is the phase diagram of production (GDP) and nominal interest rate obtained by the long-run model. Line 1 (in blue) is the growth path of "Japan as No.1", while line 2 (in red) is the path of "Japan's lost 30 years" by the joint shift of IS-LM curves.

With this phase diagram, our question above is now paraphrased as follows: How can we find a recovery path from Point J to the point of "Japan as No.1"? By running the long-run ASD model discussed in Chap. 8, we have found two possible solutions that could restore GDP to the level of "Japan as No.1" case as indicated in Table 11.1. The first solution called "Public Money Solution" is to issue public money to encourage private investment. As briefly discussed in Sect. 8.11.1 "Public Money System as Loanable Funds Case", loanable funds ASD model is used for this simulation, because the exogenous money model is applicable under the public money system. The other solution called "Debt Money (MMT) Solution" is to expand fiscal (deficit) spending further and more vigorously, as suggested by the proponents of MMT. To examine this second solution, the long-run endogenous money ASD model is used. Specifically, the government further increases the change in primary balance ratio by 0.38 (= 0.56-0.18) in year 1991.[12]

Utilizing parameter values as indicated in Table 11.1 we have run simulations and obtained two solution paths as illustrated in Fig. 11.6. Line 1 (in blue) is our goal of the Japan as No.1 growth path. Line 2 (in red) is the current Point J of Japan's lost 30 years. Line 3 (in green) is the public money solution, while line 4 (in dotted pink) is the debt money solution. As long as these two solutions are viewed in the phase diagram, both seem to restore the production (GDP) level of Japan as No. 1. Indeed, top left diagram of Fig. 11.7 confirms both solutions attain similar levels of production (GDP) around 2020, though recovery path is more cyclical under the public money solution (for reasons yet analyzed).

Using diagrams of price, money stock and government debts in Fig. 11.7, let us now compare behaviors of two solutions in more detail to find out which solution is workable and better. Let us examine the public money solution (lines 3 in green) first. As top right diagram illustrates, price fluctuates in the beginning but eventually gets stabilized. Money stock in the bottom left diagram continues to increase as public money is put into circulation, but eventually stops increasing at 2016. Government debts in the bottom right diagram does not increase at all and stays at zero throughout the period. This is simply because government does not need to borrow from banks under public money system. Instead, it can issue its own public money at interest-free. This is the public money solution we have proposed in the above-mentioned books.

Table 11.1 Two solutions out of Japan's lost 30 years

Public Money Solution (issue Public Money)	$\Delta PM = 30$ starting at t = 1995 for 21 years to subsidize $\Delta I = 55$ (until 2015)
Debt Money (MMT) Solution (increase Gov. Debts)	(Aggresive Fiscal Policy) $\Delta PB = 0.56$ ($\leftarrow$ 0.18) at t = 1991

[12] Recall from Sect. 8.13 that our long-run endogenous money ASD model assumed the primary balance ratio = 1.28 (= 1.1 + 0.18) in order to simulate the case of Japan's Lost 30 Years. Therefore, Δ PB = 0.56 means that the government's primary balance ratio is 1.66 (= 1.1 + 0.56), implementing a fiscal expansion of 1.66 times the current year's tax revenue.

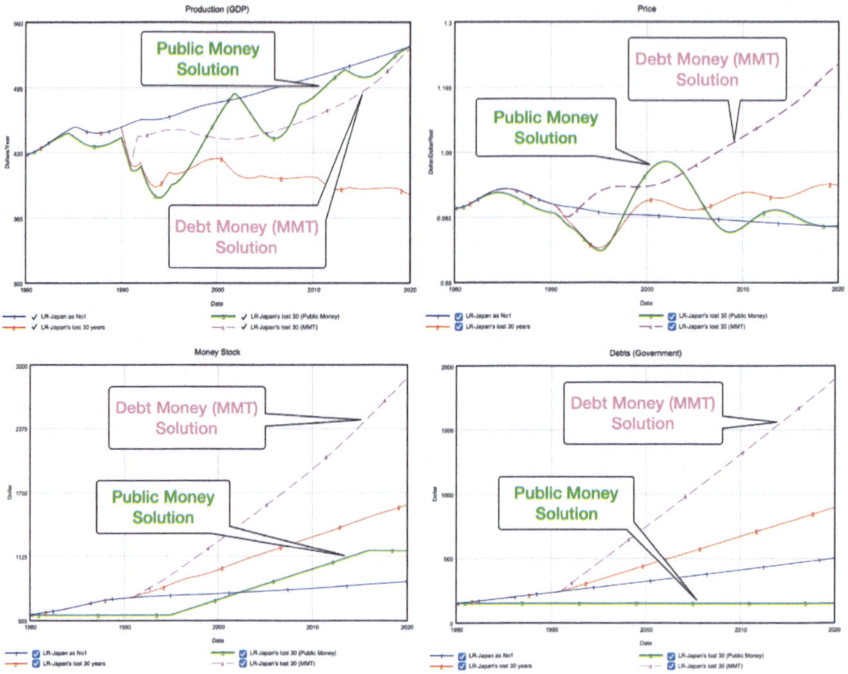

Fig. 11.7 Solutions of Japan's lost 30 years—GDP, price, money stock and government debts

On the other hand, MMT followers in Japan have claimed that Japan could have gotten out of the Lost 30 Years if the government had made more aggressive fiscal spending policy by issuing government bonds. To examine their claims we have run the long-run ASD model of endogenous money as shown in Fig. 11.7. Indeed, the debt money solution (lines 4 in dotted pink) demonstrates in the top left diagram that the production (GDP) gets restored to the level of Japan as No.1 (line 1 in blue). Hence, this debt money solution of MMT seems to be working as well as the public money solution. Yet, due to this debt money solution, money stock (line 4 in dotted pink) in the bottom left diagram continues to increase exponentially, which in turn causes rapid inflation as demonstrated by the price behavior in the top right diagram.

To be worse, government debts (line 4 in dotted pink) keep accumulating as shown in the bottom right diagram, driving government to a debt hell. This is consistent with the on-going "debt-hell" situations in Japan and the US as Figs. 6.1 and 6.2 show. These economies are indeed following the debt money (MMT) solution and experienced rapid inflation in recent years as a result of reckless fiscal expansion. Eventually the government is forced to levy higher taxes to pay interests to bankers, which in turn widens income inequality between bankers and non-bankers. In short, debt money (MMT) solution is shown here to be unsustainable and inequitable. The failures have been already analyzed as the critical flaws of MMT in Yamaguchi and Yamaguchi (2021b, Chap. 3). The failures are now comprehensively demonstrated by the long-run endogenous money ASD model. Though our model is simple and generic, it has proven that debt money (MMT) solution as a typical Keynesian fiscal policy is shown to be flawed and cannot be a sustainable macroeconomic policy.

Summary: MMT Hides System Design Failures of Debt Money

We have so far demonstrated that the seven claims of MMT are all false, and analyzed a new (4th) scenario that our nations will be destroyed eventually if MMT is practiced. In a nutshell, MMT is a false theory that hides system design failures of debt money by defining corporate, household, and government debts (borrowing from banks) as the issuance of money (IOUs). What are the system design failures of debt money? They are summarized as the following four points (Yamaguchi, 2013, Chap. 20).

1. Fractional reserve banking ("counterfeiting money") system endogenously creates debt money out of nothing and destroys it, which makes the money supply unstable and repeatedly causes business cycles such as inflation (bubble), deflation (depression), and unemployment.
2. Debt money system increases government debts and forces fiscal austerities such as consumption tax hikes and welfare budget cuts in order to repay the debt, afflicting the people and depriving their nation of its wealth. Public debts grow exponentially, eventually leading to the debt-end.
3. Compound interest on private and public debts create a financial system in which the rich ("1%") become richer, resulting in the built-in unfair income inequality in favor of 1%.
4. To pay for the principal and compound interest on debts, producers are forced to expand their production at the cost of environmental preservation. The forced reproduction will destroy the earth's ecosystem, leading to an unsustainable society and destructive futures of our planet.

These system design failures cannot be overcome as long as the policy of debt money by MMT is practiced. To overcome these design failures, we must transform the current system and make transition to the public money system.

11.5 MMT's Job Guarantee Program as "Fixes That Fail"

As if MMT is aware of the economic and social problems caused by the system design failures of debt money, its proponents have also proposed policies to overcome them. Its typical policy is "employer of last resort" program, also called "Job Guarantee Program" Wray (2012, p. 221). Main features of this program are the following two points:

(1) Government spending under this program increases during recessions and decreases during booms, thereby playing a role of built-in economic stabilizer.
(2) Wages paid under this program will function as a *de facto* minimum wage and improve working conditions in the private sectors.

This socialist (leftist) employment program, which supposedly "guarantees full employment and minimum wages" at all times, sounds like a great policy proposal and universally appealing. So what is the problem with this program?

Problem 1: Job Guarantee Program Is A Symptomatic Treatment.

Why does unemployment, especially involuntary unemployment, always occur in the first place? MMT does not try to address the root cause of the problem, but rather assumes that if unemployment occurs, it is sufficient for the government to provide temporal relief by hiring people and rescue them. This is a symptomatic treatment based on an event-level analysis of the problem, which is often pointed out in systems thinking as "Fixes That Fail" archetype. In fact, such symptom-correcting "quick fix" is known to exacerbate the problem. As the first of four design failures, we have pointed out that debt money system is a system that causes business cycles persistently such as inflation, deflation (recession) and unemployment. We have obtained simulation results that this business cycles can be mitigated by transitioning to public money system (Yamaguchi, 2013, Chap. 18). In other words, the transition from debt money to public money system is the fundamental solution that overcomes the pitfalls of macroeconomic management by symptomatic treatment.

Problem 2: Job Guarantee Program Increases Government Debts and Leads to Default.

What kind of jobs will the government provide through this program? The well-known critique of Keynesian fiscal policy is that it ends up offering the unemployed workers jobs akin to digging a hole to pay for them in times of a recession. Jobs that the government provides during a recession are more or less unproductive jobs like this. In such cases, the policy appears to be effective because it temporarily fills the output gap and increases employment. Yet, behind it is the continuous accumulation of government debt and most of them would be wasteful without contributing to the GDP growth. Such useless fiscal policy were the root cause of the Japan's lost 30 years. Politicians and finance bureaucrats may have felt satisfied that they were doing a good job of stimulating the economy with annual fiscal stimulus packages. However, as a result of this policy, the debt-to-GDP ratio has risen to an astonishing 250% by 2021 according to the OECD data. MMT might argue again that there is no problem here because government debt is an increase in private sector assets. But we have already refuted this falsehood above.

MMT calls this program the Green New Deal, referring to the New Deal policy proposed by the President Roosevelt (Democrat) after the Great Depression. Although it sounds appealing, it is essentially not different from the unproductive policies of Keynesian hole-digging. Implementing such wasteful policies will surely create another nightmare of "lost 40 years" in Japan, in which only government debts will increase while GDP stagnates. In contrast, the policy proposed under the public money system is an economic revitalization program that centers on supporting private companies in turning non-regular (part-time) employees into regular employees through subsidies and tax incentives provided by public money, thereby stimulating private-sector business activity, not the public sector or banks. At the same time, it is a program to support the industrial transformation necessary to achieve sustainable and equitable growth. Details are discussed in Chap. 14 with causal loop diagrams.

Problem 3: Job Guarantee Program Stops Innovation and Stalls Society.

This job guarantee program advocated by MMT, in a sense, creates an unproductive and lazy society, just like the one caused by the "universal basic income". Who, among the workers employed by the government's job guarantee program, is willing to take leadership and risks, and innovate? The more passive the work environment gets, the less entrepreneurial, risk-taking, and change-making motivation will emerge from such workplaces. MMT's Job Guarantee Program is just another money pit. As already mentioned, this will eventually plunge the government deeper and deeper into debt hell, and the economy will head toward hyperinflation and default. The cure is worse than the disease!

There is also a danger that the government will eventually control people's life. As with the basic income, when people become dependent on the government for their jobs and income, they are less likely to disobey the authority, making it easier for the government to control the people. Thus, power will become more concentrated in the hands of the government. On the other hand, the public money policy that we propose in Chap. 14 will spur innovation, promote welfare, and generate national progress. It is a policy that encourages strategic investment in areas such as the following categories:

- Public investment in education and research as human and future investment including tuition-free higher education system.
- Investment for constructing 21st century infrastructures such as advanced IT networks, decentralized web, sustainable energies, and safer transportation system.
- Universal medical and healthcare and other social welfare programs.

Problem 4: Job Guarantee Program Treats Labor Market as a Part of Exchange Markets of Goods and Services.

Why does unemployment occur in the first place? Public money system proposes a fundamental system design to build a society in which such unemployment does not occur. The root cause of unemployment is that labor market is linked to the goods and services market, so that once an imbalance occurs in the goods and services market, then workers are laid off simultaneously. What if labor were not exchanged in the market as it is in the goods and services market?

Suppose, for example, employees working in a small family-owned business. In this case, even if sales temporarily decline due to the recession, employees, as members of the family, would not be immediately laid off and become unemployed. Examples of these family-owned types of organization in a large scale are cooperative business enterprises (Coops), ESOP (Employee Stock Ownership Plan) companies, and many Japanese companies that practiced Japanese management of life-time employment. As we have analyzed Chap. 4, the collapse of bubbles caused by the debt money system has led to the abandonment of Japanese management, and shifted into non-regular employment, which eventually stagnated consumption, and caused the Japanese economy into the lost 30 years.

Haven't we somehow been brainwashed by economics to accept the labor market as a natural part of the market economy, where human labor is bought and sold like slaves? Western economic textbooks have built their theories on goods and services and the labor market as interchangeable markets all on the same level. For instance, labor is considered to be painful and leisure is pleasure, but since workers cannot obtain leisure without selling their labor, they regard labor as a necessary pain to bear. On the other hand, corporate managers can dismiss workers easily as if they were disposing of their assets or goods. As a result, wages are the price of labor (pain), and managers can force workers to do any kind of labor (pain) as long as they are paid for it. And those wages are determined by the supply and demand in the labor market. If workers want to be employed, they must accept low wages. People all over the world are now heavily influenced and brainwashed by such market principles of Western microeconomics.

On the contrary, labor used to be regarded in Japan not as pains, but as the path to self-salvation and bliss through the concentration on the productive work. Workers put all their energy into improving the quality of products they produce and services they provide. They believed that focusing on their productive works (as dynamic Zen) is the way of reaching self-salvation and obtaining bliss in life. On the other hand, managers also used to work hard every day, believing that providing better work environment is their right path ("Tao") of management to their self-salvation and bliss. Kaoru grew up being surrounded by these Zen-like or Japanese view of work environment and ethics. He spent his youth during the period of economic growth when Japan rose again from the ruins after World War II, followed by the income doubling era from 1960 to 1970 (with average annual growth rate of 7–8%), and the era of high economic growth from 1971 to 1990 (with average growth rate of 4–5%). Indeed, he grew up in an environment where the Japanese management (lifetime employment, seniority system, strong employee benefits, etc.) has been everywhere as a natural way of life.

As such, he still cannot forget the shock he received in his graduate course of microeconomics at Berkeley. In the class he was taught that labor, like goods and services, can be exchanged in the market any time, and workers can be fired whenever they are no longer needed. The labor market environment in the U.S. seemed to have become a battlefield, as proposed by microeconomic theories. Rather, it would be more accurate to describe that microeconomics is the study of economics that reflects this modern-day slavery-like labor market directly into the field of economics. In other words, economics has been charged with legitimizing and brainwashing innocent students to accept the reality of this disposable labor where bankers and financiers can exploit labor as they wish through their monopoly power of money.

Kaoru was not even aware of the existence of such an American-style labor market until he came to Berkeley to study economics. He was indeed ignorant at the time and believed that Japanese management practice was a universal practice such that once new graduates are hired by companies, they will be employed for life and can work there for the rest of their life if they wish so. The American-style labor market and the microeconomic theories that reflect it were a great intellectual shock to him while he was studying in the United States. Since then, he began to ask himself whether he should construct an economic model based on the view that labor is the source of suffering and wages are its compensation, or whether labor is the path to self-salvation and bliss and wages are the reward and fruits for those who seek such a path. As an academic economist, the task of modeling labor and its market became a heavy and painful choice.

When the theory of public money was finally completed, he was relieved of this burden. Labor is by no means a part of exchange markets at the same level as goods and services. He became convinced that labor must be the path to bliss through self-salvation. It can be practiced and must be realized with a new system design of public money. This is our vision of new national economic rebuilding. With public money, we must liberate people who have been brainwashed by economists under the influence of international bankers. From the next chapter we will discuss how to achieve this economic rebuilding and Make All Nations Great Again (MANGA).

Part III
Solution

Chapter 12
Transition to Public Money System

In Part I and II we have broken the taboo of economics and analyzed how the Debt Money System has been the root cause of various socioeconomic problems locally and globally. According to the scientific method of system dynamics, problems that repeat and persist over time are caused by the underlying system structure. How can we fix this system design failure, then? The conclusion drawn from our analyses in Part II was that a transition to the Public Money System can solve these problems. In other words, the emphasis is on the system *redesign*. This chapter explains the process of system transition based on macroeconomic balance sheets of Japanese economy as an example.[1]

12.1 Three Goals of System Transition

Prerogative to Issue Currency as Public Money

Who should issue money in place of the privately-owned central bank and commercial banks? The right to determine the unit and media (form) of money, to issue it, and to regulate its quantity has been the indispensable power historically granted to the state, along with legislative, administrative, and judicial powers. Thus, the issuance of legal tender as public money is the prerogative of the government that represents the public under the separation of powers.

The Constitution of Japan enacted after the World War II similarly established the legislature (Diet), the executive government (Cabinet), and the judiciary (Supreme

[1] Yamaguchi (2013, Chap. 21) provides a generic description of transition process from debt money to public money system. Readers are suggested to obtain monetary data of their local economies and apply the Japanese case described in this chapter to their home countries.

K. Yamaguchi and Y. Yamaguchi, *Public Money*,
https://doi.org/10.1007/978-981-97-6564-5_12

Court). However, the Constitution, which was outlined by the GHQ (as discussed in Chap. 4), does not stipulate which branch of the government possesses the monetary power and issue its national currency. It may come as a surprise that the monetary system, on which the system of government is built, is not stipulated in the Japanese Constitution.[2]

On the other hand, Section 8 of Article 1 of the Constitution of the United States grants the power to issue money to the legislature as follows:

> The Congress shall have Power to lay and collect taxes, . . . , to coin money, regulate the Value thereof, and of foreign Coin, and fix the Standard of Weights and Measures; . . .

However, under the Federal Reserve Act enacted in 1913, the sovereign monetary power of the US has been hijacked by the Federal Reserve System.

Likewise, the Constitution of the Republic of Turkey (founded on October 29, 1925) stipulates the power and authority to determine the issuance of money along with other rights granted to the legislature. Thus, in Turkey, where Kaoru used to teach in Ankara until recently, the power to issue money is vested in the parliament, yet the exclusive power to issue banknotes is currently delegated to the central bank under the Turkish central bank law.

In this sense, Japan's current Constitution has a major loophole regarding the fourth power of the state, i.e., the right to issue and regulate nation's currency. Consequently, as if to fill the void left in the separation of power, the debt money system has been established in Japan where an independent central bank, which is nothing more than an authorized corporation granted with banking license under the Bank of Japan Act, issues most of the nation's currency (M_0) and controls the financial system. Therefore, it is reasonable for Japan to specify the right to manage its own currency under the legislature in its constitution. However, it is also possible to make the transition under the current laws without making the constitutional amendment.

Three Goals of System Transition

How can we achieve a smooth transition to public money system? There are three major steps in achieving this goal:

1. Establish the Public Money Administration (PMA) under the legislature. Then, nationalize the central bank and merge it into the Ministry of Public Money (MPM) that is newly established under the executive branch.
2. Raise the required reserve ratio to 100% for all demand deposits of banks.

---

[2] During the postwar Japan there was also consideration of stipulating the authority of the Diet (legislature) to issue currency in Article 76 of the MacArthur Draft. However, Article 76 of the MacArthur Draft was ultimately rejected (Watanabe, 2012, p. 29). In any case Japan's monetary system has developed around the old Currency Act, enacted in 1897, and currently instituted under the "Act on Currency Unit and Issuance of Coins" (Act No. 42 of 1987), which replaced the old Currency Act (Act No.16 of 1897); and the Bank of Japan Act (Act No. 89 of 1997).

3. The PMA regulates the total quantity of money in circulation in order to stabilize prices (rate of inflation) within a range set forth by the law.[3]

Reorganization of Monetary Authority

Under the debt money system, the central bank (monetary policy committee) determines the level of interest rates in an effort to stabilize prices and the economy. Under the public money system, the Public Money Administration (PMA) determines the total quantity of money stock. In its regular meetings, the PMA reviews economic and financial conditions and assesses the potential risks of supplying (expanding) new money against its long-run goals of price stability. Specifically, the PMA decides how much new money to issue to meet the budget deficit when fiscal expenditures exceed revenues or how much money to withdraw from circulation when revenues exceed expenditures.

As the first goal of system transition, therefore, the Bank of Japan (BoJ) will be nationalized and integrated into the Ministry of Public Money, which will be in charge of implementing public money policy decided by the PMA. As discussed in Chap. 2, the BoJ is currently an authorized corporation whose 55% of its capital stock is owned by the government (Ministry of Finance) and the rest is listed on the Tokyo Stock Exchange. This peculiar nature of the BoJ (as an independent central bank) has been the source of uncertainty in the conduct of national economic policies. Therefore, to eliminate this dysfunctional element in the current organizational structure, the BoJ will be delisted immediately after the government acquired 100% of its shares, dissolved in accordance with Article 60 of the Bank of Japan Act, and promptly incorporated into the Ministry of Public Money during the initial phase of the transition.

The Ministry of Public Money (MPM) to be created for this transition is a new administrative body established under the executive branch (the Cabinet of Japan) by merging the BoJ's head office in Tokyo, local branch offices as well as foreign offices in New York, London, Paris, etc. The MPM will take over the current departments of the BoJ and their business operations as they are. Thus, all BoJ employees will become public servants at this point and their employment status will be changed to those of national government employees.

The financial assets, liabilities, and net assets currently held by the BoJ will be transferred to the MPM as deemed necessary and appropriate. At this point the BoJ will be transformed into the Public Money Vault (PMV) discussed in Chap. 11. Note that the treasury operations, which are now handled by the BoJ at the instruction of the Ministry of Finance (MoF), will be carried out within the PMV's balance sheet managed by the MPM, not by the MoF. This division of tasks, administrative areas and procedures is critical in ensuring transparency and accountability through

[3] Yamaguchi (2015) proposed the Public Money Act in the original Japanese book. However, the details of the law will differ from country to country. Therefore, we did not translate the draft of the bill in this book, which was tailored to the Japanese legal setting.

regular oversights by the legislature concerning the responsible implementation of monetary policy decided by the independent PMA.

In summary, monetary authorities in the current debt money system will be reorganized in the public money system as follows:

Monetary Policy Committee ⇒ Public Money Administration (PMA)
Bank of Japan (Central Bank) ⇒ Ministry of Public Money (MPM)
BoJ's Regional & Foreign Offices ⇒ Local Currency Bureau of MPM

MPM assists the PMA in the conduct of monetary policy and all other tasks necessary to accomplish its duties, including banking supervision, publications of policy committee minutes and economic statistics formerly compiled and published by the Bank of Japan. Other departments of MPM will be in charge of production and circulation of physical coins, notes and Electronic Public Money (EPM), which will be detailed in the next Chap. 13.

To compare implementations of the public money system in Japan and the US, the Federal Reserve System is the equivalent of the Bank of Japan, Federal Open Market Committee (FOMC) is the equivalent of the BoJ's Monetary Policy Committee, the twelve regional Federal Reserve Banks (FRB) are the equivalent of the BoJ's regional branch offices, and the United States Department of the Treasury is the equivalent of the Ministry of Finance of Japan.

Accordingly, monetary authorities of the US would be reorganized as follows:

Federal Open Market Committee ⇒ Public Money Administration
Federal Reserve System ⇒ Department of Public Money (DPM)
Federal Reserve Banks (FRB) ⇒ Local Currency Bureau of DPM

The name such as "PMA" is not particularly important. It could also be called "Currency Commission" as Fisher did, or "Public Money Policy Committee". What is important is the governance system that ensures the independence of the PMA from other branches of the government or any other private entities.

Members of the Public Money Administration

Figure 12.1 illustrates the governance structure of the public money system in the Japanese implementation case. First, the Diet shown at the top assigns (as the highest organ of state power) the authority to issue legal tender to the PMA. For separation of powers, PMA must be established as an independent committee under the legislature. This governance mechanism ensures the commission is isolated from daily political pressures while avoiding fiscal dominance by other branches of government in fulfilling price stability objective.

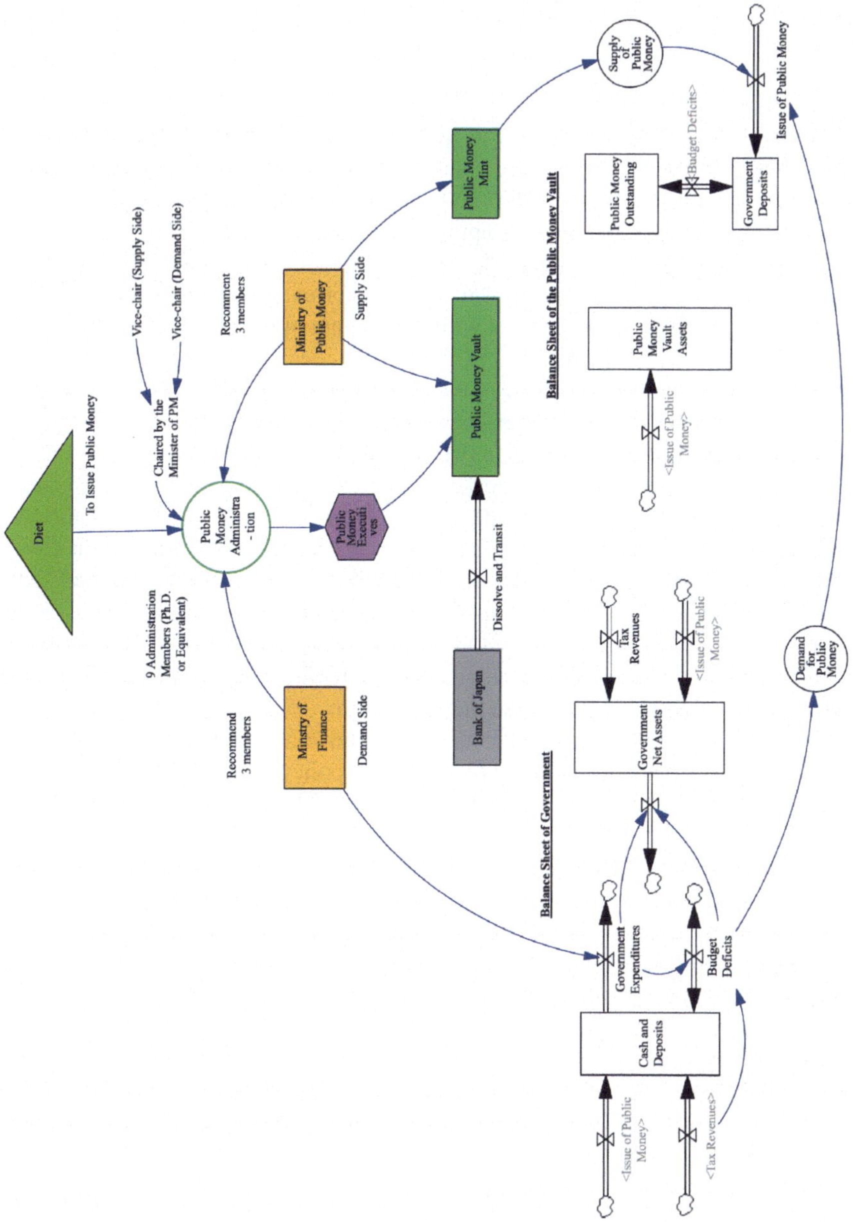

Fig. 12.1 Organizational structure of the public money system

Just as important as the independence of PMA is its internal structure and division of roles that balance the power within the monetary policy committee. In the proposed implementation for Japan, the PMA is composed of nine members, which is the same number as the current BoJ's Monetary Policy Committee. The PMA is chaired by the Minister of Public Money, who is the head of the MPM. The chair of PMA has a fixed-term of 5 years (renewable; same for other members) and cannot be removed once in office unlike other ministers.

There will also be two deputy chairs in the PMA, each selected from the Ministry of Public Money (MPM) and Ministry of Finance (MoF). Of the remaining six members, three will be nominated by the MPM and three by the MoF, respectively. All nine voting-members of the PMA are to be appointed by the government (Cabinet) as soon as the post opens. And the Diet must discuss and approve the candidates before their final appointments.[4] This is no different from the current procedure where the BoJ Governor is appointed by the Cabinet with the consent of the House of Councillors and the House of Representatives.

Such member composition creates a clear division of role within the policy committee and the administrative domains they represent. In other words, the two deputy chairs will represent the demand side (MoF) and supply side (MPM) of the PMA respectively, and be responsible for the decisions on the final amount of public money to be issued or withdrawn from circulation jointly.[5] Specifically, the four members on the supply side (vice-chair and three members nominated by MPM) and the four members responsible for the demand side (vice-chair and three members nominated by MoF) would sit in a round table and discuss the appropriate amount to be issued or withdrawn based on the fiscal data submitted by the demand side. This separation of PMA into the demand and supply sides is the first condition of governance mechanism required under the public money system.

As a second condition to ensure the responsible governance, transparency of both information and decision processes of public money policy has to be fully guaranteed to the public. In particular, the demand side of the PMA needs to publicly disclose all fiscal information to justify their demand for additional money issuance (in the case of fiscal deficit). Macroeconomic simulation models that form the basis of committee discussions should be made available for public scrutiny. By incorporating the administrative areas of MPM and MoF into the organizational structure of the PMA, the appropriate amount of public money that contributes to the welfare of society and economic growth will be determined in an open forum (under the watchful eye of the public). The chairperson of the PMA acts as the facilitator of this process but takes the lead (as the Minister of Public Money) only when the debate is so heated that the vote becomes a four-way tie. Under such cases, the chairperson will be ultimately responsible for the total supply of money to be injected or withdrawn.

---

[4] As the criteria for potential candidates of PMA members, candidates must hold doctoral degrees or have equivalent academic backgrounds in the related fields.

[5] To reflect interests of the entire society, non-voting members may be additionally commissioned to participate in the PMA discussion and report on the state of business as representatives from various sectors of the economy, including agriculture, manufacturing, and non-financial service sectors.

The Resignation Clause of Public Money Act

Handing over the right to issue money to the government would be so dangerous it would lead to hyperinflation. Take a look at the history of hyperinflation in Weimar Republic during 1921–23 and the more recent case of Zimbabwe during 2007–09. The Economics and Banking establishment has long argued that this is why central banks should manage the currency instead of the national governments. However, as the history of the Great Depression, the Japanese bubble, and even the on-going expansion of money stock in the US and Japan (Figs. 3.3 and 3.4) shows, it is precisely in the debt money system that a stable money supply as required by the real economy cannot be achieved. In other words, the rationale for *central bank independence* is nowhere to be found, either theoretically or empirically.[6]

One may still wonder what will happen if, hypothetically, excessive money is issued under the public money system? We cannot eliminate the possibility of collusion between the supply side and the demand side. How can we insert additional layer of safety mechanism to prevent unintended inflation? The public money system has a built-in mechanism to stop excessive currency issuance through what we call "inflation resignation clause". Specifically, to guarantee price stability even under such possibility, a third governance condition must be clearly stated as in the Article 8 of the Public Money Act proposed in Yamaguchi (2015):

> Minister of Public Money shall resign, without exception, whenever the rate of inflation as measured by core CPI overshoots beyond the inflation target range as set forth in this act (e.g. ±5%) for 5 consecutive months compared with a corresponding period of the previous year.

The choice of specific index such as Consumer Price Index (CPI), the specific items and composition of the price index, the tolerance range of price fluctuation (±5% in the example), and the consecutive tolerance period (5 months) shall be determined by the legislature when it passes the Public Money Act on the basis of domestic economic conditions.

It is also possible to set multiple levels of inflation tolerance ranges (e.g. two levels), with a longer tolerance period (e.g. 5 months) for the smaller range (±5%) and a shorter tolerance period (e.g. 3 months) for the larger range (±10%). This would give an early signal to the policy committee members to take precautionary measures as soon as the latest inflation rate breaks the lower inflation target range, even if a majority of PMA members are reluctant ("doves") to curb inflation.

If the chairperson does not resign in violation of the price stability clause, then, the Minister of Public Money (as the chair of PMA) may be impeached in accordance with a resolution of the legislature. To make such a clause more certain of its effectiveness, it may be possible to have not only the chairperson to resign, but

---

[6] There are literatures analyzing the correlation between "central bank independence" (although its definition varies by authors) and inflation or economic growth, etc. However, they do not show (nor base their arguments on) causal relationships, nor do they analyze the structural fragility brought about under the debt money system.

also the two vice chairs at the same time. This could further weaken the potential collusion between the supply and demand sides of the PMA.

Some may prefer that the Public Money Act itself should automatically trigger the resignation clause without going through such a roundabout procedure. The potential risk of providing for the compulsory resignation by law is that the price statistics on which such a decision depends may be manipulated (just as electoral voting system in some of the most economically advanced nations are not entirely free from human errors and potential manipulation). Therefore, one idea to avoid such risk in Japan's bicameral legislature would be to have the Minister of Public Money dismissed by a joint special resolution of both the House of Councillors (six-year term, no dissolution) and the House of Representatives (four-year term, subject to dissolution) as an additional safety mechanism to ensure stability even under such extreme case of distrust and failure.[7]

We have presented how to establish the public money system using Japan as an example. Readers are encouraged to apply the institutional framework discussed above, or tailor it to meet with particular needs of their countries. In terms of regulating monetary power under the constitutional government, it must be the legislature that ultimately holds accountable for failures of monetary policy. Since the legislature is represented by the constituents through voting, the public money system would bring monetary power back to the control of *We the people*. In this way, public money system would achieve a mechanism of governance that is the exact opposite of the current debt money system controlled by the vested interests. This will set the institutional foundation for the system transition, which is described below.[8]

12.2 System Transition Process

Let us now turn our focus on the process of transition based on Japanese macroeconomic balance sheets. To do so, it is necessary to classify the economic entities and

---

[7] Article 69 of the Japanese Constitution states: "If the House of Representatives passes a non-confidence resolution, or rejects a confidence resolution, the Cabinet shall resign en masse, unless the House of Representatives is dissolved within ten (10) days."

[8] In case of a monetary union such as the Eurozone, two directions are generally envisioned for the system transition: (1) the monetary authority of the European Central Bank (ECB) is returned to each member state, or (2) transfer the ECB's authority under the European Parliament while maintaining the monetary union. Case 1 is in effect a disintegration of the eurozone, which involves reconfigurations of its payment and settlement systems. Given that 20 years have passed since the economic integration, Case 2 may be considered preferable option in terms of ease of the transition. In case 2, however, the EU member states will need to be politically integrated into, say, the United States of Europe, which in turn establishes its own pan-European federal government and federalize the ECB into its executive branch. Which direction to be adopted is a matter of political decision by voters in each member state. Some EU citizens prefer less centralization of power into the government while others prefer it. Case 1 will be achieved by implementing three conditions of public money system at each nation state, while case 2 will be achieved by implementing them at the EU level.

group them into four sectors: public money vault, government, banks, and private sector (households and producers), and describe the flow of funds among these four sectors. We will therefore create a balance sheet for each sector capturing their financial assets, liabilities, and net assets in line with the state of the Japanese economy as of 2018, and discuss changes in their balance sheet as we take the following seven transition processes. The numerical numbers attached to each account item on the balance sheets correspond to the transition process numbers listed below.[9]

(0) The End of the Debt Money System (Financial Balance Sheets as of 2018).
(1) Exchange 100 Trillion Yen of Bank of Japan Notes in Circulation for newly issued Public Money (Notes and EPM) with a 10% premium.
(2) Create Government Deposits (assets) by issuing 1,000 Trillion Yen of Public Money as Net Assets.
(3) Redeem 500 Trillion Yen of Government Bonds held by Bank of Japan with Government Deposits.
(4) Redeem 200 Trillion Yen of Government Bonds held by Banks with Government Deposits.
(5) Redeem 300 Trillion Yen of Government Bonds held by Private Sector with Government Deposits.
(6) Secure 100% Reserves of Banks through Public Money Lending Facility
(7) Birth of Public Money System as A New Nation (Transition completed)

(0) The End of the Debt Money System (Balance Sheets as of 2018)

The classification of money in Fig. 2.1 shows the total amount of money in Japan as of 2018 as follows.

$$\begin{aligned}
\text{Base Money } M_0 &= \text{Cash} + \text{Reserve Deposits} \\
&= 112 \text{ trillion yen} + 394 \text{ trillion yen} \\
&= 506 \text{ trillion yen} \\
\text{Money Stock } M_1 &= \text{Cash} + \text{Demand Deposits} \\
&= 112 \text{ trillion yen} + 719 \text{ trillion yen} \\
&= 831 \text{ trillion yen} \\
\text{Money Stock } M_3 &= \text{Money Stock } M_1 + \text{Time Deposits} \\
&= 831 \text{ trillion yen} + 595 \text{ trillion yen} \\
&= 1,426 \text{ trillion yen}
\end{aligned}$$

Of Japan's total money stock (M_3) of 1,426 trillion yen, 1,421 trillion yen (99.7%) is debt money, and public money (coins) only constitutes about 5 trillion yen (0.3%) as part of cash. As we have analyzed in Chap. 4, the existence of this debt money

[9] Since the original chapter in the Japanese book (Yamaguchi and Yamaguchi, 2021b) was written in 2019, monetary data for the economy as of 2018 were used for numerical examples.

is the root cause of virtually all the economic problems that became evident during Japan's Lost 30 Years. In this chapter, we will discuss how this debt money can be readily replaced and transformed into public money as if by magic. To that end, let us begin by considering how the debt money has been created out of nothing. To simplify our discussion, let us round down the fractional amount of debt money into the following figures.

$$\begin{aligned}\text{Base Money } M_0 &= \text{Cash} + \text{Reserve Deposits}\\ &= 100 \text{ trillion yen} + 400 \text{ trillion yen}\\ &= 500 \text{ trillion yen}\\ \text{Money Stock } M_1 &= \text{Cash} + \text{Demand Deposits}\\ &= 100 \text{ trillion yen} + 700 \text{ trillion yen}\\ &= 800 \text{ trillion yen}\\ \text{Money Stock } M_3 &= \text{Money Stock } M_1 + \text{Time Deposits}\\ &= 800 \text{ trillion yen} + 600 \text{ trillion yen}\\ &= 1,400 \text{ trillion yen}\end{aligned}$$

The balance sheets in Fig. 12.2 are created by simplifying account items of each sector into financial assets and liabilities corresponding to the issuance of debt money based on the above figures. Let us begin our discussion of the transition process by briefly explaining these balance sheets and looking at how Japan's debt money (bank deposits) was created out of nothing.

Bank of Japan The BoJ has issued 500 trillion yen of base money (M_0) as a result of its corresponding purchase of 500 trillion yen of JGBs (financial assets) from banks through regular open market operations and the large-scale asset purchase program (QE) since 2013. Of this amount, 100 trillion yen is circulating as BoJ notes, and the remaining 400 trillion yen is held in reserve deposits from banks.

Banks Based on the reserve deposits of 400 trillion yen deposited with the Bank of Japan, banks have created demand deposits of 700 trillion yen and lent to the private sector. If the current required reserve ratio is 1%, banks could lend up to 40,000 trillion yen. Therefore, as long as there is a demand for funds from the private sector, banks can lend (create deposits) almost unlimited amount to the private sector (ignoring other regulations, such as capital adequacy requirement). This fractional reserve banking system is the root cause of current financial instability. Banks also hold government bonds of 200 trillion yen as financial assets, which they have purchased by lending the same amount to the government.

Government The government's accumulated debts are 1,000 trillion yen, of which 500 trillion yen are owed to the Bank of Japan, 200 trillion yen to the banks, and 300 trillion yen to the private sector (mainly insurance and other non-banking financial

Bank of Japan B/S

Assets		Liabilities	
(0) Gov.Bonds	500	100	(0) Banknotes
		400	(0) Reserves
		0	(0) Gov.Deposits
		Net Assets (= 0)	
		0	(0) Initial Net Assets
(0) Total Assets	500		

Banks B/S

Assets		Liabilities	
(0) Reserves	400	700	(0) Demand Deposits
(0) Gov.Bonds	200	600	(0) Time Deposits
(0) Bank Loans	700	Net Assets (= 0)	
		0	(0) Initial Net Assets
(0) Total Assets	1,300		

Total Net Asset: 0 (= - 1,000 + 1,000)

Government B/S

Assets		Liabilities	
(0) Gov.Deposits	0	1,000	(0) Bonds Issuance
		Net Assets (= -1,000)	
		-1,000	(0) Initial Net Assets
(0) Total Assets	0		

Private (Households & Producers) B/S

Assets		Liabilities	
(0) Banknotes	100	700	(0) Debts by Banks
(0) Demand Deposits	700		
(0) Time Deposits	600	Net Assets (= 1,000)	
(0) Gov.Bonds	300	1,000	(0) Initial Net Assets
(0) Total Assets	1,700		

M0 = 100 + 400 = 500
M1 = 100 + 700 = 800
M3 = 100 + 700 + 600 = 1,400

Fig. 12.2 Balance sheets of Japan's financial assets and liabilities in 2018

institutions). As a result, the government's net financial assets are negative 1,000 trillion yen. If the interest rate on government bonds is 1%, an additional budget of 10 trillion yen (about 80,000 yen per capita) would be required ever year for interest payments. The government collects this amount through taxes and pays 70% of it as interest to the Bank of Japan and banks as interest every year.[10]

Private (Households & Producers) The private sector borrows 700 trillion yen from banks to obtain 700 trillion yen as demand deposits, which, together with 100 trillion yen in BoJ notes, is used to settle daily transactions to the tune of 800 trillion yen. This total amount constitutes money stock M_1 in Japan. In addition, the private sector holds 600 trillion yen in time deposits. The sum of M_1 and time deposits becomes 1,400 trillion yen, which is the total money stock M_3. The private sector also holds another 300 trillion yen in financial assets in the form of government bonds, which it has lent to the government. The private sector's total financial assets are 1,700 trillion yen, and after subtracting debts from banks, the private sector's financial net worth is 1,000 trillion yen.

The above balance sheet analysis of financial assets and liabilities reveals the following characteristics and essence of the debt money system.

[10] Interest payments are omitted from the financial asset balance sheet prepared here. If readers are interested in the relationship between interest and built-in income inequality in detail, please refer to Yamaguchi (2013, Chap. 9) titled "Interest and Equity", and Yamaguchi and Yamaguchi (2024).

Essence of Debt Money System (1): Money Stock As Total Debts

$$
\begin{aligned}
\text{Money Stock } M_3 &= 1,400 \text{ trillion yen} \\
&= \text{Total Private and Government Debts from Banks} \\
&= 700 \text{ trillion yen} + 700 \text{ trillion yen}
\end{aligned}
$$

Of the total government debts outstanding (1,000 trillion yen), the debt from banks is 700 trillion yen after deducting the debt from the private sector (= 1,000 − 300 trillion yen). The total debts of 1,400 trillion yen, which is the sum of this 700 trillion yen of government debt and the private sector's debts of 700 trillion yen from banks, is equal to the Japan's total money stock M_3. As we have already demonstrated in Chap. 3, "Your money is someone's debts". In other words, debt money is created out of nothing at interest by someone's borrowing from banks. Conversely, if no one borrows money, the money necessary for economic activity will not be created. Once the debts are paid off, the money disappears and economic activity stops.

Essence of Debt Money System (2): Total Financial Net Asset is 0

$$
\begin{aligned}
&\text{Total Financial Net Assets} \\
&\quad = \text{Bank of Japan (0 trillion yen)} + \text{Banks (0 trillion yen)} \\
&\qquad + \text{Government } (-1,000 \text{ tril. yen}) + \text{Private Sector } (1,000 \text{ tril. yen}) \\
&\quad = 0 \text{ trillion yen}
\end{aligned}
$$

The total financial net assets of the Japanese economy as a whole will be 0. In other words, if the debt money system is laid bare in a simplified balance sheet of financial assets and liabilities as in Fig. 12.2, it is exposed as an enormous zero-sum game where someone's financial assets are someone's financial liabilities. The more the net assets (interest income) of the BoJ and banking sector increases, the more the private sector's net assets decrease through tax collection. Income inequality and wealth concentration are built-in as system design (Yamaguchi and Yamaguchi, 2024).

As we have thoroughly criticized in Chap. 11, proponents of MMT claim that the more the government ("they") borrows, the more the private sector ("we") increases its financial assets (deposits) by the same amount, and the more "we" become rich. So it is better to let "them" (the government) print more government bonds and borrow more money in order for "us" (the private sector) to get rich. The reason why this MMT's claim is false is evident from the fact that the total financial net assets of the entire economy will always become zero and does not increase at all when viewed from this financial balance sheets. An increase in the private sector's net financial assets by 1,000 trillion yen means that the government's net financial assets will simultaneously become negative 1,000 trillion yen in excess of its debt obligations.

In Chap. 4 we have observed how the Japanese government has increased its debts to prop up the money stock during the lost 30 years. As a result, a huge amount of interest on massive government debts has been taxed by the government from private net assets and forced into the hands of the bankers ("1%"). The debt money system is a zero-sum game with the above two essential features. It is a built-in system that widens the income gap and inequality.

Will the "99%" of the public still support the continuation of this debt money system? We must quickly free ourselves from these nightmares of the debt money system. What can we do about it, then? Specifically, we must eliminate the following three adverse effects of debt money system and shift to the public money system:

a. Convert interest-bearing debt money (BoJ Notes) to interest-free public money (Notes and EPM).
b. Eliminate government debts by redeeming its bonds with public money.
c. Raise the required reserve ratio of demand deposits to 100%.

(1) Exchange 100 Trillion Yen of Bank of Japan Notes for Newly-Issued Public Money (Notes and EPM) with a 10% Premium

We will now depart for the public money system. First, the legislature must pass the "Public Money Act of Japan" as discussed above and establish the legal and institutional framework for transitioning to public money system. To this end, we hope that elected members of the legislature will overcome the "divide and rule" tactics waged on the public under the debt money system (as analyzed in Chap. 10), and that this bill will be passed in a bipartisan manner as soon as possible. Therefore, we will assume in the following discussion that the Bank of Japan has already been reorganized as the Public Money Vault, and that the infrastructure is in place to allow the Public Money Administration to issue public money in coins, notes and in electronic form.

Let us now verify the transition process one by one. Transition process (1) through (6) should be read with reference to the financial balance sheets shown in Fig. 12.3. The numbers attached to each account item on the balance sheet correspond to the transactions that will be considered in the transition process (1) through (6). (0) represents the initial condition (account balance) in Fig. 12.3, corresponding to the financial assets, liabilities and net assets of each sector in Fig. 12.2.

Transition process (1) consists of the following three steps.

① The Public Money Administration issues 110 trillion yen to exchange the 100 trillion yen of BoJ notes currently in circulation with a 10% premium and delivers it to the Public Money Vault (the former BoJ). The purpose of the 10% premium is to promote the conversion for public money while stimulating the economy with the net positive effect of 10 trillion yen in new money (cash). This 110 trillion yen is first recorded as both financial assets and net assets on the balance sheet of the Public Money Vault, which are shown as Public Money and EPM. Then, the premium payment of 10 trillion yen is subtracted upon the conversion. New amount

Public Money B/S

Assets		Liabilities	
(0) Gov.Bonds	500	100	**(0) Banknotes**
(3) Bonds Repayments (CB)	-500	-100	(1) Banknotes Withdrawal
(1) Public Money & EPM	110	400	**(0) Reserves**
(1) Banknotes Withdrawal	-100	200	(4) Bonds Repaymets (Banks)
(1) Premium Payments	-10	300	(5) Bonds Repayments (Private)
(2) Public Money (D)	1,000	100	(6) Public Money Debts
(6) Public Money Loans	100	0	**(0) Gov.Deposits**
		1,000	(2) Public Money(D)
		-500	(3) Bonds Repayments (CB)
		-200	(4) Bonds Repaymets (Banks)
		-300	(5) Bonds Repayments (Private)
		Net Assets (= 100)	
		0	(0) Initial Net Assets
		110	**(1) Public Money & EPM**
		-10	(1) Premium Payments
(6) Total Assets	1,100		

Government B/S

Assets		Liabilities	
(0) Gov.Deposits	0	1,000	**(0) Bonds Issuance**
(2) Public Money(D)	1,000	-500	(3) Bonds Repayments (CB)
(3) Bonds Repayments (CB)	-500	-200	(4) Bonds Repaymets (Banks)
(4) Bonds Repaymets (Banks)	-200	-300	(5) Bonds Repayments (Private)
(5) Bonds Repayments (Private)	-300	Net Assets (= 0)	
		-1,000	(0) Initial Net Assets
		1,000	**(2) Public Money (D) Issuance**
(6) Total Assets	0		

Banks B/S

Assets		Liabilities	
(0) Reserves	400	700	**(0) Demand Deposits**
(4) Bonds Repaymets (Banks)	200	300	(5) Bonds Repayments (Private)
(5) Bonds Repayments (Private)	300	600	**(0) Time Deposits**
(6) Public Money Debts	100	100	**(6) Public Money Debts**
(0) Gov.Bonds	200		
(4) Bonds Repaymets (Banks)	-200	Net Assets (= 0)	
(0) Loans	700	0	(0) Initial Net Assets
(6) Total Assets	1,700		

Private (Households & Producers) B/S

Assets		Liabilities	
(0) Banknotes	100	700	**(0) Debts by Banks**
(1) Banknotes Withdrawal	-100		
(1) Public Money & EPM	110		
(0) Demand Deposits	700		
(5) Bonds Repayments (Private)	300		
(0) Time Deposits	600	Net Assets (= 1,010)	
(0) Gov.Bonds	300	1,000	(0) Initial Net Assets
(5) Bonds Repayments (Private)	-300	10	(1) Premium Receipts
(6) Total Assets	1,710		

Fig. 12.3 Financial balance sheets of the transition process (1) through (6)

of public money can be issued as paper-based currency called Public Money Notes, or in electronic form called Electronic Public Money (EPM). The issuance ratio of public money notes and EPM shall be adjusted by observing the demand for these exchanges in the market. Accordingly, the conversion of cash takes place as follows:

$$\text{BoJ notes (100 tril. yen)} \Longrightarrow \text{Public Money Notes or EPM (110 tril. yen)}$$

The design of the new public money may consist of a variety of designs featuring beautiful landscapes of the nation, etc. Another idea would be to publicly solicit currency designs from the 47 prefectures and use local features or prefectural flowers. Furthermore, the conversion of cash will be accelerated if a campaign is conducted to offer some kind of benefit to those who use the new public money with local designs locally. The new public notes will then stay in the local area and their circulation speed (velocity of money) would increase. In this way, public money will indeed become local currency and bring about regional economic revitalization. It will also increase the people's attachment to their local economies and new national currency issued as public money.

② Conversion can be made at the local branch offices of the Public Money Vault located throughout Japan (former 32 branches and 14 domestic offices of the Bank of Japan), as well as at the counters of banks and other depository financial institutions. Exchange for new public notes is limited to the BoJ notes in circulation as of the start date of the conversion. After the start date, all money withdrawn from ATMs and savings accounts will be carefully prearranged to be made only in public money. The information on the conversion for public money will be publicly announced in advance. However, information on the start date of the exchange with premium will be kept confidential until just before the start date begins in order to prevent the last-minute withdrawal. To ensure fairness in the payment of premiums, it is also a good idea to set an upper limit on the amount of new money that can be exchanged per person eligible with appropriate nationality. All funds needed to secure 100% reserve will be provided to banks through public money lending facility as explained in transition process (6) below.

③ As a result of the exchange process described above, the 100 trillion yen in banknote holdings would be reduced to zero on the private sector's balance sheet, leaving 110 trillion yen in Public Money and EPM as assets. The difference of 10 trillion yen would be the increase in the private sector's financial net assets. This completes the conversion and liquidation of the banknotes.

(2) Create Government Deposits by issuing 1,000 Trillion Yen of Public Money as Net Assets

① In order to redeem the outstanding government bonds of 1,000 trillion yen, the Public Money Administration issues 1,000 trillion yen of public money, which will be transferred to the government. As a result, 1,000 trillion yen of Public Money (D) is recorded as an asset on the PMV's balance sheet and the corresponding 1,000 trillion yen is simultaneously recorded as Government Deposits as a liability. "D" stands for Deposits, indicating that these currencies are issued digitally on the real time gross settlement system taken over from the former BoJ (BOJ-NET). Therefore, there is no need to develop a new system upon transition to public money system.

As in case (1), the formal bookkeeping of this transaction is to first record the 1,000 trillion yen as financial assets and net assets, and then, at the time of transfer to the government, to record the same amount as the government deposit (liability) on the PMV's balance sheet. The double-entry bookkeeping of all public money issuance must begin with recording them first as financial assets and net assets on the PMV's balance sheet, which is managed separately from other ministries and government institutions. However, to simplify the description, this process is omitted here and the government deposits are immediately recorded as liabilities.

② The government immediately records this as the financial net assets of its balance sheet and at the same time makes deposits in the Public Money Vault. As a result, the government's negative (financial) net assets disappear like a magic and become zero. When the government issues bonds and borrows money, it incurs debt and it must be recorded as a liability. On the other hand, when public money is delivered (appropriated) to the government for its use in fiscal policy, it is recorded as financial net asset. The issuance of government bonds and the issuance of public money are similar in that they both result in the creation of government deposits. Yet, the journal entries are decisively different in the debt money system and the public money system. Government bonds are liabilities because they are interest-bearing debt obligations of the government, while public money is legal tender issued based on the sovereign monetary power of the Public. Accordingly, when the government receives it, it becomes interest-free net assets.

(3) Redeem 500 Trillion Yen of Government Bonds held by the Bank of Japan with Government Deposits

① From here, we will look at the process of redeeming government bonds using government deposits of 1,000 trillion yen that were issued as public money. First is the redemption of 500 trillion yen in government bonds held by the PMV on its balance sheet (former Bank of Japan). The entire amount of bonds (asset) will be redeemed using 500 trillion yen in government deposits (liability) on its balance sheets. As a result, government bonds will be reduced to zero, and government deposits will also be reduced by 500 trillion yen (eliminated by offsetting).

② On the government balance sheet, simultaneously, government deposits and government bonds will each decrease by 500 trillion yen.

(4) Redeem 200 Trillion Yen of Government Bonds held by Banks with Government Deposits

① Next is the redemption of 200 trillion yen of government bonds held by banks. On the Banks' balance sheet, the government will redeem the entire amount of 200 trillion yen held by banks in a lump sum and transfer the same amount to the reserve deposits account of banks at the PMV. Normally, government bonds are to be redeemed sequentially on the redemption date. This may not be necessary, however, for transitioning to the public money system, and bond redemption can be done all at once to minimize unnecessary interest costs.

② Correspondingly, in the balance sheet of the Public Money Vault, the government deposits of 200 trillion yen will be reduced and the same amount will be recorded in the reserve deposits of the banks.

③ As a result of the government bond redemptions, in the government balance sheet, government deposits and government bonds will be reduced by 200 trillion yen.

(5) Redeem 300 Trillion Yen of Government Bonds held by Private Sector with Government Deposits

① Finally, the government will redeem 300 trillion yen of its bonds held by the private sector in a lump sum, and transfer the amount to the deposit accounts held at banks via the Public Money Vault. This bond redemption can be done either in a lump sum or sequentially according to the maturity profile of each bond. As with the repayment to the banks, the sequential bond redemption will result in a higher interest burden that is unnecessary.

② The redemption of the government bonds will result in an increase in reserve deposits and the corresponding demand deposits of the private sector by the same amount on the banks' balance sheet.

③ In conjunction with this, on the balance sheet of Public Money Vault, government deposits will decrease by 300 trillion yen and record the same amount in reserve deposits of the banks.

④ Simultaneously, the government balance sheet will also record a decrease of 300 trillion yen in government deposits (asset) and government bonds outstanding (liability), respectively.

As a result of the transition process (3) to (5), the government's outstanding bonds (debt) of 1,000 trillion yen will be immediately paid off using 1,000 trillion yen in government deposits. The government's balance sheet of financial assets, liabilities, and net assets will be all cleaned up and reduced to zero.

(6) Secure 100% Reserves Through Public Money Lending Facility

① Reflecting the transition process up to this point, the demand deposits, which are liabilities of private banks, amount to 1,000 trillion yen, However, the corresponding reserve deposit is 900 trillion yen, leaving banks with reserve deposit shortfall of 100 trillion yen. Under the public money system, banks must always secure and maintain 100% reserve deposits against demand deposits. Therefore, the Public Money Administration issues additional 100 trillion yen and delivers it to the Public Money Vault, which can be used to lend the same amount to banks without interest and collateral (public money lending facility). On the balance sheet of the Public Money Vault, 100 trillion yen of Public Money Loans are recorded as assets, and the same amount is transferred to the banks (as Public Money Debt), which are then recorded as reserves of banks (liability). Note that the lending to the banks through public money lending facility is used solely for the purpose of achieving 100% reserves at the time of the transition from the debt money system.

② In this way, the reserve deposits of banks will become 1,000 trillion yen and 100% reserves will be secured for all demand deposits. On the bank's balance sheet, reserve deposits of 100 trillion yen are recorded as assets, and at the same time, the same amount of Public Money Debts are recorded as a liability. In this way, under the public money system, banks would always be required to maintain 100% reserve deposits with the Public Money Vault, making them impossible to create "deposits" to extend new loans.

(7) Birth of Public Money System as a New Nation

Transition to the public money system has now completed successfully through the above process (1) through (6). As mentioned already, both Fisher and Friedman thought that the transition would be easy. Yet, they did not seem to have shown actual transition processes based on macroeconomic balance sheets. In this book we have empirically shown how easy and practical the actual transition is, starting from the current state of debt money system in Japan as of 2018. This is "the birth of a new nation" we are proposing.

Let us now take a look at how this public money balance sheet was born anew from the 2018 debt money balance sheet. For this transition process, the Public Money Administration has issued two types of public money: notes and electronic public money (EPM). First, 110 trillion yen of public money were issued, either in the form of physical notes or EPM, to replace the old Bank of Japan Notes. Next, 1,000 trillion yen were issued electronically (in EPMs) and transferred to the government's deposit account.

The remaining 600 trillion yen in time deposits held by private sector should also be converted from debt money to public money. To be more precise, public money (legal tender) that cover this 600 trillion yen of debt money (functional money) must also be issued and recorded on the balance sheet of the Public Money Vault. Accordingly, the Public Money Administration should have issued a total amount of 1,710 trillion yen of public money for the transition to be fully completed. However, since this would add more transaction steps and complicate the explanation, we have assumed that the 600 trillion yen of public money is already in circulation and exists in banks' deposit account ledgers (databases), and omitted this transition step from Fig. 12.4. Excluding the issuance of 600 trillion yen of time deposits, the actual issuance becomes 1,110 trillion yen.

Figure 12.4 shows financial balance sheet of Japan's macroeconomic sector just after transition process (7) was completed and the birth of a new nation has finished under the public money system. The figure shows total public money issuance of 1,110 trillion yen, excluding 600 trillion yen in time deposits. The total financial net assets are 1,110 trillion yen, consisting of 100 trillion yen from the Public Money Vault and 1,010 trillion yen from the private sector. In other words, the total amount of public money issued becomes the total financial net assets of the economy as a whole. The issuance of public money brings to our minds the image of a new system such that pure and innocent energies (interest-free public money) are wiping out all debt money and the debt money system is swept away, just as the two gods Inazagi and Izanami in the Japanese mythology swirled the spear (Ame-no-nuboko) into the chaos and consolidated the islands of Japan. This is "the birth of a new nation" that we are proposing. We hope the readers will also remember the origins of their countries and the spirit of their founders, as we move together toward a new bright future that become possible with public money system.

Public Money B/S

Assets			Liabilities
Gov.Bonds	0	0	Banknotes
Public Money & EPM	0	1,000	Reserves
Public Money(D)	1,000	0	Gov.Deposits
Public Money Loans	100	Net Assets (= 100)	
		100	Public Money & EPM
Total Assets	1,100		

Government B/S

Assets			Liabilities
Gov.Deposits	0	0	Bonds Issuance
		Net Assets (= 0)	
Total Assets	0		

Private (Households & Producers) B/S

Assets			Liabilities
Banknortes	0	700	Debts by Banks
Public Money & EPM	110		
Demand Deposits	1,000	Net Assets (= 1,010)	
Time Deposits	600	1,000	Initial Net Assets
Gov.Bonds	0	10	Premium Receipts
Total Assets	1,710		

Banks B/S

Assets			Liabilities
Reserves	1,000	1,000	Demand Deposits
Gov.Bonds	0	600	Time Deposits
Loans	700	100	Public Money Debts
		Net Assets (=0)	
Total Assets	1,700		

Total Public Money	1,110	(= 1,000 + 110)
Total Net Assets	1,110	(= 100 + 1,010)

M0 = 110 + 1,000 = 1,110
M1 = 110 + 700 + 300 = 1,110
M3 = 110 + 700 + 300 + 600 = 1,710

Fig. 12.4 (7) Birth of public money system as a new nation

Money stock after the transition to the public money system becomes as follows.

$$\begin{aligned}
\text{Base money } M_0 &= \text{Cash} + \text{Reserve deposits} \\
&= 110 \text{ trillion yen} + 1,000 \text{ trillion yen} \\
&= 1,110 \text{ trillion yen} \\
\text{Money stock } M_1 &= \text{Cash} + \text{Demand deposits} \\
&= 110 \text{ trillion yen} + 700 \text{ trillion yen} + 300 \text{ trillion yen} \\
&= 1,110 \text{ trillion yen} \\
\text{Money Stock } M_3 &= \text{Money Stock } M_1 + \text{Time Deposits} \\
&= 1,110 \text{ trillion yen} + 600 \text{ trillion yen} \\
&= 1,710 \text{ trillion yen}
\end{aligned}$$

From the balance sheet analysis, the following three essences of public money system emerge.

Essence of Public Money System (1)

$$\begin{aligned}
\text{Base money } M_0 &= \text{Money stock } M_1 \\
&= 1,110 \text{ trillion yen}
\end{aligned}$$

In the public money system, money is no longer created out of nothing by banks. All base money M_0 circulates as money stock M_1 and is used for daily transactions. In other words, the second of the three transition goals is achieved. Demand deposits held by private sector will be 100% backed by bank reserves. In the debt money system as of 2018, base money M_0 was 500 trillion yen, while money stock M_1 was created out of nothing by private and government debts and swelled to 800 trillion yen. The difference of 300 trillion yen is functional money M_f. Historically, this functional money caused monetary expansions and contractions, and has led to bank runs, bubbles, and economic fluctuations. With the transition to the public money system, this functional money M_f disappears and the root causes of such economic maladies will be eradicated.

Essence of Public Money System (2)

$$\begin{aligned}\text{Money stock } M_1 &= \text{Total Issuance of Public Money}\\ &= 1,110 \text{ trillion yen}\end{aligned}$$

As the transition to the public money system progresses, M_1 will become equal to the total amount of public money issued. The debt money will be eliminated, and all circulating medium become public money. As a result, the quantity of money in circulation is stabilized, and the Public Money Administration can optimally adjust the quantity of money in circulation.

Essence of Public Money System (3)

$$\begin{aligned}\text{Total Issuance of Public Money} &= \text{Total Financial Net Assets}\\ &= 1,110 \text{ trillion yen}\end{aligned}$$

The total financial net assets of Japanese economy as a whole now consists of 100 trillion yen of the Public Money Vault and 1,010 trillion yen of the private sectors; that is, in total 1,110 trillion yen. This total amount always matches the total issuance of public money M_0 of 1,110 trillion yen. In other words, although financial net assets move among sectors as a result of economic activity, the total financial net assets are equal to the total amount of public money issued. The additional public money issued by the Public Money Administration will directly increase the financial net assets of the economy as a whole. In the debt money system, the total financial net assets always end up with zero, and the system always ends up being a zero-sum game. Hence, the additional issuance of debt money never increase the economy's net financial assets. As an example, government bonds additionally issued by the government did not increase the financial net assets of the economy as a whole, and never enriched the economy.

A note should be made here about the money stocks M_1 and M_3 after the transition. Compared to the debt money system, M_1 increased by 310 trillion yen, from 800 trillion yen to the total 1,110 trillion yen. M_3 has also increased by 310 trillion yen; that is, from 1,400 trillion yen to 1,710 trillion yen. The breakdown of this increase is 10 trillion yen in premium payments and 300 trillion yen in redemptions of government bonds held by the private sector. The current Japanese economy is suffering from a lack of demand, so it can afford to absorb this increase in 310 trillion yen of additional money stock with its potential production capacity. Therefore, the

310 trillion yen increase in the money stock that will accompany the transition can be expected to induce domestic demand and increase GDP by the same amount and, in turn, stimulate the stagnant economy. If inflation should occur, prices can be stabilized by withdrawing public money directly out of circulation. This is an efficient monetary policy that becomes possible in the public money system.

Figure 12.5 illustrates money stock after the system transition is completed. Compare this with Fig. 3.7 that shows money stock under the debt money system. Demand deposits and time deposits are now circulating as legal tender (EPM) and can no longer be created by banks as functional money. Withdrawal of public money shown at the bottom of the figure refers to the complete withdrawal of currency from circulation into the Public Money Vault, not to the withdrawal associated with tax collection by the government. Under the public money system, banks and the government are regarded as currency holders on the same level as the rest of the private sector from the perspective of the PMA (*cf.* Fig. 13.3 also). Note that this figure shows EPM are issued and circulate as electronic cash, which provides both the protection of privacy and payment finality. If EPM users want to avoid risk of losing them or having them stolen, they can easily transfer them into their bank accounts. Once EPM is deposited with banks, they will circulate as demand or time deposits as shown. Time deposits in the public money system become the loanable funds of banks, which was incorrectly assumed by the mainstream Keynesian (exogenous money) theory and misapplied to macroeconomic analysis of the debt money system as discussed in Chap. 9.

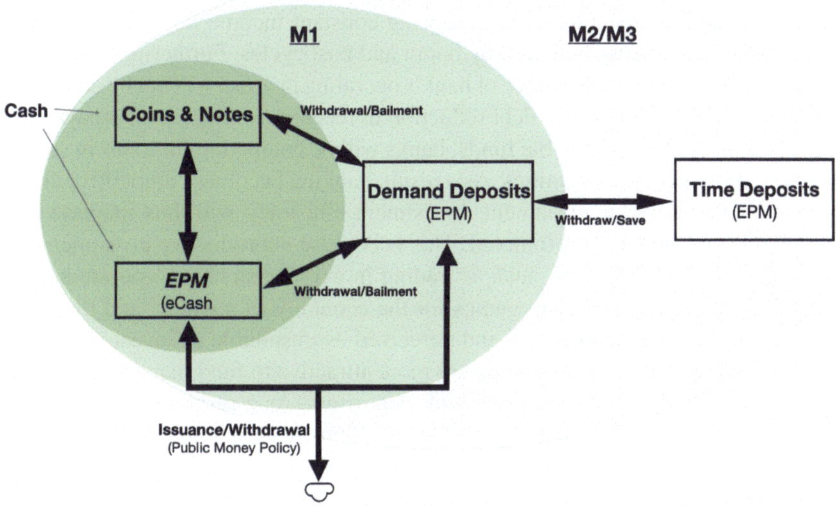

Fig. 12.5 Monetary aggregates under the public money system

12.3 New Economic Landscapes of Public Money

As we shift from debt money to public money, the system structure will change, and naturally the behavior of the economic system changes. This is the way of thinking in system dynamics. How will the behavior of the system change along with this structural change, and what will the economic landscape look like after the birth of new nations? Here, let us briefly take a look at the new economic landscapes under the public money system with reference to Table 9.2.

New Economic Landscape 1: Monetary Stability Base money M_0 issued by the Public Money Administration becomes money stock M_1. As a result, money stock becomes stable and permanent. Money, once they are issued, will continue to circulate and supports economic activities. M_1 would no longer be created and destroyed endogenously as in the debt money system, and the economy would no longer be subject to recurring bubbles, recessions, inflation, deflation, mass unemployment. Prices will stabilize and our life will become more prosperous.

New Economic Landscape 2: Financial Stability Just as water flows from high to low, surplus funds generated from savings and loan repayments will begin to be directed to real productive investments and expected to generate new economic values. This is because, under the public money system, there will be a clear distinction between truly risk-free and risk-bearing bank accounts that could lose value when banks fail on investments. Depositors will thus become more conscious of their choice in which bank to entrust their savings for how much. Banks will no longer have to pay interest for demand deposits. Conversely, they can charge custody service fees, thus ensuring constant income flows and business stability without being bothered by boom and bust cycles. Furthermore, demand deposits, which are stable source of bank's operating income, will not be destroyed even if companies prioritize debt reduction in recessions. Since loan repayments are the source of new loanable funds, banks will be competing for loans in search of new investment opportunities. As a result, banking becomes competitive under a true market-based environment. Investment efficiency will thus increase and economic growth will be promoted. This is because unproductive investments in financial asset transactions, such as trading in existing stocks, corporate bonds, and real estates are zero-sum games for the economy as a whole, and they will eventually become unattractive and perceived as unsuitable as investment portfolio. Conversely, real investments are more attractive to fund managers because they can share the investment risk with depositors. As a result, competition for loans among banks will intensify, and loans will increase not only to large corporations but also to small and medium-sized enterprises (SMEs). As a result, not only city banks but also small and medium-sized local banks, credit banks, and credit unions will be revitalized. The efficient allocation of funds will be achieved.

New Economic Landscape 3: Stabilization of Employment Under the stable supply of money and the revitalized banking sector, capital will begin to flow equally to SMEs as well as large corporations. Companies will be able to practice stable management and make long-term investments under the stable price level. This will sustain economic growth and in turn stabilize employment. Under the public money system, worker-centered employment characterized by Japanese management of lifetime employment, family allowances, and employee welfare will be realized again, as it used to be in the 1970s and 80s when "Japan as Number One".

New Economic Landscape 4: Resolving Government Debt Crises The government is now freed from the debt burdens of 1,000 trillion yen and will finally be able to operate sound fiscal policies in line with primary balance. Fiscal budget will no longer be constrained by accumulated debt, as it has been in the past, and the government will be able to enhance social welfare and social security budget, and formulate future-oriented industrial policy and growth strategies. In case additional budget is required, the Ministry of Finance will request the Public Money Administration to increase the budget. If it is determined that new money can be issued in line with price stability objective, the PMA can issue additional public money to the extent that it does not cause inflation. The debt repayment with public money will not cause recession, unemployment, wage cuts, inflation, or a contagious recession. It also avoids the worst-case scenario in which financial institutions go bankrupt due to insolvency caused by a plunge in bond prices (as analyzed in Chap. 6). Thus, there is nothing to lose by paying off national debts. Furthermore, since recessions are not transmitted to other economies, nations can implement this debt redemption as a prescription for revitalizing their own domestic economies. Only when countries make the transition in parallel can the global debt crisis be avoided.

New Economic Landscape 5: Elimination of Income Inequality Income inequality is currently a major social issue around the world. Of course, it can be attributed to individual ability as well as to the environment in which one is born, but that is not the issue here. We are referring to income inequality among classes in capitalism under the debt money system. The main class categories are bankers and financiers who receive interest income, capitalists (shareholders) who receive dividend and land rent income, managers who receive salaries, and workers (employees) who earn wage income. Unlike the current debt money in circulation, public money is not created as interest-bearing money. They are always issued at interest-free. As a result, the forced transfer of interest income to private banks will be stopped, and the gap between interest income of bankers and financiers and other non financial income of the rest of the public (1% vs 99%) will be eliminated. However, as analyzed in Chap. 10, the international bankers and financiers are also major shareholders of multinational corporations, and it is practically difficult to separate interest income from dividend income in this sense. They further increase their financial (unearned) income through the mechanism of exponential growth by reinvesting their financial income in stocks, securities, and real estate. Yet, it is still not difficult to conceptually distinguish between the two. Thus, under the public money system, the outer loop of control by "compound interests" in Fig. 10.4 can be cut off, and the gap between bankers and the rest of the classes can be eliminated. This is why the priority, called "leverage point" in system thinking, for eliminating the adverse effects of the capitalist economy is to first and foremost establish the public money system in place of the debt money system. However, the income disparity, such as unearned income vs. wage income, rooted in the classic class conflicts between capitalist and workers cannot be resolved simply by transitioning to the public money system. In order to solve this type of inequality, it is necessary to eliminate the inner loop of control by "equity ownership" by further transforming the system structure into the *MuRatopia Economy* discussed in the final Chap. 15. MuRatopia is an alternative economic system that replaces the equity *ownership* system of capitalism with the equity *possession* system of self-management, consisting of (cooperative) companies that have extended the family social organization into jointly owned democratically-controlled business enterprises.

New Economic Landscape 6: Sustainable Development Unsustainable economic development, including environmental pollution and destruction, is closely linked to the way money is created and spent under the debt money system. Debtors such as producers, households and governments around the world are constantly forced to pay interests. The only way to pay the interest is to reduce costs and increase sales as much as possible. Under such circumstances, they have no choice but to reduce costs and budgets, and give up investments that could otherwise have been easily afforded to protect the environment. The quickest way to reduce costs is to keep environmental investments as low as possible and pass them on to social costs. The dumping of pollutants, for example. In other words, the problems of environmental degradation are inseparable from the debt money system. Even in the public money system, interest payments associated with investment occur between creditors and debtors. However, the risks associated with investment are shared fairly among three parties involved: the providers of funds (savers), financial intermediaries (banks), and producers (borrowers). Thus, environmental destruction caused by unilateral and compulsory transfer of investment risks will be reduced. In this way public money system would break the chain of such environmental destruction. It is crutial to recognize that environmental problems are inseparable from the way current monetary system works. Trying to conserve the environment without reforming the debt money system is a symptomatic remedy that may temporarily wipe away the festering wounds. Public money system can finally unite countries to tackle environmental conservation and sustainable development as a urgent matter tasked to the international community.

System Transition Roadmap

We have now observed six new economic landscapes that will unfold after the birth of the new nation. Transition to the public money system that brings about these new economic landscapes is the hope for a brighter future for those of us who have suffered economically during the "lost 30 years," and it is a path to salvation. We have developed the following roadmap for implementing these seven transition processes based on the Japanese case outlined in this chapter, assuming that the publication of this book will generate broader support for this system transition. Strike while the iron is hot![11]

2023–24 Issue 110 trillion yen of public money and exchange it for BoJ notes. At least begin a pilot experiment of the proposed EPM payment system (Process 1).

2024–25 Issue 1,000 trillion yen of public money to create government deposits (Process 2). Then, immediately redeem 500 trillion yen of government bonds held by the Bank of Japan with the public money (Process 3).

2026–27 Redeem 200 trillion yen of government bonds held by banks with the public money (Process 4).

2028–29 Redeem 300 trillion yen of government bonds held by the private sector with the public money (Process 5).

2029–30 Secure 100% reserves by lending 100 trillion yen to banks (Process 6).

In order to visualize this roadmap and verify its feasibility, we have created a simple transition model based on accounting system dynamics method. Due to space limitations, the explanation of the model itself is omitted here, and only the simulation results are shown in Fig. 12.6. The model starts with 500 trillion yen of base money M_0 (line 1) and 800 trillion yen of money stock M_1 (line 2) in 2022.[12] These two lines in due course become equal and 100% Money will be realized in 2030 at 1,100 trillion yen (Essence 1 of Public Money System).

In the same year, money stock M_1 will be equal to the total public money issuance of 1,110 trillion yen (line 4). It will be stable thereafter and keep circulating (Essence 2 of Public Money System). Since the issuance of 110 trillion yen in public money in 2023, the total amount of public money issuance (line 4) has always been equal to the total financial net assets (thick line 5). From the year 2025, it stays at 1,110 trillion yen (Essence 3 of Public Money System).

Figure 12.7 shows how the outstanding government debts are redeemed in the background according to the transition steps. The redemption of government bonds is simulated by assuming lump-sum repayments. Government bonds held by the BoJ are redeemed in 2025 (line 2), those held by banks are redeemed in 2027 (line 3), and those held by the private sector are redeemed in 2029 (line 4). As a result, in 2029, the government debts of 1,000 trillion yen will be paid off fully and faithfully, and the government debts will be zero (thick line 1). Of course, banks and the private sector may wish to keep their bond holdings to maturity and continue to receive interest during that time. In such a case, the period of debt repayment will be longer

[11] We have specified the starting year of transition to 2023 when we started writing this book. It was originally set to be the year 2021 when our Japanese book was published in 2021. Readers may change the starting year and initial values according to their appropriate timing and economic condition upon planning the transition processes for their economies.

[12] Note that the monetary data as of 2018 were used in the figure instead of 2022 in order to simplify explanation. Readers may use the data of 2022 for further details of transition processes.

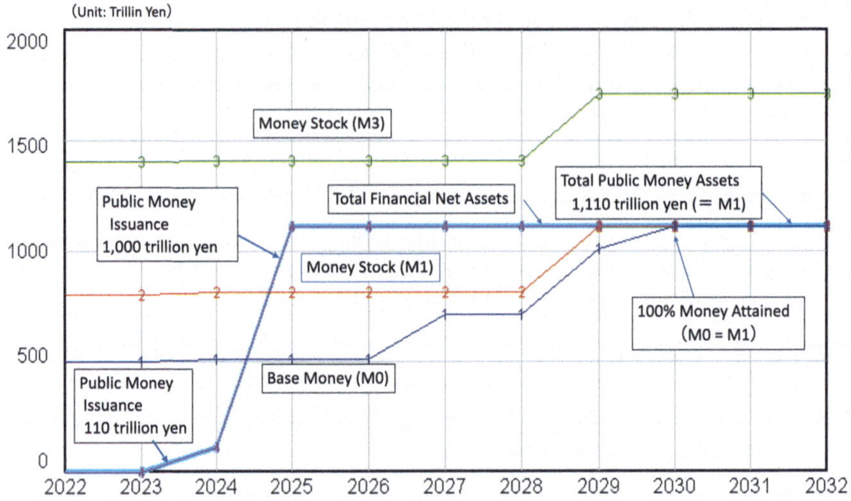

Fig. 12.6 Money stock, public money and financial net assets in transition

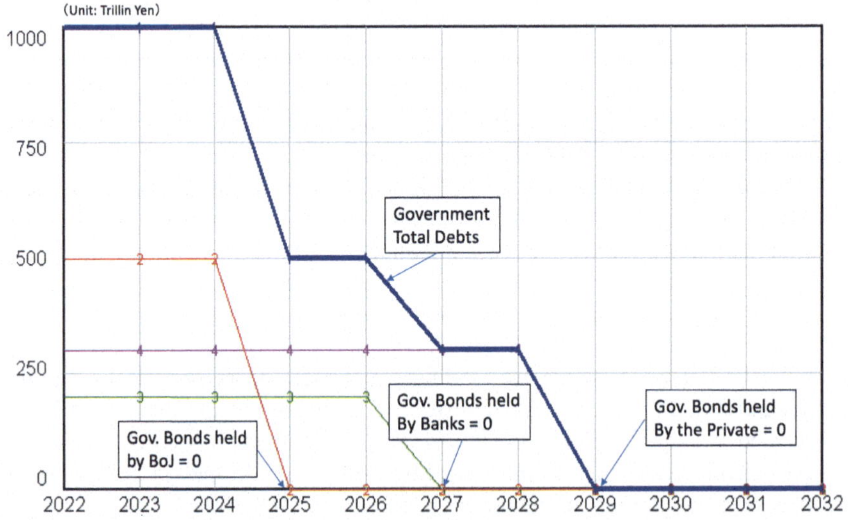

Fig. 12.7 Simulation of redemption of total government bonds

than what is shown in the figure. For example, in the case of bond redemption with a 5-year maturity (20% per year), the simulation results show that the repayments of government debts will be delayed after 2055. If the public wish to eradicate their national debts faster, they can do so as already explained, saving trillions of unnecessary interest costs.

In any case, the government will finally be freed from the absurdity of having to collect about 10 trillion yen in interest on its debt (about 80,000 yen per capita) as taxes every year, which is paid to banks and other bondholders. In this way our government will finally come back to us and truly become *the government of the people, by the people, for the people.*

Chapter 13
Electronic Public Money and Uniform Tax System

In Chap. 12 we have proposed the issuance of Electronic Public Money (EPM) to convert banknotes during transition to the Public Money System. What is EPM? How does it differ from Central Bank Digital Currency (CBDC)? And what can we do with it? The Public Money Initiative presented in the next Chap. 14 is a set of policy programs designed to overcome Japan's Lost 30 Years using EPM as the principal source of public fundings. Before we discuss such policy proposals, let us first clarify the difference between EPM and CBDC in this chapter. Specifically, we will discuss why we need EPM instead of CBDC to preserve our privacy and freedom in the digital age, and how we can simultaneously simplify the present tax system that has become unwieldy complex, inefficient and unfair by introducing Uniform Tax System in parallel with EPM.

13.1 EPM Is the Money of Futures

Classification of Money by Medium

Money is information of value. As such, a *medium* is needed for it to be recognized and to register who it belongs to (ownership). Table 13.1 classifies public money and debt money according to types of media.[1] It shows how money has taken different forms in various parts of the world in different times in history. There are three elements that determine the specific form of money; (1) unit of value, (2) medium and (3) type of issuance, which is closely related to the issuer as we have seen through various historical examples of money in Chap. 2.

The *electrum* coins issued by the Kingdom of Lydia were public money made of an alloy of gold and silver. The practice of metal coinage was carried over to the Roman Empire, whose currencies consisted of gold, silver, bronze and copper.

[1] Adapted from Yamaguchi and Yamaguchi (2017a).

K. Yamaguchi and Y. Yamaguchi, *Public Money*,
https://doi.org/10.1007/978-981-97-6564-5_13

Table 13.1 Electronic public money (EPM) as money of the futures

Classification of Money by Media

Issuance	Public Money	Debt Money (at interest)	
Non-metal Goods	Shell, Cloth (Silk) Wood, Stone, etc.		
Metallic Coinage	Coins (Gold, Silver, etc.)	Gold, Silver Ingots (Precious Metals as Bank Reserve Assets)	
Paper & Polymer Notes	Public Money Notes	Central Bank Notes (Gold Certificates)	Private Bank Notes (Deposit Certificates)
Electromagnetic Memory (Digital Money)	Public Money Deposits	Central Bank Reserve Deposits	Private Bank Deposits (Credits & Debts)
	< **EPM** > issued by PMA as Electronic Cash	< **CBDC** > by Central Bank as Base Money	< Digital Tokens > appeared since 2008 (Bitcoin, etc.)
Fiat Status	Legal Tender		Functional Money

During the time of the Crusades, the Knights Templar formed a financial network that functioned like a trust bank on the pilgrimage route, giving rise to the wider usage of *deposit money* issued by the institutions.

As commercial trades expanded in the Age of Discovery, states began to adopt purified form of gold and silver as the medium of money. Although there are several factors that affect which types of metal become relatively precious over the others, such as the discovery of new refining techniques or new veins of gold, etc., gold and silver coins are easily identifiable, generally hard to forge (durable), their total supplies are verifiably limited, and thus their authenticities were uniformly recognized across territorial borders and commercial areas. As such, these metals fulfilled the requirements for medium of money better than non-metallic goods (commodity), and become more widely accepted than non-metallic money used in indigenous societies such as silk, wood sticks or stones.

The Rise of Fractional Reserve Banking and Debt Money

The invention of double-entry bookkeeping techniques around 14th century led to the rapid development of commerce and merchant banking, particularly in affluent cities in Europe such as Florence, Genoa and Venice. By this time, bankers were engaging in fractional reserve banking as well as other financial transactions including underwriting government bonds and subscribing for loans for war finance. With the Age of Discovery, the emphasis shifted from trades in the Mediterranean, the North Sea and the Baltic Sea to trades in the West Indies (the new continent) and East Indies (the Orient) via the Atlantic Ocean. The European center of commerce and finance moved from Antwerp to Amsterdam, and to London. Through wars and political revolutions during the subsequent centuries, the societies gradually began to be structured around the precursor of modern nation states. By the second half of the 17th century, bankers and goldsmiths in Europe were not only acting as bailees of deposits entrusted to them, but were increasingly using those funds for making loans at interest.

In 1656, King Karl X Gustav of Sweden authorized the creation of nation's first publicly chartered bank, which, as we saw in Chap. 2, later gave birth to the oldest central bank. In 1694, the Bank of England was established as a joint stock company. The need for efficiency soon brought about the standardization of the weight and purity of gold coins. Issac Newton became the Master of Royal Mint in 1699, and the Kingdom of Great Britain switched to the *de facto* gold (specie) standard in 1717. The British Pound is a typical example of a unit of weight that became a monetary unit. And its abbreviation (lb.) sees its origin from the ancient Roman unit of weight for precious metals called *libra*.

Around this time paper money began circulating in the British colonies when the State of Massachusetts-Bay issued the paper currency in 1690. In response, the Britain passed several Currency Acts that limited and eventually banned the issuance of colonial paper money (*Bills of Credit*) in order to protect the British merchants and creditors from being paid in the depreciated currency. This policy created political tension and led to the American Revolution. In particular the front of a four-dollar notes issued in 1778 in North Carolina read: "*A Lesson to arbitrary Kings, and wicked Ministers.*" Many of these colonial paper currencies were issued as public money with specific redemption date, upon which the bearer could redeem in Spanish silver dollars or gold species as specified on each bill.

The Age of Central Bank and Private Bank's Debt Money

The concept of self-regulating economy advocated by Adam Smith has effectively helped bankers to limit the state intervention into their businesses. Central banks were established one after another in the 19th century. Currencies in each state began to be unified as these central banks were given monopoly powers over the issuance of banknotes. This was how the present debt money systems were established first in Europe under the gold standard. These bankers (court Jews) helped finance wars and made loans to the sovereign heads of the states and nobilities. Over the generations these bankers and financiers expanded their wealth, established multiple business interests and acquired social status.

Aristotle observed that money is only a creature of law. However, money in Europe around this time were largely circulated as commodity money, where monetary value was still tied to the intrinsic value of the medium (gold) due to the lack of authority and the public trust around governments.

The gold standard was officially adopted in the UK in 1816, and the British sovereign–gold specie–began to be issued a year after. During the period of industrial revolution, certificates of deposit and other debt securities issued by private banks circulated as a means of payment. The number of private country banks skyrocketed around this period. Gradually, however, financial system began to be centralized in Europe. First, the Austrian National Bank in Vienna was given the exclusive note issuer status in 1816, followed two years later by the Danish National Bank. Bank of England (BoE) notes were made legal tender of England and Wales, which were convertible to gold. The BoE was finally given monopoly issuance by the Bank Charter Act 1844 under the Peel government.

After a century of political battle over the creation of a central bank in the US, the Federal Reserve System was finally established just before the World War I. Due to the extension of railways and the development of industry, the US economy had already overtaken the British empire by the end of the 19th century. The US Dollar rose to its prominence after the financial crisis associated with WWI and solidified its status as the world's reserve currency after the Bretton Woods Agreement in 1944. Finally, with the suspension of US dollar-gold convertibility in 1971, the international monetary system has switched from commodity-backed system, in which monetary value was tied to the intrinsic value of medium, to fiat money system in which money exists separately from the unit of weight of the medium without direct backings by the commodity.

In this way we can use Table 13.1 as a mariner's compass to locate where we are right now in the long history of money and human civilization. As discussed in Chap. 3, today the majority of money is dominated by the debt money issued by central bank and commercial banks at interests. Money situated in the lower half of Table 13.1 are all *digital money*. Under the present debt money system, central bank and commercial bank "deposits" are simply monetary claims (credits) and repayment obligations (debts) originated from depositors, banks and borrowers.

Invention of Bitcoin and Digital Tokens

Table 13.1 also gives us a glimpse of what the future of money may hold. That is, how money may change its form as the next step in its evolution. In fact, a radical invention has recently occurred that has fundamentally changed our approach to design money of the future. The invention was called *Bitcoin* by its inventor (Nakamoto, 2008), whose identity is still the subject of debates.[2] Coincidentally, this invention took place just as the world was about to be taken by storm of another financial crisis in 2008.

---

[2] Concerning the identity of Satoshi Nakamoto, there has been a long debate as to whether he or she is a Japanese origin as the pseudonym suggests or if it is a group of people. An internet post (Evanhatch, 2021) observed that Leonard H. Sassaman, an American self-taught technologist and cryptographer, might have been the central individual, who was a doctoral student at the time at the Computer Security and Industrial Cryptography (COSIC) group at KU Leuven under the supervision of Dr. David Chaum. Chaum is also a renowned American cryptographer that originally came up with the precursor of the concept of Blockchain–core design element of Bitcoin system–in his UC Berkeley doctoral dissertation (Chaum, 1982), and later developed the *DigiCash* in 1994, the world's first electronic cash payment method based on his blind signature scheme (Chaum, 1983).

Bitcoin is a new type of intangible asset where transactions are recorded on the digital ledger (database) called *blockchain*, which are maintained on a *peer-to-peer* network of computers called *nodes*. Nakamoto (2008) designed the system so that new units of Bitcoin are generated without relying on any single entity, while preventing the double-spending problem. Specifically, new units of bitcoin are allocated to a node that successfully validated incoming transactions by finding a solution to a cryptographic problem that requires computationally intensive operations. Because of this unique approach to create a new asset that can be transfered everywhere over the Internet, it opened up a new category in our classification table as *Digital Tokens*.

People became enthusiastic about this invention of the century. Some hoped that it would be the next world currency, replacing the US dollar and other national currencies controlled by the central banks. Bitcoin was also dubbed 'digital gold' by its advocates because its total supply is pre-determined in the software that runs the Bitcoin network, a feature that makes it more transportable than traditional gold, according to Bitcoin enthusiasts. Since the emergence of Bitcoin, thousands of other digital assets called *Altcoins* (alternative coins) have been created.

Digital tokens in our classification include Bitcoin and all other types of tokens that have been created and maintained by each network, including Altcoins that rely on other type of database than blockchain. Because bitcoin was named "peer-to-peer electronic cash system" by its inventor, these blockchain-based digital tokens began to be called virtual currency, cryptocurrency and so on, without much care in their use of the terminology. The characteristics of digital token is that the ownership and transfer of each unit of asset is enabled by the cryptographic verifications. Just as we classified different types of money currently in circulation in Chap. 2, the same taxonomy should be applied to these digital tokens; that is, whether they are public money or debt money (obverse definition), and legal tender or functional money (reverse definition).

From the reverse side of the definition, bitcoin must be distinguished from legal tender (currency), because one can refuse to accept it in payments. In fact bitcoins are still bought and sold primarily for speculative tradings on crypto exchanges, and do not function like money as bank deposits (functional money) do. Therefore, it is an another asset category that does not fit into the classification table of money to begin with. However, since there were retailers that accepted bitcoin occasionally and there are a number of crypto asset exchanges providing custodial services to convert them into bank deposits and *vice versa*, digital tokens are classified as a complementary category under the functional money in Table 13.1. The same principle applies in general to other digital tokens (Altcoins), which use different security models and network consensus algorithms.[3]

[3] Digital tokens could further be classified into permission (private) or permission-less (public) types, depending on whether a validator node is required a permission to join the network consensus that finalizes transfers of assets (transaction settlement). Permission-type systems are adopted to achieve better performance, such as higher transaction throughputs and low latency. For the purpose of this chapter, however, the distinction between these two types of system architecture does not affect our discussion.

13.2 EPM Versus CBDC

Digital Tokens Won't Solve the Problems of Debt Money

In Part II we have analyzed that the current debt money system has structural defects, systematizing monetary and financial instability, accumulation of government debts, income inequality and inflation. It was thus anticipated that digital tokens would still suffer from the structural defects of the debt money system and cannot solve the problems due to their dependence on it (Yamaguchi and Yamaguchi, 2017a).

As a result, the use of digital tokens as a means of settlement has been very limited and mostly a subject of speculative trades (zero-sum games). The price of bitcoin (BTC) came close to that of a troy ounce of gold first in November 2013, reaching above 1,000 USD per BTC. Yet it soon halved in value in 2014 and another waves of boom-bust followed in 2017, 2021 and so on. Digital tokens such as bitcoin have no intrinsic value, which makes them inherently volatile.

This nature of (unbacked) crypto-asset created by no single entity accountable to the public makes them unreliable for ordinary households and businesses, let alone for governments to use them as money. Unfortunately most of digital tokens have since failed to provide significant use cases as the alternative money, nor did they address problems of the debt money system. Even if bitcoin or other forms of digital tokens gain public trust and become new currencies, there still remains a possibility that they would be exploited as base money for private banks to create new "deposits of bitcoin" out of thin air unless fractional reserve banking is properly regulated. Meanwhile, central banks around the world began to actively prepare for their own version of electronic money, which they call Central Bank Digital Currency (CBDC). We have not discussed whether the design failures of debt money system could be fixed if CBDC is introduced. To do so, we need to first define what CBDC is and how it might be introduced.

What Is CBDC? What Will It Look like?

As we can see from the classification table, we have been using digital money for quite some time. In Japan, for instance, major city banks began operation of online deposit ledger systems back in the 1960s. The Zengin System–Japan's interbank payment clearing network–was established in 1973, the same year when the SWIFT was established in Belgium. Bank of Japan began operation of its own settlement system in 1988. Thus, private bank deposits and central bank reserves, which account for most of money in circulation, are already in digital. In this sense, CBDC has been around for more than 40 years in Japan.

The new type of CBDC that central banks are now planning to introduce is the so-called retail CBDC. Unlike the existing central bank digital currency, i.e., reserves, which are used primarily for means of settlements among financial institutions, retail

CBDC is designed so that it can be used by the general public similar to banknotes. In fact retail CBDC will most likely be a digital version of banknote in terms of payment finality. As an example, the National Bank of Cambodia, in collaboration with a Japanese Fintech company Soramitsu, is one of the earliest central banks that has introduced its own integrated retail payment system in 2020 called Bakong, which uses Hyperledger Iroha Blockchain.

In Cambodia's case, verified users can download the Bakong payment application on their smartphones and start sending and receiving money. Retail CBDCs in developing countries, including the one in Cambodia, has social benefits. For example, there are many citizens who possess mobile devices but do not have access to bank accounts. Also, the usage of US dollar is relatively high in these developing countries. With the new payment application installed on their phones, CBDC can drive financial inclusion and use of domestic currency, creating a win-win situation. In just three years since its introduction, Bakong users have exceeded 10 million, reaching approximately 60% of the population.

In developed nations, however, the majority of citizens have bank accounts usually in multiple institutions that provide mobile banking services. Additionally, their retail payment infrastructures are already at satisfying level with instant payments available 24 h 7 days a week.[4] Consider the case of Japan, for instance. Bank of Japan and private sectors have continuously made improvements in both domestic and cross-border payment services over the past decades, yet the economy has been suffering from the prolonged stagnation. Thus, the benefits of introducing retail CBDC becomes vague compared to those in the developing nations.

The question then becomes, what are the benefits of retail CBDCs? Why are central banks in developed economies now constructing the narrative that our society needs CBDC more than ever to adapt itself to the fast-changing needs in the digital age? The supporters of retail CBDCs claim that they would effectively prevent money-laundering and deter criminal activities. Therefore, introducing CBDC will help maintain the law and social orders. In addition, they say CBDCs could improve settlement speeds and allow micropayments, thus easing the payment of government subsidies (such as universal basic income). They say it can also be utilized to fine-tune monetary policy, impose a carbon tax on individuals and integrate it with social credit system. It is as if central banks see it as opportunities to implement a tool of social control.

[4] Of course there are things that can still be improved, such as the level of service fees that are high barriers especially to micropayment business models, stifling innovations.

The Danger of Losing Privacy and Freedoms

Whatever their true purposes may be, what concerns many people with the introduction of retail CBDCs is the issue of privacy. In order for it to be a means of deterring criminal activities, transactions made with retail CBDC must be fully "transparent" and "programmable" by definition. That means the issuer of retail CBDCs will be able to monitor and analyze transactions in real time, and when deemed necessary, the authority can seize funds by freezing the user's CBDC accounts. Depending on the distribution model, private banks that stand between the issuer and the end users will need to administer profiling of every CBDC accounts, just as banks conduct KYC (Know Your Customer) for Anti Money Laundering/Countering the Financing of Terrorism (AML/CFT).

Concerning the privacy of retail CBDCs, central banks and authorities have been careful about how they portray what retail CBDCs should look like. For example, in June 2023, the European Commission (EC) published a proposal for regulating the establishment of what they call "Digital Euro" that is planned to be issued by the European Central Bank as retail CBDC (European Commission, 2023). The EC surely acknowledges that "the initiative fully respects the fundamental rights enshrined in the Charter of Fundamental Rights of the European Union (*ibid.*, p. 10)" such as the right to liberty (Article 6) and the freedom to conduct a business (Article 16). The document then states that "initiative provides for a high level of privacy for off-line digital euro payments (*ibid.*, p. 4)" that is consistent with the EU data protection laws and conformity with the AML/CFT framework. However, it also states that digital euro will NOT accommodate full anonymity of physical cash, i.e., privacy is *conditional.*

This is a contradiction as there is no such thing as the middle ground when it comes to protecting privacy; whether retail CBDCs will come with the same level of privacy as physical cash or not. Despite the public's concern, the Digital Euro will not likely to protect the privacy of its users. That is very concerning.

When CBDCs become ready, its promoters will likely to try to convince the general public that appropriate regulations will separate the role between the administrator of CBDC system and the law enforcement so that no single authority will be in a position of obtaining information that link the end user's identity and transactions. However, if the retail CBDC is designed so that authorities can retroactively probe transactions made by specific accounts, there is always a potential for misuse and abuse of power through arbitrary interpretations of laws and regulations. History is abundant with such examples.

The world has just witnessed how the authority nullified the fundamental rights of its citizens. The government of Canada, for example, made the draconian decision that it could shut down and freeze bank accounts of those who protested against the government action during the Covid-19 lockdown without court order in the name of "Public Health Emergency". If the authority is able to monitor every payments and if it can program currency in such ways to work (or not work) in certain transactions, total surveillance society will be established, obliterating our personal privacy and undermining economic freedoms. When economic freedom is lost, the rest of freedoms get lost. In such a society, there will be no such thing as the Bill of Rights.

First Scenario: Retail CBDC as Digital Panopticon

It is now clear from the classification Table 13.1 that CBDC has to be discussed *vis-a-vis* EPM since they are in the same category in terms of the media. EPM is a new digital currency issued by the Public Money Administration as electronic cash (see next Sect. 13.3). Hence, the remaining question is: Will CBDC fix the system design failures of debt money? More specifically, if central banks introduce retail CBDCs, what kind of change will it bring to the fractional reserve banking?

In the Cambodian case, the central bank is responsible for operating the back-end core settlement system so as not to conflict with other business operations of commercial banks. Therefore, the structure of debt money system remains as it is. Central banks that are now planning to introduce retail CBDCs, particularly those of G7 nations, have been actively conducting research on its pros and cons, and are now figuring out what to do with the banking privilege they have protected for the last centuries. The answer is rather straightforward. There are only two scenarios beyond the introduction of retail CBDCs.

As discussed in Chap. 3 (Fig. 3.7), 99% of money stock is currently created through two faucets. The first faucet is the issuance of reserves when central bank purchase financial assets or provide loans to financial institutions. These central bank reserves are interchangeable with bank notes and government-issued coins (public money). And the remaining money is created by private banks. Therefore, the first scenario after the introduction of CBDC is a case where fractional reserve banking system is left untouched and retail CBDC will circulate in parallel with coins, banknotes and commercial bank deposits. Of course, exchangeability with cash will be guaranteed for a while. This is certainly the scenario assumed in the Digital Euro initiative discussed above.

However, if physical cash usage declines, it is possible that they will be replaced by retail CBDCs. In a society where CBDC becomes the chief means of payment, the authority will gain a tool to control what people can eat, read, watch, and to whom they can communicate with, by controlling what can be purchased with CBDC. And there are myriads of social control that could be introduced on top of retail CBDCs, such as the social credit system in China or universal basic income. Consequently, CBDC issued as "programmable currency" will not be just another type of debt money. It becomes worse than the conventional banknotes in terms of privacy and freedom. Just as anyone on food stamps gets told where and how much they are able to spend their vouchers, retail CBDCs will degrade to vouchers that are mutable by any metric set by the authority.

Second Scenario: Retail CBDC as Self-Destructive Future

In any case what's crucial from the monetary system standpoint is that, under this first scenario, total money stock would still be the sum of private and public sectors' debts as analyzed in Chap. 3; *Your CBDC is someone's debt.* However, if another financial crisis occurs as discussed in Chap. 6, people will try to withdraw their bank deposits with safer retail CBDCs. The difference from the classic type of bank run is that users would try to convert their demand deposits into retail CBDC online without needing to line up to cashing machines on streets, making the bank run even faster and contagious.

Under such circumstances, central banks will need to set a cap on the amount that each user can convert their commercial banks deposits into retail CBDCs. This will in turn create the need to verify the identity of every user during the onboarding phase and link them to their CBDC accounts (apart from the AML/CFT purposes). Of course, such digital bank runs could be prevented without tying identities by setting a cap on the maximum balance that can be held per CBDC account. However, this would greatly reduce the convenience of retail CBDCs as both means of payment and store of value. That is why there will always be a need to link CBDC accounts with the identity of each user as long as digital currencies are issued along with fractional reserve banking system. This also explains why central banks have been actively working on integrating the ID system with their real-time gross settlement systems.

At this point the public scrutiny will likely be directed at the fractional reserve banking system, in which private banks are allowed to create money out of nothing. Central banks will then be driven to the point where they will have no choice but to put an end to it by themselves. This will inevitably lead to a gradual increase in the reserve ratio, which is currently at around 0–10% in G7 nations. This is the second scenario after the introduction of retail CBDCs. When 100% reserves are eventually reached, the second faucet of deposit creation in Fig. 3.7 will be closed, thus eliminating the structural cause of boom-bust cycles and the source of instability. Ironically, this arrangement will accomplish the second goal of transition to public money system discussed in Sect. 12.1. The major difference from the public money system, however, is that money must still be supplied as *someone's debt.* Who's debt will it be, then?

Since banks become genuine financial intermediaries under the 100% reserve requirement, their loanable funds must be made out of savings. Thus, under this second scenario, money needs to be issued by the central bank against government debt.[5] Of course, since the government has no other choice but to pay interests to the

---

[5] In many nations fiscal laws prohibit central banks from making loans to the government and underwriting bonds. Therefore, for new money to be issued under the second CBDC scenario (with the 100% reserve ratio), central banks will need to purchase treasury bonds directly from private sector bond holders. Under such condition, government bonds held by the central bank would be similar to traditional Consols, which are a type of perpetual debt with no fixed maturity to be redeemed and only interests are paid periodically. Thus, we may expect to see that the government

central bank out of its tax revenue, those interest on public debt must be paid for by taxes on citizens and businesses. Then, the public criticism will eventually turn to the fundamental question, "Why doesn't the government issue its own digital currency instead of retail CBDC?"

At this point, our choice will precisely become EPM vs. CBDC as Fig. 13.1 shows. And the rational choice will be to introduce EPM to protect privacy and freedom. That is perhaps why central banks, particularly in developed nations, are now hurrying up to prepare for their version of retail CBDCs before the majority of population realize on the real issue and demand central banks to be fully nationalized.[6]

Introducing EPM as Peer-to-Peer Electronic Cash

As we have examined above, retail CBDCs cannot fix the design failures of debt money system. If anything, there's a high chance that retail CBDCs could be misused as the ultimate means of control and become the worst form of money. Consequently, the benefits of retail CBDCs are minimal compared to EPM. If we take into account the historical evolution of money in Table 13.1 and rationally observe the current situation where debt money system is on the verge of collapse, we are naturally led to the conclusion that EPM is the money of the futures.

How should EPM be introduced then? The success of EPM as money of the future depends on whether it will serve as real cash that are secure and easy to use for everyone. Characteristics of cash as a payment method is that they are final and can be paid off-line while offering full anonymity. Figure 13.1 illustrates EPM issued as online electronic cash (e-cash) using digital token technologies.[7]

Public money still widely in circulation today is government-issued coins. Therefore, to introduce EPM in Japanese Yen (e-JPY), it is legally sufficient to make a minor amendment to Article 5 of the "Act on Currency Unit and Issuance of Coins". Specifically, the underlined section shall be added as follows:

Article 5 The seven types of coins are 500 yen, 100 yen, 50 yen, 10 yen, 5 yen, 1 yen, and electronic money (variable denomination).

will amend the law at some point to bypass such cumbersome step and allow the central bank to directly issue currency (as debt money) to finance government deficit. At such point, the difference between public money (EPM) and debt money (CBDC) comes down to whether the newly issued currency is recorded as net asset or liability on the issuer's balance sheet (as discussed in Sect. 9.5).

[6] In most countries where the central bank is nationalized, interest payments on government debts held by the central bank are paid back to the treasury after deducting its operational costs. In such cases, CBDC will be as close as possible to EPM, except for its governance.

[7] EPM issued as token-based money should not be confused with retail CBDCs, which are likely to be issued as account-based money. Typical examples of account-based money are bank deposits where balance of each account is linked to the account holder's identity information. Therefore, all transactions are tracked by the system administrator. On the other hand, payment by cash is made by transfer of ownership of token money (payment objects) without the need to provide identity information for verification. The system only needs to verify the authenticity of payment object just as we check the authenticity of physical cash. EPM is thus a digital currency that emulates the legal ownership of token money.

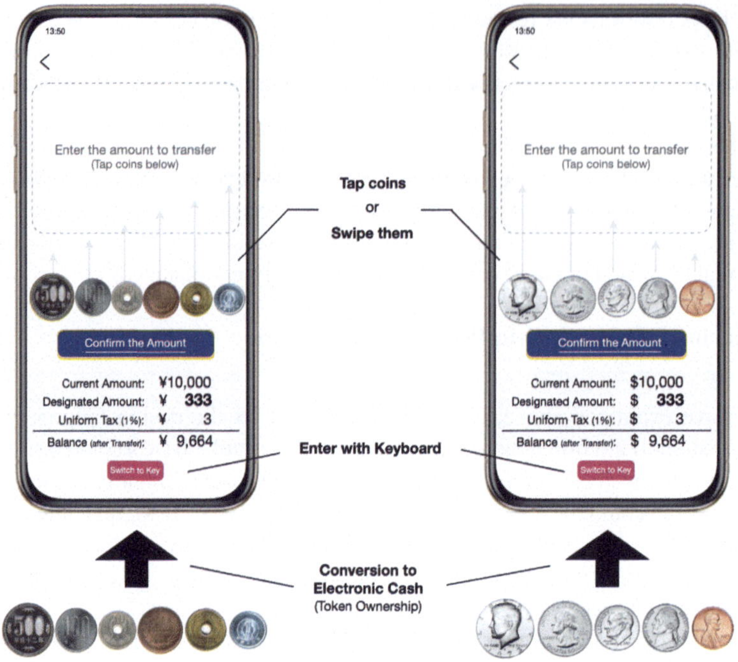

Fig. 13.1 EPM as peer-to-peer electronic cash (Left: Japanese Yen, Right: US Dollar)

13.3 EPM System Design Requirements

In order to enhance usability of EPM as true *peer-to-peer electronic cash*, EPM wallet should be designed so that users can choose from at least two modes of payment; (1) Network mode where users can transfer and receive EPM over a communication network, and (2) Proximity mode where users can exchange EPM as if they were handing over coins from person to person.

In proximity mode or "cash drop" mode, we envision a situation where payer and payee can exchange EPM simply by holding up their devices (digital wallet) close to each other using technologies such as Near-field communication (NFC). QR code payment should also be supported as one of the default payment option that users can select under the network mode. If it's technically feasible, it would be ideal for EPM to support offline payment. However, the need for offline implementation is not high since physical cash (coins and notes) would still remain in circulation as shown in Fig. 12.5. Accordingly, both network mode and proximity payment (cash drop) mode assume online environments.

It would not be difficult to support other use cases such as mobile contactless payment against POS terminals in retail stores, similar to contactless debit and credit cards embedded in our smartphones. Users can also transfer EPM directly to their bank accounts using network mode (through Bank APIs). Other use cases such as micropayments and conditional payments for decentralized applications (dApps) can be readily built via standard API provided by the EPM system. Supporting ubiquitous access to EPM would open up various business applications that were previously infeasible on existing payment infrastructure.

Following Yamaguchi (2013, Chap. 22), let us summarize the design requirements of EPM system by classifying them into two categories; requirements as (1) monetary system and (2) payment system. Let us first discuss general design requirements of EPM as a monetary system.

13.3.1 EPM as Monetary System

(1) Supply Adjustment Rate Public Money Administration (PMA) is the sole issuer of public money and tasked with regulating the total supply of currency toward price stability. The amount of new issuance or withdrawal is determined by the PMA with full transparency and accountability as described in Chap. 12. When the economy gets inflationary, the PMA is responsible for withdrawing a portion of EPM by raising *supply adjustment rate*.

(2) Uniform Tax Rate With the introduction of EPM the government can set a *uniform tax rate* on all EPM transactions and automatically collect them as *public service fees*. The introduction of uniform tax rate will simplify the present national tax system that has become highly fragmented and inefficient. As detailed in the next Sect. 13.4, this uniform tax is expected to save significant amount of costs and labor in both public and private sectors, while increasing efficiency of taxation, minimizing tax-related frauds and closing tax loopholes. Raising *supply adjustment rate* pulls back excess money directly to the PMV, while raising *uniform tax rate* transfers EPM directly to the treasury as fiscal revenues. EPM protocol must be able to accommodate such controllability of total supply.

(3) Privacy Protection Privacy of physical cash means that parties involved can keep their identity and transaction data from being revealed to anyone other than payer and payee themselves. Comparing with the level of privacy offered by physical cash, many of the existing digital tokens (including bitcoin) reveal transaction meta data and not quantum-resistant. If EPM were to be widely accepted and support various use cases, it must offer the same level of privacy as physical coins do, while ensuring that they meet the objectives of AML/CFT policy. One such idea may be to set an upper limit on the amount that can be transferred per transaction (during a specified period). Another idea is to set a certain threshold between low-volume transactions that come with full anonymity guaranteed at system level (i.e., by technology, not by regulations that can be nullified *ex post*) and high-volume transactions with partial anonymity.[8]

---

[8] "Partial" in the sense that they are subject to criminal investigations and, when necessary, identity can be disclosed by law enforcement upon due process including court orders.

13.3.2 EPM as Payment System

For EPM to be used as national digital currency, it also has to be convenient and secure. These requirements differ from those of monetary system and involve technical considerations. Below we list three requirements as a payment system.

(4) **Low Transaction Latency** Cash payments complete in a matter of few seconds. EPM payment has to be as fast as existing retail payment methods. Otherwise, the public would not consider EPM as an usable option.

(5) **Scalability and Availability** Transactions in countries with high population could easily exceed tens of thousands per second at peak times. Therefore, EPM system must be designed so that it can adequately accommodate increasing number of transactions as the economy grows. The possibility of large-scale communication failures due to major earthquakes, solar flares, cyber or electromagnetic attacks by hostile entities cannot be ruled out. As our economy becomes more dependent on digital payment systems, social consequences will also increase. Availability of EPM system must be met at the highest level as a critical national infrastructure.

(6) **Security** EPM has to be securely stored in every device (digital wallet) and transferred among users. EPM must also ensure security against man-in-the-middle and cryptanalytic attacks as well as those by quantum computers. With careful design and testing, technologies that are available today should allow governments to incorporate various security enhancements while meeting other performance requirements. Biometric authentications, such as facial recognition used in our mobile devices, may be considered as an additional layer to prevent end users from paying unintentionally or prevent others from spending EPM maliciously.

Decentralized Architecture of EPM as Payment System

Under the "conditional privacy" currently discussed with respect to the privacy of Digital Euro (retail CBDC), the monetary authority will be left with the power to trace all transaction history and, when needed, freeze CBDC accounts. After all, government regulations can be changed. As Edward Snowden's disclosure of the NSA's spy program has revealed, there are loopholes in cyberspace. As the draconian action taken by the Canadian Government during the COVID-19 lockdown has made us clear, there are exceptions in emergency. In an extreme case, payment systems themselves could be harmful if it falls into the hands of bad power.

As indicated in Chap. 12, EPM can be issued immediately in the form of (reserve) deposits on the interbank settlement system taken over from the central bank. However, those deposits (account-based money) do not provide privacy. What happens, then, if the issuer of EPM became corrupted? Even under the public money system, there is no guarantee that regulatory capture will not occur. One might wonder how a

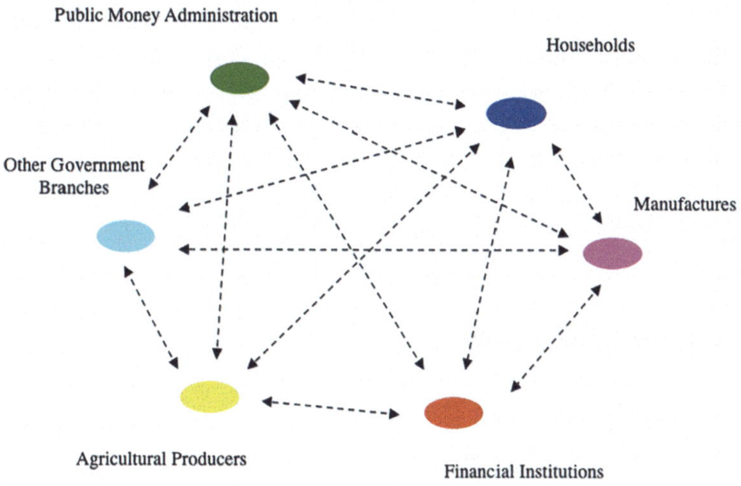

Fig. 13.2 EPM system maintained as a peer-to-peer network

digital currency issued by a government that spies on its own citizens and "allies" can protect the privacy of its users and function as power-neutral public infrastructure?

There is only one way to protect privacy in the face of these political uncertainties. Provide EPM with unconditional privacy by issuing it as electronic cash (e-cash). We call this design principle as *Privacy by Default*. One approach to issue EPM as e-cash is to incorporate the currency issuer (PMA) as one of nodes comprising the overall EPM payment network as illustrated in Fig. 13.2.[9] Under this decentralized system architecture, the PMA would only have the role to jointly validate transactions with other nodes as the administrator of payment system. This makes it impossible to unilaterally change the system configuration without the consent of other network participants from the private sectors (including traditional banks and payment service providers). Specifically, the PMA would only have an authority to oversee the list of validator nodes that jointly form the EPM network.

Is it technically feasible to build such a payment system? One promising approach that could enable EPM as e-cash is to build a system based on mixing network technology. However, distributed computing has the drawback of latency, which is the time required to process and finalize payment transactions. Bitcoin is a good example. On the Bitcoin network, it takes an average of 10 minutes to generate a block that contains transactions (though this is a deliberate design to prevent forking of the blockchain). And the speed at which BTC transactions are finalized is significantly slower than the existing centralized systems. This has forced users to choose between privacy, speed, and other conviniences such as security.

However, recent technological innovations have solved these trilemma among security, speed and privacy. In fact, digital tokens have emerged that take this

---

[9] Adapted from the original figure in Yamaguchi and Yamaguchi (2017a, Fig. 6).

approach, such as the XX coin proposed and developed by Dr. David Chaum–who is also the inventor of mixing network–and his team. If EPM payment system can provide privacy and high throughputs in a decentralized network, it can also ensure availability and resilience as a national critical infrastructure. It would also make it more difficult for governments to target their own citizens or other countries based on their power over the payment system. It will realize an ideal system that fulfills the requirements of EPM as monetary and payment system.

13.4 Uniform Tax System

Rethinking Tax System for the 21st Century

Taxation has been an essential element of society. Revolutions and uprisings in history were primarily due to dissatisfaction with heavy taxes. One of the primitive forms of taxation practiced from ancient times is the poll tax, which is levied on every (adult) citizen regardless of one's tax-bearing capacity. As such, poll tax has been considered to be the most common form of bad taxation.

Many proposals and attempts have been made to improve taxation. Income tax is closely related to war finance and establishments of modern nation states. It was first introduced in the Great Britain in 1798 (the French Revolutionary War), the United States in 1861 (the American Civil War), and Japan in 1887 (prior to the Sino-Japanese War). In the US, the constitution was amended to include income tax months before the passage of the Federal Reserve Act in 1913. Irving Fisher, while working zealously for monetary reform in the 1930s and 1940s, also proposed the (consumption) expenditure tax with his brother.[10]

After the WWII, consumption tax was introduced in France in 1959 as a value-added tax (VAT) and has since been introduced in over 160 countries, making it one of the most widely adopted form of taxation along with the income tax. Instead of VAT, the United States adopts sales and use taxes at state and local (municipality) levels and excise taxes at federal, states and local levels. In most nations, the present

[10] His motivation behind the proposal was to avoid the double taxation in income tax and tax-induced bias towards saving, which may hinder capital accumulation and economic growth. Fisher (1937a, b), Fisher and Fisher (1942) showed the feasibility of expenditure tax based on a method to indirectly calculate an individual's total consumption using double-entry bookkeeping principles. Based on the Fisher's idea, Kaldor (1955) proposed the expenditure tax. India and Sri Lanka have subsequently made attempts in 1950s and 1970s to introduce expenditure taxes based on the Kaldor's proposal. However, unlike income tax, which allows withholding at the income source, it becomes challenging to obtain accurate information on the taxable amount from someone else other than taxpayers themselves. Since it is also easy to underreport the amount of consumption expenditure, taxpayers must report income and savings to determine the amount of consumption expenditure as the difference between the two. Due to its complexity and administrative burdens of the tax return scheme, the expenditure tax were subsequently abolished in both nations.

tax systems comprise of a mixture of income and consumption taxes, and other taxes on properties, gifts and inheritance.

In Chap. 4 we have discussed that one of the structural causes of declining (real) wages in Japan was the series of tax reforms implemented during the last 30 years (along with labor liberalization implemented as part of the structural reform). Changes in tax policies benefiting the wealthy and large corporations are not problems unique to Japan. Financial liberalization and the removal of restrictions on capital movement since the 1980s have allowed multinational enterprises to move freely in and out of national borders. To secure tax revenues under the globalization, countries have shifted heavier tax burdens on labor and consumption, which are less likely to flow out of the country, instead of financial assets and corporate profits, which tend to flow out of the country when taxed. In addition, incentives to attract foreign companies and prevent outflows of capital to other countries have led to competition among nations to lower corporate tax rates and establishment of offshore tax havens.

While international capital movement itself is not a bad thing, the excessive globalization that has promoted the elimination of restrictions on it has led to the erosion of tax bases, and the resulting shift in tax burdens has diminished the perceived fairness in the existing tax system. To prevent the international double taxation and thwart profit shifting in cross-border transactions, countries have come up with various deductions, exemptions, tax credits, and transfer pricing taxation, which only made the overall structure of tax system more complicated like a patchwork. When a system gets complex, there will be loopholes that will be exploited. This is the reason why there is a growing dissatisfaction and distrust in the way the tax system is currently structured. With the introduction of EPM, we now have the opportunity to fundamentally simplify the entire tax system and make it fairer for everyone.

What Is Uniform Tax? How Does It Work?

Uniform Tax is a new form of direct national tax that can be introduced in parallel with EPM (Yamaguchi and Yamaguchi, 2017a). The tax is automatically assessed and collected whenever EPM is used in payments. It is called *uniform* since governments that issue their own currencies can unify all existing taxes into a single comprehensive Uniform Tax. In our proposed implementation discussed below, a single, fully flat and proportional tax rate is applied, which is the simplest one.

Suppose Bob owns a successful business and married to his wife Alice. Bob just got a monthly salary of $5,000 and wants to buy his wife a present. Assuming that the uniform tax rate (UTR) is effective at 1%, $1 would be collected for $100 payment of EPM. $10 would be collected for purchases of $1,000 and so on. Let's say Bob bought a present worth of $333 and 1% of UTR is applied on the total amount of EPM that Bob paid ($333) at the retail store, which is the taxable base for the particular transaction. Of course Bob can directly give her money instead of buying the present. In that case, the EPM app will calculate the necessary amount to be sent based on the effective UTR so that Alice will receive exactly the amount Bob wants to give to her. In either case, the EPM system recognizes the payment and automatically collect $3 (1%) as shown in Fig. 13.1. In this way, the uniform tax is automatically imposed on all payment transactions, regardless of whether they involve exchange of goods and services.

The same principle of taxation applies to all other payments Bob and his family make. Of course, if they think it is absurd to pay tax when giving a pocket money for their children, they can simply give them in coins and notes. If the Bob and Alice's total monthly average expenses were $4,000, the family would pay $40 in uniform tax or $480 annually (= $4,000/month × 1% × 12 months/year). That's all what the couple will be paying for their national (federal) tax under this new tax system.

The same principle also applies to companies or any other legal entities. Let's say Bob's company pays him monthly salary with bank deposits. His company will be paying the uniform tax according to the payroll payments. In the above case, the uniform tax on Bob's payroll would be $600 (= $5,000/month × 1% × 12 months/year) annually. Similarly, whenever his company make other expenditures such as purchases of raw materials and electricity bills, the EPM system recognizes every payment transaction and automatically collects them at the payment source, while fully protecting the privacy of both payer and payee. Bob's company would no longer need to pay income tax or any other national (federal) taxes.

Let's compare this to the income tax. For simplicity, let's assume that the Bob's company had annual domestic sales of $10 billion and a 25% margin. Furthermore, Bob's company has no overseas operations or permanent establishments in foreign tax jurisdictions. Assuming that Bob's company does not receive nor pay interest, dividends or rents, its net profit before taxes would simply be $2.5 billion. Now, assuming that there is no other income that is deductible or tax-exempt, the net profit of $2.5 billion would be the taxable income his company would bear. If the legal corporate tax rate is 20%, the taxable income would be $500 million (= $2.5 billion × 0.2).

On the other hand, the 25% operating margin in the above example means a 75% cost ratio. So the Bob's company would have spent $7.5 billion in total expenses to realize the $10 billion sales revenue in that year. Now assuming for simplicity that all these expenses were paid during the same year, then, if the uniform tax rate were constant at 1%, Bob's company would bear $75 million of uniform tax annually. That's all what his company would pay for the country.

The simplicity of uniform tax lies in the real-time automatic assessment and collection of tax at the event of payment. This will eliminate the need for filing tax returns, freeing individuals and businesses of enormous tax compliance costs and reducing the government's administrative costs. As with all existing tax systems, uniform tax system is vulnerable to evasion when physical currency is freely available to the taxpaying public. However, it would be much more impractical to avoid the uniform tax since the only way to do so is to make all payments with physical cash.[11] Thus, the larger the business grows and payments become, the less practical such tax avoidance becomes. Accordingly, the uniform tax system will also address the problems of double taxation[12] and base erosion and profit shifting (BEPS) by multinational corporations.

Uniform Tax as Principle of Equitable Distribution of Tax Burden

The most important feature of uniform taxation on payment transaction is that the burden is equally and broadly distributed to all participants in the national economy. Whenever EPM (currency) moves, i.e., when economic activity takes place, the tax burden will be universally distributed according to the amount of each payment. In other words, the basic argument for a uniform tax is that, rather than trying to determine the appropriate tax base that is fair to everyone based on their income or amount of money spent on consumption (or the wealth possessed or inherited), the burden should be defined, assessed and enforced based on the actual tax-bearing capacity of each economic entity as evidenced by the amount of their total expenditures.

Under the new uniform tax system, a flat-rate tax is levied equally on all voluntary payments made by all economic entities. Hence, the same egalitarian principle of distributing the tax burden applies to all economic entities regardless of social classes. This means that the uniform tax system does not differentiate tax payers between (1) *nature of transaction* such as payment or transfer, (2) *type of expenditure* such as real or financial transactions, (3) *individual attribute* such as men and women, young and old, (4) *occupation* such as farmers, freelancers, business owners, employees, diplomats or parliamentarians, and (5) *type of legal entity*, such as private individuals, hereditary peers, for-profit corporations, religious institutions, nonprofits or charitable organizations. By adapting the concept of taxation to monetary flows representing economic activities in this way, the current national tax system that have become highly complex and opaque for non-expert will be radically simplified, transparent and neutral.

11 There are of course some ways to "police" such evasion of uniform taxation. One practical approach is to impose higher tax rates on the use of physical currency than digital currency (EPM) each time it leaves and enters the banking system.

12 Also known as "tax on tax", the double taxation is a deficiency of the present tax system due to its fragmentation and complexity. In Japan the example of double taxation includes the application of a general consumption tax (national tax) to a portion of (1) gasoline tax (consisting of national and local taxes), and (2) petroleum and coal tax. In addition, corporate income is first subject to taxation at the corporate level and then taxed as dividend income when distributed to shareholders, resulting in double taxation. With uniform tax, companies and individuals equally share the tax burden proportionately only up to the amount of each payment transaction. Hence, double taxation will be eliminated.

Uniform Tax as Public Service Fees
Because of these characteristics, the uniform tax can be viewed as *public service fees* collected by the government for the provision and maintenance of public utilities and social capitals (infrastructures) that facilitate and protect the national economy. In this sense, the uniform tax is truly a universal form of flat tax that replaces all existing national taxes, including taxes on income, consumption, private wealth and properties. Due to such nature, it could also be called *cash flow tax* or *economic activity tax* depending on how we see it.[13] Because of the comprehensiveness of its broad tax base (total money flows in a given period), uniform tax also embodies the characteristics of all existing taxes levied on "flows" (consumption, income, etc.).

EPM Supply Adjustment and Uniform Tax Rates

Figure 13.3 illustrates the relationship between the EPM supply adjustment and uniform tax rates described in Sect. 13.3.1. There is a clear distinction between fiscal policy and public money policy. In the former, currencies that are already in circulation are collected as uniform taxes and flow back into the government's treasury accounts at the center, and re-injected into the economy through government's expenditures. These government consumption (C_G) and investment (I_G) will add to the national income of that period immediately.

Public money policy, on the other hand, changes the total supply of money and is conducted under a clear policy objective to stabilize prices. Specifically, the PMA decides the amount of new issuance or withdrawal based on its current supply (which PMA knows) and demand submitted by the Treasury. EPM supply adjustment rate is a control valve for this purpose.

Uniform Tax as Fiscal Policy Instrument
Using the bathtub analogy, public money policy is equivalent to adjusting the amount of hot water in a tub, which is money stock M^s. Fiscal policy accelerates the velocity of circulation V just like stirring water. In contrast to the present system, where M^s fluctuates endogenously due to bank lending and debt repayment, price level P is

[13] Uniform Tax was originally inspired by Bitcoin transaction fee and proposed along with issuance of EPM (Yamaguchi and Yamaguchi, 2017a). However, after researching previous studies when writing this chapter, we learned that Dr. Edward L. Feige had proposed a similar idea called "Automated Payment Transaction (APT) Tax" (Feige, 2000), which turns out to be the closest precedent to our proposal. In fact he anticipated that it would be the government's duty to issue and provide electronic cash in order to prevent the proliferation of privately issued digital tokens designed to evade the APT tax. His proposal, however, seems to be limited within the scope of tax reform and proposes to collect it directly on transactions going to and from every bank account by inserting new software into the existing two-tier payment system (consisting of interbank payment network connected to central bank settlement system). In this regard, APT proposal fails to address the fundamental problems of the underlying debt money system discussed in this book. After Dr. Feige first presented the idea at a conference in Buenos Aires in 1989, six Latin American countries tried it. Brazil adopted a plan similar to the APT tax called "Bank Transaction tax" between 1993–2007 along with existing taxes, which has been reported to be relatively successful (see Cintra, 2009).

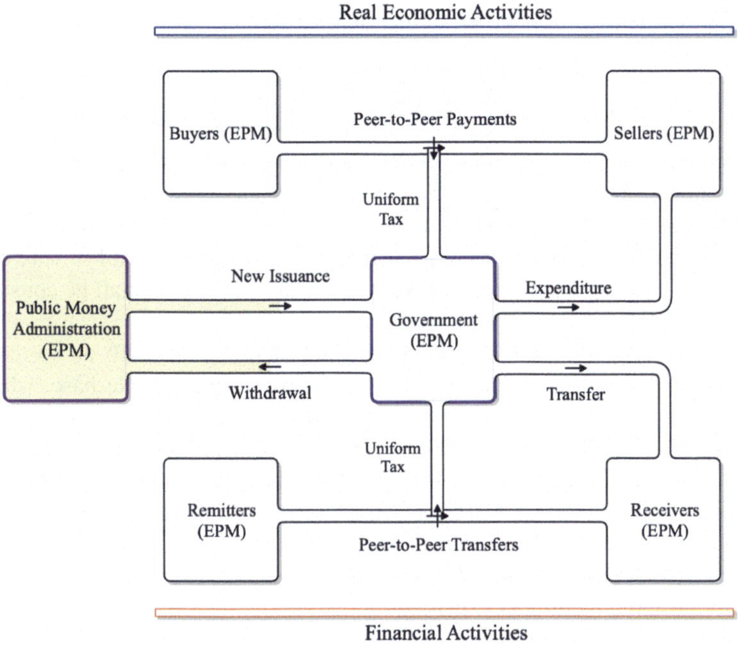

Fig. 13.3 EPM supply adjustment and uniform tax rates

generally proportional to M^s under the public money system. Therefore, the role of PMA is to control P by adjusting M^s to keep the inflation rate within the inflation tolerance range set by the law.[14]

In case of an inflationary trend, the PMA withdraws purchasing power (M_1) out of circulation. If inflation momentum is strong and persistent, the PMA may further raise the EPM supply adjustment rate. During the adjustment or contractionary phase of an economic cycle, new money may be injected through fiscal policy. In this way, the PMA is in a position to oversee the supply and demand necessary to achieve its price stability objective. Uniform tax system allows the public to know its revenues in real time (through fiscal data disclosed through the PMA) so that it also incentivizes finance bureaucrats to fine-tune fiscal policy according to the needs of the society. In this sense, uniform tax becomes more efficient and enhances government transparency.

[14] We have discussed in Part II that the velocity of money circulation V in real economic transactions has been stable historically. The Friedman's rule-based monetary policy through fixed growth rate of money stock ("K-percent rule") would be effective under the exogenous public money system.

Initial Estimate of Uniform Tax Rate: Case for Japan

Uniform tax can be introduced once the transition to public money system is completed. As uniform taxes begin to flow into the treasury, income and all other national taxes can be abolished overnight to avoid unintended double taxation. Once the total revenue from uniform taxes reach the total government expenditures, all other general taxes can be removed and unified into one national tax. Whether the government should continue to use special tax (e.g. custom duties), or whether uniform tax should also "absorb" the local government taxes (state taxes in the US) shall be considered carefully in light of the economic situation.[15]

How can we determine the appropriate level of UTR, then? To do so requires a simple arithmetic. Specifically we need to estimate total taxable base. which is the total volume of transactions made by EPM (national currency), and compare it against the desired level of fiscal revenues or expenditures. Let's consider the case of Japan. The Zengin system–Japanese Interbank Payment Clearing Network–processed approximately 2,800 trillion yen of domestic fund transfers in 2012, out of the demand deposits of about 600 trillion yen. This includes all payment transactions among non-banking sectors including business-to-business payments and households consumption and government expenditures.

In addition to payments made by bank deposits, there are roughly 100 trillion yen of BoJ notes outstanding. Although there is no publicly available data on how much payment is actually made by BoJ notes annually, they are used mostly for final consumptions at retail stores. Given that Japanese households consumption expenditure has been 300 trillion yen (Fig. 4.4), let us assume that roughly 250 trillion yen are made in cash at maximum, which is the same as assuming that the average velocity of BoJ note is 2.5 times per year, or roughly 84% of households consumption is made by cash (note that Japan's cash usage is relatively high). In total, about 3,050 trillion yen ($= 2,800$ trillion yen $+250$ trillion yen) of payment transactions are made annually in Japan with its nominal GDP hovering between 500 and 550 trillion yen for the last 30 years.

The government's general tax revenues is about 55 trillion yen and its expenditures are about 100 trillion yen. Given these preminary estimates, a uniform tax rate (UTR)

[15] In the US case, for instance, since there is an excise tax (at the federal, state, and local levels) and a sales tax (at the state and local level), introducing uniform tax would result in double taxation upon consumption expenditure. Therefore, at the state and local level, the sales and excise taxes need to be abolished immediately upon the transition, and local tax systems should be restructured around taxes other than transfer tax that would be covered by the uniform tax. Uniform tax system accordingly does not abolish the concept of tax mix, whereas the APT tax proposal by Feige (2000) assumes the integration of all federal taxes and some of the state taxes. For simplicity and cost efficiency, the latter seems preferable. However, that requires some mechanisms to distribute the national (federal) tax revenues to each state's budget according to a certain predefined criteria based on geolocation data. It not only increases the reliance of local governments and municipalities on the central government, disagreements on the distribution criteria at the state levels may create fissures and frictions between constituents that may make the introduction of APT tax at the national level difficult or appear less fair. Under the uniform tax proposal, the local governments and municipalities should continue to administer their local tax systems and maintain their own tax revenues.

of 3.3% (single, proportionate) would sufficiently cover the current level of annual expenditures without incurring fiscal deficits; that is, 3,050 trillion yen/year × 0.033 = 100 trillion yen/year. Compared with the current consumption tax rate effective (10%) as of 2022, our preliminary estimate of UTR would be far smaller, about one third of the consumption tax rate.

On the other hand, the BOJ-NET–the BoJ's real time gross settlement (RTGS) system–processed on average about 150 trillion yen per business day in 2018. This amounts to 54,750 trillion yen annually. This settlement volume should already include the interbank payments reported by the Zengin system (2,800 trillion yen/year). However, the order of magnitude is different by one digit. Most of the difference between these two data is most likely due to the wholesale transactions among financial institutions including transfers of property rights, foreign exchange and stocks. Because of the two-tier structure of the current payment system, these payment transactions by central bank reserves only show up as inter-account settlements processed on the central bank's RTGS system. Therefore, for the estimation of the uniform tax rate, the latter figure shall be used as a more appropriate reference data for our estimation.

Assuming that transactions stay at the current level, the UTR of around 0.183% would sufficiently cover the government expenditure, that is, 54,750 trillion yen/year × 0.00183 = 100 trillion yen/year. Compared with the current consumption tax rate once again, the estimated UTR should be about a factor of 55 smaller than the 10% tax rate! In the case of US Dollar, the total payment volume (taxable base) would be much larger. Accordingly, UTR for the US government would be much smaller.

These numbers themselves should provide enough reason for the majority of population to make transitions to the public money system. Nevertheless, one might be concerned that imposing taxes on financial transactions would stifle the markets and economic activity. Indeed, this sort of criticism has been directed towards financial transaction tax (FTT). Certainly, short term speculative transactions, particularly those seeking marginal profits with high-frequency trading (HFT), would decline. However, the marginal tax rate is small relative to price fluctuations that typically occur during trading process. Overall, uniform tax will serve to reduce the volatility of prices in financial markets, as Tobin tax or any variation of FTT aimed for.

This is the characteristics of uniform tax as an economic activity tax. A single flat-rate tax levied on all voluntary payment transactions hits the broadest conceivable tax base, thus requiring the lowest conceivable marginal tax rate. In both cases the actual UTR required will likely be even lower as the economy is reactivated and velocity of money increases through the Public Money Initiative proposed in the next Chap. 14.[16]

---

[16] Due to its wide tax base, the economic growth expected from adoption of the uniform tax shall cover the expected increase in the government expenditure without a significant rate increase. Even if the total transaction volume fell by 50% after the transition to 27,375 trillion yen, the UTR of 0.0036 would be enough to cover the current government expenditure of 100 trillion yen (= 27,375 trillion yen/year × 0.0036) in the Japanese case. Therefore, even large and unexpected fiscal expenditures, such as the one mobilized during the COVID-19 pandemic, would require only a rate increase at the one-hundredth decimal place. This tax rate stability and budget elasticity is another

The Fairest, Simplest and Most Transparent Tax System

Let us summarize characteristics of uniform tax in comparison with income and consumption taxes. Uniform tax enhances fairness, simplicity, neutrality, clarity, international consistency and adaptability.

1. **Fairness** of taxation can be considered from several aspects; those with equal economic power should bear the tax burden equally (horizontal fairness), and those with greater economic power should bear more (vertical fairness). In addition the intergenerational fairness has increasingly become important. For example, in Japan, the combination of the baby boom generation, the increase in average life expectancy and the recent decline in birthrates have resulted in a rapidly aging demographic structure, which may lead to inequality in the level of tax burden that needs to be paid over a person's lifetime depending on when he or she is born. Intergenerational equity means that the tax burden should be shared not only by the working generation but also by a wide range of members of the society.

   Characteristics: With respect to vertical fairness, income tax allows for a progressive burden in accordance with the income level (bracket) through a progressive tax rate and various deductions and exemptions. On the other hand, with regard to horizontal fairness, there is a risk of differences in the assessment of tax base depending on the type of income and other factors, which could lead to differences in the tax burden even among those in the same income level. There are also differences in income sources and resulting tax-bearing capacity. Thus, identifying a truly equitable tax base has been a longstanding unresolved issue in income taxation. There is also the issue of intergenerational fairness, especially in aging societies such as Japan where tax burden may be skewed toward working generations.[17]

   Unlike income taxes, the burden of consumption tax is distributed equally and borne proportionally to the level of expenditure (horizontal fairness). As such, tax burden may become regressive with respect to the income level (vertical unfairness). However, the characteristic of consumption tax is its ability to distribute the burden not only to the working population but also to a wide range of members of society (intergenerational fairness).

   Under the uniform tax, the principle of distributing tax burden is fundamentally different from that of income tax. The tax burden is shared equally among all economic entities with the same level of expenditures (spending power). Compared to the consumption tax, uniform tax burden is distributed more universally (comprehensively) and proportionally among all economic entities. To further

feature of the uniform tax, and also beneficial in terms of neutrality to the economic activities. One may worry that the loss of discipline among politicians could lead to rapid fiscal expansion. However, all they will be doing by raising UTR is to increase the velocity of money circulation. Under the public money system, fiscal expansion will not increase the total quantity of currency.

[17] There is another problem that effective income tax rate actually applied becomes less for those with higher incomes once it reaches a certain level with the help of various tax evasion schemes.

enhance the vertical fairness of the uniform tax, one may argue for a progressive tax rate. However, that is not necessary because those with higher spending power conduct a disproportionate share of total transactions in the economy. Accordingly, in terms of fairness of the uniform tax, those with higher spending power would bear a disproportionate burden despite its single flat rate tax structure.[18]

2. **Simplicity** of taxation means that the tax collection should be kept simple in order to reduce costs borne on the side of taxpayers and administrative costs on the side of tax authority. In addition to reducing the administrative and compliance cost, simplicity is important to raise the public's understanding of tax.

   Characteristics: The progressive structure of income tax rate and various standards for deductions and exceptional provisions make income tax highly complex. The administrative burden of year-end adjustments are demanding and inconvenience of tax returns persists. On the other hand, consumption (VAT) tax has few exceptions and relatively simple. However, taxpayers (businesses) have to classify their transactions into taxable and non-taxable transactions, which is a heavy burden for them. The apparent simplicity of consumption tax is only limited to its flat rate structure. In reality it is also complicated. Furthermore, since the current tax system combines these two taxes, tax is levied twice; when income is earned and the remaining income is spent on consumption.
   Uniform tax is collected automatically at the payment source, making it the simplest and most convenient form of tax for taxpayers and the authority. For individuals who have been forced to file complicated income tax returns, elimination of income tax will simplify the laborious process, especially for small and family-owned businesses. Corporate income tax will also be integrated into the uniform tax, which will not only reduce the burden on corporate enterprises, but also save significant amount of labor spent of unproductive duties.

3. **Neutrality** means that a tax should minimize interference with the resource allocation function of the market, and that the tax burden is not biased toward any particular economic activity or entity. Along with fairness, neutrality is critical to ensure that the tax system as a whole is as free as possible from distortions to economic activity.

   Characteristics: Income taxation, if highly progressive, can undermine incentives to work and undertake entrepreneurial risks. In addition, income taxes are non-neutral with respect to people's choice between current consumption and saving, and can act to discourage their willingness to save. Taxation on consumption is

---

[18] Each country shall define the specific type of transactions for tax exemptions. For example, the uniform tax need not apply to transactions involving payments between national and local governments and private parties, such as survivor pensions, unemployment insurance benefits, and local tax payments. Uniform Tax should also be exempt from transactions such as the purchase of basic necessities for individuals and households on public assistance. However, these exemptions should be kept simple and clear, and within the scope of public interest in order to eliminate arbitrariness in taxation decisions (see "4. Clarity" below).

neutral to incentives to work and conduct businesses as it does not tax income realized from productive activities. It is not progressive with respect to income levels. However, the impact of consumption tax hike may become strong during recessionary phase, such as discussed in the context of Japan in Chap. 4.
Uniform tax is the most neutral form of taxation conceivable because the tax burden is imposed proportionally on all payment transactions and not biased toward any particular industry, economic activity or entity.

4. **Clarity** means that taxation should be obvious for the tax bearer, allowing for non-arbitrary judgement in the assessment and enforcement of tax. Clarity also has to do with simplicity and transparency.

   Characteristics: There are exceptions to income tax, which could lead to differences in the assessment of taxable base. This may lead to a lack of clarity and distrust of the system among taxpayers. On the other hand, consumption tax has a relatively clear form of taxation, although problems such as double taxation have arisen. In comparison, uniform tax is the clearest form of taxation conceivable.

International Aspect of Uniform Tax System

Cross-Border Consistency and Adaptability

Tax system reflects the national history, culture, and economic structure. However, if the differences in tax items and burdens between countries become too far apart, it could hinder the international competitiveness of a country's industries and economic vitality. In an era of globalization and e-commerce, it is also necessary to ensure that national tax systems maintain international consistency and can adapt to the changing needs of the society. As more countries adopt the uniform tax system, it works to provide a level playing field at the international level.

Characteristics: Consumption and income tax rates differ from country to country. On other hand, uniform tax is also levied on all cross-border transactions, regardless of nationality of transaction parties. Thus, governments that adopt the uniform tax system can expect additional tax revenues from the internationalization of their national currencies. As a result, there is another incentive for governments to implement sound monetary policies that contribute to their sustainable economic developments. As more countries adopt the UTS, the more consistent their tax systems will become, and the harder it becomes to evade taxes internationally.

Implications for Tax Avoidance and Evasion

Over the years the wealthy individuals and multinational corporations have cleverly avoided the tax through loopholes while the majority of citizens and SMEs suffered from the increased tax burden imposed by the tax reforms. Uniform tax will equally allocate tax burden on all entities conducting payments with particular national currency. As a result no one will be able to evade tax anymore, even if multinationals and wealthy individuals abuse tax shelters, paper companies, tax havens or off-shore trusts, unless they manage to transport heavy stacks of physical cash for cross-border payments.

Furthermore, the more countries adopt uniform tax system, the more it will be difficult to avoid the uniform tax. And there will be no need to establish a supranational tax authority either, which has been discussed as a solution to address the problem of base erosion and profit shifting by transnational enterprises. Thus, uniform tax will also eliminate the need to give up national sovereignty. This is why EPM and uniform tax system is the fundamental solution that address many of economic problems while preserving the financial privacy of citizens and their national sovereignty.

Conclusion

In this chapter we have proposed a parallel introduction of Electronic Public Money (EPM) that protects the privacy and Uniform Tax (UT) that significantly enhances fairness, simplicity, clarity, and efficiency of national tax system. It will provide an effective policy tool to control tax revenues and is more neutral than all of the existing taxes in its potential impact on the economy. A uniform tax system would be ideal not only for industrialized countries, but also for developing countries that wish to attract foreign direct investments while strengthening domestic industries and drive economic development. By introducing a uniform tax, national governments no longer need to track the income of individuals and businesses for tax purposes. Thus, citizens would have no reason to provide more personal information than necessary. This is why money and tax systems reform must go hand in hand in order to maximize equity and fairness of our economic system, all while preserving our privacy and freedoms in the digital age.

Chapter 14
Public Money Initiative

Public Money Initiative is a set of fiscal policy programs designed to stimulate the Japanese economy and save the nation from its Lost 30 Years using public money as principal source of fundings. However, the socioeconomic problems currently facing Japan are not unique to Japan. Other countries are also experiencing or beginning to experience similar issues such as declining birthrates, shrinking local economies, aging public infrastructure, and lack of investments in science and technology research. Therefore, we believe that the Initiative proposed in this chapter will also be of interest to readers outside Japan. This chapter starts with outlining the problem of aging society, which is the most serious issue Japan is currently facing but has not been focused in this book yet. Then it discusses specific programs proposed by the Initiative and analyzes how each program will interact with one another based on causal loop diagrams. Finally, we will discuss how the Initiative proposed as a short-term solution to bring the economic revival will also serve as a foundation for tackling the problem of aging society as a long-term solution toward sustainable futures.

14.1 Population Decline Toward 22nd Century

Japan's demography shows that its working-age population (aged 15–64) reached its peak at 87.16 million in 1995. Around 2004–2005, the number of births per year exceeded the number of deaths and the total population peaked at 128 million in 2008. After that, it had remained flat until around 2010 and the natural decline of the total population began in 2011. In other words, Japan had already entered a demographically standstill society in the late 2000s, and is currently in the process of accelerating its pace as one of the world's fastest aging societies. If the population decline continues as projected, it is estimated to decrease to a level between 64 million and 37.7 million people in 2100.

K. Yamaguchi and Y. Yamaguchi, *Public Money*,
https://doi.org/10.1007/978-981-97-6564-5_14

If consumption cannot be expected to increase, the domestic private demand begins to decline. In such scenarios, the shrinkage of the economy itself will be inevitable. Accordingly, Japan will be sooner or later forced to rely on massive immigrants if she wants to maintain her current GDP level as the world No.3.

To explore such future scenarios, we have run our ASD macroeconomic model of Japan, first, by applying birthrate data and six population cohort among ages between 0–14, 15–21, 22–44, 45–64, 65–79 and 80 plus over, and then estimated death rates of all cohorts. Next, with these estimated results, we have applied total fertility data and estimated initial population of all cohorts and total population dynamics. Total fertility rate (TFR) applied here is defined as the average number of children that are born to a woman over her lifetime.

Figure 14.1 is the summary of our simulations of Japan's population dynamics. Line 1 (blue) in the embedded figure of Total Fertility indicates actual fertility data between 1980 and 2020. TFR in Japan was 1.26 as of 2022. On the basis of these data, the Figure successfully shows the behavior of total population dynamics (line 1) against the actual population data (line 5) till 2020.

By extending these results into the future, we have further obtained that Japan's sustainable total fertility rate that can sustain its total population is 2.1 as shown in the embedded figure. Compared with this sustainable level, Japan's total fertility rates (line 1) turned out to be far below since 1980, indicating that Japanese population is sooner or later destined to decline. In fact, our simulation showed that Japan's population peaked at 129 million people in 1999 (line 1 in the main figure), then begins to decline until the current year of 2024. Although our simulation shows that the peak of demographic change is about 10 years earlier than that of the actual data, we decided to use it as it captures the overall trend.

What will happen if the fertility rate remains the same as the current TFR of 1.26 as of 2022? We have extended the simulation beyond this century to the middle of the

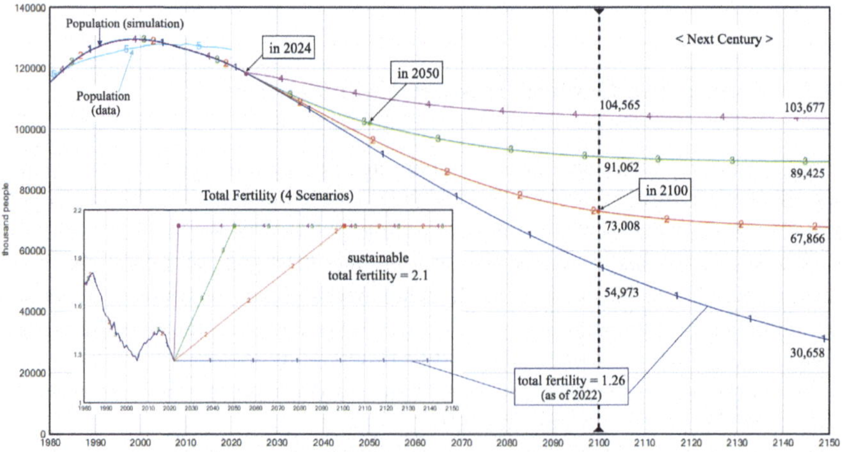

Fig. 14.1 Counter-intuitive behaviors of Japanese population dynamics

next century: the year 2150. Line 1 of Fig. 14.1 illustrates that Japan's total population continues to decline all the way to about 55 million people in 2100 and furthermore to about 31 million people in 2150. This means that total population of 31million people projected in 2150 will be about the same size as the total population of Nepal in 2022, which is ranked 49th in the world. Simply assuming that productivity per capita will be maintained at the current level, the simulation implies that Japan's economic scale shrinks to the 24% of the current level in terms of population.

Our simulations reveal the dismal future to the Japanese people with this unprecedented pace of population decline. Japan may need at least 100 million population if she wishes to maintain her current level of production and the living standard. How can we sustain such level of population, then? The answer is to restore the sustainable total fertility level of 2.1 as a national policy target.

With these considerations in mind, we have run three scenarios for TFR; line 2 (red), line 3 (green) and line 4 (pink). Line 2 attains this sustainable fertility level gradually by the end of this century in 2100. Line 3 tries to attain it by the middle of this century; that is, in 2050, while line 4 attains it as early as possible in 2024. Corresponding lines 2, 3 and 4 in the main figure show population projections under three simulations. To our surprise, in all cases population continues to decline. Even if the sustainable total fertility is attained now (line 4), total population will decline to 105 million people in 2100.

This implies that a mere attainment of sustainable fertility is not enough to stop population decline. In fact, in simulation 2, population continues to decline to 68 million people by the middle of next century, while in simulation 3 it decreases to 89 million people in 2150. Only in simulation 4 it stabilizes around 104 million people. When we think about the population decline, we tend to intuitively (linearly) assume that it will soon stop if the fertility rate is raised to a sustainable level. However, these simulations show quite the opposite and entirely counter-intuitive. It takes more than a century to attain sustainable population after fulfilling our target policy of sustainable total fertility.

Considering the current TFR of 1.26 as of 2022 and the dismal circumstances surrounding Japan's economic stagnation, it seems to be a very difficult task to attain the sustainable total fertility of 2.1 in this century. Structural reforms have forced many young Japanese into precarious, non-regular employment, forcing them to work longer hours while their salaries barely grow. Even if we could luckily attain a sustainable TFR by the end of this century (line 2), it takes another century to stabilize the population.

The only hope against this dismal future is to implement the Public Money Initiative and achieve sustainable total fertility policy as soon as possible. Only then Japan could sustain its population around 100 million people as projected above. Thankfully, through systems thinking, we have identified the fifth loop of birthrate and population in the Initiative presented below. This Initiative, which is intended to solve the Japan's Lost 30 Years as the short-term solution, turns out to lead to the sustainability of population as the long-term solution. Let us now explore the Initiative and its five programs in the next section.

14.2 Five Programs of Public Money Initiative

What can we do with public money? What kind of policies should be implemented to overcome Japan's Lost 30 Years? This has been our main question since the publication of *Public Money* (Yamaguchi, 2015). The Public Money Initiative answers these questions in a simple way. In December 2016, about a year after its publication, Kaoru organized a mailing list of the Public Money Forum. The number of participants gradually increased and hot discussions on various topics related to public money were held everyday. Some people even made their visits to the author's home from all over Japan, and each time the discussions went on late into the night. Most of the forum members who participated in the online forum were not economists. However, as the lively discussions took place, all participants came to the conclusion that the monetary issue is not a topic to be left to economists alone. Rather, it is a topic that is inseparable from our daily lives and must be understood by everyone.

The Public Money Initiative was born out of such engaged discussions and evolved into the current version presented in this chapter. The intended effects of its economic policies on our society may be compared to the effects of medical treatments on our bodies and the state of our health. Specifically, the Initiative proposes the following five programs.

1. Basic Health Recovery Program

- Provide all citizens with uniform allowance of 200,000 yen for four years (which roughly amounts to the average monthly salary in early 20s).
- Compensate for the victims of the Fukushima nuclear power plant disaster and confine the radioactivitive wastes by gathering wisdoms of the world.
- Rescue the victims of COVID-19 mRNA vaccinations by gathering the wisdoms of scientists and medical doctors with a conscience worldwide.
- Reduce the consumption (VAT) tax to zero, immediately.

2. Physical Fitness Enhancement Program

- Make non-regular employees regular employees and practice MuRatopia management such as lifetime employment, democracy at work place, employee stock ownership, etc.
- Guarantee minimum wage (e.g. 1,500 yen per hour).

3. Long-Term Human Potential Improvement Program

- Make tuitions free at national and public universities and provide the equivalent amount of scholarship grants at private universities in order to reestablish a nation founded on science, technology, arts and culture.
- Pay off all existing student loans with public money.
- Support the enhancement of human power both physically and spiritually.

4. Wholesome and Cultured Living Program

- To guarantee "the minimum standards of wholesome and cultured living" as set forth in Article 25 of the Japanese Constitution,

  (a) Households raising children are to receive benefits equal to the difference between their current income and 3 million yen (households with zero labor income are eligible for benefits by earning income from jobs provided or introduced by the government or local government).
  (b) Enhance social welfare for prosperous and fulfilling life of the elderly.

- Promote preventive medicine and preventive health insurance systems, and healthy nutritious diets through local agricultural products.

5. Friendship Diplomacy Program with Neighbors

- Advance coexistence and co-prosperity with neighboring countries through mutual-support and peace-making activities such as environmental conservation, free trade of industrial products, and enhanced ODA (Official Development Assistance).

Policies to be Decided by Direct Referendum

In addition to the above programs, important policies whose influence extends to future generations and which are controversial among the public will be decided by national referendum in a direct democratic manner, and will not be included in the program proposals in this initiative. For example, for or against restarting nuclear power plants, national security-related laws, casino laws, seed laws, etc. Once the public money system is established, the social and economic environment will be expected to change drastically for the better. Therefore, these policies can be decided by referendum under such a new environment.

14.3 Systems Thinking of the Initiative Programs

Simply listing the above five programs of the Public Money Initiative would be like a political party's campaign pledge, and would have little appeal to the readers. In order to be appealing, they need to be clearly defined in terms of priorities, how each program affects one another to create synergies, and so on. What, then, should be the highest priority among the above five programs? From the analysis in Part II, the program that "makes non-regular employees regular employees and practices MuRatopia management" should be given the highest priority.

Reviving "Japanese Management" Is the Top Priority

Why? Kaoru studied at UC Berkeley and taught economics at California State University, Hayward (renamed to East Bay since 2005) and the University of San Francisco in the 1980s when Japan was hailed as "Japan as Number One". In those days, the Japanese semiconductor industry was in fierce competition with Silicon Valley. And by the late 1980s it had surged to overtake the U.S. as the world's market share leader by country, accounting for half of the global market as briefly mentioned in Chap. 4. Wherever he visited, he was asked: "What is Japanese management? Please tell us about it." He had never before felt such a pride in being a Japanese at the time.

Japanese management is a form of labor and employment policy characterized by lifetime employment, seniority, family allowances and benefits, employee welfare, and so on. It was generally recognized at that time that Japanese management was the driving force that enabled Japan's rapid economic growth. At UC Berkeley, the International Economic Roundtable, led by Professor Laura Tyson (Director), was actively researching Japanese management and the industrial and trade policies of the Ministry of International Trade and Industry (MITI). Another Japanese graduate student who was also studying at the same Graduate School of Economics at Berkeley was participating in this project, and Kaoru was indirectly aware of the research project through him. Against this backdrop, Kaoru became convinced that the Japanese management would soon become the mainstream in the world of corporate management, rather than the inhuman shareholder-oriented management favored by Western companies in which workers are traded in the labor market as if they are exploitable commodity under the capitalist system. The Japanese management must become the universal model of economy that would save workers and redeem the world, he strongly believed.

However, after the burst of the bubble in 1990, the economic model based on Japanese management was thoroughly destroyed by structural reforms. Since then, the economy has been groaning in the "Lost 30 Years" of zero growth. Looking back, what Professor Tyson and her colleagues were studying at the Round Table was not the spread of Japanese management in the U.S., as Kaoru had expected at that time. On the contrary, they must have been studying how to collapse Japanese management, introduce the American business school-style management to Japan, and increase shareholder profits by making labor market more flexible. In fact, as soon as President Clinton was in office, Professor Tyson was appointed to the President's Economic Advisory Board (1993–95) and to the chair of the National Economic Council (1995–96). And simultaneously, strategies such as the destruction of Japanese management and industrial structure began to be implemented through Japan-US Structural Impediments Initiative (SII) and trade negotiations as discussed in Chap. 4.

Part of this grand economic strategy was the rush to establish the American-style business schools (MBA programs), which was brought to Japan during the Clinton presidency. As one of these MBA schools, graduate school of business was opened at Doshisha University in Kyoto in 2004. And Kaoru, working on the new ASD macroeconomic modeling at Haas School of Business, UC Berkeley, as a visiting scholar, was invited as a full-time professor at the Doshisha Business School.

However, Kaoru could not keep up with the efficiency principle and market fundamentalism of American business school-style management that prioritize the economic interests of shareholders (capitalists) and bankers (financiers). In the fall of 2009, he has launched the world's first Green Business Program (Green MBA) with "public money" and "Japanese management" as its two pillars as the program director at Doshisha Business School. Fortunately, this Green MBA program was quickly gaining international recognition and Kaoru's interview article appeared in English business school magazines. He was also invited to give a speech about the program at the Asia-Pacific Business School Directors' Conference. In March 2013, just as the new Green MBA program was getting off the ground, Kaoru was suddenly fired from Doshisha University after being criticized that "Professor Yamaguchi has been teaching biased economics" during one of the faculty meetings. His academic dream of establishing the Green MBA program was shattered. But he has never given up his dream to this day, believing that "Where there is a will, there is a way".

So, how exactly was Japanese management destroyed? First of all, as we saw in Chap. 4, the Agency Worker Law was enacted in 1986, just before the collapse of the bubble economy. Trade unions have been watered down and the working environment that had been protected by lifetime employment has fallen apart. In 1996, the scope of dispatched workers was expanded to 26 industries. And in 1999, dispatch labor business was fully liberalized in principle and strengthened. At this point Japanese management was almost completely destroyed. The final step in this process was the revision of Agency Worker Law that was enacted in April 2004, which removed the term limits on worker dispatching to the 26 industries.

As a result, the so-called "Lost Generation", the term that refers to the generation born in the 1970s, whose job-hunting coincided with the post-bubble recessionary period, have been thrown into the raging competitive society without being able to experience the warmth of Japanese-style employment and the efficiency of production. Consequently, Japanese people now live in a society where new agency businesses are making profit out of dispatching labors (a modern-day human trafficking) and getting fat in collusion with the government's globalist policies of structural reforms.

How can Japan overcome the Lost 30 Years and regain the "Japan as Number One", then? The answer is simple. Rewind the screws of globalism that has been wound up over the past three decades. This is not an impracticable theory nor a paper plan, because the success of Japanese management has already proven its effectiveness when companies practiced it actively in the 1970s and 80s. This is the reason why the top priority must be to use public money effectively to re-establish the Japanese management and regain the control over the economy.

Systems Thinking of "Japan as Number One"

From here, we will analyze the initiative programs by applying the causal loop diagram (CLD) explained in Chap. 6 and analyze such national strategy.

Figure 14.2 illustrates a central part of the causal loop diagram created to apply systems thinking to the initiative programs. The positive sign (+) surrounded by a round arrow is a loop identifier and indicates that the loop is a positive (reinforcing) feedback loop. It turned out that all four of them are positive feedback loops in this diagram. Specifically, they are referred to as (1) Regular Employment loop, (2) Living Environment loop, (3) Growth Engine loop, and (4) Participatory Workplace loop, respectively. Let's look at them one by one.

In the regular employment loop, when the number of regular employees increases along with economic growth, real wages and income will increase, which increases consumption, boosts domestic demand, and further drives economic growth. Indeed, this becomes reinforcing feedback loop such that

$$\underline{\text{Economic growth } (+) \rightarrow \text{ Regular employees } (+)} \rightarrow \text{Real wages } (+)$$
$$\rightarrow \text{Income}(+) \rightarrow \text{Consumption } (+) \rightarrow \text{Domestic demand } (+)$$
$$\rightarrow \text{Economic growth } (+).$$

The positive signs (+) attached to variable names denote that the cause and effect in the causal relationship change in the same direction. For example, Consumption (+) indicates a causality in which an increase in Income (cause) leads to an increase in Consumption (effect). And a decrease in Income leads to a decrease in Consumption. In a growing economy, this positive feedback loop is spinning in the direction of expansion.

The living environment loop is derived from the regular employment loop, starting from income (+) → private housing investment (+) → domestic demand (+). The growth engine loop is another derivative of the regular employment loop, starting from domestic demand (+) → corporate capital investment (+) → economic growth (+). These three positive feedback loops are core economic growth drivers that work for any market economy. During the period of high economic growth from the 1960s and the "Japan as Number One" period from the mid-1970s, these positive feedback loops reinforced each other and drove the phenomenal growth of the postwar Japan.

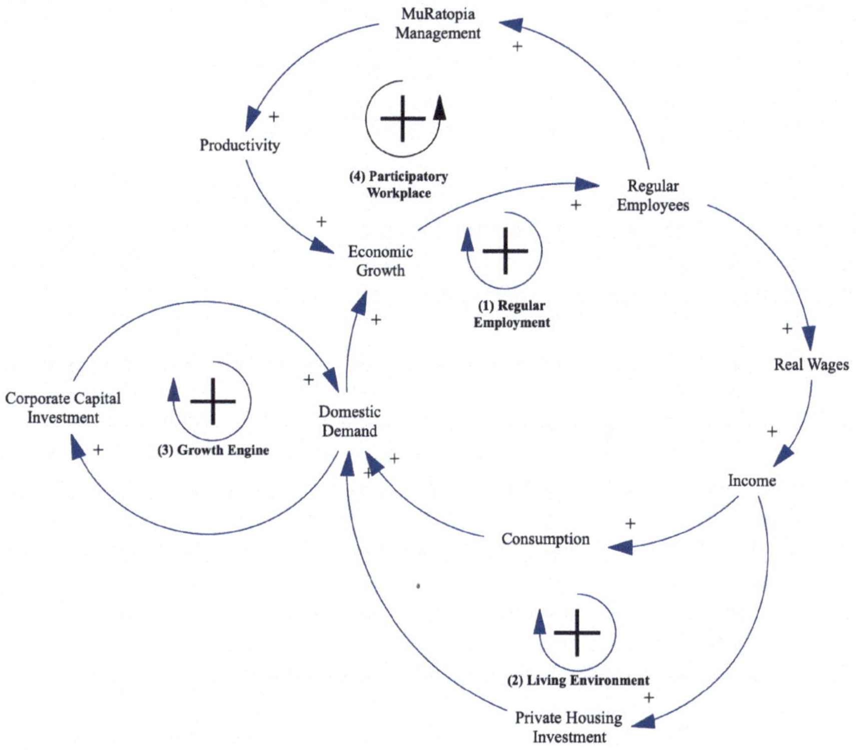

Fig. 14.2 Systems thinking of "Japan as Number One"

Furthermore, when Japan had been growing fast during 1960s through 1980s, the fourth positive feedback loop of participatory workplace played an important role as follows:

$$\underline{\text{Economic growth } (+)} \rightarrow \text{Regular employees } (+)$$
$$\rightarrow \text{MuRatopia management } (+) \rightarrow \text{Productivity } (+)$$
$$\rightarrow \text{Economic growth } (+).$$

MuRatopia management is a term used to describe business management that practices Japanese management under the public money system. We will discuss it in detail in the final Chap. 15. It is this positive feedback loop that has driven Japan's miraculous growth and enabled to build a socioeconomic model characterized by welfare capitalism analyzed in Chap. 4. And it is this loop that we think is missing in the Western capitalist economies. Application of systems thinking analysis has successfully identified this feedback loop of participatory workplace that has been indispensable to Japan's postwar economic success.

Systems Thinking of "Japan's Lost 30 Years"

Japan's Lost 30 Years refers to the 30 years of economic stagnation starting from 1990 when the bubble burst to the present. From a systems thinking perspective, it can be analyzed that the positive feedback loop of regular employment that supported Japan's high economic growth up to that point was forced to turn into a negative feedback loop. Specifically, the structural reforms imposed by the U.S. government has broken the regular employment loop. As a result, the negative feedback loop of Non-Regular Employment has emerged and began to rotate in the opposite direction, causing the economy to stagnate.

Figure 14.3 illustrates this newly added Non-Regular Employment loop created by the introduction of labor market deregulations. This negative feedback loop is indicated by a negative sign (–) surrounded by a round arrow, and behaves as follows. As firms increased the number of non-regular employees in order to reduce labor costs, real wages and income declined and stagnated. As we saw in Fig. 4.6 in Chap. 4, the number of regular employees decreased by 290,000 from 34.52 million to 34.23 million from 1989 to 2018, while the number of non-regular employees increased by 13 million from 8.17 million to 21.17 million. In fact, the increase in the number of workers during the lost 30 years was entirely due to non-regular employment! This negative feedback effect worked to suppress or even reduce consumption, pulling down domestic demand and slowing down economic growth.

In other words, this non-regular employment loop is shown as follows.

$$\underline{\text{Economic growth (+)} \rightarrow \text{Non-regular employees (+)}} \rightarrow \text{Real wages (-)}$$
$$\rightarrow \text{Income (+)} \rightarrow \text{Consumption (+)} \rightarrow \text{Domestic demand (+)}$$
$$\rightarrow \text{Economic growth (+)}.$$

The negative signs (-) attached to variable names indicate that the causal relationship changes in the opposite direction. It does not mean that the variable itself will decrease. For example, the meaning of Real wages (-) indicates that an increase in Non-regular employees decreases Real wages, and vice versa.

The only difference between the regular employment and non-regular employment loops is the underlined part where the causal relationship from Economic growth (+) diverges to Non-regular employees (+) in the latter. As mentioned above, due to the labor market deregulations, the causal relationship of "Regular employees (+) → Real wages (+)" was broken, and replaced with "Non-regular employees (+) → Real wages (-)". As a result, non-regular employment loop was brought into the economy as a negative feedback loop. Thus, the economy has fallen into a negative deflationary spiral of increased non-regular employees → decreased real wages → decreased income → decreased consumption → decreased domestic demand → decreased economic growth, leading to the 30 years of economic stagnation despite aggressive monetary and fiscal policies. As a result, the number of non-regular employees increased from 19.1% to 38.2%, almost 40%. The rationale behind labor market

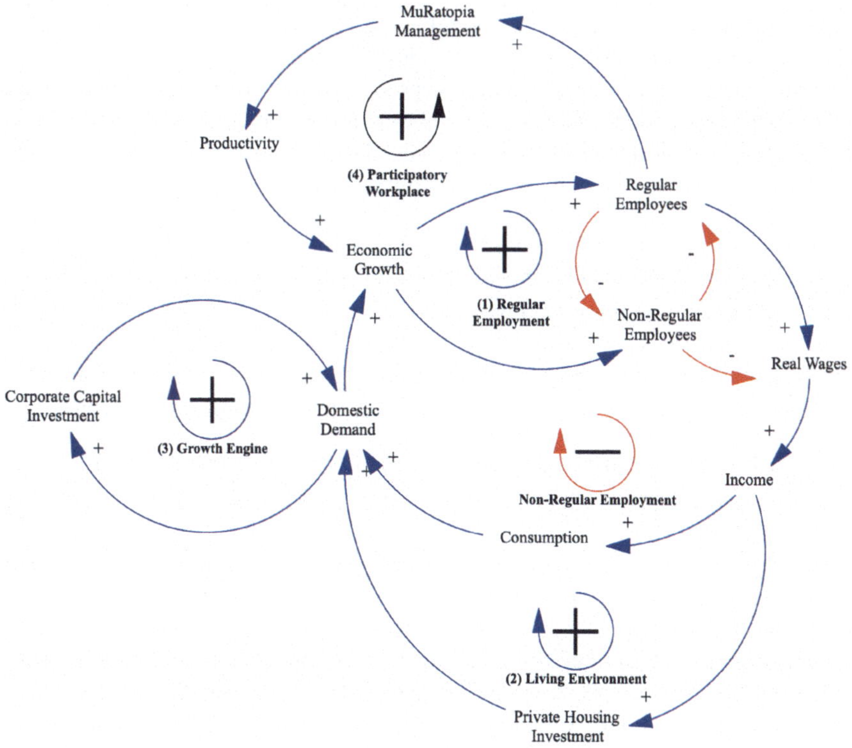

Fig. 14.3 Systems thinking of Japan's lost 30 years

liberalization was that such reforms would improve economic performance and lead to recovery, as it would reduce the costs of hiring and firing workers, enhance labor mobility, and increase job creation. None of these happened in Japan unfortunately. What it all did was indeed a horrible destruction of Japanese management.

To be worse, this non-regular employment loop causes another negative feedback loop to appear such that (read "MuRatopia" as "Japanese" below)

Economic growth (+) → Non-regular employees (+)
→ Regular Employment (-) → MuRatopia management (+)
→ Productivity (+) → Economic growth (+).

In other words, the participatory workplace loop that drove "Japan as Number One" began to rotate in an opposite direction such that the increased non-regular employees are no longer feel a sense of belonging to their companies, and begin to pay less attention to the quality of goods and services. As a result, productivity drops, which could undermine the international competitiveness of Japanese companies, and further worsen economic growth in the long term. In this way, the positive feedback loop of participatory workplace has turned into a negative feedback loop, destroying Japanese management and causing Japan's lost 30 years.

Furthermore, two positive feedback loops such as the Living Environment loop and Growth Engine loop, which are derived from this non-regular employment loop, also turn into negative feedback loops. Specifically, the living environment loop starts to behave as follows (showing a segment of the loop):

$$\text{Decrease in income } (+) \rightarrow \text{Decrease in private housing investment } (+) \rightarrow \text{Decrease in domestic demand } (+).$$

The growth engine loop, spurred on by the combined effects of the two negative feedback loops (non-regular employee and living environment), now becomes

$$\text{Decrease in domestic demand } (+) \rightarrow \text{Decrease in corporate capital investment } (+) \rightarrow \text{Decrease in domestic demand } (+).$$

In this way, these two supposedly positive feedback loops began to reverse through non-regular employment loop, dragging down Japan's economic growth. Private-sector housing and corporate capital investment slowed down. As a result, domestic demand dropped even further, bringing Japan's economic growth to a complete halt.

Viewed from the perspective of debt money analysis in Chap. 3, private debts of producers and households, which had been steadily expanding until around 1990, stopped and began to decline. In other words, private sector investments such as corporate capital and housing investments, which have been the growth engine of the economy, began to decline and stagnated completely. In order to stop this reverse cycle, Japanese government increased its debt vigorously by issuing treasury bonds. As a result, the decline in Japan's money stock was narrowly avoided. Yet government spending went into unproductive investments, producing no multiplier and spillover effects, leaving only debts to accumulate. Consequently, the government debts continued to increase, and driving the nation and its entire economy into the present "debt hell" situation.

From the systems thinking analysis here, the root cause of Japan's lost 30 years became clear. The (1) regular employment loop, which was a positive feedback loop, was cut off by the structural reform, and the non-regular employment loop, which turned out to be a negative feedback loop, was forcefully brought into the economy and stagnated the domestic demand. Consequently, the (2) living environment, (3) growth engine and (4) participatory workplace loops, have all begun to spin in reverse and suppressed the rotation of the growth engine loop. This was why the Japanese economy became stagnant and why monetary policies supported by government deficits did not work. By applying systems thinking in this way, a path to recover from the lost 30 years also becomes clear.

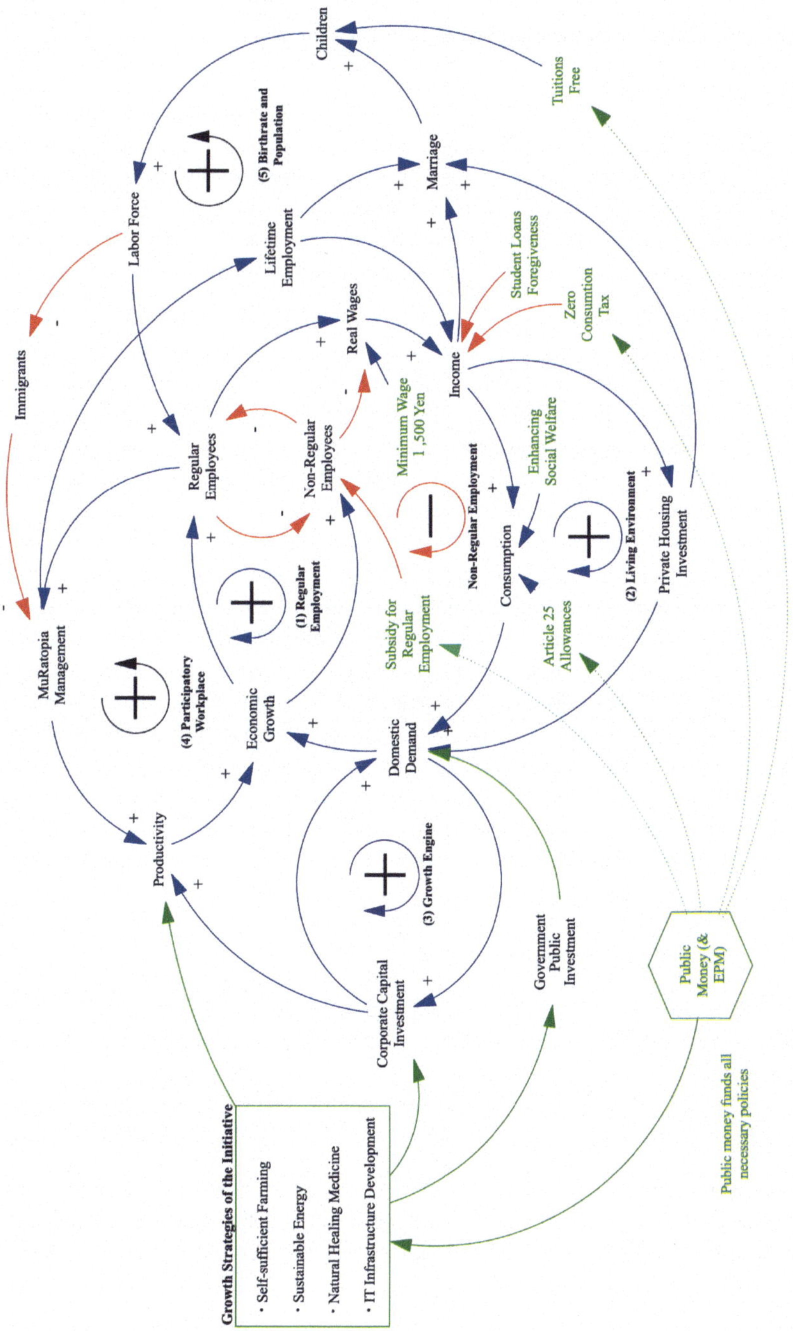

Fig. 14.4 Causal loops diagram of the public money initiative

Systems Thinking of Regaining from "the Lost 30 Years"

Figure 14.4 shows an expanded diagram of Fig. 14.3. From here on, we will use this expanded diagram to consider a new economic growth strategy to regain from the "lost 30 years" with public money. The underlined parts below indicate the corresponding programs proposed in the Public Money Initiative. From a systems thinking perspective, our strategy is to find positive feedback loops and expand them so as to create synergy effects for regaining economic growth.

1. *Regular Employment Loop*
   Introduce Subsidy for Regular Employment to support companies and organizations with public money to cover additional wage costs needed to convert non-regular employees into regular employees. Actual operation of the subsidy programs are left to companies and the government in charge of the concerned sector. As a result, the number of non-regular employees will gradually decrease and the positive feedback loop begins to rotate once again.
   It is desirable to abolish the series of labor market deregulations implemented as part of structural reforms at the same time. However, if companies convert non-regular employment into regular employment with the subsidy, the Agency Worker Law will gradually become ineffective and meaningless. Therefore, there is no need to confront head-on the vested interest groups benefiting from the deregulation. There is no need to worry about inflation either, since the regular employment subsidy will increase wage income, which in turn will increase consumption, which will eventually lead to an equal amount of GDP growth. "Public money spending first" that we discussed in Chap. 11 will increase private income and then generates a net increase in real output (physical goods and services) by the same amount. Thus, the alleged "spending first by the government" advocated falsely by MMT is only possible and valid with public money.
   Our initiative proposes the following programs of public money spending to reinforce the regular employment loop.

   - Minimum Wage of 1,500 yen as a program to raise real wages.
   - Zero Consumption Tax and Student Loan Forgiveness as a program to expand income.
   - Article 25 Allowances and Enhancing Social Welfare as a program to stimulate consumption.

   As a result of these various reinforcement programs, the regular employment loop will begin to rotate faster, stronger and more stable. The Japanese economy will attain sustainable growth and development, and the Sun will begin to rise again.

2. *Living Environment Loop*
   Once the regular employment loop begins to rotate again, the "living environment loop" will begin to rotate normally such that increase in income (+) → increase

in private housing investment (+) → increase in domestic demand (+). To promote housing investment and reduce the burden of long-term mortgage loans, it would also be effective to introduce a program to compensate the interests on housing loans with public money. Unlike corporate capital investment, housing investment cannot and should not be expected to contribute directly to economic growth. Therefore, it would be unfair to impose interest on borrowings for such housing investment. Public money should be used to cover the interest cost. Figure 14.4 does not describe this housing investment support program, so readers are encouraged to fill in the missing connections. In this way, once the core causal loop diagram is completed, we can add as many supplementary programs as we wish into the feedback loops. This is the analytical strength of systems thinking.

3. *Growth Engine Loop*
As the regular employment loop begins to rotate, the "growth engine" loop also starts to rotate normally such that increase in domestic demand (+) → increase in corporate capital investment (+) → increase in domestic demand (+). This is main engine of growth, where demand generates demand. During the lost 30 Years, this loop turned into the opposite direction, dragging down economic growth. As a result, the money stock accumulated in the corporate sector lost its destination for investment. As of 2018, approximately 460 trillion yen of funds (demand deposits) were retained internally and stacked up idle. When the "growth engine" loop begins to rotate normally, huge amounts of retained funds begin to be directed toward corporate capital investments.
Further strategies are needed to ensure that these retained earnings are channeled into productive sectors instead of unproductive ones. To do so, we need to direct this engine of growth into promising investment that will further accelerate the pace of growth and digital transformation, support research in technology and help grow new industries. Below is the new economic growth strategy programs that we are proposing in the public money initiative.

   - Natural and Organic Farming
   - Sustainable Energy
   - Natural Healing Medicine and Treatment
   - IT Infrastructure Development

   Here we only list the program items due to space limitations. However, we encourage readers to use their imagination to flesh out these programs to reinforce the growth engine loop. These programs will simultaneously increase corporate productivity, leading to further economic growth and further strengthening the regular employment loop.

The above three loops become the core loops of the Public Money Initiative for regaining from the lost 30 years.

Let us further examine the programs and surrounding loops that reinforce these core feedback loops using Fig. 14.4. Once the regular employment loop starts to rotate, the following two derivative loops will emerge.

4. *Participatory Workplace Loop*
   As workplaces begin to be filled with regular employees, participatory workplaces will develop that eliminate external shareholder's control and prioritize workplace democracy and corporate social responsibility. As a result, the workplaces, where workers spend most of their lives, become the "path to bliss through self-salvation", resulting in higher productivity and further economic growth. In order to elevate such an economy to a more universal concept, Kaoru called it "MuRatopia Economy" in his Ph.D dissertation at Berkeley (later published as Yamaguchi, 1988), whose concept will be explained in detail in Chap. 15.
   In other words, the Participatory Workplace loop becomes the positive feedback loop that enhances productivity through healthy market competition, job security and worker's fulfillment as follows:

   $$\begin{aligned}&\text{Regular employees } (+) \rightarrow \text{MuRatopia management } (+)\\ &\rightarrow \text{Productivity } (+) \rightarrow \text{Economic growth } (+)\\ &\rightarrow \text{Regular employees } (+).\end{aligned}$$

   When this loop begins to rotate, the influence of external shareholders on management begins to be eliminated, democracy at workplace will be further practiced, and the wage gap between shareholders (capitalists) and employees will be rectified.
5. *Birthrate and Population Loop*
   As the number of regular employees increases and lifetime employment is promoted under MuRatopia management, it becomes easier for workers to secure their own home, thus private housing investment increases. As a result, combination of these two feedback loops create a better social environment for marriage, which will eventually lead to an increase in the number of children and future labor force participation, further increasing the number of regular employees. Thus, this birth rate and population loop becomes the following positive feedback loop:

   $$\begin{aligned}&\text{Regular employees } (+) \rightarrow \text{Real Wages } (+) \rightarrow \text{Income } (+)\\ &\rightarrow \text{Marriage } (+) \rightarrow \text{Children } (+) \rightarrow \text{Labor force } (+)\\ &\rightarrow \text{Regular employees } (+).\end{aligned}$$

   This birthrate and population loop also derives another positive feedback loop via MuRatopia management as follows:

   $$\begin{aligned}&\text{Regular employees } (+) \rightarrow \text{MuRatopia management } (+)\\ &\rightarrow \text{Lifetime employment } (+) \rightarrow \text{Marriage } (+) \rightarrow \text{Children } (+)\\ &\rightarrow \text{Labor force } (+) \rightarrow \text{Regular employees } (+).\end{aligned}$$

This birthrate and population loop is reinforced also by an another feedback loop via private housing investment as follows:

Income (+) → Private housing investment (+) → Marriage (+).

program that reinforces this loop is the Tuition Free program in the initiative. As money begins to flow to SMEs, local economies will be revitalized simultaneously. It is as if new blood circulates throughout our body, invigorates the health of local communities, and reactivates the whole nation. In this way, domestic real investment increases, which in turn expands domestic demand and boosts GDP. Of course, GDP is just one indicator of development and excessive reliance on it should be avoided.

Furthermore, the need to accept immigrants will decrease. This will eliminate friction in the workplace caused by cultural differences, further enhancing MuRatopia management. In other words, the Participatory Workplace loop will be reinforced by the Birthrate and Population loop as follows.

Labor force (+) → Immigrants (-) → MuRatopia management (-)

Seven Subsidy Programs

In this chapter we have identified the five positive feedback loops that become crucial for Japan to regain its lost 30 years. Reinforcing these feedback loops are the subsidy programs proposed under the Public Money Initiative. Specifically, we have discussed the seven underlined subsidy programs and considered how they work in synergy using systems thinking.

a Subsidy for Regular Employment
b Minimum Wages of 1,500 yen per hour
c Zero Consumption Tax
d Student Loans Forgiveness
e Article 25 Allowances
f Enhancing Social Welfare
g Tuition Free

There may be some missing loops that could not be covered here. We encourage readers to continue systems thinking, and expand Fig. 14.4 further with papers and pencils. By applying systems thinking we can design macroeconomic policies from an entirely different viewpoint. It is said that our cerebrum gets pleasure from synaptic connections between individual neurons. The programs of the Public Money

Initiative, thus connected by systems thinking, will be a great source of our energy toward a bright future.

14.4 The Initiative for Sustainable Humanity

By applying systems thinking, we have identified five positive feedback loops out of the Public Money Initiative to regain "Japan's lost 30 years" ; that is, (1) regular employment loop, (2) living environment loop, (3) growth engine loop, (4) participatory workplace loop, and (5) birthrate and population loop. From these analyses, we found that our short-term solution of five positive feedback loops includes the fifth loop of birthrate and population that leads to the long-term solution. This means that Public Money Initiative provides not only the solution out of the lost 30 years, but also a foundation to the long-term sustainability of population. In other words, making a transition to the public money system and implementing the Public Money Initiative must be the solution of socioeconomic sustainability of humanity, not only for Japan but also for All nations.

Figure 14.5 illustrates the same four scenarios as shown in Fig. 14.1, in terms of birthrate figure here. Japan's birthrate peaked at 1,840 thousand people in 1984, then began to decline by its half of 932 thousand people in 2022. If the total fertility rate is fixed at the current level of 1.26, annual birthrate continues to decline to 210

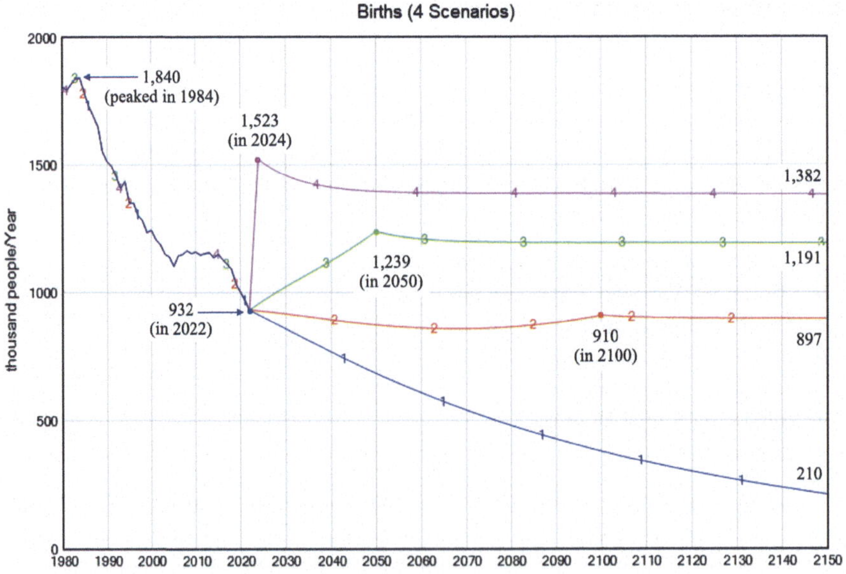

Fig. 14.5 Birth rates under four scenarios and sustainability

thousand people in 2150, which leads to the total population of 30 million people as discussed in Sect. 14.1 (Scenario 1).

Scenario 4, on the other hand, is to attain the total fertility rate to the sustainable level of 2.1 as soon as in 2024. In terms of birthrate, this implies that annual birth rate has to increase to 1,523 thousand people in 2024, and be maintained at the level of 1,382 thousand people toward the next century (line 4 in pink). Only then Japan's long-rem population is sustained around 103 million people. Scenario 3 shows that if birthrate is increased to 1,239 thousand people (which is equivalent to sustainable total fertility of 2.1) in 2050 and maintained around the level of 1,191 thousand people (line 3 in green), then long-term population is sustained around 89 million people as shown in Fig. 14.1.

Only if the Public Money Initiative is implemented scenario 4 (or scenario 3) can be attained thanks to the (5) birthrate and population loop. That is to say, any single-handed government policy to combat declining birthrates turns out to be "the fixes that fail" according to our systems analysis. To attain the long-term sustainability of population, we have to initiate the Public Money Initiative as soon as possible. This is our "Public Money" solution proposed on the basis of systems thinking.

Chapter 15
MuRatopia Economy

The goal of this book is to present *the systems solution to end national debt, banking crises, built-in inequality, inflation and control by CBDC*. We have so far spent much of our energy to analyze the root cause of these problems as system design failures of debt money, and concluded that transition to the public money system is the solution. However, the solution would not be sufficient unless we achieve the MuRatopia economy that will end the present globalism.

15.1 Globalism as *Divide and Rule* Tactic

Globalization vis-á-vis *Globalism*

Globalization itself is an irreversible process in the course of social evolution. In a world where technologies overcome our physical boundaries and information travels around the world instantaneously, mechanisms and institutions of politics, economy, culture and other spheres expand beyond national borders.

What is Globalism *vis-á-vis* Globalization, then? It is considered in this book as a "divide and rule" tactic that has been used repeatedly to establish the authoritarian *supra-national government* with a single world currency. As discussed in Chap. 11, such a political vision is a topic that has been publicly discussed by many heads of the international banks and organizations for many decades. Indeed, for those who control the international banks that make up the top 25 control holders in the "network of global corporate control" listed in Figs. 10.6 and 10.7, national borders and domestic regulations are nothing more than "structural barriers" that constrain the free movements of capitals, resources and labor that they could otherwise exploit more efficiently.

Who are advocating the Globalism, then? The power structure analyses developed in Chaps. 9 and 10 have led us to a working hypothesis that they are a small but highly influential network of academics, financiers, religious and political elites. As

K. Yamaguchi and Y. Yamaguchi, *Public Money*,
https://doi.org/10.1007/978-981-97-6564-5_15

system dynamics researchers, however, we are not interested in who these globalists are because, as the science of complex systems tells us, if the underlying system structure is redesigned and transformed, problems (system behaviors) caused by the original dysfunctional system will also be solved (see Table 9.2). Places to intervene in a system are called *leverage points*. In systems analysis they are the true points of power as they represent "nearly effortless way to cut through and leap over huge obstacles" (Meadows 1999, p.1).

"Pay No Attention to That Man Behind the Curtain"

What is wrong with their Globalism, then? According to our observation, the globalists seem to possess an ultimate political agenda aiming to control every aspects of our society and enslave *We the People*, billions of us, under their autocracy by depriving freedoms of speech and economic activities. As analyzed in Chap. 10, their primary tactics to expand their power have been to implement *divide and rule* strategy and maintain the debt money system.

Examples of their "divide" tactics are: religious divisions such as protestants vs. catholics, Judaism vs. Islam; racial divisions such as white vs. black, Jews vs. Gentiles; ideological divisions such as capitalism vs. communism; political divisions such as conservatives (the right) vs. liberals (the left); and more recently, gender divisions such as majority vs. LGBT minority, pro-life vs. pro-choice, and the list goes on. Globalists do not care about the underlying issue as long as they can foster distrust and enmity between local groups and create lasting divisions that will prevent alliances that challenge their status quo.

In this way, globalists has kept *We the People* divided into opposing camps and let them fight one another in an attempt to profit themselves towards advancing their political agenda. Their "divide and rule" tactics over the last centuries have been to distract people from recognizing the root of the problems; system of control through money, which is the source of their power. As the famous scene from the *Wizard of Oz* vividly captures, the globalists have used loudspeakers (media) and all kinds of theatrical equipments (smokescreens and explosions) to tell us, "pay no attention to that man behind the curtain!" From systems standpoint, however, those men behind the curtain are less important. Individuals and corporate names change over time. What matters is to end the system of control through which the Wizard of Oz has created fear and illusion of power among the people.

Do Not Mistake the Leverage Points!

Accordingly, transitioning to public money system must be the *first* step in our global effort to end this "divide and rule" tactics of the Globalism. In Chap. 12 we have shown how to transition from the debt money system through the Japanese case. Yet, the transition to public money system would not be *sufficient*, because globalists have another source of unearned income through dividends and rents even under the public money system. Thus, globalists can exercise their control over business management as long as the equity ownership system remains in their hands. Accordingly, there is a need to discuss how to stop their control through the equity ownership system in this last chapter.

15.2 Transition to the Self-Managed Business

From Equity Ownership to Equity Possession

Even under the public money system, globalists can exert ownership by purchasing shares and control business management as capitalist shareholders. To stop this business control, equity ownership has to be replaced with *equity possession*. In the original design of MuRatopia economy, which Kaoru conceived as a reunification process of workers and capitalists, etc., the concept of *equity possession* was first introduced against equity ownership (Yamaguchi, 1988).

What is *equity possession* that distinguishes from equity ownership in a capitalist economy? It consists of three principles as the following excerpt explains.

> A capitalist economy as a social institution presupposes a modern concept of private ownership. The essence of this concept is the exclusive right to dispose of a private property by its legal owner. In other words, no other person can exercise such a right of disposal without the permission of the legal owner, even if the other person is actually in a state of possessing the property. Hence this concept allows the exclusive and absolute right of property disposal by its private owner *beyond time and space*. A capitalist economy would not function without this legal system of private ownership. For instance, an exchange of a commodity in a market presupposes its owner, because the exchange is nothing but a transfer of private ownership.
>
> In comparison, possession refers to the exclusive right to dispose of a private property by those who are in a state of its actual management, and thus who are sharing it. In other words, possession is a private ownership which is *confined by time and space*. Private ownership only *here* and *now*–this is possession. In this sense if possession is imposed in private ownership, no legal owners of the property can exercise their right of disposal from outside or from past into future. ⋯ This is the essence of possession. And *possession* is the only institutional and legal requirement of property management which is imposed in the MuRatopia economy. To be more specific, for the case of production units this institutional requirement of possession consists of the following three principles:
>
> **Principle 1** Automatic possession of the production units at the time of participation. When co-workers join MuRatopian organizations, they automatically become possessors of the production units and join self-management in a democratic manner. Moreover, no co-workers are dismissed against their will.
>
> **Principle 2** Automatic dispossession of the production units at the time of departure. When co-workers leave MuRatopian organizations, they automatically dispossess the production units and lose control over self-management from outside. Dispossession also occurs at their death, and no one can inherit their possessions unless that person himself or herself joins the organizations.

Principle 3 Possession of the production units as a niche.
Everyone in the MuRatopia economy is entitled to freely create or seek the fittest niche or habitat in the form of possession, but no one is allowed to derive economic benefits from possession itself. In other words, sales of the production units are, under this principle, nothing but a change in the form of possession without payment, and thus the production units as physical stocks are continuously self-managed, accumulated or destroyed by new possessors. Hence, co-workers can only derive economic benefits from production and exchange of net flows (= consumption and investment goods), but not from exchange of stocks or the production units themselves (Yamaguchi, 1988, Pages 171–173).

Once these three principles of possession are institutionalized into business organizations, shareholders (capitalists) as owners of business entities cannot participate in management decisions unless they work as co-workers. In other words, shareholders are still entitled to receive dividends, but their voting rights are confined only to its co-workers as members of MuRatopian organizations. Yet non-worker (non-member) shareholders can still vote against management indirectly by selling their stocks in the market. In this way direct control by outside shareholders over management will become obsolete and business workplaces become *self-managed*; that is, participatory democracy at workplace is realized. Transition to the self-managed business becomes the sufficient condition to end the economic tyranny under the current shareholder capitalism as Globalism.

15.3 MuRatopia Economy Beyond Globalism

As discussed in Chap. 9, economics since Adam Smith's *The Wealth of Nations* (1776) has coined three different economic systems such as capitalism, socialism and communism under the debt money system, which gave rise to the present Globalism. International bankers and globalists have fully utilized these conflicting views to "divide and rule" the world, and expanded their control over businesses and industries under their power-hungry Globalism platform.

When public money system and self-managed business are attained, globalists will lose their means of control through debt money and equity ownerships. Accordingly, they can no longer exercise *divide and rule* tactics. Such fundamental changes will empower each and every person and allow their natural creativity to flourish. *We the People* begin to enjoy true diversity as if various flowers and animals coexist in meadows, hills and everywhere on this planet.

To describe a new unified view of three schools in economics of the industrial age such as Walrasian (neoclassical), Keynesian and Marxian economics, Yamaguchi (1988) proposed the MuRatopia economy that is based on the equity ownership of means of production (capital) and its management against the equity ownership of the capitalist economy. However, the original concept of MuRatopia economy entirely lacked the analysis of debt money system when Kaoru first introduced it in the 1980s as discussed in Sect. 9.2. Accordingly, we must redefine the MuRatopia economy

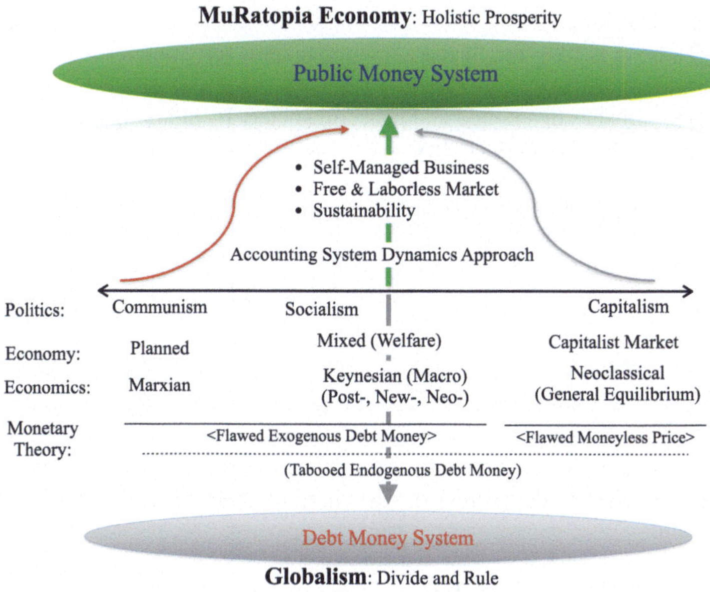

Fig. 15.1 MuRatopia economy as the alternative beyond globalism

as the system that has the following four pillars (features) against the Globalism as illustrated in Fig. 15.1.

Four Main Pillars of MuRatopia Economy

Pillar 1 Public Money (transition from debt money)
that fixes system design failures of debt money; that is,
(a) alleviates repeated business cycles of boom and bust, built-in inflation and deflation, recession and unemployment, etc.,
(b) reduces government debts to zero, and
(c) eliminates built-in income inequality between bankers (debt money lenders) and non-bankers (debt money borrowers).

Pillar 2 Self-Managed Business (transition from equity ownership)
that ends the globalism by abolishing equity ownership control;
that is,
(d) establishes participatory democracy at workplace, and
(e) eliminates income inequality between shareholders and capitalists (equity owners and employers) and workers (employees).

Pillar 3 Free & Laborless Market (transition from capitalist labor market) that
(f) eliminates capitalist labor market in which wage labor is traded

like slavery, and
(g) advances free speech and authentic market activities.

Pillar 4 Sustainability that
(h) establishes diversified and peaceful society by attaining the following three levels of reproducibility:

- Physical reproducibility
- Social reproducibility
- Ecological reproducibility

Yamaguchi (2004a) defined and analyzed sustainability as physical, social and ecological reproducibilities using system dynamics modeling method. Indeed the Public Money Initiative proposed in Chap. 14 is shown to provide a foundation toward the sustainability of humanity as a socio-economic sustainability; that is, physical and social reproducibilities of sustainability could be met under the public money system.

Competitive Advantages of MuRatopia Organization

Business entities similar to MuRatopian organizations include companies such as the ones that practice Japanese management and the Mondragon Corporation (cooperatives) in the Basque region of Spain. These organizations share the same purpose with MuRatopian enterprises in terms of social responsibility-oriented management that values employee enrichment, while preventing control and takeover by outside shareholders. The fundamental difference is that the Muratopian enterprises are based on the premise of public money system.

The transition to public money system will stabilize the economy and establish a stable business environment, which will give these companies a competitive advantage over pure capitalist (joint-stock) companies controlled by outside shareholders. The reasons are obvious. First, the lifetime stable employment and equitable distribution and use of corporate profits will enable workers to take ownership of their own companies and work actively throughout their lifetime, making them more productive and efficient. Of course this does not constrain freedom of occupation.

Second, because they are self-managed, MuRatopia enterprises are able to maintain competitive prices (when necessary) by allowing wages to vary elastically in response to business cycles, while eliminating the influence of outside shareholders who demand short-term dividends. It is precisely in the current information age that the MuRatopia economy thus redefined will replace the capitalist economy and take us to a new era of holistic prosperity.

15.4 What is MuRatopia?

So far we have not explained the concept of MuRatopia itself. To see how it was explained originally, let us quote a paragraph from (Yamaguchi, 1988) below:

> We will call such a re-unified future economy *MuRatopia economy* where co-workers work co-operatively in communes, communities, local organizations, and global organizations in harmony with nature. The Japanese word *mura* literally means village. I have envisioned the future society in the spirit and practice of a Japanese village where village people live in a self-sufficient community, help each other co-operatively at the busiest time of harvest, and respect nature's way. The one character word *mura* may also be considered as consisting of two different characters: *Mu* and *Ra*. *Mu* implies "nothingness" or "emptiness"–the most fundamental concept of Zen Buddhism, and *Ra* means "being naked" or "having no possession". Accordingly, I have associated the implication of *Mu* (nothingness) and *Ra* (no possession) with *mura* (village), because I have further envisioned the mind of future society in the combination of these concepts. - *topia* is from the Greek *topos*, which means place. Hence, the word *MuRatopia* is now coined to describe our new social design. (Yamaguchi, 1988, pages 170, 171).

The name of MuRatopia was thus coined in 1988 by combining three words: Mura, Mu and Ra as illustrated in Fig. 15.3 below. In this final chapter of the book, let us refine the concept of MuRatopia by reflecting recent archaeological discoveries. In this way the concept of MuRatopia becomes a more universal vision based on the "Mura" (village)–a minimum social unit of sustainability– that has been nurtured in the Japanese archipelago since ancient times.

Mura (village) as a Sustainable Social Unit Throughout History

According to the recent archaeological excavations, Japanese villages described above turned out to have existed throughout human history. For example, a knife made of Obsidian (approx. 7 cm long and 3 cm wide) found at the foot of Mt. Akagi in Gunma Prefecture turned out to be one of the oldest tool known to mankind, about 30,000 years old. The artifact demonstrated a culture of polished stone tool in the Neolithic Age. Furthermore, Jomon Pottery–the world's oldest earthenware–was found at Oh-hira Yamamoto I Site in Aomori Prefecture in northern mainland Japan, which turned out to be around 16,500 years old.

These artifacts convinced historians of the need to recognize the existence of a new civilization that started around 17,000 years ago in the Japanese archipelago, which they named the "Jomon civilization" (Onagi, 2022). In fact, compared to the Sumerian civilization, which has been known as the oldest civilization that suddenly appeared in the historical region of southern Mesopotamia (now south-central Iraq) around 7,500 years ago, this Jomon civilization is even older.

The Jomon civilization continued through 3,000 years ago, when wood burning (causing temperature of 800–1,000 degrees Celsius) was replaced with Yayoi earthenware technology of charcoal burning (causing temperature of 1,200–1,500 degrees Celsius) around 3,000 years ago. In this way, the world's oldest Jomon civilization existed for 14,000 years from around 17,000 years ago until 3,000 years ago.

So far, 95,531 archaeological sites have been investigated and Earth Puppet of 15,000 bodies have been discovered, including *Jomon Goddess* excavated at Nishinomae Site in Yamagata Prefecture (4,700 years ago) and *Jomon Venus* at Tanahata Site in Nagano Prefecture (ca. 4000 years ago). Surprisingly, no lethal weapons has been found in these sites, which implies that Jomon civilization developed no culture of homicides and no slaves (class hierarchy). Its social system consisted of families, villages (brothers and sisters, relatives), surrounding fields for harvests and countries. Village (mura) had been a sustainable social unit throughout Jomon civilization. Accordingly, our imagination of the villagers such as quoted above can be extended over the Jomon civilization, that is, "village people live in a self-sufficient community, help each other co-operatively at the busiest time of harvest, and respect nature's way."

For most of its history since ancient times, people have been living peacefully on the Far East islands as peace-loving villagers. Indeed, one example of how they have developed a mentality of respect over generations is reflected in the first article of the Seventeen-Article Constitution enacted by Prince Shotoku in 604 AD, which reads: "Be mindful of harmony and do not fight each other". Lifestyles of villagers originated from the world's oldest Jomon civilization could be said to have spread all over the world throughout history among various civilizations to follow. In this sense, village (mura) must be a core social units, together with the peace-loving spirits of villagers, when we design our new economy for sustainable futures.

Mu (nothing) as Symbolic Conceptualization of Eastern Civilization

Eastern Civilization, following the Jomon civilization, is symbolized by Buddhism which originated with the teachings of Buddha Shakyamuni around 2,500 years ago. The key concept of (Zen) Buddhism is "Mu", which means "nothingness" or "emptiness". We understand the essence of its philosophy to be as follows. Whenever we say this is my hand, my leg, my idea, etc., we are referring to them as if they are not Myself. Similarly, whenever we say "I want to be successful and rich", there exists no such Myself (Ego) whose desire is to be successful and rich. Nowhere! Because my desire is not Myself. Thus, we are nowhere and nothing. Hence, our attachment to such desires as if it is "real" is nothing but an illusion and a source of sufferings in case of its failure. In order to be relieved from such sufferings, then, we have to enlighten Myself so that my desire (as my parts) is different from Myself and nothing. This is a core teaching of the Buddha and Buddhism.

We could explain this teaching in terms of mathematical logic of set vs. subset. My parts (such as bodies and desires) are subset of the whole set of Myself. Thus, the whole set is nowhere within the subset. In case the whole set of Myself is identified as a whole set1, then we can create a new subset1 consisting of the previous subset and the whole set1. In this case, Myself becomes a new whole set2 consisting of subset1. And the new whole set2 of Myself is, again, nowhere within the subset1. In this way, the whole set of Myself cannot be captured indefinitely as long as we cling to the subsets. It becomes "Mu".

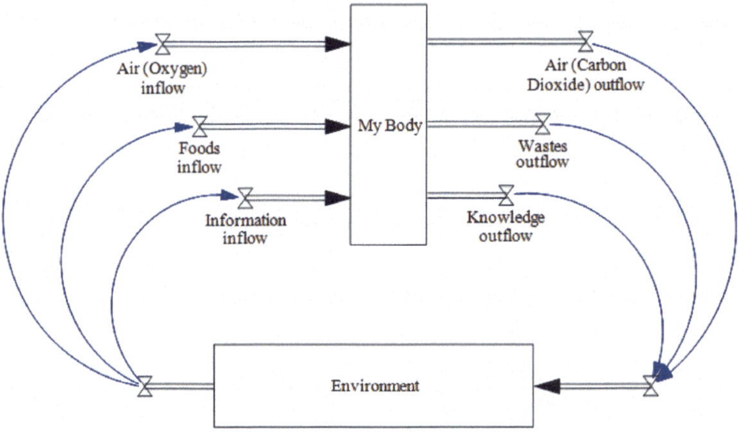

Fig. 15.2 Where is myself in my expanded body (environment)? Nowhere!

Let us expand our search for Myself. So far we have only considered "set and subsets" as stocks at a moment in time. Yet, our body has to be actually living in order to cause such desires. In other words, our body has to hold constant inflows of air (oxygen), foods and information, and outflows of air (carbon dioxide), wastes and knowledge as illustrated in Fig. 15.2. That is, to sustain our life our body has to be a living system of inflows and outflows. Our body as a system has to be further connected to the environment. Thus, our body and environment jointly become our new subset in order to be able to say "I want to be successful and rich". In this way, sustainable environment becomes inseparable from our body itself for a blissful life. Indeed, it must be a part of our expanded body. This is why sustainable environment is included as one of conditions of sustainability in the MuRatopia economy discussed above. Where is Myself in our expanded body, then? Again, nowhere.

Ra (naked) as Symbolic Conceptualization of Western Civilization

Western Civilization, following the Jomon Civilization, may be symbolized by the *Venus de Milo*, an ancient Greek sculpture, that was created during the Hellenistic period between 150 and 125 BC, around 2,150 years ago. It was carried on to the Renaissance period as the revival of Hellenism, being symbolized by the *Birth of Venus*, a painting (1485) by Sandro Botticelli, then *David*, a masterpiece sculpture (1504) created by Michelangelo, and the *Last Judgment*, a fresco (1512) painted by Michelangelo that covers the whole altar wall of the Sistine Chapel in the Vatican City.

The key concept of Western civilization symbolized by these artistic works is "Ra", which means "nakedness" or "born naked". That is, we are all born naked by nature (or created by Gods) as free and equal individuals.

MuRa as Unifying Holism of Eastern and Western Civilizations

The Heart Sūtra is a popular sutra in Mahāyāna Buddhism. Especially in Japan, it is often chanted at the Buddhist funeral. Even in our daily conversation in modern Japanese, the following part of the heart sutra is often quoted as an essential wisdom of Buddhism:

Form is Emptiness, Emptiness is Form.

Since this translation may be too abstract to understand, we'd like to quote the essential part of the heart sutra from another translation as follows:

This Body itself is Emptiness
and Emptiness itself is this Body.
This Body is not other than Emptiness
and Emptiness is not other than this Body.
The same is true of Feelings,
Perceptions, Mental Formations,
and Consciousness.[1]

Applying our "set vs subset" interpretation of Mu and Ra, we could interpret this sutra as follows: this body (subset of my parts) is not Myself, that is, nothing (whole set of Mu). Yet, out of nothing (Mu) we are born naked (Ra), which gradually grows into our parts of this body. That is, Ra is considered to be this body. Then, the first four lines of the above translation can be interpreted as follows:

This Body itself (Ra) is Emptiness (Mu)
and Emptiness itself (Mu) is this Body (Ra).
This Body (Ra) is not other than Emptiness (Mu)
and Emptiness (Mu) is not other than this Body (Ra).

In other words, the essence of the Heart Sutra can be compactly described as "Ra is Mu and Mu is Ra". The new concept of "MuRa" is thus born as a symbolic conceptualization of Holism that unifies Eastern (Mu) and Western (Ra) civilizations. Moreover, Mura (village) has been a sustainable social unit throughout our history, across East and West, from the Jomon Civilization. Hence, the concept of MuRatopia is born as a place where East and West are unified as illustrated in Fig. 15.3. MuRatopia as new holism will transcend beyond theism such as monotheism, polytheism, animism and atheism, and provides a room of true diversity and wholeness. We are living with all kinds of sufferings daily and need salvation constantly.

Hence, in terms of salvation, the beliefs system of MuRatopia (consisting of Jomon, Eastern and Western Civilizations) may be classified as follows:

- Jomon Civilization: Salvation through Sun-Nature & Ancestor Worship.
- Eastern Civilization: Inner Salvation through Meditation to the Enlightenment.

[1] https://plumvillage.org/wp-content/uploads/2014/09/2014-Thich-Nhat-Hanh-New-Heart-Sutra-letter-cc.pdf.

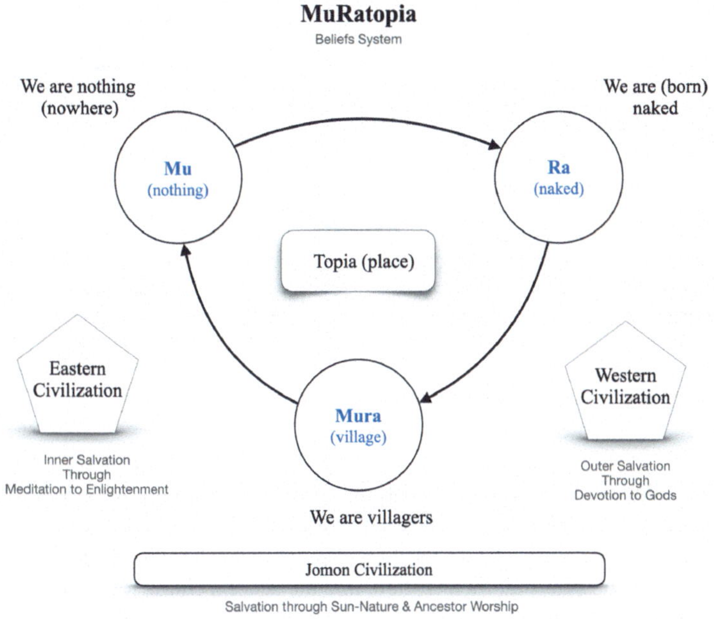

Fig. 15.3 MuRatopia as global villages of holism

- Western Civilization: Outer Salvation through Devotion to the God(s).

Whichever belief system we live with, we have to respect one another as co-inhabitants of MuRatopia, because our spiritual life is part of diverse beliefs system in MuRatopia. This is the holism we need to aim for better futures.

15.5 Hugging Civilizations with MuRatopia

Holism of unifying Eastern and Western civilizations discussed above does not imply dominance of one civilization over the other through "Clash of Civilization" (Huntington, 2002). Rather, it implies co-existence of diversified civilizations and cultures, as if they are hugging one another with mutual respect. In other words, we pose that this new holism will emerge along with the MuRatopia economy that consists of four pillars such as public money system, self-managed business, free & laborless market and sustainability. Figure 15.4 illustrates relations between civilization and economy throughout human history in terms of money, a main theme of this book. According to the monetary criterion, human history may be broadly divided into the ages of the following four economies.

Pre-Money Economy where commodities such as shells, hemp clothes, silks, stones might have been used as medium of exchange within local villages throughout

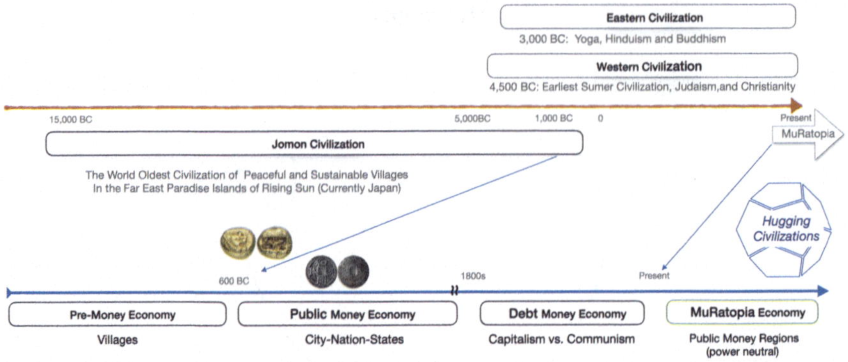

Fig. 15.4 Hugging civilizations with MuRatopia

Jomon civilization. The term "Pre-Money" is used here in the sense that there is a possibility that archaeological research will establish the existence of a means of exchange of some kind. In fact the Japanese word for money "*kahei*" consists of the first character (*ka*) that means shell, and the second character *hei* implies cloth (hemp, silk, etc.). This fact indicates that they had been widely used as medium of exchanges among villagers within and across villages since ancient times.

Public Money Economy where public money of various media were issued without interest by public entities such as kings and government and used for economic activities in city-states and nation-states. That is, public money and birth of city-nation-states become inseparable.

Debt Money Economy where private banks issued debt money and loaned it at interest. Lending and borrowing of debt money thus became the dominant economic activities and means of control since as early as the Middle Ages.

MuRatopia Economy Public money and electronic public money (EPM) are issued at interest-free to support free economic activities of *We the People* under decentralized social systems. Hence, public money in this economy becomes entirely *power-neutral*, which is contrary to what neoclassical economics used to have brainwashed us, saying that "money is neutral".

15.6 Public Money First and Now!

Why should public money be a theme for everyone? In this book we have concluded that the peaceful world of holism as hugging civilizations can be realized by erecting the four pillars of MuRatopia economy. However, the majority of the public is still unaware that they are living under the system where 99% of money has been taken over and controlled by debt money. The collapse of Japanese bubble and the subsequent Second Great Depression since 2008 evidenced the lesson learned from the Great Depression that the debt money system is the root cause of national debt, banking crisis, built-in inequality and inflation. It is crucial to raise this awareness of debt money

Start by talking about this "money problem" with people around you. Build a bottoms-up movement and bring this problem to the attention of legislators as the top national priority. The choice between public money and debt money is a matter so fundamental that it will determine whether *We the People* control our own futures or become slaves of the debt money. Crisis is an Opportunity.

Thank you for patiently traveling with us up to this point. Let us now begin our new journey toward MuRatopia, and Make All Nations Great Again with Public Money!

Bibliography

Allen, W. R. (1993). Irving fisher and the 100 percent reserve proposal. *Journal of Law and Economics, 36*(2), 703–717.

Aristotle (1934 [350]). *Nicomachean ethics (translated by H. Rackham)*, volume 19 of *Aristotle in 23 Volumes, Loeb Classical Library (Original work published 350 BCE)*. Cambridge, MA: Harvard University Press.

Arrow, K., & Debreu, G. (1954). Existence of an equilibrium for a competitive economy. *Econometrica*.

Backhouse, R., & Laidler, D. E. W. (2004). What was lost with is-lm. *History of Political Economy, 36*(5), 26–56.

Backhouse, R. E., & Laidler, D. E. W. (2004). What was lost with is-lm. *History of Political Economy, 36*(Supplement), 25–56.

Barro, R. J. (1976). Rational expectations and the role of monetary policy. *Journal of Mountary Economics, 2*(1), 1–32.

Bernanke, B. S. (1994). The macroeconomics of the great depression: A comparative approach. NBER Working Paper Series 4814, National Bureau of Economic Research.

Bernanke, B. S., & Blinder, A. S. (1988). Credit, money, and aggregate demand. *American Economic Review, 78*, 435–439.

Black, J. (2021). Chester A. Phillips and the forgotten history of bank credit. Doctoral dissertation, Universitat de Barcelona.

Brady, M. E. (2017). The is–lm debacle: An analysis of nearly nine decades of errors committed by economists attempting to deal with j m keynes's (not hicks's) is-lm analysis in the general theory. Available at SSRN. https://doi.org/10.2139/ssrn.2960817

Bundesbank, D. (2017). The role of banks, non-banks and the central bank in the money creation process. Article from the monthly report, pp. 13–33, Deutsche Bundesbank.

Cagan, P. D. (1956). The monetary dynamics of hyperinflation. In M. Friedman (Ed.), *Studies in the Quantity Theory Of Money* (pp. 25–117). Chicago: University of Chicago Press.

Chandler, L. V. (1971). *American Monetary Policy, 1928–1941*. New York: Harper and Row.

Chaum, D. (1983). Blind signatures for untraceable payments. In D. Chaum, R. L. Rivest, A. T. S. (Eds.), *Advances in Cryptology: Proceedings of Crypto, 82*, 199–203.

Chaum, D. L. (1982). *Computer Systems Established, Maintained and Trusted by Mutually Suspicious Groups*. PhD thesis, Computer Science. Berkeley: University of California.

Cheney, D. W., & Grimes, W. W. (1991). *Japanese technnology policy: What's the secret*. Council of Competitiveness: Technical report.

K. Yamaguchi and Y. Yamaguchi, *Public Money*,
https://doi.org/10.1007/978-981-97-6564-5

Chossudovsky, M., & Marshall, A. G., editors (2010). *The Global Economic Crisis – The Great Depression of the XXI Century*. Global Research Publishers.

Cintra, M. (2009). *Bank transactions: pathway to the Single Tax ideal; The Brazilian experience with a bank transactions tax (1993-2007)* (2nd ed.). Munich Personal RePEc Archive.

Cohen, J. (1972). Copeland's moneyflows after twenty-five years: A survey. *Journal of Economic Literature, 10*, 1–25.

Cutts, R. L. (1990). Power from the ground up: Japan's land bubble. *Harvard Business Review*, May–June issue.

Das, R., Wexler, P., Pirooznia, M., & Elhaik, E. (2017). The origins of Ashkenaz, Ashkenazic Jews, and Yiddish. *Frontiers in Genetics*, 8. https://doi.org/10.3389/fgene.2017.00087

Dawson, J. C. (1996). *Flow-of-Funds analysis: A handbook for practitioners*. Sharpe: M.E.

Debreu, G. (1959). *Theory of Value*. Yale University Press.

Douglas, P. H., Fisher, I., Graham, F. D., Hamilton, E. J., King, W. I., & Whittlesey, C. R. (1939). A program for monetary reform. Unpublished paper. Included in the Editor's Appendix to "100% Money by Irving Fisher", ThaiSunset Publications, 2011.

Dyson, B., Greenham, T., Ryan-Collins, J., & Werner, R. (2010). Towards a twenty-first century banking and monetary system. Joint Submission to the Independent Commision on Banking.

European Commission (2023). Proposal for a regulation on the establishment of the digital euro.

Evanhatch (2021). Len Sassaman and Satoshi: a Cypherpunk History. https://evanhatch.medium.com/len-sassaman-and-satoshi-e483c85c2b10

Feige, E. L. (2000). Taxation for the 21st century: the automated payment transaction (apt) tax. *Economic Policy, 15*(31), 474–511.

Felisini, D. (2017). *Alessandro Torlonia: The Pope's Banker. Palgrave studies in the history of finance* (1st ed.). Cham, Switzerland: Springer.

Fischer, S. (1977). Long-term contracts, rational expectations, and the optimal money supply rule. *Journal of Political Economy, 85*(1), 191–205.

Fisher, I. (1920 [1911]). *Purchasing power of money–Its determination and relation to credit, interest and crises*. New York: The Macmillan Company, New & revised edition.

Fisher, I. (1932). *Booms and Depressions-Some First Principles*. New York: Adelphi Company.

Fisher, I. (1933). The debt-deflation theory of great depressions. *Econometrica, 1*(4), 337–357.

Fisher, I. (1937a). Income in theory and income taxation in practice. *Econometrica, 5*(1), 1–55.

Fisher, I. (1937b). A practical schedule for an income tax: How income may best be defined for income tax purposes. *The Tax Magazine, 15*(7), 379–390.

Fisher, I. (1945 [1935]). *100% Money: Designed to keep checking banks 100% liquid; to prevent inflation and deflation; largely to cure or prevent depressions; and to wipe out much of the national debt* (3rd ed.). The City Printing Company, New Haven. First edition published in 1935 by Adelphi Company, New York.

Fisher, I., & Fisher, H. W. (1942). *Constructive income taxation: A proposal for reform*. New York and London: Harper and Brothers Publishers.

Forrester, J. W. (2013). Economic theory for the new millennium. *System Dynamics Review, 29*(1), 26–41.

Friedman, M. (1987). Monetary policy: Tactics versus strategy. In J. A. Dorn & A. J. Schwartz (Eds.), *The Search for Stable Money: Essays on Monetary Reform.* Chicago: University of Chicago Press.

Friedman, M. (1992 [1960]). *A program for monetary stability* (10th ed.). New York: Fordham University Press.

Friedman, M. (2006 [1970]). The counter-revolution in monetary theory. In K. Matthews & P. Booth (Eds.), *Issues in Monetary Policy: The Relationship between Money and the Financial Markets* (pp. 171–183). Reproduced in Appendix 2. John Wiley & Sons Ltd.

Friedman, M., & Schwartz, A. (1963). *A monetary history of the United States 1867–1960*. Princeton University Press.

GAO. (2011). *Federal reserve system-opportunities exist to strengthen policies and processes for managing emergency assistance*. The United States Government Accountability Office (GAO): A Report to Congressional Address.

Garner, W. D. A. (2016 [2010]). *Who really owns your gOLD?: How the Jesuits use gold economics to control humanity* (4th ed.). Adagio Press, USA, first edition published in 2010.
Hansen, A. H. (1949). *Monetary theory and fiscal policy*. McGraw-Hill Kougakusha, Ltd., Tokyo, international student edition.
Harding, R. (2019). 'Japanification' stalks the US and Europe. Financial Times, Tokyo, October 21, 2019.
Heinrich, H. W. (1931). *Industrial accident prevention: A scientific approach*. New York: McGraw-Hill Book Company.
Hicks, J. (1937). Mr. keynes and the "classics": A suggested interpretation. *Econometrica*, 5(2):pp. 147–159.
Hicks, J. R. (1980). Is-lm: An explanation. *Journal of Post Keynesian Economics, 3*(2), 139–154.
Hidalgo, C. A., & Hausmann, R. (2009). The building blocks of economic complexity. *In Proceedings of the National Academy of Sciences, 106*, 10570–10575.
Himino, R. (2005 [2003]). Kensho BIS Kisei to Nippon [BIS Regulations and Japan–An Examination]. Kinzai Institute for Financial Affairs, Inc., Tokyo. Second edition.
Horn, R. V. (2014). Henry simon's death. *History of Political Economy, 46*(3), 525–535.
Hughes, B. (2002). *The secret terroritsts*. Truth Triumphant, P.O.Box 1417 Eustis, Fl. 32727, USA.
Huntington, S. P. (2002). *The clash of civilizations*. Simon & Schuster.
Ishii, M. (1996). *Dare mo kakanakatta Nippon Ginko-Erito Shudan no Mewo Ooitakunaru Jittai (Bank of Japan Nobody Wrote-Shocking Inside Stories of An Elite Group One can Hardly Look At)*. Tokyo: Appuru Shuppan.
Ishii, M. (2001). *Nippon Ginko no Haiboku-Ushinawareta 10 nen no Haishin (Defeat of the Bank of Japan-The Betrayal of the Lost Decade)*. Tokyo: Kodansha.
Ishii, M., & Werner, R. A. (2003). *Fukuinichiginno kikenna sugao (The Bank of Japan under Toshihiko Fukui)*. Tokyo: Appuru Shuppan.
Ito, T., & Hoshi, T. (2020). *The Japanese economy* (2nd ed.). Cambridge, MA: MIT Press.
Kaldor, N. (1955). *An expenditure tax*. London: Allen and Unwin.
Keen, S. (2014). Endogenous money and effective demand. *Review of Keynesian Economics, 2*(3), 271–291.
Keynes, J. M. (1936). *The general theory of employment, interest, and money*. London: Macmillan and Co.
Keynes, J. M. (1971 [1930]). A treatise on money. In T. R. E. Society (Ed.), *The Collected Writings of John Maynard Keynes*, volume 5. Macmillan, London.
Knight, F. (1933). Review of alvin hansen's economic stabilization in an unbalanced world. *Journal of Political Economy, 41*(April), 242–45.
Knight, F. H., Cox, G. V., Director, A., Douglas, P. H., Hart, A. G., Mints, L. W., Schultz, H., & Simons, H. C. (1933). Untitled memorandum on banking reform. dated march 16, 1933. Published in Appendix in R. J. Phillips, The Chicago Plan and New Deal Banking Reform, New York: M.E. *Sharpe, 1995*, 191–199.
Koo, R. C. (2009). *The holy grail of macroeconomics – Lessons from Japan's great recession*. John Wiley & Sons (Asia) Pte. Ltd., Singapore, revised and updated edition.
Kriesler, P., & Nevile, J. W. (2016). Is-lm and macroeconomics after keynes. In J. Halevi, G. C. Harcourt, P. Kriesler, & J. W. Nevile (Eds.), *Post-Keynesian Essays from Down Under, volume 1: Essays on Keynes, Harrod and Kalecki of Theory and Policy in an Historical Context*. London, UK: Palgrave Macmillan.
Krugman, P. R. (2015). The rage of the bankers. *The New York Times*.
Kydland, F. E., & Prescott, E. C. (1977). Rules rather than discretion: The inconsistency of optimal plans. *Journal of Political Economy, 85*(3), 473–491.
Lebor, A. (2013). *Tower of basel: The shadowy history of the secret bank that runs the world*. New York, USA: Public Affairs.
Lee, K.-S., & Werner, R. A. (2018). Reconsidering monetary policy: An empirical examination of the relationship between interest rates and nominal GDP growth in the U.S., U.K. *Germany and Japan. Ecological Economics, 146*, 26–34.

Lietaer, B., Arnsperger, C., Goerner, S., and Brunnhuber, S. (2012). *Money and sustainability–The missing link. A report from the club of rome EU chapter to finance watch and the world business academy*. Triarchy Press.

Lucas, R. E. (1972). Expectations and the neutrality of money. *Journal of Economic Theory*, 103–124.

Lucas, R. E. (1976). Econometric policy evaluation: A critique. In K. Brunner, A. Meltzer (Ed.), *The Phillips Curve and Labor Markets. Carnegie-Rochester Conference Series on Public Policy* (vol. 1, pp. 19–46). New York: American Elsevier

MacLeod, H. D. (1866 [1856]). *The theory and practice of banking (vol. 1* (2nd ed.). London: Longmans, Green, Reader, and Dyer.

Mahmud, S. F., Yamaguchi, K., & Yülek, M. A. (2017). *Money matters: Some puzzles*. Peter Lang Gmbh, Frankfurt a. M.: Anomalies and Crises in the Standard Macroeconomic Model.

Mahmud, S. F., Yamaguchi, K., & Yülek, M. A. (2020). Chapter 6: Beyond dsge: An accounting system dynamics modelling approach. In Z. Iqbal, T. Akin, N. E. Maghrebi, & A. Mirakhor (Eds.), *Handbook of Analytical Studies in Islamic Finance and Economics, volume 4 of De Gruyter Studies in Islamic Economics, Finance and Business (chapter 6* (pp. 139–168). Berling, Boston: De Gruyter Oldenbourg.

Mankiw, N. G. (2007). On textbook writing. Greg Mankiw's blog, March 4th, 2007. http://gregmankiw.blogspot.com/2007/03/on-textbook-writing.html [Accessed: December 13, 2023].

Mankiw, N. G. (2016). *Macroeconomics* (9th ed.). New York: Worth Publishers, A Macmillan Education Imprint.

Marshall, A. G. (2010). *Crisis is an opportunity: Engineering a global depression to create a global government*. Montreal, Quebec: Center for Research on Globalization.

Marx, K. (1965 [1867]). *Capital* (vol. 1-3). Moscow: Progress Publishers.

Marx, K. and Engels, F. (1969 [1848]). Manifesto of the communist party. In *Marx/Engels Selected Works* (vol. 1, pp. 98–137). Moscow: Progress Publishers.

McCarty, B. (2020 [1922]). *The suppressed truth about the assassination of Abraham LIncoln*. Washington, D.C.: Lutheran Library.org.

Mcleay, M., Radia, A., and Thomas, R. (2014). Money creation in the modern economy. Quarterly bulletin q1, Monetary Analysis Directorate, Bank of England.

Meadows, D. H. (1999). *Leverage points: Places to intervene in a system*. Hartland, VT: The Sustainability Institute.

Meadows, D. H., Meadows, D. L., & Randers, J. (1992). *Beyond the limits*. Post Mills, Vt: Chelsea Green Publishing.

Meadows, D. H., Meadows, D. L., Randers, J., & Behrens, W. W. (1972). *Limits to growth-A report for the club of Rome's project on the predicament of humankind*. New York: Potomoc Associates-Universe Books.

Meadows, D. H., Randers, J., & Meadows, D. L. (2004). *Limits to growth-The 30 year update*. Vermont, USA: Chelsea Green Publishing Company.

Minsky, H. P. (1982). *Can it happen again?* Sharpe, Armonk, NY: Essay on Instability and Finance. M.E.

Mints, L. W. (1945). *A history of banking theory in Great Britain and the United States*. Chicago, IL: University of Chicago Press.

Mitchell, W., Wray, L. R., & Watts, M. (2019). *Macroeconomics* (1st ed.). Red Globe Press.

Modigliani, F. (1944). Liquidity preference and the theory of interest and money. *Econometrica, 12*(1), 45–88.

Mullins, E. C. (1983). *Secrets of the federal reserve–The London connection* (1st ed.). Bankers Research Institute.

Nagoshi, K. (2019). *Postwar political party's history of sectret funds: Genealogy of "Dependence" inscribed in U.S. and Russia's official archives (in Japanese)*. Shinchosha.

Nakamoto, S. (2008). Bitcoin: A peer-to-peer electronic cash system, https://bitcoin.org/bitcoin.pdf

OECD (2019). "General government debt" (indicator), https://doi.org/10.1787/a0528cc2-en [accessed on 31 March 2023].
Onagi, Z. (2022). *Jomon Civilization-The truth about history erased from textbooks around the world (in Japanese)*. Tokyo, Japan: Bio Magazine.
Palley, T. (2017a). A theory of economic policy lock-in and lock-out via hysteresis: rethinking economists' approach to economic policy. *Economics: The Open-Access, Open-Assessment E-Journal*, 11(18):1–18.
Palley, T. I. (2017). The theory of endogenous money and the lm schedule: prelude to a reconstruction of islm. *Brazilian Journal of Political Economy, 37*(1), 3–22.
Phillips, C. A. (1920). *Bank credit: A study of the principles and factors underlying advances made by banks to borrowers*. New York: Macmillan.
Phillips, R. J. (1995). *The Chicago plan & new deal banking reform*. Sharpe Inc, London: New York, M.E.
Posner, G. (2015). *God's bankers: A history of money and power at the Vatican*. Simon and Schuster.
Prestowitz, C. V. (1990 [1988]). *Trading places: How we are giving our future to Japan and how to reclaim it.* Basic Books, New York, paperback edition.
Quiggin, J. (2012). *Zombie economics–how dead ideas still walk among us*. Black Inc.
Richardson, G., Komai, A., Gou, M., & Park, D. (2013). Stock Market Crash of 1929. Federal Reserve History; www.federalreservehistory.org/essays/stock-market-crash-of-1929 [accessed: February 14, 2024].
Robinson, J. (1973). What Has Become of the Keynesian Revolution? In J. Robinson (Ed.), *After Keynes* (pp. 1–11). Basil Blackwell.
Rochon, L.-P., & Rossi, S. (Eds.). (2017). *Advances in endogenous money analysis*. Cheltenham, UK: Edward Elgar Publishing.
Samuelson, P. A. (1948). *Economics: An introductory analysis*. New York: McGraw-Hill.
Schewmmann, M. (2015). *Putting a stop to ficticious bank accounting; with a plan to redeem the US and Euro Area national debts*. IICPA Publications.
Schumpeter, J. A. (1934). *The theory of economic development: An inquiry into profits, capital, credit*. Interest and the Business Cycle: Harvard University Press, Cambridge, Massachusetts.
Schumpeter, J. A. (1987 [1954]). *History of economic analysis* (1st ed.). Routledge, London.
Shirakawa, M. (2019). World has learned wrong lessons from 'Japanification'–Governments should focus on raising productivity, not on specter of deflation.
Smith, A. (1838 [1776]). *An inquiry into the nature and causes of the wealth of nations*. Edinburgh: Adam and Charles Black.
Soddy, F. (1926). *Wealth, virtual wealth and debt: The solution of the economic paradox* (2nd ed.). George Allen & Unwin, second Edition published in 1933.
Spaulding, E. G. (1869). *History of the legal tender paper money issued during the great rebellion being a loan Without interests and a national currency*. Buffalo, New York: Express Printing Company.
Sterman, J. D. (2000). *Business dynamics-Systems thinking and modeling for a complex world*. New York: The McGraw-Hill Companies.
Stiglitz, J. (1997). *Economics* (2nd ed.). New York: W.W. Norton.
Stiglitz, J. E. (2003). *Deflation, globalization and the new paradigm of monetary economics. A speech given at the expert group on recent developments in international finance, foreign exchange subcommittee, council on customs, tariff and foreign exchange (on April 16th, 2003).* Retrieved from https://warp.ndl.go.jp/info:ndljp/pid/1022127/www.mof.go.jp/singikai/kanzegaita/giziroku/gaic150416.htm [accessed on December 3rd, 2023] National Diet Library: Web Archiving Project.
Stinnett, R. B. (2001 [1999]). *Day of deceit: The truth about FDR and pearl harbor*. Simon & Schuster. Originally published in 1999 from The Free Press.
Sutton, A. C. (2010 [1976]). *Wall street and the rise of hitler: The astonishing true story of the American Financiers who bankrolled the nazis*. Clairview Books.

Sutton, A. C. (2012 [1974]). *Wall street and the bolshevik revolution: The remarkable true story of the American capitalists who financed the Russian communists*. Clairview Books, reprinted edition.

Suzuki, Y. (2019). Tsukuda-kun wo shinobu (in memory of my friend tsukuda). Published from the author's personal webpage.

Taylor, J. B. (1993). Discretion versus policy rules in practice. *Carnegie-Rochester Conference Series on Public Policy, 39*, 195–214.

Teitelbaum, R. (2020). Conspiracy Theorists Ask 'Who Owns the New York Fed?' Here's the Answer. Institutional Investor (February 24th 2020). https://www.institutionalinvestor.com/article/2bsx0wq4jdzo82fk8nhfk/culture/conspiracy-theorists-ask-who-owns-the-new-york-fed-heres-the-answer [accessed: March 24th, 2022].

Tobin, J. (1963). Commercial banks as creators of 'money. Discussion papers 388, Cowles Foundation for Research in Economics, New Haven, Conneticut.

Tymoigne, E., & Wray, L. R. (2013). Modern money theory 101: A reply to critics. Levy Economics Institute Working Paper No. 778, 57 pagers.

Vitali, S., Glattfelder, J. B., & Battiston, S. (2011). The network of global corporate control. *ETH Zurich, Switserland*. http://arxiv.org/pdf/1107.5728.pdf

Vogel, E. F. (1979). *Japan as number one: Lessons for America*. Harvard University Press.

von Hayek, F. A. (1966 [1929]). *Monetary Theory and the Trade Cycle*. Augustus M. Kelley Publishers, New York, reprint of 1933 english edition, london: jonathan cape; originally published in german in 1929 edition.

von Mises, L. (1953 [1912]). *The theory of money and credit* (2nd ed.). Yale University Press, New Haven. English translation by H. E. Batson.

Warburg, P. M. (1930). *The federal reserve system: Its origin and growth* (Vol. 1). New York: The Macmillan Company.

Watanabe, A. (2012). [Operational status of currency system in japan] Wagakuni no tsukaseido no unyojokyo ni tsuite (in japanese). *Finance* (pp. 18–31).

Weintraub, E. R. (2014). Mit's openness to jewish economists. In *MIT and the Transformation of American Economics* (pp. 45–59). Duke University Press.

Werner, R. A. (1995). [Create a Recovery Through Quantitative Easing] Keiki Kaifuku Ryoteki Kinyukanwa Kara (in Japanese). Nihon Keizai Shinbun (Nikkei), September 2.

Werner, R. A. (2003). *Princes of the Yen: Japan's central bankers and the transformation of the economy*. Sharpe: New York, M.E.

Werner, R. A. (2005). *New paradigm in macroeconomics: Solving the riddle of Japanese macroeconomic performance*. Basingstoke: Palgrave Macmillan.

Werner, R. A. (2016). A lost century in economics: Three theories of banking and the conclusive evidence. *International Review of Financial Analysis, 46*, 361–379.

Wray, L. R. (1990). *Money and credit in capitalist economies: The endogenous money approach*. Edward Elgar Publishing.

Wray, L. R. (2004). *Credit and state theories of money: The contributions of A*. Mitchell Innes: Edward Elgar Publishing, Northampton, Massachusetts.

Wray, L. R. (2012). *Modern money theory*. New York, USA: Palgrave Macmillan.

Yabe, K. (2014). *Why Japan can't stop US bases and nuclear power plants? (in Japanese)*. Tokyo: Shueisha International.

Yamaguchi, K. (1988). *Beyond Walras, Keynes and Marx – Synthesis in Economic Theory Toward a New Social Design*. American University Studies. Peter Lang Publishing, Inc., New York.

Yamaguchi, K. (2003). Principle of accounting system dynamics–modeling corporate financial statements. In *Proceedings of the 21st International Conference of the System Dynamics Society*, New York. System Dynamics Society.

Yamaguchi, K. (2004b). Money supply and creation of deposits : SD macroeconomic modeling (1). In *Proceedings of the 22nd International Conference of the System Dynamics Society*, Oxford, England: The System Dynamics Society.

Yamaguchi, K. (2005). Aggregate demand equilibria and price flexibility: SD macroeconomic modeling (2). In *Proceedings of the 23nd International Conference of the System Dynamics Society*, Boston, USA. The System Dynamics Society.

Yamaguchi, K. (2006). Integration of real and monetary sectors with labor market: SD macroeconomic modeling (3). In *Proceedings of the 24th International Conference of the System Dynamics Society*, Nijmegen, The Netherlands. The System Dynamics Society.

Yamaguchi, K. (2007). Balance of payments and foreign exchange dynamics: SD macroeconomic modeling (4). In *Proceedings of the 25th International Conference of the System Dynamics Society*, Boston, USA. The System Dynamics Society.

Yamaguchi, K. (2008). Open macroeconomies as a closed economic system: SD macroeconomic modeling completed. In *Proceedings of the 26th International Conference of the System Dynamics Society*, Athens, Greece: The System Dynamics Society.

Yamaguchi, K. (2009). Logical vs Historical Time in A Price Adjustment Mechanism. In *Proceedings of the 27th International Conference of the System Dynamics Society*, Albuquerque, New Mexico, USA: The System Dynamics Society.

Yamaguchi, K. (2010). On the liquidation of government debt under a debt-free money system: Modeling the American monetary act. In *Proceedings of the 28th International Conference of the System Dynamics Society*, Seoul, Korea: The System Dynamics Society.

Yamaguchi, K. (2011). Workings of a public money system of open macroeconomies: Modeling the American monetary act completed. In *Proceedings of the 29th International Conference of the System Dynamics Society*, Washington D.C., USA: The System Dynamics Society.

Yamaguchi, K. (2012). On the monetary and financial stability under a public money system: Modeling the American monetary act simplified. In *Proceedings of the 30th International Conference of the System Dynamics Society*, St. Gallen, Switzerland: The System Dynamics Society.

Yamaguchi, K. (2013 [2004]a). Modeling long-term sustainability. In M. Quaddus, & M. Siddique (Ed.), *Handbook of Sustainable Development Planning: Studies in Modelling and Decision Support* (chapter 4, pp. 61–90). Edward Elgar Publishers, Cheltenham, UK; Northamton, MA, USA, second edition.

Yamaguchi, K. (2014). From debt money to public money system – Modeling a transition process simplified. In *Proceedings of the 32nd International Conference of the System Dynamics Society*, Delft, Netherlands: The System Dynamics Society.

Yamaguchi, K. (2015). *Public money-Modern version of the Chicago plan that liquidates government debt (in Japanese)*. Tokyo, Japan: Toyo Keizai Shinpo-sha.

Yamaguchi, K. (2022 [2013]). *Money and macroeconomic dynamics – Accounting system dynamics approach*. Japan Futures Research Center, Awaji Island, Japan. First edition published in 2013. Edition 6 published in 2022. Available at: http://www.muratopia.org/Yamaguchi/MacroBook.html

Yamaguchi, K., & Yamaguchi, Y. (2016). Heads and tails of money creation and its system design failures – Toward the alternative system design. In *Proceedings of the 34th International Conference of the System Dynamics Society, Delft, The Netherlands*. System Dynamics Society.

Yamaguchi, K., & Yamaguchi, Y. (2017a). Public money, debt money and blockchain-based money classified – EPM as money of the futures. Working paper no.01-2017, Japan Futures Research Center, Awaji Island, Hyogo.

Yamaguchi, K., & Yamaguchi, Y. (2021a). Accounting system dynamics modeling of money stock as debts-Theory and case analysis of Japan. In R. Y. Cavana, B. C. Dangerfield, O. V. Pavlov, M. J. Radzicki, & I. D. Wheat (Eds.), *Feedback Economics, Comtemporary Systems Thinking*. Switzerland: Springer Cham, Cham.

Yamaguchi, K., & Yamaguchi, Y. (2021b). *Introduction to public money (in Japanese)*. Tokyo: Shueisha International.

Yamaguchi, Y. (2021). Money stock as total debts–A case study on the financial accounts of the United States. Working paper no. 01-2021, Japan Futures Research Center.

Yamaguchi, Y., & Yamaguchi, K. (2017b). Peer-to-Peer public money system – Focusing on payments. In *Proceedings of the Second Asia-Pacific Region Conference of the System Dynamics Society at theNational University of Singapore*, Boston, USA: The System Dynamics Society.

Yamaguchi, Y., & Yamaguchi, K. (2022a). The endogenous money IS-LM model of the debt money system (Part I) – A paradigm shift in macroeconomics. JFRC Working Paper No. 01-2022 http://muratopia.net/research/papers/EndogenousIS-LM.pdf

Yamaguchi, Y., & Yamaguchi, K. (2022b). The endogenous money IS-LM model of the debt money system (Part II) – Loanable funds vs. engogenous money. JFRC Working Paper No. 02-2022 http://muratopia.net/research/papers/EndogenousIS-LM(Part2).pdf

Yamaguchi, Y., & Yamaguchi, K. (2023). The long-run endogenous money ASD model of the debt money system (Part III) – Paradigm shift in economics as a science. JFRC Working Paper No. 02-2023 http://muratopia.net/research/papers/EndogenousASD(Part3).pdf

Yamaguchi, Y., & Yamaguchi, K. (2024). The long-run endogenous money-interest ASD model of the debt money system (Part IV) – Built-in unfair income distribution and inflation. JFRC Working Paper No. 01-2024 http://muratopia.net/research/papers/EndogenousASD(Part4).pdf

Young, W., & Zilberfarb, B. Z. (Eds.). (2001). *IS-LM and modern macroeconomics. Recent Economic Thought*. Dordrecht, Netherlands: Springer.

Zarlenga, S. A. (2002). *The lost science of money: The mythology of money-the story of power*. New York: American Monetary Institute.

Index

K. Yamaguchi and Y. Yamaguchi, *Public Money*,
https://doi.org/10.1007/978-981-97-6564-5